By the same Authors

THE RISE OF AMERICAN CIVILIZATION

AMERICA IN MIDPASSAGE

By the same Authors

THE RISE OF AMERICAN CIVILIZATION

AMERICA IN
MIDPASSAGE

by

CHARLES A. BEARD
& MARY R. BEARD

Illustrated from drawings by
WILFRED JONES

LONDON
JONATHAN CAPE

FIRST PUBLISHED 1939

PRINTED IN THE UNITED STATES OF AMERICA
BOUND BY A. W. BAIN & CO. LTD., LONDON

Nel mezzo del cammin di nostra vita. . . .

Prefatory Note

The quotations on pp. 693 ff. are from *U. S. A.*, published by Harcourt, Brace and Company; copyright, 1930, 1932, 1933, 1934, by John Dos Passos. Quotations on pp. 715 f. are from *Conversation at Midnight*, published by Harper and Brothers; copyright, 1937, by Edna St. Vincent Millay. To Harcourt, Brace and Company we are indebted for the privilege of making quotations from the works of Kay Boyle, Archibald MacLeish, Carl Sandburg, and Lewis Mumford. To the Vanguard Press we are under obligations for similar privileges in connection with the works of James T. Farrell. With respect to quotations from other contemporary sources, we have cited the names of authors and their works and desire to express here our appreciation of the considerations extended to us by members of the Republic of Letters and their publishers.

C. A. B.
M. R. B.

New Milford, Conn.
Winter, 1938

Contents

Contents

AMERICA
IN MIDPASSAGE

AMERICA IN MIDPASSAGE

CHAPTER I

The Golden Glow

AFTER the long and toilsome rise, American civilization reached, at the summer solstice of Normalcy, the high plateau of permanent peace and prosperity — in the general opinion of business organizers, bankers, guardians of the National Shrine in Wall Street, bondsalesmen, grateful holders of stocks, lawyers, doctors, editors, writers, columnists, artists, architects, actors, philosophers, economists, scientists, engineers, teachers, professors, women of the leisure class, the aristocracy of labor, and the politicians of the right direction. Notes of jubilee drowned the plaintive cries of farmers and the queasy doubts of querulous critics. According to the golden appearance of things, ingenuity would create novelty upon novelty, gadget upon gadget, to keep the nation's machines whirling; inevitably outlets would be found for the accumulations of capital and the torrents of commodities; and employment would be afforded for laborers befitting their merits and diligence. Articles for comfort and convenience, devices for diversion and amusement were multiplying with sensational rapidity, giving promise of a satisfaction even more gratifying. Corporations were swelling in size, holding companies were rising to dizzy heights, the tide of liquid claims to wealth was flooding in. Since, it was thought, the morale of the nation was grounded in ineradicable virtues and sustained by a beneficent religion, American civilization was well fortified against all varieties of untoward experience.

Reassured by the solidity of business, educators drove ahead with plans for buildings, campuses, and endowments still more magnificent, to fit the youth of the land for entering upon the heritage prepared and guaranteed by their ancestors. Pouring out from the seats of learning, hopeful graduates, with diplomas in their hands and benedictions on their heads, looked forward in confidence to security in the professions, services, polite callings, or dainty domesticity. For consumers there were to be automobiles, radios, electric refrigerators, silk stockings, lingerie, and cosmetics, if necessary on the installment plan, with no payment down. Wherever, in the worst of excellent circumstances, unfortunates required succor, an appeal could be made to private philanthropy that the homeless might have their shelter and the hungry their bread.

This permanence and beneficence seemed doubly guaranteed by a strong government, under the watchful guardianship of nine impeccable judges soon to be housed in the resplendent Palace of Justice at the national capital. Under political institutions inherited from prudent forebears and solidified by respectful practice, the people ruled through laws of their own making, within the fixed limits of the Constitution; and as it had been it might ever be. No powerful faction challenged the form of government or threatened the vested rights of property. Nowhere in shadows lurked a Catiline. The continental home of the nation, with its outlying possessions, was guarded by an army and a navy whose renown had never been darkened by defeat in war. Relations with other governments were now pacific. Having disclaimed pretensions to larger empire, the United States could face the future without fear of perilous conflicts upon land or sea. Foreign trade was increasing in volume, as loans were granted to impoverished or backward economies abroad, stimulating domestic industries, expanding employment, swelling the coffers of bankers and capitalists with commissions and profits, and adding the bonds of interest to the ties of international humanity. With the older generations still remembering the last armed contest, and the new generation not old enough to lust after its experience in another, the weary nations of the earth were ready to renounce war as an instrument of national policy and enter upon an endless age of peace. So, at least, it seemed in the generality of opinion.

§

This generality of opinion was incarnate in Calvin Coolidge, President of the Republic. Looking out upon the scene, he pronounced it fair and good. He had been elected by a triumphant majority against all opposition in 1924, and as he contemplated the coming years he saw every reason for exulting in their promises. In his own personality he typified the virtues which were celebrated on ceremonial occasions as the unfailing sources of prosperity and accumulation: thrift, prudence, and simplicity. There was firmness in his character, suggesting the granite of the Vermont hills amid which he had been reared. And his virtues were widely acclaimed by Americans of his generation in the plenitude of their wealth. His crisp and homely aphorisms excited pleasure in the drawing rooms of Park Avenue and in the exclusive clubs of Chicago and San Francisco. Stories of his passion for economy in private and public expenditures were told and retold in Palm Beach, Newport, and Aiken at Lucullan feasts typical of the golden age. When he set his face like flint against high taxation of the rich and demanded a reduction in public outlays, he heightened their confidence in the future of the country and its institutions. When he scolded critics in Congress, scorned the appeals of progressives, and braved the laughter of the amused minority, he added to the assurance which resisted the spirit of innovation in matters economic and political. As long as Calvin Coolidge stood on guard at the White House with the executive veto, those who shared his sentiments could maintain their faith in the bright image of today and tomorrow.

In case an executive veto failed to block any objectionable measure driven through the Congress of the United States by the tumult of democracy, the Supreme Court remained as the ultimate bulwark under the aegis of the Constitution. Its personnel, carefully selected, offered a guarantee of caution and conservatism. Over that tribunal presided William Howard Taft as Chief Justice, a jurist with long political experience. As a candidate for the presidency on two occasions and as President for four years, he had fully certified his views to the whole country. After a period of retirement, following his conflict with the Progressives and his defeat in 1912, he had been elevated to the supreme bench by President Harding. The general conceptions of the Constitution and the rights of property entertained by the Chief Justice were shared by three colleagues — Justice Pierce Butler, formerly a mighty railroad lawyer in the West, Justice George Sutherland, once a leader of the Republicans in the Senate, and Justice Edward T. Sanford, who had come to his post from a lower court. These three had also been nominated by President Harding with due reference to their qualifications. With them were affiliated, in matters of essential doctrine, Justice Willis Van Devanter, distinguished by a career of services in the

Republican party and chosen for the bench by Taft while he was President of the United States, and Justice James Clark McReynolds, whom President Wilson had translated from the office of Attorney General — making a safe majority of six against almost any piece of legislation deemed unfriendly by the leading beneficiaries of the great prosperity.

The weight thus provided for the scales of justice was somewhat balanced by three members of the Court who constantly warned their brethren against substituting their economic predilections for the provisions of the Constitution. Old and crowned with honors, Justice Oliver Wendell Holmes led this group; he had been chosen by President Theodore Roosevelt for the purpose of tempering the harshness of corporation law with the humanity of jurisprudence. Akin to Justice Holmes in spirit was Justice Louis D. Brandeis whose work in labor and social legislation President Wilson had recognized by appointing him to this permanent position on the bench. The third member of the triumvirate was Justice Harlan F. Stone, elevated by Coolidge, the youngest of the nine in point of service and differentiated from his two colleagues by varied experiences as dean of the Columbia University Law School, practitioner in New York City, and Attorney General of the United States. Though these three Justices, powerful in learning and in gifts of expression as they were, could by no means dominate the Court, in time of sharp division they could dissent; and again and again one or more of the three did dissent with reasoned and pungent arguments against decisions of the majority affecting gains, profits, and incomes, especially in respect of statutes violating the Social Statics of Herbert Spencer. But on such occasions they could not issue orders in the name of the Court. That function was reserved to the majority.

While President Coolidge was in the White House and the Supreme Court was dominated by Justices of kindred conceptions, insurgents in the national legislature could do little or nothing to dim the light of the fair prospect. The elections of 1926 had given the Republicans a safe working majority in the House of Representatives. In the Senate remained the apostles of Normalcy: James E. Watson of Indiana, David A. Reed of Pennsylvania, Reed Smoot of Utah, and Francis E. Warren of Wyoming. In all the main points of doctrine President Coolidge could rely upon their orthodoxy. On the face of things there were forty-eight Republican members in the Senate, forty-seven Democrats, and one Farmer-Labor spokesman. But appearances were somewhat illusory. Among the Senators nominally of his own party, with whom the President had to work, were Smith W. Brookhart, a radical agrarian from Iowa; James Couzens, an independent millionaire from Michigan; George W. Norris, the indomitable radical from Nebraska; and Robert M. La Follette, Jr., heir of his father's devotion to democracy and a strong defender himself. The presence of these men in the Senate meant that every policy presented by President Coolidge would be mercilessly examined, if not torn to tatters in debate. But, after all, they were a minority and they could accomplish little in the line of positive action. They could combine with Democrats in pushing investigations of the oil scandal that had marred the Giant Masquerade during Harding's administration and in approving inquiries into other forms of coöperation between the Government and business enterprise; yet, while the bright hues of prosperity lay upon the cities, few people were really disturbed by incidents of scandal and corruption, as the election of 1924 had demonstrated.

§

Given his scheme of values and outlook upon life, his background and purposes, President Coolidge was obliged to devote special consideration to matters of national finance and economy. In this domain he found the situation on the whole excellent though open to improvement by the exercise of prudence.

At its peak in 1919, the interest-bearing debt of the United States had stood at the staggering sum of $25,700,000,000 in round numbers. At the close of the fiscal year in 1928 it had been reduced to $17,318,000,000. At the same time the Treasury reported that the surplus of revenues over expenditures for the fiscal year amounted to nearly $400,000,000 — of which a part was from non-recurring sources. "We are striving, as always," said the President to the federal officials responsible for budget estimates, "to pave the way for further reduction of debt and of taxes. This in itself necessitates unremitting effort to hold the level of our expenditure program." At the existing rate of debt retirement, the Treasury could count on a trivial debt at the end of fifteen or twenty years.

Moreover the present burden was offset, in the calculations of that department, by the obligations of foreign governments to the amount of nearly $11,000,000,000, all evidences of World War debts. Belgium, Estonia, Finland, Great Britain, Hungary, Italy, Latvia, Lithuania, Poland, and Rumania had delivered their bonds to the Treasury. Greece, Czechoslovakia, and Yugoslavia were on the point of depositing their pledges, and the war debt-refunding agreement with France was in process of successful negotiation. Among the great powers indebted to the United States, only Russia was set down as a recalcitrant defaulter. With debt retirement proceeding rapidly, with a surplus for the fiscal year, and with the bonds of great powers in hand or on the way, President Coolidge and his Secretary of the Treasury, Andrew W. Mellon, reviewed achievements with pride and looked forward with composure, in matters of public finance.

The sphere of business which President Coolidge surveyed at the close of 1928 likewise presented attractive prospects. Experts who watched the barometers of "free" enterprise cited impressive gains over the previous year, in check transactions, the advance of railway shares on the market, and the material appreciation in industrial stocks. The

New York Exchange reported that the volume of operations for the twelve months exceeded the total of the previous year by nearly fifty per cent and the total of 1926 by almost eighty per cent. Collaterally, brokers' loans for dealings in stocks had broken into a "new high" and interest rates were rising. It was with some justification in "facts and figures" that President Coolidge, in his final annual message to Congress, rejoiced that the country was in an "era of prosperity more extensive and of peace more permanent" than ever before in its history. To this prosperity, he admitted, there might be perils; but not while his policies were cherished and continued by the nation. "The main source of these unexampled blessings," he insisted, "lies in the integrity and character of the American people."

When President Coolidge found one sector of business enterprise, namely high-seas shipping, less prosperous than others, he suggested ways and means of amelioration. Under his guidance Congress lent the financial assistance of the Federal Government to that needy industry, by passing the Merchant Marine Act of 1928. Under this measure the Postmaster General was authorized to award contracts for the carriage of mails to all ports not covered by the coastwise shipping laws. But instead of paying shippers a fixed sum per pound of mail transported, as under previous legislation, he could now allow them a certain amount for every mile traveled on the outbound voyage from the United States, regardless of the quantity of mail on board. Although the rates varied according to the tonnage and speed of the ships, the maximum payment could run as high as twelve dollars per nautical mile. Besides making generous grants to shipowners for the carriage of mail, the Government continued the practice of lending money at low rates of interest for the construction and repair of vessels, and permitted operators to employ naval officers on leave with half-pay from active service. This Act, as a commissioner of the Shipping Board explained, offered to the shipping business the most lucrative subsidy in the world. As later investigations disclosed, the statement proved correct, indeed startlingly correct. Lest some mistake occur in the matter of lucrative returns, Congress provided that the Government should continue to operate at its own loss the "pioneer lines" that were not paying their expenses, and then transfer them to private owners as soon as a profit appeared on the balance sheets.

§

That the masses in cities and rural regions might dwell in the effulgence of the golden glow, leaders in business enterprise offered stocks and bonds to "investors" and country banks. Investment houses, often affiliated with great banking institutions, established branches all over the country, tied together by leased wires for instant communication. They organized selling forces, headed by high-powered drivers who "pepped up" salesmen by their florid orations on the "merits" of the "securities" offered to the public, and by promising bonuses and promotions for success in disposing of stocks and bonds.

Young men fresh from academic groves, Bachelors of Arts in one thing or another, were recruited by the tens of thousands and drilled into rank and file salesmen for the highways and the byways. On trains, in airplanes, and by automobile, they sped hither and yon looking for customers. To some were assigned "the big game" — men and women who could buy shares in thousand lots and bonds by the block. To others was given the task of visiting small cities and towns, dangling prizes before little bankers, and charming men and women into exchanging their cash or prime securities for the new offerings that often promised higher rates of interest and better opportunities for profits than old and seasoned paper. Flaming youth seemed to have unlimited economic opportunities at least, selling liquid claims to wealth. With banks and brokers establishing special departments to take care of women as customers, college girls found a new avenue of equality stretching out before them.

Apparently impatient over the volume of security issues that accompanied the construction of new plants and the expansion of old industries, enterprising men of affairs set feverishly about the manufacture of additional stocks and bonds by the formation of holding companies. In the field of electric power, for example, such a company would buy a controlling interest in a number of concerns engaged in the actual operation of electric plants. It did not operate itself; it merely "held." The money for this transaction the company acquired by selling its own stocks and bonds to the eager public so eloquently described in the financial columns of the newspapers. Not content with simple operations, imaginative financiers formed super-holding companies, that is, corporations which united holding companies based upon control over operating concerns. As imagination expanded, holding company was piled upon holding company until the pyramid threatened, like the Tower of Babel, to pierce the heavens. Nor was ambition limited to single industries. One financial skyscraper, through an intricate network of holding concerns, gathered under its top concern railways, terminals, trucking companies, coal mines, orange groves, real estate developments, office buildings, a hotel, a bridge, a ferry, a heat, light, and power plant, a dock, and a winter resort, in addition to a number of enterprises more difficult to classify. Nothing that Lemuel Gulliver saw in Brobdingnag, not even corn as tall as trees, was more fantastic in conception and appearance.

As the structure of a holding company rose and expanded, it was customary for its directors to "write up," that is, inflate, the actual value of the subsidiaries acquired and to issue stocks or bonds, or both, founded upon the new "values." Since, in the field of public utilities, the holding company operated usually in two or more states, it was almost entirely free from the control, such as it was, exercised by state utility commissions charged with responsibility for assuring the public that stocks and bonds represented tangible wealth or the requirements of prudent investment. So emancipated, operating hither and yon, the holding company could add almost any nominal values it liked to the real and tangible values attached to underlying property. It could float and advertise stocks and bonds resting on hopes, speculations, and other intangibles, within the loose and vague boundaries set by the law of fraud, as liberally interpreted by the courts.

Not even in the days of The Octopus had financiers been able to get control over so much property by selling the securities of their companies to the public and using the money to purchase widely scattered and numerous minor concerns. To the wealth acquired by this process was added income derived from "servicing" the subsidiaries, controlling the salaried positions in the lower companies, and dominating the purchase of their supplies. Seldom if ever had the "natural forces of free enterprise" been so freely unleashed to gather in the investor's money and lay duties on the consumer's dollar. With prosperity mounting as on the wings of the morning there seemed to be no limit to the volume of liquid claims to wealth that could be issued and sold to the public, or to the profits that could be gathered in from the sale of paper and the management of underlying properties. Financiers, bankers, brokers, operators, and manipulators walked on air, sailed the skies, exuded the optimism of everlasting progress in their line of enterprise.

While this towering structure of paper claims to property was rising higher and higher, giving gapers and gazers the vertigo, the governors of the country laid no profane hands upon it. They "let it alone" with all the severity demanded by the stiffest defender of liberty. They did not seek to regiment the financiers, to dictate to them, to interfere harshly with the market in bonds and stocks. From the point of view of free enterprise, which was bound in the inexorable nature of things, as orthodox economists taught, to "release productive forces" and make everybody as

prosperous as humanly possible, the legal conditions prescribed for business by government were ideal, or almost
ideal, especially when taken in conjunction with the tariffs,
bounties, and subsidies added to heap up the measure.
Indeed the governments of many states vied with one
another in giving business enterprise the freest range that
fancy could conceive within any bounds of government.
As practically all the corporations, super-corporations, and
holding companies, which led in this upward rush toward
the sky, derived their charters — that is to say their authority to do "business" — from state governments, politicos in
these little domains, often corporation lawyers themselves,
smoothed the path for incorporators. Although a majority
of states exercised a control more or less strict over the formation of companies, others imposed no restrictions worthy
of mention and actually invited financiers to come in and
secure authority to behave as they pleased.

Lest the advantages of the liberty available be missed by
financiers, lawyers and enterprisers in the states of freedom
advertised the merits of their commonwealths' in blatant
words. A document of invitation carried by The Scientific
American positively shouted to all whom it concerned : "In-
corporate in Arizona. Complete in 1 day. Any capitalization, least cost, greatest advantages. Transact business anywhere. Laws, by-laws, and forms free." Another beckoned
from the pages of System : "Charters — Delaware best,
quickest, cheapest, most liberal. Nothing need be paid in.
Do business and hold meetings anywhere. Free forms." It
was on the basis of evidence clear and abundant that a witness declared before a Senate committee in 1937 : "States
have turned loose upon the other states a flock of corporate
vultures — I use that phrase deliberately and after mature
consideration — to prey upon the economy and people of the
other states." Although W. Z. Ripley, in his Main Street and
Wall Street, carefully described this procedure in detail, his
report to the nation made little, if any, impression on business men, beyond stirring up a storm of protest against his

conclusions. After all, the Lords of Creation naturally supposed that they understood corporate enterprise better than a mere professor. At least, they could afford, in practice, to ignore his animadversions.

The financial columns of great dailies announced in huge headlines and flashing descriptions a wide variety of new issues of stocks and bonds. They drew attention to the bonds of foreign governments offered at prices to yield six or seven per cent, or even "better." Why be content, salesmen asked, with a miserable three or four per cent on American Liberty bonds? If the people were squeamish about investing in foreign paper, of course they could get American real estate bonds paying five, six, or seven per cent — first mortgage bonds at that, guaranteed or unguaranteed, both equally "sound" and based upon "valuations" made by reputable firms of engineers and accountants. To investors inclined toward an elastic rate of return, rather than fixed interest, in order that they might share in the progressive prosperity, stocks in bewildering array were tendered — common stocks, Class A stocks, Class B stocks, preferred stocks of the first and second order, all sponsored by houses of the highest standing, with powerful New York banks as "trustees." If the investor desired "the security of diversification" he could buy stocks in railroads, utilities, foods, drugs, automobiles, and all the other prime industries of America. If perchance he distrusted his own judgment in making choices, he could purchase shares in investment "trusts," organized by solid old banking houses or their affiliates. These trusts were directed by "experts" who bought the securities of ten, twenty, fifty, or more "selected" industries and invited inexperienced men and women to benefit from corporate wisdom by acquiring shares resting on fractions of many holdings.

While some of the securities so tendered were proclaimed gilt-edged, others were more or less covertly acknowledged to be "a bit speculative." Yet was anything really speculative in an age of rising and endless prosperity? At all events there were investors who wanted more than the fixed interest of a first-mortgage bond or the modest dividend of a conservative corporation. They were eager to take a chance or their latent desires could be awakened by skilled psychologists in salesmanship. So even the oldest and most honorable banking houses or their affiliates brought out issues that might rise ten or fifteen points or might not, as events would disclose. Although advertisements of such prizes were often expressed in guarded language, the names of the sponsors obscured the warnings. Lines of fine print in the trust indenture, drawn by astute lawyers, often provided legal and moral exculpation for the issuing houses in case of a wreck.

But who read fine print, or understood its terms, if read? Nor was it always to the interest of salesmen to draw the attention of prospects to the stipulations of an indenture that reduced the equity of the stock to a position far removed from real value, indeed to a position of mere hopes founded upon possible, though not probable, contingencies. If salesmen did duly warn their customers, their side remarks must have fallen on deaf ears. Why not? After all, miracles were happening every day. Radio Corporation of America, which had once been tossed around at a few dollars a share, was at ninety-four dollars a share in March, 1928, and was destined to rise to $549 a share the very next year.

To this enchanting scene all the more appearance of solidity was given by the magic of the sponsorship. A majority of the men who led in the grand flotations and operations represented the flower of American culture, if their training in universities was an index of that culture. Certainly they were not the Daniel Drews, the Diamond Jim Bradys, the Russell Sages, and Hetty Greens of the Gilded Age, ruthless plungers, cut-throat competitors, and grim crushers of the weak who had risen from the bottom or near it, under the jungle law of tooth and claw. Of the fifty men rightly classified by Frederick Lewis Allen among the Lords of Creation as the "most powerful or influential in the Wall Street of 1929," at least forty were college men. A majority of the forty came from Harvard, Yale, Amherst, and the Massachusetts Institute of

Technology, from New England institutions, from the home of Federalism where fortunes had been augmented by the manipulation of papers since the establishment of the Constitution and the funding of the old state and continental debts. The Harvard quota, the largest of all, included such "wizards of finance" as J. P. Morgan, Thomas Lamont, George Whitney, George F. Baker, Jr., and Vincent Astor. The men of collegiate culture were, of course, often jostled by, or associated with, men who had climbed up from the bottom of the economic ladder — John J. Raskob, the Van Sweringen brothers, Clarence Dillon, and Samuel Insull, for example. But neither the jostling nor the association had tarnished the finish, the erudition, or the virtuosity of the university graduates at the top. The consideration which they enjoyed in all exclusive circles, their good taste, their correctness of dress, their respect for religion, property, and monogamy, their widely-known professions of rectitude, combined to give strength to the popular faith in the solidity, promise, and trustworthiness of their financial and business transactions.

§

Nor was the domestic scene alone fair with prosperity and assurance. To President Coolidge and those who shared his vision the foreign outlook was almost equally gratifying. Being no Caesar or Marcus Aurelius, Coolidge was neither restive with the longing to enlarge the American empire nor seriously troubled by its present size and problems. So he settled down contentedly within the ample reaches bequeathed by the navy and its affiliated interests in business and politics. The phantom of Philippine independence raised by the Democrats had been banished for all time, it seemed, by the results of the presidential election in 1920. That form of American intervention in China, known as the Open Door, was apparently working smoothly, subject to no threat of an overt nature, at least from Japan now entangled in the treaties and naval limitations of the Washington Conference.

In the Caribbean, as in the Far East, President Coolidge, as head of the navy, was able to pursue a steady course despite occasional protests by recalcitrant Senators against the use of marines — in Nicaragua, Haiti, and Santo Domingo. To such opposition he replied laconically, in terms that seemed axiomatic to those who regarded them as axiomatic, that "American lives and interests" must be protected everywhere.

That the President desired no friction with Mexico, however, was evident in the chill reception which he accorded to the importunities of interventionists who called for a war on that country in defense of American "rights." During his career in the Senate, Albert B. Fall had clamored for action in Mexico, but he was now out of the Senate; moreover he had resigned from the post of Secretary of the Interior and was under indictment for fraudulent transactions in oil consummated during his tenure of office. In the face of continued demands for strong policy from other interventionists, President Coolidge appointed Dwight W. Morrow, of the House of Morgan, ambassador to Mexico in 1927, with the expectation that he would adjust disputes by measures short of war. To protect the existing territorial American empire was one thing. To extend it by expensive adventures was no part of President Coolidge's program.

While peace reigned within the territorial empire, the dominion of foreign commerce was expanding and presumably could enlarge forever on the basis of free enterprise. From year to year, with some fluctuations, sales to other nations increased in absolute amounts, although not relatively in ratio to exportable production. The fact that commodities of export were shifting from agricultural produce to manufactured goods, with direful repercussions for labor on the land, merely confirmed the optimism of leaders in business enterprise as they forged ahead in their struggle with European and Oriental competitors. Between the years 1900 and 1930, agricultural exports fell from 66.2 per cent of the total export of the United States to 31.8 per cent of the total, while non-agricultural products, machinery and machine tools leading, rose from 33.8 per cent of the total to 68.2 per cent. In the calculation of promoters all this advance was due to the prowess of American manufacturers, bankers, and salesmen and no visible limits to everlasting expansion blurred the future. In the initiative of business men the regular politicos exulted and upon it, they were sure, the nation might safely rely.

The fact that American business men were building branch factories abroad in the staple lines of industry also lent apparent confirmation to assurance by giving Americans what was proudly called a grand "stake" in the fortunes and economy of other mighty nations. To overcome the barriers of foreign tariffs or meet the competition of cheaper foreign labor, manufacturing concerns established branches in Canada, Ireland, Great Britain, Europe, Latin America, and the Far East. If fortresses could not be taken by frontal assault, they could be occupied by boring within the walls. Besides going after foreign competitors on their home grounds, American business men bought the stocks of foreign industrial concerns, thus winning a minority voice, if not majority control, and sharing in any profits that accrued. By 1929 American private investments of the direct type in manufacturing, merchandising, mining, smelting, and other enterprises abroad amounted to the fine-appearing total of $7,477,735,000; and the structure, to the Lords of Creation, looked as substantial as the battlements of heaven.

Supplementing the billions directly invested in tangible commercial and industrial property abroad — property owned by residents of the United States — were billions invested in the bonds of foreign governments and the securities of foreign corporations. At the end of 1930 this type of portfolio investment, representing "interest capital," embraced a total of $7,204,218,000. Within its scope came national, dominion, provincial, and municipal bonds of governments in Europe, Canada, South America, Asia, Oceana, the West Indies, Mexico, Central America, and Africa. According to an official estimate as of January 1, 1931, the total of direct and portfolio investments, combined with minor items, reached the stupendous sum of $15,170,028,000. When to this aggregation was added the $11,000,000,000, owed to the Government of the United States by foreign governments on the World War account, the American "stake abroad" in the fates and fortunes of other countries amounted to about $26,000,000,000 in round numbers. Here, at least, were paper claims which accountancy viewed as a part of the national wealth, as signs of power and prosperity. "Evidences" of such claims were to be found in trust funds for widows and orphans, in the vaults of local banks, in the treasuries of universities, and in the strong boxes of American citizens who had "bought into" American economy triumphant abroad.

The billions poured from the United States into other countries enabled foreigners, financially handicapped, to buy American commodities ranging from wheat to machines by the shipload and thus gave a powerful stimulus to American production. With these billions in money went the high-powered salesmen of private concerns and the commercial agents of the Federal Government, including under the head also ambassadors, ministers, consuls, and naval attachés. As the money and men spread over the earth, the slow-going British and the still more leisurely Orientals were pushed and jostled by the representatives of American enterprise. From Copenhagen to Belgrade, from Tokyo to Singapore, from Liberia to Cape Town, and across the seas to Adelaide, loans of American money were consummated and the goods of American industries were deposited. A map of the world showing trade journeys, the stations visited, and the capital accounts registered resembled a universal commercial empire.

If it was not, like the old Roman Empire, marked by one government and one peace, with proconsuls ruling the provinces, it was at least assured the protection of the United States navy and it seemed as solid to its promoters and beneficiaries as economic and military power could make any system of human affairs. A few obscure and fretful Americans presumed to suggest the hazards of defaults and repudiations, but their warnings were as naught compared with the averment of men mighty in practical affairs that the stake abroad was founded on the integrity of business and the good faith of governments.

§

With industries humming, stocks soaring, and the empire of American trade expanding, with Europe still weary from the great blood-letting of the World War, the prospects of peace seemed as flattering as the opportunities for commercial advantage. Indeed, the time appeared ripe to effect a closer integration of "world economy" on terms satisfactory to American business. In the spring of 1927, amid the plaudits of peace advocates, a world economic conference, composed of the representatives of fifty nations, including the United States, assembled at Geneva and established, optimists said, "a landmark in the progress of international coöperation." As a representative of the Department of Commerce explained, it was "the first comprehensive gathering of the nations of the world for the purpose of consulting upon a wide range of economic problems and difficulties, with the double objective of seeking means for the removal of the obstacles in the way of the revival of general prosperity and of establishing such principles in economic affairs as would help to remove the causes for international friction and ensure world peace." The discussions of the conference covered a wide range, though on vital matters its conclusions were reserved. It recommended that the nations stop raising tariff barriers and set about lowering them, saving the "legitimate" interests of the various countries and their workers. In respect of American policy that declaration, with the qualifications, could be regarded as affirming convictions already entertained.

With the idea of providing more safeguards for the peace deemed essential to the success of commercial enterprise in all forms, President Coolidge called for an international naval conference to be held at Geneva later in the same year, 1927. Alleging that the conference might hinder the work for disarmament apparently going forward through the League of Nations, France and Italy declined to participate; but the representatives of Great Britain, Japan, and the United States did assemble at Geneva to discuss restrictions which had been deferred by the Washington Conference held during the Harding administration, namely, limitations on cruisers, destroyers, and submarines. Through many weeks the delegates argued at Geneva and then, in August, broke off negotiations without reaching an agreement on these implements of the sea power.

Although the conference did not work out according to expectations, American newspapers came to the rescue and dispelled the temporary gloom by laying the blame for the deadlock and failure on Britain. So instructed by the press, the American nation could find gratification in its good intentions and look forward to bringing Great Britain to reason at a succeeding convention. Nor was this confidence shaken three years later when a Senate investigation disclosed the lobbying and propaganda financed by American shipbuilding and other interests at Geneva for the purpose of defeating the proposed naval limitations.

If at the moment naval armaments could not be limited and relief granted to taxpayers, at any rate the glow on the horizon could be heightened by a verbal declaration in favor of world peace. And when it was made, President Coolidge declared it "the most important act" of his administration. The transaction came about in this manner. On April 6, 1927, the tenth anniversary of America's entrance into the world war, the French foreign minister, Aristide Briand, announced that France was prepared to enter an engagement with the United States outlawing war between the two nations. Although the Department of State in Washington hesitated, advocates of peace rallied to the proposal and, after mature consideration, Frank B. Kellogg, the Secretary of State, countered the French suggestion with a grand plan for widening the outlawry of war by means of a general treaty pledging all nations to pacific methods in the conduct of their relations.

After negotiations had cleared the way, representatives of Great Britain, France, Germany, Italy, Japan, the United States, and other powers signed at Paris in the summer of 1928 the document known as the Briand-Kellogg Pact, or the Kellogg-Briand Pact. Their pledge of eternal peace bound the signatories to "condemn recourse to war for the solution of international controversies and renounce it as an instrument of national policy in their relations with one another." Over their signatures, the nations agreed that the settlement of their disputes "of whatever nature or of whatever origin shall never be sought except by pacific means." This Pact the Senate of the United States ratified in January, 1929, and President Coolidge appended his signature, in America, at a special ceremony.

It was not only President Coolidge who rejoiced. To all appearances the Pact was the true outlawry or renunciation of war for which the war-weary peoples had long yearned. The language of the document was clear and luminous. Diplomats had given it their blessings and through them responsible governments had plighted their word of honor. A ritualistic solemnity had enveloped the completion of the ratification in the United States. By collateral statements on and off the records, it was true, the leading signatories laid restraints upon its terms. Great Britain, for example, reserved her special interests, France certain continental obligations, and the United States the responsibilities of the Monroe Doctrine. No method was provided for "implementing" the Pact by coercive measures directed against offenders, and hence the effort of any foreign office to apply its shining language in practice might well involve it in difficulties. Nor did the Pact proscribe in any respect a defensive war, that is, a war for the defense of national territory against invasion, or, presumably, national interests, however defined and anywhere.

But these reservations put little or no damper on the warmth of the popular enthusiasm which the Pact evoked, except among the unbelievers to whom the Pact really meant nothing at all. How could such appearances be deceptive, such dignity disingenuous, such trumpeted honor merely cynical? In the age of boundless optimism, with stocks skyrocketing every day, commerce increasing, profits soaring, the very suggestion seemed both unwarranted and invidious.

§

Although their views and actions little affected the vision of fair prospects at home and abroad, there were doubters and critics in Congress not entirely content with the theory and practice of the great promotion. Among the matters that engaged the attention of recalcitrant members, including Republicans as well as Democrats, two were of major significance — the disposition of natural resources still belonging to the Federal Government and the state of agriculture. The first presented a double aspect. Immediately involved were pending inquiries into corrupt relations among oil companies, directors of the Republican party, and officials of the Government during the Harding regime. Already the Senate investigation committee under the leadership of Senator Thomas J. Walsh had laid bare specific transactions which showed beyond question that Albert B. Fall, as Secretary of the Interior under Harding, had engineered the leasing of two great oil reserves to Harry F. Sinclair and Edward L. Doheny on terms that promised immense profits to their respective concerns. Already it had demonstrated by indubitable evidence that Secretary Fall had suddenly grown affluent after the transactions in oil and that he had received money from both of the gentlemen who had closed advantageous bargains with the federal administration.

At the very time a court of law was supplying news on the personal progress of Mr. Fall, the Senate committee was adding new chapters to the oil scandal. In February, 1928, a son-in-law of Fall was forced to confess that Harry F. Sinclair had given him a large block of Liberty Bonds and a substantial sum in cash to be transferred to his father-in-law. But, the witness insisted, the money represented payment for an interest in Fall's ranch properties which were to be used as "a gentleman's riding and hunting club." For a moment the skeptics naturally assumed that there had been some connection between the transfer of bonds and cash to Fall and the oil lease that he had granted to Sinclair. In April, 1928, however, a trial jury thought otherwise. After two hours' deliberation it acquitted both Fall and Sinclair of the charge that they had conspired to defraud the Government of the United States. Although Respectability probably vented a sigh of relief, Senator Norris, commenting on the verdict, remarked for public benefit: "We ought to pass a law that no man worth $100,000,000 should be tried for a crime. That at least would make us consistent."

The clean bill of health which the acquittal of Fall and Sinclair seemed to give to the Party of Prosperity was marred for another brief season when the Senate committee of investigation pursued the oil matter a little further and drew into its dragnet Will Hays, a high counselor of the Party. Mr. Hays had been chairman of the Republican national committee during the campaign of 1920 and had served for a time as Postmaster General under President Harding. Before the case of Fall and Sinclair had been decided in their favor — while the presidential election of 1928 was coming into sight — the Senate committee discovered, through an examination of Mr. Hays, a trail leading from the oil transaction straight to the Republican national committee that had taken charge of the campaign for the election of President Coolidge four years previously. As Mr. Hays and his brother had been of counsel for one of Sinclair's oil corporations before the quest for normalcy began in 1920, and had maintained close personal and business relations with Sinclair subsequently, the discovery was of temporary inconvenience to the guardians of law and order.

On the witness stand in March, 1928, Mr. Hays admitted that he had received from Sinclair in 1923, after the oil scandal had broken, $185,000 in Liberty Bonds as a contribution toward discharging the deficit of the Republican treasury. This was in addition to the $75,000 in cash given by Sinclair to the Republican campaign fund of 1920. In the course of its investigation, the Senate committee also received testimony to the effect that Mr. Hays had turned some of the Liberty Bonds over to prominent Republicans in exchange for cash to be placed in the party chest; and that the Secretary of the Treasury, Andrew W. Mellon, when tendered a block of these bonds, had rejected them and handed his check to Hays for $50,000 as a gift. On the Senate witness stand, Secretary Mellon explained his rejection of the bonds on the ground that "they had come to me for a purpose which did not suit me," but added that he had not, at the time, deemed it necessary to inform the Senate committee of the transaction, merely because Sinclair's bonds had been presented to the fund of his party.

Having traced oil money to the Republican treasury, the Senate committee recalled Mr. Hays to the stand and asked him point blank some relevant questions. At a meeting held in December, 1923, the Republican national committee had made preparations for the Coolidge presidential campaign that was to start actively in a few months. Did the Republican directorate then know about the receipt of the large contribution to the party funds made by Sinclair, the oil magnate? Would Mr. Hays have ventured to tell the party committee about this contribution?

To such pertinent queries Mr. Hays replied in language befitting his state of mind: "I don't think that that situation would have — I hardly know. I don't know whether that would have — the status of that investigation [the Senate committee's] would have involved, if there had been a big contribution at that time, as you say — $135,000. I don't assume that the status of that investigation was such that it would have affected the minds of the committee. I don't know. Sinclair was regarded, I think, as a rich man. . . . They [the members of the Republican campaign committee] did not regard it as you [Senator Walsh] did. I assume that must be so. I think that time — but this is far-fetched, guessing at the minds of men, as Mr. Mellon said, but at that time I rather think, as he said, that the state of mind of the committee would probably have been one, while not of indifference, but not of great concern, because I don't think they knew much of about what you recognized or you thought was fact."

Although Mr. Hays' facile treatment of embarrassing questions left uncertain the degree of awareness among the members of the Republican committee, two impressive facts were placed on record : Liberty Bonds from Sinclair had helped to pay off the Republican deficit in 1923 and had aided in clearing the way for a vigorous campaign to elect President Coolidge to succeed himself the following year. The silence of President Coolidge on the point led many citizens to assume that he could have had no knowledge of the transaction, unless perchance, in the routine of things, Secretary Mellon had seen fit to give him some information concerning the business. So, in the generality of Republican opinion, the President was completely exonerated.

That President Coolidge had lost neither command nor prestige as a result of the inquiry into oil and campaign funds, that he was not to be deflected from his fixed policies by such revelations, was demonstrated later in the year during a contest over the disposal of federal water power at Muscle Shoals, where a great plant had been developed for war purposes during the Wilson administration. In accordance with his conception of sound economy, Coolidge proposed to turn this power over to private interests, openly and on terms not too onerous for profitable operation.

In response Congress completed on May 25, 1928, the passage of a joint resolution rejecting this program and substituting another of its own construction. The resolution provided for continued government ownership and operation of the power plant, the addition of new units, the granting of

preference to municipal and other public bodies in the sale
of current, and use of surplus power in the experimental
development of nitrates. But this was merely an empty
gesture against the enjoyment of the golden glow. As Congress adjourned shortly after the adoption of the joint resolution, President Coolidge had an opportunity to ignore it
under the ten-day rule of the Constitution, and he took full
advantage of his opportunity. He made no direct public
comment on the measure. He did not veto it and return it to
Congress for reconsideration. He simply smothered it with a
"pocket veto" and treated the protest of its sponsor, Senator
Norris, with disdain.

§

When the cloud of agrarian unrest, larger than any man's
hand, rose above the scene so perfect to all beneficiaries,
President Coolidge was equally successful in preventing a
deluge. Unquestionably this shadow was ill-boding. Since
the collapse of war prices in 1921, agriculture had been sinking toward or below the level of subsistence, despite the fair
prospects offered by the empire of business, banking, and
investment. Between 1920 and 1933 "one farm in every four
was sold for debts or taxes." The increase of tenancy, already
long in process, was speeded up to a startling momentum. If
the loss of homes and employment, if distress and discouragement, had any meaning in terms of humanity, the plight of
agriculture was certainly tragic. If urban economists knew
little about it and cared less, those financiers who watched
the failure of country banks by the hundreds every year
could not escape taking notice of rural ruin. Moreover there
were business leaders connected with farm implement industries who felt the jars of agricultural decline through their
skins if not through the study of statistical tables. Certainly
two among them, George N. Peek and General Hugh S.
Johnson, associated with the Moline Plow Company, knew
that plows could not be sold to bankrupt farmers and they
had agrarian sympathies besides. With whirlwind zeal a few

men of great energy threw themselves into the growing farmers' movement and helped bring it to a focus in the farm bloc in Congress.

By this time the tactics of the agrarians in their battle with capitalists had radically altered. Greenbackism had been smothered in 1876, free silver had been covered by an avalanche in 1896, and victory in those years had given Republican managers a strong sense of security. But inflation, attacks on banks, criticism of railway rates, and assaults on the trusts, which had brought nothing but defeats to agrarians, were now put aside by the agricultural bloc for a new weapon, for an onslaught on the whole philosophy and practice of business enterprise as sponsored by President Coolidge and the Republican directorate. Under the general theory of the business system, capitalists, farmers, and industrial workers on the whole received as their reward shares of the total product rightly and justly proportioned to their respective contributions. This assumption the agrarians now overruled. In fact at a farm conference called by Henry C. Wallace, the Secretary of Agriculture, in 1922, a resolution had been adopted directing Congress and the President to "take steps immediately to reëstablish a fair exchange value for all farm products with that of other commodities."

In short, powerful spokesmen of powerful agrarian interests repudiated the whole price mechanism of the capitalist system. They declared that in the exchanges of the so-called "free market" farmers did not receive in return for their produce an equivalent in commodity values; that the market was "rigged" against them; that capitalism was draining the wealth of the soil into the cities; that the policy of the Government facilitated the process of exploitation; and that the Government must intervene positively to put a stop to this perversion of fair price adjustments. The agrarian challenge on this level was persistent and pervasive.

And it had some support from economists of the schools, though rarely had American economists displayed the militancy of their British colleagues and demanded a complete system of laissez faire, including free trade among nations. All of them who had the courage of their convictions admitted that farmers were selling most of their great staple products at prices determined under the pressures of the world market and were buying their manufactures in the domestic market protected against foreign competition by high tariffs. That was obvious enough and the orthodox solution was to abolish the protective tariff. But agrarians knew that this entrenched privilege could not be broken, even if they desired to break it. So they adopted the view that they were robbed by a one-sided price mechanism and proceeded to formulate counter measures based on that interpretation of the American system.

Taking their cue from those protected manufacturers who sold most of their output at home behind the tariff wall and unloaded the rest abroad as best they could, the agrarians formulated their program, later incorporated in the McNary-Haugen bill, on a kindred philosophy, with variations in details. Like the beneficiaries of protective tariffs, they called upon the National Government for aid. They demanded the creation of a federal farm board endowed with large powers and supplied with a huge revolving fund of cash. With the aid of the board, they proposed to dump on foreign countries the "surplus" in several great staples and to force higher prices for the remainder in the home market. For the purpose of covering losses on sales abroad and putting a check on agricultural production, they devised an equalization fee to be paid by the farmers enjoying this form of federal assistance. To the utter surprise of urban philosophers who contemplated the pageant of industrial prosperity with satisfaction, the agrarians were able to push the McNary-Haugen bill through Congress in 1927. Metropolitan editors seemed unable to explain the phenomenon save in terms of agrarian fanaticism — as a mental disease. Recovering their self-possession, however, after the first outburst, they called upon the President to cure this evil at once and for all time by a resounding veto.

President Coolidge responded with alacrity in a long message condemning the bill in gross and detail and stamping it with a firm veto. The measure was unconstitutional, he declared. It was an adventure in government price fixing — "an economic fallacy from which this country has every right to be spared." The equalization fee deprived farmers of property without due process of law. It was, indeed, "a tax for the special benefit of particular groups" — differing apparently in this respect from the schedules of protective tariff acts. When Congress, unconvinced by the President's condemnation, repassed the McNary-Haugen bill the following year, with some changes in detail but not in principle, once more the President countered by a veto. This time he expressed his disapproval in language of increased acerbity, revealing the volcanic emotion with which he contemplated this form of government intervention in "natural economy." Yet, after the bill was vetoed, he doubtless looked upon the agrarian incident as one of the passing, if customary, inflammations of politics.

Having blocked the agrarian movement, assured domestic tranquillity, and protected American interests abroad, President Coolidge delivered a kind of farewell address to the world in a speech on Armistice day, 1928. America, he said, had saved Europe "from starvation and ruin," after the war. American citizens need not apologize "to anybody anywhere" for any failure to discharge their duty in defense of world liberty. The settlement of the war debts had been made on "the merciful principle" of ability to pay. In any event, Americans could doubtless "better afford to lose them than our debtors could afford not to pay them." As if addressing himself to advocates of the League of Nations, he declared tartly: "We have given of our counsel when asked." The United States had desired a limitation of armaments, but foreign governments would limit only the class of combat vessels "in which we were superior" while refusing limitations on the class in which they were superior. "We are against aggression and imperialism." Our overseas possessions, except the Canal Zone, are a burden, not an advantage. "We hold them not as a profit, but as a duty." Our course is set. We should pursue it "with due humility," and meet our responsibilities "in accordance with the requirements of conscience and righteousness."

§

Naturally it was in the cities that the Coolidge system shone with the brightest lustre. If agrarians grumbled over the President's veto of the farm relief bill, his popularity appeared undiminished among industrialists and financiers. In the cities it was generally agreed, in the spring of 1928, that he could have the renomination for the asking. However, as long ago as the previous summer, he had spoken the cryptic words: "I do not choose to run." Just what the words meant his friends were not sure and politicians had difficulty in interpreting them. Did he mean that he would not be a candidate again in any circumstances or merely that he did not choose to wage a personal contest for renomination? In the uncertainty, his senatorial opponents in February, 1928, adopted a resolution, proposed by Senator La Follette, protesting against a "third term." Yet so strong was the public sentiment for the President that his friends fostered a "draft Coolidge movement" even after he had requested local party managers to refrain from pressing his candidacy. Whether he genuinely preferred retirement to private life or whether he wished to set his party free to express itself on the point of another term, while secretly hoping that it would choose him on its own volition, remained among the secrets of State.

Whatever the meaning of the President's cryptic words, other Republicans certainly felt competent to wear his mantle. Among the aspirants Herbert Hoover, Secretary of Commerce since 1921, led from the very start. In the final test at the Republican convention he received the accolade as the man best fitted to preserve American institutions, sustain the empire, and continue the promotion of trade throughout the earth. Lionized as a great engineer, a successful man of business, a world-famous humanitarian, he also enjoyed the reputation of being an efficient administrator. Who among all the members of the President's entourage was better equipped to keep the heavens radiant and assure the unbroken progress of American civilization?

Moreover Mr. Hoover had the proper background for a telling appeal to forty million voters in a popular election: he symbolized the American tradition of the poor boy rising by his own initiative to the highest office in the gift of the nation. Born in Iowa, he wore the aura of the soil and typified the democracy of the Middle West. With this advantage, easily recalled for addresses to farmers, he had made his spiral ascent from lowly beginnings, through student days at Stanford University, to participation in professional and promotional enterprises connected with mines, railways, and metallurgy in Mexico, Italy, Great Britain, China, Russia, and other foreign countries. He had acquired a competence and was residing in England when the world war broke out in 1914. Either on his own motion or at the suggestion of the British government, Mr. Hoover accepted the chairmanship of a commission formed for the relief of Belgium and in that position he rapidly became a world figure. When the United States entered the war, he served the American Government in many capacities: as administrator, technician, economist, and adviser. Foreign governments also called upon him for aid.

Appointed Secretary of Commerce by President Harding shortly after the conclusion of the war, Mr. Hoover made that Department a beehive of activities associated with the promotion of business enterprise, and he sponsored a monument to his achievements in the form of a massive building to house its army of employees. Assisted by a huge staff of experts he collected information on "trade opportunities" abroad and disseminated it among American business men seeking foreign markets for their commodities. For the prosperity of domestic business he had been no less solicitous. At the same time he had escaped the animosity of agrarian leaders;

though it was privately known that he had no sympathy with farm relief of the McNary-Haugen type — that his opposition was positively violent — his official duties had not compelled him to inscribe his antipathy in black and white on the public record.

All nature seemed conspiring to make Herbert Hoover the ideal candidate to succeed President Coolidge. Here was an outstanding business man for a business empire, a vigorous exponent of prosperity through private liberty and government promotion, a man of world experience to deal with nations that had just renounced war as an instrument of national policy, a humanitarian famous from the Volga to the Yangtze. Who knew better how to keep the ways open for expanding trade, dissolve clouds of doubt and danger, and coöperate wisely with private and public beneficence in enhancing the values of American civilization? That many huckstering politicians in his party feared and disliked him, that the huge Vare-Grundy machine in Pennsylvania supported him, made little difference in the crucial hour when enthusiasm carried him to triumph in the Republican convention of 1928 on the very first ballot, with 837 votes out of 1089.

To reach the White House, however, Mr. Hoover had to run a gauntlet flanked by Democrats ardently engaged in promoting the interests of their candidate, Alfred E. Smith, governor of New York, astute in the ways of politics, and popular with the "liberals." For a while it seemed that Democratic leaders might seek victory in exploiting the malodorous oil scandals, but they soon put a soft pedal on such tactics. Neither President Coolidge nor his Secretary of Commerce, Mr. Hoover, had been directly involved in those diversions and the Democrats might find the bomb exploding in their own hands. After all, a stew was brewing in Tammany Hall and Mr. Smith had long been associated with that institution, though he had never been publicly involved in the turmoil and turpitude that had marked its history and was himself no more open to scandalous attacks than the

Republican candidate. A far greater handicap to Mr. Smith's campaign in a country overwhelmingly Protestant was his loyal membership in the Catholic Church. Even Southern Democrats found it hard to approve that religious affiliation and extremists were inclined to see in his nomination a new Popish plot.

But Mr. Smith had a certain advantage in the laurel of liberalism that wreathed his head. He had been a sponsor of social legislation in the state of New York, both as a member of the Assembly and as governor. With the help of expert advisers he had learned to clothe his natural sympathies for plain people in the language of social workers. He had defended and befriended public education. In times of public hysteria no official had been stancher in the defense of civil liberties. He had kept "red baiters" in leash and pardoned men accused of advocating radical doctrines. He had fought for the public ownership of water power sites in the Empire state, led in the reorganization of state administration, and displayed talents in the conduct of public business. Moreover he had a "humorous way with him" that caught the fancy of the crowds and, besides, he had been, from the start, an outspoken opponent of the prohibition imposed on the sale of alcoholic beverages.

Although the campaign offered to the people a choice between two distinguished personalities, the platforms of the two parties presented no sharp antithesis of policy. Both agreed that the lamp of prosperity must be kept burning and fed by the same kind of oil that had been regularly used with such success. On the old issue that had long divided the parties, namely, the tariff, there was almost perfect agreement, save in details of phraseology. The Republicans, of course, stood their ground. Echoing their old traditions, the Democrats spoke of tariff duties that would "permit effective competition, insure against monopoly, and at the same time provide a fair revenue." But these words were balanced immediately by the declaration that the measure of the tariff rate must be the difference between the cost of production at home and abroad, "with adequate safeguard for the wages of the American laborer."

In his campaign speeches Mr. Smith insured business men against "any sudden or drastic revolution in our economic system which would cause business upheaval and popular distress," and promised to protect "to the very limit . . . legitimate business enterprise as well as American labor from ruinous competition of foreign-made goods produced under conditions far below the American standard." As if to bind the assurance, the Democrats selected as chairman of their national committee John J. Raskob, a rich industrialist who poured his own money into the contest.

Of the vexatious question raised by the agrarians, the parties were wary. The Democratic platform indulged in generalities on the point and the Republicans were also circumspect. But during the campaign Mr. Smith approved the principles of the McNary-Haugen bill, including the equalization fee. Though Mr. Hoover disliked everything savoring of the agrarians' plan, including a plank endorsing farm relief which had been defeated in the Republican convention, he promised to farmers higher tariffs and the creation of a farm board empowered to deal with surpluses in some fashion. In so doing, he did not surrender, however, his opposition to crop and price controls; he simply gave his supporters in the Republican party "talking points" for the campaign.

Nor did a definite contradiction appear in the positions of the candidates and parties on the irksome question of prohibition. Both platforms promised bone-dry enforcement as demanded by reverence for the Constitution. But Mr. Smith telegraphed the Democratic convention, after the nomination was safely clinched, that he favored "fundamental changes" in the prohibition laws, which, while preventing the return of the saloon, would "secure real temperance, respect for law, and eradication of existing evils." To all such irritants Mr. Hoover responded, in language a bit vague, by declaring himself against the repeal of the prohibition amendment and promising an inquiry into abuses and methods of correction.

So it seemed that, while the two candidates agreed on the merits of the golden glow and on the necessity of warding off all storm clouds, Mr. Smith believed in enlivening the scene by assuring alcoholic beverages to all participants in American civilization who cared to establish psychological conditions favorable to a fuller enjoyment of its benefits.

Although no statistical analysis could separate the "causes" for the division of ballots in the election, it was significant that Mr. Smith carried two states in the North, Massachusetts and Rhode Island, in which the Catholic vote was numerically powerful; and lost all the "normally" Democratic states in the South, except Alabama, Arkansas, Georgia, Louisiana, Mississippi, and South Carolina. Superficially, the election had the appearances of a Republican and Protestant landslide. Yet an examination of details revealed the strength of Governor Smith's popularity. Fifteen million votes were cast for him as against 8,300,000 polled by the Democratic candidate, John W. Davis, and the 15,700,000 votes gathered by President Coolidge in the election of 1924. From one point of view this was an immense personal tribute. The huge plurality against Governor Smith was doubtless due, in a large measure, to the unusual outpouring of hitherto negligent voters. While exact information was not forthcoming on the motives of voters, that manifestation could be ascribed with some justification to the personal qualities of Mr. Hoover, to his vigorous stand against repealing the Prohibition Amendment, and to the general belief that the existing guardianship of prosperity should not be disturbed. As to the perpetuation of the golden glow Mr. Smith could offer no more assurance than Mr. Hoover; indeed, not as much assurance.

§

On assuming Coolidge's place in the White House, President Hoover likewise beheld alluring prospects of "prosperity more extensive and peace more permanent." During the campaign, he had seemed to be aware of poverty and distress

in the United States, even under the high fulfillment of industrial success, and had expressed the hope that during his
administration the remaining blots on the economic landscape would be removed by a continuance of Republican
policies thus far so happily advanced at home and abroad.
To this expectation he had adverted in his inaugural address:
"The large purpose of our economic thought should be to
establish more firmly stability and security of business and
employment, and thereby remove poverty still further from
our borders."

If that statement of the case did not concede the existence
of dire poverty within the United States, it recognized spec-
tral forms somewhere on the borders. And in keeping with
this admission President Hoover early promised, and in fact
did later invite, the coöperation of experts in economics,
medicine, public health, and social work with a view to perfecting "the means by which government can be adapted to
human service," especially in the "development of those processes which directly affect public health, recreation, education, and the home." Indeed all through his speeches, messages, and addresses, he emphasized the responsibility of civic
leaders and public officials for strengthening the economy and
improving the social organization upon which political and
economic institutions rest. Though often regarded as a mere
heir of Coolidge policies, President Hoover was a thinker and
actor in his own right. After six years of relative quiescence,
save in matters of negation, an unwonted stir in the White
House followed his inauguration in 1929.

Nevertheless the broad frame of political philosophy within
which President Hoover confined his operations of thought
and action in official affairs did not differ essentially from that
of his predecessor. He opposed the agrarian contention that
the price mechanism of business enterprise robbed farmers of
wealth to which they were entitled by economic efficiency
and social justice. As Secretary of Commerce, he had joined
the Chief Executive in promoting the expansion of American
trade and investment in all parts of the world with the aid of

government agencies. As President, he retained his faith in capitalism and foreign trade. He also shared the doctrine advanced by Coolidge that American dollars invested abroad and American citizens residing there were as much a part of the nation as if in the United States and were, therefore, entitled to the protection of the National Government. In the main, policies so conceived and carried out had brought and would maintain prosperity, he believed; if refined and made more scientific they would drive poverty further from American shores. But beyond such forms of intervention, assistance, and protection, in his opinion, the Government should not go. Other activities savored of "state socialism" which he spurned root and branch. Hoover's rejection of crop control in agricultural legislation and his veto of a new Muscle Shoals bill providing for government ownership and operation made his position clear beyond dispute. In other words, business men could count upon the tenacity of President Hoover's resolve to uphold what they called "free enterprise."

Toward other social questions Hoover did not assume, however, a negative attitude. Personally and as a national leader, he lent official encouragement to the efforts of private associations attacking problems of poverty, sickness, and delinquency. He created and sponsored conferences or committees on unemployment, medical care, law enforcement, economic tendencies, and social trends. On all types of civic coöperation, sometimes called "voluntary socialism," he bestowed his blessings. "Our people," he said in his first inaugural, "have in recent years developed a new-found capacity for coöperation among themselves to effect high purposes in public welfare. It is an advance toward the highest conception of self-government."

Moreover such coöperation, he thought, should receive the active support of government. "Progress is born of coöperation in the community, not from governmental restraints. The government should assist and encourage these movements of collective self-help by itself coöperating with them."

The Department of Commerce under his leadership had affiliated itself with business interests in innumerable relations. Now, as chief executive of the nation, President Hoover proposed to foster private associations and to assist them in promoting the general welfare. Quite rightly was it said at the time that the President had "the sociological outlook" and in itself this marked a certain change in the intellectual climate of the White House, if indeed not a transition to something else.

The official measures which expressed President Hoover's scheme of political thought at the outset of his administration were aimed at continuing domestic and foreign policies along lines set by his predecessors. Since the opening of the Harding regime, the Republicans had been making legislative concessions to farmers, amplifying the loan and credit system, and regulating market and stockyard practices. During his campaign Hoover had offered something more. Whatever interpretation had been put upon his words, he meant no positive government interference with production and prices. That would have been to fly in the face of "the natural and free price mechanism" upon which prosperity was supposed to depend for its very existence and perpetuity. His creed the President made perfectly plain to the special session of Congress called in the spring of 1929 : "We must not undermine initiative. There should be no fee or tax imposed upon the farmer. No governmental agency should engage in the buying and selling and price fixing of products."

The outcome of congressional deliberations, amid which the administration overcame an agrarian bloc in the Senate, was the Agricultural Marketing Act of June, 1929. The law provided for a federal farm board, conferred upon it large powers, and placed in its hand a revolving fund of half a billion dollars. Among other things the board was authorized to lend money to coöperative marketing associations, to aid in coördinating the work of such associations, and to set up "stabilizing corporations" for the purpose of storing, holding, and marketing certain commodities in the interest of higher price levels. In establishing this machinery, President Hoover and his supporters rejected the old agrarian demand for some form of crop control designed to prevent the ruin of the whole structure by a flood of "surplus" commodities.

Given the nature of the new administrative machine and its powers, only one favorable condition could have prevented a failure and the waste of the half-a-billion dollars, namely, an improvement of agricultural prices on the world market. That improvement did not occur. On the contrary farm production remained on a high level, the prices of produce fell rather than advanced, and the heroic, almost frantic, efforts of able men on the farm board were in vain. Millions of dollars designed to stabilize the market passed into the hands of private operators who were little if anything more than speculators. After a year's experience with the attempt to raise prices without reference to supply, it became painfully evident in Washington that the farm board was stuck fast in a maze. Soon agrarians were pointing to their former prophecies and girding themselves for a new law designed to combine crop control with price adjustment. The income of farmers in 1931 was far far below the return of the previous year.

Second on the program was the tariff. Republican leaders had declared that the rates were not high enough and during the campaign of 1928 industrialists had paid large sums of money into the Republican campaign fund in lively hopes of favors to come. Nor were they without some justification in events. Their European competitors, partly with the aid of American investors and bankers, had rehabilitated their industries and were prepared for a vigorous price war. New times, new circumstances.

In his campaign, Hoover had advocated a special session of Congress to make "limited changes in the tariff" and deal with agricultural relief. When Congress took up the revision of the customs duties, however, it did not confine itself to limited changes. In accordance with historic practice, the framing and adoption of the Hawley-Smoot tariff bill was accompanied by bitter wrangling in Congress. As usual, Democrats loudly condemned upward revisions in general and voted discreetly on particular items, such as sugar, textiles, and steel. In the end the bill made 1125 changes in the existing revenue law, of which 890 were upward, ranging on the average from thirty-one to thirty-four per cent.

When the bill finally emerged from Congress in June, 1930, it was greeted by protests in many quarters. Finance capitalists wondered how foreign debtors could force interest and installments over the high barriers thus erected. A large body of professors, offended by its schedules, filed a formal objection against this "perversion" of economic principles deemed inviolable. Undoubtedly the measure was for the President an unpleasant dose and after signing the bill he issued a studied defense of his action that savored of apology. But whatever Hawley and Smoot thought of his plea in abatement, they could rejoice that their tariff law was placed on the books.

After helping to throw the weight of the Government on the side of higher protection for industrialists, on their plea that it was necessary for a continuance of prosperity, President Hoover turned to applying another axiom of his economic philosophy, namely, that of keeping the Government out of any business that would yield a profit. The occasion for a practical demonstration of this axiom arose in connection with a power problem inherited from the previous administration at Muscle Shoals. When the goblin of "public power" reappeared, the President immediately bent his efforts to promoting the private ownership and operation of the government's property in the Tennessee Valley. If that end could not be achieved he was determined to prevent, at all costs, the production and distribution of electricity by direct government action. Any such step, the President insisted, would imprint the bar sinister of socialism upon the unblemished escutcheon of American politics. Yet the task to which he set himself called for watchfulness and labor on his part, for Senator Norris was augmenting, day by day, the forces resolved upon public ownership and operation of the power resources and facilities in controversy.

In this struggle, President Hoover's burden was increased by the stubbornness of the men whose enterprise he sought to favor: the price offered for Muscle Shoals by private capitalists had been so low and the terms of purchase so onerous that they annoyed even conservative Senators who shared Hoover's economic philosophy. His task was further complicated by revelations brought out at periodic hearings before the Federal Trade Commission and incorporated in the ensuing reports — revelations which dealt with the propaganda and lobbying tactics of the electrical utility concerns. It was shown that they had secretly subsidized newspapers and slipped their doctrines quietly into editorial columns. They had surreptitiously hired leaders in women's clubs, college professors, and publicity experts to promote their cause. To the chests of political parties they had contributed huge sums for election purposes. The "red badge" of communism they had deliberately pinned upon their opponents to discredit men and women who refused to accept their program wholesale. Some of their undercover activities were so gross that the more reputable utility magnates were themselves flustered; and metropolitan newspapers, normally inclined to belittle congressional inquiries, felt compelled to deplore such behavior.

Making effective use of these revelations, Senator Norris delivered in the upper house documented speeches that brought new recruits to his side; men accustomed to oppose his program now shrank from the appearance of evil which even seeming to favor the utilities implied. Under his leadership, Congress again passed, in 1931, a resolution providing for government operation of the power plants in case they could not be leased to private concerns within a year and on specific terms. For a moment the radiance of the golden glow was overcast.

While the Muscle Shoals measure was still pending at the capital, President Hoover made a public statement in which he treated the whole business as trivial and chid the national legislature for giving so much time to a matter of such slight importance. Having failed to defeat the resolution in Congress, he resorted to Coolidge tactics and applied the veto when it came to his desk. The bill, he said, would help to destroy "the initiative and enterprise" of the American people — the very source of prosperity and progress. The conditions imposed would make it impossible to find a responsible lessee among the concerns that might bid for the property. Enormous and unknown expenses would be involved in modernizing the plants. The resolution had provided that members of the government control board must believe in the wisdom and feasibility of the objects contemplated by the proposal. This, insisted the President, would make it impossible to find worthy men to accept positions on the board. Having disparaged and denounced the whole project, Hoover countered it with a proposal of his own. He advised Congress to authorize the creation of a commission empowered to lease the Muscle Shoals plant "in the interests of the local community and agriculture generally."

Taken in connection with the contemporary revelations by the Federal Trade Commission, the argument and tone of the President's message raised the political temperature in Congress, but not enough votes were marshaled to pass the measure over his veto. His opponents could merely prepare to take the issue to the country in the coming congressional election.

Although Hoover pleased business interests by signing the Hawley-Smoot tariff bill and by opposing government operation of power plants using public waters, he was not an extremist. He recognized that organized labor had a place in American economy and consequently set his approval on the Norris-La Guardia anti-injunction bill in March, 1932. This project had been no part of the official Republican program, although it bore the names of Republicans. In precise language the Act declared that employees should be free from coercion by employers and should have the right to bargain collectively through agents of their own choice. It outlawed "yellow dog" contracts in labor relations — contracts binding employees not to join trade unions. It forbade federal courts to issue restraining orders or injunctions contrary to the public policy so pronounced or contrary to any of the particularized stipulations of the Act, including provisions for open hearings in which the rights of employees were to be safeguarded. Carefully drawn with the aid of legal experts, this law marked an important stage in the development of federal labor legislation in the interests of collective bargaining. As such President Hoover accepted it, despite the protests of certain manufacturers who had worked against it openly or covertly during its progress through Congress. It did not, of course, "put the Government into business," but it lent government aid to the promotion of collective bargaining in business and was therefore somewhat alien to official normalcy. Nor was it exactly calculated to sustain the pristine liberty of enterprise.

§

In the field of foreign relations deemed normal, President Hoover, generally speaking, was loyal to the policies of previous Republican administrations. Like President Coolidge, he disclaimed the intention of overt aggression against any Latin republic to the south. Just before his inauguration he made a good-will tour of South America and after assuming office he took steps in the direction of friendly cooperation. From Nicaragua, he withdrew all the marines, except a "nucleus" engaged in training native guards. In 1930 a commission was sent to study conditions in Haiti which had been under American control since Wilson's administration. On the basis of its report Hoover announced that the natives would be aided in establishing "self-government" and that in due course diplomatic forms would be substituted for dominance through armed forces. Notwithstanding a number of trying incidents in relations with

Mexico, Hoover insisted on pacific adjustments in every case. Rattling the sword was foreign to his nature and poor economic policy in addition. To allay any possible doubts, his Secretary of State, Henry L. Stimson, publicly declared that the Monroe Doctrine, "far from being an assertion of suzerainty over our sister republics, was an assertion of their individual rights as independent nations." It was only by indirection, under the Platt Amendment, that the State Department sustained the cruel and despotic regime of Señor Machado in Cuba where American bankers and investors had enormous loans and credits at stake.

In respect of the Far East no equivocation was permitted. In that sphere, the doctrines of empire and intervention bequeathed by Admiral Mahan, Theodore Roosevelt, John Hay, and Henry Cabot Lodge were preserved and developed. When Congress enacted a bill in 1932 providing for the contingent independence of the Philippines, Hoover interposed with a veto. When the measure was repassed by the requisite two-thirds majority, he must have found pleasure in seeing it rejected by the Philippine legislature. Speaking of the Philippines, Warren Gamaliel Harding had said that "we ought to go on [there] with the same thought that impelled Him who brought a plan of salvation to the earth. . . . He gathered his disciples about him and said, 'Go ye and preach the gospel to all nations of the earth.'" In his veto message Hoover re-echoed these sentiments.

When Japanese armed forces invaded Manchuria in 1931, tore the province away from China, and proceeded to organize a puppet state under the dominion of Tokyo, that other formula of American policy in the Orient, the Open Door, confirmed by the Nine-Power Pact of 1922, was invoked by the Hoover administration. In January, 1932, the Secretary of State, Henry L. Stimson, dispatched to Japan a formal note calling attention to the Nine-Power Pact which declared respect for the administrative and territorial integrity of China and reaffirmed the doctrine of equal trading privileges. The note, in addition, curtly informed the Japanese foreign office that the United States "does not intend to recognize any situation, treaty, or agreement which may be brought about by means contrary to the covenants and obligations of the Pact of Paris" — the Kellogg renunciation of war as an instrument of national policy.

This stroke of state won hearty approval from two sources. The emphasis on Open Door interventionism appealed to American economic interests in the Far East and the ringing invocation of the Peace Pact expressed the pacific sentiments so widely entertained in the United States. The combination was powerful. Yet it was thwarted by the governments of Great Britain and France which failed to support the American position. The League of Nations toyed nervously with the dilemma and ended with a weak gesture. In the circumstances Japan defied the State Department of the United States, withdrew from the League of Nations, and held fast to her pound of flesh. Yet President Hoover laid claim to an achievement: "Above all I have projected a new doctrine into international affairs, the doctrine that we do not and never will recognize title to possession of territory gained in violation of the peace pacts."

From the Coolidge regime the Hoover administration had inherited an inflexible opposition to the recognition of Soviet Russia, a confidence in the approaching collapse of its economic system, and a tenacious will to avoid lending countenance to its ideology. This disapproval of Russia's attitude toward private property was reinforced by objections to the default on her foreign debts. To the Hughes formula of official non-intercourse with Soviet Russia, Hoover steadfastly adhered — a course which affected relations with Europe in general and particular.

The Coolidge administration had also transmitted a friendly interest in the World Court and a program for joining that tribunal, the appropriate papers for which President Hoover laid before the Senate, without however pressing hard for ratification. Retaining an interest in the

League of Nations, which sprang presumably from his warm
attachment to the concert of powers, the President made a
number of amiable overtures in that direction. In proceedings of the League which bore immediately upon American
economic interests or upon humane proposals, he participated
through official or unofficial delegates or observers. In
fact he went as far as he could, safely, in helping to uphold
the prestige of the League and sharing its counsels, while
being careful to disavow, in the language of Harding's time,
all American entanglements.

The crowning act of the Hoover administration in the
line of normalcy for foreign relations was the negotiation
of the London treaty of 1930 applying naval limitations to
cruisers, submarines, destroyers, and airplane carriers as
well as to the battleships restricted by the Washington
conference. An effort to accomplish this design had been
made at Geneva three years before, while Coolidge was at
the head of affairs, but that conference was unable to reach
an agreement. At Washington in 1922 the United States
had sacrificed ships. At Geneva an adjustment required
sacrifice on the part of Great Britain, and British naval
experts would have none of it. Their obstinacy, coupled with
that of American admirals and the propaganda of American
shipbuilding interests, eventuated in a deadlock, while
Japan looked on with Oriental satisfaction. But in 1930 circumstances were more propitious. The Labor premier, Ramsay Macdonald, was then directing the British government
and, after a personal visit from the British prime minister,
Hoover took the steps necessary to assure a conference in
London.

More astute than Wilson had been in 1918, Hoover associated with the American delegation two powerful Senators
— David A. Reed of Pennsylvania and Joseph Robinson
of Arkansas, leader on the Democratic side. After about
four months of haggling at London, the American, British,
and Japanese delegations arrived at an agreement respecting
cruisers, destroyers, and submarines for a term of six years.

In addition they revised the Washington settlement by suspending the replacement program and adopting a holiday for battleship construction until 1936. To this phase of the naval holiday, France and Italy also agreed.

Taken collectively, the details of the treaty marked merely a possible restriction on the expansion of naval expenditures, not a reduction in accordance with the expectations of peace advocates. But in explaining the agreement to the country, President Hoover expressed deep satisfaction: "The most vital feature of its great accomplishments for peace is the final abolition of competition in naval arms between the greatest naval powers and the burial of the fears and suspicions which have been the constant product of rival warship construction."

Nevertheless, in carrying through his program for limiting sea armaments and easing international tension for a freer flow of world commerce, Hoover found it necessary to overcome powerful shipping and naval interests at home. When the London treaty was laid before the country and the Senate for consideration, the customary gale blew against this "surrender to Great Britain," this "betrayal of American interests." The Hearst press, abetted by a few Senators including Hiram Johnson, was especially scurrilous. The Navy League sprang into unwonted activity. It issued broadsides against the treaty, and came very near to charging President Hoover with treason in "jeopardizing American national security." The passions of the Daughters of the American Revolution were also enlisted against the project. With this opposition a number of American admirals were in hearty accord. If their position forbade them to come out openly in the press, they took full advantage of the opportunity to aid their friends quietly and to voice their dissent at hearings opened by Senate committees. Owing to the volume of vocal and printed protests, the outlook for the treaty was gloomy at first and the Senate adjourned without acting upon the question of ratification.

Then Hoover and his supporters brought their strategy

to bear on the conflict. The President called a special session of the Senate to meet in July for the consideration of the
London treaty. Hearings were held on the proposal by the
Senate committee on foreign relations and the Senate committee on naval affairs; and the prime interests and ideas on
both sides were thoroughly explored. Under the questioning
of Senator David A. Reed the issue was narrowed to its
substance : the London treaty fell short of the Navy Board's
requirements "only with respect to the armament of three
ships" and the armament of these three ships "with six-
inch guns instead of eight-inch guns."

When Admiral Jones insisted that the point of the eight-
inch guns was "vital," Senator Reed confronted the Admiral
with a letter he had written a year before declaring that
"there are conditions under which a six-inch gun unit would
be of more value than an eight-inch gun unit." Additional
probing disclosed the fact that the advantages of either type
of unit would depend largely upon the weather and the
fighting conditions, which no Admiral could possibly foresee.
When Admiral Chase opposed the treaty before the Senate Committee and insisted upon discussing technicalities,
Senator Reed bored into the Admiral's mentality. The
Senator asked the Admiral whether he had ever commanded
the fleet. The answer was, "No." He asked the Admiral
whether he had ever been to sea on an eight-inch gun cruiser
or seen one at target practice. Again the Admiral answered,
"No." Then Senator Reed put to him the question : "Do
you know how thick the armor on its turrets is ?" When the
Admiral replied, "I do," the Senator shot back : "How thick
is it on the *Salt Lake City* class ?" Thereupon the Admiral
had to confess : "I do not recall the exact thickness now,
sir." Although this type of inquisition may not have been
entirely just to the admirals, it helped to weaken their prestige and prepare the way for the ratification of the treaty
by the Senate.

From another angle, broadsides were let loose upon the
opponents of the London treaty. In 1929, while President

Hoover was preparing for the London conference, it became known through a suit at law brought by one W. B. Shearer against shipbuilding companies that he had been a kind of paid lobbyist for them at the Geneva conference two years previously. In September the President publicly condemned propaganda designed to "create international distrust and hate," called upon shipping interests for an explanation, directed the Attorney General to consider taking action in the matter, and invited a Senate committee to go "to the very bottom" of the strange business. Under a Senate resolution a subcommittee of the committee on naval affairs started an inquiry into the activities of Shearer that ran through the autumn and winter, and brought powerful personalities and interests out into the open.

The Senate inquisitors were none too keen in their searching and repeatedly failed to press revealing questions, but they spread upon the public record one of the most unsavory stories in the long history of American scandals. The investigation showed that shipbuilding concerns and allied interests had hired Shearer to represent them at Geneva, that he had done all he could to defeat any settlement there, and that after the breakdown of the conference he had been employed as lobbyist general for big naval appropriations and merchant marine subsidies. Sworn testimony disclosed Shearer preparing propaganda articles for the Republican campaign committee in 1928, calling peace advocates traitors, attacking Charles E. Hughes as a betrayer of his country, writing speeches for representatives of the American Legion and the Daughters of the American Revolution in aid of a big navy and merchant marine, serving William Randolph Hearst as a propagandist for $2,000 a month, and maintaining confidential contacts with the Navy Department. Under direct questioning, distinguished figures in shipping circles — Charles M. Schwab, E. G. Grace, and C. L. Bardo, soon to be President of the Manufacturers Association, for example — twisted, turned, confessed inability to remember, or sought to put disreputable actions in the best possible guise.

Incidentally the Shearer inquiry threw the spot-light on the interests that had lobbied for the Jones-White Merchant Marine Bill enacted during the Coolidge administration. In that "enterprise" Shearer had been employed and had served his employers faithfully. On the record of the Senate subcommittee was placed a letter from C. L. Bardo, vice president of the New York Ship Building Company, which put the lobby costs for this bill at $150,000, including $30,000 for "publicity and advertising," "$26,000 for "services of experts," and $23,000 for "hotel expenses in Washington." Speaking of the undercover achievement, Mr. Bardo said in his letter: "This activity was carried on in the interests of the shipper, shipbuilder, shipowner, and suppliers of materials used in ship construction." Since heavy expenditures had been incurred in securing legislation advantageous to these interests, Mr. Bardo called upon several beneficiaries to pay the bill: for instance, the General Electric Company, the Bath Iron Works, the Worthington Pump and Machinery Company, and the American Brown Boveri Electric Corporation.

All this and more, combined with Senator Reed's grilling of naval experts, temporarily aroused a certain moral indignation in the country and facilitated the ratification of the London Naval Treaty. On July 21, 1930, the Senate set its seal of approval on the document by a vote of fifty-eight to nine. "It will renew again the faith of the world in the moral forces of good-will and patient negotiation," said Hoover, "as against the blind forces of suspicion and competitive armament."

§

For nearly ten years, it so came about, great business interests, to whose ingenuity and initiative the prosperity of the golden glow was attributed by admiring editors and publicists, pursued their course of "free enterprise" without encountering insurmountable barriers. They demanded higher tariffs and their demand was granted. They called for a material reduction in the heavy taxes on large incomes, to release money for the expansion of industry, and their argument was accepted. They besought the Government to refrain from producing electric power on the public domain and along navigable waters and distributing it directly to consumers, and their beseeching was heeded. Under the easy laws of indulgent states, they formed corporations, investment trusts, and holding companies, ever larger and more intricate in structure; they issued stocks and bonds at pleasure within the mild terms of generous legislation — without submitting their accounts and valuations to the scrutiny of federal inquisitors. They wanted to be let alone; and in all those years not a single major statute adversely affecting their rights of property was written in the law books of the Union.

Abroad as well as at home, business interests enjoyed the favor and protection of a benevolent government. Throughout the insular possessions of the American empire they reaped the benefits of preferential tariffs drawn against alien competitors. Peace they deemed necessary to the pursuits of civilian trade; for nearly ten years peace reigned; and it was sealed by an almost universal pact renouncing war as an instrument of national policy. Soldiers, sailors, and marines guarded their outposts in troublesome places beyond the jurisdiction of the United States. Ships from a powerful navy sailed the waters of seven oceans fulfilling the pledge of the Navy Department to keep the sea lanes open and promote American commerce. A corps of alert agents from the Department of Commerce scoured every nook and cranny of the world in the service of business interests, hunting opportunities for them to sell goods, lend money, and invest in foreign mills, mines, and stores. If difficulties arose, willing ministers, ambassadors, and consuls intervened on behalf of American nationals. A representative of the State Department spoke truly when he declared to an assembly of exporting merchants that the Secretary of Commerce, Mr. Hoover, "is your advance agent," and the Secretary of State, Mr. Kellogg, "is your attorney"; and he might well have added that the navy is a guarantee that your advance agent and attorney will speak as men having authority even in the distant places of the earth. In the economy of things, those who were let alone in their ways had eager and obedient servants, when, in any hour of stress, they needed aid and protection under the power and renown of the Republic. Not without visible evidence and plain reason did they pronounce their world good and look forward with confidence to its perpetuity.

CHAPTER II

Dissolutions

EARLY in the autumn of 1929, while Congress was seeking to strengthen the colors of the golden glow by raising the tariff still higher, out of the sky came flashes of lightning and rolls of thunder that were heard around the world and harrowed the guardians of the National Shrine with "fear and wonder." On September 5, there was a wild break in stocks on the New York Exchange; and Roger Babson, watcher of business indices, predicted that "sooner or later" a general crash would bring a decline ranging from sixty to eighty points. September 24, news of another sharp explosion in the market sped over the wires; the next day a check was announced; three days later a steep downward slide sent alarms in every direction. September 29, Arthur Cutten, the great plunger in speculations, a specimen from ancient times, issued a proclamation that he was "a bull on stocks" and that even twelve billion dollars in brokers' loans for speculative purposes "would not be unduly large." October 3 and 4, occurred the largest breaks of the year, followed by a few days of hesitation and a cable from London in which

Charles E. Mitchell, of the National City Bank, exclaimed in dulcet tones: "American markets generally are now in a healthy condition." The report was an exaggeration. When on October 16 a committee of the Investment Bankers Association admitted that speculation had reached a danger point and that many stocks were far above their intrinsic values, industrial and utility equities swept downward in an avalanche. For a week rallies and breaks alternated, with a drop ranging from five to ninety-six points on October 23. A great fright was creeping over the realm of high finance and brokers were calling for more margins as selling orders poured in from the provinces.

At eleven o'clock on the morning of Thursday, October 24, came a shock that was soon felt in the four corners of the earth: for a number of stocks listed on the New York Exchange no buyers could be found at any price. And on all securities, including these very stocks, member banks of the Federal Reserve system had outstanding loans to brokers and dealers amounting to $6,634,000,000 — a sum larger than the average volume of money in circulation throughout the United States during the preceding year. Evidently in this hour the "situation" was portentous for the bankers themselves. For months they had sat in their offices lending money for the great game at the National Shrine, accepting as security the stocks in which manipulations were carried on. Now the very paper in their hands was swiftly becoming valueless. But if they called their loans suddenly, they would accelerate the precipitous decline of "values" already under way.

They were, in other words, caught between two fires and some ingenious action was necessary if they were to save themselves. About noon Thomas Lamont, of the J. P. Morgan Company, summoned the representatives of four great banks to the throne room at Broad and Wall Streets, and allowed news of the event to be flashed to the press and brokers' houses from the center to the circumference of the American empire. Were Lords of Creation to assume dominion, stop the downward course of stocks, and rescue the sinking? With bated breath, victims of the pinch awaited an answer.

About 1:15 of that very day, it arrived, or something taken for an answer came. With a firm stride, Richard Whitney, floor operator for the Morgan Company, walked to the trading post for United States Steel in the Exchange and bid 205 for a large order of Steel shares, which stood at the moment at 193½. The effect was electric. Reports of the order ran out over the wires to newspapers and brokers from one end of the country to the other. Before the calming effect of this news had passed, floor traders under instructions from bankers began to make offers for stocks that in the morning of that day had found few buyers or none at all. With the swiftness of wind, stocks rallied.

A miracle had taken place under the command of the masters of economic destiny. So, at least, it appeared. After a meeting of the Federal Reserve Board in the afternoon, attended by Secretary Mellon, the Treasury announced that "business is fundamentally sound" and that the troubles were due to "bear raids." From far and wide reverberated echoes so uniform that they seemed inspired. The financial wizard of the Cleveland Trust Company, Leonard P. Ayres, poured into eager ears the explanation that the crash was a "security panic, with no economic basis. . . . A rally tomorrow is in order." From his point of observation and interest, Charles E. Mitchell saw "nothing to worry about." Not to be outdone in the transmission of glad tidings, President Hoover added his reassurance: "The fundamental business of the country, that is, production and distribution of commodities, is on a sound and prosperous basis." With a confidence omniscient, the president of the Equitable Trust issued a ukase: "There will be no repetition of the break of yesterday. I have no fear of another comparable decline."

Indeed the tone and unanimity of the auspicious chorus could not have been more perfect if all had been prearranged. The president of the American International Corporation, as if expressing the surmises of sound business everywhere, gave special thanks: "I think we are all indebted to the four gentlemen who met on the corner yesterday and through their action steadied the whole situation." In an oration that filled two solid columns of print, Charles Schwab explained that the country was prosperous and that the steel business was good. From Philadelphia came a solemn confirmation by Samuel Vauclain, of the Baldwin Locomotive Company; from Chicago, the corroboration of George M. Reynolds, of the Continental Illinois Bank and Trust Company. To such reports ostentatiously spread over the pages of the next morning's papers was added an authentic statement that a consortium of six members, representing great banks, had been formed, not to push up prices, "but to furnish a cushion of purchasing power against the recurrence of any such condition as Thursday." With the perspicacity customary in such circumstances, newspapers and stock dealers spoke affectionately of "the Big Six" as "Saviors of the Market." Heaving sighs of relief, brokers went about their business as usual on Friday morning, October 25. The market steadied and rose.

For the unsophisticated public, including brokers and speculators, the marvelous act of prestidigitation had been exhilarating, if mystifying. The Lords of Creation were in their places after all. But just what had the Big Six done? When questioned by eager reporters, Thomas Lamont replied that he did not know, although in the following January he allowed some inklings to escape. Whatever it was, the possible results became evident in a very few days after their act of thaumaturgy. As the market steadied, the bankers concerned had an opportunity to call in enough loans to save their margins of security and thus avoid heavy losses themselves, while slowly feeding into the markets the stocks they had bought, perhaps at a profit for the participants. Whether they took full advantage of their opportunity the records of history did not disclose. But one thing was certain. If "Saviors of the Market," they were not "Saviors of Mankind," for they soon refused to hold the promised "cushion" under falling prices. When the roar of the storm was renewed four days afterward, they cast off the role as "Saviors," even of the Market, stepped swiftly aside, and let the hurricane rage. Had they merely saved their own skins on October 24? Were they really Lords of Creation after all? Or were they lords who deliberately declined to exercise their prerogatives? Or were they merely bannerets and Sancho Panzas? Had the rejoicing over their feat been merely the conquest of reason by delusion? The haruspex of the National Shrine made no reply. On October 29, events vouchsafed the answers.

On that day, shortly after the New York Stock Exchange opened, the bottom almost fell out of the buyers' market. Only sellers appeared in force and they dumped hundreds and thousands of shares into this well-nigh bottomless pit at any prices that were offered. Down, down, down, dropped prices as the throng of brokers milled and shouted around the posts of the specialists who were supposed to have buyers for all comers. Out in the streets early editions of newspapers announced the calamity. Worried by the scare-headed reports, small holders and large rushed to increase the flood of selling orders. Over humming telephones brokers called upon their customers for more margins before it was too late. As the volume of business swelled through the day, wires were blocked with messages that could not be delivered in time to save speculators from a complete sell-out. When at last the gong rang out the closing hour, stock tickers were far behind in their reports, brokers' offices were in a pandemonium, and efforts to reach distracted victims with final news were still being made, in vain. It seemed, to use Edmund Burke's phrase, that "the architects of ruin" had completed their work. In the tumult of the day a record turnover of 16,410,000 shares was registered and the average price of fifty stock leaders fell almost forty points. Amid the repercussions of the explosion, bankers and brokers gathered in little groups, plunged to and from hurried conferences, seeking explanation, hope, and policy in preparation for the morrow.

Day after day during the remaining months of the year rallies alternated with collapses at the National Shrine, as optimism vied with despair in the bosoms of buyers and sellers. Entries chosen from the financial chronology in the American Year Book help to represent the starkness of the oscillations and the tumultuous emotions of personalities. October 30, "stocks rally as Rockefellers announce they are buying stocks." November 6, "stocks break 5 to 66 points." November 8, "trading quieter, prices lower." November 12, "violent collapse in stocks." November 13, "stocks break with great violence." November 15, "recovery in stocks." November 21, a White House conference announces large construction expenditures and Henry Ford makes a statement in Washington; "stocks advance." December 3, "Hoover's message to Congress expresses optimism, covering all aspects of trade and industry. Stocks rally while message reaches New York." December 12, "stocks decline in the widest break since November 12." December 13, "after further dip, market rallies sharply in late trading." December 19, "stocks decline in brisk trading." Through the rest of the winter declines, rallies, and dullness marked the course of fear and indecision. In the spring of 1930 decision turned to distrust. May 2, "wave of liquidation on stock exchange." May 3, "another violent break in stocks." June 6, "market weak." June 7, "another sharp break." June 8, "stocks break heavily." June 10, "recovery in stocks." For men and women whose affections were centered on such values, the alternation of faith and doubt was heart-rending. In the place of wild enthusiasm had come utter dejection. The mightiest Julius had fallen and "the sheeted dead did squeak and gibber in the Roman streets."

§

Within a few months after the first explosions on the Stock Exchange, underlying forces and realities were revealed in the events and conditions of industry, agriculture, and social living. Neither records nor figures permit, nor does the character of written discourse allow, an accurate description, a photographic portrayal in full proportions of the total drama running through four turbulent years — the scenes of unfolding distress with all the human tragedy and comedy that accompanied the gigantic pageant. Yet a part of the story was told in the cold and forbidding figures that registered those aspects of the drama susceptible of mathematical enumeration.

With some appropriateness a beginning could be made with the downward rushes of the stock market. Between September, 1929, and January, 1933, according to the Dow-Jones index of stock prices, 30 industrials fell from an average of 364.9 to 62.7 dollars per share. A group of 20 public utilities stocks dropped from 141.9 to 28.0 dollars per share. Twenty railroad stocks declined from an average of 182.0 to 28.1 dollars per share. Other indices recorded the same catastrophe. According to The New York Times index of 50 stocks (25 industrials and 25 railroads), the average price fell from 300.52 to 58.65 dollars per share. A compilation by the Standard Statistics Company (Inc.) of 421 stocks (351 industrials, 37 public utilities, and 33 railroads) based upon an index number of 100 as the 1926 monthly average, showed a decline from 225.2 to 49.1 from September, 1929, to January, 1933. According to the same source and during the same period, the index of 20 New York bank stocks fell from 357.8 to 67.9.

High among the indices of changing economic status and personal distress throughout the country were the increasing suspensions of banks. In mere financial crashes of this type there was, to be sure, little new. Between 1920 and 1929 about 5,000 banks with deposits of $1,500,000,000 had collapsed, but those failures had occurred mainly in rural regions and reflected principally the economic misfortunes of farmers and their dependent merchants. Now the normal rate of suspensions leaped upward. Between June 30, 1929, and June 30, 1930, 640 banks suspended, as against 549 for the previous corresponding period. During the next fiscal year 1553 banks closed their doors, tying up over a billion dollars in deposits, as compared with $345,000,000 in the previous season. For the first ten months of 1932, the number of bank suspensions was 1199 and the impounded depositors' funds amounted to $605,000,000.

If this marked a turn in the tide, a promise of restoration, as contended by financiers, the thought brought no consolation or relief to the millions of people whose savings were caught in the vise and whose prospects of full recovery were at best dubious. Moreover as the season of calamity advanced, banks in great cities — New York, Pittsburgh, Washington, Cleveland, and Chicago — went under, with detonations that sent tremors throughout the financial system. If such institutions could explode, where did safety lie and what disaster could come next?

Scarcely less significant than banks in the generality of economic indications were the railroads. Their tracks penetrated every region, city, and important community of the country. Their car loadings registered in a large measure the output of industrial plants and the movement of goods. Their passenger receipts reflected the activities of business life, the economic power of multitudes to travel and enjoy leisure, and the condition of hotels, resorts, even whole towns and regions, dependent upon travelers. And now for three successive years, railways reported a decline in the movement of goods and passengers and a shrinkage of earnings. Early in the depression weaker lines began to default on their bonds and pass into the hands of conservators or receivers. During the first four years of the cataclysm in transportation approximately 45,000 miles of railway passed under the jurisdiction of trustees, receivers, or bankruptcy courts. Before a positive check appeared in the precipitous descent, great systems had become derelicts — for example, the Wabash; the Chicago, Milwaukee, and St. Paul; the Chicago and Northwestern; the Missouri Pacific; the St. Louis and San Francisco; and the New York, New Haven and Hartford. Finding their

revenues diminishing, railroad managers reduced their purchases of locomotives and materials, discharged employees by
the thousands, and reduced the working hours of operatives
kept in service. Only by acute management and with the aid
of loans from the Reconstruction Finance Corporation did
huge companies, such as the New York Central and the
Baltimore and Ohio, manage to survive. In other words a
twenty-billion dollar industry was crippled in vital parts and
the ramifications of its recession spread in every direction.

In other divisions of the economic system, disequilibrium,
as certain economists called it, superseded ideal poise. In
January, 1931, the United States Steel Corporation reported
that its earnings for the previous December were the lowest
for any month since February, 1915. In the spring of 1932
came the smash of Samuel Insull's "two billion dollar empire" in public utilities and the collapse was followed by the
flight of the magnate to Greece. In the autumn the real
estate bond house of S. W. Straus and Company in New York
City went into a receiver's hands, leaving millions in bonds
outstanding, most of them in default. This breakdown was
soon succeeded by the failure of older and more conservative
establishments of the same kind. All in all, it was estimated,
at least six billion of the ten billion dollars in "sound real
estate securities" dropped into default and millions were sold
by the victims at prices ranging from six to fifteen cents on
the dollar. In the aggregate, business failures for the first
nine months of 1932 were reported as 23,798 against 20,311
for the corresponding period in 1931 and 16,030 for the same
period of 1929.

In a survey published by the Guaranty Trust Company,
an institution not given to pessimistic statements, the workings of the American system were set forth in bald terms:
"Measured by almost any of the accepted standards of economic welfare, the year 1932, taken as a whole, was a period
of deeper depression than 1931. The production and distribution of commodities were at lower levels; unemployment was
greater; the earnings of business enterprises were smaller and

losses were larger, and commercial failures were more numerous. Prices in general continued to decline, although the downward trend was interrupted by an advance during the third quarter of the year. Distress among the farming population was increased by the further drastic decline in prices of agricultural commodities." In this darkened sky, the one star of hope to which the survey could point was a falling off in the number of bank failures. But given the state of business and agriculture in general, this reversal of a single trend may have meant merely that the house-cleaning of weaker institutions was drawing toward an end. However interpreted, the fair prospect that Calvin Coolidge had acclaimed in 1928 was sadly marred and the Lords of Creation, deemed "the rulers of America" a short time before, were powerless to restore its aurorean lineaments.

Upon industrial workers the dissolution of prosperity fell with terrific weight. Even in the perfect time of President Coolidge's prosperity, the number of unemployed, it was estimated, averaged about 2,000,000 a year. No precise figures of unemployment were available as crashes on the Stock Exchange followed one another with startling sharpness; but according to the reckonings of William Green, president of the American Federation of Labor, industrial workers were rapidly "deflated." In April, 1930, 2,954,000 persons were out of work; by October, 1930, the number had increased to 3,924,000; by October, 1931, the total unemployed had risen to 6,801,000; and by October, 1932, the total stood at 10,908,000. During the first two months of 1933, the number rose to 12,000,000, and less reliable estimates placed it even higher. The Federal Reserve Board's unadjusted combined index of factory employment (with the monthly average of 1923–1925 as 100) catapulted from 105.4 in September, 1929, to 58.1 in January, 1933; and this was regarded as a conservative reckoning.

The social consequences of unemployment were quickly registered in the clamor for relief in the great industrial centers. A survey of 126 cities, made in 1932, representing

56 per cent of the urban population of the United States, reported relief aid to 823,894 families in May, 1932, as against 386,151 families of the previous year. Relief expenditures of New York City set at approximately one million dollars in October, 1929, rose to nine and a half millions in February, 1933. The Committee on the Costs of Medical Care reported "appalling" conditions in the South where the incomes of the people in ten southern states were so low that they were unable to purchase adequate treatment.

While industrial workers slid down hill, the descent of farmers was expedited, despite President Hoover's Agricultural Marketing Act. During the post-war decade the value of farm property decreased by twenty billion dollars; more than 450,000 farmers lost their farms; farm tenancies increased by more than 200,000; and the gross annual farm income dropped from sixteen to eleven billion dollars. Then came the crisis of 1929. Between that year and 1932 farm values suffered another decline of thirty-three per cent and the gross annual income of farmers shrank fifty-seven per cent. Between 1920 and January, 1933, the prices received by farmers for their produce fell from an index number of 205 to fifty-one. Measured by the same index the prices of goods the farmers bought dropped only from 206 to 105 during that span of years.

Though industries slumped, profits diminished, unemployment increased, and farm distress intensified, the burden of private and public debts, once deemed evidences of national prosperity and confidence, remained nominally fixed; and it was an Atlas burden. In a statement placed before the Senate Finance Committee investigating economic conditions, Irving Fisher of Yale University estimated the total debts owing in the United States in 1929 at 234 billions of dollars as compared with the 362 billions reckoned as the total wealth of the United States. According to a compilation of the National Industrial Conference Board, the total interest-bearing debt was estimated at $154,761,000,000 in 1929. This death grip on economy embraced a farm indebtedness of approximately twelve and a quarter billions, a steam-railroad debt of twelve and three-quarter billions, a total public debt of over thirty billions, a corporate debt of close to seventy-five billions, and individual indebtedness (other than farmers') of twenty-five billions. After three years of deflation and liquidation, the debt still totaled 134 billion dollars according to a study of the Twentieth Century Fund released in the spring of 1933. During the same period the national income had fallen from eighty-five to forty billions of dollars.

All these blows of misfortune were borne for many months with a remarkable fortitude. Then a definite change in temper took place in the spring of 1932. In May the railway brotherhoods presented a plea to President Hoover, containing an ominous emphasis. "Mr. President," it stated, "we have come here to tell you that unless something is done to provide employment and relieve distress among the families of the unemployed, we cannot be responsible for the orderly operations of the railroads of this country — that we will refuse to take the responsibility for the disorder which is sure to arise if conditions continue. . . . The unemployed citizens whom we represent will not accept starvation while the two major political parties struggle for control of government. . . . We are not Socialists, we are not Communists, nor are we anarchists. . . . There is a growing demand that the entire business and social structure be changed because of the general dissatisfaction with the present system. We cannot longer ignore this situation."

First in the West and rapidly throughout the country, whole communities turned to barter in the effort to provide relief and break the business stagnation; to force a resurgence in exchange of goods and services. More than 144 organizations in scores of communities in 29 states were reported by Stuart Chase to be turning to barter, to "wooden money," to self-liquidating printed scrip. As 1932 drew to a close, farmers were "on the march" to prevent foreclosure sales, to stop the production and sale of commodities until a fair price was assured, to end tax sales, to cut down the principal of farm mortgages, and to reduce the interest rates. The law was either reluctant or unable to cope with them and violence broke out here and there. In the East, industrial labor was growing equally restless. In a statement published in the January issue of the magazine, Nation's Business, William Green declared: "The American trade-union movement has been patient. . . . We gave government every opportunity to produce a remedy. We gave management every opportunity to produce a remedy. We gave finance every opportunity. . . . We agreed to refrain from drastic action if employers would refrain from drastic action. . . . Finally, after three years of suffering we, the organized workers, declare to the world, enough; we shall use our might to compel the plain remedies withheld by those whose misfeasance caused our woe."

§

During the early stages of the stock market collapse, prognosticators and soothsayers in high finance, almost without exception, from Irving Fisher of Yale University to Andrew W. Mellon, Secretary of the Treasury, took the position that the downward course of stocks had little or no relation to the real state of transactions in industry and agriculture. With droning reiteration, they insisted that "business, that is, the production and distribution of commodities," was sound; that only "the lunatic fringe" of speculators was affected by the decline in paper values; and that the mass of the people would remain secure in their homes and employments. "The nation will make steady progress in 1930," maintained Secretary Mellon in his words of good cheer on New Year's Day, ". . . I see nothing in the present situation that is either menacing or warrants pessimism." From President Hoover in the White House early in May, 1930, came the message: "We have now passed the worst." And in October came confirmation: "The income of a large part of our people has not been reduced."

In the lush days of the rising market it had been generally assumed that stock prices bore a close relation to the condition and movement of actual production and distribution. Indeed the very justification for the market itself had been that it performed a vital function in bringing capital funds into business enterprise; that it served as a place for the adjustment of prices to business realities and through the knowledge and intuition of brokers kept a fair equilibrium in the relation of liquid claims to intrinsic values. Now this justification in terms of classical economy seemed to be rudely cast aside, and the conclusion was drawn by persons in high places that the stock market was a kind of "racket" where speculators had engaged in reckless operations, bearing no reasoned relations to the actual transactions of business itself. Such a verdict coming from leaders in banking, industry, and politics served to unsettle the faith of the people in the merits of the National Shrine and the authenticity of the auspices. In time this loss of faith was to plague many authors of the idea.

With their hearts chilled by repeated disappointments, pontifices among the Lords of Creation took a second line of prognosis. Industries were actually slowing down, dividends were really being passed, and unemployment was rapidly increasing. Facts sinister and brutal were visible to the blindest of prophets. Then what could be said about them? The answer made in the second line of prognosis was that industrial depression had in fact come upon the country, that there had been several such setbacks in American history, and that the nation had always come out of them into a bigger and better prosperity. "I believe," said Secretary Mellon as the year 1930 wore on, "that just as soon as much of the products in the market at present are disposed of, the business depression will better itself. Curtailment of output, without question, will correct the present condition within a short time." This rested upon actual experience and had the ring of practicality. The oil, aluminum, and other industries in which the Secretary was heavily interested were already retrenching, laying off workers, reducing the surplus on the market, and thus preparing for the correction of conditions, as correction was understood.

By the middle of 1931, President Hoover himself was convinced that the stock market gyrations revealed at least a certain unsoundness in business, a shrinkage of production and distribution, a reduction in the people's income. Speaking to the Indiana Editorial Association on June 15, he too took the second line of prognosis, with trust in Providence as a form of re-insurance. The blight of the depression, he said, "stretches from all quarters of the globe to every business place and every cottage door in our land." But "depressions are not new experiences, though none has hitherto been so widespread. We have passed through no less than fifteen major depressions in the last century. We have learned something as the result of each of these experiences. From this one we shall gain stiffening and economic discipline, a greater knowledge upon which we must build a better safeguarded system. We have come out of each previous depression into a period of prosperity greater than ever before. We shall do so this time. . . . Surplus money does not remain idle for long. . . . Whatever the immediate difficulties may be, we know they are transitory in our lives and in the life of the nation. We should have full faith and confidence in those mighty resources, those intellectual and spiritual forces which have impelled this nation to a success never before known in the history of the world. Far from being impaired, these forces were never stronger than at this moment. Under the guidance of Divine Providence they will return to us a greater and more wholesome prosperity than we have ever known."

§

Accompanying the declines and dissolutions in domestic economy were widening fissures in the empire of overseas finance and commerce that had also presented glowing prospects on the morning when President Coolidge left the White

House. From day to day came the news that foreign countries had defaulted on bonds bought by American investors
with such avidity under the advice and pressure of bankers
and their salesmen. By the close of 1932 more than a billion
dollars' worth of bonds in American hands, it was officially
estimated, were frozen, representing losses in Austria, Bolivia,
Brazil, Bulgaria, Chile, Colombia, Costa Rica, Cuba, Ecua-
dor, El Salvador, Greece, Hungary, Panama, Peru, Uruguay,
and Yugoslavia. Soon billions invested in Germany were in
default or in a paralysis which brought a steep decline on the
market, as frightened investors sought to save something
from the wreckage. Although the bonds of Italy and Poland
escaped default, they staggered downward in prices amid the
great fear. As European dictators closed in on the economies
of their respective countries, American owners and investors
entangled in fixed properties were glad to effect settlements
which let them out of the debris holding some of their capital
intact. With wry faces Americans who had lent money to
German municipalities for the construction of model dwellings saw their bonds in real or virtual default, while millions
of their countrymen still lived in substandard houses, in
shacks, and in crude shanties pieced together by the unemployed.

The downward swoop in foreign commerce was likewise
disconcerting to guardians of that once expanding empire. In
1929 the export of merchandise reached the towering value
of $5,240,995,000 under the stimulus of lavish lending abroad.
In 1932 it totalled only $1,611,000,000. Since American in-
vestors, irked by defaults on old loans, were in no mood to
throw good money after bad, the outlook for lifting the export
total was not encouraging. Moreover foreign governments
were building barriers against the influx of goods, sometimes
for purely fiscal ends and at other times for the deliberate
purpose of curtailment or exclusion. France, for example,
made horizontal increases against selected countries under
the device of an "exchange compensation tax." In aid of
such limitations other governments employed a quota sys-

tem, fixing the specific amounts of particular commodities for which entry was to be allowed. Partly on fiscal and partly on commercial grounds, foreign governments also resorted to a control of currency exchanges in such a manner as to restrain the import of commodities. Building on earlier legislation of a restricted character, the British government practically abandoned its historic "free trade policy" in 1932 and went over to a general scheme of protection, under which preferences were devised for British possessions. Meanwhile Latin-American governments that had generally maintained uniform tariff fronts against all countries began to negotiate special agreements with selected countries, offering concessions in exchange for concessions — a privilege of which Great Britain was not slow to take advantage.

In other crises, a serious decline in exports had chiefly affected American agriculture, for in former times the major portion of the export had been composed of farm products. But in 1929 non-agricultural products, including manufactures and machinery, constituted far more than one-half the total export. This shift, so significant for domestic politics, had been recognized by leaders in the formulation of American policy. As early as 1926, Herbert Hoover, speaking then as Secretary of Commerce to exporters in New York, gave his interpretation of the trend: "Foreign trade has become a vital part of the whole modern economic system. . . . In peace time our exports and imports are the margins upon which our well-being depends. . . . The great problem in our foreign trade, however, is the export of goods in which we compete with other nations — but if we are intelligent we should be able to command our share of them. Our most competitive group is that of manufactured goods, and expansion of the exports of our manufactured goods is of the utmost importance to us. As our population increases we shall consume more of our foodstuff. . . . If we are to maintain the total volume of our exports and consequently our buying power for imports, it must be by steady pushing of our manufactured goods."

With the aid of American loans and the drumming agents of the Federal Government, business men had pushed the sale of "our manufactured goods." And in the crisis of the depression they, as well as farmers, were caught in the shrinkage of international trade. In earlier days exporters and importers, especially on the Atlantic seaboard, had been the chief promoters of foreign commerce, on which they thrived under the comforting phrases of classical economics. In 1930 powerful manufacturers catering to foreign markets, disturbed, if not wrecked, by the slump, joined the importers and exporters in the search for a way out of the dilemma presented by the decline in the sale of finished goods abroad. If, for example, textile industries engrossing the home market could still rejoice in the protection afforded by tariff barriers, manufacturers of automobiles, cigarette-making machinery, and typewriters, for example, had no need of it and could be vocal on the side of "getting foreign trade started again." But all their drumming could not restore the boom of former days; neither could reason nor a fairy's wand.

§

As thousands of constituents mourned over defaulted foreign bonds in their strong boxes, as receivers for banks in calamity excavated from their vaults paper in the form of Peruvian sixes or Cordoba sevens, a great clatter arose in the "provinces" where, as Dwight Morrow of the Morgans once explained, bankers had distributed such "securities." From the "provinces," the clamor reached Washington. How had this ruin come to pass? What did it all mean? Who was responsible for the downfall of "values" and "investment opportunities"? Responding to the cries of pain and wonder, the United States Senate ordered its finance committee to investigate the whole business "at the earliest possible moment," and authorized the committee to apply the penalties of the law to witnesses who failed to comply with the summons or refused to answer "any question pertinent to the investigation."

On December 18, 1931, the inquiry opened. Great men among the Lords of Creation were called before the committee and invited to explain the amazing rise and decline of foreign financing — such as Thomas Lamont, of J. P. Morgan; Otto Kahn, of Kuhn, Loeb; Charles E. Mitchell, of the National City; Winthrop Aldrich, of the Chase National; Clarence Dillon, of Dillon, Read; James Speyer, of Speyer and Company; Joseph Swan, of the Guaranty Company; and Frederick Strauss, of J. and W. Seligman. To these experts in finance were added representatives of the Departments of State and Commerce, under whose sympathetic auspices the foreign lending had been so effectively advanced, and Professor Edwin Walter Kemmerer of Princeton University, "the magic money doctor," who had helped to put "on a sound footing" some of the foreign governments whose finances were now in difficulties. If these gentlemen could not enlighten the Senate and the country, where did hope of enlightenment rest?

In the more than two thousand pages of testimony and documents, the history and existing state of things were more or less exposed to public gaze and astonishment. Despite much confusion, forgetfulness, bickering, and hesitation, several lines of relevant fact and opinion were developed. Under what conception of things had come about all this money lending from which calamities had eventuated? Were the bankers, engaged in promoting foreign loans, thinking of economic advantages for the people of the United States? Or were they thinking of something else? Otto Kahn answered categorically that the object of the promoting banker "is and must be beyond all other things America's prosperity, not merely from the point of view of a patriotic and decent citizen, but from the point of view of his own pocket. The international banker's profit, even in the case of foreign bonds, is made in this country, and not abroad." He was, in other words, not solely actuated by private interest.

While conceding that in specific cases the business of foreign lending might have been "overdone," Thomas Lamont said: "I should think that American commerce had in the long run benefited very greatly by these loans." Bankers had supplied capital to European countries denuded by war; they had aided in the rehabilitation of foreign industries; they had contributed to stabilization abroad; they had assisted in restoring "the normal course of commerce." Returning to the main issue, the effect of foreign loans upon the United States, Mr. Lamont was emphatic: "I go so far as to say that not only have they contributed very materially to the maintenance during those years of our foreign trade, but that they have contributed very materially to the capacity of the borrowing governments to enable them to discharge their obligations when due, and punctually, to the United States Government." If the bankers, in the pursuit of profits, had made genuflections to graven images, they had, it appeared, also served patriotism.

The broad and pleasing generalizations uttered by such men of expertness and authority as Otto Kahn and Thomas Lamont were allowed by the Senate committee to pass as authentic evidence, as if disposing of the issue. But when Charles E. Mitchell, of the National City Bank, declared that "foreign investments very largely control the volume of the export business of the United States," that they should have "a sound basis of desirability to the most critically patriotic of Americans," and that the banking interests concerned deserved praise, not criticism, the committee called for proof instead of assertion. Senator Couzens asked Mr. Mitchell what proportion of the billions invested abroad went into the manufacture of goods that had formerly been made in the United States. The witness confessed: "That I cannot answer, sir." The Senator then asked the banker whether it was not a fact that American capital had gone to foreign countries and engaged there in manufacturing to avoid paying their tariff duties on American goods. To this the banker responded in the affirmative. By open confession, therefore, exported capital had to some extent cut into the production and profits of domestic industries, and had not contributed to American prosperity and patriotism obviously, if at all. Following this thread, the Senator inquired "what percentage" of the total exported capital was employed in cutting down domestic business. The banker admitted that he did not know. Since it took knowledge to establish the validity of a generalization, the bankers failed to substantiate their thesis of automatic beneficence and patriotism, though they refrained from introducing Adam Smith's "invisible hand" of God to save their argument.

After the testimony of exporting bankers had raised some doubts respecting the national advantages derived from all this lending of money to foreign countries, Francis P. Garvan, speaking for the Chemical Foundation, laid before the Senate committee a list of American loans that had been made to competing chemical concerns abroad. Referring to the chemical industry specifically, Mr. Garvan gave his view of what had actually happened: "These international bankers . . . have been persistently borrowing the savings of the American people and, for the bribe of huge commissions, have been loaning these savings to the international chemical cartel, or its constituent companies, or allies, the cartel whose success is necessarily based upon the destruction of our industry and our independence. . . . Our chemical industry is faced not only in our own country, but throughout the world, with competitors whose pockets are filled with American savers' money, and, with the ability to extend long-time credit based thereon, competitors who either never intend to repay their loans, or who intend to buy them up in a depreciated market at ten or twenty cents on the dollar."

For the protagonists of the Hawley-Smoot tariff bill so recently enacted, Mr. Garvan's particular figures and specific contentions in the name of American industry were almost, if not entirely, sufficient to dissolve the overarching hypothesis of beneficence supplied by the bankers. Even for disinterested parties given to cool appraisals of policies, the facts and arguments presented to the Senate committee on foreign lending made untenable the complacent optimism and basic assumptions of the financiers. Other questions were then in order.

How had the headlong rush into money lending occurred? Who was responsible? Clarence Dillon supplied his answer: the capital exported was "surplus" capital — wealth not needed at home — and bankers had merely channeled the outward flow. Senators were not convinced. One member of the committee thought the outward flow of capital was largely due to the higher rates of interest offered by agents and bankers for foreign governments — six, seven, and even eight per cent for "gold bonds." Another member insisted that by promoting foreign loans at higher rates of interest, the bankers had perhaps contracted credit at home and exerted a deleterious influence in slowing down domestic enterprise. But Mr. Dillon held fast to his thesis: "It is a question of surplus, because this country would use its own money." That the outflow would tend to raise the domestic interest rate, he conceded, but he clung to the idea of the "surplus" to the end. In some respects this idea gave consolation to citizens who had suffered under the bankers' theory of patriotism and beneficence: the bonds in default represented surplus capital after all — money and goods not "needed" at home. If this discovery did not entirely ease the pains of bondholders, it at least made the bankers' case appear more defensible to themselves.

While the problem of beneficence and patriotism in foreign lending was being examined, a subsidiary question arose: How did it happen that so many bond issues had been offered to American investors? Some illumination was obtained by the Senate committee in the immediate hearings and a dazzling light was focused upon the question by a later inquiry into the general subject of banking and finance. That all or nearly all the exporting bankers had sent or kept agents abroad searching fervently for opportunities was already well known, but no exposition of detailed methods had been made. In quest of information on the point, Senator Hiram Johnson asked one of the investment bankers, Frederick J.

Lisman, to explain how his fraternity went about floating loans in Peru. Mr. Lisman replied that several banking houses were engaged in sharp competition to get the favors. That was, in fact, the state of affairs "all over Latin America." The purpose, continued the witness, was "to satisfy the public demand for securities." Yet it was not the sole purpose: "Bankers do not knowingly float bad loans. But the purpose is to do a good business at a profit." Incidentally it was brought out in connection with a Peruvian loan that one of the banking houses had paid a large amount to promoters who arranged the deal behind the scenes and transferred to the son of the President of Peru the sum of $415,000 for his "services" in the course of the flotation. Moreover the Senate investigation unearthed the fact that another loan had been issued for a South American republic after federal officials had pointed out the unsoundness of the transaction — a warning that came true in a default.

§

Especially pertinent to an understanding of the bankers' tactics were the revelations respecting the financing of investments in Cuba whose freedom and independence had been guaranteed when the United States began the "war of liberation" in 1898. By the opening of 1931 the direct investments in that little island alone amounted to $935,706,000, and among them were huge loans to the Cuban government, engineered by three powerful banking houses of New York City — the Chase National, the J. P. Morgan Company, and the National City. Although, for reasons of weight or none at all, the Senate committee did not explore the methods by which the Morgan Company got a share of the business, it did inquire rather closely into the operations of the Chase National group, especially into the fifty million dollar loan of 1928.

At the time the transaction was consummated, Cuba was in the iron grip of a military dictator, Machado, news of whose bloody regimen had been circulated far and wide through the press in the United States. Was Carl J. Schmidlapp, the spokesman of the Chase National interests, aware of the fact? Senator King asked him directly whether he knew that Machado had arbitrarily extended the terms of Cuban senators and congressmen and that "to accomplish his end he had suppressed all political parties and was governing by military rule?" Mr. Schmidlapp answered: "No." Did Mr. Schmidlapp know that Machado had a rather large standing army? "I had not given it a thought one way or the other," responded the banker. "I did not know what the Army of Cuba was."

With reference, however, to some details of the financing, the banker had a little knowledge. He was aware that the Chase National had employed José Obregon as manager of the Cuban branch of the Bank, first at $12,000 a year and then at $19,000, and he was acquainted with the fact that Obregon was a son-in-law of Machado, the military ruler of Cuba. He also confirmed a report in the hands of the Senate committee to the effect that a commission of half a million dollars was paid over to Obregon, as bank manager, for distribution among the participants in the syndicate connected with the flotation. Was Machado's son-in-law employed by the Chase National merely on account of his talents as a banker? Mr. Schmidlapp was not asked to develop that topic; nor did he vouchsafe specific information.

But on this point his New York house had some data. A year previously one of its representatives had written in respect of Obregon: "As we know, from any business standpoint he is perfectly useless. He has neither any ability for banking, nor has he the slightest ability in negotiating, which was something which we thought it might be possible to build him up to do. . . . From what I could gather in listening to some of the Cubans' talk is that Joe [Obregon] has very little standing with the President [Machado], and I think this is probably true. On the other hand, where the rub comes in is that if we do not pay him his salary, the President

[Machado] would have to give him an allowance, and in times as hard as these this might be fairly difficult to do." The writer of this note on the managerial ability of Obregon also informed his concern that Machado was using public funds illegally and that the State Department in Washington was "worrying" about it. With such and similar transactions the promotion of American investments had proceeded in the days of prosperity and "the free market."

§

Through the evidence elicited at the hearings on foreign loans and at subsequent inquiries, it was possible to get microscopic glimpses of pecuniary enterprise at work, but no complete and accurate picture of the whole operation was constructed. Charles E. Mitchell, of the National City, had said in explanation of his role : "Many of us have found real inspiration in the fact that in the issuance of this large volume of foreign loans we were playing a part in the development of American trade and industry. That was our first motive always." This was a lofty sentiment and it was confirmed by the testimony of Thomas Lamont and Otto Kahn. Yet neither the bankers who answered the call for information nor the Senators who heard the testimony were able to present a balance sheet covering all the transactions. They did not establish, on a basis of figures, the thesis that the sequences flowing from the multitudinous operations in foreign lending, including bankers' commissions, augmented the wealth of the United States. The bankers had operated in a system with which they were familiar, according to methods they deemed appropriate, under economic theories they accepted without severe scrutiny. That much was certain. Nevertheless no demonstration proving the case of beneficence was made. Nor was it possible to make one from knowledge available.

Other things stood crystal-clear in the record. There had been a fierce competition among rival banking houses. In the course of competition, some of them, banks of high standing in the world of finance, though by no means all, had employed politicians, or the relatives of politicians, in foreign countries, to press American money upon restive governments. Huge commissions and douceurs had been paid to the intermediaries. Adverse reports on the financial condition of potential borrowers had been suppressed and concealed from the American investors to whom securities had been offered. Warnings from experts in the service of the United States Government had been stifled or ignored. Little consideration had been given to the actual destination of American money poured into foreign countries. Millions had been spent on a great highway in Cuba, on a gilt-domed capitol in Havana, and on unproductive public works in Peru.

These things were matters of common knowledge in enlightened circles. Yet, on the whole, bankers had been indifferent to the use of funds, so long as the bonds of borrowers were drawn in correct legal terms. Nor had they paid much attention to the tyrannical acts of dictators whom they helped to keep in power by lavish contributions of American money. Bankers might buy foreign politicians and supply them with cash, but they usually deemed it none of their business to make sure that this money went into prudent enterprises to enrich the borrowing nations and thus add guarantees to the securities they offered to the American public. Though heavily involved in the intrigues of foreign politics, they conveniently forgot politics. The responsible agent of the Chase National Bank confessed himself unaware of facts known even to casual readers of metropolitan newspapers : that Machado had violated the constitution of Cuba, had suppressed all opposition, and was running in a tyrannical course, which finally led to his overthrow and flight. Innocence more magnificent had seldom been displayed by men associated with pecuniary enterprise.

The Senate committee had put the question to the Lords of Creation : How did it happen ? And it had received some answers. On the basis of these responses, the Chairman,

Hiram Johnson, exclaimed that it was necessary to devise legislation "which would preclude the possibility of any such outrageous and shameful activities being indulged in again in this country, to the detriment of our people." But what kind of legislation? The committee asked Professor Edwin Walter Kemmerer, the distinguished expert in finance, for light on the problem. The Professor granted that when bonds got into the hands of commercial banks, trust funds for widows and orphans, and the endowments of educational institutions, the value of such securities became "affected with a great public interest." In view of the tales that had already been told, that much did seem obvious. Could the Professor offer some conclusions on the matter of remedial legislation? He could not: "No, sir; I have no conclusion except the feeling that something should be done. . . . I suppose in the course of a short time we will go ahead again and repeat the same mistakes." That was an admission: there really had been some "mistakes." A Senator interposed: "People forget yesterday." The Professor replied: "They may remember yesterday, but they forget the day before." Bankers had testified that the people were clamorous for new issues of bonds in the days of the golden glow. The Professor evidently imagined that in time they would be on the war path again urging bankers to furnish more "investment opportunities." Apparently history would repeat itself, till doomsday.

Unable to get any unconfused light from the science of economics or from the sociology of the banking fraternity, the Senate committee devised more "hasty legislation," of a negative character. By a statute, called the Johnson Act, Congress in 1934 made it unlawful to sell in the United States the bonds or securities of any foreign government, or its subdivisions, which had defaulted on the payment of obligations to the Government of the United States. This was not the type of legislation deemed "constructive" by economists and bankers. It left none of that freedom which permitted creditors to help in lifting good but unlucky debtors to their feet by new advances of funds. What it represented was the temper of a multitude of American citizens who found themselves either completely ruined by foreign lending or in some degree of economic misfortune as a result of the bankers' excursions into operations that "benefited the United States." News of the excursions as disclosed by the Senate committee, even though cautiously handled by metropolitan papers, reached the outlying regions of the country. A few citizens naturally inclined to forget continued to remember and nursed for a time a terrible wrath against the bankers. In fact, some caustic commentator set in circulation the frightful word "banksters."

§

Supplementing the bulky volumes of testimony and papers laid before the public by the Senate committee engaged in investigating foreign loans was a remarkable document dealing with the influence which American investments in branch factories abroad had exerted on American industry and enterprise at home. Did this capital poured into foreign countries add to or diminish the wealth of the United States? In this connection the Senate did not call the Lords of Creation before a committee and ask them to elucidate the problem. By resolution it merely instructed the Department of Commerce, which had been eagerly promoting this form of foreign enterprise, to disclose "the extent to which American capital invested in manufacturing in Europe constitutes a competitive menace, directly or indirectly, to the industries carried on in the United States." In compliance with the instructions, the Department set its experts at work on the issue presented and in 1931 they reported their findings and lack of knowledge, under the heading American Branch Factories Abroad.

This response to the call of the Senate was accompanied by a statistical elaboration that must have been impressive to manufacturers of many commodities whose outlets abroad had recently been drastically narrowed, either by American branch factories in foreign countries or by other forces less discernible. But the response was not an answer. "In view of the constantly increasing exports of the commodities figuring largely in the branch-factory movement," said the experts, "it is impossible to ascertain the effect of the branch factories on our export trade." If there was a slight euphemism in the reference to constantly increasing exports in 1931, the language was at all events explicit. Yet the experts conceded that "there is a certain amount of competition between the branch factories and the parent plants in the United States as regards neutral markets." How much? "The full extent of this competition cannot be ascertained" from the available statistics.

What of the future for American manufacturers and industrial workers affected by this outpouring of capital abroad? The Department of Commerce was as non-committal, if not as lyrical, as the bankers: "The movement is intimately connected with the general industrial development of the United States and its future progress is likely to be determined primarily by the availability of capital and the economic policies of foreign countries." Such was the capacity for insight possessed by the great Department of Commerce so heavily endowed in financial resources and so well equipped with expert personnel by Secretary Hoover and his chosen successor. Perhaps the report represented all that intelligence and knowledge could accomplish. Even if true, it instigated queries among the people's representatives on Capitol Hill and added to the perplexities and quandaries of the people themselves in the very deeps of the crushing depression.

§

While the invisible empire of investment in foreign countries was being drawn into question, doubts were rising in respect of the visible empire in the Philippines. In conjunction with the poetry of the white man's burden, manifest destiny, and moral obligation, claims had been made from the beginning that this was also a paying proposition in itself and a stepping stone to greater commerce on the mainland of Asia. At the very outset of empire building in 1898, seekers after world power for the United States had declared that the American people were producing more than they could consume, that outlets for "surplus" manufactures and farm produce must be found, and that imperial expansion would bring the necessary openings. Unless we expand, it was said, we burst. Expansion came. And after thirty years' experience, ample time for a fair test, a balance sheet of the operations containing all the economic items susceptible of "numerical expression" showed a net loss of about four million dollars a year, apart from the cost of extra naval defense. Individual interests in the United States had made high profits. The American people as a whole had not found the promised outlets for goods and taxpayers had been compelled to shoulder heavy additional burdens. Such was the outcome of all the blare, oratory, trumpeting, boasting, and pluming of the great adventure.

As the tariff legislation of the United States facilitated the import of sugar, coconut oil, copra, and other agricultural products from the Philippines into the United States in return for manufactures, it was the American farmers who felt, or said they felt, the adverse effects of empire. Manufacturers, money lenders, and merchants had profited a little from manifest destiny but farmers gradually arrived at the conviction that the experiment in expansion was carried on largely at their expense. Gradually American industrial workers reached the conclusion that they too had a case against imperialism. Out of affectionate consideration for "our little brown brothers" and for other reasons, the ports of the United States had been thrown open to immigration from the Philippines and in many divisions of industry Filipinos were cutting into American standards of living, especially on the Pacific Coast.

When the great depression deepened, the pressures of

agrarian and labor interests were exerted in Congress against the pressures of industry, commerce, finance, the State Department, and the naval bureaucracy. There had been, it was true, opposition from the former sources since the beginning of the imperial adventure, but the capitalistic interests had been able, on the whole, to win and hold the favors of federal legislation and administration, and to retain the solicitude of the Navy Department. By 1930 the tables were turning and at a series of congressional hearings a real inquest was conducted into the economic merits of empire.

Outside the committee rooms of Congress, opposition to independence for the Philippines was voiced by those interests and newspapers that had long supported the adventure in imperialism and advocated coöperation with Great Britain in European politics. The lyricism of doing good to them that sit in darkness was revived and applauded once more. The specter of Japan seizing the emancipated Islands was raised again. Responsibility for aiding Great Britain in maintaining the balance of power in the East was reëmphasized in poignant language by publicists.

That the United States could not, single-handed, overcome the naval power of Japan in her own waters, save in a long, costly, and bloody war was conceded. That Great Britain might not throw her weight on the side of the United States in such a conflict was admitted. Nevertheless to seek an escape from the pretext for this war was contemptuously described as the policy of "scuttle and run." Experts in "sea power," "Pacific relations," "international coöperation," "world affairs," and the pomp and circumstance of "grand politics" sought to educate the hinterlanders of the United States. Ingenious devices for heating patriotism and making it identical with imperialism were employed. If the attitude of the metropolitan press represented general American opinion and resolve, then the tempest raised in Congress by agrarian and labor leaders would soon subside.

But music from the chorus of imperialism failed to enchant all the politicians in Washington. In December, 1932, Congress passed a bill for granting independence to the Philippines at the end of ten years on various terms and conditions, including popular approval of the proposal in the Islands. The following month President Hoover vetoed the bill and, in a message to Congress and the country, reviewed the arguments. He did not repudiate entirely the vague idea of ultimate independence. His attention was rather concentrated on the methods of the measure in question. It might project the Philippine people "into economic and social chaos, with the probability of breakdown in government, with its consequences in degeneration of a rising liberty . . . so carefully nurtured by the United States at the cost of thousands of American lives and hundreds of millions of money." To the pleas of the agricultural interests in the United States undoubtedly supporting the bill, Hoover offered a rebuttal: "We are trustees for these people and we must not let our selfish interest dominate that trust." Crouching in the neighborhood was a covetous Japan. "Nor has the spirit of imperialism," the President said, "and the exploitation of peoples of other races departed from the earth." Indeed seldom before had the official thesis of dollar diplomacy been expressed in wider and nobler terms than in Hoover's veto message. Yet it too failed to convince the agrarians. Congress carried the measure over the veto, and in a little more than a year after the Philippines had rejected the first tender, a modified bill was signed by another President and placed upon the statute books of the land.

§

Amid the uproars, investigations, recriminations, alarms, distresses, and curses that accompanied the course of the depression, President Hoover was called upon to formulate measures for coping with the flying debris of the crisis. Coupled with the already existing emergency in agriculture, the industrial calamity set for Hoover dilemmas which Coolidge had escaped, fortunately for his reputation as a statesman. Moreover it changed from week to week, adding the complications of development to those of the original dissolution.

Viewed from the White House, the business depression went through three stages. At first the stock market débâcle in the autumn of 1929 was regarded as affecting mainly speculators and paper jugglers, leaving American business untouched or at least fundamentally sound. The clouds would soon blow over. However, destiny willed otherwise. As the depression deepened, great banks locked their doors, industries slowed down, unemployment became obviously appalling, and misery thickened, it was conceded by the administration that something serious had happened and was happening. For this state of affairs President Hoover devised formulas and took actions deemed appropriate within the frame of his social philosophy. The depth of the depression was due, in his opinion, to the backlash of the World War. In other respects it was only another periodical crisis and would soon be merely as a tale that is told. By the spring of 1932 he was convinced that the crest of the wave was broken, that business was returning to "normal," that his measures had been effective, and that nothing novel or experimental was needed to facilitate "recovery."

In the beginning of the ordeal, none was clairvoyant enough to foresee how far the industrial depression would go, what havoc it would carry in its train — not even the President of the United States and the Lords of Creation who "ruled America." Was the market crash a harbinger of an economic breakdown or merely a drastic readjustment of liquid claims and paper manipulations? In common with economic leaders called greatest and best, President Hoover at the outset took the position that the industrial structure was sound and that the plunges of stock prices were passing flurries. Confidence in this belief seemed to be the preëminent need. Acting on that assumption, the President summoned to the White House outstanding leaders in manufacturing, transportation, agriculture, utilities, and labor organization and

asked them to adopt measures of private procedure calculated
to keep economic enterprises running on an even keel and
wages for buying power flowing steadily. He also announced
the creation of a continuing council of business men charged
with the duty of watching the trends in national economy
and bringing about the coöperation of interested parties in
the maintenance of production on a high level.

What more was to be done by the Government of the
United States, if anything? What did precedents and economic philosophy have to offer in the dilemma? Was the
President merely to follow precedents or to make them? As
a basis of judgment Hoover had access to records of experiences in three major panics — 1837, 1873, and 1893, as well
as the teachings of minor disturbances. Two of the major
panics had occurred under Democratic auspices and one
under Republican authority. A little less than one hundred
years before 1929, Martin Van Buren had taken office under a
comforting sun of prosperity and in his inaugural address had
spoken confidently of the valor of the people, referred to
exhaustless resources, and paid tribute to the blessings of free
institutions. Nevertheless, within a month a devastating depression started and ran for more than six years, scattering
bankruptcies, unemployment, misery, and starvation in its
wake. What then did President Van Buren do? First, he
read the people a lecture on their follies. He told them that
their troubles were chiefly due to excessive issues of bank
paper and the enlargement of credit facilities, to heavy investments in unproductive lands, to the creation of fictitious
values, and to "the rapid growth, among all classes, especially
in our great commercial towns, of luxurious habits founded
too often on merely fancied wealth, and detrimental alike to
the industry, the resources, and the morals of our people."

Having read the people this lesson, Van Buren, speaking in
the name of the Government, disclaimed all responsibility
worthy of note for the hardships in which the people found
themselves plunged. "All communities," he said, "are apt
to look to government for too much. Even in our own coun-

try, where its powers and duties are so strictly limited, we are prone to do so, especially at periods of sudden embarrassment and distress. This ought not to be. The framers of our excellent Constitution and the people who approved it with calm and sagacious deliberation acted at the time on a sounder principle. They wisely judged that the less government interferes with private pursuits the better for the general prosperity. . . . Its real duty . . . is to enact and enforce a system of general laws commensurate with, but not exceeding, the objects of its establishment, and to leave every citizen and every interest to reap under its benign protection the rewards of virtue, industry, and prudence." In reality, of course, the framers of the Constitution had created a government designed to interfere extensively with economic affairs, but by 1837 the Democratic fiction of the Constitution had been substituted for the truth of the business; and only disgruntled old Federalists and Whigs were likely to challenge Van Buren's constitutional theory.

Having opened with a false premise in respect of the Constitution, Van Buren proceeded to his conclusion : "If therefore I refrain from suggesting to Congress any specific plan for regulating the exchanges of the country, relieving mercantile embarrassments, or interfering with the ordinary operations of foreign or domestic commerce, it is from a conviction that such measures are not within the constitutional province of the General Government, and that their adoption would not promote the real and permanent welfare of those they might be designed to aid."

After stoutly refusing aid to business and commerce, Van Buren, in silence, left to the strained mercies of private charity the unemployed of the urban centers, whose miseries are so graphically described in the pages of Horace Greeley's reminiscences. The example set by Van Buren, with modifications in detail, was followed by President Grant and President Hayes during the panic that began in 1873 and by President Cleveland twenty years later. Apart from proposals bearing on the Treasury, their innovations in policy consisted mainly of measures intended to contract currency and credit, as suggested by experienced bankers, and the use of federal troops in industrial disputes. Such in broad outlines was the system of theory and practice which served as a precedent and ideal for President Hoover when another great depression opened in the autumn of 1929.

But Hoover rejected this policy of negation, so foreign to the spirit of social welfare, engineering, and promotion, and embarked upon a program of positive action designed to mitigate, if not prevent, the evil consequences of the depression. Though his program, as a matter of course, came within the framework of his experience and social philosophy, it was none the less radical in its implications, for it marked a departure from the renunciation of his predecessors. It accepted a responsibility on the part of the Federal Government for breaking the clutches of the crisis and for seeking ways and means of overcoming the violent fluctuations of such cyclical disturbances. Instead of greeting the visitation with the old cry, "God wills it," or "Nature decrees it," Hoover invoked intelligence and took action in conquering the periodical "black death" which had so often disrupted industrial processes. In so doing he drew upon himself the easy criticism of those who said that he did not do enough or did the wrong thing, but such strictures in no way obscured the fact that he broke from precedents and made precedents in the discharge of his duties as Chief Executive of the United States.

§

Although Hoover developed the features of his program seriatim as the course of the depression unfolded, in their completed form they displayed economic consistency. As Secretary of Commerce, he had formulated a project for expanding the construction of public works to absorb workers discharged from private employment during industrial contraction. In accordance with this scheme, now as the President, he appealed to state and local authorities to coöperate with the Federal Government "in the energetic yet prudent" expansion of public works enterprises. Resorting to a world war precedent, he recommended, and Congress provided for, the creation of the Reconstruction Finance Corporation in 1932, endowed with the power to make loans to banks, railroads, exporters of agricultural products, and to farmers for crop production, all under specific terms as to security. Legislation easing credit for debt-burdened farmers and slowing down foreclosures was supplemented by a measure which set up a system of discount banks authorized to make loans to home owners in peril of losing their shelter. With a view to stimulating enterprise through "reopening credit channels," the discount facilities of Federal Reserve banks were enlarged and hitherto ineligible paper was admitted as the basis for advances to member banks. In addition, Hoover urged upon Congress a revision of legislation "to restore confidence in railroad bonds," to afford more adequate safeguards for depositors in banks, and to curtail federal expenditures in various directions.

All these elements of the President's program dovetailed together in a reasoned pattern that conformed to a conception of economics widely held if not dominant. Under this conception the economic entrepreneur supplies, in addition to management, the necessary capital, and his capital set in motion creates wealth — producers' goods and consumers' goods — and gives employment. To take care of an increasing population, extend employment, and raise standards of living, an appropriate expansion of capital in the form of accumulations, money, and credit is likewise indispensable to a steady operation of economy. "Normally" the provision of capital through savings and the drive of the profit motive automatically keep the economic mechanism running smoothly and in the best possible manner. Whatever the "causes" of a business depression, it is accompanied by a tightening of the money market and a slowing down of enterprise. Hence in harmony with the conception, the Government can give an impetus to the sluggish mechanism by expanding the credit facilities offered to entrepreneurs and by adding to the buying power of labor through wages paid on public works. It is true, as Democratic critics alleged, that this policy meant giving special aid to "men at the top" of the system, but it also implied the belief that the benefits of such aid would rapidly percolate to the bottom of the social pyramid. If so, would the benefits be realized in fact and be diffused rapidly enough to convince the expectants at the bottom that the remedy was sufficient?

On this question the fate of President Hoover's administration mainly turned. In the beginning many Democrats and some insurgent Republicans vigorously denied the general efficacy of the cure, though they accepted its essential features. In line with historic use and wont in politics, they harassed the administration by criticizing details and by imputing to it the primary desire to aid capitalists in banking, railway, and other enterprises. After the Democrats captured the House of Representatives in the mid-term elections, the sniping at the President grew in intensity. As the number of unemployed increased and economic distress became more acute, members of Congress insisted upon direct federal aid to the jobless and brought up proposals directed to that end. Precedents for this action they found in previous grants to sufferers from earthquakes, famines, floods, and droughts. As chairman of the American Relief Administration, Hoover had supervised the disbursement of $100,000,000 appropriated by Congress in 1919 for relieving misery in Europe and at one time the Administration had ten million pitiable Russians on its roll of dependents. In view of such examples and the rising distress in America, congressional leaders rallied in increasing force to the idea of making federal appropriations for the relief of the unemployed through state and local agencies.

Such proposals, however, did not harmonize with President Hoover's sense of propriety and he condemned them. "I am opposed," he said bluntly in 1931, "to any direct or indirect Government dole." He announced himself as equally opposed to any scheme of federal unemployment insurance and killed by a pocket veto a bill providing federal aid for employment exchanges. When Congress attempted to appropriate twenty-five million dollars for relief, to be distributed by the Red Cross, administration forces were thrown athwart the effort. When Congress seemed persistent, the chairman of the Red Cross defiantly announced that his association would refuse to disburse any money appropriated to it from federal resources. Only under terrific pressure did Hoover consent to sign a bill authorizing loans to state agencies for relief work and self-liquidating projects — in July, 1932, while the presidential campaign was in progress. When a number of veterans, "the bonus army," poor and hungry, marched on Washington and settled there to promote "adjusted compensation" legislation, he employed federal troops to rout and disperse them; their tents were burned and blood was spilled. Congressional dissent from his relief policy, especially in the forms made manifest, he denounced as playing politics with human misery, and to the end of his term he continued to insist that direct aid for the unemployed was a duty of localities and private charities. This position, he argued, was necessary to "the maintenance of the American system of individual initiative and community responsibility."

§

Insofar as he was called upon to meet emergency problems in international relations, President Hoover also kept well within the circle of his economic philosophy. When great banking houses in Vienna fell into dire straits in the spring of 1931 and their difficulties were followed by bank failures in Germany, it became evident that Germany could not continue to pay both reparations to the victorious Allies and installments on the debts owed to private investors abroad. Besides the billions in long term loans made to Germany in the period of expansive prosperity, there were short term credits amounting to hundreds of millions which had been extended by British and American bankers in quest of high interest returns. Clearly the Germans had overborrowed and when pinched by the depression they could not meet their obligations.

While the contingency was painful to the creditors, it was no surprise to German economists and statesmen. For a long time common rumor in Berlin had intimated that in the next crisis foreign banks and investors would call upon their respective governments to forego reparations or public debts in the interest of private money lenders. And the crisis came in 1931. Although the United States Government had refused to admit an official connection between German reparations and payments on the debts owed by the Allies, American bankers knew that an economic connection existed or could be established through pressure politics. Indeed the whole structure of reparations and inter-governmental debts interfered with the business of bankers engaged in floating foreign loans in the United States and likewise with export and import business in general. Well aware of this obvious relation, one of them had earlier hired a propagandist to tour the Middle West and convert the hinterland to the gospel of public debt cancellation — in the interest of private debts. The forgiveness of debtors — "our Associates in the War for Democracy" — had a pleasant moral connotation and it would clear the way for more private loans and trade abroad, with compensatory commissions thereunto attached.

Having been occupied as Secretary of Commerce in promoting foreign commerce and money lending, President Hoover clung to the belief that these economic activities were indispensable to domestic prosperity. "In peace time," he had said in 1926, "our exports and imports are the margins upon which our well-being depends. The export of our surplus enables us to use in full our resources and energy. . . . The making of loans to foreign countries for productive purposes not only increases our direct exports but builds up the prosperity of foreign countries and is a blessing to both sides of the transaction." So molded by experience and instructed by his philosophy, Hoover reached the conclusion that a moratorium on inter-governmental debts would be advantageous to private recovery, when the German crisis broke over his head.

Although Congress was not in session, the President communicated with individual members by wire and, receiving favorable responses, he proposed to all the countries concerned, in June, 1931, a moratorium for one year on inter-governmental obligations. Italy and Great Britain quickly agreed. Somewhat stunned by the suddenness of the proposition, France balked for a time and insisted on coupling provisos with her acceptance. Reacting rapidly to private hopes, the prices of stocks leaped upward on the New York Exchange, only to sink back again after a second thought had come to the brokers. When Congress ratified the moratorium at its next session in December, it held stubbornly to the old contention that the public debts owed to the United States by foreign governments would have to be paid. For importers, exporters, bankers engaged in lending money abroad, and advocates of American participation in the European concert of powers this was a grave disappointment.

In the end, most of the applause that had greeted the moratorium in metropolitan centers was blanketed by complaints of Senators and Representatives from the unconverted regions. Not without a display of resentment did Congress finally ratify the temporary concession to the foreign governments and the rumor spread that the American taxpayers had been outwitted by the bankers again. An action that had been welcomed as a wise and generous gesture was now characterized in Democratic quarters as another ingenious stroke designed to aid "the men at the top," in the hope that benefits would seep down to the base of the social pyramid.

§

President Hoover's measures, taken collectively, were not swiftly followed by results sufficiently patent to silence the accumulating protest and criticism. And for bitter criticism, especially of the political type, he was ill-prepared by practice. As a promoting engineer, particularly in the Orient, he had been accustomed to giving orders to employees who obeyed with alacrity and asked no irritating questions. As the head of great international relief enterprises he had possessed large powers, dispensed huge sums of money, received the unstinted praise of multitudes whose woes he had alleviated. This is not to say that he had encountered no abuse or buffets of fortune; but certainly, until he sought the Republican nomination in 1928, his political experience had been restricted to bureaucratic administrations. With the recorded history and practice of great politics his acquaintance was not, to speak moderately, equal to his knowledge of private affairs.

Moreover, the give-and-take, the squabbles over spoils, the personal mischiefs, the hateful disagreements and equally intense love-feasts of petty politics were alien to his spirit and his conceptions of values. The ancient rule of "going along" he could not accept. He had entered high official life by the front door. The post of Secretary of Commerce had come to him as a reward for outstanding services and accomplishments in war and peace, not as a political job. With backslapping, huckstering, and growling members of Congress he was never at ease. To strong dissent of any kind he was sensitive and he was inclined to regard even remonstrances, if pertinacious, as a form of bumptiousness. His trials and vexations were not more onerous than those of some other Presidents, but his capacity for treating them lightly or humorously was smaller than that of politicians who had battled their way upward to the White House along the arduous path of party hustle and tussle. His tenacity was little tempered by their flexibility. Entangled in his own limitations, he could not, like Lincoln, tell stories and laugh loudly when Democrats in the House hawked at him and members of his party in the Senate harassed him. He had never acquired the art of symbolizing his opponents in the lineaments of cold-blooded greed, cunning, or futility, whether they deserved it or not, and was both astonished and grieved to see himself so portrayed.

Besides suffering from the cruel thrusts of ordinary politics, President Hoover was the victim of hard circumstances — the dissolutions and heartburnings of the economic depression. No President or party had ever fully escaped the political effects of such convulsions. Though at the head of triumphant Jacksonian Democracy, Van Buren was overwhelmed in 1840 by a resurgence of the shattered and impotent Whigs. In the middle of the depression that opened in 1873, the popular verdict was against the Republicans under whose auspices it had opened, and it is highly doubtful whether Hayes was even victorious in the electoral college. Cleveland was repudiated by his party in 1896 and the Democrats were driven from office by a Republican revival.

Now, in 1932, the nemesis was to overtake the Republicans. They had been in power when the panic began and, not without some justification, they incurred the charge of responsibility for it. When the sun of prosperity rose they had generally taken credit for the event; the good fortune, they claimed, had been due to their prowess. As their candidate, Herbert Hoover had promised to continue their beneficent policies and had expressed the hope that such poverty as remained might thus be banished from the land. If the Republicans had once caused the sun to rise, why could they not do it again? If they could not, their alleged powers were delusive and their bold front was a sham. They were victims, not makers, of history. Such at least was the tenor of the popular verdict. With a thirst for alcohol rising as the depression deepened, President Hoover, an advocate of prohibition, was caught in a grip of forces too tenacious for his strength and ingenuity. If, as Phillip Guedalla has said, the final position of a statesman in history depends upon the nature of his exit from the stage, the circumstances of Mr. Hoover's departure were certainly ungenerous to his undoubted merits and talents. Necessities that could not be

broken closed in upon him and his party during the onward
sweep of the economic catastrophe.

§

Outside the circles of Republican theorizing and Democratic nagging, an immense upsurge of private inquiry and
thought, in the fashion of American democracy, inundated
the country with critical dissertations and new plans. Beyond the dispute in words lay the fact that the ponderous
machine covered by President Hoover's economic philosophy
had slowed down to less than half its potential speed, strew-
ing bankruptcies and human casualties from the center to
the periphery of society. Above the optimistic prophecies
of trade promoters was heard the crash of foreign markets,
as bonds went into default and the grand stake abroad
shriveled. Over against the promises of ever-expanding outlets for American "surpluses" in the wake of empire rose
mountains of "surpluses," for which no sales could be found.
Furthermore the pressure of imports from imperial possessions bore heavily upon already demoralized domestic markets for agricultural produce.

From every angle of vision undeniable signs of the deepening
depression thrust themselves into the range of observation —
machines idle, engines rusting, locomotives weather-beaten
on grass-grown sidings, ships without cargoes tossing mourn-
fully at anchor, tractors silent in deserted fields. In that province especially assigned by tradition to women were tokens
of decay: empty cupboards, ragged clothes, unpainted
houses, stinking jungles of wood and tin in the very shadows
of the centers of culture. Newspapers, journals and books
teemed with stories of wandering men and women, boys
and girls adrift, ruined homes, deserted families, leaders of
finance poring over balance sheets of wrecked hopes, and, on
the slabs of city morgues, bodies of suicides finding in death
a security against want denied in life. Although high officials
knew about these things, private citizens, especially teach-

ers and relief workers, thrown daily into close contact with them, were acutely disturbed by them. For a time even the firm assurance of economic optimists — their faith in the "natural course," the "invisible hand," and "the long run" — was shattered.

After many months had elapsed and oft-repeated promises of prosperity "just around the corner" had grown stale, a profound searching of minds and hearts brought forth ideas never before expressed so widely in the high places of American power. Throughout the year 1931, as signs of havoc spread, the volume of indignant protests and demands mounted. On March 27, Daniel Willard, president of the Baltimore and Ohio Railroad, speaking at the fiftieth anniversary of the Wharton School in the University of Pennsylvania, laid squarely before the assembled dignitaries the problem presented by enormous productive capacity on the one side and unemployment and dire need on the other. The gravity of this condition and its challenge to their intelligence he emphasized in positive terms. The system that made it possible for five or six million people to be idle and vainly searching for work, he declared to the professors and benefactors, was unsatisfactory and had failed in one important respect. Placing himself in the position of a working man in the peril of starvation for himself and his family, the master of railway management shot a bolt of horror into Respectability by asserting : "While I do not like to say so, I would be less than candid if I did not say that in such circumstances I would steal before I would starve." Governors of law and order could scarcely believe their ears.

On June 3, 1931, Matthew Woll, acting president of the National Civic Federation which had so long combatted liberals, whether red or pink, addressed an open letter to James W. Gerard, who had recently drawn up the famous list of "sixty-four rulers of America." The appeal urged Mr. Gerard to call a national industrial congress for the purpose of framing plans for overcoming the crisis, applying economic powers rationally, and giving permanent security to the

nation. "We need," Mr. Woll declared, "to meet the cold-
blooded communist five-year plan with a warm-blooded ten-
year plan of democratic idealism woven into the very pattern
of our national fabric." In language even more pointed,
Mr. Woll laid before the country in a radio broadcast the problem which Daniel Willard had presented at Philadelphia a
few weeks earlier. "It is unthinkable," he exclaimed, "that
America can consent to face such a problem, with all of its
physical, mental, and moral endowment, and permit itself
to be found sitting idly, waiting for the 'ferment' to settle,
quiescent, hoping somehow we will 'muddle through.'" Rejecting the economists' confidence in the inerrant efficiency of
the slow-moving price mechanism, Mr. Woll called upon the
leaders of industry and labor to plan, establish, and assure an
economic system of abundance and security. Time might pronounce the design chimerical, but the thought and feeling
which it expressed flowed into the currents of opinion and
inclination that were to make history.

A few days later, June 11, 1931, Nicholas Murray Butler,
addressing the American Club in Paris, under the title of Progress and Poverty, described the revolutionary consequences
of mass production in labor displacement and warned his
audience that this alone, apart from the devastation of the
world war, would have produced a crisis in our economic and
social life. With labor unemployed, the power of consumption destroyed, and democratic forces at work in society, the
western world suffered from a "lack of competent, constructive, courageous leadership, political, social, and economic."
There was the puzzle. And what was the answer? "The universal answer of the office-holding class is 'Wait.'" On this
form of statecraft, Dr. Butler dryly commented: "Gentlemen, if we wait too long somebody will come forward with a
solution that we may not like. Let me call your attention to
the fact that the characteristic feature of the experiment in
Russia, to my mind, is not that it is communist, but that it is
being carried on with a plan in the face of a planless opposition. The man with a plan, however much we may dislike it,

has a vast advantage over the group sauntering down the road of life complaining of the economic weather and wondering when the rain is going to stop." Later in the same year Dr. Butler, in expounding the same philosophy, analyzed the chief presuppositions of orthodox economics, framed a long list of specifications for reform, and concluded with a vigorous appeal for action to fortify the foundations of our social and economic order. As if remembering the old aphorism "with what little wit the world is governed," Dr. Butler remarked ironically : "If, as Junius wrote to the Duke of Bedford, we cannot be safe, we may at least cease to be ridiculous!"

In the autumn of 1931 a special commission of the Federal Council of the Churches of Christ issued a message of criticism and proposal to be read to congregations on Labor Sunday. The document drew a gruesome picture — of men and women tramping the streets in search of work, crowding into churches and police stations seeking relief, standing in bread lines, waiting in the vestibules of charitable societies. At least twenty times since 1855 the country had passed through business depressions, it stated. Are we to endure this forever? it asked. When prosperity returns are we to drift and repeat again this story of frustration and agony? There are grave imperfections in an economic system which makes possible the awful contrast of vast fortunes and breadlines. A new conception of the position and needs of workers in the modern world is necessary, and the best minds of the nation must be applied to the reconstruction and planning of our social and economic life on sound religious principles. In a spirit of renewed dedication, the Council declared: "The facts of the situation themselves constitute a challenge to the churches to assume their rightful place of ethical leadership ; to demand fundamental changes in present economic conditions ; to protest against the selfish desire for wealth as the principal motive of industry ; to insist upon the creation of an industrial society which shall have as its purpose economic security and freedom for the masses of mankind, 'even these least, my brethren' ; to seek the development of a social order which shall be based upon Jesus' principles of love and brotherhood."

About the same time the bishops of the Protestant Episcopal Church, in a pastoral letter, proclaimed to the faithful that "the contrast between individual want and collective plenty cannot be accepted as in accordance with the will of God." The resources of the earth are unimpaired, and multitudes dependent upon doles and charity constitute an arraignment of the present economic system. Our "acquisitive society," they said, stands bewildered in the presence of a crisis precipitated not by physical catastrophe, "but apparently by the competitive, profit-seeking principles upon which, it has hitherto been assumed, general prosperity is based." Immediate relief must be given, but that is not enough. Society must see that such a crisis does not occur again. Though the Church cannot advocate a particular method, it calls upon employers "to labor for the adoption of a plan or plans which shall coördinate production and consumption, insure continuity of employment, and provide security of income to the workers of the nation. . . . The profit-seeking motive must give way to that of service." To economic distress and political unrest are added the aggravations of force in international relations : "We, with the cave man, still depend upon force, the only difference being that his club has developed into vastly more efficient agents of destruction." This, too, is in violation of Christian principles and contrary to the Christian attitude from its beginning. Throbbing with emotion, this mingled condemnation and constructive appeal rang through the Protestant Episcopal Churches and awakened echoes from Maine to California.

It was one thing for the clergy, somewhat removed from the turmoil of the marketplace and committed by faith to ethical principles, to arraign the economic order and demand measures of planning and protection against such afflictions. All this Great Business might take with a grain of salt, for it had long been accustomed to seeing men who lacked knowledge of practice indulge in theorizing. But on Sep-

tember 16, 1931, a distinguished industrial leader, Gerard
Swope, of the General Electric Company, startled Respectability by an address on planning delivered to the National
Electrical Manufacturers Association, at the Hotel Com-
modore in New York City, the very citadel of the Lords of
Creation. In language more restrained than that of the
clergy, he dwelt upon the sad plight of willing workers seeking employment, yet insisted that the presence of this condition in such periods of depression "detracts nothing from its
wrongness." Then, with a deliberation evidently studied,
Mr. Swope warned his brethren in business enterprise:
"That industry must evolve and make effective those measures which will first ameliorate and ultimately eliminate
these conditions must be the reaction of everyone who gives
thought to what is taking place. Industry must do this thing,
because it will surely be done." In other words, if industry
did not order its household, society would act through its
government. Having pointed to the handwriting on the wall,
Mr. Swope put forth the elements of a plan designed to
stabilize industry and employment, rationalize and purify
business management, and safeguard workers against the
vicissitudes of economic stresses and strains. Two months
later, Mr. Swope amplified his original plan in an address
before the Academy of Political Science in New York City,
thus giving economists a vision of things unnoted in the
classical scheme under the "invisible hand" of Providence.

At the meeting of the Electrical Manufacturers Association
before which Mr. Swope laid his original design, Owen D.
Young was present and spoke in support of the general purpose underlying it. His address was brief and pointed. Its
staccato sentences were punctuated with caveats to the Lords
of Creation. "To the insistent calls for industrial leadership
in these disorganized times," he told them, "there has been a
discouraging silence." Academic theses had been submitted
to the country, but they were far removed from practical
application. Now Mr. Swope, "after previous conference
with his associates in the electrical manufacturing industry,"

submits a plan definite in terms and bearing the testimonial of practicality. It is not free from criticism. It raises grave questions of public and business policy. But alternatives must be faced. Three courses are open. We can do nothing and accept the "system of intensified individualism which, because of its disordered action, necessarily brings great peaks of prosperity and valleys of depression." We can place positive responsibilities upon industry for planning and stabilization. We can acquiesce in government action, "providing the means for employee protection through the power of taxation." These are the three positions, with some possible compromises, which every citizen should consider. "What is the answer? Which shall it be?" Although caution marked Mr. Young's periods, there could be no doubt that he was deeply moved and felt oppressed by the gravity of the national crisis.

On the day following the publication of Mr. Swope's plan in the newspapers near and far, industrial leaders, editors, publicists, politicians, professors, and clergymen started a torrent of comment and debate. Samuel Vauclain, of the Baldwin Locomotive Works, replied tartly: "I don't believe in it," but the judgments of business leaders were on the whole favorable. Speaking as president of the United States Chamber of Commerce, Silas Strawn pronounced the scheme "excellent" and in line with plans then being projected by his association. Dr. John A. Ryan, of the National Catholic Welfare Conference, commended the objects of Mr. Swope's plan as admirable, but thought that business men in general did not have "sense enough" to form the trade associations required by the proposal unless compelled to do it by law. How could it be done by law "under our Constitution"?

As usual, the politicians, recognizing the dynamite in the plan, were circumspect. Many Democrats, according to their scheme of thought, surmised that some tinkering with the sacred text of the anti-trust laws was in the offing, although other Democrats promised to weigh and consider Mr. Swope's proposition. Senator Simeon Fess, chairman of the Republican national committee, observed that the plan was "constructive" and ventured the opinion that it would be studied with care by government economists and industrial leaders. Speaking for the agrarian interests, Senator Smith W. Brookhart made caustic suggestions and exclaimed : "I am glad to see a great business manager conceding the collapse of the capitalistic system !" Whatever unfolding time might reveal — action, escape, repudiation, or oblivion — it was certain that Mr. Swope had shaken the pillars of Respectability for the season and thrown a burning brand of thought into the very center of complacency.

Meanwhile there were stirrings among the officers of the American Federation of Labor. The traditions of the Federation had been, in the main, conservative. It had accepted the imperatives of the capitalist system and within that framework had sought to win for labor what was loosely called "a fair share" of the product of industry. But now the product to be shared had fallen to about half its former volume and good trade unionists by the thousands wandered helplessly among the throngs of the unemployed, sat disconsolately on park benches, or moped in kitchens or chimney corners. Moved more by this spectacle than by any economic theories, the executive council of the Federation prepared for the convention, in October, 1931, a long report on the industrial system and measures of relief and prevention to be taken.

In this document the council rejected the academic hypothesis that the automatic workings of the price system brought justice, efficiency, and beneficence. It referred to the unequal distribution of wealth, in fact; to the lack of buying power among the people; and to the trials visited upon the country by the depression : "This unequal distribution of the nation's income throws the industrial mechanism out of balance." The President of the United States should call a national economic conference; planning and coördination should be projected by a national economic council; all the facts of business enterprises should be public property;

a federal labor board should collect statistical information on which to base constructive policies. Like organized business, organized labor shrank from a government control too stringent; yet it assigned to government a kind of directive role in stabilizing and assuring the full operation of economic processes. Although its program of action was not far removed from that of President Hoover, the Federation had ostensibly forsaken the essential principle of historic capitalism — the automatic attainment of the highest possible prosperity through the deterministic operations of the acquisitive instinct.

Without waiting for business men of Wisconsin to grapple resolutely with the panic somehow acknowledged to be associated with their system, Governor Philip La Follette, in November, 1931, summoned the state legislature in a special session. In a resonant message he presented the issues as he saw them. "We are in the midst of the greatest domestic crisis since the Civil War," he opened. "In this crisis, people are divided broadly into two groups: one opposes, and one favors, collective action to meet the emergency and to guard against its recurrence in the future." For ten years business has tolerated the deflation of agriculture. It has failed to put its own house in order. Capital has controlled our business machine and enjoyed the lion's share of the return from its operation. In 1929 "the top rung of our federal financial ladder, comprising 504 individuals," reported net incomes of over two million dollars apiece. They are not "worth" it for "the kind of leadership they have given us." Then followed a caustic etching of the contrast between concentrated wealth and the miseries engendered by the depression.

Having pictured indubitable features of the calamity, Governor La Follette submitted a program of legislation. It embraced the extension of public ownership, the stabilization of private business, unemployment insurance, the provision of machinery for community planning, a drastic revision of banking practices, and the equalization of the burdens of taxation. The struggle would be rough, the Governor told the legislators, but a government that had sent four million men to war could put five million persons to work. A government that had squandered billions for destruction could spend billions for enterprises of peace to insure a richer life. Simply stated, we are engaged in the "age-old struggle of mankind to build a better world."

In December, 1931, shortly after the legislature of Wisconsin had begun to wrestle seriously with the Governor's proposals, the United States Chamber of Commerce made public a report of its committee "on continuity of business and employment." The document was the outcome of a long study made on the demand of the Chamber for a project dealing with unemployment distress and for "a rational program of production and distribution to be initiated by business itself." While accepting the fundamental principles of capitalism, the report expressed grave doubts respecting the universality of its automatic beneficence. It pointed out the perils of speculative activity, war, and depressed agriculture. The freedom of individual action which might have been justified in the relatively simple life of the past century "cannot be tolerated today," for the unwise action of a single individual may adversely affect the lives of thousands. "We have left the period of extreme individualism and are living in a period in which national economy must be recognized as the controlling factor." The calamities of the time have been overemphasized, but the call to action is inescapable. "To an onlooker from another world, our situation must seem as stupid and anomalous as it seems painful to us. We are in want because we have too much. People go hungry while our farmers cannot dispose of their surpluses of food; unemployed are anxious to work, while there is machinery idle with which they could make the things they need. Capital and labor, facilities for production and transportation, raw materials and food, all these essential things we have in seeming superabundance. We lack only applied intelligence to bring them fruitfully into employment. This condition has led to a host of suggestions for national planning."

Though moderate in language, the report to the Chamber of Commerce was severe in its criticism of past methods in business enterprise. On the constructive side, it proposed the creation of a national economic council, under private auspices but including representation from the United States Department of Commerce. This council should employ experts of high competence, study the structure, functioning, and trends of business, lay bare the operations of the market place, and supply information for the guidance of enterprises. Under relaxed anti-trust laws, business concerns should be permitted to enter into contracts "for the purpose of equalizing production to consumption," and conducting business "on a sound basis." The formation of trade associations, the provision of unemployment reserves, private unemployment insurance, and other elements of planning, as suggested by the project of Gerard Swope, were brought under review. Immediate relief should be provided by private charity and by state and local government; proposals for federal appropriations should be opposed; but business enterprise has obligations pertaining to stabilization and continuity of employment — obligations created by a faulty functioning of the automatic system. There must not be delay, the Chamber's report insisted. "Time presses."

By the time the report to the Chamber of Commerce reached the public, a sub-committee of the Senate committee on manufactures, under the chairmanship of Robert M. La Follette, Jr., had held hearings on a bill to establish a national economic council. In the course of its proceedings, the subcommittee took the testimony of distinguished men of affairs, such as James A. Farrell, of United States Steel; Albert H. Wiggin, of the Chase National Bank; Alfred P. Sloan, of General Motors; and Charles E. Mitchell, of the National City Bank. It called upon eminent economists for their analysis and exposition of the severe contraction in business and for ways and means of mitigation and escape: upon Wallace B. Donham of the Harvard Business School, John M. Clark of Columbia University, and Virgil Jordan, formerly chief economist for the National Industrial Conference Board, for example. Spokesmen of labor, management, and social reform also laid their views before the subcommittee in language deliberately measured, yet revealing indignation at a system that permitted the stark contrast between potential plenty and evident misery and degradation. Day after day, Senator La Follette inquired and probed, seeking from great men of affairs and from close students of economy the clue to the deep mystery: How did it all happen and what is the way out?

At one end of the scale, Albert H. Wiggin answered for the philosophers of the "unconscious, automatic functioning of the markets." Is it possible to stabilize our industrial activity to any degree? "I do not think so." Did investment bankers contribute materially to the inflation and explosion in the security business? They were trying to supply what the customers wanted. Were they merely interested in the profits to be obtained from mergers and the issuance of securities under their auspices? "I should think so." Did the investment banker's incentive for profit affect his attitude toward the issuance of large security issues? "No banker intends to issue a security that is not going to be absorbed by the investing public. In other words, he is in business for profit and to make money." What is the way out? "Revival of business in the United States depends upon: (1) rapprochement between France and Germany; (2) reduced reparations; (3) reduced interallied debts; and (4) reduced tariffs."

Near the close of this hearing, Senator La Follette remarked: "Your counsel is one really of despair, then." Mr. Wiggin answered: "Human nature is human nature. Lives go on. So long as business activity goes on we are bound to have conditions of crisis once in so often." The Senator thought a moment and then commented: "The capacity for human suffering is unlimited?" The great man of affairs answered: "I think so." To clinch his contentions, Mr. Wiggin handed to the subcommittee a statement by Doctor

Benjamin Anderson, economic adviser to the Chase National Bank, who, the witness explained, is "highly respected. . . . He is a university man and a man of great intelligence. He is conscientious, and gives the truth of the situation." The learned Doctor's statement, when read into the record, proved to be a swift summary of the classic doctrine of laissez faire : let us alone and rely upon the unconscious, automatic functioning of the market. Thus an ancient code was repeated by rote and incorporated in a government document.

Against this classic theory, formulated by a learned Doctor and presented by one of the Lords of Creation, Senator La Follette set the statistics showing the functioning of the market as compiled by E. A. Goldenweiser, director of research and statistics of the Federal Reserve Board. In the form of graphic charts, Mr. Goldenweiser displayed the violent fluctuations of production and employment during the glorious age of prosperity from 1919 to 1931. As they stared at these charts, the Senators tried to see in the steep peaks and deep valleys the "equilibrium" of unconscious and automatic markets. Apparently equilibrium in reality did not conform to theory, even in a rough approximation.

By other economists, also respected and conscientious, "the truth of the situation" was presented in terms quite unlike the philosophy of the unconscious offered by the Chase National Bank. While rejecting the idea of iron regimentation in communist forms, they pointed out a long list of abuses in the capitalist system — abuses that did not square at all with the capitalist doctrine of "let us alone." Letting them alone, in fact, had not ended grave dislocations and suffering. The "unconscious" men in the market places should wake up, acquire a realistic knowledge of industrial processes, and substitute managerial intelligence for mere pecuniary interest and the automatic, acquisitive instinct. There had been reckless and ruinous financing of uneconomical projects. There is now a maldistribution of wealth that curtails buying power. Business must plan within the limits of exact knowledge ; government must deal boldly with rash banking and credit inflation and with swollen incomes and inheritances. If some economists seemed to be satisfied that this was the best possible world, others were ostensibly applying the sharp edge of analysis to capitalism, its methods, and its calamities. While the news of the hearings was flowing from the press, the reading public learned something about the kind of thinking that was going on among those in high places who were supposed to be exercising their brains.

§

As the distressful year of 1931 wore into the distressful year 1932 and preparations for the presidential campaign approached, the climate of opinion was vibrant with asserting, searching, doubting, hoping, and planning. Wherever confident citizens assembled in comfortable homes or paneled offices, the phrases of business inherited from times past ran current. Capital, the fruit of thrift and saving. Freedom of movement for capital and labor. Individual initiative, the paramount reliance. The profit motive, the source of prosperity. Restoration of equilibrium through the price mechanism. The natural order. Freedom of the markets. Business cycles. Readjustments. Best system in the world. Bigger prosperity after every panic. Recovery around the corner. No government interference. Loans from the Treasury for banks, railways, and insurance companies in distress. Charity and state and local relief for the unemployed. No starvation. The crazed public in quest of opportunities for investment. War, the cause of troubles. No limit to the suffering of humanity. I should not think so. I do not remember. I cannot recall. It may have been. To some extent, possibly. Technical correction by decline in stock prices. The American system. We may look forward without anxiety. Of such conceptions singly or in combinations was composed the thought of Respectability as it moved toward the quadrennial election geared by the Constitution of the United States to the movement of the planets.

Other words resounded in emphatic reiteration among clergymen, teachers, doctors, engineers, labor leaders, social workers, politicians, and business men who were not as certain in conviction as the members of Respectability. Our acquisitive society. Stark contrast between plenty and misery. Unbalance. Disequilibrium. Defects in capitalism. Rigid prices. Economics of scarcity. Tragedy of waste. Maldistribution of wealth. The absurdity of want amid plenty. Stealing preferable to starving. Challenges to the social order. Security of employment. Palaces and breadlines. Misery and luxury. Instability of industry. Parity of agriculture and industry. Bankruptcies and suicides. Crisis in government and economy. War on depression and poverty. Betrayal of fiduciary trust. Fraudulent securities. Control by corporations. Collective action. They guessed wrong. Economic planning. National planning. The folly of fatalism. Robber barons. Business must act. Government must act. Unendurable. Ridiculous. Insult to intelligence. Never again. Where now are the Lords of Creation?

If some of these words and phrases were intended to be coldly descriptive, all directly or by implication fanned the blaze of emotional insurgency. The recital of facts riddled the validity of old formulas. Ideas laden with revolutionary suggestions, once limited to groups obscure and unimportant, raced like wildfire from one end of the country to the other, adding intellectual ferment to the physical hardships that attended economic dissolutions.

CHAPTER III

The Referendum in the Crisis

WITH the inexorability of time the presidential election, as prescribed by the chronology of the Constitution, drew near, and politicians made ready for a great referendum on leadership, personalities, policies, measures, and the state of the nation. As the hour of decision approached, scanners of the horizon searched for portents in experience and philosophy. Despite signs of an upturn in economy, the shadows of dissolutions lay heavily upon the landscape, rural and urban. Slogans tinctured with radicalism were uttered in all parts of the country. Under powerful and respectable auspices comprehensive plans had been put forward for overcoming the ills of the panic and preventing such black plagues in the future.

In the circumstances many prophets forecast an immense diversion of political loyalty from the major parties that had long held the affections of the voters. Would history repeat itself? The panic of 1873 had been followed by violent agitations, the rise of a militant, if small, labor movement, and the rapid spread of the Greenback party. Indeed that

113

faction polled approximately a million votes in the congressional elections of 1878 and threatened to split both Republicans and Democrats. In the wake of the next crash, in 1893, had come a renewal of labor disputes, the Pullman strike of 1894, the emergence of Eugene V. Debs as a socialist leader, and the capture of the Democratic party by populist ideas and enthusiasm.

Such were some of the "lessons" from American experience available to prognosticators, but they were not the sole guides to the making of forecasts in 1932. The fate of Russia in the immense collapse of 1917 had indicated that at least on one occasion exponents of the Marxian theory had guessed right or had been fortunate in the turn of events. What had once been a mere scheme of dialectics debated in pot-houses and parlors now commanded a more general consideration, even from practical persons not at all given to speculations. According to the teachings of Marx, the economic breakdown, which started in 1929, might eventuate in something more serious than defaults, bankruptcies, doles, soup kitchens, and reform. Under his explanation of history, capitalism was not an everlasting order of things; it was a system always in process of development, marked by a growing concentration of wealth and control, by a falling rate of profit, and by periodical crises as inevitable features of its motion in time.

These crises, ran the Marxian theory, would increase in intensity and devastation until, at some point in coming years, capitalism would reach the end of its profitable expansion and the final cataclysm would occur. At that conjuncture the workers, triumphing over capitalists, would ring the death-knell of the profit system, usher in socialism or communism, celebrate humanity's "spring into freedom," and close history. Whether this prophecy was to be viewed with despair or delight, Americans were constantly told by the Marxists that the great depression was the beginning of the end. Or, if the crash did not culminate in the triumph of a Stalin, it might eventuate in the dictatorship of a Mussolini; fascists welcomed that eventuality. At all events, as the election approached, the air was charged with the feeling that strange things could "happen."

It was not necessary for voters to believe in any of the radical theories afloat to be impressed by the insistent demand for immense efforts in national planning and action to overcome the crisis and erect safeguards against its return. Leaders in churches, education, engineering, business enterprise, and the American Federation of Labor had advanced and defended more planning and less laissez faire. They had called for it in addresses, programs, and manifestoes during the previous year, 1931. They had discoursed on "our acquisitive society," the inadequacy of the profit motive, the contrast between potential plenty and actual scarcity, the necessity of industrial or government action to prevent the recurrence of such ruin, and drastic modifications in the prevailing system of economic use and wont. In 1931 Dr. Nicholas Murray Butler, responsible head of a great university, had said: "The period through which we are passing . . . is a period like the fall of the Roman Empire, like the Renaissance, like the beginning of the political and social revolutions in England and in France in the seventeenth and eighteenth centuries. . . . It is in some ways more powerful than them all; and it holds more of the world in its grip than any of them, but it certainly resembles them in its epoch-marking character." That America must "face the future" with rational plans for social security was a wide conviction, the need for which was proclaimed in the pulpit, on the platform, in gatherings of "experts," from business and professional forums, in conventions of the people, in the press. And in this ferment of opinion, pulsating with intense emotion, preparations for the national referendum on the crisis opened in the spring of 1932. But in spite of all the scanning, exploring, debating, and planning, in circles high and low, politicians betrayed little interest in theories and projects. They were primarily concerned, it seemed, with the instant need of things.

Trained in the earthly school of practice, Democratic managers, to whom belonged the function of criticism and opposition, felt reasonably certain that the exasperations of the day would be ascribed to the party in power and that victory would come to them by default, if they said little about their intentions and made no mistakes in the choice of a candidate or the conduct of the campaign. Under the regime prevailing in the Solid South, many of the most experienced and astute of the Democratic politicians were men who had seen long service in Congress and had held their seats despite the reverses of their party during the age of Normalcy. Well acquainted with the demands of Southern planters, manufacturers, real estate agents, lawyers, bankers, and cotton brokers, they were accounted hardheaded and not given to apocalyptic visions.

The object of their hearts' desire was to oust from power the party that had monopolized the choice places for twelve years. And their Northern associates in the mechanics of politics were equally eager for such a fray. Since the retirement of Woodrow Wilson, "deserving" Democrats from Northern cities and fields had gathered few luscious plums from the fruitful tree in Washington. As the skilled craftsmen of the trade assembled around the table of strategy, they took some note, however, of that "lunatic fringe," called liberal, whose support might be necessary for the acquisition of desirable things; but most of them could be placated by small jobs. All the omens, then, seemed to be auspicious for a Democratic triumph.

§

While the Democrats were gathering their forces, the Republican convention assembled at Chicago, renominated President Hoover and Vice President Curtis, formulated their defensive explanation of unhappy events, and projected their program. The existence of an economic depression and widespread suffering the Republican platform frankly admitted, and then proceeded to an elucidation of the calamity which laid little or no responsibility at the door of the party. The depression was world-wide; hence, according to the implications of the thesis, it was no mere national phenomenon to be ascribed to Republican policies. When trouble first appeared in undeniable form, President Hoover had averted many misfortunes "by securing agreement between industry and labor to maintain wages and by stimulating programs of private and governmental construction." When "the great drought of 1930" intensified the hardships of the people, they were mitigated by the mobilization of resources for physical relief, through the ministrations of the Red Cross. Under the presidential leadership a nation-wide organization was effected to grapple with the situation. Thus the general welfare had been maintained, argued the platform, by a combination of Republican management and policy with popular patience and courage — until the spring of 1931.

When the revolving earth brought the spring of that year, "the possibility of a business upturn in the United States was clearly discernible." Unhappily a series of unexpected tragedies then upset the calculations. Where could responsibility be placed? The Republican platform answered: "Suddenly a train of events was set in motion in Central Europe, which moved forward with extraordinary rapidity and violence, threatening the credit structure of the world and eventually dealing a serious blow to this country. The President foresaw the danger. He sought to avert it by proposing a suspension of intergovernmental debt payments for one year." But the strain was too great for the credit machinery of Central Europe. Disintegration continued "until in September Great Britain was forced to depart from the gold standard. This momentous event, followed by a tremendous raid on the dollar, resulted in a series of bank suspensions in this country, and the hoarding of currency on a large scale."

To avert the new perils flowing from the conduct of other

nations, President Hoover again took swift and effective action. Under his initiative the National Credit Association came into being and mobilized credit resources in aid of banks; the Railroad Credit Corporation was created; the capital of the Federal Land Banks was increased; the discount facilities of the Federal Reserve System were enlarged; and the power of the Reconstruction Finance Corporation was thrown into the breach. So a foundation was again laid for recovery. At this juncture, delays in Congress and the consideration of new and unsound measures, obviously fostered by Democrats, had kept the country in a state of uncertainty and offset much of the good otherwise accomplished. Undismayed by such carping opposition, Hoover had enlarged his program, supported loans to needy states for purposes of relief, and proposed the creation of a federal relief fund to aid states during a temporary failure of financial resources. In short, foreign governments and Democrats were the principal scapegoats.

Having dumped the causes of the national calamity at other doors, the Republicans made tenders to all interests. Financiers were informed that public expenditures were to be drastically reduced, Hoover's unbalanced budget brought into better equilibrium, the gold standard maintained, and the banking structure repaired. Moreover the depositing and investing public was remembered: federal supervision over the Reserve system was to be widened and made more stringent. Affiliates of member banks, which had led in the flotation of securities, should be examined and required to make reports, until information was developed for a more permanent solution of the problem they had presented. Home owners were to receive additional assistance. The policy of federal aid to agriculture was to be continued and broadened. Manufacturers and farmers could confidently rely upon the maintenance and extension of the protective principle. Consumers of electric power should have the benefit of federal supervision over interstate transmission of current. Labor was reminded of the many favorable laws passed under Republican auspices. That was history. For the present and future : " Collective bargaining by responsible representatives of employers and employees, of their own choice, without the interference of any one, is recognized and approved." The language of the pledge did not make it clear whether an outside organizer for the American Federation of Labor was to be banned, but at all events there was something for the consideration of labor. Moreover the platform commended "the constructive work" of the United States Department of Labor.

As if bidding for the support of Americans who adhered to the collaboration of the world powers for peace, the Republican platform proposed an ambient policy. Membership in the World Court should be accepted. The American delegation was "laboring for progress" in the reduction of armaments at Geneva. The Republican administration had acted in harmony with the League of Nations in the interests of peace. With pointed reference to Japan's seizure of Manchukuo, it had announced that it would not recognize any situation, treaty, or agreement brought about in violation of the Kellogg Pact. In continuation of this policy, Congress should enact legislation authorizing the calling of an international congress in case of any threat that the terms of the Pact would not be fulfilled. As for "our neighbors of Latin-America," they may be sure that "we have no imperialistic ambitions." Aid had been given to Nicaragua in the solution of its troubles, the number of marines stationed there had been reduced, and services of supervision over Haiti were being rapidly abridged. But the isolationists were not neglected : there had been no entanglement in the Sino-Japanese dispute during the consistent maintenance of treaty rights and international obligations, and it had been made patent to the League of Nations "that American policy would be determined at home."

Far down the line in the Republican program, after highways, crime, narcotics, and civil service, came the plank on the Eighteenth Amendment. If the sense for news values

was a gauge of the primary public interest in the very throes
of the depression, this plank was the most important concern of the people, for The New York Times placed the
prohibition pledge of the Republicans on its first page and
relegated the rest of the party document to page fifteen.
Although a strong bloc at Chicago demanded an outright
repeal of the Amendment, Hoover's managers forced the
adoption of a middle course. The issue of prohibition repeal
was to be resubmitted to the voters and repeal, if it came,
was to be restricted by safeguards in favor of temperance :
the Federal Government was to protect dry states against
the invasion of the liquor traffic from other states and it was
also to prevent the return of the saloon. The proposal,
Hoover remarked, did not "dictate to the conscience of any
member of the party"; it guaranteed that "in no part of
the United States shall there be a return of the saloon system with its inevitable political and social corruption, and its
organized interference with other states."

Having announced and justified their faith, the Republicans shot sarcastic barbs at their opponents : "The vagaries
of the present Democratic House of Representatives offer
characteristic and appalling proof of the existing incapacity
of that party for leadership in a national crisis. Individualism running amuck has displaced party discipline and has
trampled underfoot party leadership. A bewildered electorate has viewed the spectacle with profound dismay and
deep misgivings." Unable to agree upon any grand policy,
the Democrats in Congress, according to the Republican
interpretation, had only found some unity of action around
"the pork barrel." Between the helpless citizens and the
evils threatened by such measures "a Republican President
stands resolutely," and "the people, regardless of party,
will demand his continued service." Insurgent Republicans
had also given the administration anxious days and nights.
They were not mentioned by name, but they were told that
coherent party action was necessary for the adoption of
"well-planned and wholesome" legislation. Apparently

identifying the Republican party with the nation, the platform sought to impress upon Senators and Representatives "the inflexible truth that their first concern should be the welfare of the United States and the well-being of all of its people, and that stubborn pride of individual opinion is not a virtue." After a recapitulation, the platform closed as follows: "The Republican party faces the future unafraid! With courage and confidence in ultimate success, we will strive against the forces that strike at our social and economic ideals, our political institutions."

§

In his acceptance address, President Hoover spoke with evident concern of the blights that had fallen upon the country, his efforts to cope with them, and the pledges of the party platform. Here and there he commented upon and amplified its terms, strongly commending its analysis, criticisms, and proposals. After all it was his work and came entirely within his frame of social and economic reference. For the first stage of the panic, over-production, reckless speculation, and abuse of financial power had been mainly responsible; for the second, the renewed outbreak of the "insidious diseases" left by the world war. "Two courses were open. We might have done nothing. That would have been utter ruin. Instead, we met the situation with proposals to private business and the Congress of the most gigantic program of economic defense and counter-attack ever evolved in the history of the Republic. We put it into action. . . . No government in Washington has hitherto considered that it held so broad a responsibility for leadership in such times." Yet more work remained to be done. Millions were still unemployed. Farmers' prices were below a living standard. Other millions were haunted by fears for their future. "No man with a spark of humanity can sit in my place without suffering from the picture of their anxieties and hardships before him day and night." If reëlected, the President promised that he would carry forward the work of reconstruction within the limits of the American system.

Among the generalities and pledges of Hoover's address were a few words that bore upon the agricultural problem — so fateful to his career: "The farmer was never so dependent upon his tariff protection for recovery as he is at the present time. We shall hold to that." To this particular constituency these remarks were gratifying, but insufficient. In fact, to belligerent farmers they were hollow, without meaning. Farmers were demanding measures more drastic, especially control over price-depressing surpluses. What had Mr. Hoover to say on that proposition? No such scheme could come within the scope of his economic and social philosophy. "No power on earth," he admonished the nation, "can restore prices except by restoration of general recovery and markets. . . . There is no relief to the farmer by extending government bureaucracy to control his production and thus curtail his liberties, nor by subsidies that bring only more bureaucracy and ultimate collapse. I shall oppose them." To militant agrarians gathering for the fray, this was unpalatable — all the more so as coming from a President who had created a huge bureaucracy for the promotion of commerce and housed it in a costly building, who had approved lucrative subsidies for shipping and aviation. Admittedly he expressed his conviction and with courage for his words cost votes where votes were needed. "Not regimented mechanisms, but free men, is our goal," the President declared. . . . "This is my pledge to the Nation and to Almighty God."

With their interpretation of history exhibited in the platform, the lines of the drama written, and the stage set for the play, the Republicans faced the problem of presenting their candidate to the public in appealing form. This enterprise offered difficulties. For months Charles Michelson, clever and vitriolic agent of the Democratic National Committee, had been daily, almost hourly, picturing the

President to the country as a bewildered, baffled, futile man, hard of heart and indifferent to human sufferings. Nor were things going well in the councils of the President's party. Few of the seasoned veterans in Republican politics felt in perfect rapport with Hoover. Whatever ingenuity his ways revealed, it was not exactly their type of ingenuity. Stalwarts who had affection for Normalcy disliked Hoover and were free in expressing their contempt in the lobbies and salons of Washington. Other Republican members of Congress, such as Senator La Follette, Senator Norris, and Senator Cutting, had joined with Democrats in defeating or mutilating measures drafted in the White House, and their designs had encountered numerous retaliations at the hands of the President. Bringing them into line proved to be an impossibility. Yet as the bitter jealousies of Napoleon's generals were often stilled in the presence of battle and sudden death, so the antipathies among most opponents in the President's party were momentarily put aside as the managers joined in what journalists call the "build-up" of their candidate. Fortunately for the cause, Hoover's intimates were extremely loyal; in their eyes he was a great figure, unappreciated but of heroic stature — the type required by the exigencies of the trying times.

As presiding officer at the Republican convention in Chicago, the Honorable Bertrand H. Snell, leader of his party in the House of Representatives, had presented the thesis, the antithesis, the synthesis, and the deus ex machina. For many years, he said, under "progressive, forward-looking, constructive Republican leadership" the country had prospered and reveled in the felicity of security. It was true that "the invisible but ghastly pestilence of world-wide economic depression" had descended upon the land. How had that untoward event occurred under such leadership? "It is the ghost of the World War stalking over the earth." At this point, when the grand old party of Abraham Lincoln was wrestling with a fate not of its own making, the Democratic party had got control of the House of Representatives.

And with what consequences? "Uncertainty about the future increased; confidence all but disappeared; business continued to slow down. The country was thrown into a state of mind approaching chaos. No one could foretell what the Democratic majority would propose or would do next. There followed a period of anxious waiting, of trembling inactivity."

Speaking with the authority of a Representative who had witnessed at first hand the political operations in Washington, the Honorable Mr. Snell gave the country his picture of Democratic capacity. So long as they followed the guidance of President Hoover "all was well"; but, "when they started casting about for a program of their own, they became mired. They began with a blaring of trumpets." They organized a policy committee to arrange a program "to put the world back into joint." They called in their members of Congress, "all of their defeated candidates for President, and all their other master minds." Yet "not all of these geniuses combined were able to evolve a plan because no two of them could agree upon any plan." Confusion and open revolt followed the effort. "The Democratic party has as many wings as it has candidates and certainly its candidates are legion. These wings do not flap together; they flap against each other. The Democratic party is a mob of feuds and factions, unable to bring order out of the chaos in its own ranks." How could such a motley crowd maintain order in government? "The nation is to be asked to accept confusion as national policy and disorder as a rule of government." That chaos the people cannot want or endure. "They want a party in control that has a program, knows where it is going, and has the courage of leadership."

At the head of this fraternity stood President Hoover, "the pilot who keeps eternal vigil on the bridge of the ship of state. . . . No man living or dead has had to grapple with such gigantic problems at home and abroad. No man living or dead has fought world-wide economic adversity with so stout a heart and so deep an understanding." George Washington "as an engineer solved stupendous and vexatious problems for the benefit of mankind. . . . President Hoover's mind is the mind of an engineer. He first gets his facts and then he acts. . . . Sureness of decision, solidity of formation, and enduring construction by using tested materials is ingrained in the education and thought processes of an engineer. These traits are governing in all decisions on all questions. Herbert Hoover, the engineer President of the United States, is solving, and will solve, stupendous and vexatious problems, as did our first engineer President, for the benefit of our mankind. . . . With indomitable confidence and courage, with faith in our Commander-in-Chief, and with a comradeship of purpose to meet every foe of the republic, foreign or domestic, let us press onward, shouting the great American battle cry: 'Forward to victory!'"

This delineation of Herbert Hoover as "the great engineer" in the White House applying rationality to the process of government was surely dexterous and yet it did not evoke popular enthusiasm. Nor was it a complete picture of the man. Already the phrase, "great engineer," had become the subject of ribald jest among indecorous journalists. So to the rescue of Republican politicians was brought the subtler and more ingenious artistry of the man of letters, William Allen White. In making an appeal to millions of women voters and their no less sentimental brethren in search of mercy as well as omniscience, the portrayal of a giant endowed with the strength of technology was inadequate. It left the humanity of the President out of the reckoning and needed correction. The task of retouching the picture Mr. White therefore undertook in an editorial that was scattered broadcast as a pamphlet by the Republican campaign committee under the heading: "Hails Genius of Hoover." Writing at the close of the session of Congress in the summer of 1932, with the record before him, Mr. White was in command of hard facts, as well as the superlatives of his craft, and he rose to the heights of the occasion.

How had the devastating calamity come upon America?
Mr. White gave his answer to the question: the President
and his advisers "early last year decided that this depression
was part of a world-wide phase of after-war adjustment in
civilization." Against this thing, President Hoover had
formulated his program. The establishment of the Reconstruction Finance Corporation was "the greatest fiscal
measure ever adopted by any government in all times." Had
the President failed to secure its creation "not a bank in
America would be open today and our commercial system
would be paralyzed." Other measures of a supporting nature had been pressed through Congress under executive
leadership — for balancing the budget, effecting economy in
expenditures, and saving the homes of debtors. No other
President had ever won as much "in any other eight months
in the history of this nation. He has won constructive, necessary legislation of a wide, important scope, and in some cases
of an almost revolutionary character." It was not perfect,
but without Hoover's guiding brain more errors and weak-
nesses would have crept into legislation. There in monolithic
form stood the monument of national salvation.

Fearful that the people were unable to appreciate the
man so incarnate in the deed, Mr. White sought to enlighten
them further: "President Hoover's leadership is not vocal.
He cannot address the American people. His strength is in
conference. He cannot make public sentiment and thereby
coerce Congress. Roosevelt and Wilson worked that way; so
did Lincoln. But Hoover's talent is a different talent. He
can convince individual men, small coteries of men, groups
that can be reached by his voice, that are impressed by his
sincerity, that are carried along by the resistless logic of his
position. . . . Hoover cannot appeal over Congress to the
masses."

So constituted by nature, the President, in Mr. White's
drawing, was at the mercy of unscrupulous or less scrupulous
men. "Hoover's method," he explained, "involves a
struggle with individuals, with militant minorities, with

mean and selfish groups that seek party or factional advantage. Moreover Hoover's method leaves the public at the mercy of demagogues. . . . So Hoover stands alone. He has fought this good fight for eight long grinding months which have torn his heart out, wracked his body, tattered his patience, but he has won. . . . He may have to wait for history to give him the laurel, but he has won it. . . . America has had no other President who has done in eight months such Herculean work for the salvation of his country as Herbert Hoover has done since December 1931. . . . Here is a rounded man, human, subject to the foibles of humanity, but strong, clean, brave and wise, a leader worthy of the times." In short, Hoover was the personification of kindness in strength, of humanism combined with rationality, the wracked and heart-torn savior of America in a time of great crisis — a picture drawn by a friend who had seen the man within the President, the victim of mean, selfish, factional, and demagogic assaults. That the portrayal was eloquent not even the most carping critics could deny. Would history accept it?

§

With the depression still in full swing and President Hoover standing firmly on his program, the Democrats made ready for the choice of their candidate. Assuming that the laurel would not wither on election day, many aspirants looked with longing eyes upon the prize of nomination. Governor Albert Ritchie, of Maryland, entertained hopes. Backed by William Randolph Hearst and Senator William Gibbs McAdoo, John Nance Garner gathered a quota of delegates for the convention. Naturally eager to remove the sting of his defeat in 1928, Alfred E. Smith cast about somewhat unobtrusively for support and his friends came to believe that in an hour of deadlock the crown might go to him. Newton D. Baker was mentioned. But in the process of capturing delegates, Governor Franklin Delano Roosevelt, of New York, early spurted ahead.

When the Democratic convention assembled, Governor Roosevelt had the largest following — an impressive number, though not the two-thirds made necessary by the rule of the party. If that gave him hope, it provided no assurance. Champ Clark had possessed a majority of the delegates in 1912, but Woodrow Wilson, powerfully aided by William Jennings Bryan, had wrested the honor from him almost at the moment of his victory. Failing in an effort to change the two-thirds rule, Governor Roosevelt's managers made a skillful maneuver behind the scenes. Delegates pledged to Mr. Garner were shifted to Governor Roosevelt, thus guaranteeing his nomination, and by courtesy, if not by trade, Mr. Garner was selected as the candidate for Vice President. When William Gibbs McAdoo announced in the convention that California would vote for Roosevelt, some cynics cried in unison: "What price California?" But after the answer came, all was forgotten in the jollification of comradeship; or rather, almost all, for in the bitterness of his soul, Alfred E. Smith, having failed to receive the nomination, could scarcely bring himself to support the choice of his party.

In contrast with the Republican platform, the Democratic pronouncement was a paragon of brevity. Save in minor particulars, it was, however, far less explicit. Apart from a few points, it presented no direct alternatives to the Republican promises of salvation. The Republicans had represented themselves as the victims of inexorable history not of their own making and as heroic figures beating back the cruel tides of adversity that flowed from other shores. As a matter of interpretation and tactics, the Democrats rejected this explanation of recent events and drew bold outlines of the villain in the drama.

"The chief causes" of the unhappy state of the nation, the Democrats declared, "were the disastrous policies pursued by our Government since the World War, of economic isolation, fostering the merger of competitive business into monopolies and encouraging the indefensible expansion and contraction of credit for private profit at the expense of the public. Those who were responsible for these policies have abandoned the ideals on which the war was won and thrown away the fruits of victory. . . . They have ruined our foreign trade; destroyed the values of our commodities and products, crippled our banking system, robbed millions of our people of their life savings, and thrown millions more out of work, produced wide-spread poverty and brought the Government to a state of financial distress unprecedented in time of peace." Although Republicans as such were not mentioned in this bill of indictment, they had been in control of the Government since the world war. Hence there was no doubt about the location of "those who were responsible." And, the Democrats declared, "the only hope" of improvement, of restoration, of bringing the nation back to the proud position of domestic happiness and leadership in the world "lies in a drastic change in economic governmental policies."

And what "drastic changes in economic governmental policies" were proposed by the Democrats? They fell into two groups: the one, involving a resort to old policies; and the other, departures from traditions in the form of new policies. First, there was to be "an immediate and drastic reduction of governmental expenditures . . . to accomplish a saving of not less than twenty-five per cent in the cost of Federal Government" and a call upon the states to make a zealous effort to achieve a proportionate result. Second, the federal budget was to be balanced annually and revenues raised "on the principle of ability to pay." In the pruning of expenditures, a navy and army "adequate for national defense" were to be maintained, but the facts must be surveyed to the end "that the people in time of peace may not be burdened by an expenditure fast approaching a billion dollars annually."

Paying tribute to historic Respectability, the Democrats advocated "a sound currency to be preserved at all hazards," and, remembering Populism, they approved "an international monetary conference . . . to consider the rehabilitation of silver and related questions." The anti-trust laws were to be strengthened and impartially enforced — for the benefit of labor and the small producer and distributor. With reference to foreign trade there must be "a competitive tariff for revenue," a fact-finding tariff commission free from executive interference, reciprocal trade agreements with other nations, and an international economic conference to restore international trade.

Aside from the reference to a competitive tariff for revenue, the meaning of which was far from clear, the Democratic platform so far presented few flat contradictions to the tenders made in the Republican pronouncement. Whatever may have been the content of the phrase "competitive tariff" in the minds of the authors, it offered no unequivocal promise of a revision downward, either general or selective.

Taking up another theme which had long agitated business men, the Democrats wrote into their platform a clause advocating "the removal of government from all fields of private enterprise." Thus they repudiated the socialistic stigma and endorsed a motto which had entranced chambers of commerce for many years. That fitted well into the project for strengthening and enforcing the anti-trust laws in the manner proposed by Woodrow Wilson in his New Freedom. But, as if recalling such recent legislation as the Act for the distribution of electric power at Boulder Dam and the approval of such invasions of the business field by the Republican platform, the Democrats added a proviso: there was to be no competition with private enterprise "except where necessary to develop public works and natural resources in the common interest."

Under the head of old policy came also the Democratic promises touching assistance for the unemployed: "We advocate the extension of federal credit to the states to provide unemployment relief wherever the diminishing resources of the states make it impossible for them to provide for the needy; expansion of the federal program of necessary and useful construction affected with a public interest, such as adequate flood control and waterways." In no way did this pledge depart from the program initiated by President Hoover, endorsed by his party, and offered to the future. Nor was there anything new in the Democratic plank advocating "the spread of employment by a substantial reduction in the hours of labor, the encouragement of the shorter week by applying the principle in government service." Just how the reduction in the hours of labor was to be effected was left to the imagination of the voters. Certainly the language of the clause carried no implication that the thing advocated was to be realized by direct federal intervention in the processes of industry. On the contrary, the reference to a possible example set by the federal service indicated a platonic wish, rather than a specific act of Congress making a curtailment of hours mandatory throughout the nation, if necessary in defiance of the states.

Coming to "drastic changes" which they had promised, the Democrats incorporated in their platform a few items that at least implied novelty. Republican leaders had referred provisions for unemployment and old age to business enterprise itself. The Democrats left the issue to the states: "We advocate unemployment and old age insurance under state laws." This was positive and constituted the only direct bid to labor contained in the platform, apart, perhaps, from the promise to prosecute the trusts. As if recurring to the age-long effort to unite agrarians in the South and the West, the Democrats devised their offering to agriculture, cautiously and yet with inferences that might be fundamental; they favored "effective control of crop surpluses so that our farmers may have the full benefit of the domestic market" and "the enactment of every constitutional measure that will aid the farmers to receive for their basic farm commodities prices in excess of cost."

Just what did that mean in 1932? The Republican platform recognized the problem of controlling farm production and favored a national policy for diminishing the acreage under production by the withdrawal of marginal lands. Did

the authors of the Democratic pledge mean that, if victorious, the Democrats would enact federal legislation providing
for crop control? And what kind of legislation for farmers
was deemed to be "constitutional," as the platform delimited
its own promises? No clue to the reply was given until the
candidate, Franklin D. Roosevelt, later put a gloss on the
confession of faith by espousing the agrarians' program for
effective crop control under the stimulus of contributions
from the national treasury.

To the Republicans in possession of the Federal Government, the Democratic platform attributed perversions of
the economic system, which had robbed millions of their
savings, thrown millions out of work, and produced widespread poverty. By implication, the capitalist system itself
was essentially sound. Only Republican abuses had brought
on the great catastrophe. But how were such evils to be corrected and avoided for the future? The Democrats offered
several panaceas. The "investing public" was to be protected by requiring all persons and concerns offering stocks
and bonds for sale to file with the Government and carry in
their advertisements: "true information as to bonuses, commissions, principal invested, and interests of the sellers."
Though a similar proposal had been made by the Industrial Commission in 1900, under the administration of
President McKinley, the dust of neglect had gathered upon
it. Now the Democrats promised action and went further.
They advocated the regulation of holding companies which
sold securities in interstate commerce, the regulation of
exchanges in securities and commodities, the severance
of security and investment affiliates from commercial banks,
and additional restrictions on the power of Federal Reserve
banks to permit "the use of Federal Reserve facilities for
speculative purposes." In line with Republican recommendations, the Democrats also proposed federal regulation of
the rates of utility companies operating across state lines.
By cutting off certain excrescences that had grown on the
American economic system, the ills and worries of the time

were to be banished, it seemed, restoration and recovery assured, and the great ideal of Jefferson, the founder of the party, attained: "Equal rights to all; special privileges to none."

Somewhat outside the circle of economic enterprise — outside agriculture, industry, and labor — stood the question of Prohibition, the burning issue of the hour judging by the salvos that greeted references to repeal in the convention at Chicago. Here the Democrats were explicit, in part: "We advocate the repeal of the Eighteenth Amendment." The Republicans had merely promised to submit an amendment allowing the states to deal with the liquor problem in their own way. The Democrats dared to flaunt the word "Repeal." The Republicans had called for legislation protecting the dry states and fending off the return of the saloon. The Democrats invited the states to enact laws that would promote temperance, "effectively prevent the return of the saloon," and bring the liquor traffic under control. The Republicans had pledged to the states the aid of the Federal Government in upholding prohibition where it existed and in safeguarding citizens everywhere against the return of the saloon. So, too, the Democrats demanded that "the Federal Government effectively exercise its power to enable the states to protect themselves against importation of intoxicating liquors in violation of their laws." Those who read and compared the language of the two platforms discovered differences in words which were microscopic rather than the sharp oppositions of black and white, except for the Democratic promise to repeal the Volstead Act.

However much or little the Democratic platform differed from the Republican program on the issues of domestic affairs, its declarations in direct matters of foreign policy certainly stuck close to tradition and practice. The tender of reciprocal trade agreements was an old Republican device that had been advocated and tried with results little more than pitiable. Like the Republicans, the Democrats favored entering the World Court, consulting with the powers on threatened violations of the Kellogg Pact and other treaties, international agreements for the reduction of armaments, and insistence upon the payment of the debts owed to the United States by foreign governments. In substance this was a vow to continue the policies of President Hoover, with such elements of Woodrow Wilson's "idealism" as had been incorporated in the old body of diplomatic formulas. Yet on one point, the Democrats were peremptory: "independence for the Philippines." For both parties that had once been an academic matter; now it was emerging from the realm of platitude into the sphere of action and hence the Democratic reiteration of the old slogan had a reality not hitherto attached to it.

§

With the country in distress, with agriculture wracked by more than ten years of ruinous prices, mortgage foreclosures, and bankruptcies, with a platform ambiguous enough for any occasion, what image of their candidate did the Democrats present to the country? By ingenious minds it was formed for the opening pages of their "campaign book." Franklin Delano Roosevelt was a descendant of early Dutch settlers on his father's side and of "equally fine colonial ancestry" on his mother's side. For capturing the Irish, Italian, and German vote that was fortunate and it offended no Anglo-Americans. Franklin was born "in a fine old home overlooking the Hudson River, surrounded by trees and looking across a field where the hay had been cut for over a hundred years. His godfather was Elliott Roosevelt, the only brother of Theodore." The fact was not mentioned but it was true that, relatively speaking, Gaius Sempronius Gracchus, younger son of Tiberius and Cornelia, was also well born. Still, "even those who know" Franklin D. Roosevelt best, "often wonder that one man can so perfectly understand the viewpoint of the dirt farmer and the city laborer, the man in the street and the one in high places — and can so quietly, impartially, firmly, uphold the rights of each and achieve a fair deal for all." That was a problem in social psychology and the Democratic image-makers supplied the solution.

The solution? "As a boy young Franklin roamed the woods, read in the well-stocked library, rode horseback, and took a child's eager interest in all that pertained to the management of a large and prosperous farm." He sailed boats on the water, traveled abroad, cycling from country to country. "At school he broke athletic records, kept up his classwork without difficulty but without enthusiasm." Evidently no academician, no bookworm, was offered to the people. "Early taught by his illustrious cousin Theodore" the lesson of good citizenship, young Franklin began to preach the doctrine. Meanwhile he "did not neglect more personal interests, and soon after graduation [from Harvard] he married Miss Anna Eleanor Roosevelt, his distant cousin and the favorite niece of the President. Theodore Roosevelt gave the bride away, dashing from a St. Patrick's day parade to the ceremony. With typical Roosevelt enthusiasm, the young wife threw herself whole-heartedly into her husband's interests." Elected to the state senate "by a strong rural vote," the young knight "won his spurs as an aggressive liberal leader" and helped to defeat an old-guard candidate for the United States Senate "to the dismay of seasoned politicians, including the famous Charlie Murphy of Tammany Hall." Made an Assistant Secretary of the Navy by Woodrow Wilson, Mr. Roosevelt had done his full part in "helping to win the war," keeping on good terms with the 125,000 workers employed on Navy projects.

After the close of the world war, Franklin D. Roosevelt was a national figure. As the nominee of his party for Vice President in 1920, he campaigned over the country "by car, train, and airplane." Stricken by the tragedy of desperate illness, he had battled his way through the trials and had emerged crippled but fit for public duties. Believing whole-heartedly "in a Progressive Democratic party," he had nominated Alfred E. Smith at the convention of 1924 and again in 1928. In aid of Mr. Smith's candidacy, he "proved his friendship . . . to the hilt by consenting to run for Governor of New York." Despite the Republican landslide he carried the state in 1928 and was even more triumphantly reëlected two years later. As Governor he "sponsored the most intelligent and constructive program for helping the farmer that the state has ever known." To labor, "organized and unorganized," he proved himself a reliable friend, by advancing a program of labor legislation. As Governor, he also strengthened the laws providing for old-age insurance, took direct action to reduce the volume of unemployment, and called an extraordinary session of the legislature to deal with the pressing issue of relief for the impoverished. He had given the consumer "a fair deal," demanded from public utilities "fair service at reasonable rates," and managed to put teeth into the state laws "that really protect the poor man, and the obscure man, whether he be farmer, small business owner, or city apartment dweller."

Now Franklin D. Roosevelt has been called to a campaign for the presidency. What will he do to cope with the cataclysmic upheavals? "Roosevelt is for fundamental measures which will prevent the recurrence of the present economic disaster. He is for a substantial lowering of the tariff — which will allow a flow of goods between countries; as well as for the building up of the home market by a reduction in the differential between the farmers and the industrial workers; and by giving the industrial workers security of wages through unemployment insurance . . . holding himself equally responsible to every section, every class, and every citizen." When tendered the Democratic nomination, he had "electrified the convention" by a spectacular flight from Albany to Chicago, broken traditions by accepting the honor then and there, and dedicated himself "to a new deal for the American people."

Beside the word-picture of Franklin D. Roosevelt as a personality and statesman, the Democratic campaign managers placed an etching of his colleague in the campaign, John Nance Garner. Mr. Garner, in the revered American tradition, was born in a log cabin. Though an offspring of colonial pioneers, his grandmother, born Katherine Walpole, had descended from "the Walpoles who produced the English prime minister." After a boyhood in field and forest, Mr. Garner made his way upward through country schooling and a training "in the Methodist faith, to which he still adheres," through "one term at Vanderbilt University," to success in the practice of law, publishing, banking, and local offices, and finally to a place in the Congress of the United States. There he worked against the "autocracy" of Speaker Joseph Cannon, wrestled with the Goliath of Finance, Andrew W. Mellon, advocated graduated income and inheritance taxes to ease the burdens of the poor and make the rich bear their share, and served as a "watchdog of the treasury." In Congress, Mr. Garner labored against "the iniquitous features of the Hawley-Smoot tariff act," voted against the Eighteenth Amendment, and valiantly sought to "balance the budget." Acting contrary to local religious convictions, Mr. Garner, without counting the cost, had enthusiastically supported the candidacy of Alfred E. Smith in 1928 as the "regular" nominee of the party. As leader in the House of Representatives, he entered the lists against President Hoover on the ground "that the small business man and the individual merited as much consideration in the way of government loans as the banks, insurance companies, and railroads."

Their portrait of Mr. Garner as a symbol of Americanism, the Democratic campaign managers supplemented by his own confession of faith in the form of a letter of acceptance. "There are just two things to this Government as I see it," said the candidate. "The first is to safeguard the lives and properties of our people; the second is to insure that each of us has a chance to work out his destiny according to his talents. . . . In my opinion nearly all of our civic troubles are the consequence of Government's departure from its legitimate functions. . . . Government is not a pedagogue, nor a parson, nor a pied piper. . . . Had it not been for the steady encroachment of Federal Government on the rights and duties reserved for the states, we perhaps would not have the present spectacle of the people rushing to Washington to set right whatever goes wrong." The economic distress through which the country is passing cannot be wholly explained by "outside influences over which we have no control." These are contributing factors but the major causes can be found in the legislation and policies of Republican leaders. On the doorstep of the Republican party lie the unbalanced budget and mounting expenditures. The Democrats? They have promised a twenty-five per cent reduction. "That pledge will be redeemed." Their tariff plank is "equally definite and constructive, and must have a strong appeal to industrialists, farmers, labor, and business men who all suffered by the wrecking of our foreign trade under the embargo rates." There, the Democratic managers said in effect, is John Nance Garner's explanation of the depression and his frame of economic reference for salvation.

§

In his address of acceptance, delivered in person before the Chicago convention, Mr. Roosevelt presented his interpretation of recent history, his analysis of automatic market operations, and his overarching hypothesis for policy. During the period of expansion "there was little or no drop in the prices that the consumer had to pay although . . . the cost of production fell very greatly; corporate profit resulting from this period was enormous; at the same time little of that profit was devoted to the reduction of prices. The consumer was forgotten. Very little of it went into increased wages; the worker was forgotten; and by no means an adequate proportion was even paid out in dividends — the stockholder was forgotten." Where did the corporate surpluses go? "First, into new and unnecessary plants which now stand

stark and idle; and secondly, into the call money market
of Wall Street, either directly by the corporations, or indirectly through the banks. Those are the facts. Why blink
them?" In the hour of lamentation, the Republican administration had come to the aid of the interests at "the top of
the pyramid," on the old assumption that benefits would leak
down to those at the bottom. In reality, "never in all history have the interests of all the people been so united in a
single economic problem. . . . Statesmanship and vision,
my friends, require relief to all at the same time."

According to this economic interpretation, the managers
of the unconscious, automatic market had consciously and
willfully manipulated it, and the Republican administration
had sprung to the aid of the men at the top. "And there we
are today!" exclaimed Mr. Roosevelt. What now is to be
done to cure and avoid? Governments must economize.
The Eighteenth Amendment must be repealed though the
return of the saloon must be prevented. Daylight is to be
let through securities offered to the investing public. The
avenue to employment is to be partly opened by well-planned
public works as self-sustaining as possible. Agriculture is in
a slough of despond. "Final voluntary reduction of surplus
is a part of our objective," but emergency measures are necessary to repair the immediate damages. "Such a plan as that,
my friends, does not cost the Government any money, nor
does it keep the Government in business or in speculation."
So far as the actual words of the farm bill are concerned, "the
Democratic party stands ready to be guided by whatever
the responsible farm groups themselves agree on." For
mortgaged home owners and farmers, credit is to be eased.
The "primary responsibility for relief rests with localities
now, as ever"; yet the Federal Government has a continuing
responsibility that will soon be fulfilled. In these terms
Mr. Roosevelt set forth his view of "the recent history and
the simple economics, the kind of economics that you and
I and the average man and woman talk." "Woman," it
seemed, was not to be forgotten either.

While laying emphasis on domestic economy, Mr. Roosevelt took into account its contacts with world commerce. Republican leaders of the nation had erected "an impregnable barbed wire entanglement around its borders through the instrumentality of tariffs which have isolated us from all the other human beings in all the rest of the round world." On their part, the Democrats had made their tariff offer and Mr. Roosevelt approved: "I accept that admirable tariff statement in the platform of this convention. It would protect American business and American labor." Leaving aside specifications of the protection to be afforded, Mr. Roosevelt continued: "By our acts of the past we have invited and received the retaliation of other nations. I propose an invitation to them to forget the past, to sit at the table with us, as friends, and to plan with us for the restoration of the trade of the world." Yet agriculture is to have "a reasonable tariff protection; . . . the same protection that industry has today." Thus, although the Democratic managers had been careful in their portrait to remove all academic taint from their candidate, he himself seemed to proclaim the formula of historic internationalism so assiduously and stoutly propagated by the schoolmen — that dream logic belied by all the tariff acts of the leading nations since the fateful year 1918. However, the dream logic of Mr. Roosevelt was safeguarded by qualifications — protection for American business, American labor, and American agriculture.

§

When the parts of the two major platforms bearing upon specific economic issues were superimposed and all were rearranged with reference to any scheme of economic thought and corresponding reality, their similarities were striking. They presented essentially the same structure, the same elements, the same interpretation of American culture and history. Both accepted as permanent the continuance of the prevailing ownership and distribution of real and intangible property and promised to take the government out of business. Both accepted the imperative of the profit motive as the prime motor in setting and keeping real property in action to produce wealth, with the contingencies of opportunity, risk, losses, and insecurity inseparably attached. Both assumed that the automatic pressure of competition would prevent "artificial" prices, hold down "exorbitant" profits, and estop perilous concentration of wealth. Both assumed that a "fairly" just distribution of wealth would occur through the automatic and unconscious operation of the price and wage mechanism in the marketplace, sustaining the continuous circulation of commodities and the equilibrium of economy. The perdurance of all American culture, including mores, folkways, and ethical sentiments, was likewise taken for granted by the two platforms; in other words, there would be a continuity of what John R. Commons called "duty, performance, forbearance, and avoidance" on the part of those who possessed little or no real or tangible property under the prevailing system of tenure, use, and wont. No doubt, duties, performances, forbearances, and avoidances were as necessary to functioning economy as property, real and intangible, but owners could count on nonowners fulfilling these obligations without making sociological disturbances.

In formulating their articles of faith, therefore, the makers of the two platforms departed from the political philosophy bequeathed by the Fathers of the Republic, rejected even the implication of development, and adopted the equivalence of the schoolmen in economics, who knew no history or excluded it from their conception of reality as injecting irrational vagaries into the symmetry of rationality — the "natural" order. James Madison had foreseen a time when the great mass of the people would be without property of any kind; when the statesmen of America would find all their wisdom tested. Thomas Jefferson had contemplated the arrival of that contingency. Daniel Webster had propounded a similar philosophy of politics and economics. But neither

the Republicans nor the Democrats took note of it in making
their platforms, if indeed they had ever heard of it.

Their conception of things allowed for no development
in American history, making fundamental alterations in the
distribution of real and intangible property, effecting an
increasing concentration of control, adding to the number of
tenants and sharecroppers, drawing in its wake a rising population of industrial workers and white-collar employees.
There were no inexorable tendencies in American history, no
tendencies as real and ruthless as the operations of the price
mechanism, reshaping from top to bottom the configuration
of actuality with which politicians were supposed to deal.
Judging by the intimations and implications of their platforms, both parties believed that American history had been
closed; that the future, near and distant, would repeat some
period of the past unnamed; that the function of politics
was to "recover" and "restore." What situation? That
of 1928, 1914, 1896? To this question there was no answer,
for "practical politicians" apparently deemed it irrelevant.

Yet there were stresses and strains in the perfect system
of equivalence and equilibrium. Idle workmen and women
on breadlines and dispossessed farmers could see and feel
them. Even many scholastics admitted as much privately,
if not publicly. From what sources had sprung dislocations
in the symmetry of the automatic? If the platform makers
were to be accepted as authorities, the main sources were
four in number. Some willful men had violated the rules of
the economic game by seeking to avoid the discomforting
effects of competition, by refusing to hand out their rewards
of profit to consumers and wage earners. This was, however,
a passing phenomenon not inherent in the economic system, a
kind of evil spirit that could be vanquished by legislation. A
second source of disequilibrium was the economic breakdown
in foreign countries, which threw obstructions into the
smooth-running machinery of the American equilibrium.
Akin to crashes in foreign economies was war — a strange
thing presumably unconnected with the forms, operations,

and passions of domestic and foreign economies. The fourth source of disturbances in the equilibrium was the willful intrusions of government into the mechanism of private economy — into the "natural" circulation of goods and into the "natural" operations of the price and wage system in the domestic and world market. Both party platforms promised to beat back these intrusions, more or less, but the Democratic platform especially emphasized this interpretation of the disequilibrium and in substance implied that the policies and actions of the party, if victorious, would be encompassed by that frame of reference.

§

With the platforms so drawn and the issues so formulated, the campaign of the major parties ran along in customary channels. The great debate, if at times heated, never roared up into a thunderous dispute. It was marked by no such frenzy and violent language as the contest of 1896, waged in the midst of a depression less devastating in its social effects. The Democratic candidate awakened no fears comparable to those raised by the militancy of William Jennings Bryan. No turbulent strikes, such as the Pullman struggle of 1894 or the Pittsburgh upheaval of 1877, frightened the John Hayses and Henry Cabot Lodges of 1932. In contrast a strange calm reigned everywhere, as if the memory of Sam Adams, Daniel Shays, and John P. Altgeld had perished from the earth.

The Republican candidate, Herbert Hoover, spoke with gravity, in a style sober and dignified, sometimes lacking in limpidity. In the nature of things, he was compelled to take the defensive. After all, whatever mighty things he had in fact accomplished, the plague of the depression still lay heavily upon the country, despite some evidences of lifting. That was not an achievement to which he could convincingly point with pride. He could say that without his labors things would have been far worse, but there was little popular appeal in that observation. Men of large affairs, the Lords of Creation, were able to appreciate the theory and practice of his administration and his program for the future. Yet even they were not united. Many, if not all of them, had been engaged in stock pools, manipulations, and "churnings," and Hoover had openly ascribed a large part of the country's troubles to their activities, especially to their efforts to make money by selling stocks "short." As a result Hoover had few ardent friends in Wall Street, which was supposed to be the nerve center of the economic system that he was striving to resuscitate.

On the Democratic side, the candidate also carried on a decorous campaign with touches of geniality rather than the vindictiveness of the crusader. This seemed in keeping with Roosevelt's character and it was good strategy besides. With encouraging reports coming from every direction, his party managers knew that their chief problem was to avoid "making mistakes," that is, declarations too precise and likely to alienate voters by clarifications and specifications. Only one major point in his platform did Roosevelt amplify by a commitment affecting the resentments and designs positively cherished by millions of voters, namely, the control of surpluses in agriculture.

After the veto of the McNary-Haugen farm bill and the failure of President Hoover's Farm Board to stem the downward flux of prices, a group of men in the Department of Agriculture had evolved a plan for balancing the agricultural output. In the autumn of 1931 M. L. Wilson, of the Montana State Agricultural College, had launched a campaign to enlist the support of business men and farmers for a scheme of control known as "the domestic allotment plan." Under this scheme there was to be no dumping of surpluses abroad; nor any government interference with the open market prices, such as Hoover had sponsored at a great cost to the Treasury and with negative results. On the contrary, under the domestic allotment plan, farmers were to cut surpluses by paring down production, and were in return to be given benefit payments, in addition to the open market prices —

payments proportioned to each producer's share of the domestic consumption of the commodities listed as human food. By the summer of 1932 a multitude of business men, especially merchants relying on a local trade and manufacturers of farm supplies, had become convinced that this domestic allotment plan was the only hope for barring the road to ruin.

As Governor of New York, Roosevelt had taken a genuine interest in agriculture and had devoted messages and addresses to the exposition of agricultural difficulties in his state. But the domestic allotment scheme applied particularly to the producers of great staples in the West and South, rather than to dairy and miscellaneous farming in the East, although the latter too was in a semi-paralyzed state. To most stock brokers, men of affairs, and other members of the middle class in the East, this agrarian project was as mysterious as Egyptian hieroglyphics. Perhaps, generally speaking, they looked upon it as an invention of "crack pots," a device of farmers to get something that did not belong to them under the American Economic System, but its contours gave them no sleepless nights.

Eventually, compelled by his function as campaigner to examine innumerable proposals and hear all views, Roosevelt gave careful consideration to the domestic allotment plan as presented to him by Rexford Tugwell, then professor of economics at Columbia University. Having explored the details of the project, Roosevelt decided to support it openly. In September he went into the very heart of the agrarian West and in a ringing speech at Topeka, Kansas, he espoused, in general terms, the very principles of crop control which were soon to be written in the terms of the Agricultural Adjustment Act. At last the agrarians had broken through the barriers of equivocations and had won a definite commitment on their program. Like a forest fire the news spread among farm leaders in village, hamlet, and field. Without unduly affronting capitalists and trade unionists, it was to bring a deluge of rural votes in the Middle West, the old stronghold of Homestead Republicans.

Any trepidation started among men in high places by
Roosevelt's acceptance of a positive agrarian program was
offset in part by a statement from William H. Woodin included in the Democratic book of faith. This document had
a peculiar significance for the discerning. Mr. Woodin was
the president of the American Car and Foundry Company.
He was so intimately acquainted with the J. P. Morgan Company that his name was included in its "preferred list" of
friends who received opportunities to buy stocks at prices
below those paid by the "investing public." This fact was
not known outside the inner circle in 1932 and was not
revealed to the country until after the election; but it was
doubtless no secret to the Morgan associates when Mr.
Woodin issued his campaign manifesto. The document itself
was skillfully designed to allay the "fear" that Roosevelt's
policies were inimical to big business. The suggestion, explained Mr. Woodin, was absurd "unless by big business is
meant bad business"; and certainly no man in a high place
admitted that he was engaged in bad business, as innumerable congressional investigations made plain. "By tradition
and training," as Mr. Woodin set forth the personality of the
candidate, "he is antagonistic neither to the rights of invested capital nor to the rights of those whose capital is their
industry, self-respect, and ability to produce. To his thinking
there is no distinction to be drawn between the classes and
the masses."

Although caution and moderation marked the campaign
conducted by the two major candidates, there were charges
and counter-charges, rumblings and grumblings that must
have left their impressions upon public sentiments after the
election had passed. On behalf of the Republican party it
was drummed into the heads of the people who listened that
the triumph of the Democrats meant more ruin in American
economy. While the Democratic campaign book assured
big business that it had "absolutely nothing to fear" from
Roosevelt's policies, Democratic spellbinders made such
savage assaults on "the wickedness of Wall Street and mag-

nates in finance" that some voters were doubtless led to expect material changes in the system of acquisition and enjoyment. In this expectation they were confirmed by the vituperations of two manipulants who had enormous followings: Senator Huey P. Long of Louisiana and Charles E. Coughlin, priest of the Little Flower in the diocese of Detroit. Both were ardent supporters of Mr. Roosevelt's candidacy. The Senator fulminated in the South against great riches and reiterated one theme: "Share our wealth." In the North, Father Coughlin concentrated his wrath on bankers, capitalism, and communism and demanded a government currency having the semblance of fiat money. While the Democratic candidate put no official seal of approval on the philosophy of these preachers to the multitudes, he derived electoral benefits from their audiences; the hopes and alarms which they raised entered into the tumult of emotions associated with the national referendum.

Given the formulations of the major parties and the character of their campaigns, given wide-spread unemployment and actual misery among industrial workers, the signs seemed propitious for socialists and communists of all schools and persuasions to make, if not an immense diversion, at least a larger showing than in any previous contest. The United States, they thought, might be entering the final crisis which would pave the way for their triumph. They knew, to be sure, that the main body of labor in the United States was unorganized and that orthodox trade unionists wanted a larger share of the profits, not an overturn of the capitalist system. But in the turmoil of 1932, when even skilled craftsmen were tramping the streets, socialists and communists could imagine that "objective realities" had altered the psychology of American industrial workers and prepared them for a break with the past.

Although the great majority of socialists in the United States had one faith and one prophet, they disagreed among themselves over the precise interpretation of the Word according to Karl Marx and the right line of tactics to be followed. Above all they were divided over the methods of practice. Would the triumph of labor over capitalism come everywhere in a crisis, through violence, and by means of a dictatorship? If so, it was argued, then this must be the universal creed and appeal. Or were tactics appropriate for the despotism of the Tsar wholly inappropriate in the United States, with its democratic institutions and freedom of discussion?

True to tradition established when it was founded in 1900, the Socialist party rejected the dogma of automatic violence and endorsed political methods for achieving its ends. Yet even the Socialist party, in presenting Norman Thomas as its candidate, accepted the hypothesis that if labor encountered violence from the other side a response in similar terms might be a historic necessity. Inclined to spurn Socialistic tactics as supine, Communists chose other devices. But they were split into factions, for the unity of their creed and procedure had been shattered by the victory of Stalin and the downfall of Trotsky in Russia. Hence Communists failed to present "a united front" behind the candidate of the Communist party, W. Z. Foster.

Whatever issues, if any, were decided by the referendum, the numerical result was overwhelming. The total popular vote rose nearly three millions above that cast in 1928, showing, even when increase of population was discounted, that strong currents of popular sentiment had been set in motion. The tables of the preceding election were almost reversed. Hoover received 15,758,901 votes and carried only six states — Connecticut, Delaware, Maine, Pennsylvania, New Hampshire, and Vermont. With a popular vote of 22,809,638 Roosevelt carried forty-two states. A detailed analysis of the balloting by counties revealed that, on the whole, the old centers of disaffection which had supported William Jennings Bryan in 1896 threw their weight to Roosevelt in 1932. It also revealed the fact that counties and cities which had long been set down in the statistics of politics as "rock-ribbed Republican" experienced upheavals that were almost volcanic. For example, every county in Indiana that had given Bryan a majority in 1896 went Democratic in 1932, and other counties that had been reckoned as Republican since the civil war shifted over into the Democratic column. Despite this crack in the alignment of the major parties, the combined Socialist and Communist vote, with women nationally enfranchised in the meantime, was only 987,000 in round numbers as against nearly one million cast for Eugene V. Debs in 1912.

After the storm of the campaign had blown over, many citizens who had voted for Roosevelt doubtless had visions of things to be done by the incoming Democratic administration. In some respects the Democratic mandate was emphatic, especially with reference to the agrarian program. In other respects it was clouded by uncertainty. The concatenation of federal actions later known as "the New Deal" was not forecast in its entirety; nor were several parts of the coming program foreshadowed at all. It could not be correctly said, therefore, that the country had voted for a New Deal any more than it had voted for the emancipation of slaves in 1860, or for a war on Spain and imperialism in 1896. Indeed, the American electorate had seldom, if ever, voted for anything positive. Yet, as in the case of Lincoln's election, startling events occurred between the November poll and the March inauguration — events which conditioned, if they did not make necessary, actions not contemplated in the referendum.

CHAPTER IV
Detonations

AMID the celebrations of victory, Democrats prepared to
divide the spoils, in accordance with a venerable
tradition. Having watched history "repeat itself,"
Senator George W. Norris described the process: "The professional politician is mainly interested in jobs. He deals in
political jobs and sells them across the political counter much
as the merchant sells calico and boots and shoes." The
practice covered petty posts in villages as well as lucrative
places in city, state, and national governments, and nothing
in the Democratic campaign of 1932 presaged any substantial
interference with the normal course. The platform, it is true,
contained a few pledges that could be interpreted as com-
mands; the candidate had committed himself to the agrarian
program and given hints of action in other directions. But
equivocation was always possible in fulfillment, and Roosevelt was generally regarded as "an amiable man" who would
not ride too hard when entrusted with the reins. Had the
American financial system been as sound as Hoover alleged
during the campaign, had there been no mighty dislocation

150

in economic forces at home and abroad since the summer of 1932, had history stood still or proved reversible, the administration of Franklin D. Roosevelt might have pursued an unvarying routine as Democratic politicians expected. The lush spoils of office might have been distributed with customary rejoicings and sore disappointments; a number of mild "corrective" statutes might have been placed upon the books in a leisurely fashion; and the era of the New Freedom might have been in some respects duplicated.

§

Unknown, however, to the makers of small politics, perhaps known only to a few men on the inside of financial operations, a swift and apparently inexorable shift had been taking place in the incidence of liquid claims to wealth, especially bank deposits. As Berle and Pederson later pointed out, in their illuminating study of Liquid Claims to National Wealth, the very term "liquid claims" was relatively new in economic thought despite the fact that "from 1900 onward these claims had constituted a larger and larger percentage of the fixed or non-liquid wealth of the country." Between November, 1929, and November, 1932, an immense collapse had occurred in the values behind those claims called stocks and bonds, and thousands of banks, mostly small in size, had been caught in the roaring flood of bankruptcy. Nevertheless, banks in general, particularly large institutions in the great cities, had seemed to stand like rocks of Gibraltar, sentinels of power looming high in the dusk of the little gods. Business was sinking, unemployment was mounting, misery was spreading. But mighty banks revealed no flaws. In round numbers their resources amounted to seventy-one and a half billions in 1928, seventy-two billions in 1929, seventy-four billions in 1930, and over seventy billions in June, 1931. What their ledgers showed on June 30, 1932, while the campaign was in progress, the public did not know for, contrary to custom and significantly, the announce-

ment of the official figures was long withheld — a delay lasting until January, 1933. After all, what preoccupied persons,
engaged in ordinary politics or in deriving history from
memoirs, ever paid any attention to the statistical tables of
financial reports dealing with changes in intricate economic
relations?

As a matter of fact, between June 30, 1931, and June 30,
1932, bank resources had dropped from seventy billions to
fifty-seven billions, and bank deposits had declined about
twelve billion dollars. This new configuration of liquid claims
had come about through innumerable individual actions,
each perhaps conscious, resulting in a general economic
situation which no one had foreseen, deliberately willed, or
purposely effected. If some persons had dimly divined an
approaching pinch, the public certainly had no suspicion of it
in June, 1932, or on election day in November of that year.
Individual bankers knew only too well that the value of the
papers in their portfolios was shrinking as railways went into
the "hands of custodians," to use the phrase more polite than
that of plain bankruptcy, as real estate mortgages plunged
into default, and as the golden certificates of towering holding companies shriveled like autumn leaves in a fire. Individual depositors were also aware that they were withdrawing
deposits to meet expenses as the days of unemployment and
unprofitable business went on. But the sum of individual
actions, the totality of banking resources, was beyond the
knowledge of the generality, and perhaps even of the Lords
of Creation. If a few leaders in finance suspected that
trouble was coming, they were disposed to take comfort in a
transcendent faith : the "invisible hand" makes public good
out of private transactions consummated in the interest of
individuals.

In the circumstances, as the campaign drew to a close,
little attention was paid in the country at large to the news
on October 31, 1932, that the governor of Nevada had proclaimed a banking holiday for twelve days in order to save
a chain of banks in the state. Their real estate assets were

frozen and their depositors were withdrawing money. Although for the moment an avalanche was averted in Nevada, neighboring states became nervous. Was it a local disorder that could be insulated? Or was it the beginning of a general dissolution? In the shouting of the election, the event received scant notice east of the Hudson River where, some imagined, the history of America was all made. Artists in coloring and makers of beautiful letters in Greenwich Village could still cash checks on metropolitan banks, if they had balances.

But even the illuminati must have been alarmed when in January, 1933, newspapers published figures compiled by the Comptroller of the Currency showing a steep drop in banking resources and bank deposits. Certainly "men in high places" and such politicians as gave attention to public business suffered dizzy spells as they ran their eyes down the columns of digits, mere ink and yet so fateful in terms of human life and political management. It may have been "silly," as Henry Seidel Canby, expert in polite letters, once remarked, to make "the attempt to interpret even business solely by statistics of supply and demand, profit or loss." Even so, the "inside development of the American nation" between January, 1932, and March, 1933, was not to be "found in American novels and plays," as Mr. Canby intimated in using his broom on "the economic interpretation of history." At least, some of it was registered in the reported shrinkage of liquid claims to wealth during the fifteen months previous to the inauguration of Franklin D. Roosevelt on March 4, 1933, and news of the disagreeable fact jarred complacency from Montauk Point to Catalina Island.

While the detonations of the report by the Comptroller of the Currency were still reverberating, their oscillations were accelerated by the figures of the quarterly release made by the Reconstruction Finance Corporation on February 3, 1933. Here, too, were indisputable statistics associated with supply and demand, profit and loss. They showed that the Corporation had authorized, between February, 1932, and December,

1932, loans to 5,582 banks and trust companies and that the loans actually made during the period amounted to $850,000,000. Next on the list of borrowers from the Corporation stood the railroads. Powerful lines as well as powerful banks were evidently in trouble, for it was not the function of the Corporation to assist concerns that could carry their own loads. Now it began to dawn upon the people that banks were in serious straits and that railways, whose bonds were stacked in the vaults of savings banks, universities, foundations, and insurance companies, were struggling for existence and positively gasping for credit. Beyond cavil, vital parts of the American System were far from "sound," according to any conception of that term, and depositors hastened to withdraw from banks more money for expenses and hoarding.

In the meantime, banking "incidents" multiplied in the provinces. On January 20, 1933, the legislature of Iowa enacted a law authorizing the Superintendent of Banking to assume the management of any bank and operate it for a year without instituting a formal receivership. This was also a sign of the tornado, as afterwards discovered, but the country, accustomed to the bankruptcy of rural banks in the era of Coolidge prosperity, could easily regard the event at the moment as just another episode. Although Iowa was a part of the Union, who in the high places of the omniscient and omnipotent East gave much thought to acts of the Iowa legislature? Nor did the press of the financial metropolis appear to be seriously disturbed when on February 4, 1933, the governor of Louisiana, hearing that certain banks in New Orleans were in peril, proclaimed a general banking holiday. Yet that was also another straw in the wind. According to a story in circulation the dictator of the state, Huey P. Long, had once prevented, at the point of a pistol, a group of bankers from going into liquidation. His political power was still unbroken in February, 1933. Then why did he eventually allow things to come to a dire pass among the bankers of his state? Perhaps, after all, the emotions of a dictator were futile before a stampede of events to be interpreted in economic terms. Still, as far as the nerve centers of the industrial Northeast were concerned, Louisiana, like Iowa, was far away and Confidence might act as insulation.

Hopes arising from that source were dashed, however, when news that could not be pushed far back into financial columns announced that the governor of Michigan had proclaimed on February 14, 1933, a banking holiday for a week throughout the state. Yet circumspection marked both the proclamation and the press reports: the action had been taken for the purpose of enabling "some of the larger banks in Detroit to meet the situation." In the ordinary course, this might have passed as an adequate explanation. But coming on top of the Comptroller's report from Washington, the revelations of the Reconstruction Finance Corporation, and explosions in Nevada, Iowa, and Louisiana, the news from Michigan jangled the American System from center to periphery.

From state to state banking holidays spread, for no one in authority seemed to want the "automatic and unconscious" operations of the marketplace to follow the process of liquidation to its logical and cleansing finality, in preparation for an upturn. Still, as proclamations of banking holidays rattled from state capitals like shots of machine guns, the strong banks of New York, Chicago, Philadelphia, and other great centers continued to operate, their grim walls showing no fissures. Could they withstand the drain of their correspondent banks and weather the gale without government intervention? That question was definitely answered. At 4 : 20 on the morning of March 4, 1933, the governor of New York declared a limited two-day moratorium and when nine o'clock arrived the doors of banks in great centers of finance remained shut. Throngs collected in the neighboring streets vaguely hoping for — something.

So it came about that, when President Hoover rode along Pennsylvania Avenue with Franklin D. Roosevelt to the inauguration, the huge mechanism of American finance had almost ceased to function. In forty-seven of the forty-eight states, banks were either closed completely or, with few exceptions, were doing business under severe restraints as to the withdrawal of deposits. By the hour for beginning the interpretation and application of the mandate received in the preceding November, profound alterations had been made in the resources and functioning of banking interests. Whatever the cause, no matter where the responsibility lay, facts, real facts, fraught with brutal consequences, threatened the nation with cataclysm. Philosophers, psychologists, and public relations counselors could no more conjure them away than could the bankers and politicians who stood aghast in their presence. Lords of Creation, Pillars of Society, Peers of Respectability gathered for hurried and whispered conferences amid the magnificence of their clubs and offices. Home owners, bond holders, "investors," bank directors brooded over defeated calculations. Silent crowds of the idle and unemployed flooded and ebbed through the streets of the cities, wondering, puzzled, and bewildered, rather than revolutionary in spirit. If, as Ralph Waldo Emerson had said, "Whiggery is the great fear," the banking collapse of March, 1933, awakened another great fear — one that staggered the heirs of Whiggery and everybody else. No words, spoken or written, could fully describe the confusion and fright. Those who went through it were powerless to enclose their sensations in a rationality of language that could reproduce it in the feelings of succeeding generations.

§

For the frightful crisis in banking affairs, men in high places had, as always, an explanation which was also in the nature of an alibi. Francis C. Sisson, president of the American Bankers Association, had formulated the escape in an address to his assembled colleagues during the previous October: "The blame for this situation rests with state laws and public supervisory agencies, not with legitimate members of the banking fraternity." Although the word "legitimate" opened to them the path for a successful flight, the implication of the formula was clear and positive: government, not the bankers, must bear the blame. And in a sense that was true. Since the days of Andrew Jackson, under the theory of states' rights and laissez faire, banking had been left largely under the supervision of state governments and the multiplication of local banks had been encouraged. Bankers had successfully prevented the Federal Government from establishing control over the currency through a public bank of issue in Washington and, tenaciously clinging to the Jacksonian tradition, the Congress had refused to give a semi-private corporation a position of centralized dominance. Under this policy, or lack of policy, a reckless struggle for business had long prevailed among thousands of independent banks, despite the creation of a national banking system during the civil war and the subsequent strengthening of that separate device. The truth was that for more than a hundred years bankers had distrusted the politicians and the politicians had distrusted the bankers, both with good reasons in theory and experience.

Out of this antagonism had come a condition of highly competitive banking, in which a large number of state and federal institutions, singly or in small combinations, fought for depositors and borrowers in accordance with the Darwinian conception of life and society, transplanted from England and enthusiastically advanced in the United States during the gilded age, while the economists steeped in that philosophy were insisting that all economic activity except consumption is production. Banks were established in small towns where the amount of available business did not justify the venture. Federal banks were given the power to issue notes on the basis of paper securities and thereby inflate the currency on the shaky foundations of tenuous claims to wealth. In the thirst for profits, loans were made on real property at swollen values, on the bonds and stocks of pyramided corporations at fantastic valuations; and billions were poured into the stock market to finance speculation in paper tokens which fell little, if any, short of pure gambling in unknowable futurities. Presumably each banker was partly conscious of what he personally was doing but there was no conscious control over the entire process — either in the hands of the Federal Government or of a single national corporation. And it so happened in the more or less blind competition that Adam Smith's "invisible hand" of Providence failed to effect an outcome in the "general interest." When, in the contraction of resources and deposits, the results of millions of individual transactions came together in a total process, the consequence was a convulsion. That much was painfully evident, whatever the correct apportionment of "blame."

Perhaps even then the part of the public that possessed any knowledge of banking or did any thinking on the subject might have accepted the bankers' explanation and alibi — "all the blame rests on government," if other relevant facts had not been exhibited contemporaneously. According to the official thesis of the bankers, constantly reiterated, their transactions, though motivated by the natural desire for profit, were collectively in the public interest, that is, they helped to sustain and to promote the production and distribution of real wealth. Did the private conduct of the "legitimate members of the banking fraternity" correspond in reality to their official thesis? Did practice conform to theory? While everything had been going smoothly such questions might have seemed impertinent to bankers, but grueling adversity now suggested an inquiry.

Moved by curiosity, if nothing more, the Senate of the United States passed, in the spring of 1932, a resolution instructing its committee on banking and currency to make an investigation "with respect to the buying and selling, and the borrowing and lending, of securities upon the various Stock Exchanges," and to report on the subject. Although sponsored mainly by dissidents, the resolution had support also among the more conservative Senators. President

Hoover himself had been harrowed and vexed by "short selling" on the exchanges, which seemed to be arbitrary and likely to arouse more fear among the people, multiplying the physical afflictions of the times. Hence the resolution was carried through the Senate despite the usual cries against "rocking the boat" and "making attacks on private rights guaranteed by the Constitution."

Acting under its instructions the Senate committee opened its hearings on April 11, 1932, and held periodical sessions until June 23, producing at each hearing sensational evidence bearing on the official thesis of the bankers. For reasons deemed sufficient, the committee suspended its operations on June 23, remained quiescent during the campaign season, and then resumed proceedings early in 1933. Through the rest of the year, the committee pursued its searching inquiry — after February 21, with the assistance of a skilled prober, Ferdinand Pecora.

In the course of the investigation the committee called before it once more the veritable Lords of Creation and asked them to explain to a tormented public how the stock and banking crisis had really happened. Representatives were summoned from the mightiest banks and the most Napoleonic brokerage houses: for example, J. P. Morgan and Company; Kuhn, Loeb; Lee, Higginson and Company; National City; Dillon Read; and Chase Securities Corporation. Before the committee appeared the famous figures of the legitimate banking and trading fraternity, keepers of the National Shrine now a bit tarnished by wear, while accounting experts examined their books and files of correspondence.

From day to day, in restrained and yet sagacious tones, counsel and members of the committee asked witnesses to verify documents, to authenticate matters of record, and to explain just how the practices of bankers and traders conformed with the official thesis that all lawful acquisitive actions redounded to the public interest. Never before in the history of the country had the anatomy, morphology, intelligence, morals, and functioning of the banking and stock-trading business been so fully laid bare to national gaze and understanding. Even the metropolitan papers, accustomed to treat congressional investigations with contempt or to "play them down" by relegation to inside columns, were moved to place reports from the committee rooms on their front pages under startling captions. Some odors simply could not be confined. So, during the months previous to the inauguration of Franklin D. Roosevelt and during the tempestuous weeks that followed, the nation was literally rocked by revelations, confessions, admissions, and even apologies from the highest men in the highest places — the Lords of Creation, the men who, according to James W. Gerard, "ruled America."

In the voluminous testimony and documentation incorporated in the bulky volumes of the committee's report, the story was told of just what bankers and traders had been doing, under their official theory of serving the public interest. No economist saw fit to integrate all the revelations of transactions so recorded into a system of institutional economics and contrast them with the hypothetical fictions of schoolmen, but fragments of the capitalist system in operation were made so vivid by the Senate committee's exposition that even country bankers could grasp their significance, as they looked ruefully at their blocks of defaulted bonds and their piles of depreciated stocks. In the hearts of the millions of "investors," with unsystematic minds, who had gambled in stocks during the frenzied days, particular items from the committee's investigation awakened poignant emotions and outraged feelings. They were cut to the quick as tales of special stock pools and raids — Kolster Radio Corporation, Indian Motorcycle, Anaconda Copper, German bonds, and Radio Corporation — blazed into the front pages of their favorite and trustworthy newspapers. All this exposure, no less than the sight of closed banks and the experience of personal losses, contributed to the tumult of opinions and passions in the sweep of which the Roosevelt administration began its work and moved forward to its future.

Page after page of sworn testimony showed that mighty men among the Lords of Creation had formed "pools" for particular stocks and bonds, run up the prices of securities, poisoned the news of financial columns by the bribery of reporters, drawn unwary sheep into the pen of bulls and bears and sheared them as the bottom fell out of liquid claims to wealth. Theoretically the stock exchange had been viewed and celebrated as an unconscious marketplace where the prices of stocks and bonds found, or tended to find, their "natural" level, as sellers offered and buyers purchased securities according to their individual judgments on values. Insiders had long known about pools and manipulations to their own advantage but, in the days of the Golden Glow, ordinary investors, sober or frenzied, had vague, if any, ideas relative to that subject. On the whole the impression reigned that "legitimate members of the banking fraternity" had nothing to do with such manipulations, in fact discountenanced them as injurious to sound business. But after the Senate committee started its inquiry, innocence gave way to knowledge and a sense of double outrage developed — over personal losses incurred at the game and the prestidigitation practiced at the expense of simple, if greedy, players.

A few examples will illustrate processes too vast for a description short of the original full hearings. In 1928 the earnings of the Kolster Radio Corporation dropped in the direction of zero and the directors were disquieted; but a way of flight from ruin by unloading the wreck upon the public was quickly discovered. Rudolph Spreckels, chairman of the company and chief stockholder, called in the aid of George Breen, "the hero of a hundred pools," gave him options on Kolster stock, and set him in motion. Mr. Breen thereupon engaged the interest and cupidity of a number of prominent stock brokers and hired a newspaper publicity man to prepare the people for another opportunity to "invest in America's prosperity." In a short time news of "highly favorable developments" in Kolster business was circulated among brokers and insinuated into the financial columns of the press. With "public interest" receptive, Mr. Breen and his enlisted brokers started "the big push" — buying and selling huge blocks of Kolster stock, all the while managing to raise the price as eager watchers rushed to share in "a good thing." In the course of this "unconscious and automatic" market operation, the price of stock was lifted from seventy-four to nearly ninety-six, over twenty points, as the insiders gradually sold out their holdings. When they withdrew from "the killing," Kolster stock slid down to its "natural" value, reaching five or six dollars a share in December, 1929. Then in January, 1930, the bubble burst; the company went into the hands of receivers.

About two years after the wreck, the Senate committee exhibited to the country the outlines of this transaction in institutional economics. The naive public had lost millions of dollars in the "business" adventure. Mr. Spreckels had received more than nineteen million dollars for stock that proved to be worthless. One company of brokers collected $182,760 in fees from operations. The hero of the pool, Mr. Breen, reaped a profit of $1,351,152.50, according to his own testimony. The publicity expert's reward was $40,000 — a small sum for such effective labors; yet, as he had ventured no money at all in the "enterprise," his entrepreneur's risk had been negligible.

Perhaps the most diverting feature of this demonstration in productive economy was Mr. Breen's elaborate defense of the process and his own action. It had all been legitimate. He had not manipulated the market. He had merely sought to "stabilize" it, he declared. Since, however, the stock under his care had risen twenty points and then fallen to almost nothing within a year, his adroitness in the art of maintaining an economic equilibrium was, to say the least, not impressive. In fact, his stabilization theory, when presented to the Senate committee, was received with raucous laughter. And for Lords of Creation, in a time of political uncertainty, laughter was as inauspicious as anger.

If the Kolster Radio farce could be discounted as a play

Harry Guggenheim, Thomas E. Bragg of a Stock Exchange
firm, and Charles E. Mitchell, head of the National City
Bank and its investment affiliate. With the aid of his institutions, his colleagues, his brokers, his high-powered selling
agents throughout the country, Mr. Mitchell bought and
sold Anaconda stock, churned the market, ran up prices,
"stabilized" the boiling market somewhere between 60 and
135, and sold out to "investors." Before many months
passed Anaconda stock plunged downward to about four
dollars a share. The public's losses were estimated at
$160,000,000 and the profits of legitimate members of the
banking fraternity were correspondingly large, temporarily
at least. Although the Senate committee did not elicit from
proud witnesses all the details of the public services rendered
by the pool, or even get an admission that there had been a
pool, its discoveries were as salt rubbed on the wounds of
thousands of investors who had once believed the glorious
yarns spun by the National City's agents and "investment
counselors." Discounting all allegations of deliberate conspiracy against the public, substituting the word "stabilization" for "manipulation," still there seemed to be justification for Arthur M. Wickwire's phrasing in the Weeds of Wall
Street: "The Anaconda crushes its prey."

Akin to the formation of a pool was an operation known
as price pegging, which took place especially in connection
with the flotation of new issues of stocks or bonds. Its immediate purpose was to hold up the price of a security to the
offering figure until the distributors had succeeded in selling
the issue to the investing public, for a drop under the offering
price or even weakness made prospective customers skittish.
Such an operation was well illustrated by the case of the
German bonds issued on June 12, 1930, through a syndicate
under the leadership of the J. P. Morgan Company. The

inside of this business transaction in "the automatic and un-conscious" market was unfolded by the Senate committee early in its inquiry. The witness was Richard Whitney, president of the New York Stock Exchange and head of a brokerage house — destined to an assignment in Sing Sing prison a few years later.

Under insistent examination, Mr. Whitney explained the process to the lay public. From June 12, the day of the public offering, to July 2, 1930, the syndicate operated in the market, buying and selling the German bonds and keeping the price on a level with or above the offering price of ninety. This operation Mr. Whitney's house had carried on "under order . . . through J. P. Morgan and Company." On July 2, after the syndicate had disposed of the entire issue to investors, it "pulled the plug," to apply the characterization of the Street, and let the securities take care of themselves. Almost immediately the price sagged below ninety, and on the day of Mr. Whitney's explanation the German bonds were selling at thirty-five or thirty-six cents on the dollar.

To the undiscriminating public, especially that portion which held the depreciated German bonds, this looked very much like a pool. To those experienced in the art of practice, as distinguished from the logic of theory, on the contrary, it was not a pool; nor was it in any way unusual. Indeed, Mr. Whitney made it clear to the Senators from the "provinces" that it was "an absolutely usual and customary method of merchandising and distributing securities." Although men familiar with the folkways and mores of business readily agreed, innocence was appalled to read about it in the morning papers. The factual description of the operation, coming so shortly after the collapse of this "prime security," made a galling impression upon holders of the "sound, gold bonds." The public learned how the selling agents who had given investors the privilege of personal suggestions in June, 1930, had been working for a syndicate which was holding up the price temporarily by operations in the market, that is, until the bonds were unloaded and the plug could be pulled. Mr. Whitney would not concede that his market transactions had made an "artificial" price; his purpose had merely been "to maintain a price." But again the audience at his hearing failed to understand, and in a few days the laughter of wiseacres, even in far-away village stores, was rising over the new phrases: maintaining a price, rigging the market, pulling the plug, protecting investors, and letting prices find their natural level.

The effervescence provoked among small investors by the news of stabilization, pools, price maintenance, and plug-pulling was almost turned into venom when they received a detailed explanation of another practice in "the automatic and unconscious market," known as "the cut in." This short and pointed phrase meant "giving our inside clients a chance to buy our securities at a price below that offered to the public." In the nature of things every great banking house had its heavy depositors, borrowers, and friends. Among the friends might well be old schoolmates, neighbors, members of the same social set, as well as directors of other banks and corporations able to reciprocate by extending similar privileges. In the nature of things also a few of the friends might be men high in the councils of the political parties — either casual acquaintances or leaders with whom contacts had been made in the "natural course" of transactions or otherwise. All this had been customary and conventional from time immemorial. Even corner store magnates had received from the village bank considerations not extended to hard-bitten farmers and penniless proletarians. Nevertheless the anatomy and morphology of the system had never been exposed until the Senate committee performed deft operations on it in the presence of the assembled representatives of the entire press, all on edge to peep behind the curtain.

Although the system was general, the Senate committee chose to illustrate it specifically by examining the practice followed by the House of Morgan. Its counsel and agents in searching the files of that firm came across lists of distinguished American citizens who had been given opportunities to buy securities at prices below those reigning in the market-place. Partners of the House, despite pertinacious questioning, refused to admit that the lists had any special significance apart from the regular business of merchandising and distributing securities. Their more generalized explanation was that the lists contained the names of men of means who could well afford to participate in the risks and advantages of investment. Just how and by whom in the House of Morgan and under whose final authoritative decision the lists were perfected, the witnesses failed to make clear. Some individuals there enrolled were personal friends. For what reasons other names were placed on the list witnesses were at a loss to explain. In several instances they could not recall any reasons. Certainly, they insisted in substance, there was nothing sinister in the lists, no design to influence anyone, especially any of the politicians who appeared on the books. It was, as they saw it, merely business, normal business, and their sincerity on the witness stand seemed transparent. They objected to calling the lists "preferred" or even "selected." They chose to describe them simply as "lists."

Without emphasizing the refinements, explanations, and purifications introduced into the evidence by the Morgan partners, managing editors blazoned on the front pages of their papers the names of influential men chosen from the Morgan "lists" — with supplementary annotations. In skeleton form the registers presented to readers of newspapers made an imposing schedule of personalities that could be arranged in the following order:

Charles Francis Adams, former Secretary of the Navy under President Hoover

Newton D. Baker, former Secretary of War under President Wilson

Bernard M. Baruch, philosopher general of the Democratic party

Charles D. Hilles, co-manager, with J. Henry Roraback, of the Republican party

J. R. Nutt, former treasurer of the Republican National
  Committee

William H. Woodin, then Secretary of the Treasury under
  President Roosevelt — the business leader who in 1932
  had assured good big business that it had nothing to
  fear from The Chief

Norman H. Davis, Ambassador to the World under President
  Hoover and under President Roosevelt

William G. McAdoo, former Secretary of the Treasury under
  President Wilson and Senator from California

Henry E. Machold, former chairman of the Republican party
  in New York and a utility magnate

Frank L. Polk, Under-Secretary of State under President
  Wilson

Silas H. Strawn, former president of the United States
  Chamber of Commerce and distinguished Republican
  leader in Chicago

Owen J. Roberts, Republican from Pennsylvania, Associate
  Justice of the Supreme Court of the United States,
  appointed by President Hoover

General John J. Pershing, Commander of the A. E. F. in the
  War for Democracy

Wallace B. Donham, head of the Harvard School of Business

John J. Raskob, chairman of the Democratic National Committee, recent manager of Alfred E. Smith's campaign

John W. Davis, former Democratic candidate for President,
  counsel for the House of Morgan

Calvin Coolidge, former President of the United States.

Selected and annotated names from the Morgan "lists,"
crowned by fitting headlines, fastened attention upon the
ways of the Street. No qualifying elucidations could overcome the immediate effect of the news. In vain did George
Whitney, Thomas Lamont, and other partners from the
House of Morgan, courteously and modestly explain that
they had no thought of political influence in selecting such
friends of the House for investment opportunities. Hour
after hour Morgan partners, under the glare that blazed on
witnesses, responded in well-modulated, never angry or
impatient, voices to questions about the list and its implications. Special circumstances, never political, they contended, were sufficient to account for the appearance of each

name in the lists; the thought of political influence or any other kind had never occurred to them. If in a tabulation, political connotations were attached to the selected names, that was purely fortuitous — no part of any design framed by the House of Morgan. Charles Francis Adams just happened to be the father-in-law of a young Mr. Morgan. Calvin Coolidge had voluntarily sought the advice of the House in solving his investment problems. Senator McAdoo had been merely a warm friend of a former partner. Newton D. Baker was simply a man of Cleveland — the home of the Van Sweringen Brothers for whom the Morgans had done a large, if not profitable, business. Giving such men advance opportunities was just business, customary business.

In time, perhaps, the patient elucidation of the Morgan partners might have overcome the insinuations and innuendoes of the doubtful and the cynical. But the effect of their even-tempered exegesis was partly vitiated by what seemed to be lack of knowledge on their part which was not convincing to a public stung by losses into incredulity. When Mr. Pecora asked Mr. George Whitney whether John J. Raskob had something to do with the Democratic National Committee, the witness replied: "I don't follow such things." Mr. Pecora inquired of him whether Henry E. Machold had not been chairman of the Republican committee in New York for many years and Mr. Whitney replied: "Why, I don't know, Mr. Pecora. You seem to be suggesting that we have these listed with their political offices. Well, I don't know." Was not Silas H. Strawn president of the United States Chamber of Commerce? In response, Mr. Whitney confessed innocence: "I really don't know." Why had J. R. Nutt subscribed to Allegheny stock through the Morgans when he was a friend of the Van Sweringens in his home town? Mr. Whitney: "I don't know, sir. I just don't know." Rarely did Mr. Whitney appear to find knowledge of such matters in his mind. When informed by Mr. Pecora that Cornelius N. Bliss had once been treasurer of the Republican national campaign committee, Mr. Whitney re-

sponded: "So I heard." To astounded reporters who knew
the answer to every question of the kind, Mr. Whitney's
want of familiarity with political events and personalities
seemed almost miraculous. How could so distinguished a
citizen be so slightly informed about matters of public interest and common knowledge? How could great men in the
House of Morgan be so great and yet apparently so limited
in acquaintance with practical affairs?

If the introduction of other evidence had not intervened,
the explanations of the Morgan representatives respecting
the so-called "preferred" lists, coupled with protestations
of artlessness in matters political, might have been more
generally accepted. However, other evidence was presented
and suspicions regarding protestations of devotion to "sound
banking practices" were raised by the revelation of a letter,
dated February 1, 1929, to one of the gentlemen on a "list,"
William H. Woodin, at the moment of the Senate hearing
May, 1933, Secretary of the Treasury under President
Roosevelt. This letter from a member of the Morgan House,
written to Mr. Woodin in 1929, gave him the privilege of
purchasing 1,000 shares of Allegheny stock. It explained
that the stock "is not the class of security we wish to offer
publicly" and that the House was giving some of "our close
friends" a chance to buy shares at the cost to the firm,
namely twenty dollars a share. By way of special assistance,
the Morgan partner furnished Mr. Woodin additional information: "I believe that the stock is selling in the market
around $35 to $37 a share, which means very little, except
that people wish to speculate. . . . There are no strings
tied to this stock, so you can sell it whenever you wish. . . .
We just want you to know that we were thinking of you in
this connection." After this letter had been placed in the
record, Senator Townsend asked the Morgan witness, Mr.
George Whitney, when he sold most of his own Allegheny
shares and received the answer: "I really do not know. I
sold some, but I do not remember how many." Thereupon
the committee's counsel placed before the witness a copy

of his income tax returns for 1929 disclosing that he had sold that year 8,145 shares at a profit of $229,411.32.

When the text of the letter and reports of the hearings pertaining to it reached the pages of newspapers, they formed for the public a definite image of the kind of business transacted by the House of Morgan. The partners again sought to show that this was merely one among numerous transactions which had proved to be sound for investors and that it could easily be distorted. Yet the Morgan Company had sold privately to its close friends a stock of such a dubious character that the House would not sponsor the paper publicly. It took cognizance of the fact that "people wish to speculate." It informed Mr. Woodin that he could have the stock at twenty dollars a share, that it was selling at from fifteen to seventeen dollars above that price, and that he could sell his allotment whenever he wished to do so, clearing by the transaction perhaps $15,000 or more. In short, the stock was not good enough for the Morgans to issue openly, but it was being fed out privately to the speculative public and close friends of the House were given an opportunity to make "easy money" by unloading on the people who "wish to speculate." That may not have been the Morgans' notion of themselves, but it was an image that appeared to conform to the evidence they had presented. Even Walter Lippmann protested, with chaste restraint: "The testimony has shown that at least in the period under investigation, that is to say, in the years of the great boom, the House of Morgan had not only not exercised a wise restraint upon the speculative craze, but participated in it and profited largely by it."

Besides forming pools, pegging prices, and giving favors to close friends, legitimate members of the banking fraternity, with notable exceptions, had used high pressure methods in inducing the "people who wish to speculate" to keep up their activities. One Chicago investment house, which had sold large blocks of Insull securities, paid for a radio program of instruction delivered to the people in their homes. The program was conducted by a soft-voiced broadcaster known to the radio audience as "The Old Counselor." On inquiry it was discovered that "The Old Counselor" was a professor in Chicago University who was paid fifty dollars a week for his services of instruction and that "everything he delivered" was written in the office of the investment bankers who were unloading "securities" which proved to be almost if not entirely worthless. Far out on the Pacific Coast, another professor acted as an old counselor to the people, by making broadcasts praising the securities of a New York real estate house that later went into bankruptcy and ruined thousands of small investors who had sought safety in its "first mortgage gold bonds."

These disclosures, coupled with revelations of the ways in which electrical utility companies had employed professors in their propaganda, led to questions about the character of scholars in the universities. Querulous curiosity also extended to political matters when it was discovered that the program conducted by the Chicago professor known as "Old Counselor" had opened with an introductory address by a Republican member of the House of Representatives, at the time chairman of the banking committee, and that the Honorable Member had rendered this service at the request of the head of the investment house engaged in selling Insull securities.

Whatever the effect of revelations respecting the salesmanship of a few professors, it was trivial in comparison with the excitement aroused by an exposition of the methods employed by stock manipulators in "poisoning" the "financial news" of reputable papers. Early in the Senate committee's proceedings, Fiorello H. La Guardia entered its chamber with a trunk full of papers and presented sensational evidence to the effect that deceiving the public by false news had been a regular part of the market proceedings carried on by insiders. From evidence in the possession of Mr. La Guardia the public learned that pool operators, in preparing what was euphoniously called "balloon ascensions" for people who wished to speculate, had paid large sums in cash or stocks to financial writers on newspapers of the highest standing.

When one of the gentlemen implicated in such phases of business enterprise was asked to explain his methods, he replied: "I employed newspapers." The counsel for the Senate committee sought to correct him: "You mean writers, I suppose." His response was illuminating: "I don't know what they were. I would give them a copy of an article and sometimes it was in the paper and sometimes it wasn't." Canceled checks issued to writers for their labors in behalf of balloon ascensions showed that reporters on the papers representing the Cream of Respectability had so stooped to serve private interests: the Wall Street Journal, the Evening Mail, the Financial American, The New York Times, The Herald Tribune, and The Evening Post, for instance. Thus even great publishers had been deceived on occasion by their own employees. While in justice to themselves and their readers, they immediately got rid of their unfaithful servants, millions of readers were introduced to the hidden potentialities of financial "news."

In the examination of the National City Company, the affiliate of the National City Bank, the structure and methods of high-pressure selling were uncovered in detail. The men associated with this institution were no mere operators in particular pools and deals. They had a grand system, at the head of which stood Charles E. Mitchell, long deemed a titan of the "legitimate" banking fraternity. The National City Company had divided the country into nearly seventy districts and had established offices in all the important centers of business. The several parts of this empire were tied together and united with the main headquarters in New York by more than eleven thousand miles of private wires. Salesmen in the respective districts were stimulated to high tension by "sales contests" in which large prizes went to the agents who sold the most shares or bonds of particular issues. A special division of the Company combed the automobile registrations, tax lists, and other evidences of property ownership for "prospective customers" or, as things often turned out, prospective victims. By this process new names were constantly added to the roll of persons upon whom selling agents could call in search of investors; in one year, 1928, at least 122,000 new "opportunities" were furnished to the selling force.

Among the securities relentlessly pressed upon prospective customers was the stock of the National City Bank in small or large lots. From day to day the National City Company sent "flashes," or telegraphic dispatches, to its agents, instructing them in the matter of objectives and procedures for the immediate future. In one of those flashes, called "Loaves from Crumbs," headquarters advised its salesmen to observe whether clients had small balances in their accounts accruing from other transactions and, if balances were discovered, to induce such clients to buy one or more shares of National City Bank stock. In any particular case the balance might be less than the amount required for one share. In that instance, salesmen were informed: "You can have the customer put up the remaining cash. If you will continue this practice, it will not be long before each client and you will be agreeably surprised by the shares of the National City Bank stock that he will have accumulated. By using the crumbs of cash resulting from exchanges to buy the new stock of the National City Bank and continuing that practice as opportunity arises, you will work these crumbs into a loaf of substantial size with consequent advantages to the client, the National City Company, and yourself." The advice was frequently taken. Customers bought shares at figures ranging as high as $579 and later were surprised, not agreeably, by seeing them fall to twenty-five or thirty dollars a share. Indeed one day after Charles E. Mitchell had described this type of business to the Senate committee, many former clients in the room declared that they had lost all their savings in helping the Company to make loaves from crumbs.

§

If the bankers' description of their high-pressure selling system actually seemed formal when inscribed in the records of the Senate committee, their operations had a human interest which was illustrated by the injection of a customer or, it would be truer to say, a victim of the bankers' new legitimacy. Some of "the people who wish to speculate," as the Morgans explained the frenzy of the time, were not in truth desirous of embarking upon a career of speculation. One of them was Edgar D. Brown, of Pottsville, Pennsylvania, to whom M. R. Werner has given literary immortality in his volume on Privileged Characters. Mr. Brown had by careful management accumulated about $100,000, partly invested in sound government bonds. Suffering from ill-health, he decided to leave his home town for California. Who was to look after his property during his absence? While pondering that question, he chanced upon an advertisement in a magazine of national circulation, suggesting that anyone about to take a long trip would do well "to get in touch with our institution." This tender of assistance made to the public came from the National City Company. The idea seemed excellent. Here was a great company advertising in a great magazine. So Mr. Brown answered the appeal to reason and very soon a district representative of the Company called upon him in the beneficent guise of an investment counselor. After taking an inventory of Mr. Brown's securities, the counselor wrote to headquarters about the prospects. That was the beginning of a beautiful friendship with the National City Company.

Being an American, Edgar Brown of Pottsville, Pennsylvania, was not averse "to making a little money" by having papers shuffled to and fro in the market, but he was also cautious. At first he insisted that the Company buy bonds for his account and no common stocks. The customer was to be pleased. The Company sold his prime securities, bought bonds yielding a higher rate of interest (of which the Company had plenty on hand), and induced him to borrow money from its twin concern, the National City Bank, at the market rate, for the purpose of buying more high-yield bonds. For a time all seemed to go like a whirl-wind — on paper; Mr. Brown appeared to have his capital doubled or better — on paper. Then the high-yield bonds began to decline as plugs were pulled out or the cruel truth about foreign bonds crept around in esoteric circles. Mr. Brown was alarmed. Thereupon his investment counselor from the National City Company carefully explained: "That is your fault for insisting upon bonds. Why don't you let me sell you some stock?" Mr. Brown consented. Exactly how the transition in finance was made does not appear in the record. Mr. Brown swore that he had never told the coun-selor to buy any particular stocks. But, whether his memory was faulty or not, Mr. Brown soon found "his" Company buying stocks for "his" account fast and furiously, churning them up and down and around and around, and selling him the "favorite" securities of the Company, which was active in syndicates and pools. For a time that seemed to go well, although Mr. Brown had difficulty in keeping track of his papers in the flurry of the great commotion.

Although Mr. Brown was now enjoying the salubrious climate of Los Angeles, he apparently kept his eyes on the stock market reports and discovered in September, 1929, that the prices of his "securities" were dropping. In some trepidation he visited the Los Angeles branch of the National City network for the purpose of saving what he could by selling his liquid claims to wealth. On his arrival at the office of the Company, he was besieged by many counselors. "I was surrounded at once," he told the Senate committee, "by all of the salesmen in the place, and made to know that was a very, very foolish thing to do. . . . I was placed in the category of the man who seeks to put his own mother out of his house." Local counsel was supplemented by a telegram from his counselor in Pennsylvania, who got his address in some mysterious way: "National City Bank now 525. Sit

tight." Despite the advice, Mr. Brown continued to urge
upon the Company the sale of his stock, only to be informed
by his counselors that he was foolish and that the market
would rise, despite the troubles of the day. Sales pressure,
he learned, did not work in reverse. The Company refused
to sell his stocks as long as he had a chance to save something from the wreck.

While Mr. Brown of Pottsville, Pennsylvania, and Los
Angeles, California, was still beseeching and vacillating, the
bubble burst in Wall Street on October 29, 1929. Then the
National City Company, without stopping in the hurry to
consult the restive client, sold his Bank stock at $320 a
share, in good time "to get out" itself. It also disposed of
his securities and paid off his debts at the National City
Bank. In the final moments of affliction, his Company
could obtain no more loans for him to save the paper on
which he had been told to "sit tight." After the storm was
over, Mr. Brown found himself at the bottom of the economic
ladder, where he had started in his youth, entirely stripped
of his savings. His status he graphically described in a letter
to the New York headquarters of his Company: "I am now
40 years of age — tubercular — almost totally deaf — my
wife and family are depending on me solely and alone and
because of my abiding faith in the advice of your company
I am today a pauper." The chief of headquarters may have
laughed or cried, but he lent Mr. Brown no more money.
Down and out Edgar Brown made his way back from the
sunny climate of California to Pottsville, Pennsylvania,
where old friends found an appropriate place for him, "clerk-
ing for the poor board."

§

While engaged in forming pools and syndicates, giving
"our friends" inside opportunities to buy stocks below the
market, buying the affections of newspaper reporters, and
turning droves of salesmen loose on prospective customers,
some legitimate members of the banking fraternity came to

the conclusion that their services to their own institutions were so valuable as to warrant extra compensation over and above the stated salaries. In many cases the special rewards took the form of bonuses voted by grateful directors. In the case of the National City Company, the process was regularized and standardized by the establishment of a "Management Fund" for the benefit of low-salaried executives, most of whom received about $25,000 a year. The Fund was supplied by pouring into its chest a fixed percentage of the Company's earnings. Semi-annually the high officers assembled around the Fund and each one wrote on a secret ballot just what proportion of the total amount each of his respective colleagues should receive, leaving his own name off the list. On the basis of the ballot, the Fund was divided. As Charles E. Mitchell was the head of the National City Bank as well, he deemed it advisable to create another such Fund for that institution. Between 1923 and 1930, the Combined Funds so divided amounted to more than nineteen million dollars. And it happened in the balloting of appreciative colleagues that Mr. Mitchell received on the average about one-third of the distribution.

On the witness stand before the Senate committee, Mr. Mitchell explained this system prevailing at the headquarters, to which Mr. Brown of Pottsville, Pennsylvania, had appealed in vain for aid. The Fund was a valuable device in personnel administration, Mr. Mitchell thought, for it helped to hold the loyalty of executives who might otherwise have been dissatisfied with $25,000 a year and have accepted more attractive posts in other financial institutions. "It establishes," he said, "an *esprit de corps* and an interest in one officer in another officer's work that is to me most noticeable." Indeed, in appreciation of his services to the National City institutions, Mr. Mitchell's own salary, apart from the Fund, had been raised from $100,000 a year to $200,000 in 1931, amid the debris of the depression. To Senator Couzens, the total picture looked peculiar. He asked Mr. Mitchell whether giving each individual officer "a split" had

not inspired "a lack of care in the handling and sale of securities to the public." To this insinuation the banker replied:
"I can readily see from your point of view, that that would
seem so. . . . At the same time I do not recall seeing it
operate that way." Thereupon, the Senator diagramed his
view: "You would not see it. Only the customers would see
it after they had gotten their securities." Perhaps Mr.
Brown, of Pottsville, Pennsylvania, lately of California, had
already seen it. At all events, the directors of the National
City institutions retired Mr. Mitchell from his dual post,
after the facts that they had long privately known had become public property.

§

The perfect meeting of Simplicity and Respectability
occurred, however, in the Kreuger and Toll affair which was
reviewed in the Senate committee's chamber on January 11
and 12, 1933. That enucleation of the difference between the
economic practice of business men and the economic theory
of the schoolmen was especially dramatic on account of the
personalities entangled in the transactions, the number of
shorn investors involved, and the hundreds of millions drawn
into the whirlpool. Moreover it made an international
uproar. European investors, bankers, lawyers, accountants,
and manipulators, as well as American counterparts, had
been caught in the ascension, explosion, and descent. The
central figure of the drama, once revered as the Grand
Symbol of the Age, and then damned in suicide as the most
gigantic liar and swindler of all ages, was Ivar Kreuger,
appropriately a specialist in an incendiary product — the
inflammable match — among other things.

In European countries the humble match had been seized
upon by impecunious governments as a source of indirect
revenue collected through a public monopoly. The article
was in universal use. By monopolizing it, a government
could add to each pack of matches a tax so small as to be
almost impalpable and yet yield enormous sums in the aggre-

gate. Furthermore a beggared government, in need of immediate millions, could collect in advance by issuing bonds against the revenues to be obtained from matches — for ten, twenty, or thirty years. In the United States, where matches were used by prodigal citizens in billion quantities, they formed a big item in industrial production. On the continent of Europe the match was so important that the fate of states-men might hang upon its potentialities for revenue.

With a genius little short of the miraculous, Ivar Kreuger divined the possibilities of the match, among other things, on two continents. From one end of Europe to the other, he approached poverty-stricken governments with offers of huge loans to be secured and liquidated through public monopolies. To befuddled premiers, dictators, and secretaries of treasuries, casting feverishly about for money with which to pay bills, arm soldiers, and build battleships through painless taxation, he seemed a veritable godsend, a wizard, a wonder-worker. Wherever he went in Europe the doors of chancelleries and treasuries flew open to receive him. The biggest and mighti-est welcomed him, dined in state with him, bowed to his lightest wish. To ordinary business men, who had to seek letters of introduction, wait unnoticed in antechambers, prostrate themselves in quest of opportunities to sell goods or float loans, Ivar Kreuger was more than a wizard: he was the Supreme, Invincible, High Potentate among the very Lords of All Creation — the most brilliant star in the uni-versal firmament of business. Compared with Kreuger, Montagu Norman of the Bank of England or J. P. Morgan, the American Napoleon, dwindled into an obsequious courtier seeking favors in the very Throne Room of Sovereignty. When Kreuger came to the United States to deal in matches — and other things — he came as a conqueror to command. And he did command.

With his bases of action and manipulation in Sweden, France, Holland, and the United States, Kreuger organized at least 140 companies, some independent, others intercon-nected, all tied into his personal network. Among his many concerns, the Kreuger and Toll Company and the International Match Corporation were of special interest to American investors and speculators. Through these concerns about $250,000,000 worth of debentures and participating debentures were issued in the United States and their securities were listed for trading on the New York Stock Exchange.

In the indenture for a fifty million dollar issue of "secured sinking fund gold debentures" of the Kreuger and Toll Company, devised in March, 1929, a special provision allowed the Company to substitute new stocks and bonds for stocks and bonds originally pledged as security for the loan, provided that the par value and interest returns on the substitutes equaled 120 per cent of the debentures and the interest requirements. Obviously this clause permitted Kreuger to substitute "shaky bonds" for good bonds, if the substitutes had the requisite par value and were at the moment paying their interest. But the provision which assured to Kreuger this liberty of shifting securities underlying the debentures was explained on the ground that it was necessary for the conduct of so great an international business, with changes taking place constantly in its relations with governments. Perhaps it was. Even so, the original bonds posted as security were dubious to any banker with insight, for they included such paper as Latvian six per cents, Greek eight and one-half per cents, and Ecuadorian seven per cents; and in the course of time Kreuger substituted Yugoslav bonds for bonds of the French Republic.

The sponsoring house for a huge block of these debentures was Lee, Higginson, and Company, founded in Boston in 1848 and regarded as one of the soundest and most conservative banking houses in the United States. Although it had established a branch in New York City, it was such a pillar of Boston honor and intelligence that it commanded respect and confidence throughout the country. The partner of the house most intimately associated with the flotation of the debentures was Donald Durant who, after leaving college, had worked his way up from the position of "office boy" to that of high responsibility in the Company. Was Mr. Durant "acquainted with the mechanism and legal conditions under which the security business is conducted generally abroad"? He had had, he replied to the inquisitor, "something to do indirectly with various issues for foreign companies, but had never had any experience with the operation of an office abroad."

Since the underlying securities for the debenture issue were foreign government papers, the counsel for the Senate committee asked whether he was "fairly well acquainted with political conditions abroad." Mr. Durant answered that he had never pretended to be an expert on political conditions. They were important? "Perhaps important in the getting of foreign issues, of foreign Government bonds, but the bond speaks for itself as an obligation," he contended. Mr. Durant was a director of the Kreuger and Toll Company which issued the debentures in the United States? Yes. Had he attended any meetings of that Company? None between 1929 and 1932 — the year of the flotation and the year of the disaster.

But the Lee, Higginson Company did not issue the debentures without aid. It was assisted by "participating houses" with imposing lists of directors — Kreuger and Toll; Clark, Dodge, and Company; Brown Brothers and Company; the Guaranty Company; the National City Company; Dillon, Read; and the Union Trust Company of Pittsburgh. Among the directors of these sponsoring houses loomed such impressive figures as Jerome D. Greene, John Henry Hammond, C. H. Sabin, P. A. Rockefeller, James A. Stillman, N. F. Brady, Richard B. Mellon, and David A. Reed. Around the nucleus of powerful participating houses were grouped members of the syndicate which sold to the American public the Kreuger and Toll five per cent "secured sinking fund gold debentures." The bare list of syndicate members, including no references to their directors, filled almost six pages of fine print in the Senate committee's record. It embraced such magnates of business as Lehman

Brothers, the Manufacturers Trust Company, the J. P. Morgan Company of New York City, the Union Trust Company of Cleveland, the Mellon National Bank of Pittsburgh, the Shawmut Corporation of Boston, the First National of Detroit, Cassatt and Company of Philadelphia. In all, there were more than three hundred active sponsors, participating in the operation of selling and in the profits arising from the success of the venture.

Distributed geographically, the members of the syndicate fairly well covered the continental domain of the United States from Bangor, Maine, to Seattle, Washington, from San Francisco, California, to Miami, Florida. Indeed nothing short of the entire list of cities and towns in which one or more banks and other responsible concerns offered Kreuger and Toll debentures to their customers could convey a correct impression of the magnitude of the enterprise : Daytona Beach, Jacksonville, Miami, Tampa, Atlanta, Baltimore, Jersey City, Newark, Albany, Auburn, Buffalo, Cooperstown, Elmira, Geneseo, Glens Falls, Gloversville, Jamestown, Johnstown, New York City (more than seventy firms), Ogdensburg, Rochester, Syracuse, Troy, Utica, Watertown, Canton (Ohio), Cincinnati, Cleveland, Columbus, Dayton, Toledo, Youngstown, Braddock (Pennsylvania), Erie, Masontown, Norristown, Philadelphia, Pittsburgh, Sharon, Wilkes-Barre, Charleston (South Carolina), Norfolk (Virginia), Richmond, Washington (D. C.), Bridgeport (Connecticut), Hartford, New Haven, Bangor (Maine), Portland, Boston, Lowell, Pittsfield, Springfield, Providence, San Francisco, Aurora (Illinois), Champaign, Chicago, Evanston, Moline, Peoria, Quincy, Rockford, Indianapolis, La Porte, South Bend, Clinton (Iowa), Davenport, Des Moines, Muscatine, Sioux City, New Orleans, Detroit, Jackson, Kalamazoo, Lansing, Minneapolis, Saint Paul, Kansas City, St. Louis, Lincoln, Omaha, Lead (South Dakota), Sioux Falls, Memphis, Dallas, Houston, Salt Lake City, Seattle, Spokane, Beloit (Wisconsin), Janesville, Madison (four banks), Milwaukee, and Monroe.

In each of these places, one or more institutions enjoying public confidence offered the securities of Kreuger and Toll to friends, acquaintances, and prospects. To widen the network, banks and investment concerns in large cities allowed correspondents in surrounding regions to share in the general distribution. Given such favorable circumstances, the big sale was a complete success and widows, orphans, colleges, and investors by the thousands, as well as speculators, found themselves in possession of "secured sinking fund gold debentures."

Shortly after the syndicate withdrew its support and the plug was pulled in the spring of 1929, Kreuger and Toll securities seemed to waver. They crumbled in the great crash of the autumn. Still, the Lee, Higginson Company had a certain faith in the "equities" and in January, 1932, when Kreuger and Toll American certificates were selling at six cents on the dollar, the Company sent out a circular, entitled "An Undervalued Security," which contained the following suggestion : "Taking into consideration facts alone and not general apprehension unsupported by facts, they represent, in our opinion, an interesting commitment from the standpoint of price in relation to intrinsic value. . . . Unless one lacks all faith in the future of the world, and in the preservation of its economic structure, it seems obvious that these assets will not continue to be valued as they are at the present time" — one prognosis that proved to be correct. Ivar Kreuger evidently had a similar faith or some kind of faith in the world, for in the same month, January, 1932, he arranged with a New York brokerage house to borrow a million dollars, secured by Kreuger and Toll stocks, for the purpose of "stabilizing" the market. A representative of the house declared to the Senate committee that the Lee, Higginson Company had knowledge of the arrangement. Whether it did or not in fact, the brokerage house churned the market in accordance with the contract signed by Kreuger. It was engaged in churning when the dénouement came about two months later.

On March 12, 1932, Ivar Kreuger died suddenly in Paris where directors of Kreuger and Toll, including Donald Durant of Lee, Higginson, had assembled for a meeting with him planned to discover, among other things, the meaning of some mysterious transactions now suspected. When the news of Kreuger's death reached Mr. Durant, he cabled his partners in New York: "For partners only Oak died very suddenly today not public yet please say nothing until announced here." And before Kreuger's death as a suicide was announced in the United States, European speculators unloaded a large amount of Kreuger paper on American "investors."

After the news broke in New York and all the capitals of the world, lawyers, accountants, security-holders' committees, and other interested parties started an exploration of Kreuger's companies, accounts, transactions, and "miracles." Forty volumes could scarcely hold the documents and findings. The evidence contained in their pages placed Kreuger among the most colossal manipulators of all times, ancient and modern. His financial reports and balance sheets on which American business men had trustingly relied were peppered with fraud; his reported earnings were three, four, or five times above his real earnings. During a period of eighteen years the actual operating profit of one group of filiates, for example, was apparently about 150,000,000 kroner, before interest on bonds, and yet dividends amounting to 668,000,000 kroner had been paid. Neither the height nor the depth of Kreuger's operations could be fully reckoned. Investors merely knew that they had lost heavily.

How had it been possible for Kreuger to secure formidable statements, declarations, balance sheets, and other "evidences" of "intrinsic values" upon which trusting business men in America had relied in urging prospects and customers to invest in his secured sinking fund gold debentures? With great ingenuity and display of details, the mystery was explained to the Senate committee by an accountant who had investigated about 140 of the wizard's concerns. Kreuger had formed two companies for the special purpose of fixing up the reports that "demonstrated" his high financial standing — the Continental Company and the Dutch Kreuger and Toll. "Those," explained the accountant, "he kept well under his thumb with creatures of his own in charge, and auditors, and he knew that he could get a certificate from them at any time of anything he wanted. And that is where he buried his stuff. . . . The whole structure was honeycombed with irregularities."

As if unable to take it all in, Senator Costigan inquired: "They were clearing houses for manipulation?" To this the accountant laconically replied: "Well, they were sinks." Reluctantly, a representative of the New York Stock Exchange admitted that he and his colleagues responsible for listing Kreuger "securities" on the Big Board had accorded to a foreigner privileges not granted to Americans and had been snared by "the greatest swindler of all time." Sponsors, leading bankers, managers of the Stock Exchange, men who had been supposed to know what they were doing, all stood naked under the sign of their defeat — Credulous Ignorance — from Bangor to Seattle, from San Francisco to Dallas and Miami.

§

Capping the testimony displaying lack of insight and mistakes in judgment were disclosures showing that great bankers had not been paying federal income taxes in recent years. Here again their activities were entirely "legitimate." The law levied taxes on capital gains and permitted deductions for losses. When the promoting bankers were making large profits, they paid large taxes on incomes. When they incurred losses, they deducted losses from earnings. If their losses exceeded earnings for the year, they owed no taxes to the Government. Under the law, losses had to be realized; that is, the holder of a $1000 bond which fell to $60 could not deduct his loss unless he sold his bond and "took his loss" in fact. Presumably it was the intention of the lawmakers that losses so established should be bona fide; in other words, that the seller should actually dispose of his bond in the market and be permanently rid of it.

Yet under the terms of the law a practice had grown up of selling securities to friends and relatives, deducting the losses, and then buying back the same paper at the expiration of a few months at or near the same price. In keeping with this practice the owner of a home or a farm might have sold his property to his wife at a loss and taken the loss out of his income tax, if he had thought of it and the revenue officers had accepted the transaction as bona fide. But small investors, unlike bankers and manipulators, were not all familiar with the niceties of the law and, when they read in the newspapers that many Lords of Creation had paid no income taxes at all in 1930, 1931, and 1932, they found difficulty in making fine discriminations.

Within the letter of the law, the devices employed in incurring losses that could be deducted from incomes were various. Albert Wiggin, of the Chase National Bank, had three "personal," or "family," corporations to which he could sell or from which he could buy securities, as occasion might suggest. He also had similar corporations chartered in Canada. If he was about to make a profitable sale of stock, he could transfer the transaction to one of his Canadian corporations and thus show no taxable profit actually arising within the jurisdiction of the United States. By employing such legitimate methods, Mr. Wiggin, as he remarked, "saved" a tax of $440,000 on a profit of $4,000,000. Charles E. Mitchell, of the National City Bank, was so adroit and multifarious in consummating transactions of this kind that legal action was brought against him by the Government. With the aid of Max Steuer, called the Prince of Juries, Mr. Mitchell convinced twelve men tried and true that all had been lawfully done; but the Government later recovered large sums from him in the form of back taxes. Otto Kahn testified that he had reduced his taxes for 1930 by selling securities to his daughter and had bought them back a few months later. He had cut his taxes and yet remained, financially speaking, in possession of the same property — all as permitted by the letter of the law.

A similar elucidation of the perfectly legitimate process was made by another expert in finance. At the end of the year 1930 this expert sold certain shares publicly in the market. His wife borrowed money from him on her personal note and bought a similar amount of these shares. "There was no agreement nor any understanding between us," he testified, "that I should any time later on repurchase these shares from her or any of them. I intended the sale to be a complete and final disposal of these shares, and she understood it to be so. . . . I was advised that under these circumstances I was fully within my rights in deducting from my income return for the year 1930 the amount of the loss sustained." A few months later, however, things seemed to be "slipping." Indeed they might get worse. "I talked to my wife about this, and we both felt that it was not wise that she should continue to carry this debt against stocks. Therefore, I purchased the stocks from her on April 8, 1931, at the original price and she thereupon paid her loan. The note was surrendered and marked 'paid.'" All this was entirely proper within the terms of the law and accepted as such by the Treasury Department of the United States under President Hoover. Yet, when millions of investors were smarting under their losses and income-tax payers were learning of their own carelessness in taking advantage of their rights, such revelations by the Senate committee had a tendency to aggravate, rather than allay, popular irritations.

§

The innumerable transactions disclosed by the Senate committee, taken collectively and arranged with reference to any coherent theory of political economy, did not seem to square with doctrines of business long taught in the schools and accepted by the Mentors of Society as good always and everywhere. Since the time of Adam Smith it had been widely held that legitimate business transactions, under the invisible hand of Providence, had kept economy in motion, produced and distributed wealth, and redounded to public welfare. This broad principle had been worked out into a system, an American System, which bankers and men of affairs were supposed, at least by professors and school children, to observe in practice. Its elements could be simplified in the following terms. Individual industry brings earning. Thrift effects savings. Savings supply capital. It is the function of capital to set enterprise in motion, under the profit incentive. Enterprise in motion creates and distributes wealth in the form of valuable goods. Bankers lend their depositors' money on sound securities to aid capital in setting enterprise in motion, and they float securities for the same purpose. Business men to whom such funds are lent manage real property employed in production, with fiduciary consideration for investors entitled to reward for thrift and saving. The stock exchange is a place where bona fide securities are listed after examination and where investors are furnished a true and open market for buying and selling securities at their intrinsic or natural level. The participants in this System know what functions they are performing. Presumably, they know what they are doing and, as Thomas W. Lamont phrased it, they regard their transactions as in the main "wholesome." For about fifty years this was the general conception of the System, expounded by economists, popularized in public schools and Sunday schools, celebrated by men of affairs at banquets, and repeated by business and professional women at some of their conventions.

In many respects the practices described to the Senate committee offered strange contrasts to the pure word of this theory. Untold billions had been accumulated, not by labor and thrift, but by organizing holding companies, investment trusts, corporations, pools, price manipulations, and balloon ascensions on the basis of inside knowledge — knowledge withheld from stockholders and the general public. At the same time "poisoned financial news," bought and paid for by the insiders, had been concocted to mislead investors. Untold billions in capital had been used, not to set enterprise and labor in motion, but for purposes far removed from the creation of real goods. Billions had been collected to form holding and investing companies which merely bought stocks in going concerns at inflated values, often from and through insiders. Millions had been employed to get control over industries and railway companies with a view to making a profit in fees, commissions, and purchases, rather than to enlarging their real capital — plants, trackage, and terminal facilities.

Millions had been diverted to consolidating banks and other concerns through stock purchases and directorships, thus increasing the powers of control and manipulation. Banks had been lending money in the boom years but not merely for the purpose of enlarging plants and setting wealth-creating enterprises in motion. They had lent money to big speculators in the stock market, to the creators of hidden pools, to the organizers of mergers bearing no relation to any increase in real capital, that is, to plant extension or more efficient operation of existing plants. Many a business man supposed to be safeguarding his investors' interests had been found wrecking the property over which he was supposed to preside, speculating in the market in the securities of his own concern, forming secret pools against stockholders and investors. Eventually Lords of Creation whose superior wisdom and knowledge the populace had been taught to respect were forced to confess publicly that their System did not harmonize in practice with the theory of business enterprise : "Let us alone and we will produce wealth, distribute prosperity, and employ the idle."

Pools, syndicates, plug pullings, balloon ascensions, poisoned news, "favors to our friends," high-pressure salesmanship, management funds, and bonuses had not come inexorably out of the automatic, unconscious market. Schoolmen droning economics in the classrooms might still hold that such activities were productive because they were not forms of consumption ; but participants in the deeds were not asleep at the time. Wide-awake and astute men, with the aid of wide-awake and astute lawyers, had *ex proprio motu* and with full knowledge, created and operated such devices for their own end — making a profit. Such undertakings did not spring from the realm of the unconscious. The men who carried them on doubtless had little inkling of the distant consequences or total outcome of their labors. Probably they had learned from history just what statesmen and historians had learned — nothing or at best very little. Nevertheless the evidence presented to the Senate committee made it indisputable that these men had done all these things deliberately. They had their explanations, justifications, homilies, and moralities to unfold in a way that, in their opinion, absolved them from responsibility for the misadventures and reverses of their operations. Some of them seemed to have only hazy ideas as to the meaning of pools, balloon ascensions, and other practices known even to the errand boys of the Stock Exchange. Yet none of them contended that their acts had been performed unconsciously or automatically.

According to an old maxim, every idea which gets possession of civilization begins as a rank heresy and ends as a crass superstition. Could it be that the once heretical American System had become a superstition ? At all events clergymen, professors, editors, columnists and other promoters of law and order, from circles which had long defended the System on the basis of its Theory, now began to question its Practice in vigorous inquiries. Some of the promoters of law and order were obviously horrified by the Senate findings with respect to the things which the Paragons and Pillars of the System had been doing. Even such well-poised commentators as Walter Lippmann and Mark Sullivan were moved to deviate slightly from their fixed line in discussing the course of events. And misgivings expressed in pulpits, on the platform, and in the press seeped down to the listening and reading multitude. The inside history of their heroes and their investments had repercussions among farmers and other homeowners in peril of losing the very roofs over their heads. Through the tabloids, if through no other channels, the derelicts of industry got inklings of errors in high places affecting their own struggle to keep soul and body together. If, in moral standards and lust for money, the people in general were akin to the Lords of Creation, that possible resemblance merely burdened them with the sting of a common defeat. Judging by critical comments, the spirit of black distrust was succeeding the spirit of unquestioning faith.

§

It was fortunate for the possessors of good things in 1933 that William Randolph Hearst had reversed the role filled by his yellow press during the opening years of the century. Once he had thundered against plutocrats, railway magnates, stock gamblers, monopolists, and the "Plunderbund." In flaming editorials his papers had scourged "the money changers in the temple" with the vigor and wrath of ancient Jewish prophets. Indeed he had gone so far as to permit one of his writers to hint at assassination as a method for disposing of one major leader of the time. By 1933, however, for reasons best known to himself, he had shifted over into the conservative fortress. He had supported Coolidge and dined with him in the White House. He had approved the Democratic candidate in 1932, for there was little in the Democratic platform or campaign speeches to which he could take exception. Appealing to the populace for readers, he had advocated large expenditures for public works to give employment and he had condemned President Hoover's opposition to direct federal grants in aid of the idle and the hungry.

In the main, Mr. Hearst's emotions were conservative in 1933. Instead of turning his engines of denunciation against the possessors of special privileges, he employed them in defending things he had formerly denounced and applied his energies to pillorying and flaying critics and doubters as

"Reds." The most charitable explanation of this reversal was that Mr. Hearst had grown old. Certainly that was enough. Voltaire had once remarked that the strength of the English church rested upon the fact that it made no man a bishop until he had become so aged that avarice was his sole motive. At all events Mr. Hearst, who had formerly made men tremble over their possessions, now seemed to tremble himself. And the country witnessed the spectacle of the man whom Theodore Roosevelt had charged with being an accessory to the death of President McKinley transformed into the man praised, wined, dined, and flattered by the spiritual descendants of Marcus A. Hanna, the paragon of conservatism in the age of McKinley.

Though the Hearst press swung to the side of "yellow" reaction, it would have been a marvel of history if no leaders had arisen to express the sentiments and resentments of the multitudes who were unemployed or fretted by deposits frozen in banks, homes or farms in peril of foreclosure, bonds in default, stocks evidently worthless. It would also have been a marvel if no demagogues had taken advantage of the opportunity to elevate themselves into places of influence and authority. Both appeared upon the scene and it was not always easy to distinguish the one from the other.

From ancient times, it is true, a connotation of evil had been associated with demagogues. In the fourth century before Christ, Aristotle had called the demagogue the man who flatters the people as the sycophant flatters the tyrant. The people were "too ready" to listen to him — "the worthless fellow" opposed by "the better class." At least the demagogue was a trouble-maker. "Revolutions in democracies," declared the Greek philosopher, "are generally caused by the intemperance of demagogues who either in their private capacity lay information against rich men . . . or coming forward in public they stir up the people against them." Yet Aristotle did not regard the demagogue as an evil genius springing out of a vacuum, with no justification or right on his side. "Constitutional governments and aristocracies," he explained, "are commonly overthrown owing to some deviation from justice in the constitution itself."

In classic theory, therefore, it had not been entirely a case of black against white — the villainy of the demagogue against the excellence of "the better class." The judgment of subsequent history likewise had been mixed. Jefferson, the hero of agrarians, had been denounced as a demagogue and atheist by "the wealth and talents" of his time. Nor had the planting aristocracy looked upon Lincoln and his "greasy mechanics" as the symbols of perfect chivalry. With historic lines of demarkation so loosely drawn it was impossible in 1933 to make a distinction universally acceptable. Nevertheless, if violence of language and the promise of impossible gifts were the signs of demagogy, then the United States had three masters of the art engaged in whipping up opposition to the Lords of Creation and their System — Huey P. Long, Father Charles E. Coughlin, and Dr. Francis E. Townsend. Each in his way was a man of singular power. Each addressed himself to a special audience and employed his own language and symbols of martial array. But, if the character of their following was the test of their intention, all appealed to misery and discontent with the economy and government of "the better class."

Huey P. Long, son of a poor farmer, born in 1893, belonged in origin to the class upon whose support he depended for power. By energy of will and strong native talents he had made his way through a toilsome youth and meager education to a position at the bar. Early in his career as a lawyer he had encountered the Standard Oil Company, and its ruthless obstruction, he said, had kept him from entering the millionaire circle. Had he been taken into the fold of the mighty his annals might have been those of many a poor boy who had marched from poverty to riches. Be that as it may, Mr. Long became an inveterate foe of the "corporate interests" and their politicians in Louisiana. Gathering strength in the progress of his denunciations, he managed to find a place for himself on the state commission charged with the regulation of public utilities. In 1928 he was elevated to the office of governor by a large popular vote.

As if learning from Machiavelli, Governor Long sharpened and turned against his foes the weapons they had employed against him. He brought the state legislature under his dominion. He drove his opponents out of office, by "ripper" legislation when necessary. Their places he filled with his obedient servants — some of them men whose vision of a political heaven was a kingdom in which corruptionists enriched themselves according to the formula of the Orleanist monarchy in France.

Whatever the character of his council, from start to finish the Governor remembered his constituents, so long neglected by "the better class" which he had evicted from political dominion. Under his direction the public school system was strengthened, free books were provided for pupils, farmers and villagers were "lifted out of the mud" by a network of improved roads and bridges, and the state university of Louisiana was raised to a higher standard of proficiency. Naturally all this improvement cost huge sums of money and to meet the bills the Governor laid heavy taxes on corporations and public utilities while exempting small homesteads from public levies. Even his irreconcilable foes had to acknowledge that, despite his ruthless methods, the Governor had materially aided poor whites and negroes in their galling struggles with ignorance and poverty.

Reaching out like Alexander for new worlds to conquer, Governor Long entered the campaign as a candidate for the United States Senate in 1930 and was elected. By this time he had attracted national attention and started to work out his economic program for the country. "I had been in the United States Senate only a few days," he said, "when I began my effort to make the battle for a distribution of wealth among all the people a national issue for the coming election." At the Chicago convention, Senator Long took special note of one sentence in Franklin D. Roosevelt's acceptance speech : "Throughout the Nation, men and women, forgotten in the political philosophy of the Government of the last years, look to us here for guidance and for a more equitable opportunity to share in the distribution of national wealth." This became Senator Long's keynote: "Share our wealth." With his wonted vigor, tireless and almost superhuman, he threw himself into the campaign for the election of Governor Roosevelt to the office of President, assailing the rich as despoilers of the people and demanding legislation that would strip them of power and force a new distribution of wealth. Just how this reallocation was to be effected, the Senator did not make very precise. His citations from the Old Testament seemed to indicate that he imagined it possible to divide railways, industrial plants, and corporate property as the ancient Jews had divided land and cattle. Yet, if his economic theory was somewhat obscure, there was no doubt about the effectiveness of his appeal and the magnitude of the following he secured.

Soon after President Roosevelt assumed his duties in the Spring of 1933, Mr. Long opened his barrage in the Senate. When he spoke, he ridiculed, snapped, gesticulated, and bellowed. News that he was to address his colleagues and the nation brought huge crowds to the galleries. Rarely had a Senator lashed out with such fury at banks, bankers, stock brokers, investment houses, and the Lords of Creation in particular and general. No invisible ties imposed caution upon his tongue. Dominant over his own local machine, sustained by the spoils of office and the perquisites, he could spurn the peace-offerings of corporations and "the better class" in his state. Senators of his own party, less secure in their seats, knew this and, as he scourged the money changers, named names, or made insinuations, they sat silent in their places, some aghast, others afraid.

When the Senate committee engaged in investigating stock exchange practices disclosed the fact that President Roosevelt's Secretary of the Treasury, Mr. Woodin, had been on the "preferred lists" of the J. P. Morgan Company, Senator Long made an impassioned speech declaring that "the

Treasury Department of the United States should be ousted
from the House of Morgan." After Collier's Weekly had
begun a war on him, Senator Long entered the chamber of the
Senate committee, subjected Thomas W. Lamont to an inquisition, and sought to show that Mr. Lamont's ownership
of stock in a concern that controlled Collier's Weekly had
some connection with the attack published in its pages.

Shaking his finger at the witness, Senator Long persisted in
his effort to drive Mr. Lamont into a corner and make him
confess that through his financial interest in the Crowell
Publishing Company he had exerted pressure upon editorial
policies. Again and again, Mr. Lamont explained that his
relation with the concern as a stockholder was merely
financial and that he had not influenced in any respect the
nature of the articles printed in its various publications, not
so much as an article in the Woman's Home Companion or
the Farm and Fireside. Again and again he patiently informed the Senator that he was not even familiar with
editorials and articles which had appeared in the pages of the
Crowell magazines. "I haven't control of any of those papers, Senator Long," Mr. Lamont insisted quietly. "You
see, Senator Long, my connection with the Crowell Publishing Company is simply a financial connection . . . I hold such
stock as I hold in that company for the purpose of the dividends that I gain through it, I hope." When thus informed
that the witness was interested in the dividends rather than
in the intellectual output of the industry, Senator Long hurled
at Mr. Lamont the retort: "I see. Thank you," provoking
hilarity among the reporters and auditors in the chamber.

To the end of the hearing Mr. Lamont preserved his com-
posure. Without raising his voice, he tried to make the
Senator believe that the connections of the House of Morgan
or its partners with men who happened to be in politics or
the publishing business was incidental to financial transactions and in no way designed to influence political or editorial
convictions or policies. Between the things which Mr. Lamont explained and the things he said he knew nothing

about, Senator Long swelled in exasperation until he reached the point of explosion. In every respect the scene was indicative of a change in popular temper: a member of the House of Morgan had been treated with indignity by a Senator of the United States, a thing inconceivable in the age of the golden glow.

The second mighty malcontent of the season, Father Charles E. Coughlin, priest of the Royal Oak parish in the diocese of Detroit, pastor of the Shrine of the Little Flower, built up his dominion of power largely through the radio. Branching out from a local station over which he delivered sermonettes on religious and moral subjects to his parishioners, Father Coughlin organized a radio league of his own in 1930, bought time on other radio stations, and delivered a series of broadcasts on political and economic issues, in which he named names and fumed at men in high places. Swiftly he gathered an immense audience. One of his outbursts against President Hoover, it was reported, brought 1,200,000 letters from his auditors. Denunciations of the Morgan Company, Andrew W. Mellon, Ogden Mills, and Eugene Meyer as "the four Horsemen of the Apocalypse" evoked cheers from the hundreds of thousands. When great banks closed their doors in Detroit early in 1933 and the streets of the city were jammed with men and women crying for their money on deposit, Father Coughlin loosed a torrent of invective against bankers and politicians. Inasmuch as enormous audiences listened to his addresses, his stinging monologues "made news." So the press felt compelled to repeat them for its multitudinous readers and the nation fairly writhed under the priest's brazen denunciations.

Although Father Coughlin held rather close to Senator Long's keynote, his program contained distinctive elements. Being a Catholic, he employed for his coverage the humane sentiments expressed in the noblest encyclicals issued at Rome on social questions. The special objects of his censure were bankers, brokers, and "their politicians." The emancipation from their despotism was to come from "a living annual wage, nationalization of banking and currency and of natural resources, private ownership of all other property, control of private property for the public good, government banking, congressional control of coinage, steady currency value, cost of production plus a fair value for agriculture, labor unions under government protection, recall of non-productive bonds, abolition of tax-free bonds, social taxation," and other devices.

These proposals, it was evident, stemmed largely from the creed of American populism, with its attachment to the direct owners of small properties and its enmity for high finance and large enterprise. They were familiar, but in this case familiarity did not breed contempt, for auditors by the million heard with rapture their own desires so lustily stated. Clearly addressed to small home owners, debt-burdened farmers, and laborers — to men and women struggling on the verge of subsistence — the appeal penetrated every region and substratum of society. Commanding an audience so large and so constituted, on doctrines so formulated, Father Coughlin at first threw his weight on the side of the Roosevelt administration. He was among the councilors invited to Washington and stood ready to cheer as well as to scoff. How much havoc he could play with party regularity in 1933, none of the adepts could divine and as the months of the year slipped by they had to walk warily.

Less imposing in personality, no orator at all, was Dr. Francis E. Townsend, the third mighty malcontent who brought heavy pressure on Washington as the Roosevelt administration picked its way, now resolutely, now cautiously, amid the broken fortunes of the depression. Dr. Townsend was a quiet, soft-voiced physician of humble origins. For long, weary years, he had served poor patients generously in the Black Hills. At length, in search of a milder climate, he had migrated to Long Beach, California, where he found a minor post in the department of health. When the panic struck the nation in 1929, he and his little family were safe enough themselves but the sights and sounds of the catastrophe were too much even for his schooled patience. Through his window, one day, according to his own account, he saw three old women sorting over the contents of a garbage can in the street, searching there for their daily bread. Like Paul on the road to Damascus, Dr. Townsend beheld a sign and heard a call. With the wrath of an indignant prophet, he loudly cursed a world in which old women were compelled to search for food in the wastes of a city — so loudly that his outburst lifted his wife to her feet in alarm. This was America, land of the free and home of the brave, the land of great wealth and rugged individualism — indeed! Under the stress of tumultuous emotions, Dr. Townsend evolved a simple plan of salvation.

About his scheme there was nothing revolutionary, nothing as radical as the program of Senator Long or the proposals of Father Coughlin. It called for no knowledge of Marx's dialectics or Spengler's technics; nor of the automatic market or marginal utility. Aged people simply ought not to starve or resort to garbage for their bread. An old-age pension, Dr. Townsend thought, would prevent that, and many states had pension systems, of a kind, already in effect. It should, however, be a generous pension — two hundred dollars a month; no less. But that could not stand alone. The country was in financial straits and industry was running on a low level of production. Consequently Dr. Townsend had to add another drive to his system: each recipient of a two hundred dollar pension must spend it all within a month. Such an enormous stream of cash would set all sleeping enterprise in rapid motion, he thought, keep it in motion, and stimulate new enterprise. The aged poor were to be saved from disgrace and poverty; the problem that had baffled the world's statesmen was to be solved swiftly and painlessly. With economic energies engaged at full blast, the revenue for the pensions could be painlessly derived, by a sales tax, a transactions tax on consumption. The wealth of the rich would not be threatened. Consumers would pay and the American System, unchanged in form, would run at top speed.

In vain did economists try to explain voluminously that the transactions tax would really fall upon the poor whose buying power was already scant and that a pension of even thirty dollars a month would cost four billion dollars a year. Dr. Townsend retained his fixed idea and in the highways and byways preached his gospel of economic salvation. From one end of the land to the other, Old Age Revolving Pension clubs were formed by the thousands and members assembled in conventions. Contributions were collected in dollars, dimes, and pennies. Old men and women, believing that pensions were almost at hand, sold their earthly possessions and emptied the returns into the treasury for the good of the cause. Very soon the whole country was laid out into districts, each with its directing headquarters, and a central office was established in Washington, well-staffed by publicity experts. Petitions to Congress were drafted and it was alleged that at least twenty-five million signatures had been secured before much time had elapsed. As the movement acquired enormous funds for propaganda, it recruited orators, manipulators, and clever managers of the news.

Having organized an immense constituency, the Townsendites concentrated a heavy pressure on the politicians. Candidates for Congress were questioned privately, heckled at public meetings, and driven into commitments. While the uproar was at its height, the directors of the movement could claim a strong nucleus of followers in the House of Representatives. In many districts even conservative Republicans had to make bows of approval. Added to the noise raised by Senator Long and Father Coughlin, the shrill voices of the aged poor deepened the tension of the national capital as the Roosevelt administration formulated its policies, while taking account of the necessities likely to be presented in coming campaigns.

§

Domestic anxieties were augmented in the spring of 1933 by foreign news. At the end of three years the detonations

of the panic appeared to be expanding rather than diminishing throughout the world; but in the general wreckage communist Russia forged ahead, enlarging production and employment, while capitalist nations blundered around aim-
lessly. In 1933 the Soviet Republic brought to a close its first
five-year plan with a paean of triumph, and announced the
opening of the second concerted effort on a scale more vast.
The arch-conspirator, Leon Trotsky, with his feverish designs
for a quixotic world revolution, had been expelled, his faction
suppressed, the Stalin regime consolidated, and the demonstration of efficient socialism in one country acclaimed as
in progress. From any point of view the spectacle was impressive. The left-wing intelligentsia in the United States
now spoke knowingly of five-year plans realized, not romantically of utopian dreams as of old. The middle classes were
moved to mild curiosity at least and read the New Russian
Primer by the thousands. If the red-baiters in turn were
stirred to greater activity, that could be interpreted to mean
that communism was really on the march. Even President
Hoover had felt compelled to refer to five-year plans, if only
to discredit all planning as Bolshevik in origin and intention.
Marx had emerged from a hole in a corner and hovered as a
hope or a menace over places high and low.

Still, Russia was far off and could be discounted as a bit
oriental in its ways and values. Besides, communist formulas — for instance, law of capitalist development, thesis,
antithesis, and synthesis, inevitable breakdown of capitalist
economy, dictatorship of the proletariat, and the spring into
freedom — had a strange sound in most American ears.
The phrase "materialist dialectics" was a puzzle propounded
in drawing-rooms for sheer entertainment. Had the preachers of ideology been confined to the Kremlin or the banks of
the Volga, the rolling reverberations of their voices might
have faded away unheard in Jersey City, in the Rocky
Mountains, in sunny California. It so came about, however,
that while the celebration of Russia's first five-year plan was
in process, nearer events in central Europe announced the

triumph of another ideology, equally dogmatic and equally Bolshevik in method, whose rise to power could not be ignored in any part of the United States.

For fifteen years Germany had been struggling through the mess left by the war, under a constitution that was in many respects a model for the world. Despite endless difficulties and the harsh impositions of the Versailles Treaty, sober and steady Germans had managed to keep their political machinery running, especially with the aid of lavish loans, long-term and short-term, from American and British capitalists. But the old military party, tolerated and favored by the Weimar republic, continued to smart under the stings of defeat, and found it more pleasant to discover scapegoats in democrats, socialists, and Jews than to accept the disconcerting fact of its own failure. Militarism still lived and its devotees became positively frantic as they contemplated their impotence. To the unrest of the officer class was united the violence of war veterans from the trenches. They chafed at the restraints of civilian life, even when they could secure regular employment, and they turned to murder and civil war during discouraging days of enforced idleness. All through the years which Coolidge found so blessed with prosperity, German veterans unadjusted to civilian life had been drawing together in the National Socialist Workers Party under the direction of a powerful demagogue, Adolf Hitler.

In opposition to this growing military concentration, German democracy developed only factionalism, betraying confusion in purpose and method. Cursing democracy in terms as lurid as those employed by Hitler's Nazis, Communists fought Socialists in the streets and occasionally voted with Hitler's party in the Reichstag. Frightened by communism and socialism alike, great landlords trembling for the safety of their estates and capitalists anxious over the future of their heavy industries cast about for any port in the storm. Terrified ladies made lavish contributions to Hitler's exchequer. So, when the full fury of the economic panic broke in Germany in 1929, there was no democratic unity to cope with the gathering forces of reaction. Backed by his marching men, Hitler, in January, 1933, came to terms with Franz von Papen on "a national concentration" representing landlords, heavy industries, and Catholicism, foe of all "irreligious" radicalism. From a conference with President von Hindenburg, now in the last stages of senility, the two conspirators emerged with a commission to form a government composed of Hitler as chancellor, von Papen as vice chancellor, and a cabinet weighted by landlords and big industrialists.

Within two months Germany had slipped into despotism. On February 4, a month before the inauguration of Roosevelt in Washington, von Hindenburg signed a decree prohibiting public meetings and silencing the press. A few weeks later the Reichstag building, dedicated to the German people, was gutted by fire — perhaps an event symbolizing Nazi contempt for democratic institutions. February 28, Hindenburg suspended all the fundamental rights guaranteed by the Weimar constitution, imposed severe penalties on open opponents, and put the country into a state of siege. Although Hitler's party received less than a majority of the votes cast in an election on March 5, it was able, by unity of will, to ride rough-shod over the divided opposition. March 23, a docile Reichstag met and enacted legislation which in substance put an end to the last pretences of constitutional government and placed a formal sanction on government by dictatorial decree — government by despotism. Now terrorism moved swiftly. All opposition parties were suppressed. Trade unions and coöperative societies were destroyed. Jews were barbarously persecuted. Liberal critics, even of the German race, were beheaded, shot, or imprisoned. Like Mussolini's Fascists, Hitler's Nazis began their march over "the rotten corpse of liberalism and democracy," as they termed it — a march that was to end in tyranny, armed to the teeth, triumphant, invincible at home, feared abroad. "Let contemptible democracies beware!" ran the cry along the Berlin-Rome axis.

Meanwhile, across the Pacific, the fire lighted in China by Japanese militarists continued to burn. The efforts of President Hoover and Secretary Stimson to quench it had been without avail. Great Britain and France had refused to join them in united action against the violator of the Kellogg Pact. Almost without let or hindrance the Japanese consolidated their position in Manchukuo, pressed westward and southward, operated around Peiping, made "deals" with local war lords, and bombed their way down toward the Yangtze. In Tokyo all the old Liberals who had coöperated with the League of Nations and sought an orientation toward the Anglo-Saxon world were driven from power. Some died. Others were assassinated. A few fled. The remainder with rare exceptions took refuge in silence. Their last line of defense had been destroyed in 1924 when the Congress of the United States passed the Exclusion Act, slammed the door in the face of the Japanese nation, making no effort to spare its feelings. Like a bolt from the heavens had come the answer. "Asia for the Asiatics!" rolled the war shout from Yokohama to Dairen. With their power and prestige enhanced, militarists and navalists took charge of the government in Tokyo, polished their weapons, and prepared to tear up four-power pacts, nine-power pacts, and all the other kinds of pacts that stood in their way. The little candle of democracy, which had flickered in the national capital of Japan, sank into a dying sputter. Over this development, Rome and Berlin at least could strut. Was tyranny, one of the oldest forms of government, to be the last?

During the closing months of his administration, President Hoover watched the course of events with growing anxiety. His defeat in the election had left him with no mandate for action, and inability to fathom his successor's plans added to his perplexities. In domestic affairs the tension of the economic distress remained taut. In foreign affairs the question of the inter-governmental debts was pressing. Great Britain and France asked for a re-opening of the settlements, and France prepared to default on her obligations. The disarmament conference at Geneva was in a state of suspended animation, and on its idle talk Germany had heaped ridicule. A world economic conference had been called and experts were laying out the agenda, but the prospects for "appeasement" were slight. The Hoover-Stimson doctrine applied to Japan in the Manchukuo affair was hanging in mid-air and the Council of the League of Nations was maneuvering for an escape.

In an effort to bridge the gulf, President Hoover, after the election, invited Governor Roosevelt, his successor, to confer with him on the issues of the moment and on November 22, 1932, they held a desultory discussion without arriving at a program of joint action. The following January, Secretary Stimson took up the matter of foreign affairs with Governor Roosevelt. Apparently he gained the impression that the incoming President would adhere to the policy of refusing to recognize territorial changes made in violation of the Kellogg Pact. Later in the month President Hoover and Governor Roosevelt again conferred in the White House, and again failed to arrive at any major decision. Although a statement was issued to the effect that the incoming administration would be glad to discuss the debt question and other matters with British representatives, the pronouncement merely confirmed a platitude. Admittedly the conference was futile. If the misadventure gave President Hoover an opportunity to shift some of the responsibility for the banking crisis of February upon his successor, Governor Roosevelt was able to retort that it would have been folly to assume responsibility without power.

§

Such, in bald outline, with meager illustrations, were the maladies and tumults surrounding the Roosevelt administration when it entered upon its duties in March, 1933, and began to thread its way in the maze. Banks closed. Unemployment increasing. Grievances deepening. Uncertainty

206 AMERICA IN MIDPASSAGE

spreading. Farmers, tenants, and share croppers groaning. Bread lines lengthening. "The better class" bewildered and bespattered by the revelations of congressional inquiries. Investors full of wrath over the duplicity of their former counselors. Malcontents sowing the wind. Communists jeering. Fascists sneering. Old-line Democrats in Congress bewildered by problems and spectacles never yet beheld in a world they never made. Republican managers reduced to helplessness. A majority of Senators and Representatives committed to only one positive program — the hoary program of currency inflation in some form. The country and the national capital beset by alarms. The optimism of 1928 succeeded by pessimism. There was, to be sure, more good humor and less hatred than the amount of distress suggested, but even merry-makers could scarcely escape thought of the vortex. Was the crisis merely another episode in the long history of calamities — a passing shadow? Or was it the beginning of profound changes in American life? With the future veiled, only guesses and surmises were possible on March 4, 1933.

CHAPTER V

Reformation and Salvation

THRUSTING immediately at the fright induced by stresses and strains, President Roosevelt, in his inaugural address on March 4, 1933, called upon "a stricken Nation in the midst of a stricken world" to put aside fear and move forward to the conquest of the depression "as a trained and loyal army willing to sacrifice for the good of a common discipline" under the leadership that had just been placed in his care. This could be done in accordance with the terms of the Constitution, which "is so simple and practical that it is possible always to meet extraordinary needs by changes in emphasis and arrangement without loss of essential form." It was to be hoped that "the normal balance of Executive and legislative authority" would be wholly adequate to cope with the task that confronted the country; but the "unprecedented demand and need for undelayed action may call for temporary departure from that normal balance of public procedure."

Unequivocally the incoming President described the sweep of the depression, ranging from the collapse of eco-

207

nomic values to despair among "a host of unemployed citizens." There was no doubt about all that. "Only a foolish optimist can deny the dark realities of the moment. . . . Plenty is at our doorstep, but a generous use of it languishes in the very sight of the supply." Guilt was implied and the President passed judgment. "Primarily this is because rulers of the exchange of mankind's goods have failed, through their own stubbornness and their own incompetence, have admitted their failure, and have abdicated. Practices of the unscrupulous money changers stand indicted in the court of public opinion, rejected by the hearts and minds of men. . . . They know only the rules of a generation of self-seekers. They have no vision, and when there is no vision the people perish. Yes, the money changers have fled from their high seats in the temple of our civilization. We may now restore that temple to the ancient truths. The measure of the restoration lies in the extent to which we apply social values more noble than mere monetary profit." Thus the sentiment of dedication was sweetened for sinners by the idea that the primary scapegoats were the money changers — from whom investors had bought Allegheny common, Kreuger and Toll secured, sinking fund gold debentures, and other symbols of wealth in the riotous days of the prodigal son.

There must be a program. "There must be a strict supervision of all banking and credits and investments; there must be an end to speculation with other people's money; and there must be provision for an adequate but sound currency." That was an echo of Woodrow Wilson's New Freedom, especially soothing to the heirs of populism. But President Roosevelt did not stop with currency reform. "Our greatest primary task is to put people to work." There must be a wiser use of our great natural resources, a better balance of industry and agriculture, an increase in the value of agricultural products, protection for mortgaged homes and farms, a curtailment of government expenditures, a unification of relief work, and national planning for public utilities that have a definitely public character. In foreign relations we must follow "the policy of the good neighbor." No efforts will be spared to restore world trade by international adjustments. Yet such trade relations, "though vastly important, are in point of time and necessity secondary to the establishment of a sound national economy. I favor as a practical policy the putting of first things first." In such terms the President's program was outlined.

The next step from talking was action. We must act; we must act quickly. We must act together. We are dependent upon one another; we must give as well as take. We must bend to discipline, for without discipline "no progress is made, no leadership becomes effective. . . . This I propose to offer," pledging the supremacy of the larger good. "With this pledge taken, I assume unhesitatingly the leadership of this great army of our people dedicated to a disciplined attack upon our common problems." The Constitution permits it, for it is so framed that the Government can meet every stress. Measures required by the stricken nation will be laid before Congress, and proper efforts will be made to secure a speedy adoption.

In case Congress fails to adopt or devise appropriate measures and the emergency continues to be critical, "I shall not evade the clear course of duty that will then confront me. I shall ask the Congress for the one remaining instrument to meet the crisis — broad Executive power to wage a war against the emergency, as great as the power that would be given to me if we were in fact invaded by a foreign foe. . . . We do not distrust the future of essential democracy. The people of the United States have not failed. In their need they have registered a mandate that they want direct, vigorous action. They have asked for discipline and direction under leadership. They have made me the present instrument of their wishes. In the spirit of the gift I take it."

In supporting the constitutional provision for a strong President, Hamilton, long before Roosevelt's day, had said in the sixty-ninth number of the Federalist: "Every man the least conversant in Roman history knows how often that republic was obliged to take refuge in the absolute power of a single man, under the formidable title of 'Dictator.'" The provision had been tested in war in 1861 and 1917. Now it was to be tested in time of peace. Or was it? Could an invocation of force command the energies of the nation for constructive purposes, for the building of a civilization? The future lowered over the present.

"This is a day of national consecration." With these words President Roosevelt had opened his inaugural address — words which were, in the process of editing, omitted from the definitive edition of his works published five years later. Having begun on this note, and having disclosed his resolve to act, to wield great powers in an attack upon calamity, the President, in bringing his address to a close, called for divine aid: "In this dedication of a Nation we humbly ask the blessings of God."

The ideas, "consecration" and "dedication," peculiarly fitted the popular mood of the hour. They suggested that the task to be undertaken had a sacred character; they throbbed with religious fervor. For centuries the preacher, Hebrew and Christian, in calling sinners to account, had reminded them of their wickedness and pointed out the narrow way leading to righteousness. Things had been done that should not have been done. Things that should have been done had been left undone. After years of reckless living, the nation had fallen upon evil days. A consciousness of sin was abroad in the land. The future was uncertain and even greater adversity might be hidden behind the morrow. "People are like . . . little children quarrelling, crying, and then straightaway laughing," Marcus Aurelius, Emperor of the Romans, had said in the second century of the Christian era. On March 4, 1933, in the United States, they were quarrelling and crying. They might be laughing again, as soon as a ray of prosperity broke through the clouds; but at the moment they were grieved, afraid, and repentant. Even the voice of the opposition presses and benches could be neither scornful nor ribald in the presence of the débâcle or of the Chief

Executive scourging the wicked and seeking a road to the promised land.

Without waiting for Congress to assemble on March 9 to consider the state of the nation, in accordance with his official summons, President Roosevelt squared away for action on the Sunday following his inauguration. His advisers found sanction for government by decree in the unrepealed provisions of a war statute, enacted in 1917, giving the Chief Executive almost plenary control over foreign exchanges, gold, silver, and currency. Under the authority of this legislation President Roosevelt issued, at one o'clock in the morning of March 6, an order closing all the banks in the United States from Monday, March 6, to Thursday, March 9; and on the day of expiry he extended it "in full force and effect until further proclamation." During the holiday all banking transactions were suspended, except those specifically authorized by the Secretary of the Treasury, with the approval of the President.

This decree, completing the closures already made under state authority, was designed to stop runs on banks and maintain the status quo until new legislation could be enacted by Congress — legislation safeguarding "sound" institutions, providing more currency, and establishing procedures for salvaging as far as possible the banks that were really in financial straits. If any lawyers were inclined to ask what constitutional authority the President had over state banks in time of peace, their question had no practical effect. With amazing unanimity, national leaders rallied to the support of the Executive's proposals. A conference of governors assembled at the White House on Monday, March 6, threw aside political affiliations, expressed confidence in the President, and urged all the people to coöperate with him "in such action as he shall find necessary or desirable in restoring banking and economic stability." On the instant the Constitution of the United States had acquired an extraordinary flexibility and the rights of sovereign states over banking had been, for practical purposes, abrogated.

When Congress gathered in special session on March 9, the Chief Executive was cautious. He did not propose anything specific and radical, such as nationalizing banks of issue. He merely laid before Congress a message calling for blanket authority over banks and the draft of a bill conferring it. With an alacrity suggesting spontaneous combustion, excited Representatives and Senators rushed the draft through the two houses and placed it on the President's desk before the close of the day. Neither Lincoln in 1861 nor Wilson in 1917 had been granted drastic powers with so little haggling and bickering. That "democracy can act," in accord with its normal processes, in a crisis, had been conclusively demonstrated.

The new legislation gave the President authority in time of war or "any other period of national emergency" to resort to extraordinary measures in respect of currency and banking. It empowered the Treasury to compel the surrender of all gold coin, bullion, and gold certificates in exchange for other coin or currency issued under the laws of the United States. Conservators for national banking institutions were provided. National Banks were allowed to raise cash by the sale of preferred stock, and arrangements were made for permitting both national and state institutions to borrow from the Reconstruction Finance Corporation. Steps were taken to expand the currency for immediate needs in the form of "circulating notes" issued to Federal Reserve banks on the basis of federal obligations and other prime paper.

In appearance the Act was an emergency measure, but President Roosevelt was looking beyond the exigencies of the day. In his mind it was "to mark the beginning of a new relationship between the banks and the people of the country." The Act was not the nationalization of banking and currency that had been demanded by one wing of Jacksonian Democracy. It drove no money changers from the temple. On the contrary it gave the support of public credit to bankers while establishing the supremacy of the Federal Government over gold. Time was to amplify the meaning.

Under the authority of the emergency legislation, during an inquiry into the soundness of institutions in difficulty, the Secretary of the Treasury permitted the gradual resumption of the banking business. By the end of May nearly thirteen thousand banks were reported open without restriction. As they held almost ninety per cent of the total amount on deposit throughout the United States, it seemed that the immediate emergency had passed. Viewed superficially, the remaining problem was one of determining the fate of state and national banks yet in a dubious position. Nevertheless other fiscal events of major significance for American economy were soon set in train.

Among them was the modification, if not the abandonment, of the gold standard as the basis of the monetary system — a violation of the fundamental principle written into law in 1900, four years after the "battle of 1896 for the salvation of the country." By the legislation of 1900 a certain weight and fineness of gold was made the foundation of the American dollar and all other currency was made exchangeable in terms of gold. Two essential elements were embraced in the system : gold, a privately owned commodity in general circulation, was chosen as the substance on which the dollar rested and all paper money could be freely exchanged for that precious metal. While gold certificates issued by the Government had a certain priority, possessors of other paper currency could nominally demand gold in exchange. The "free" movement of gold thus established for internal economy was also extended to international transactions and gold circulated "freely" among the nations in the operations of their commerce.

Although this gold system, as far as the United States was concerned, was little more than thirty years old, it had become embedded in American business thought and in popular psychology. Actually it had acquired some of the characteristics of a fetish, a sacred thing, absolutely indispensable to the functioning of industry and commerce on any level of efficiency. To touch it or to threaten it was to

profane the very altar of Fortune. It was true that Great
Britain, the modern originator of the gold standard for
universal purposes, had abandoned it, or at least cut loose
from it, but the major portion of American economists
seemed to regard the British revision as a temporary procedure, and in any case no guide for American policy.

Whether Great Britain had been "forced" off the gold
base or had voluntarily "gone" off made little difference.
The fact remained and it impinged upon American policy.
Either from necessity or as a matter of policy, the United
States gradually followed the British example in some
respects, as the Chief Executive became convinced that gold
was not, after all, a veritable pillar of heaven. "Gradually"
is the correct word, and "in some respects" must be attached
to it. The very closing of the banks on March 6, 1933, impaired the gold standard, for citizens could not then demand
gold for any gold certificates which they held. The gold
standard was further impaired when the banks were reopened, for they were forbidden to pay out gold or gold certificates. Another step was taken on April 5 when the President issued an order prohibiting the hoarding of gold and
requiring the delivery of all gold coin, bullion, and certificates
to Federal Reserve banks on or before April 28, with minor
exceptions for industrial and other purposes. A supplement
to this measure, in August, prohibited all private holdings of
gold and all private transactions in gold. Thus two phases
of the gold system were destroyed, namely, private ownership of gold coins or bullion and free transactions in that
metal.

With transactions in gold hampered by the banking crisis
and forbidden by executive order, Congress faced the issue
of public and private contracts calling for payments in gold
values. Previous to 1933 it had been a practice of governments and private concerns in the United States to stipulate
that their bonds and other evidences of indebtedness which
they sold were payable in gold coin "of the present standard
of value." Obligations running into the billions contained

this "gold clause." After March 6, however, it became impossible to fulfill all such contracts.

Of course, fulfillment had always been a mere matter of theoretical probability. Now it had become even theoretically impossible. President Roosevelt recognized the fact. Congress agreed and by a joint resolution, effective June 6, 1933, it folded the mantle of law over the fact and the theory. It declared that the right to require the payment of gold obligations in gold was "against public policy" and that such obligations could be lawfully satisfied by payment in any coin or currency "which at the time of payment is legal tender for public and private debts." Looking to the future, Congress prohibited the issuance of new obligations containing the gold clause. In short, in the emergency, one of the "most sacred elements" in public and private contracts was swept aside by national legislation. Had the spirit of Daniel Shays returned or was there a necessity that knew not law?

While "the eternal foundations of sound economy" seemed to be dissolving like vapory figments of the imagination, the agrarian interests in Congress grew bolder and made a concerted drive on the retreating Old Guard of the Gold Army. The ghost of 1896 had not been buried after all. The Senate and the House were crowded with members who could recall Bryan's picture of mankind crucified on a cross of gold; but for forty years advocates of inflation and free silver had been baffled by the protagonists of sound money. Now in an hour of crisis their victory seemed to be in sight. If it had not been for the opposition of President Roosevelt, they might have exploded the gold works then and there.

In the circumstances they were able to do no more than declare their sentiments and confer upon him powers to be used at his discretion. Appropriately, they incorporated their principles in the farm relief law of May 12, 1933, known as the Agricultural Adjustment Act. Their main purposes were declared to be to offset the effects of depreciated foreign currencies on American foreign commerce, to maintain a parity among the currency issues of the United States, and to meet the economic emergency by an expansion of credit.

For the attainment of these ends, the President was authorized, not commanded, to use the Federal Reserve System in purchasing and holding obligations of the United States in an aggregate sum of $3,000,000,000. If this device could not be applied, then the President might direct the Treasury to issue three billion dollars' worth of legal tenders for the purpose of meeting the maturing obligations of the Government or purchasing its obligations in the market. Attacking their principal foe, gold, the agrarians empowered the President to reduce the weight of the gold dollar by fifty per cent at most, and to fix the weight of the silver dollar at a definite ratio to the gold dollar. Notwithstanding the defeat of efforts to force the coinage of silver at the ratio of sixteen to one, the President was authorized to accept a certain amount of silver from foreign debtors and issue silver certificates against it. Later the silver faction was able to force through a measure declaring that, in the monetary system of the United States, silver shall constitute one-fourth in value as against three-fourths in gold, and directing the Treasury to buy silver within a certain price range per ounce, store it, and issue silver certificates. Nevertheless its declaration of sentiments was in fact largely academic — a threat, not an achievement — since President Roosevelt did little or nothing under the inflationist sections of the Agricultural Adjustment Act.

After all, William Jennings Bryan was dead. A Kerensky might be on the horizon of fervid imaginations, but no Bryan was there any more. When Congress recovered from the first shocks of the crisis and came to formulating the Banking Act of 1933, conservatives took the lead and steered close to their well-known headlands. An inducement was made to bring more state banks into the Federal Reserve System, by permitting federal banks to open branches in states which gave a similar permission to their own banks. Stricter supervision was established over banks, holding companies, and affiliates, and banks were required to cut loose, within a year, from affiliated security concerns. In this way, it was hoped, some patent abuses in the investment business would be eliminated. With a view to holding down speculation, while providing accommodations to business and commerce, the Federal Reserve Board was given large powers over the purchase and sale of eligible paper by member banks. To remove fears and lure money out of hoards, a temporary scheme for insuring deposits up to a certain amount was put into effect.

Despite some alarms on the right, the Banking Act of 1933 was conservative from start to finish, from the standpoint of agrarian inflationists. The limited power to issue currency was still vested in private hands. Banks of issue were not nationalized. Private banking was not confined to commercial business. The original compromise between centralization and states' rights was preserved in its essential features.

A search for some overarching hypothesis of consistency to explain the various currency and banking measures led to the White House rather than to Capitol Hill. In Congress every action took the form of an adjustment of interests. The Chief Executive, on the other hand, gave out a series of statements that had the merits of a certain congruity, especially in relation to the basic rights of property. He was seeking, he declared, to "restore commodity price levels," to facilitate the payment of public and private debts "more nearly at the price level at which they were incurred," to effect a balance in the price system "so that farmers may exchange their products for the products of industry on a fairer exchange basis." The question whether the measures adopted would accomplish the posited ends might be debated, but here at least was a clear objective. Beyond these adjustments in the price system, President Roosevelt looked to stabilization — the establishment and maintenance of a dollar "which will not change its purchasing and debt-paying power during the succeeding generation." In appearance this was the time-worn scheme for overcoming the calamities of depression by currency manipulation, but other measures of the administration made it plain that the day for pure and simple reliance on any such device had passed.

In the process of seeking to raise the price level and stabilize it, President Roosevelt had to take account of international aspects of the currency system. Here, too, he was positive as to objectives. He declared that the dollar had too long been at the mercy of accidents in international trade, the internal policies pursued by other nations, and political disturbances in other continents. "Therefore," he said, "the United States must take firmly in its own hands the control of the gold value of our dollar. This is necessary in order to prevent dollar disturbances from swinging us away from our ultimate goal, namely, the continued recovery of our commodity prices. . . . My aim in taking this step [of buying and selling gold] is to establish and maintain continuous control. . . . We are thus continuing to move toward a managed currency." Whether it was possible, in fact, to manage the domestic price system and at the same time cushion it against the shocks of foreign-trade oscillations was a matter of dispute among schoolmen. Nor was it easy, if at all feasible, to find out whether multitudinous practices did indeed conform to the controlling hypothesis of policy. Even so, the departure from the conception of the "free" market, national and international, with gold as the unit of exchange, seemed to close an epoch.

While making much ado over the alleged expulsion of money changers from the temple and the revision of the currency and banking system, Congress turned to public finance. "Our government's house is not in order," President Roosevelt declared to the special session called in March, 1933. He reminded it of the Democratic promise of economy and warned the members that "too often in recent history liberal governments have been wrecked on rocks of loose fiscal policy." Well aware of log-rolling propensities among Senators and Representatives, he demanded and received a broad authority to reduce payments to war veterans and to cut, within certain limits, the salaries of government employees. Proceeding under the provisions of the Economy Act, the President effected changes, consolidations, and reductions which, it was estimated, would bring savings amounting to nearly a billion dollars in the next budget. Collaterally, federal revenues were raised by new taxes, on legalized beer, gasoline, new capital stock, and excess profits. After conventions in the requisite number of states had ratified, in December, 1933, the twenty-first amendment, repealing prohibition, Congress joined state legislatures in a scramble to derive heavy revenues from alcoholic beverages.

Taking the position that emergency peace expenditures, like war expenditures, constituted a class in themselves and should be at least partly financed by bond issues, Roosevelt proposed to set up a double budget. Outlays for emergency purposes were to be met by borrowings, and the budget of ordinary or current expenditures was to be balanced by curtailments in expenditures and increases in revenues. As a matter of fact the Government of the United States had never possessed a budget which clearly separated capital outlays from current running expenses. From the beginning Congress had made appropriations from tax revenues to pay for roads, waterway improvements, lighthouses, buildings, and other public works of various kinds. Some states and many cities had established the distinction and had regularly borrowed money for public improvements and emergency outlays, often making provision for meeting interest and installment charges as they fell due. But Congress had not followed these examples. Nor had the Government of the United States ever set up a capital balance sheet, showing on the one side the federal debt and on the other its real and intangible properties which could be deemed offsetting assets. For example, the money borrowed for the Reconstruction Finance Corporation was properly placed under the head of federal debt, but the securities pledged by private concerns with the Corporation as collateral undoubtedly formed assets of some value that belonged, with equal propriety, on the credit side. Accordingly, there was a promise of more realistic finance in Roosevelt's proposal. However, he did not work it out in detail or apply it with precision. Despite all the pledges, mounting deficits marked the dealings of Congress and the Administration.

In connection with the "purification" and readjustment of the financial system, Congress laid its hands on the National Shrine in Wall Street by extending federal control over the issue of certain types of securities for which a high degree of market freedom had hitherto existed. The scheme of control was embodied in the Securities Act, approved May 27, 1933, and later given a more permanent form in the Securities and Exchange Act. In part the legislation expressed the indignation of investors and speculators who had suffered losses in the pools, peggings, balloon ascensions, and other operations of the great boom. In part also the law had a bearing upon banking, currency, and the functioning of economy in the broadest sense of the term.

Although it was not easy to draw the legal line between "honesty" and "fraud" in security transactions, between sober judgment and absurd hopes, the revelations of past transactions made by the Senate committee on banking and finance created an overwhelming sentiment in favor of additional protection for investors. Irrespective of the intention, the drafting of merely protective features was difficult. The determination of the kinds of new liquid claims to wealth that actually represented real wealth called for prognosis no less than diagnosis. Additional complications sprang from the fact that banking was entangled in the process of issuing stocks and bonds : many liquid claims in the form of securities were employed as the basis for the expansion of the currency by members of the Federal Reserve System. That the raising of capital funds by the sale of securities bore some relation to the forms and operations of industry was also undeniable. Was it possible, by positive restrictions on the freedom of the market, to compel banks and sellers of securities to discharge the function which they had been supposed to perform : that of acting as mediators between investors and productive enterprises in need of capital goods? The situation was perplexing and Congress struck out pragmatically.

After exempting from the operations of the Act a long list of securities, such as government bonds and commercial paper of limited scope, Congress stipulated that other securities must be registered with the Federal Trade Commission, later the Securities and Exchange Commission especially created. In all cases registration was to disclose specific information respecting the nature, sponsorship, and substance of the paper tendered to the public. Among the items of information required were the names, addresses, and functions of the persons connected with the "issuer" of the security, including directors and officers of the corporation concerned, underwriters, persons owning more than ten per cent of the stock, salaries paid to officers and directors, and commissions paid to participants.

From personnel, Congress turned to substance. It called upon the issuer for information respecting the funded debt already outstanding, the amount and purpose of the security offered, properties to be acquired by the capital raised, material contracts arising in connection therewith, balance sheets, profit and loss statements, and articles of incorporation. Subject to exceptions and modifications, foreign securities were brought within the same frame of control. For the benefit of investors, essential parts of the information filed with the Commission were to be made matters of public record. Remedies at law were provided against participants guilty of making untrue statements or concealing facts essential to the broad purposes of the Act. Heavy penalties were set for persons who transgressed the law, subject to judicial safeguards in case of violations due to justifiable conditions or the fallibility of human judgment. To protect American holders of foreign securities, Congress provided for the creation of a semi-private Corporation of Foreign Security Holders empowered to look after the interests of investors whose paper was in default.

During the debates on the original bill in Congress and outside, protests were lodged against the severity of the restrictions proposed against violations of the liberty long enjoyed in pecuniary transactions — the liberty deemed essential to dynamic enterprise. In the light of available information respecting the spoliation of investors in the age of Coolidge prosperity, few critics were brash enough at first to demand complete laissez faire in the grand style. Yet many were ready to insist that the restraints of the bill would deprive industry of needed capital, paralyze the enterprise of bankers and initiators, and slow down the process of recovery. In the theory of business enterprise, room had always been made for the element of risk; the mechanical laws of economics did not work perfectly; at the side of or in the interstices of the network composed of going concerns lay possibilities of chance that might result in either profit or loss.

Indeed there were a few economists who maintained that, in the regime of corporate management, this operation of whirling Fortune's wheel was the chief function left to the business man. If losses ensued, they must be accepted. If the divination was correct, new and great enterprises might rise, enriching individual promoters and adding to the sum total of national wealth. It mattered little that the modern devotee of Fortune used other people's money. It was the function that counted.

Vibrating between the idea of economic law and the conception of economic chance, with freedom for business ingenuity and risk, Congress tossed to and fro over the terms of the securities bill. In the end it declared that numerous economic activities traditionally regarded as a part of the free system should be forbidden, but that some leeway should be granted to pecuniary enterprise under the protection of the courts. When the provisional legislation was recast in the Securities and Exchange Act of 1934, its restrictions were tightened and enforcement was entrusted to a special body, the Securities and Exchange Commission.

§

All the modifications in banking, currency, and security legislation left untouched a question of wider and deeper popular interest: What about unemployment and poverty? At no time during the formulation of these modifications did the Roosevelt administration itself take the ground that such cleansing and readjustment of system would be automatically followed by a speeding up of industry and agriculture to the highest possible tempo. Theorists and practitioners who considered this subject were divided on the prospects. Without designating the time and place at which any free and automatic market had actually maintained the highest possible level of economic activity, one group maintained that some of the restrictions imposed by the banking and security legislation really impeded the proper flow of capital into the production and distribution of goods. Another group, squaring its economic philosophy with the New Freedom of President Wilson, was inclined to insist that, with abuses and excrescences cut off, the industrial mechanism would speed up under its own momentum.

But other ideas were afloat and other interests were vocal in the political forum. Free market or no free market, millions of unemployed on the ragged edge of awful hunger and local officials struggling with the cruel realities of human wretchedness clamored for "relief." Price mechanism or not, business men, represented by the United States Chamber of Commerce, demanded the right to balance production and consumption and to eliminate the unfair practices so obtrusive in the competitions of the marketplace. Farmers had received their pledge in the campaign and were impatient for redemption. While all the ideas and interests were interrelated, each set had its particular defenders and proceeded on its own assumptions as to the nature of American economy and things deemed desirable.

Could the idle be put to work? For unemployment and pauperism on such a large scale, respectable economic theory had no systematic place. In the realm of gentility a primary assumption had long prevailed to the effect that, in the main, idleness and poverty were due to defective minds or bodies, or to congenital improvidence; and in the current saying, as in other popular aphorisms, there was an element of truth. But with ten or twelve million people unemployed and many on the verge of hunger, if not actually starving, the situation was bothersome even for aphorists and economists. If phrase-makers were willing to let nature take its course, as doing nothing had been rhetorically described, politicians were in no position to adopt the maxim. As elected persons they had a public responsibility of some kind that was not imposed on private persons, for instance on the issuer of Kreuger and Toll secured, sinking fund, gold debentures. Being politicians, presumably they had to be on guard against undermining the national morale — the very foundation of government and economy.

In dealing with unemployment and immediate relief, President Roosevelt and Congress had before them other considerations bearing upon the central issue — how to put people to work by prying economy out of the slough and setting it in motion. Time and again in history governments had done little or nothing while multitudes died in famines and floods; for example, in Russia and China. If, in the theory of experts, a repetition of such allegiance to "natural law" was possible in the United States, no such probability appeared in the calculations of politics. With little or no positive guidance from theoretical economics of any reputable school, the President and Congress sought to grapple with the scheme of things entire, under the pressure of powerful interests, right, left, front, rear.

The legislative measures and executive actions which followed in swift succession during the spring and summer and autumn of 1933 showed a resolve to prevent starvation, if necessary even by the dole so generally abhorred. Nevertheless there was a growing recognition of the fact that the rigors of the law for paupers in the historic style were inapplicable. Even legal provisions for the immediate relief of the destitute, save hurried grants for food and clothing, expressed more than the traditional righteous psychology of alms giving associated with the stigma of pauperism. Two or three million unemployed persons might deserve nothing, but the suspicion of total depravity and disgrace could hardly apply wholesale to twelve or thirteen millions. Brushing aside the warning against "pauperizing" the people, Congress enacted the Emergency Relief law, approved May 12, 1933, which made available half a billion dollars to aid the states in coping with their relief obligations. Under the terms of the Act, the Federal Emergency Relief Administration was established and $250,000,000 granted to the states — a part to be proportioned to each state's outlay for the purpose and a larger part to be allocated to the states on the basis of their requirements without reference to their own expenditures. Besides distributing money in aid of relief, the Emergency Administration bought huge quantities of food and clothing that "glutted the market" and distributed them through the network of state and local agencies in all parts of the country. "While it isn't written in the Constitution," President Roosevelt explained, "nevertheless it is the inherent duty of the Federal Government to keep its citizens from starvation." Though the proposition violated an earlier dictum by President Van Buren and had a strange ring for constitutional lawyers, in that hour of alarm even Respectability had little patience with black-letter lore.

To the main body of the American people, however, doles were detestable. Something frightful lurked in the prospect of ten million citizens sunk in the morass of permanent pauperism, sustained by meager grants of money and commodities. Subsequent familiarity with the horror, coupled with the high cost of providing honest work, might induce willingness to accept the dole, but in 1933 opposition to the very idea was almost universal. "Work, not doles!" was the cry heard on all sides. In response to this preference, Congress sought to create work under public auspices. By the Unemployment Relief Act of March, 1933, it authorized the President to employ citizens in constructing and maintaining works of a public nature in connection with the natural resources of the country. Under this authority the Citizens Civilian Conservation Corps was organized and more than 300,000 young men, housed in well-built camps, were set to work combating forest fires, soil erosion, floods, and plant pests, planting trees, making trails, and cutting fire lanes on the public domain — state and federal. In November, 1933, with employment still lagging, President Roosevelt created the Civil Works Administration, allocated to it $400,000,000 for the coming season, and instructed it to provide occupations for about four million people on highways, community projects, and other hastily devised activities, ranging from social work in nursery schools to traveling theatrical performances. When charged with employing people on wasteful and futile undertakings, representatives of the administration replied that the hostility of business enterprise to all forms of public competition made it impossible to utilize the unemployed in the creation of wealth. If there was irony in the paradox, there was practical economics as well.

§

If large-scale pauperism and permanent doles were to be avoided, industry and agriculture had to be operated at fuller capacity. Of this the Chief Executive and Congress were fully aware. So, while trying to meet the obvious and menacing needs of millions unemployed, they sought to adjust the "unbalanced" economy of the nation, prod it into swifter motion, stabilize it, and aid it in providing opportunities for earning a livelihood "in the normal channels of private enterprise." In the realization of this broad purpose, two great statutes were enacted and put into force: the farm relief, or Agricultural Adjustment Act of May 12, 1933, and the National Industrial Recovery Act of June 16, 1933. Although it was later the fashion in uninformed circles to ascribe these measures to academic theorists and to characterize them as "hastily drawn," the facts in the case belied the imputation. Each measure in truth conformed to some kind of economic theory — the theory of hard-bitten practitioners.

The provisions of both statutes had behind them accumulations of precedents. What is more: academicians did not make the precedents or dictate the provisions. The Agricultural Adjustment Act, for example, had been in process of formulation for years; only a few detailed specifications were wanting in the spring of 1933. Except for the labor section, the National Industrial Recovery Act embodied the system of thought officially set forth by the United States Chamber of Commerce; and representatives of that powerful body participated actively in the drafting of the bill. It was in keeping with the facts, therefore, to say that the two statutes gave legal expression to the economic doctrines of organized agriculture and organized business enterprise. The section of the Recovery Act accorded to labor could scarcely be regarded as an exception to this rule, for it was written to forestall special legislation in that line, rather than to establish new policy in labor relations. In the original draft no such provision was incorporated; labor was at first left to fend for itself. Only when Congress seemed on the verge of enacting a thirty-hour bill did the draftsmen of the Recovery Law bring themselves to accept collective bargaining in industry. The sheer truth was that agriculture and business were striving to break through an impasse which they had created for themselves or, more accurately, which history had prepared for both.

For farmers, the Government was to enlarge buying power by an adjustment of prices and production. Lest there be a misunderstanding of their economic theory, the authors of the Agricultural Act set it forth explicitly in Title I. Their purpose, they said, was to establish and maintain a balance between the production and consumption of agricultural commodities and to assure appropriate marketing conditions.

The balance so determined was to be of such a character that it would "reëstablish prices to farmers at a level that will give agricultural commodities a purchasing power with respect to articles that farmers buy, equivalent to the purchasing power of agricultural commodities in the base period." For tobacco the base period chosen was from August, 1919, to July, 1929, and for other farm produce from August, 1909, to July, 1924.

In this underlying conception of agricultural prices there was an element as old as the republic. When Federalists and Jeffersonian Republicans were battling over power, John Taylor of Caroline County, Virginia, had contended in an elaborate treatise that high finance, with its tariffs, bounties, and "paper," violated the laws of "natural exchange" and created a constant unbalance against agriculture. After the lapse of more than a hundred years an effort was being made to redress the unbalance, real or imagined, by employing the powerful instrumentalities of the Federal Government. The Federal Marketing Act of the Hoover administration had honored the theory and accomplished no favorable results. Another tack was to be taken now.

The devices adopted by the Agricultural Adjustment Act were simple. The prices of "basic agricultural commodities," such as wheat, cotton, field corn, sugar beets, and pork products, were to be raised by curtailing production and controlling market operations. Production quotas adjusted to effective demand were to be established on the basis of statistical calculations. For the purpose of holding output within the limits of the quotas, each farmer affected was to make his pro rata reduction and in return for his action receive a subsidy from the Government precisely determined by the degree of the curtailment. Nominally there was no compulsion. Practically the inducement was sufficient to bring about almost universal compliance. Such, in substance, were the mechanics of the Act, with many variations in detail and many stipulations collateral in nature. Of necessity the project would cost money; provisions for revenue were therefore incorporated in the statute itself — unhappily for the sponsors of the bill, as they learned three years later when the Supreme Court declared the law invalid. Chief among the sources of finance were taxes on the processing of commodities, such as grinding wheat into flour, taxes on domestic products grown in excess of quotas, and customs duties on certain imported farm commodities. To all appearances, at the time, the statute was "water-tight" and the funds were assured for enforcement.

At last producers on the land were to try out a reform devised to fit their interpretation of things. Although millions of farmers were affected by the law and a great diversity of agricultural and processing interests was drawn within the scope of its terms, the Agricultural Adjustment Administration put the statute into force with extraordinary swiftness and universality. Throughout the country, at farmers' meetings in villages and counties, agents of the Administration explained the complexities of the Act, determined the reduction quota of each producer, drew up the contract, and had it duly signed. Field agents visited the farms listed in the program, surveyed the land taken out of cultivation, checked up on other adjustments, and made sure that changes in crop rotation or land uses conformed to the terms of the law. After all these preliminaries were over, the Agricultural Administration in Washington scrutinized the millions of reports and sent checks on the Treasury to farmers for their compliance with agreements.

Nothing just like it had ever been done in the history of American agriculture, not even in the midst of war. In times past, steel barons had cut production by "dinner table agreements," but the sheer act of swinging millions of farmers into serried lines was little short of magic, at least to the theorists of farm individualism. The insularity of regimentation was also overcome. Through a combination of cotton and tobacco with corn and wheat a union of Southern and Western hearts was effected, such as Calhoun and the statesmen of the planting system had sought in vain to secure nearly a hundred years before. However viewed, the mere accomplishment was a tribute to the skill and power of the Secretary of Agriculture, Henry A. Wallace, George N. Peek, head of the Agricultural Adjustment Administration, and their capable assistants.

Before the Agricultural Adjustment Administration, under the direction of Mr. Peek, could set in full operation the elaborate machinery for organizing the production of farmers, Congress sought to grapple with the problem of the idle industries and unemployed workers. How could employment be provided and wage levels maintained? In the search for an answer, Congress came to grips with two formulas for dealing with the issue. Spokesmen for labor, with Senator Hugo Black of Alabama in the vanguard, proposed to reduce by law the hours of work per week throughout the country, while upholding the wage levels. From one point of view this was a project for dividing the existing amount of employment. The second formula for economic salvation was that devised by the United States Chamber of Commerce. Under its interpretation of events, the long-drawn-out economic distress was mainly due to savage competition which destroyed profits all around; and the exit from the dilemma lay in balancing production with effective demand while establishing "fair competition" or "fair trade practices" under the authority of the Federal Government. Both formulas rested on the assumption or conviction that Congress could, in point of constitutional law, nationalize trade and labor practices under its power to regulate interstate commerce, or, as the liberalizing lawyers put it, "the flow of interstate commerce." More than one statute resting upon that general prerogative had been enacted in times past and sustained by the Supreme Court. Doubts still entertained on the question of its validity were set aside in favor of action.

As a result of a compromise both formulas were employed in drafting the National Industrial Recovery Act — a measure for a limited type of national planning, approved by the Chief Executive on June 16, 1933. Although the two operating theories really implied a restriction of production, the first section of the Act proclaimed the grand purpose to be the acceleration of productive enterprise. It referred to the "widespread unemployment and disorganization of industry." It declared a national emergency to exist. How the automatic, self-adjusting market of capitalist economy could ever be "disorganized" Congress did not attempt to explain in the preamble nor in the body of the law. It accepted disorganization as fact. Indeed, at the moment, it did seem to be a fact.

Having announced the emergency, the first section of the Act set forth the economic objectives of Congress: "to remove obstructions to the free flow of interstate and foreign commerce . . . to provide for the general welfare . . . to induce and maintain united action of labor and management under adequate government sanctions and supervision, to eliminate unfair competitive practices, to promote the fullest possible utilization of the present productive capacity of industries, to avoid undue restriction of production (except as may be temporarily required), to increase the consumption of industrial and agricultural products by increasing purchasing power, to reduce and relieve unemployment, to improve standards of labor, and otherwise to rehabilitate industry and to conserve natural resources." In commenting on the purposes of the Act, Roosevelt referred to its emergency features and to the objective of planning "for a better future, for the longer pull."

A breach had been made in the predominant theory of a successful economy. Undoubtedly a mosaic of many ideas, the opening section of the National Industrial Recovery Act broke with the economic assumptions that had long prevailed in Congress. For many years a few students of technology had been insisting that the going economy of the United States fell far short of the total productive capacity available in the scientific and natural resources of the country. Thorstein Veblen had underlined the thesis. But to most theorists this truth, so obvious to those with eyes to see, had seemed esoteric as compared with the habitual recitations of school-men in economics; while Congress, representing "practical" persons, had proceeded on a tacit assumption that the anti-trust laws merely reaffirmed the law of gravitation in business enterprise. Hence it was a daring intellectual adventure when Congress recognized that "the present productive capacity of industries" was not fully utilized. A second interruption was made in use and wont by the declaration that an increase in "purchasing power" would lead to an increase in the consumption of industrial and agricultural commodities. Had not academicians taught their pupils that, in the automatic and unconscious operations of things, the wages of labor were rather naturally adjusted to the contributions made by labor to the total production of wealth? Strange phraseology had crept into a statute of the United States.

The practices of industry were to be codified and con-trolled. In giving effect to the alleged purposes, the Recovery Act authorized the formation of associations, or groups, in each trade and industry. Such organizations were to be truly representative and open to all individuals or concerns entitled to membership. Any association properly organized under the Act had the authority to adopt "a code or codes of fair competition for the trade or industry or subdivision thereof." A code duly drawn, after affording the interested parties ample opportunity to be heard, went to the President for his scrutiny and when approved had the force of law for all members of the industry in question. To expedite the process of industrial organization, the President was em-powered to draft and impose a code upon any trade or in-dustry that failed to establish its own constitution. Recog-nizing the fact that it would take time to devise codes, Congress also authorized the President to license business enterprises and enter into arrangements with individuals or concerns willing to put into immediate effect accepted stand-ards of hours, wages, working conditions, and fair trade practices. In short, Congress conferred on trades and industries the right to organize; gave the President authority to bring into line the laggards that failed to exercise the right; and permitted him to recognize officially individuals and concerns which conformed to the new standards of work, wages, and fair competition.

Under the terms of the Act, a code for a trade or industry had to contain certain features. It set the business practices for the entire group and might provide for a uniform system of accounting and reporting. It could even go to the extent of prescribing the use of plants and equipment and indirectly the prices of goods and services. Although price fixing was not expressly authorized, a certain amount of price adjustment flowed inevitably from the agreements as to hours, wages, and competitive actions. So far the code fit the formula proposed by the United States Chamber of Commerce.

But in carrying the bill through Congress a concession was made to organized labor: a special clause of the law (Section 7-a) provided that every code, agreement, and license should contain three conditions respecting industrial workers. Employees were to enjoy the right to organize and bargain collectively, to designate their own representatives, and to be free from interference by employers in the choice of their agents. No employee could be required to join a company union or to refrain from affiliating with an organization of his own choosing. Within the scope of the code each employer had to comply "with the maximum hours of labor, minimum rates of pay, and other conditions of employment, approved or prescribed by the President."

However, in placing legal or political restraints upon the economic war of all against each and each against all, Congress encountered two danger signals: international competition and the antitrust laws. Beyond the horizon was the cheap labor of teeming millions in Europe and Asia. How could American cotton spinners paying a dollar a day or more in wages survive a flood of imports from Japanese mills where working girls were paid twenty-five cents a day or less? For this contingency, a Democratic Congress, without so much as a salute to free trade, made provision, by empowering the President to restrain or forbid the importation of goods and articles which rendered "ineffective" or "seriously" endangered the maintenance of any code or agreement. Thus domestic economy was sheltered against "cut-throat" competition from foreign sources. Next came a consideration of the Sherman and Clayton Acts, prescribing the law of competition at home. With scarcely a shudder among the congregation of faithful trustbusters in the national legislature, a clause was incorporated in the Recovery Act exempting codes, agreements, and licenses duly adopted and approved "from the provisions of the anti-trust laws of the United States." For more than forty years statutory supplements to "the laws of nature" had been on the books. Now they were to be set aside — for the emergency anyway and the immediate life of Title I of the Recovery Act, namely, two years.

At last the path was cleared for an experiment in the kind of national planning proposed by the United States Chamber of Commerce. To supervise and press forward the gigantic process of organizing trade, industry, and labor, the National Recovery Administration was established under the direction of General Hugh Johnson, who combined a limited amount of homely wisdom with the irritating methods of a drill sergeant. Leaders in commerce, industry, and trade unionism rolled into Washington. Amid much confusion and table pounding, codes were drafted, approved, and put into effect. Wrangles within and between trade associations were heard and decisions rendered. To every individual and concern that complied with the terms of the appropriate code an emblem — the Blue Eagle — was awarded. Like a sudden rash, Blue Eagles burst forth in the windows of shops, on the walls of factories, and in the advertisements of merchants.

As demonstrations of good-will and a determination to set business going, monster parades were held in large cities, headed by political and economic dignitaries. Blaring bands and cheering throngs greeted the new day of national cooperation in "breaking the panic's back," putting people to work, and restoring profits to enterprise. At Washington, labor boards, advisory boards, code authorities, and mediation boards were created to scrutinize or administer the millions of details. The whole country was laid out in districts, recovery boards were established in the states, and local bodies were organized — all to promote "the fullest possible utilization of the present productive capacity of industry." Within a year, more than four hundred codes were completed and put into effect, covering about ninety per cent of American business enterprise and approximately twenty-two million wage and salary workers. Considered merely in itself, this was a gigantic manifestation of human effort directed to the achievement of economic ends on a national scale.

§

At the same time, as if convinced that these great measures for lifting agriculture and industry out of the abyss were insufficient to set economy in rapid motion, Congress sought to stimulate the process by authorizing public works of social value. Such enterprises, it assumed, would make heavy demands upon the stagnant construction industries and they in turn would supply the wages to augment the buying power of industrial workers. Thus the wheels would keep turning round and round and round. In this scheme there was no abrupt departure from custom. In fact, since 1929 state and local governments had resorted to public works as a form of activity designed to break the jam of economic quiescence. In the blueprint stage or on the horizon of engineering thought were innumerable projects for such activity under public auspices.

But state and local governments were hampered by constitutional and statutory provisions respecting the floating of loans and the letting of contracts, which either imposed blockades or long delays upon generous and rapid enterprise. Only the Federal Government possessed unlimited borrowing power and could put workers and materials in motion without encountering a tangle of legal barriers. Although it had to watch for any obstacles which the Supreme Court might discover in the federal Constitution, the country was not disposed at this time to enter upon fine-spun debates over the theories of juristic probability. Powerful interests, therefore, including the Hearst press, representatives of heavy industries, and spokesmen of the workers, urged the Roosevelt administration to take action — immediate, bold, and wholesale action — in spite of the burdens already thrown upon the Treasury.

Among the projects in public works long pending in Washington was the development of water power in the Tennessee Valley — a potential for easing the burden of labor and raising social standards, if only under the guise of war necessities, navigation, and flood control. Efforts to turn over the Muscle Shoals plant to private interests had been defeated. Efforts to develop it under public auspices had likewise been blocked by executive veto. But George W. Norris, who had led the tedious campaign for public ownership, development, and operation, was still in the Senate, as resolute as ever in defending his program. In the spring of 1933 his advocacy had been strengthened. Having deserted the Republicans during the campaign of the previous year to support the candidacy of Roosevelt, Senator Norris met a hearty welcome at the White House. Moreover Roosevelt, while governor of New York and as a candidate for the presidency, had indicated that he would seek the development of power resources under public auspices for two purposes: to force a reduction of electrical rates and to make electricity available to millions of Americans yet unserved. When Senator Norris now found Democratic members of Congress setting up hurdles in his path, he could rely upon executive assistance instead of rebuffs. His reliance was reinforced by the fact that the utility interests had, in the main, supported President Hoover for reëlection and vigorously opposed Roosevelt on this very issue. With little difficulty, therefore, the bill for the development of natural resources in the Tennessee Valley was rushed through both houses of Congress and signed by the President on May 18, 1933.

Knowing well that their measure would be challenged by utility interests in the federal courts on constitutional grounds, the draftsmen of the Act made due obeisance to constitutional authority by opening with an appropriate declaration of purposes. Among other things the Act was designed "to improve the navigability and to provide for the flood control of the Tennessee River." For that approach there were precedents in conservative legislation and judicial decisions. Strict constructionist Democrats had denied their weight, but few if any Republicans had ever entertained doubts on that score. Another purpose of the Tennessee Valley Act was "to provide for reforestation." For that, also, there were accepted Republican examples; Republican leaders had engineered through Congress the Appalachian Forest Reserve Act of 1911 which appropriated money for the purchase of lands for forests "with a view to protecting the navigability of streams." A third purpose of the Tennessee Valley Act was "to provide for the national defense" by the creation of a corporation to operate "the government properties" at or near Muscle Shoals. If the Supreme Court of the United States turned its back on precedents touching the navigability of streams, flood control, and reforestation, it was not likely to withhold from Congress the power to prepare for war. On that point even Virtue and Respectability had no reservation.

To accomplish the purposes of the Act the Tennessee Valley Authority was created and endowed with extensive powers. The Authority was composed of three members, all required to "profess a belief in the feasibility and wisdom of this Act." It was authorized to issue securities; to construct dams, reservoirs, power houses, transmission lines, and incidental works on the Tennessee River and its tributaries; to contract with commercial concerns or produce fertilizers and ingredients; to coöperate with agricultural experiment stations and farmers; and to produce, distribute, and sell electric power to private corporations, individuals, states, counties, and municipalities. In arranging for the sale of power to private concerns for redistribution, the Authority was required to make sure that the electrical rates to ultimate consumers were reasonable, just, and fair. Throughout the austere lines of the statute ran the note of a general purpose: that of "fostering an orderly and proper physical, economic, and social development of said areas," reserving to the Government of the United States the right to take full possession of the whole enterprise in the event of war.

Here, within the scope of a single statute, were fused in one project activities for which there were individual precedents scattered from the old Muscle Shoals plant to Boulder Dam and Alaska. If any particular item in the law was novel, it was the Authority's power to build transmission lines and sell current directly to individuals, and the utility interests regarded this as especially dangerous. Step by step they had been compelled to allow public regulation of their rates and services, then public construction of plants, and subsequently public operation. Now they faced public competition in the sale of electric power. It was with difficult maneuvers impending that the Tennessee Valley Authority, consisting of Arthur Morgan, David Lilienthal, and Harcourt Morgan, began work in the summer of 1933.

In some respects the Tennessee Valley development stood alone. It had its own history. Doubtless it would have come in one form or another had there been no depression emergency. It gave expression to a movement of ideas and interests which was broader in scope and really inspired the Roosevelt administration in laying out its general program of public works. Authority for the program was contained in Title II of the National Industrial Recovery Act, which empowered the President to establish a Federal Emergency Administration of Public Works and to supervise the Administrator in executing a comprehensive scheme of public enterprises. For the realization of the blueprints the enormous sum of $3,300,000,000 was appropriated by Congress.

Under the immediate direction of Harold Ickes, Secretary of the Interior and Public Works Administrator, allocations of money were made to certain classes of federal projects and to a number of undertakings planned by state and local governments. Among the allotments were grants for two giant power plants — one, the Grand Coulee on the Columbia River, approximately seventy miles west of Spokane, and the other at Bonneville, Oregon, about fifty miles east of Portland. Although far less comprehensive than the Tennessee Valley development, these engineering exploits included the generation and sale of electric power, the improvement of navigation, flood control, and the provision of water for reclamation. Whether considered as devices for stimulating construction industries and employing labor or as power projects, they raised in the Far West conflicts of interests akin to those evoked at Muscle Shoals.

Departing more radically from national precedents, the Public Works Administration responded to an appeal from a small but active minority that had made "housing the people" an issue. By decree, it created in June, 1933, an Emergency Housing Division and authorized it to promote the clearing of slum areas and the erection of low-cost dwellings. In October, a Housing Corporation was created and given power to proceed on its own motion, buy land in cities, and build houses by direct action. For this purpose it could exercise the right of eminent domain and condemn land if necessary to cut extortionate prices. In addition to carrying out its own projects, the Corporation could enter into relations with municipalities and semi-public housing corporations, allot funds to them on specific conditions, and encourage them to substitute modern dwellings for slum tenements. Thus under government propulsion building industries floundering on the borders of disaster were to be stimulated to production and at least a few blots on American civilization removed.

Over the whole business, especially over direct federal action in condemning land and building houses, hovered the usual "grave constitutional doubts," but blighted cement, brick, and lumber industries and idle masons and carpenters probably gave little heed to the agitations of lawyers when they saw the prospects of profits and employment offered by federal housing activities. Their eagerness was too exigent to permit fine discriminations in jurisprudence.

While Congress was discovering the well-known frightfulness of living conditions in cities, its attention was drawn to another familiar fact, namely, that in large sections of rural and mining regions degradation in housing was, if possible, deeper and blacker. In various respects the problem of rural housing was more baffling than that of slum clearance. A low-paid urban worker could at least spend some money each month for rent. The stranded farmer's or miner's family, unemployed and living in a shack, had little or nothing to spare for a landlord or a government housing authority. Embarking upon rural housing projects was evidently highly experimental, and Congress was mindful of the hazards. Without attempting to be specific, it allocated in the National Industrial Recovery Act the sum of $25,000,000 for the purpose of "aiding the redistribution of the overbalance of population in industrial centers . . . for making loans for and otherwise aiding in the purchase of subsistence homesteads." This authorization, which set a precedent for the later Resettlement Administration created in 1935, was followed by the construction of a "model village" in a decayed mining region of West Virginia and by other experiments of the kind. Whatever could be said for or against them they certainly revealed difficulties and helped to educate the educators and well-wishers.

Far more conventional in economic thought were the major allocations of the Public Works Administration to federal and local projects. These included grants for highways, bridges, office buildings, hospitals, schools, tunnels, soil erosion control, rivers and harbors, the construction of buildings for the Army and Navy, and the improvements of the lighthouse and airways services. States were spurred to activity along these lines by the formation of local committees, the offer of loans on easy terms, and outright gifts amounting to a certain percentage of the cost of each enterprise. Within little more than a year, at least 17,000 projects, scattered from Porto Rico to Alaska, had been approved and had received allotments of funds. The Administrator reported that ninety-nine per cent of the counties in the Union had at least one project, that nearly 700,000 persons were directly employed on public works, and that probably 1,400,000 were engaged in supplying materials for the enterprises under way. There had been an impatient, almost frantic, demand for action. Alfred E. Smith had called for a dictator to cut red tape and set things in motion. Amid confusions, uncertainties, and uproars, the Roosevelt administration displayed energy in directions so numerous as to be astounding to old-fashioned politicians.

§

While striving to relieve farmers, industrialists, and urban workers by stimulating production, the Federal Government came to the aid of debtors in town and country. From all sections came the call: "Credit, credit, credit!" During the Hoover administration, Congress had adopted the policy of saving home owners from "the natural consequences" of their debts. For that purpose it had created the Home Loan Bank System but had limited the Bank to transactions with lending institutions, which were in about as much trouble as the debtors themselves. Dissatisfied with results achieved under this legislation, the Roosevelt administration went directly into the money-lending business and formed contacts with individual debtors. By an act approved June 13, 1933, Congress established the Home Owners Loan Corporation endowed with a capital of $200,000,000 and authorized to issue bonds to the amount of two billion dollars. The Act also provided for the formation of Federal Savings and Loan

Associations, for thrift and home-financing societies, organized on coöperative principles. In accordance with its instructions, the Corporation took over mortgages on homes at lower interest rates and extended the time for payments on principal to a longer term of years.

At the moment, real estate values were so low that many mortgages on real property were selling at prices ranging from eight to twenty cents on the dollar. Bondholders were frightened within an inch of their lives. Even foreclosure, in a multitude of cases, meant slashes in the bondholders' liquid claims. Home owners heavily in debt were overwhelmed by anxiety. Banks and mortgage institutions trembled for their own safety. In the circumstances a chorus of praise welcomed the decision of Congress to hurl the Federal Government into the money-lending business. But when the prospect of private profits began to take the place of certain losses, the praise could be forgotten and condemnation substituted.

Deviating less from precedents were the activities of the Roosevelt administration in relieving farmers oppressed by debts. During the first administration of President Wilson, Congress had instituted a farm loan system, and the business had been extended under Republican auspices as agricultural prices sank in the market. Confronted by a crisis still more acute in 1933, Congress authorized federal land banks, by the Farm Relief Act, to issue bonds in the amount of two billion dollars, purchase farm mortgages, exchange bonds for mortgages, and make new loans at a rate not to exceed four per cent. Under later legislation Production Credit Corporations, Production Credit Associations, a Central Bank for Coöperatives, and regional Banks for Coöperatives were established, the formation of thrift and self-financing organizations among farmers was encouraged, and the credit of the Federal Government was placed at their disposal. By an executive order, the scattered agencies of the Government concerned with farm mortgages, loans, and credits were consolidated under the Federal Farm Credit Administration and the multitudinous activities of agricultural financing were integrated into a coherent and powerful system.

When all the details of legislation and administration were brought into a scheme of theory and practice, it became evident that the major portion of farm financing was passing out of the hands of private banks and institutions into the control of government agencies which maintained direct contact with individual farmers and farmers' associations. Although slow in coming to a focus, this development really marked a departure from historic traditions and methods. From the adoption of the Constitution until 1916, farmers had relied upon banks, mortgage institutions, and local money lenders for credits and loans. As the researches of James O. Wettereau disclosed, the first Bank of the United States, so hated by the agrarians, did little "to befriend the agricultural man." Its successors, whether national or state, had operated on the theory of "charging all the traffic will bear." In a large measure the finances of great insurance companies had been built upon farm mortgages as "premier securities." But the structure of private financing had long been crumbling, especially after the advent of Woodrow Wilson's New Freedom, and the downward swing in agriculture that followed the close of the world war shook it from top to bottom, as thousands of rural banks broke down. By 1933 thousands of farms were not worth the nominal value of the mortages recorded against them and in such circumstances even foreclosure offered little consolation to creditors.

After the private financing of agriculture had ceased to be safe and profitable, interested money lenders — individuals and institutions — were willing, indeed eager, to shift the onus of the dubious business to the Federal Government. It was now difficult, if not impossible, to collect eight, ten, or twelve per cent on a farm loan. Millions of dollars' worth of farm mortgages in the vaults of banks and insurance companies had defaulted on interest and principal and were on the way to extinction. Collection by foreclosure, even with the posse comitatus of the sheriff available to supply force, encountered physical and moral barriers. Sheriffs and governors might invoke the agencies of state power, but they could not compel anyone to buy the property of his neighbor auctioned off under the hammer of the law. Often by agreement farmers arranged that no bid above a trivial sum should be offered for livestock or a farm sold under duress; and, when the debt collector had followed due process to the end, he found himself in possession of a few dollars in "full satisfaction" of a claim for hundreds or thousands of dollars. Since the system of private economy had failed to work according to the canons of autonomism, private and institutional losers joined farmers in the demand for "relief." For the time at least, money lenders, insurance companies, endowments, and universities preferred a three per cent Federal Farm Mortgage bond to a six or eight per cent private mortgage in default and steadily sinking in value. Facing the probabilities of a total loss, High Respectability lodged few protests in 1933 against "putting the Government in the farm credit business."

§

Despite minor dissents and controversies over details, the country as a whole rallied enthusiastically to the support of President Roosevelt during the spring and summer of 1933. Companionship in misery and fear almost turned politics into a love feast. Powerful business leaders coöperated with the administration in a spirit of cheerful compliance contrasting sharply with the hostility which they had displayed toward Bryanism, Progressivism, and the New Freedom. It seemed that the concussions of the crisis had shaken their assurance in themselves and their system. The old program of "letting nature take its course" had lost its glitter. They themselves had always made use of government whenever advantages could be obtained by that method; the Coolidge and Hoover administrations had favored them by special policies and had let them alone in most of their major operations. Yet catastrophe had come upon them, under the most beneficent auspices. In the spring and summer of 1933 the Lords of Creation were distraught and for the moment had no rallying point save the Chief Executive of the nation. In due time they were to turn upon him with unrepentant anger, but in the opening months of his administration they were contrite, thankful for favors, and eager to serve. Although by late autumn an opposition composed of discordant elements began to emerge from the fog of turbulent activities, it had no program. It could harass the outposts of the New Deal but could not take the citadel.

The second session of Congress, which opened in January, 1934, the first under the Twentieth Amendment altering the date of its annual meeting, kept on the same course, despite the rumbles of vexation. Its numerous acts bore the stamp of interventionism, not of a return to "free enterprise." Government control of agriculture was increased by a mandatory Cotton Control Act which fixed the production of that commodity and made provision for enforcement by a heavy tax on output in excess of quotas. Additional relief was granted to debt-burdened farmers by the Frazier-Lemke law imposing a moratorium on foreclosures and easing the terms of settlement for debtors. Federal regulation of utilities was fortified by the creation of a Communications Commission empowered to control telegraph, telephone, and radio concerns, which had been loosely supervised hitherto by the Interstate Commerce Commission. Agrarians of the old style, who still pinned their faith to free silver, forced the President to accept a measure requiring the purchase of silver in amounts necessary to keep that metal equal to one-fourth of the monetary stocks of the Government. It also authorized him to call all silver into the Treasury, and this action he took later in the year. Although conservative Senators called the bill a form of legalized robbery, Congress ordered a transfer of the title to all gold in the Federal Reserve System to the Federal Reserve Board. This measure it supplemented by an act fortifying the earlier provisions for the insurance of bank deposits. Designs for the control of investment and stock selling processes were strengthened by the Securities and Exchange Act. To administer and apply the general principles prescribed by the law, a Commission was established, with an experienced stock speculator at the head.

Two bills passed by Congress widened the area of what was coming to be called "social legislation" — a relatively strange phrase in federal jurisprudence. One, the Railway Pension Act, instituted a pension system for railway employees and made levies on carriers and workers to supply the funds. The second, entitled the National Housing Act, was built more on hopes than substance. In conception, it represented mainly the views of bankers, real estate promoters, and the building interests. In performance, its chief outcome was to place the credit of the Government behind the construction and repair of dwellings. Severely criticized by housing reformers and little used by the supposed beneficiaries, the measure served as a kind of stop-gap rather than as a charter for rehousing activities on a national scale. More permanent in effect, perhaps, than the terms of the Act were the revelations of wretched housing throughout the United States and the awakened sense of public obligation manifest in the discussion of the bill.

In turning from domestic affairs to matters impinging on relations with other countries, Congress vacillated in its economic theory. Agitated by reports from the Senate committee that had investigated the methods employed by bankers in floating foreign loans and had inquired also into the sources of immense losses in that field, Congress again applied interventionism — a kind of punitive remedy. By the Johnson Act of 1934 it forbade, within American jurisdiction, the sale of securities of foreign governments which had defaulted on payments due to the Government of the United States. If, as was said at the time, the law was conceived in resentment rather than cunning, it undoubtedly expressed a determination to control the freedom of enterprise that had formerly reigned in the flotation of foreign loans. A mandatory bar of law stood between bankers and investors in the United States and renewed operations in the money markets of many foreign countries. Good money was not to be thrown after bad in an effort to rescue desperate debtors.

Yet the very Congress that wrote the protective tariff provision into the National Industrial Recovery Act and passed the Johnson law veered in the direction of freer trade by devising the Reciprocal Trade Act of 1934, designed to promote foreign commerce. In this case, as in previous legislation, supreme confidence was placed in the Chief Executive. The Trade Act empowered the President for a term of three years to make trade agreements with foreign governments, and, within limits, to change existing import duties and restrictions. With a view, it was alleged, to keeping "politics" out of the transactions, trade agreements so negotiated were to go into effect without the consent of the Senate. This arrangement was undoubtedly a wholesale transfer of law-making and treaty-making powers to the Executive Department, and yet such "delegation running riot" inspired no effective protest among professional guardians of the Constitution. A frontal assault on the tariff seemed to be out of the question, especially for an administration engaged in raising wages and prices at home. There was more promise for "tariff reform" in sapping and mining — a little, not much. What the ingenuity of the State Department could effect under the terms of the Act lay hidden in the uncertainty of things.

§

The word "never" is to be used sparingly in history. It could be said with due respect for the record, however, that never before had Congress in the course of two years enacted legislation running so widely and deeply into American economy. Perhaps it would be no exaggeration to declare that all the federal legislation from the establishment of the Constitution down to the inauguration of Franklin D. Roosevelt in the spring of 1933 had not flouted so materially the presuppositions of "free enterprise" and the doctrine of laissez faire.

How did this happen, and what was its meaning? Was it, as heated imaginations suggested, a revolution or the beginning of a revolution? Or did it merely bring to a closer focus theories and practices long in process of development, without marking a sharp break in the course of events? Was it an illustration of Edmund Burke's dictum that greater changes may be effected in society by accretion and accumulation over a period of years than by a sudden revolution radically executed? Or was it a tempest in a teapot that would subside when wheat sold again at a dollar a bushel, if it should do so again, and the United States Steel Corporation resumed the payment of dividends? As always, where freedom of opinion is permitted, diversity of opinion raged over such fundamental questions.

On the verdict to be reached, history threw some light. Behind each statute of the New Deal legislation lay a long series of agitations, numerous changes in the thought and economy of American society, and pertinent enactments. Except for certain sections of the National Industrial Recovery Act, not a single measure passed by Congress in 1933 and 1934 was without some more or less relevant precedent; and this Act, in departing from the philosophy of antitrust individualism, reflected conceptions that had been associated with the apparently inexorable concentration of control in industrial economy. Had there been no profound dislocations connected with the panic, the movement of ideas and interests in this economy would have continued, unless history itself came to an end. But the depression had introduced fear, uncertainty, and distress, had cut established connections loose from customary points of contact, had shaken many rigid opinions, and, to use a metaphor, had made social relations more fluid. Where everything seemed afloat, particular interests gained more liberty of action and found more companions in misery ready to coöperate. When industry was prosperous, it could defy or hold the agrarians in check.

When both branches of economy were in peril of ruin, industrialists and agrarians were readier to make concessions, truces, and combinations that rendered possible the flood of far-reaching legislation.

In this legislation was there anything revolutionary? If by revolution is meant the overthrow of one class by another, a sudden and wholesale transfer of property, then all the New Deal laws combined effected no revolution. Nor were they intended to do so. The Agricultural Adjustment Act deprived no farmer, planter, or wheat-raising corporation of land. The Recovery Act stripped no industrial concern of its tangibles. The two laws were designed to set agriculture and industry in motion without changing property holdings or property relations. The former did little or nothing for tenants, and nothing at all for mere laborers on the land. Indeed, by forcing the curtailment of crops, it reduced employment for farm laborers. If the Recovery Act made a gesture in the direction of collective bargaining, it merely referred to a principle easily violated by obstinate practice. In saving distressed banks, the Government saved depositors. The departure from the gold standard enriched gold-mining concerns. Concessions to silver swelled the profits of interests engaged in extracting that metal, thus giving value to property once stagnant or of no value. The credit and money-lending legislation was framed to protect the holders of railway, bank, and real estate securities against grievous losses, and to enable debt-burdened farmers and home owners to avoid the stringent processes of liquidation.

And all this was done by placing the credit of the Government, that is, the collective public, under disaster-ridden private enterprises, by adding billions to the national debt, by shifting the major portion of the burden to indirect taxes, including heavy excises on alcoholic liquors after the repeal of the Prohibition Amendment in December, 1933, and by postponing, in an effort to avoid, a day of reckoning. If a change in things was thus effected, it was the change of tying private interests more closely into a single network and making the fate of each increasingly dependent upon the fate of all. From the process a revolution might develop, but that would be another historical illustration of events outrunning purposes, of mankind building better or worse than it knows.

The business was too complicated, however, for any neat theory of revolutionary dialectic — the overturn of one class by another until the final day of the communist spring into everlasting freedom or the totalitarian jump into the thousand year period of the corporative state. When history was conceived not as handsprings into liberation but as the movement of ideas and interests in time, with occasional broad jumps occurring, then the events of 1933 and 1934 seemed merely to mark the dissolution of once firm assurances and a modification of many theories and practices.

Whatever the near or distant outcome might be, the New Deal legislation did indicate fundamental doubts respecting many ideas, long current, as good always and everywhere in American society. It marked a general surrender of the doctrine that poverty and unemployment come only from the improvidence of the poor and that the persons affected must take the consequences of their futile and evil lives. It repudiated the Darwinian law of the jungle by seeking to eliminate through concerted action — mutual aid — innumerable practices of competition once deemed right and just, including the shifting of capitalists' strains to labor in the form of wage cutting. For more than forty years, statesmen and demagogues alike had sought by antitrust acts to intensify the ruthless struggles of competition, on the assumption that such conflicts in economy were wholesome and that the downward pressure of competition on labor was of no concern to the State or Society.

Besides casting off the formulas of economic Darwinism, New Deal legislation brought forcibly into national thought a recognition of persistent agrarian claims, affecting the conception of a balanced economy. For more than a hundred years philosophic agrarians had insisted that capitalism and its price system, with or without the protective tariff, worked against agriculture, exploited it, drained the land of its bone and sinew, failed to do justice to labor on the soil. For more than a hundred years economic thought had been steadily growing urban in outlook. To quote a European wag, it was the work of asphalt flowers. But the crisis of 1933, the Agricultural Adjustment Act and supplementary measures thrust agrarian economy into the center of national policy.

With the powerful aid of the Government, farmers were at last enabled to imitate industrial practices in time of depression, namely, to curtail production, reduce losses, and turn laborers adrift to shift for themselves. As Secretary Wallace conceded, this was the economy of scarcity with a vengeance, but if the medicine was good for industrialists it might be good for farmers. Although it brought forth wails of disgust from urban editors, publicists, and propagandists, it called popular attention to the fundamental principles of capitalist economy and suggested a general revision. If an economy of abundance, that is, general prosperity, was ever to be established in the United States, both industry and agriculture would have to undergo some kind of transformation, escape from the bondage of the so-called "effective demand," from the periodical restriction of production to meet reduced buying power.

On a final balance sheet struck at the close of 1934 it was only in the matter of banking and currency that New Deal legislation offered the possibility of resolvent implications. The gold standard, with the interchangeability of currencies, was abandoned. For this formula, Respectability had waged a hot campaign in 1896. Then it had deemed the gold standard so nearly a command of God and Nature that few words could be too bitter or vile enough to characterize opponents. In 1933 the everlasting gold foundations slipped out from under the economy of society, leaving it very much as it was before, if no more happy and secure. By other enactments Congress declared that banks, investment houses, and stock exchanges could not be relied upon to keep business enterprise in motion, to protect the public against exploitation, and to fulfill the moral obligations of fiduciary trust. That, too, was a blow to Respectability's sense of private virtue. Had it not been for the opposition of President Roosevelt as a guardian of vested rights, Congress might have gone far beyond these measures. According to the reports of seasoned newspaper men in Washington, a large number, perhaps a majority, of the Senators and Representatives were prepared, in the spring of 1933, to abolish stock exchanges, nationalize banks of issue, and reduce the substance of fixed claims to wealth by a huge inflation of the currency.

Had the restraining hand of the Chief Executive been released, a conjuncture of physical distress and financial maladies might have culminated in that form of revolution known as inflation. The immense structure of fixed debt, public and private, with its heavy claims on the returns of real property and the wages of labor, might have been pulled down close to the earth, if not entirely liquidated. But by maneuvering, by accepting powers without using them, President Roosevelt helped to prevent that convulsion. In so doing, he probably interpreted correctly the popular judgment; for in the congressional elections of 1934 the active voters, contrary to the mid-term tradition, increased the Democratic delegations in the House and Senate, diminished the strength of the Republican opposition, and seemed to approve the course which things had taken under the management of the Chief Executive. The returns of the balloting divulged no evidences of an overwhelming demand for a program more radical or for a retreat upon the way thus far chosen. It was with renewed confidence, then, that Roosevelt announced to Congress on January 4, 1935, a broader scheme of action touching the wiser use of natural resources, social insurance, and security of homes.

By that time, however, the immense strain thrown upon the nerves, sentiments, and acquisitive instincts of individuals had begun to snap the bonds of coöperation imposed by fear, law, and administration. Indeed for that strain the people had been ill-prepared by knowledge, understanding, and acceptance of responsibilities; and their leaders, especially those trained in schools and colleges, had been no better prepared. From decade to decade it had been revealed in the census returns of industry, agriculture, and labor, that the self-sufficing homestead and community were dying and that all the interests, occupations, properties, and callings of the nation were being drawn into a tighter and tighter web of economic interdependence. The commodities and articles produced in each center or region were scattered broadcast throughout the Union in exchange for goods of use and consumption. The complete independence of the farming family that satisfied all its own wants had almost vanished. For isolated individualism, always overemphasized in American thought and teaching, was substituted an interlaced system of exchange and mutuality correctly described as collectivism.

Yet the very word that described the fact excited horror among editors, professors, teachers, school superintendents, public mentors in general, and their disciples, who, in accordance with immemorial practice, repeated by rote the axioms and maxims received from high instructors. The mental imagery of the past was employed to combat the present and the future. So the deep-seated propulsions of private interest found sanction in the phrases of Respectability for a drive to the very end of acquisition.

For a brief season, in the spring of 1933, fear — blanched fear — held these propulsions in leash and counseled unity and coöperation. This counsel was incorporated in an open letter directed to the governors' conference by a committee of representative citizens on March 6 of that year. "We are convinced," said the signers of the manifesto, "that there is throughout the nation a spontaneous spiritual uprising of confidence and hope in our chosen leader. The nature of our national crisis calls for an expression of this confidence in the combined voice of the people to show that they are behind him, alert and vocal and united in heart. Prompt and decisive action of a national scope, and in several directions, is necessary to prevent economic collapse throughout the land.

The ordinary operations of government that prevail and are suitable in time of prosperity with normal conditions may be too slow to meet adequately this emergency and avoid the danger of this economic avalanche carrying all before it." In this spirit the citizens' committee appealed to the governors and the Congress of the United States to support the President and our institutions, "thus enabling the whole people to declare in unison their confidence and faith in our President." That would, they asserted, "constitute the people's appeal to the patriotism of Congress, which we know they possess, in common with all, to coöperate with the President in taking such action as will guarantee economic stability, restore confidence, and thereby relieve unemployment and widespread distress."

This memorandum and appeal, framed during the great fear, was signed by William Green for the American Federation of Labor; Louis J. Taber, master of the National Grange; Edward O'Neal, president of the American Farm Bureau Federation; His Eminence George Cardinal Mundelein; Dr. Harry Emerson Fosdick; Rabbi Stephen Wise; Alfred E. Smith; Newton D. Baker; Dr. Nicholas Murray Butler; H. G. Harriman, president of the United States Chamber of Commerce; Daniel Willard, president of the Baltimore and Ohio Railway; and Walter Lippmann, publicist. In a few months some of the signers were to turn against President Roosevelt and his prompt and decisive actions "of a national scope," and denounce legislation of Congress apparently enacted to "guarantee economic stability." But in March they all joined in the "spiritual uprising of confidence and hope."

However interpreted, the appeal and the revolt had a bearing upon the nature of the great upheaval. Were the signers only united in support of the President until banks and financial institutions had been saved by the outpouring of public credit? Or did they deem his prompt and decisive actions "of a national scope" to be inappropriate guarantees of "economic stability?" Or were they alarmed by subsequent measures framed to "relieve unemployment and widespread distress?" Whatever the answer, the distinguished signers of the appeal for national solidarity evidently believed in March, 1933, that the crisis was national in scope and that national measures alone could cope with it; and in this belief they had a solid basis of facts evident to open eyes.

Nevertheless the high tension of unity reflected in the appeal steadily relaxed after the banks and financial institutions of the country had been saved, at least for a time, by the actions of the Roosevelt administration. Nowhere dominant was there a program of concerted and defensible unity, inspired by strong resolve and informed by realistic knowledge, to continue, expand, and apply effectively the recognition accorded to the collective character of American economy. Nowhere available was there a scheme of tested thought and moral principle to sustain such a program. Nowhere available was there a body of tried, trained, and loyal public servants to fill all the top positions of administration required to discharge skillfully the functions so suddenly imposed upon the Government of the United States. Nor did the President seem able, during the uproar and haste of the time, to draw together all the duties so suddenly assumed, assure efficiency, and explain to the nation the fullness of the designs taking shape in Washington. In such circumstances bustle and improvization characterized political action. Either because too much was undertaken or the requisite abilities were lacking or the strain was too great for private interests, the devices adopted by the administration began to disintegrate, the acquisitive instinct seized upon its opportunities for satisfaction, individualists called "chiselers" fell upon the spoils, and the "spontaneous spiritual uprising" of March, 1933, dissolved. A large part of the economic, intellectual, and moral leadership that had rallied to the New Deal melted away. The "brain trust," composed of a few intimate advisers, disbanded. Still, President Roosevelt continued to command a majority of voters.

CHAPTER VI

Interplay of Court, Congress, and President

A T the center of the national stage, President Roosevelt
enacted his role of leadership and, during the early
months of his administration, through the power he
symbolized and the force of his personality, he commanded a
public affection rarely bestowed upon a national figure in
America. Even in time of war a President of the United
States had not been accustomed to such enthusiastic coöperation from his party and his political antagonists. In the
eyes of the unemployed, the poverty-stricken, the debt-
harassed farmers and home owners, he was a Prince in shining armor leading the hosts of justice against the powers of
darkness and confusion, a Prince devoted to peace and humanity. Neither on grounds of broad policy nor on the basis
of personal antipathies did his critics marshal an imposing
opposition. In crucial matters they followed his leadership.
Such non-conformity as they mustered was sporadic, not organized. Such independence as Congress displayed ran, in
the main, to details rather than principles. Cordial to the
press, endowed with an ingratiating voice for fireside dis-

256

courses to the people over the radio, the President, during these months, seemed to hold the entire nation in the spell of his magnetism. Actions deemed mistakes by the captious were treated as the normal errors of a human being who was trying, with courage and resolution, to bring the nation out of economic distress and spiritual defeat. In the circumstances, President Roosevelt overshadowed all other personalities in the Government and all the Lords of Creation in the country.

§

At the other end of Pennsylvania Avenue, during the season of executive preëminence, sat the Supreme Court attending to matters relatively small and receiving slight consideration from the multitudes engrossed in saving their very skins. Nevertheless experts knew that the laws which went through Congress touched economic matters of vital interest and could easily be employed to raise constitutional issues. Astute lawyers were conversant with the conflicts taking shape and early began to speculate on the outcome. Had the Government pressed its cases to a decision at the autumn term of Court in 1933 the atmospheric pressure of calamity might have carried it to victory. But for many reasons, trial was postponed, perhaps above all from lack of time rather than fear of the result. Not many laymen, possibly, supposed that the Supreme Court would venture to pull down the pillars of the great fabric erected, as alleged, for the salvation of the country. Nor did all students of law. In a searching analysis of constitutional and economic complexities, Professor E. S. Corwin indicated the perils that lurked in judicial intervention of the old style, entitling his volume, significantly, The Twilight of the Supreme Court. And for a moment, the Supreme Court was content with an undramatic role. In two cases involving state legislation of the reformist type, the Court, though sharply divided, betrayed "liberal leanings" in 1934. It sustained a Minnesota statute placing a moratorium on mortgage foreclosures and a New York statute

empowering a commission to fix minimum prices for milk —
laws designed to ease the worries of debtors and farmers in
the new mode. Evidently constitutional law was viable in
both meanings of the term.

However encouraging these decisions were to the administration in Washington, the two state laws upheld by the
Court did not cut very deeply into accepted economic predilections, despite the vigorous complaints of the four dissenters — Justices Sutherland, Van Devanter, McReynolds,
and Butler. Nor, save by implication, did the two decisions
lend countenance to the legislation recently enacted by
Congress. To watchers concerned with the future, only one
thing seemed sure : since the judges were divided in opinion,
Chief Justice Hughes and Justice Roberts held the fate of
the Court, if not the New Deal, in their hands, and they
were not devoid of political acumen and experience.

As governor of New York and as the Republican candidate
for President in 1916, the Chief Justice was familiar with the
problems of power, the sweets of victory, and the bitters of
defeat. He did not cherish the illusion that the Constitution
is as unequivocal as the multiplication table. Far from it.
He had once publicly declared that the Constitution is what
the judges say it is and, despite the context which explainers
tried to use in glossing over the confession, the statement,
with or without the context, meant just exactly what it set
forth in intelligible English. The Chief Justice also knew
that the Court could sustain the New Deal legislation by
reference to the liberal doctrines of Alexander Hamilton and
John Marshall or annul it by reference to the narrow doctrines of Thomas Jefferson and John C. Calhoun. Previously,
he had referred, in secular discourse, to the wounds which the
Court had inflicted upon itself in the Dred Scott case, the
Legal Tender cases, and the Income Tax case. In brief, the
Chief Justice was sagacious, appreciative of the hazards implicit in decision either way, and not unmindful of the statesman's role in the unfolding drama.

When in February, 1935, the Supreme Court came to

grips with legal issues presented by the resolution of Congress abrogating the gold clause in private and public securities, it equivocated and was by no means categorical in its reasoning. By a five to four vote it sustained the proposition that the gold clause, in respect of railway bonds, could not be enforced and that the payment of interest and principal in legal-tender currency was sufficient. When the holder of a federal gold certificate demanded coin in accordance with the Government's pledge, the Court replied that he had demonstrated no actual damage at the moment and that the Court of Claims could not entertain his suit. When the holder of a Liberty bond demanded his gold as promised in the instrument, the Court gave him a double-barreled answer: the provision of the law overriding the gold obligation of the bond is unconstitutional, but the "plaintiff has failed to show cause of action for actual damages." If no compliment to the Roosevelt administration, the decisions were no comfort either for those defenders of the gold standard who insisted on a judicial order compelling the Treasury and corporations to discharge their gold obligations in accordance with the terms of the contracts. Part of the resolution of Congress is valid, said the Court in effect, and part of it is invalid; for the moment, if ever, nothing can be done to enforce the unconstitutional part.

For die-hards who wanted from the Court a paralyzing blow at the monetary policy of the New Deal, these decisions were disappointing. At best they offered only rays of hope — feeble rays. In their effect upon practice, as distinguished from jurisprudence, they were mere verbal concessions. Furthermore, the whole business was clouded by confusion in judicial reasonings. Although a majority of the nine judges agreed on the decisions, the majority were not united in agreeing with the opinion of Chief Justice Hughes on the most fundamental issue up for determination, namely, the power of Congress to abrogate the Government's gold pledge. Addressing himself to this question, Justice Stone declined to accept two primary propositions put forward by the Chief

Justice in bolstering up the conclusions which the majority affirmed. That left four judges united on the opinion of the Court in the particular instance. And on the other side there were four dissenters — the historic four, Justices McReynolds, Butler, Sutherland, and Van Devanter. Speaking for them, Justice McReynolds, with pungent sarcasm, charged Chief Justice Hughes with using "mere generalities or multitudes of words to distract the mind," characterized the "repudiation of national obligations" as "abhorrent," declared that the Constitution was now destroyed, and referred to "Nero," the royal prerogatives of old France, and the near "wickedness" of the administration's monetary policy. Although his printed opinion was more restrained than his oral discourse from the bench, it was blunt and furious enough to irk the majority of the judges as well as the celebrants of an alleged victory in the White House.

§

A few months passed, while speculators in jurisprudence scanned the heavens for omens. In May and June, the Supreme Court declared its twilight to be a dawn, by holding major acts of Congress null and void. Its decisions scattered consternation in New Deal circles, made the President angry, and encouraged his opponents to come into the open for a direct assault. According to a legend, it had been the custom for Louis XIV to remain in the background during a war until his generals declared a fortress on the verge of surrender, and then to ride fully caparisoned to the front in time to receive the honors. In the spring of 1935 the Supreme Court so thoroughly shattered the New Deal fortress that even little men felt that they could safely ride into the breach. Any supposition that the Supreme Court felt itself incompetent to govern was now waved aside. To all appearances, the eminent tribunal intended to employ its engines of sovereignty in handling the national crisis. It had failed at this business in 1857, reversed itself in 1871, partly succeeded in 1896; it might be more fortunate in a fourth grand effort.

The first of the three destructive decisions declared invalid the Railroad Retirement Act, which had provided a system of pensions for railway employees — an installment of the social security program already announced. Justice Roberts delivered the opinion of the Court. Before his elevation to the bench, he had lifted the curtain on his basic social philosophy in an address in 1923 to the Trust Division of the American Bankers Association, by declaring: "The business man in America today feels that he is doing business with a minion of government looking over his shoulder with an upraised arm and a threatening scowl. . . . Are we to go into a state of socialism, or are you men, and men like you, prepared to get out, take off your coats, and root for good old-fashioned Anglo-Saxon individualism?" Certainly the Railroad Pension Act ran counter to that well-known brand of "Anglo-Saxon" philosophy, and Justice Roberts found that the Constitution of the United States also ran against it. The Act, he said, was invalid. It denied due process of law, "by taking the property of one and bestowing it upon another." It violated the interstate commerce clause of the Constitution. It had no "reasonable" relation to interstate traffic or to efficiency in operating railways. Flashing through the austere texture of his jurisprudence were gleams of Justice Roberts' faith in individualism. A pension system would destroy rather than promote the loyalty of employees. It was "an attempt for social ends" to insure "a particular class of employees against old age dependency" and, therefore, invaded the rights of property. This credo was underwritten by a wealth of citations and discriminations.

In the position thus taken Justice Roberts was sustained by the four Justices who had thought the Constitution destroyed by the decisions in the gold cases. Against him were ranged four dissenters — Justices Stone, Brandeis, and Cardozo, and Chief Justice Hughes. The burden of delivering the dissenting opinion was assumed by the Chief Justice.

In an argument that equaled in vigor the discourse of Justice
Roberts, he posited axioms similarly cogent but with different
social content, drew diametrically opposed conclusions
respecting the meaning of the Constitution as applied to the
Railroad Pension Act, and sustained his reasoning by citations as thoroughly apposite. Turning abruptly on the
majority, he declared: "The gravest aspect of the decision
is that it does not rest simply upon a condemnation of particular features of the Railroad Retirement Act, but denies
to Congress the power to pass any compulsory pension act for
railroad employees." In making this assertion the Chief Justice did not correctly anticipate history; but in the spring of
1935, the decision of the majority on the Railroad Retirement
Act seemed to sound the doom of every "attempt for social
ends" to insure any class of employees against old-age dependency. The barrier raised was so high that, apparently,
nothing short of a constitutional amendment could hurdle it
and this was out of the question.

The division of opinion that marked the railway pension
case vanished when the Supreme Court came to the Frazier-
Lemke Farm Moratorium Act of 1934. Without hesitation,
eight colleagues agreed with Justice Brandeis in declaring the
statute void. Although the law, loosely drawn, had been no
official part of the administration program, it reflected the
desperate plea of debtors for relief from the letter of the bond.
Unanimous also was the opinion of the Court in the Humphrey case involving the power of the President to remove
federal officers without regard to stipulations imposed by
Congress, in respect of qualifications.

The issue in the Humphrey case was an old one. Since the
establishment of the Constitution the nature of this power
had been debated by lawyers. Practice likewise had varied.
Yet competent authorities had regarded the matter as settled
by the Meyers case in 1926, when Chief Justice Taft upheld
the removal power of the President and went out of his way
to indicate that the prerogative was almost unlimited in its
range. But the Chief Justice had then seen the problem

from the standpoint of the Chief Executive as well as of the Court, and at the moment Calvin Coolidge was safely installed in the White House.

Now in 1935 the political scene presented many new aspects and dissenters of 1926 joined newcomers in declaring that President Roosevelt could not oust a member of the Federal Trade Commission at will. The member in question, a good Republican, had been outspoken, even acrimonious, in denouncing policies espoused by Roosevelt. In taking this course he felt safe, for the law under which he held office prescribed specific conditions for removal. And the Court sustained his view. President Roosevelt, it said, could not retire Humphrey merely because they differed over policies, over a mere interpretation of the officer's duties. Friends of the President contended that he had been "tricked" by the official, that the two had agreed upon a friendly settlement, and that the Commissioner had then dared the President to remove him. Whatever the verdict on that charge, the Supreme Court narrowed an executive prerogative which many legal experts had long held to be a part of the President's constitutional authority. But the public did not get excited about this contest.

Far different was the reception accorded to the Schechter case, May 27, 1935, in which the Court unanimously agreed that the National Industrial Recovery Act was null and void. When this case reached the Court, enthusiasm for the Act was dying and difficulties of enforcement in detail were harassing the administration itself. The Act was assailed by business men who had originally sponsored it, by foes of corporations, and by a number of labor leaders. As things had developed, none of the interested parties affected by the law had been able to reap all the expected advantages. The substitution of coöperation in industry for tooth and claw had proved to be a Herculean undertaking without the mastery of a Hercules. A demand for a return to a free-for-all competition, out of which the statute had sprung as a protest and mode of escape, surged through the country. If not as unanimous as the decision of the Court, the demand was potent. In the climate of opinion so prepared, Chief Justice Hughes, with the support of all his colleagues, brushed the Recovery Act and its symbol, "the Blue Eagle," into the waste basket, with an air of finality almost imperial in its sweep.

In the opinion that supported the decision, the Chief Justice seemed to block every loophole for the regulation of procedures, hours, and wages in industries by federal law. He was not content to declare that the code-making provisions of the Act violated the doctrine of the separation of powers; that they transferred the law-making authority from Congress to the President and trade associations. Had he so limited his range, Congress could have corrected this error by modifying the statute, in accordance with many earlier decisions sustaining the quasi-legislative powers of boards and commissions. As if determined to make a complete disposal of the business, the Chief Justice, with equal force and assurance, destroyed the hours and wages provisions of the Recovery law. The determination of hours and wages in such local industries, he asserted, does not "directly affect" interstate commerce, cannot be brought about by Congress under the commerce clause, is left to the states under the Constitution. In 1931, two years before the Blue Eagle burst upon their vision, some chicken dealers had been charged with violating the federal antitrust laws by running a "racket," and the Court had held that the chicken business did affect interstate commerce. However, in the spring of 1935, the chicken business did not look the same to the judges.

News of the decision in the Schechter case startled the country. For the first time in many months the Supreme Court of the United States crowded the President of the United States off the front page of the daily newspapers. "Wall Street Hails New Deal Defeats!" shrieked a headline announcing gratification from the precincts of the National Shrine. After the report of the decision broke in the afternoon, stocks spurted upward as if the great day so longed for in the Street had come at last. The night closed in. "Regimentation" seemed buried in its darkness. But the next day came word that business men were not unanimous like the Court. New England textile manufacturers were not exulting whole-heartedly in the prospects of a free play for the low-wage mills of the South. On behalf of the American Federation of Labor, William Green issued a warning that wage-slashing under the ruling of the Court would be a signal for a series of strikes. Telegrams poured into the White House asking the President to save all that he could of the Recovery Act under the recent edict from the Palace of Justice. The day following the decision of the Court, stocks which had jumped upward shot downward "in the second heaviest trading of the year." Evidently the news of the business resurrection by judicial fiat had been exaggerated.

§

Four days later, President Roosevelt met the representatives of the press. The wonted smile had gone from his face. Off the record he gave reporters a history of judicial intervention in policies that bristled with insinuations. For the benefit of the public he stated that the Supreme Court had interpreted the Constitution in the light of the "horse-and-buggy days." He expressed a fear that the decision of the Court in the Schechter case had jeopardized the Agricultural Adjustment Act, the Securities and Exchange Act, the Social Security bill, and other social legislation then pending. In measured words he referred to the Dred Scott decision as an important factor among the events that precipitated the civil war. "With some asperity," reporters noted, the President observed that the Court "seemed to recognize mining as an instrument of interstate commerce when it supported injunction suits against miners, although the shoe was on the other foot when the question of miners' wages and hours was raised." At the close of the press conference, the inference was drawn that the President contemplated not a civil war but a constitutional war, "if the Constitution made his federal program for regulating economic conditions impossible." No special shrewdness was required to discover that then and there President Roosevelt had made up his mind to counter, in his manner and time, the destructive blast that had rolled down from the Palace of Justice.

Yet events urged caution. In speaking of the Supreme Court with asperity, in referring to its horse-and-buggy doctrines, he had touched an American holy of holies. Though conservative tradition admitted that Congress could be cursed as a "gang of criminals," or the President as "a law-breaker and a communist," the tradition commanded awe in the presence of the Supreme Court. If President Roosevelt was not well acquainted with its mandate on May 31, 1937, he was made conscious of it in a very few days. Soon after his opinions on judicial opinions became known, the Liberty League, an organization of rich men and women, formed to "save the country," issued a ukase against him personally and his leadership and against all tinkering with the sacred text. Not to be outdone by the Liberty League, Senator Borah, whose forgotten speeches were sprinkled with scathing reflections on the judicial process, delivered an impassioned oration against President Roosevelt's constitutional reasoning, defended what he called the handiwork of "Hamilton, Madison and Jefferson," and demanded the maintenance of the Constitution as interpreted by the Supreme Court. Telegrams of criticism from people who could afford to pay for them flooded the President's desk.

The opposition to his legislative policies now had a higher intellectual and moral coverage than mere economic argument — the coverage of the Constitution. Many critics of the administration who, for various reasons, had shrunk from direct assaults on explicit measures of the New Deal, could now put on shining armor in defense of the Constitution as expounded by the Supreme Court in destroying New Deal statutes. With the campaign of 1936 approaching, an appeal to the voters was in sight. The Democrats had fulminated against the Supreme Court forty years before and had been overwhelmed at the polls. It was true that the Republicans had also assailed the Court in 1860 and had triumphed in the election; but it took long memories to recall that incident. Bemused, if not frightened, by the experience, the President relapsed into silence as the storm over the Constitution continued to rage. Whether Chief Justice Hughes was a tactician might be debated. That the Chief Executive had been one could scarcely be denied.

While the President kept his own counsel on the issue of the Court, Congress went forward with his legislative program. Before closing its session in August, 1935, it passed a sheaf of bills extending the scope of the New Deal. It modified and strengthened the Agricultural Adjustment Act. It enacted the Social Security law providing for a system of national old-age pensions and insurance. Despite the positive warning of the Court in the Schechter case, Congress enacted the Wagner-Connery Labor Relations bill and the Guffey-Snyder Bituminous Coal bill — both regulating industrial processes, on the assumption that they "directly" affected interstate commerce. For the railway pension law declared invalid by the Court, a new pension law was substituted. Since pensions could not be assured under its authority over interstate commerce, Congress shifted the base of the new law to the taxing power. The new statute was doubtful in the light of some judicial decisions, but a chance was taken, and the railways finally accepted its principles. In a similar spirit, the Farm Mortgage Moratorium Act was revived, drastically amended, and placed on the books in new form. Thus the Democrats went ahead legislating. If some of them desired to settle back, enjoy the sweets of office, and lay the responsibility for quiescence on the Supreme Court and the Constitution, the majority favored continued experimentation. So more acts of Congress were to be carried up the marble steps to the throne room of the Palace on Capitol Hill.

§

When the Supreme Court reassembled in the autumn of 1935, expectancy was on tiptoes in the capital and the country. Weeks passed. From decision day to decision day, crowds eager for news turned away from the Palace of Justice in disappointment. It was rumored that the Justices were engaged in heated controversies and could come to no agreements on crucial pending measures. Not until January 6, 1936, was public curiosity gratified by an official announcement. On that day the Court, by a vote of six to three, declared null and void the Agricultural Adjustment Act, the law for which agrarian leaders had labored so long and so zealously.

The opinion of the Court was delivered by Justice Roberts. He conceded that Congress had the power to tax for the general welfare; in fact the Constitution said so in plain English. But the power to regulate and control agricultural production was a right reserved to the states and Congress could not spend the money raised by taxation to effect such a purpose. Having excluded Congress from interference with agriculture in the states, Justice Roberts painted a frightful picture of what might happen in case Congress were allowed to do any such thing. "It would be possible," he insisted, "to exact money from one branch of an industry and pay it to another branch in every field of activity which lies within the province of the states." In the manner sometimes honored by violation, Justice Roberts disclaimed all thought of passing upon the wisdom or merits of the Act; he merely "squared" the law by the Constitution and found it invalid — perhaps too long or too short or too crooked.

From the interpretation and application of the Constitution put forward by Justice Roberts there was vigorous dissent by Justice Stone, supported by Justices Cardozo and Brandeis. According to a report current in Washington deemed fairly authentic, Chief Justice Hughes originally believed the Agricultural Adjustment Act to be valid and finally went with the majority for the purpose of avoiding another close division, five to four. Such splits, already numerous, were producing doubts in the country respecting the very operating hypothesis of the Court, namely, that it was unaffected by the merits of statutes and was merely expounding the Constitution with unerring accuracy. At all events, as in many other cases in which the Chief Justice found himself aligned against the liberal constructionists, he assigned to a colleague the task of writing the opinion agreeable to Justices Butler, Sutherland, McReynolds, and Van Devanter. Whether this action represented courtesy or an ingenious maneuver, certainly the Chief Justice was not impervious to the cutting and blistering dissent read to the majority and the country by Justice Stone.

Point by point, Justice Stone followed the argument of the majority opinion, analyzing it with Ciceronian pertinacity. Under his conception of intellectual operations, it seemed a flagrant contradiction in terms to say, as Justice Roberts did, that Congress had the power to tax and spend for the general welfare and then defeat that power by applying "limitations that do not find their origin in any express provisions of the Constitution" — limitations "to which other expressly delegated powers are not subject." Justice Roberts had contended philosophically that the Adjustment Act invaded powers belonging to the states. Justice Stone replied by citing practices — a long list of federal expenditures for schools, roads, vocational rehabilitation, unemployment relief, financing agriculture, industry, and commerce, and other activities clearly within the powers of the states. Must these functions also collapse under the principle now advanced by the majority? Justice Roberts had referred to hideous abuses that might arise if the principle of the Agricultural Adjustment Act were sustained, if the exercise of such powers of government were not kept in check. This contention, Justice Stone replied, "hardly rises to the dignity of an argument."

Taking up the time-honored theory repeated by Justice Roberts that the Court merely declares the law and cannot err, Justice Stone replied that judicial power may be abused, that "Congress and the courts both unhappily may falter or be mistaken in the performance of their constitutional duty." Apparently referring to an inarticulate premise in Justice Roberts' argument, Justice Stone said prophetically : "Courts are not the only agency of government that must be assumed to have capacity to govern. . . . Interpretation of our great charter of government which proceeds on any assumption that the responsibility for the preservation of our institutions is the exclusive concern of any one of the three branches of government, or that it alone can save them from destruction, is far more likely, in the long run, 'to obliterate the constituent members' . . . than the frank recognition that language, even of a constitution, may mean what it says : that the power to tax and spend includes the power to relieve a nation-wide economic maladjustment by conditional gifts of money."

Although Justice Stone's opinion was pointed enough to make the victors wince, it was after all just a dissent. They had carried the day. In his argument before the Court against the Adjustment Act, George Wharton Pepper had closed with the exclamation : "I pray Almighty God that not in my time may 'the land of the regimented' be accepted as a worthy substitute for 'the land of the free.'" The prayer, if it had little to do with constitutional law, vibrated with the animus of the opposition. Mr. Pepper was and had long been a close personal friend of Justice Roberts; they had studied together as young men in the University of Pennsylvania, had risen together in the economics and politics of Philadelphia, and had served as colleagues in the councils of the Republican party. Indeed, Mr. Pepper had urged President Hoover to appoint Mr. Roberts to the Supreme Court and had warmly supported his confirmation. In the circumstances cynics had been inconsiderate enough to suggest that a nice sense of judicial propriety would have led Justice Roberts to refrain from writing the opinion of the Court in response to the fervid plea of his bosom friend and former political associate. But the suggestion was hypercritical and implied that a judge must necessarily be influenced by what he knows as a man and feels as a friend. In any case, the power of the Court had been vindicated and the triumph over "regimentation" had been magnificent — in the particular matter and for a time, if not for eternity.

Owing to the sweeping language of the Court in overthrowing the Agricultural Adjustment Act, there was no possibility of getting around the decision by minor modifications of the original text. Yet neither President Roosevelt nor Secretary Wallace made adverse comments for public benefit, with or without "asperity." That they had not accepted defeat, however, became evident on January 8 when the President announced his determination to attain justice for agriculture and gave out an official statement to the effect that his administration would continue the Agricultural Adjustment program or "its equivalent." Within a short time, agrarian lawyers found a loophole in the judicial barrier, and on February 29, 1936, the President signed the Soil Conservation and Domestic Allotment Act, instituting a form of crop control under a more constitutional name. Crop adjustments were called soil-erosion adjustments — to "normal domestic human consumption" as determined by the Secretary of Agriculture. As in other matters of federal and state coöperation, the states were to enforce the law temporarily, subject to the supervision of agents from the Department of Agriculture.

§

With the agrarians theoretically prostrate under the Constitution and, according to political calculations, powerless to force an amendment of the text in their favor, one great enterprise of the New Deal seemed to lie in ruins. Having disposed of the Agricultural Adjustment Act, the Supreme Court then took up the program for the Tennessee Valley and the development of water power resources under the jurisdiction of the Federal Government. Congressional control over navigable streams and falling waters on the national domain was indisputable, if readers of law could believe legal words. Neither navigable rivers nor public lands were yet regarded as objects of private property with which individuals might "do as they please." But could the Government itself utilize these power resources, build hydro-electric plants, construct transmission lines, and sell current directly to consumers? Or was it compelled by the Constitution either to let its resources go to waste or turn them over to private corporations for development? These questions had been argued directly or by implication before the Supreme Court in a Tennessee Valley case and after a tedious delay that tribunal rendered an opinion, on February 17, 1936.

Like the effort of agrarians to influence economy with special reference to their concerns, the attempt of the Federal Government to develop its power resources had involved a perennial conflict of interests. It had been marked by acrimonious debates on the floor of Congress, by voluminous investigations of utility companies, their practices, and their propaganda, and by rhetorical contests in newspapers and magazines. Billions of dollars had been drawn into consideration, and the prospects of gathering more billions in private profits had been placed in jeopardy.

During the campaign of 1932 Roosevelt had endorsed public ownership of public power resources and direct government action in their development. In so doing he had openly defied a great industry. Taking into account existing utility interests and the potentials of future expansion, the economy of power production overtopped in dollars and cents the assessed valuation of all the farms between Maine and California. Therefore, if less visible to the eye, the issue presented by the Tennessee Valley case was scarcely less significant, in material terms, than the problem raised by the Agricultural Adjustment Act; and the following enlisted by the electric power companies, if more concentrated, was probably as active in politics as the agrarians.

In the strange involution of legalistic processes the case presented to the Supreme Court in the Tennessee Valley litigation came not from a private company claiming to be damaged by federal competition. It was raised by certain holders of stock in a corporation that had made a favorable contract with the Tennessee Valley Authority for the purchase of electric power produced by its plants. Hence the case propounded two questions. Do these plaintiffs have interests adversely affected and enjoy the right to a hearing and adjudication ? If they have a standing in the Court, does the Government of the United States have a constitutional right to build the Wilson dam and enter into a contract with the Alabama Power Company for the sale of surplus energy from the plant and for other auxiliary purposes ? Three possibilities confronted the Court. It could dismiss the stockholders' plea as offering no true case for consideration, thereby postponing the day of judgment. It could assume jurisdiction and give the narrowest possible range to its decision. Or, after assuming jurisdiction it could, for practical purposes, settle the general question of public power development. Often the Court had traveled outside a particular case and prepared the way for broad rulings against the Government. Logically, if not psychologically, the reverse process was possible. Using the immediate Tennessee challenge, the Court could emancipate the Government for the pursuit of its avowed power policy.

Over the first of the questions the Supreme Court was divided five to four. The Chief Justice, who wrote the opinion, was supported by Justices Butler, Sutherland, Van Devanter, and McReynolds. He took the position that the plea presented a true case and that the Court should hear it. Justices Brandeis, Stone, Cardozo, and Roberts dissented, contending that the plaintiffs had no standing in court and that by according them a standing the Court opened the door to all kinds of collusive actions on constitutional grounds. Having assumed jurisdiction, however, the Court considered the second question and by a vote of eight to one decided that Congress had the power to construct the Wilson dam for war purposes and other constitutional ends and to sell surplus power to the Alabama Power Company. Nevertheless in its opinion, the Court hewed close to the narrow line and gave no hint that the fundamentals of the New Deal power program were valid. Though hailed in the White House and recorded in the press as a victory, the decision in itself was at best a dubious victory. In fact it could be considered as a defeat for the administration in that it flung wide the gates for endless litigation and left ample room for invalidating the essentials of the Tennessee Valley program whenever a broader question was raised for adjudication.

Any pleasure produced in the Executive Mansion by the alleged victory in the Tennessee Valley case must have been cooled by the arguments against the Government in the Guffey-Snyder coal case, which closed on March 11; and completely dispelled by a forthright decision against the validity of the law rendered on May 18, after two months of wrangling in the council chamber of the Supreme Court. Like the Tennessee Valley Act, the Bituminous Coal Act affected powerful interests and was the outcome of a long struggle to adjust them. For years the coal industry had been "sick." The competition of oil and hydro-electric plants had injured its markets. The relentless rivalry of mine owners had transformed their business into a cutthroat fight for survival and price slashing had kept the market in turmoil. Warfare among owners and sellers was accompanied by attempts of labor to prevent wage reductions and unemployment, by efforts to uphold standards of living already low and precarious, by strikes, riots, injunctions, strife with coal and iron police, intrigues, and bloodshed. Again and again the diseased industry had been investigated by public commissions. Again and again the conclusion had been reached that nothing short of collective action in the public interest could save it from wreckage, could lift it even partly out of the quagmire of the depression. Everywhere that the coal empire extended, throughout vast sections of the country, from Pennsylvania to the west, south, or north, in all the coal states, the same scenes of misery and degradation were reported. In despair, owners and miners alike had turned to Congress for help and state officials had contributed their pleas. Had there been no politics in coal, the informed opinion of the nation on the need for collective action might have been almost unanimous.

It was in line with no less than nineteen government hearings and investigations of the coal industry that Congress framed the Guffey-Snyder coal bill, which sought to stabilize the industry, adjust production to effective demand, equalize and steady prices, and substitute amicable arrangements with labor for dragging, costly, and sanguinary strikes. In the place of economic violence there was to be coöperation, with protection for the public interest; mutual aid was to mitigate the war of each against all. Familiar with this economic background the Government marshaled a battery of talents to sustain the validity of the Coal Act before the Supreme Court. On the legal side it engaged John Dickinson, Assistant Attorney General, Professor Edward S. Corwin of Princeton University, and Professor Thomas Reed Powell of Harvard, three of the profoundest students of constitutional history and law that the country could boast. Their capacities were supplemented by the ingenuity and knowledge of experts from the Bureau of Mines, especially Frederick Tryon, whose grasp of technical problems was wide and firm. The brief prepared and the argument presented were accordingly an exceptional combination of jurisprudence, economics, and technology. And a dramatic touch was added to the pleadings by the fact that Mr. Dickinson, assigned to deliver the oral argument, was a descendant of a member of the convention that had framed the Constitution of the United States in 1787.

After disposing of the legal preliminaries, the Government's brief devoted seventy-seven pages to "the legislative background" of the Coal Act, accompanied by a large graphic map showing the far-reaching interstate flow of coal from the mining regions affected to all parts of the country. Could anyone deny that every great coal-producing unit covered by the law depended on interstate commerce and was enmeshed in a national net of coal economy? From economics the brief turned to constitutional law. The Act employed the taxing power of Congress to bring producers into coöperation. Was that permissible? In a long schedule, counsel for the Government listed examples of the use of the taxing power for other than mere revenue purposes, and showed how the Supreme Court had repeatedly sustained such actions. Could Congress exercise one of its undoubted powers for a purpose not expressly set forth in the Constitution? The contention that it could not, answered the counsel, " is a fallacy which was early sought to be introduced into our constitutional thinking by opponents of a protective tariff and was answered conclusively and exhaustively by Mr. Justice Story." That was the truth of the matter; and it was a genial hint to at least four members of the Court who were committed to the proposition that a protective tariff was constitutional — a use of the taxing or regulating power for purposes not explicitly mentioned in the Constitution. Perhaps the counsel thought that a love of logic might overcome a love of something else — and resentments as well.

Supplementing the taxing power granted by the Constitution to Congress was that of regulating interstate commerce. On this point the Government brief heaped up citations showing that in many cases, especially under the antitrust laws, the Court had brought under the rubric of interstate commerce various actions connected with local industries that affected the flow of such commerce or burdened it. When miners had struck and tied up local production, they had been set down as interfering with interstate commerce. In such cases industry had not been insulated against federal action and placed entirely under state authority. Again and again strikes had been held to be within the scope of the Sherman Anti-Trust Act or of federal commerce power, on the ground that they were designed, as the Court had once said, to " control the supply entering and moving in interstate commerce, or the price of it in interstate markets." If Congress could act to enforce competition and restrain strikes, why could it not act to promote coöperation and bring about collective bargaining? Such in sum and substance was the Government's central question.

In addition to providing for coöperation among owners and collective bargaining in labor relations, the Coal Act contemplated the establishment of prices, within limits. Recently Justice Roberts had declared in the name of the Court that a New York statute authorizing the fixing of prices for milk was valid; that it did not violate the due process clause of the Fourteenth Amendment. It seemed, then, to counsel for the Government, that, in authorizing the establishment of prices in the coal industry, Congress did not violate the due process clause of the Fifth Amendment limiting federal power.

In support of this proposition they referred to the milk case and to the considerations advanced by Justice Roberts, "which made price fixing for that industry a reasonable and hence legitimate exercise of governmental power and consistent with due process." In his opinion sustaining the New York law, Justice Roberts had employed economics. "During 1932," he had said, "the prices received by farmers for milk were much below the cost of production. . . . The situation of the families of dairy producers had become desperate and called for state aid similar to that afforded the unemployed, if conditions should not improve. . . . Milk is an essential item of diet. . . . The prevalence of unfair and destructive trade practices in the distribution of milk, leading to a demoralization of prices . . . , unrestricted competition aggravated existing evils . . . , the normal law of supply and demand was insufficient to correct maladjustments detrimental to the community." After quoting these passages from Justice Roberts' earlier opinion, counsel for the Government cited parallel passages from official sources showing an almost identical condition of affairs in the coal industry. Logic might carry the Court over from milk to coal.

On the other side, counsel for the plaintiff rested their case largely on legal grounds and gave little attention to economic

or technological matters. They insisted that the coal industry was an intrastate affair and did not come within the scope
of interstate commerce. For this contention they also had the
support of some judicial decisions and applied to their case
the opinion invalidating the National Industrial Recovery
Act and the Agricultural Adjustment Act. The use of the
taxing power for purposes other than revenue-raising, they
maintained, violated the Constitution. For that also there
were judicial precedents. Passing over economic considerations, the counsel branded the Coal Act as an attempt to
establish a planned economy, to unload the troubles of the
coal industry on the Federal Government, to institute federal
control of economic life, and to promote the interests of coal
operators and miners as against the rest of the nation. As far
as the arguments against the Guffey-Snyder law were concerned, the coal industry might have been in a flourishing
state, owners and miners well content, and the Federal
Government merely trying to interfere with a sound economic
order for the purpose of regimentation. Beyond that the
opposition deemed it unnecessary to go. If the reasoning of
the Court in the opinion which invalidated the Recovery Act
still appealed to the Justices who indulged in it, then the Coal
Act, which established "a little NIRA," was also invalid.

Nevertheless when the decision was reached in the coal
case, the Court was not unanimous. Indeed it was split three
ways. A majority composed of five members declared the
entire Coal Act null and void. Congress had provided in the
law that the price-fixing and labor sections were separable
and that the nullification of one need not abrogate the other.
Speaking for the Court, Justice Sutherland refused, however,
to accept the dictum of Congress. He found the two sections
to be so entangled that when the labor provisions were thrown
out they carried along the price-fixing provisions. In respect
of the labor provisions, he was categorical: "The [labor] controversies and evils which it is the object of the Act to
regulate and minimize are local controversies and evils
affecting local work undertaken to accomplish that local

result." But Chief Justice Hughes was not entirely satisfied. Although he went with the majority in nullifying the labor provisions of the Act, he separated from them in the matter of the price-fixing provisions. For the latter he found constitutional warrant. If nothing could be done for labor under the Constitution, something might be done for mine-owners in the way of regimenting their prices. Wages might be local but prices even at the mine's mouth might be a part of interstate commerce.

To the surprise of logicians who had read the opinions of the Court in the National Industrial Recovery case, Justices Stone, Brandeis, and Cardozo dissented all along the line in the coal case, and insisted on postponing the consideration of the labor provision. In the former case all the Justices had apparently agreed that the regulation of wages was a local matter, under the authority of the states, not Congress, and had implied that the regulation of industry was also local. In this case three Justices united in sustaining the validity of all parts of the Coal Act properly before the Court. Justice Cardozo wrote their opinion. Dealing with the economics of the issue he said: "Overproduction was at a point where free competition had been degraded into anarchy. . . . There were strikes . . . with the accompaniment of violence and bloodshed and misery and bitter feeling." The price-fixing provisions of the law, he held, were clearly within the power of Congress to regulate, promote, and protect the flow of interstate commerce. As a matter of hard fact, "the complainant has admitted that 'substantially all' (over $97\frac{1}{2}$ per cent) of the sales of the Carter Company are made in interstate commerce." Turning to the labor provisions of the Coal Act, Justice Cardozo drew attention to the fact that the issue was not before the Court. "What the code will provide as to wages and hours of labor, or whether it will provide anything, is still in the domain of prophecy. . . . The complainants have been crying before they are really hurt." The validity of the labor clauses he desired to postpone to the day when it could be properly reviewed.

When the three-forked thunderbolt fell in the Court room on May 18, 1936, one thing was clear amid the confusion : the Court had nullified the entire Coal Act. Lawyers for the plaintiff rejoiced. Foes of the New Deal were convinced that one more spike had been driven into the coffin of this spectre and that preparations could be confidently made for the funeral services after the autumn election. Gloom settled over the lawyers for the Government. The Court had informed them that the high and rock-ribbed barrier of the Constitution stood in the way of the "progress" they were promoting. In the White House, silence reigned. Was it the silence of resignation or the calm of meditation and planning ?

Everything done that day was not done in the Palace of Justice. Masters in the coal industry and governors of great coal states had favored the Coal Act and were still resolved to overcome the anarchy of the business by coöperative processes. Labor too had a continuing interest. The hard-bitten leader of many a coal battle, John L. Lewis, did not embrace the victor in jurisprudence. "It is a tragic and ominous commentary on our form of government," he said, "when every decision of the Supreme Court seems designed to fatten capital and starve and destroy labor." And, unlike the opinions of the Supreme Court, Mr. Lewis' opinion was not mere law, logic, and rhetoric. A few months later it took the form of a $469,870 contribution from the United Mine Workers of America to the campaign fund for the reëlection of President Roosevelt. However powerful they were, whatever their inclinations, members of the Supreme Court could not duplicate that performance.

§

As things stood on the afternoon of May 18, 1936, the regulation of wages and labor conditions in industry appeared to be a right reserved to the states. Two weeks passed. On June 1, the Supreme Court, by another five to four vote, declared invalid the New York State minimum wage law for

women. The opinion of the majority, written by Justice
Butler and approved by Justice Roberts, who had upheld
the power of New York to fix milk prices, was so comprehensive in its terms as to close the door against all wage regulation, state or federal. On his side Justice Butler produced a
load of authority. He cited decisions of the Supreme Court
nullifying previous state wage laws and invalidating an act
of Congress that provided for minimum wage standards in the
District of Columbia. The fact that the New York law
immediately under consideration varied in terms from the
other statutes which had been set aside made no difference
in his reasoning. In the District of Columbia case, Justice
Butler said, "it was held that Congress was without power
to deal with the subject at all." And the ruling in that case
applied also to state laws however conceived or framed to
accomplish the same purpose. Such statutes, too, violated
the freedom of competition and contract — in relation to
employment guaranteed by the Fourteenth Amendment.
The prescribing of minimum wages for women "would
unreasonably restrain them in competition with men and
tend arbitrarily to deprive them of employment and a fair
chance to find work." If a strict respect for the immediately relevant precedents cited was controlling on June 1,
1936, then Justice Butler's decision and opinion reposed on
strong foundations.

But Chief Justice Hughes, in this instance, did not accept
the version of the majority. He found the ends of the New
York statute legitimate, the means appropriate, the Act
constitutional. This contention he rested mainly on the
ground that the law differed in principle and administration
from minimum wage laws previously held invalid by the
Court. Hence the New York statute could be sustained without repudiating and reversing earlier doctrines of the high
tribunal. "The constitutional validity of a minimum wage
statute like the New York Act," he stated, "has not hitherto
been passed upon by this Court." The Chief Justice pointed
out the features which distinguished the District of Columbia

law from the Act immediately under consideration : "We have here a question of constitutional law of grave importance, applying to the statutes of several states in a matter of profound public interest. I think that we should deal with that question upon its merits, without feeling that we are bound by a decision which on its facts is not strictly in point." Turning from the technicalities of the law, the Chief Justice referred to " the seriousness of the social problem " presented by the statistics of low wages and to the heavy burden thrown upon the taxpayers by the necessity of supplementing wages by payments from the public relief agencies. The issue might be, theoretically, one of mere law to the majority; to the Chief Justice it presented aspects of humanity.

Justices Stone, Cardozo, and Brandeis agreed with the Chief Justice in upholding the statute before them but declined to make the difference between the New York law and the District of Columbia law the basis of decision. For these dissenters, Justice Stone wrote the separate opinion. "I attach little importance to the fact," he declared, "that the earlier statute was aimed only at a starvation wage and that the present one does not prohibit such a wage unless it is also less than the reasonable value of the service." He did not think that " the vague and general pronouncement of the Fourteenth Amendment" required any such fine-spun distinctions. "There is grim irony in speaking of the freedom of contract of those who, because of their economic necessities, give their services for less than is needful to keep body and soul together." The language of the Amendment did not prevent legislation deemed reasonable and appropriate for dealing with any of those matters of public concern with which it is the business of government to deal. Is the principle of the New York law reasonable ? This question Justice Stone answered by citing the legislation of Congress, of seventeen states, and of twenty-one foreign countries, including Great Britain and the four Commonwealths. Such a legislative demonstration "precludes for me any assumption that it is a remedy beyond the bounds of reason."

How, then, could the majority of the Justices take the opposite view? Justice Stone answered: "It is difficult to imagine any grounds, other than our own personal economic predilections. . . . The Fourteenth Amendment has no more embedded in the Constitution our preference for some particular set of economic beliefs than it has adopted, in the name of liberty, the system of theology which we may happen to approve." The New York statute was reasonable. The Fourteenth Amendment, unless twisted to cover a system of economics, did not forbid it.

There were, moreover, among the Court's own rulings, many precedents to sustain the Act. Justice Stone cited them, laying special emphasis on the Nebbia case in which Justice Roberts, a short time before, had upheld a New York law that authorized the fixing of prices for milk. This decision certainly allowed government interference with freedom of contract and the autonomy of the marketplace. In his judicial opinion Justice Roberts had said that, as far as the Fourteenth Amendment was concerned, "a state is free to adopt whatever economic policy may reasonably be deemed to promote public welfare and to enforce that policy by legislation adapted to its purpose." Surely, if a state could interfere with freedom of contract in buying and selling milk, it could interfere with freedom of contract in the matter of buying and selling the labor of human beings confronted with the problem of keeping soul and body together.

So it seemed to Justice Stone. The declaration and decision in the milk case, he thought, should control the Court in the wages case. "They are irreconcilable with the decision and most that was said in the Adkins case" — the District of Columbia case. "They have left the Court free of its restriction as a precedent, and free to declare that the choice of the particular form of regulation by which grave economic maladjustments are to be remedied is for legislatures and not for the courts. . . . We should follow our decision in the Nebbia case and leave the selection and the method of the solution of the problems to which the statute is addressed where it seems to me the Constitution has left them, to the legislative branch of the government." In substance Justice Stone took the reasoning of Justice Roberts in the milk case at face value, applied it to wages as well as to milk prices, and employed it to wipe out the tangle of economic theories incorporated in previous opinions on wage legislation. He did not propose to reverse the old opinions. In effect, he maintained, they had been reversed by the Court itself in the milk case and the door had been opened for such social legislation as reasonable persons might deem appropriate to the solution of basic economic problems. By inviting Justice Roberts to examine his own record, by attributing the strict view of the majority to economic predilections, by taking down the bars set up by the Court against such social legislation, Justice Stone presented the real issues that divided the Court and the country. His strong and muscular English admitted no double interpretation.

§

However considered as a pronouncement in law, the decision of the Supreme Court in the minimum wage case struck into sentiments that had long been expressed in contests over such social legislation and were to count heavily in the approaching presidential campaign. Intransigent feminists had fiercely objected to wage regulation that applied merely to women, considered as a sex so weak as to require special protection. They did not oppose legislative measures applicable to men and women alike. What they especially feared was that minimum wages, if binding on women alone, would become maximum wages for women or would in fact, as some experience had indicated, drive women out of many employments and make their plight worse than before. Although, on different grounds, manufacturing and other private interests rejoiced with the irreconcilable feminists in the decision of the Supreme Court invalidating the New York statute, the action of the Court aroused intense hostility. For years

COURT, CONGRESS, AND PRESIDENT 285

innumerable men and women had striven to secure protective
legislation for women in industry against the opposition of
employers; now their labors had been declared vain by the
Court and a constitutional barrier had been set up against
all such forms of protectionism.

As a climax to the Court's work for the season, the minimum wage decision presented vexatious features to those
politicians who imagined that they could make the constitutional division correspond to the partisan division in the
presidential campaign. Republicans in general had praised
the Supreme Court for invalidating New Deal statutes and
had sought to identify President Roosevelt's policies with
assaults on the Constitution and with attacks on "the independence of the judiciary." In fact it had been the fashion
for newspapers to treat judicial decisions in the language of
the sporting page and to speak of "victories" and "knock
outs." After the defeat administered to the Guffey-Snyder
coal law, The New York Times summed up the play to date
under the heading, "Court's New Deal Score." In the great
controversies of the law, the New Deal had been twice upheld,
once ambiguously, and eight times repudiated, all unquestionably and on major issues.

But the minimum wage decision did not run against any
policy peculiar to the New Deal. For many years Republicans as well as Democrats, spurred on by women who
championed the idea of improving the weak economic position of their sex by law, had sponsored such legislation applicable to women and children. Out of the Court's adverse
ruling no mere partisan case could be made. Nor did the
foes of the Roosevelt administration venture to celebrate
it as a triumph of constitutionalism over haste, waste, folly,
and communism. Even to them it did not demonstrate the
inerrancy of judicial decisions — the truth of the proposition
that the Supreme Court could never be wrong in its constitutional interpretations. If it could be wrong in one case, why
not in another or many others?

For politicians who hoped to make a clear-cut constitu-

tional issue in the coming campaign, the decision in the
New York case was rendered all the more troublesome by the
dissent of the Chief Justice. It is true that minimum wage
legislation affected mainly small employers, the owners of
laundries, petty concerns, and sweatshops, that it touched
adversely few powerful business interests; still, in respect of
the constitutional question, that made no difference. Either
the judges knew the Constitution and interpreted the document correctly or they might be wrong all along the line in
glossing the vague language of the fundamental law. Now,
at the end of a season in which the Court had ruled almost
uniformly against the New Deal, the Chief Justice had
dissented from the decision and opinion put forward by the
majority. His language had been restrained. He had not
attributed to them economic predilections. He had not even
suggested that they tortured the Constitution by reading
their own theories into its language. He had stuck close to
the technics of jurisprudence. But the general public was
not given to making subtle distinctions in its judgments. It
understood simply that the Chief Justice had declared the
majority to be wrong in its constitutional law. Even The
New York Times, never associated with revolutionary ideas
save in the historical sense, said editorially that the minimum wage decision "is unfortunate in more than one
respect."

Events had so shaped affairs that at the very end of the
judicial season, at the very opening of the presidential campaign, the issue of "saving the Constitution" was blurred for
party managers by a decision and opinion in a matter that
was of slight concern to the major economic interests. Up to
that time the Supreme Court had declared the New Deal
unconstitutional in eight "first-rate" cases, sustained it
actually in one gold-clause case, and given it limited approval
in the Tennessee Valley case. Yet when analyzed, the
"score" was not as perfect as it looked on its surface. In only
one major case against the New Deal had the opinion of the
Court, as distinguished from the decision, been unanimous,

and that opinion dealt with the farm mortgage moratorium which President Roosevelt had not officially sponsored. In four of the eight vital decisions against the administration, the Court had been divided in opinion either seven to two, six to three, or five to four. Where doctors of equal learning and competence differed about a major operation, the patients and their intimate friends could hardly avoid making choices. While readers of sporting pages and helpers at filling stations probably did not go into such recondite matters as "the reasoning necessary to the decision of the case," they could scarcely scan newspapers without noting that the "score" of the Supreme Court was a subject of animated debate. Added to the disagreement in the minimum wage case, the divisions of the Court in official New Deal cases made it impossible for political engineers to make the Constitution of the United States exactly identical with the constitution of the Republican party. Even men and women of little learning could easily discover discrepancies in any such hypothesis.

Yet in the early summer of 1936 the jubilation of Roosevelt's critics was almost rapturous. Huge and fundamental sections of the New Deal had been declared invalid and, if there was strict logic in the reasoning of the majority of the judges, other sections awaiting trial were also foredoomed to destruction. Powerful economic interests, affected by actions of Congress and the President, had sought and received ultimate protection at the hands of the Supreme Court under the aegis of the Constitution, so difficult to amend. Nothing seemed to remain save the obituary of the New Deal and the vindication of the Supreme Court in the coming referendum.

§

While the Supreme Court, proceeding from its own major premises, was crushing New Deal measures in the logic of law and critics of the New Deal were celebrating, the Roosevelt administration kept on its course, promoting new legislation although somewhat bewildered by the mazes of constitutional law. Whether deemed magnificent or petty, the exercise of negative functions by the Court left the positive responsibilities of governing with the President and Congress. Though the Court had spoken, the problem of unemployment remained immense and pressing. And in his message of January 4, 1935, President Roosevelt had formulated a more systematic policy for dealing with this dilemma. Among the prime objectives of the administration he placed security of livelihood through the better use of natural resources, security against the major hazards of life, and security for homes. He proposed that the Government quit the "business of relief," restore to states and communities the care of the feeble and dependent, and provide work for able-bodied men and women still excluded from opportunities in private enterprise.

For guidance in the provision of public employment, the President laid down seven principles : all work must be useful ; compensation must be above the dole level and yet not high enough to discourage individuals from entering private employment ; projects should be chosen with a view to employing directly a large amount of labor ; projects should compete as little as possible with private business ; arrangements should be made for tapering off public work as rapidly as private enterprise could absorb the unemployed ; the location of projects should be determined with reference to the amount of local unemployment and the plans devised by the National Resources Board. In response Congress authorized the appropriation of $4,800,000,000 for relief and unemployment. The supervision of expenditures was vested in the Works Progress Administration, headed by Harry Hopkins who assumed the duty of organizing work projects and handling the remaining subsidies for local relief.

Considered in terms of financial responsibility and human needs, the Works Progress Administration was a stupendous enterprise, beset by almost insurmountable obstacles. Millions of unemployed had to be classified according to talents,

aptitudes, and previous training. Their geographical distribution had to be determined, connections established with
state and local agencies, projects created for the several
occupations, supervisors engaged, and the numerous undertakings scrutinized. Nothing of the kind had ever been done
anywhere on such a scale and in such a spirit. That private
interests, local politicians, and petty parasites would seek to
fasten themselves upon the enterprise was to be expected.
The possibility that it would be used to build up machines
for the Democratic party in every community in the country
was recognized. Indeed suggestions that a non-partisan or
bi-partisan administration be instituted were made early in
the history of the experiment. But, apart from all such
knowledge and from the issue of wisdom or unwisdom in
attempting public relief, millions of people were, in glaring
truth, unemployed and without the means of livelihood.
The Works Progress Administration represented a national
effort to avoid the mere dole, to overcome the moral degradation and the deterioration of skills associated with prolonged
idleness, and to provide occupations offering a semblance of
self-respect. In any case the Federal Government had moved
far way from the policies pursued in previous panics and
depressions.

Associated in spirit with the assumption of immediate
responsibility for the unemployed, but looking to the future,
was the enactment of the Social Security law of August 14,
1935. By this measure Congress set up the framework for a
national system of old-age and unemployment insurance,
rounded out a national scheme for old-age pensions, and made
various provisions for health, welfare, and security, in coöperation with the states. For the attainment of its objectives,
Congress exercised its powers of taxation and appropriation.
To create a fund from which to pay old-age insurance to
certain classes of persons over sixty-five years of age, it laid
a tax on employers and employees, beginning in 1937 and
supplying accumulations to be drawn upon in and after 1942.
Provision for insurance against unemployment, for the bene-

fit of given classes of employees and for fixed periods of time, was made by the imposition of a federal excise tax on the payrolls of employers. The tax, however, was a mere device to compel the states to act, for it was stipulated that whenever a state created a system of unemployment insurance, within the frame of the national law, employers could make substantial deductions from the federal levy. Likewise conditional were the terms of the Act pertaining to old-age pensions. These terms authorized federal grants to states, up to the amount of fifteen dollars a month per person, for the purpose of encouraging state governments to give pensions to all needy individuals over sixty-five years of age, with the sum of thirty dollars a month regarded as the standard. In other words the Federal Government matched state grants, dollar for dollar, up to the maximum allowance and thus offered a stimulus to old-age pension legislation that had been developing in various parts of the country over a period of many years.

While efforts were made during the consideration of the social security measure to secure the adoption of a health insurance program, Congress was not ready for that experiment, especially in view of the hostility exhibited by members of the medical profession. In formulating the Act, Congress limited the scope of its general welfare clauses to specific grants to the states. It gave them aid in providing for needy and dependent children, promoting the health of mothers and children, especially in areas of economic distress, furnishing medical services for crippled children, maintaining public health services, and caring for homeless and neglected children. Admittedly defective in many respects, economically fantastic in authorizing the accumulation of enormous reserves in the Federal Treasury for insurance purposes, the Act none the less went a long way towards establishing some safeguards against awful hazards of fortune for approximately twenty million people. While criticized on one side for the extent of its range, it was attacked on another side for omitting millions of persons, such as employees in small concerns, domestic servants, and agricultural laborers from the insurance benefits of the law.

Treating railway employees as a special group, Congress established for them an independent pension system. After the Supreme Court invalidated in May, 1935, the pension act of the previous year, Congress sought an escape around the barrier imposed by the judicial decision. The earlier law had provided that revenues for the railway pension fund should be derived from contributions made by employers and employees. It was against this arrangement that the Court directed objections especially emphatic. Blocked in one maneuver, Congress resorted to another. By one act it granted the pension and by a second act it laid a tax on railways to provide funds for the Federal Treasury which had to foot the pension bill. It authorized the payment of graduated pensions to employees who had reached the age of sixty-five and had seen thirty years of service or had been retired for physical or mental disability.

While the social security program was still in process of formulation, President Roosevelt called on Congress on June 19, 1935, in a special message, to revise the federal tax system with a view to accelerating the movement "toward progressive taxation of wealth and of income" and "encouraging a wider distribution of wealth." Implying that wealth is not the pure fruit of individual talent and labor, the President declared: "Wealth in the modern world does not come merely from individual effort; it results from a combination of individual effort and of the manifold uses to which the community puts that effort. . . . The people in the mass have inevitably helped to make large fortunes possible. . . . The ownership of wealth represents a great public interest and a great ability to pay. . . . Our revenue laws have operated in many ways to the unfair advantage of the few, and they have done little to prevent an unjust concentration of wealth and power. . . . Social unrest and a deepening sense of unfairness are dangers to our national life which we must minimize by rigorous methods." On the basis of this social philosophy, the President suggested a heavy tax on large inheritances and on large incomes and a graduated tax on corporation incomes.

The tax message fell with a splash in the very center of national politics. In appropriate quarters it was called just a scheme for "soaking the rich." In other quarters, equally appropriate, it was hailed as a forward step toward "social justice." Senator Huey Long, then driving ahead with his share-our-wealth campaign and attacking the administration on the left flank, addressed an open letter to President Roosevelt commending this proposal. The Senator admitted that the wind had been taken out of his sails but declared consistently that if the plan were enacted into law he would "take 200,000 share-our-wealth clubs" straight into the New Deal camp. With the campaign of 1936 creeping on, this proffer of help was not to be treated as a trifle.

Other Senators, more realistic in outlook, thought the occasion fitting to reconsider the federal tax structure from top to bottom. Senator La Follette, for example, insisted that mere heavy taxes on large incomes and inheritances would not yield a revenue commensurate with the amount of political noise raised by the suggestion, nor go far toward curing the growing disease in the national budget. He countered, therefore, with a proposition to broaden the foundation of the income and inheritance taxes, to carry the tax line far down into the ranks of the middle class, and to produce revenues befitting the continuing expenditures. In the end, however, Senator La Follette was overborne. Congress did no more than raise the rates on large estates and on high incomes, make levies on the "excess profits" of corporations, tax inter-corporate dividends, and increase the rates on personal holding companies. As a revenue producer, the Act worked no wonders. As a stick to beat off the storm troops of Senator Long and Father Coughlin, it was not without force.

Among the agencies contributing to the concentration of wealth, against which the new tax program was directed, were holding companies, especially in the field of electrical utilities. Their growth and extension had been rapid in the days of the golden glow and then some of them had exploded in the days of the dissolutions, scattering casualties among millions of trusting investors. Congressional investigations had laid bare many of the questionable methods employed by financiers in promoting these corporate leviathans and had disseminated the suspicion that their sponsors had often been imprudent and in some cases deceptive, if not clearly dishonest. By the summer of 1935, the Federal Trade Commission had published in many volumes the testimony gathered during its inquiry into electrical utilities — testimony showing practices from which honorable persons might well shrink, practices intended to deceive the public, defeat reasonable legislation, and augment private profits at the consumers' expense. Persons acquainted with the documents bearing on holding companies, in particular President Roosevelt, his advisers, and informed members of Congress, knew very well that the facts in the business invited remedial action. Indeed none save the most prejudiced witnesses could dispute the necessity of federal intervention. Accordingly there was little excuse for surprise when Roosevelt put the regulation of holding companies on his program for legislation in the summer of 1935.

Shortly after the holding-company bill came before the Senate, a provision was inserted in the text calling for the dissolution by 1940 of all "intermediate concerns," that is, for an excision of many superstructures erected upon operating companies. This proposition, loosely called "the death sentence" by critics, raised a terrible din. Telegrams and letters deluged Senators and Representatives; lobbyists descended upon Washington in protest; but under the pressure of the Executive, a majority was mustered in the Senate for the measure carrying the death sentence. More amenable to the demands of critics, the House broke out in revolt and refused to approve the objectionable clause. Only after a spectacular debate, in which emotions dominated ideas, could party managers, led by Senator Burton K. Wheeler and Representative Sam Rayburn, force the House to accept the Senate's verdict against intermediate holding companies.

As finally drawn, the Holding Company Act reached out in two directions. It vested in the Federal Power Commission the authority to regulate the rates, facilities, and security issues of concerns engaged in the interstate transmission of electrical power. It stipulated that, at the end of three years, super-holding companies must be dissolved; that such corporations were thereafter to limit their operations to "single integrated systems and the business directly connected with the supply of power service to consumers." One exception was made to this rule: a holding company might continue to exist if necessary to tie together a group of operating power plants in a single region and to promote efficient operation. Inevitably the "securities" of flimsy structures sank to a low level on the stock exchanges. One section of the great American rainbow appeared to be beyond hope of restoration.

Another application of the common-law doctrine that industries affected with public interest are subject to special regulation was also made in August, 1935. For several years motor trucks and buses had been engaged in interstate traffic, utilizing the magnificent highway systems built at public expense. As usual individuals and companies rushed into the business, cutting rates, furnishing various types of service from good to bad, and often exhibiting an inability to pay damages for the destruction of lives and freight in accidents. In some respects the early history of railway transportation was repeated.

As motor traffic swelled in proportions, railways felt the keen edge of competition and lodged protests with Congress. They were strictly regulated; they could not slash rates or dodge financial responsibility; and they were heavily taxed. A large portion of their revenues went into the public treasuries from which flowed money to pay for the construction of highways. Shippers and passengers who had grievances against truck and bus lines joined their laments to the objections of railway companies. All this agitation had been going on for years, when in August, 1935, Congress took action and placed interstate buses and trucks under the Interstate Commerce Commission. It required such common carriers to secure certificates of convenience from the Commission before engaging in operations. It empowered the Commission to regulate the rates, services, issuance of securities, safety appliances, and hours of labor in this branch of transportation. In short, it put motor transportation on about the same footing as interstate commerce by rail.

A respectable tradition lent sanction to the regulation of industries affected with public interest, and shippers, passengers, and consumers approved that form of government intervention on their behalf. Government aided business with subsidies, provided tariffs for special industries, and protected property; and beneficiaries usually commended each transgression of the "natural order." A tradition that approved government interference with labor relations was also in process of development. In early days state courts had intervened to outlaw labor organizations and to penalize strikes. Gradually, over a long period of years, this practice was modified by legislation and judicial interpretations; and at length the formation of trade unions, collective bargaining, and the conduct of strikes became lawful within certain limitations, statutory and judicial. From a position of negative tolerance, circumscribed if in many respects generous, government moved to a position of positive control in the promotion of bargaining in labor relations. If direct intervention was proper in the interests of business enterprise, why not in the interests of labor? Logic offered no prohibition and the course of events, through its own compulsion, suggested an affirmative answer.

A place within the framework of law, in statutory language at least, had been given to organized labor by the Clayton Anti-Trust Act of 1914, passed during the administration of President Wilson. Lines of protection were still more firmly drawn by the Norris-La Guardia Anti-injunction Act, signed by President Hoover in 1932. This measure expressly stipulated that thenceforth workers were free to organize, choose their own representatives, and negotiate with respect to terms and conditions of employment. By the same Act the circumstances in which injunctions could be issued in labor disputes were strictly defined. And all this was done in order that workers "shall be free from the interference, restraint, or coercion of employers of labor, or their agents, in the designation of such representatives or in self-organization, or in other concerted activities for the purpose of collective bargaining or other mutual aid or protection." When the draftsmen of the National Industrial Recovery Act, in the following year, sought precedents for the clause on collective bargaining, they had only to turn to the Norris-La Guardia law and the debates in Congress for illumination and guidance. They made nothing new, out of whole cloth, in a vacuum.

Nor did the labor movement stop on the day that the Supreme Court abrogated the labor codes drawn up under the National Industrial Recovery Act. Nor was the conduct of collective bargaining relegated to the domain of private negotiation. The Clayton Act and the Norris-La Guardia Act still stood on the books. The organization of labor proceeded. And on July 5, 1935, a few weeks after the decision of the Court in the Recovery case, Congress added to the older statutes the Wagner-Connery Labor Relations Act. The new law declared that it was the policy of the United States to protect the free flow of interstate commerce by encouraging and safeguarding workers in forming associations, electing representatives, and carrying on the practice of collective bargaining. The policy so announced was then expressed in terms of positive provisions. If amazing to readers not grounded in history, it was in reality a mere affirmation of accepted legal doctrine. To the declaration of right, however, Congress added guarantees and an agency of enforcement. It forbade employers to interfere with or dominate any labor organization, such as a company union, or to refuse to bargain collectively with their employees. The administration of the Act was intrusted to the National Labor Relations Board, composed of three members, appointed by the President and the Senate. That judicial safeguards might accompany proceedings, "cease and desist" orders of the Board were made subject to judicial review. Thus an administrative agency, under judicial control, set about guaranteeing to laborers specific rights in reference to organization and collective bargaining.

In matters of procedure, the Wagner-Connery Act went beyond the labor section of the Recovery Act which the Supreme Court had invalidated. It left untouched, however, the determination of hours and wages. Responding to pressures that survived the judicial decree, Congress hunted loopholes in the close-knit texture of the judicial reasoning and was not long in finding one. The Federal Government was among industry's greatest consumers, its purchases ranging from thumb tacks to battleships. Presumably it had the power to prescribe the conditions under which its purchases were produced. So, at all events, Congress thought, for in 1936 it passed the Walsh-Healey Government Contracts Act, laying down labor terms for all producers who made contracts with the Federal Government involving amounts in excess of $10,000. Such contractors were required to pay not less than the prevailing rate of wages in the locality — in general the trade union rate; they were to maintain an eight-hour day and a forty-hour week; and they were forbidden to employ boys under sixteen years of age and girls under eighteen. In substance this law attempted to establish, within given areas of industrial enterprise, minimum standards of employment, such as the Supreme Court had destroyed the previous year in overthrowing the Recovery Act. As a supplement, Congress, by the Air Transport Labor Act of 1936, extended similar controls to common carriers by air and to all carriers engaged in transporting air mail.

As the record stood when Congress adjourned on June 21, 1936, after appropriating during its life the breath-taking sum of more than twenty billion dollars, including authorization for the payment of the Veterans' Bonus in cash, the public had notice that the adverse decisions of the Supreme Court had put no tight brake on executive intentions or legislative policies. The President had beaten no retreat. Congress had left unpassed no major measure up for consideration. It was demonstrated that judicial intervention in the course of political affairs had not stopped the movement of secular history — as the people prepared to pass judgment on the New Deal in November.

CHAPTER VII

Appeals to the Ultimate Power

THE earth turned and amid the eternal dying and becoming, which are phases of human history as well as the history of all organic life, the season came for a popular appraisal of the New Deal and a verdict upon its authors, its critics, and its future. This democratic process was provided by the Constitution to which all paid homage. Although Chief Justice Hughes, speaking as a lawyer, had declared that the Constitution is what the judges say it is, the dictum was not all-comprehensive. Before his appointment a wit had remarked that the Supreme Court follows the election returns. There was some truth in that maxim also, and yet not the whole truth. Still further back in American history the substance of the business was more correctly and solemnly described by Thomas Cooley, once a member of the Michigan Supreme Court and universally regarded as among the three or four truly great commentators on constitutional law that the country had produced, ranking with Kent and Story if not above them. Speaking of the written document, Judge Cooley remarked: "We may think that we have the Constitution all before us; but for practical purposes the Constitution is that which the Government in its several departments and the people in the performance of their duties as citizens recognize and respect as such; and nothing else is. . . . It represents at last the acts done under it." The President, Congress, and the Supreme Court had discharged their duties as they were given to see them. In the summer and autumn of 1936, citizens were to perform their duties, working their thoughts and their verdicts into the structure of the Constitution as acts "done under it."

§

In the process of appraising and deciding, personalities as well as laws, judicial opinions, and economic practices entered into consideration. This too was history. The greater the contingency, the broader the opportunity for the personality. That had been true in the days when Napoleon liquidated the French revolution into tyranny and when George Washington devoted his talents and energies to carrying the American revolution through the trial at arms to a settlement under the Constitution. It was still true. The New Deal was personified in President Roosevelt, affectionately called in wide circles "F. D." and in a circle more intimate "the Chief." Did the Republican opposition have at command a personality competent to enlist the interests, express the ideas, and consolidate the sentiments necessary to victory?

Ex-president Hoover was available. Yet, however distinguished his qualities, he had never been popular with the working politicians of his party and running against him were the memories of the panic that had come upon the country during his administration. Martin Van Buren, with all his personal charm and political skill, had not been able to recover power after the economic disaster of 1837. It was no more likely that Herbert Hoover, if regarded as an unfortunate victim of history, could accomplish in 1936 a feat which had not been achieved in the previous campaigns that had followed panics. In private relations, Hoover excited warm loyalties. On the public hustings he lacked magnetism. Over the radio he gripped few hearts. Even the experience of eight years had effected no profound alteration in his thought or his powers of cognition, making him more competent as a leader for the campaign of 1936.

In sheer prestige, of course, no regular Republican was comparable to Hoover. His former Secretary of the Treasury, Ogden Mills, possessed talents and energy, but he was a symbol of great wealth in a country that still had six or eight million unemployed men and women and with unshakeable tenacity he clung to the attitudes of 1928. To Ogden Mills supple adaptation to changing environment was a form of inconsistency and instability and, in standing still, he invited neglect. The rock of Gibraltar might be majestic, but human history was not so geologic in nature, if equally inexorable. At the opposite end of the party was Senator William E. Borah, generally regarded as progressive in tendencies. During the upheavals of other times, Borah had remained formally in the path of party regularity while displaying all kinds of irregularities in opinions and practices. As a life-long critic of great riches and concentrated industries, he had appealed to the little man in Republican ranks. On such grounds, he was classified as a radical by the Respectability. That epithet he accepted. Declaring that he intended to break the hold of the Old Guard on his party, the Senator allowed himself to be put forward as an aspirant for the nomination and was valiantly supported by Hamilton Fish, a member of the House of Representatives, who had thus far won renown principally as a "red-baiter." But Borah was old and, though still dynamic, was beyond the age line for strenuous campaigning.

Among the younger dignitaries of the Republican party Senator Arthur Vandenberg of Michigan, reëlected despite the Democratic landslide of 1934, was considered a potential candidate. In political philosophy Vandenberg claimed to be a follower of Alexander Hamilton and an exponent of the

doctrines laid down in the Federalist. In a volume entitled
Alexander Hamilton, The Greatest American, published
years before, the Senator had nominated Hamilton for that
exalted position, apparently above Washington and Lincoln.
The first Secretary of the Treasury was, he declared, "the
Master Builder of the indissoluble Union, the Gladiator who
saved the Constitution, the Founder of Public Credit, the
Architect of Policies and Institutions, the inspired Oracle of
sound American Purpose and Necessity, the Intrepid Soldier,
the Great Economist, the Most Brilliant Author, the Most
Fascinating Orator, and the Foremost Legal Luminary of his
time." This work on Hamilton, and other writings, had
helped to rank Vandenberg among "the leading statesmen
and thinkers of Michigan."

After the crisis of 1933 came upon the land, the Senator
recalled the days when Hamilton and Jefferson had been
united in Washington's cabinet and, in remembrance of their
joint labors, he had proposed a coalition of Democrats and
Republicans to overcome the forces of economic dissolution.
Failing in that objective, he supported several New Deal
measures in the Senate, including the Stock Exchange Act
and the Social Security Act, and thus revealed progressive
inclinations, while asserting the right to independent criticism. Having left the school of Die Hards without passing
the center line, Senator Vandenberg was talked about for the
presidency in 1936, but his candidacy was not pressed. Did
he smell the smoke of immediate defeat and retreat in preparation for 1940?

While Republican negotiators were casting about for the
right personality as leader, a figure rose out of the plains,
Governor Alfred M. Landon of Kansas. He too had escaped
the Democratic landslide in his own state and thus achieved
a reputation for exceptional talents. As governor he had been
prudent and industrious though he had displayed no qualities
of spectacular genius that in themselves attracted national
attention. Had fortune not favored him, Landon might have
encountered the fate of many competent governors who had

shone locally for a season on the way from obscurity to oblivion. But his neighbors thought he had the calibre of executive leadership and local newspapers spoke of him as the right man to break the entanglements of the New Deal and lead America into another period of "sanity and prosperity."

Reports flew beyond the borders of Kansas and reached William Randolph Hearst, then politically disgruntled. Unable to control President Roosevelt, he had broken away from the New Deal early in its course and flung diatribes against it in his customary style. After casting about on all sides for a man who could oust President Roosevelt from the White House, Hearst came to the conclusion that Governor Landon offered the best chance. He visited the Governor in person and afterward let loose a torrent of publicity in favor of "the strong, silent man of Kansas." Almost over night, the Governor was built up as a national paragon, with the aid of Hearst's call to his millions of readers.

Two possibilities lay before the promoters of Governor Landon's candidacy for the nomination. They could present him in the role of "the Coolidge from Kansas," as he was sometimes called, make a bid for the support of conservative Democrats already forsaking their party standard, and launch a frontal attack on the New Deal all along the line. Such tactics were not entirely fanciful, for Mr. Landon had been a business man — an independent oil producer; he had amassed a small fortune; and as Governor he had been an apostle of economy, while the Federal Government poured millions into Kansas for the relief of farmers and the unemployed. The second possibility was to present him as bidding for the approval of the progressives who had flocked in large numbers to Franklin D. Roosevelt's camp. This project, too, had merits, for in 1912 Landon had forsaken Republicans of the Old Guard and joined the insurrection led by Theodore Roosevelt. Emphasis could easily be laid on that aspect of his political career. In the end, apparently through the good offices of William Allen White, the progressive tack was taken, effectively but not brusquely enough to frighten off those who preferred the image of Calvin Coolidge.

In either role, however, Governor Landon found difficulties arising from the propaganda of his leading publicizer, William Randolph Hearst. Innumerable conservative Republicans regarded Hearst as the unregenerate Catiline of 1901. To progressive Republicans he was no less offensive, for his press daily vilified everything that savored of "liberalism." Unwilling to cast off Hearst, as William Allen White urged, Governor Landon took the incubus along with the supposed aid and carried it through the convention and the campaign.

§

When the Republicans assembled in convention at Cleveland early in June only one bond united all hearts. That was opposition to President Roosevelt and all his works — an opposition ruled by fear and hatred. In seconding the nomination of Governor Landon, Senator Vandenberg voiced this antagonism: "I belong to but one bloc and it has but one slogan — stop Roosevelt." The will to revolt was expressed even more emphatically in an address by Hoover, who condemned Roosevelt and the New Deal in implacable language and called for a holy war on them both, amid the deafening cheers of the delegates. But, if united in condemnation of action already taken, the Republicans were divided in respect of future action. Their experienced party managers were conspicuous either by absence or neglect. Charles D. Hilles, David A. Reed, Ogden Mills, and J. Henry Roraback, who had driven the steam roller over many a convention, commanded no regiments, exercised no sovereign prerogatives at Cleveland. The place of finance capital in Republican counsels was taken by the representatives of business concerns, such as E. T. Weir of the steel industry, Joseph Pew of oil, and William Bell of chemicals. Though thoroughly familiar with the economic interests laboring for the control of platform and candidate, Governor Landon's political sponsors

refused to accept dictation. They pushed aside the old practitioners whose thought had crystallized in Mark Hanna's
age and the new men whose theory of politics rested on something akin to Darwinism. Convinced that at least a tinge of
progressivism, a recognition of some changes in American
economy, must go into the platform and the proceedings,
they would brook no interference with their way.

In the end the convention adopted a platform that certainly looked more like the program of the New Deal than
like the Republican formulation of 1900, and Governor Landon was presented to the country as a kind of "liberal" by a
maneuver as clever as it was ruthless. Only in the preamble
did the platform reflect emotions shared by all the delegates.
Free citizens, it declared, today for the first time are threatened by government itself. The New Deal has "dishonored
American traditions" and "betrayed" party pledges. The
powers of Congress have been "usurped" by the President.
The integrity and authority of the Supreme Court have been
"flaunted." The rights of citizens have been "violated."
The rights of states have been torn away from them. The
country has been "dishonored" by the repudiation of "its
most sacred obligations." Witnesses have been "intimidated." Citizens have been harassed by investigations. The
New Deal has "bred fear and hesitation in commerce and
industry"; it has "coerced and intimidated voters"; it has
been guilty of "tyrannical policies." The morale of many
people has been destroyed. "Appeals to passion and class
prejudice have replaced reason and tolerance." Those were
biting words — betrayal, dishonor, usurpation, coercion, and
tyranny. Even subject to the usual discounts applied to
party platforms, they expressed the inveterate passions of
the economic conflict. A reporter described the temper of the
convention in saying that "this may be the bitterest campaign since the Civil War."

When the platform makers turned from preamble to
planks, from criticism to proposals for action, divisions broke
out in the convention and irreconcilable contradictions in

matters of policies became manifest. The first plank pledged the party to resist all attempts to impair the authority of the Supreme Court and bound it to uphold the independence of the judiciary against the encroachments of the legislative and executive branches of government. Yet in a subsequent paragraph, the platform favored state legislation and inter-state compacts to abolish child labor and sweatshops and to protect women and children in the matter of wages and working conditions. "We believe," the Republicans de-clared, "that this can be done within the Constitution as it now stands."

That declaration was made on June 11. A few days before, the Supreme Court had held the New York minimum wage law invalid. The language of the majority in the Court had been specific and sweeping — all such legislation is unconsti-tutional. Chief Justice Hughes had tried to convince his colleagues of the majority that a particular kind of wage law was valid and his view they had rejected in language that was not open to any double interpretation. Therefore every person who had read the opinion of the Court, including Governor Landon, knew that a promise to enact minimum wage laws for women ran directly counter to the Constitution as interpreted by a majority of the judges; in substance, if not in theory, it flouted the authority of that high tribunal. As they engineered the plank into the platform, did old Progressives of 1912 who had once overtly denounced the judiciary laugh up their sleeves?

Passing from legal abstractions to the exposition of eco-nomic theory and promise, the Republicans framed their planks for business enterprise, conceived mainly as little enterprise. Assuming the correctness and continuity of the existing distribution of property and income, they proposed government protection against foreign competition and free-dom for private enterprise within the tariff walls. They promised a repeal of the Reciprocal Trade Act, as "futile and dangerous," and a return to the principle of "the flexible tariff." Yet tariffs were to be adjusted "with a view to promoting international trade, the stabilization of currencies, and the attainment of a proper balance between agriculture and industry." In the interest of free enterprise at home there was to be a vigorous enforcement of civil and criminal laws against monopolies and trusts and the enactment of additional legislation against restraints on trade. While promising greater freedom to private enterprise, the Republicans also recognized "the existence of a field in which government regulation is desirable and salutary." The location and area of the field were not fully specified. But there was a hint: "We favor federal regulation, within the Constitution, for the marketing of securities to protect investors . . . also of the interstate activities of public utilities."

More space was given in the platform to agriculture. After condemning New Deal practices, the Republicans made their own pledges: retirement of abandoned and non-productive lands; enlargement of the domain dedicated to public uses; benefits to farmers for coöperation in protecting and restoring land resources; aid in the development of new crops; protection against foreign competition; "as an emergency measure," during the agricultural depression, federal benefit payments within the means of the Federal Government, consistent with a balanced budget; ample farm credit at rates "as low as those enjoyed by other industries"; encouragement and development of coöperative marketing; aid to districts suffering from temporary disaster; removal of land banks from politics.

Thus far there was little divergence from the agrarian policies inaugurated before the New Deal and expanded under that dispensation. Respecting only one point was there a sharp departure. The Republicans promised government aid in disposing of surpluses abroad and advocated bargaining for foreign markets selectively as distinguished from granting favors all around on the most favored nation principle. Over this issue George N. Peek, former administrator of the Agricultural Adjustment Act, had parted with the New

Deal. He insisted on driving a hard bargain with each foreign country and was so extreme as to propose dumping abroad at any price. Although this was a game which two could play and retaliations were always possible, the Republicans paid tribute to Mr. Peek and his agrarian philosophy.

To the labor sector of economy, the Republicans repeated their old tender. Under the head of the tariff, they offered to protect American wage levels against "the destructive competition emanating from the subsidies of foreign governments and the imports from low-wage and depreciated-currency countries." If the tariff clause conformed to Republican history, the promise took cognizance of changed operating conditions in what economists were fond of calling "international economy." Turning to domestic aspects of labor, the makers of the platform caught the phrase "collective bargaining" from the political atmosphere. Labor must be protected in its right "to organize and to bargain collectively through representatives of its own choosing without interference from any source."

The phrasing seemed clear on its face, but analyzed in the light of contemporary usage it could have a double meaning. Did the words "without interference from any source" cover "outside agitators" from the American Federation of Labor or the Committee for Industrial Organization? In appropriate minds they did and thus in appearance lent countenance to company unions. Support for that interpretation came from the sentence immediately following, which bound the party to "prevent government job holders from exercising autocratic powers over labor." Members of the Federal Labor Relations Board might be included among such job holders. They had been supervising labor elections in industries and applying the provisions of the Wagner Act which outlawed company interference with the balloting of employees. At all events while Republican campaign orators pointed with pride to the collective bargaining plank in their platform, Democratic orators pointed with scorn to its ambiguity.

That the American system might not function perfectly even under their auspices, the Republicans recognized by pledging themselves to measures of social security. Real security, they said, could only come from increased productive capacity and for this boon they looked to "the energy, self-reliance and character of our people, and to our system of free enterprise." Nevertheless society had an obligation "to promote the security of the people by affording some measure of protection against involuntary unemployment and dependency in old age." This did not mean approval for the Social Security Act of the Roosevelt administration of course; that was subject to severe criticism; it omitted many classes of people from its benefits and was unworkable besides. Hence a more effective system should be created. In the matter of old-age pensions, the Federal Government should provide standards for the states and territories and make proportional contributions in money up to a fixed maximum. In the matter of unemployment insurance, the Republicans proposed to encourage states and territories to adopt "honest and practical measures for meeting the problems." The pages of history were really not to be turned back; the events of recent years were not in fact to be denied; but greater competence and more practical sense were to be concentrated on the public solution of the problems raised by old-age dependency and the casualties of unemployment. The automatic adjustments of free enterprise could no longer be the sole reliance.

Nor were the poor to stew in their own "improvidence," as in the days of normalcy: "The necessities of life must be provided for the needy." This function could not be left to private charities and local governments as President Hoover had thought proper. A compromise was necessary. Responsibility for relief administration should fall upon non-political local agencies familiar with community problems; federal public works should be planned on their merits and separated from relief activities; relief agents should be selected on grounds of merit and fitness; and state and local governments should bear their fair share of the cost. On such conditions the Federal Government should make grants-in-aid to states and territories "while the need exists." In this way, ran the argument, an end could be put to the "confusion, partisanship, waste, and incompetence" which had marked the course of the New Deal in coping with the social distress of the crisis.

With an easy-money faction led by Senator Borah to be conciliated, the Republicans walked more warily than they had done in 1896 when they threw out the silver phalanx bag and baggage. Now their provisions on finance, money, and banking were cautious, even in revealing secret wishes for a return to 1896. No mention was made of restoring immediately the gold standard at the old ratio or any ratio. "A sound currency" was to be preserved "at all hazards"; there must be no further devaluation of the dollar; authority to control the currency must be taken from the President and restored to Congress. The budget must be balanced "not by increasing taxes but by cutting expenditures, drastically and immediately." The taxing power should be employed for "raising revenue and not for punitive or political purposes." That was a seasoned principle which Democrats had repeatedly used in their constitutional arguments against the protective tariff, but in the urgency of this occasion its origins could be overlooked.

As in the case of domestic finance, the Republicans indulged in some circumlocution in their reference to international exchange: "We will coöperate with other countries toward stabilization of currencies as soon as we can do so with due regard for our national interests and as soon as other nations have sufficient stability to justify such action." With nearly all nations committed to managed currencies, tariffs, subsidies, bounties, quotas, or prohibitions, the prospects for stabilization on any terms were not flattering. Nevertheless the Republicans evidently felt that something had to be said on the subject, if only for the benefit of concerns engaged in the export business.

Careful as it was, the reference to international stabilization of currencies was partly offset by declarations on foreign policy, as well as on the protective tariff. Peace was mentioned: "We pledge ourselves to promote and maintain peace by all honorable means not leading to foreign alliances or political commitments. . . . We will coöperate with nations in the limitation of armaments and control of traffic in arms." Still there must be no collective affiliations. "Obedient to the traditional foreign policy of America and to the repeatedly expressed will of the American people, we pledge that America shall not become a member of the League of Nations, nor of the World Court, nor shall America take on any entangling alliances in foreign affairs. . . . We shall use every effort to collect the war debt due us from foreign countries, amounting to $12,000,000,000, one-third of our national debt." In a world rent by wars and rumors of war, the Republicans declared that the best promise of peace lay in international arbitration by free, independent tribunals, acting "in accordance with law, equity, and justice." Meanwhile national defenses must be "adequate."

Before the name of Governor Landon was placed in nomination, a telegram from him stating his position on certain items in the platform, "as a matter of private honor and public good faith," was read to the convention. Ingeniously the telegram cut left, then right. Landon expressed the hope that the promised protection for women and children with respect to wages, hours, and working conditions could be effected under the Constitution as it then stood, but declared that, in case this proved to be erroneous, he would, if nominated and elected, favor a constitutional amendment authorizing such legislation. Since the managers of both parties were chary of advocating any alterations in the text of the Constitution, Governor Landon's announcement was a boon to the progressives.

At the same time comfort was given to the conservative wing. The Governor interpreted the words "sound currency" to mean "a currency expressed in terms of gold and

convertible into gold." That much made a clangor which
awakened memories of 1896. But the iron ring was quickly
softened. The adoption of such a gold-based currency must
not be effected "until and unless it can be done without
penalizing our democratic economy and without injury to
our producers of agricultural products and other raw materials." If the gold faction could applaud one sentence,
the easy-money faction could applaud the second, for it imposed conditions upon the first. In addition Governor Landon broadened the party's plank commending civil service
reform. On these terms he was nominated by acclamation
after other aspirants had dropped out of the race and with
him was associated, as candidate for Vice President, Colonel
Frank Knox, a Chicago newspaper publisher.

§

The Democratic convention followed, late in June, at
Philadelphia — a monster demonstration in popular ebul-
lience. For two good and sufficient reasons it was held in
the Pennsylvania metropolis. By the choice of that city for a
gathering of the faithful, the political designs of the Democrats on the great Republican state might be forwarded. And
direct economic advantages were offered to the party chest.
In anticipation of great crowds and much spending, local
merchants had helped to raise a bounty for Postmaster
General Farley's treasury. Indeed it had been said by the
critical that he auctioned off the convention to the highest
bidder. Like most party rumors there was something in
the allegation; it merely fell short of the whole truth in the
premises. At all events immense crowds poured into the
city by train, airplane, automobile, bus, and boat, and the
convention, which had little work to do, was prolonged for
the purpose of giving the Philadelphia merchants "their
money's worth."

With nominations a matter of routine and no tangled
factional disputes to smooth out, the delegates stamped,

cheered, and whistled in the assembly hall, amid the blare of bands and speeches amplified by the radio, accepting the fact that their function scarcely rose above the dignity of that performed by a rubber stamp. Between sessions, delegates and visitors swarmed over the city, sight-seeing, buying, and seeking amusement in every place of diversion. Composed largely of job holders, political beneficiaries, and expectants, the convention had little to do beyond providing ratification, celebration, and jollification, with the aid of noises afforded by the machine age and of liquid refreshments made freely available by the repeal of the Eighteenth Amendment. Efforts of a small group to stage a demonstration in favor of Alfred E. Smith were whirled away like chaff in a cyclone. Enlivened by war whoops from the braves, the convention approved the platform and nominations in a rush and a roar. Even the time-honored rule requiring two-thirds of the delegates to make nominations was abrogated. In the long history of political meetings there had never been anything just like the Philadelphia assembly of 1936.

One resemblance to previous assemblies was to be noted however. As in nearly all conventions, the main business was determined by managers behind the scenes, in the relative quiet of little rooms — this time under instructions from the White House.

Being the party in power the Democrats, in accord with political usage, devoted a large part of the platform to the approval of their own works. Whereas the Republicans had surrendered to "the privileged few," the Democrats had restored the people to sovereignty, promoted recovery, and humanized the policies of the Federal Government. Putting aside the hoary maxim of anarchy plus the police constable, they had adopted as their overarching hypothesis: "We hold this truth to be self-evident — that government in a modern civilization has certain inescapable obligations to its citizens, among which are: (1) protection of the family and the home; (2) establishment of a democracy of opportunity for all the people; (3) aid to those overtaken by disaster."

Under this conception, pertinent measures of the New Deal were cited. There had been a drive on kidnapers and bandits, the platform asserted. In the same paragraph with the mention of criminals, perhaps not inadvertently, stood the words: "We shall continue to use the powers of government to end the activities of malefactors of great wealth who defraud and exploit the people." Stock speculation had been curbed; "the unholy practices of utility holding companies" had been checked. On the foundations of the Social Security Act "a structure of economic security for all our people" was to be erected. There must be an extension of rural electrification, an expansion of housing activities, a continuation and enlargement of the agricultural program, additional protection for labor, freedom for business from "the ravages of cutthroat competition," enforcement of antitrust laws against "monopoly and concentration of economic power," provision for the unemployed on "useful public projects," a currency stabilized so as to prevent "wide fluctuations in value," and an enlargement of the merit system in civil service.

When they came to foreign policy the draftsmen of the platform tried to encompass a wide range of hopes and fears. The issue presented by the League of Nations was moribund and they failed to mention it. The plan for entering the World Court had been defeated in the Senate and reference to that form of mondial collaboration was omitted. But many voters still clung to the idea of collective action among nations, allegedly in the interest of peace, and they were to be placated. On the other hand recent neutrality legislation had indicated a passionate desire in every section of the country to abstain from quarrels in Europe and Asia. The fruits of the world war and its victory had been too sour for popular digestion and "isolationists" had to be conciliated.

What then would the Democrats do? They would continue the policy of the good neighbor, work for peace, oppose war as an instrument of national policy, advocate the settlement of international disputes by peaceful means, resist aggression, foster foreign commerce, and seek by mutual agreement to lower trade barriers "which have been raised against our exports of agricultural and industrial products." In this bill of promises, one item was elusive. Just what was meant by the phrase "work for peace"? Since America was now at peace with all the world, the words could mean nothing more than generous sentiments — tenders of "good offices" to nations in trouble or on the verge. Or, if twisted, they could signify direct action in the nature of collaboration for war on the world stage. If the latter was intended, the phrase did not declare it in positive terms; nor had elections since 1920 warranted any such interpretation; nor did President Roosevelt's campaign speeches lend sanction to it.

Indeed several positive phrases in the Democratic platform presented a direct antithesis to the idea of working for peace by any collective underwriting of the status quo or the balance of power in Europe or Asia. "In the disputes of others," it declared, "we shall continue to observe a true neutrality." Whether that had been done during Italy's war on Ethiopia was a matter of dispute, but there stood the pledge. Bowing to the storm raised by the Nye investigation of the munitions industry and war financing, the Democrats said, somewhat cryptically, that they would "continue . . . to take the profits out of war." They would "guard against being drawn, by political commitments, international banking, or private trading, into any war which may develop anywhere." Nor was there to be anything quixotic in the lowering of trade barriers. "We shall continue . . . as in the past to give adequate protection to our farmers and manufacturers against unfair competition or the dumping on our shores of commodities and goods produced abroad by cheap labor or subsidized by foreign governments." In accepting the idea that international banking or private trading could draw the country into a foreign war, the Democrats went far beyond the Republican pronouncement on foreign affairs, while avoiding specifications. By offering adequate protection against cheap labor and dumping, they adopted Republican doctrines and repudiated the hypothesis of the "free international market" as representing a reality or as offering prospects worthy of any immediate or practical consideration.

High above all other issues, if in the background, was the Constitution of the United States under which Democrats had been acting and were proposing to act further. Along nearly all their front, the Supreme Court had erected barriers of interpretation against the exercise of federal power. Yet procedure on a national scale seemed to be made imperative by the very interlocking of great economic processes. "The Republican platform proposes to meet many pressing national problems solely by action of the separate states. We know," countered the Democrats, "that drought, dust storms, floods, minimum wages, maximum hours, child labor and working conditions in industry, monopolistic and unfair business practices cannot be adequately handled exclusively by forty-eight separate state legislatures, forty-eight separate state administrations, and forty-eight separate state courts. Transactions and activities which inevitably overflow state boundaries call for both state and federal treatment. We have sought and will continue to seek to meet these problems through legislation within the Constitution."

Nevertheless Democratic legislation designed to solve these problems had been riddled by decisions of the Supreme Court; and if principles announced by that tribunal were applied in the future, many remaining statutes and additional laws of similar character would be rendered invalid under or "within" the Constitution. For this reason some party advisers had insisted that the issue be taken up boldly and that a constitutional amendment be proposed. After some debate, their suggestion was discarded by the makers of the platform, perhaps on grounds of difficulty or timidity or with the thought that other devices might be employed after the election. At all events, the route of contingency was chosen: "If these problems cannot be effectively solved by legislation within the Constitution, we shall seek such clarifying amendment" as will permit the state and federal legislatures, within their respective spheres, to enact laws deemed necessary "adequately to regulate commerce, protect public health and safety, and safeguard economic security. Thus we propose to maintain the letter and the spirit of the Constitution."

The phraseology bore the stamp of "the sacred tradition," save for the word "clarifying." Suggested by a lawyer of singular distinction, a connoisseur of language, the term insinuated that Congress had ample powers already, that the Supreme Court had muddied the Constitution, and that in any event nothing beyond clarification was required. Having given this notification, the New Dealers, unlike Republicans in 1860 and Democrats in 1896, refrained from making any reference in the platform to a possible reconstruction of the Supreme Court.

On its face, until analyzed, the constitutional plank of the platform adopted by the Philadelphia convention seemed legible enough. The Democrats announced in substance that they were going ahead on lines already pursued and if necessary would seek to clarify the fundamental law of the land by an amendment. What implications, however, were contained in the term "necessary"? More than a hundred years before, John Marshall had explored its meaning in the case of McCulloch *vs.* Maryland and given his interpretation : "If reference be had to its use, in the common affairs of the world, or in approved authors, we find that it frequently imports no more than that one thing is convenient, or useful, or essential to another. To employ the means necessary to an end, is generally understood as employing any means calculated to produce the end, and as not being confined to those single means, without which the end would be entirely unattainable. . . . A thing may be necessary, very necessary, absolutely or indispensably necessary." In effect, therefore, the Democrats said that they would seek a clarifying amendment if they found it convenient or useful, provided they could not vault the judicial barriers in other ways.

Doubtless the Democratic management had in mind no purely formalistic conception of the Constitution and the Supreme Court, such as the lawyers of the Liberty League had set forth as the true and only view. To this conclusion something like positive warrant was given by the acclaim of the convention itself. Amid ripples and roars of applause, President Roosevelt's chosen spokesman, Senator Alben Barkley, of Kentucky, implied as much in delivering the keynote address — that pronouncement which, according to all realistic understanding of power politics, reveals the spirit and animus underlying the overt terms of the platform. After surveying the policies and achievements of the Roosevelt administration, the Senator came to the barriers: "But we are told by the smug and cynical apostles of the status quo that the Supreme Court has nullified some of the acts of this administration. And while anxious farmers ponder their fate, and laboring men scan the heavens for a rainbow of hope, and women and children look in vain for the preservation of their lives and health, a voice from the grave at Palo Alto [Ex-president Hoover's home] shouts: 'Thank God for the Supreme Court.' I make no attack on the Supreme Court. As an institution I respect it, and I would be both unfair and unjust if I were unwilling to accord to judges on the bench the right to their views of laws and constitutions which I claim for myself. But . . ."

Having placed judicial lucubrations on a level with his own opinions, as mere "views," the Senator proceeded to set forth his interpretation of the whole business. Some three or four outstanding acts passed during the Roosevelt administration had been invalidated, as against twenty-one acts declared null and void between 1920 and 1930. The three or four acts in question had been "conceived and consummated in behalf of labor, or agriculture, and the honest conduct of business, and designed to constitute this a government of equal rights." These were the measures "cast aside by the rigors of technicality and the application of antiquated economic predilections in the interpretation of the document." Democrats had taken a higher ground. "We have thought that under its broad and generous outlines we might rescue the people from national disaster. We have sought to treat it as a life-giving charter, rather than as an object of curiosity on the shelf of a museum." Even so, Democrats would abide by the Court's decisions and seek to shape their program "in accordance with them. But . . ." The nine eminent judges could not agree on what the Constitution means. How then could 531 members of Congress expect to agree? On occasion five of the eminent judges have said that a law violates the Constitution and four judges "equally eminent, learned, and sincere, and equally alive to the compulsions of modern life" have said that it does not violate the Constitution. "Then we are at least relieved of any obligation to underwrite the infallibility of the five whose views prevail."

Bringing the Supreme Court to the bar of popular judgment, Senator Barkley asked: "Is the Court beyond criticism? May it be regarded as too sacred to be disagreed with?" The answers he sought in American history. Jefferson did not think so. Andrew Jackson did not think so. Abraham Lincoln did not think so. With evident relish the Senator quoted the famous passage from Lincoln's first inaugural address: "If the policy of the government on vital questions affecting the whole people is to be irrevocably fixed by the decisions of the Supreme Court the instant they are made in ordinary litigation between parties in personal actions, the people will have ceased to be their own rulers, having to that extent practically resigned their government into the hands of that eminent tribunal." This conception of the Court and the Constitution, Senator Barkley buttressed by a reference to the dissenting opinion of Justice Stone in the Agricultural Adjustment case, with which Justice Brandeis and Cardozo had concurred.

What was the conception of Chief Justice Hughes? This question must have risen in the minds of the Senator's auditors. "The Constitution," said that dignitary, during the interval when he was off the bench, "is what the judges say it is." Theodore Roosevelt did not think that the Supreme Court was above scrutiny and he had used scathing words about its decisions. Governor Landon and Colonel Knox, the very Republican candidates now offered to the people, had supported Theodore Roosevelt in 1912 in a campaign of criticism. The record of practice stood out against the pure theory of the folk lore.

As he proceeded, Senator Barkley grew ironical. "The judges have decided that, under the Constitution, the Federal Government cannot lift men, women, and children out of the degradation of unconscionable hours, wages, or working conditions, because it invades the rights of the states. They have decided that the states cannot do it, because it invades the rights of private property. I presume that this progressive and logical course will soon lead us to the conclusion that private property cannot do it, because it violates the law of gravitation." A new definition of interstate commerce was needed — an interpretation bringing commodities produced in one state and consigned to another state within the scope of that term. Thereupon the Senator placed "over against the hosannahs of Hoover for the tortured interpretation of the Constitution . . . the tortured souls and bodies of men who work and pray, of women whose God-given right is not fulfilled in a sweatshop, and of children whom we have sought to restore to the school room and the playground."

In his address accepting the renomination, President Roosevelt spoke of ultimate power only in broad and general terms. He made no specific reference to the constitutional controversy; but after charging "the economic royalists" with creating a new despotism, he accused them of wrapping it "in the robes of legal sanction. . . . In vain they seek to hide behind the flag and the Constitution." However casual these words may have seemed to the generality, no adept in power politics could miss their import.

§

As soothsayers had foretold, the campaign was both lively and acrimonious. The Presidential candidates themselves as a rule kept their part of the debate on a high level but their vocal supporters were rarely so scrupulous. Allowing Vice President Garner to play a minor role, Roosevelt went on long tours and made extensive use of the radio. His rival, Governor Landon, campaigned like a veteran, traveling west to California and east to Maine, speaking in great cities, talking at country towns, appealing over the air, and mingling with throngs in the fashion consecrated by democratic practice.

As the campaign proceeded, the tension grew tighter. Although Roosevelt discussed many issues in genial speeches, he drew the lines firmly in his Madison Square address on October 31 : "For twelve years this nation was afflicted with hear-nothing, see-nothing, do-nothing government. The nation looked to government but the government looked away. Nine mocking years with the golden calf and three long years of the scourge! Nine crazy years at the ticker and three long years in the breadlines! Nine mad years of mirage and three long years of despair! Powerful influences strive today to restore that kind of government with its doctrine that that government is best which is most indifferent. For nearly four years you have had an Administration which instead of twirling its thumbs has rolled up its sleeves. We will keep our sleeves rolled up. We have had to struggle with the old enemies of peace — business and financial monopoly, speculation, reckless banking, class antagonism, sectionalism, war profiteering. They had begun to consider the Government of the United States as a mere appendage to their own affairs. We know now that government by organized money is just as dangerous as government by organized mob. Never before in all our history have these forces been so united against one candidate as they stand today. They are unanimous in their hate for me — and I welcome their hatred." After enumerating the principal measures and projects of the New Deal, the President exclaimed : "For these things, too, and for a multitude of others like them, we have only just begun to fight."

On behalf of the Republican cause Governor Landon spoke

with equal firmness, if in general with less asperity. He listed and condemned the New Deal measures in rhetoric which recalled the preamble of his party platform. But he did not align himself with mere conservative intransigence. Taking up the issue of civil liberty, in language clearer and more specific than that employed by his powerful competitor, he pleaded with the nation to keep the channels of free discussion open as the best guarantee for the perpetuity of democracy. He denounced restraints upon liberty of opinion, spurned legislation imposing special oaths upon teachers, and decried all forms of suppression and oppression. "The right of free inquiry," he declared, "is one of the essentials of free government. It is the very bed rock of democracy." Turning to the Roosevelt administration, he charged it with employing the machinery of government in propaganda designed to keep itself in power and "to bring into question the faith of the people in their way of life and in their form of government." With more than wonted verve, he quoted Thomas Jefferson's program for the University of Virginia : "This institution will be based on the illimitable freedom of the human mind. For here we are not afraid to follow truth wherever it may lead, nor to tolerate error as long as reason is left free to combat it."

In speaking of other matters Landon broke through the rigid line which Roosevelt insisted on drawing between the parties. His appeal to farmers went beyond the strict tender of his platform in promises of federal aid. Taking up the labor question, he interpreted collective bargaining more nearly in the terms of the Wagner Labor Relations Act, much to the annoyance of his followers on the extreme right. When all discounts were made, the net impression left by the Governor at the end of the campaign was that of a man who would make strenuous efforts to straighten out federal finances and to rationalize, rather than demolish, the program of social and economic legislation ascribed, not with complete justice, to the New Deal. No carping critic could find in his campaign addresses an argument for a complete return to the state of things prevailing in the days of the golden glow.

Blaring above the fray of the campaign debate was the shrill note of the constitutional issue. Elaborating their platform, Republican speakers charged their opponents, in terse, even violent, terms, with seeking to destroy the independence of the judiciary and to undermine the Constitution. In the main the answer of the Democrats was a plea of avoidance: Nothing irregular had been done. The administration had obeyed the decisions of the Supreme Court. If necessary, it would seek an amendment clarifying the sacred text. While there had been criticisms of the jurisprudence turned out by the majority of the judges, that was in accord with the Jackson-Lincoln tradition and had the sanction of time-honored practice. But such counter arguments were vague, so that the upshot of the election was inevitably controversial. Just what campaign pledge had been made by the Democrats on the court issue? Certainly it was not as transparent as President Wilson's implied promise to keep the country out of war in 1916 nor as definite as the Republican promise of prosperity in 1928; yet it gave the general impression that the method of constitutional amendment would be employed by the Democrats — only if necessary.

Against the Democratic position, Republican orators arrayed specific arguments. Though the Supreme Court had overruled most of the New Deal program, the Democrats proposed to go ahead without resorting to a constitutional amendment, unless necessary. That was no unconditional surrender to the judiciary and its Constitution. President Roosevelt had urged Congress to pass one measure in spite of doubts respecting its validity. That, the Honorable Bertrand Snell, Republican leader in the House of Representatives, had hinted, came near to the borders of an impeachable offense. The President's acrid remarks about the "horse and buggy" view of the Constitution were reiterated by critics and treated as evidence of his underlying animus against the high tribunal in the Palace of Justice. The whole legislative program of the Roosevelt Administration, they insisted, ran against the letter and spirit of the Constitution, amounted to a usurpation of powers, trampled down the rights of states.

Given this record, the refrain continued, there could be no doubt that a Democratic victory meant some kind of assault upon "the independence of the judiciary" and a re-interpretation of the Constitution under some kind of partisan pressure. In other words, Republicans informed the country, with shrewd insinuation, that the Democrats, if victorious, would in some way curb the Supreme Court; while Democrats carefully avoided exhibiting an official bill of specifications respecting their concrete intentions. Given this loose joining of issues, the Democrats could say, in 1937, with a show of justification, that the country, instructed by their opponents on the consequences of a Democratic triumph, had approved President Roosevelt's call for a re-reading of the Constitution and had given him a mandate to arrange the details of the undertaking.

In accordance with the psychology of the popular process in politics, the personalities of the candidates had a positive bearing on the outcome, entirely apart from the proposals discussed in the campaign. Whatever the intrinsic merits or defects of Governor Landon's arguments, his crusade had not advanced far when it became notorious that he was not swinging the currents of popular enthusiasm over to his side. Indeed at the outset a division over strategy added elements of weakness. One group of his advisers, including William Randolph Hearst, continued to emphasize the role of "the silent Coolidge from Kansas," and wished to rely upon the power of taciturnity in creating the image of the strong man for an hour of crisis. By keeping pen and ink away from William Henry Harrison in 1840 and confining his utterances to sententious generalities, the Whigs had been able to stem the tide of Jacksonian Democracy and gain possession of the presidency. The successful experiment might be repeated. On the other hand another group of Landon's advisers demanded an open campaign all along the line. With that idea of strategy, stern silence was incompatible. The candidate had to join the war of words, to present himself as he really was, without paint or adornment, and to pit his knowledge, thought, voice, and personality against the powers of his opponent. As the conflict proceeded, the giant once shrouded in the mystery of silence slipped out of the shades and as a sheer candidate submitted himself to popular judgment.

In the beginning of Landon's campaign, seasoned observers, Republican in sympathies, doubted whether any person enlisted under their banner could carry the country in the election. As the days of the contest ticked off, doubts increased. If the people wished to hear trenchant arguments, they were certainly not gratified by the manner of Governor Landon's speaking; his very syllables were heavy. If the people expected flaming oratory, they were disappointed; that was not in keeping with the Coolidge tradition nor was it, apparently, within the power of the Governor. The sight of the man did not magnetize audiences. His voice, in platform address and over the radio, was hesitant, even in its strength, and displayed no insinuating graces. It also lacked the resonance required for the packed amphitheater or marketplace. His reasoned counsels of prudence were burdened by awkwardness; his most effective pleas were blunted by the style of his delivery. Though long associated with plain people and following their ways naturally and without effort, the Governor did not capture "the folks" as he drove through or mingled with crowds.

Had he possessed the art rather than the substance of the popular appeal, he might have done better. Or did the people not want one of themselves in the White House now? In any case, for some reason, the solid, lymphatic man did not make headway. Perhaps no one could have done that under Republican auspices, not even another plumed knight in shining armor, if such could have been discovered and entrusted with the old banner frayed by the blasts of the depression days. Had fortune favored Alfred Landon, as it blessed Warren Harding in 1920, and had victory come to

him on the wings of Mercury, he might have disclosed great
qualities in the office of President; but that opportunity was
in neither the omens nor the necessities of the time.

On his part, President Roosevelt conducted his campaign
with improved adroitness and heightened energy. Four
years before, caution had been his guardian; the promise of
success lay not so much in saying the right thing as in avoiding the wrong thing. Now the scent of victory suggested
belligerency. Experience had brightened his wits and enlarged his knowledge. His role as the heir of Andrew Jackson
seemed to grow in his imagination and give a driving quality
to his decisions. While his speeches did not resound with
Webster's sonorous roll, or shimmer with the polished hard-
ness of Woodrow Wilson's rhetoric, his prose, although sometimes dull and repetitious, often glowed with poetic warmth
and was enlivened by the flight of speeding words. And
through all his addresses ran the strong note of democratic
humanism — the note struck in Thomas Paine's Rights of
Man, kept alive in the Middle Period by the reformers, and
renewed after the darkness of the civil war.

Endowed with a positive genius for the opalescent phrase,
clever in forming rounded sentences, agile in springing the
trap of logic, proficient in insinuation, the President sped
through the whole gamut of campaign strategy, now as if in
the thick of the fray, now as if judging it from afar. No son
of the soil or the forge himself, he nevertheless in his travels
seemed the very apotheosis of popular sentiment, as monster
throngs crowded about his car or train, evincing spontaneous
enthusiasm. If in writing his speeches the President had, as
admitted, the aid of powerful literary advisers, nearly every
passage was finally composed in his tempo, fitted his arma-
ture of thought, and expressed his gift for the artistic touch.
Personality and destiny seemed fused in a single force.

§

Before the campaign had entered the final phase, "name
calling" had become a favorite substitute for inquiry and

reasoning. By that time an array of horrid names had been created to stigmatize opponents, and they were rotated with heat and profusion. To the Democrats, Roosevelt had given a cue in the epithet "economic royalists" and they clutched at the signal, adding accusations equally invidious and more flamboyant. In the Republican appeal to national intelligence, the repertory of damnation was also varied: communists, alien ideas, enemies of the American system, foul breath of Moscow, riot of confiscation, ought to be deported to Russia, agents of the Red international, fomenters of class war, foes of the Republic founded by Washington and consecrated by Lincoln, revolutionary attacks on American democracy, undermining the Constitution, assaults on the independence of the judiciary, preachers of hate, sowers of domestic discord, demagogues. Over and over again the phrases rolled, over and over with thrumming and plangent reiteration. If Federalists, peering over the battlements of Heaven, heard their spiritual heirs brazenly defending "democracy," which only "Jacobins and atheists" had favored in 1800, they must have thought that the world had gone mad.

So continuous and heavy was the verbal barrage against him that President Roosevelt deemed it necessary to make a well-placed speech devoted to disclaiming communism and asserting his Americanism. Yet, judging by the new outburst of criticism which followed this profession of loyalty to his country, the disclaimer was without effect on the press and Republican orators. If indeed the characterizations of the President by Republican leaders and rhetoricians were really to be taken at face value, the voters chose a Communist for the office of Chief Executive and declared in favor of a full communist program in the November election.

As a matter of fact the Socialists and Communists themselves made a poor showing in both the campaign and the election. The former, with Norman Thomas again at their head, put forward an orthodox platform, dismissed the New Deal as a capitalistic illusion, and offered a few planks of immediate demands directed to farmers and industrial workers.

By a strange turn of events, the Socialists seemed, in their orthodoxy, to be on the left of the Communists and received some support from the disciples of Trotsky at the very end of the Red wing.

Presumably instructed from Moscow as to the correct party line, the Communists were very circumspect. They refrained from making a totalitarian statement of Marxism. They declared that American economy should be made "the common property of the whole people, operated fully for the benefit of all who work." If true to party tradition, this statement fell far short of proclaiming "the revolution and the dictatorship of the proletariat." With ears turned to agrarian discontent, the Communists advocated the regulation of farm prices in a manner to guarantee cost of production — a proposal in harmony with the demands of the Farm Holiday Association. In foreign affairs, they advocated reliance upon collective security, support for the League of Nations, economic sanctions against Japan, Germany, and Italy, and a prohibition on loans and sales of supplies to nations that violate the Kellogg Pact. Even William Lemke, bidding for the farmer-labor vote as the candidate of the Union party, though milder in general philosophy, was as radical as the Communists in some of his immediate demands and in his denunciations of the "concentrated wealth" that had "impoverished the masses." At the end the combined vote of the Socialists and Communists was only about one-third of their total in 1932 and less than half the number of ballots cast under the sign of the Union ticket.

§

To the power of the actors in the campaign was added the force of the stage machinery secured by lavish outlays of money. Although the Republicans had huge campaign funds at their command, there were heavy battalions on the other side. According to the careful calculations of Dr. Louise Overacker, published in The American Political Science Review for June 1937, the Democratic outlay between January 1 and December 31, 1936, was $5,194,741, about $3,700,000 below the expenditure of the Republican National Committee during the same period. Under the astute management of Postmaster General Farley, men and women were invited to dine together for the cause at the rate of $50 or $100 a plate, and Democrats holding office or in expectancy of favors-to-come accepted invitations with alacrity. An elaborate campaign book was sold at high prices, even to heads of corporations that could not lawfully subscribe to party funds. Contractors, merchants, and industrialists advertised generously in its pages, bringing more gifts of dubious legality.

To the contributions of the "economic royalists" who happened to be in the Democratic fold and the receipts from dinners and campaign books were joined "free-will offerings" from the huge army of political job holders and relief beneficiaries. Where reluctance laid a drag, discretion suggested a spur. In possession of the federal administration, as well as state, municipal, and local machines, the Democrats had official sources of funds that were wide and rich. In other times, party workers in the lower ranges had been paid mainly from contributions collected in the upper ranges. Now millions of urban and rural voters were sustained wholly or in part by money from the Federal Treasury; millions of farmers were showered with payments for not producing crops. Even allowing the whole contention that party politics did not enter into the administration of relief and agricultural adjustment at the top, the fact remained that such beneficence had been called into being under the auspices of President Roosevelt; and the beneficiaries were not likely to forget it. Not often, if ever, in the history of popular campaigns had so much money been enlisted on the side of a party whose members owned the minor share of the national wealth.

Within the category of large campaign gifts, as Dr. Overacker's analysis of the returns shows, was visible a significant shift of economic incidence. "In 1928," she says, "both major parties depended largely upon bankers and manufacturers for their contributions, although the Republicans received a larger proportion of their funds from manufacturers than did their rivals. In 1932, although the proportion of the Democratic fund coming from manufacturers dropped appreciably, Roosevelt's promises of a New Deal had no apparent effect upon the support of the bankers, who contributed as heavily as in 1928." Four years later the scene altered. "The revolt of the bankers and brokers from the Democratic party is startling. Only 3.3 per cent of the contributions of $1000 or more came from this group, compared to 14.7 per cent in the case of the Republicans."

Among the contributors to the Republican fund were representatives of "such important New York banking and investment houses as J. P. Morgan and Co., . . . Bankers Trust, Guaranty Trust, National City Bank, Chase National Bank, . . . Kuhn, Loeb, and Company, . . . and Dillon, Read, and Co." — all of which had been recently subjected to congressional investigations. Among the manufacturers, the heaviest forces, especially steel and chemicals, were thrown on the Republican side. Oil and tobacco were more equally divided. "Chain stores and mail order houses gave the bulk of this part of the Republican fund, while none of these supported the Democrats." The economic support of great publishers went with their editorials to the Republican candidates, William Randolph Hearst leading with $50,000. On the other hand motion-picture producers, theater owners, and the professionals, such as lawyers, physicians, and authors, displayed Democratic leanings. Perhaps even more portentous in terms of power was "the emergence of labor as a factor in the financing of the Democratic party and other organizations which supported Roosevelt." From this source came "the impressive total of $770,218."

After completing a microscopic examination of all recorded contributions to national party funds, Dr. Overacker made deductions evidenced by the facts: "From this analysis of the 1936 campaign funds it seems clear that the program of the Roosevelt Administration has served to sharpen the division on economic lines. The drastic reduction in contributions made by banks to the Democratic party, the increased support which the Republicans received from manufacturers, labor's support of Roosevelt, and the very large contributions which certain wealthy families gave the Republican party all point in this direction. The Republicans became more definitely than in the past few campaigns the party of 'big business.' Their campaign was the most extravagant, and probably the most wasteful, in campaign history. Captains of finance and industry poured their dollars into the fund without stint. Mr. J. Howard Pew, himself a generous contributor, probably spoke for many of them when he said: 'Considering the importance of this campaign, I have felt it a duty and a privilege to make these contributions, and I expect to make further contributions, if necessary to the cause. The American form of government, the fundamentals of our democratic society, the economic system under which our country has become the greatest in the world, are in jeopardy.' The 'haves' rose generously to the defense of a system under which their fortunes had been made."

Yet income and property were split, if unevenly. "The Democrats, abandoned by the financiers, and with less support than usual from representatives of the larger manufacturing interests, drew heavily from the legal profession and from the liquor and tobacco interests. They also had material support from two groups whose traditional allegiance seldom falters — office holders and the South, irrespective of economic interest. Without the support of these two groups, they would have been in a sad plight indeed. Lastly, they wooed the 'little fellow' diligently and to good purpose, and won substantial support from a new quarter — organized labor. The Democratic party emerged from the campaign less definitely the party of the 'have nots' than the Republicans are the party of the 'haves,' but the 'have nots' played an important role in financing its campaign." Looking to the future, Dr. Overacker asked what would happen in case of a revolt on the part of office holders and Southern conservatives. Without funds from these sources the Democrats would be compelled to depend more heavily upon contributions from labor. Was that a handwriting on the wall or merely the flicker of a passing shadow?

§

Reflecting in some measure, perhaps, the drift of campaign contributions, great newspapers operated ostentatiously on the Republican side. A conservative estimate, based upon careful surveys by the editors of The New Republic, indicated that at least seventy per cent of the metropolitan circulation, probably more, was thrown against the candidacy of President Roosevelt. The old Pulitzer organ, The St. Louis Post-Dispatch, abandoned its ancient moorings and went over to Landon. The Baltimore Sun, unable to make a clean-cut decision, repudiated Roosevelt without embracing the Republican cause zealously. Many papers nominally committed to the Democratic leader, such as The New York Times and the Scripps-Howard chain, were lukewarm, apologetic, and querulous, rather than militant, in their support. Coupled with the shift and vacillation of journalistic opinion was a manifestation of belligerence in editorial language that signified deep-seated passions. For a fair comparison in the arts of vituperation it was necessary to go back to the campaign of 1896, indeed to the campaigns of 1796 and 1800. The metropolitan press, in the main, was not only Republican in philosophy; it was almost revolutionary in its vindictiveness.

Another striking feature of the campaign lay in the fact that nearly all the columnists were about as vindictively Republican as the majority of the prominent editors themselves. Despite an air of Olympian detachment that occasionally hung over the opening words of their articles, there was little question about the nature of their subjective irritations when the final sentences appeared. Thus special powers of elucidation, innuendo, and persuasion were enlisted on the Republican side. In addition, many editors who were nominally Democratic in policy printed daily or periodical comments and homilies from one or more of the chain writers, and in this way countered their own news selections and editorials by propaganda from the other camp. The total flow of ink in the Republican cause was, therefore, greater than the total roll of Republican newspapers indicated. Such was the power of the press to be tested by the popular verdict.

For the course taken by the metropolitan press in the campaign, economic determinists had their explanation: the newspaper business is merely one phase of "big business" in an age when large capital is required for a single publishing plant as well as for a chain of plants. In support of this hypothesis they could cite the authority of The Wall Street Journal: "A newspaper is a private enterprise, owing nothing whatever to the public, which grants it no franchise. It is therefore 'affected' with no public interest. It is emphatically the property of the owner, who is selling a manufactured product at his own risk. If the public does not like his opinions or his method of presenting news the remedy is in its own hands. It is under no obligation to buy the paper. . . . Editors, except where they own their own newspapers, take their policy from their employers. . . . But for ridiculously obvious reasons, there are many newspaper owners willing enough to encourage the public in the delusion that it is the editor of a newspaper who dictates the selection of news and the expression of opinion. He only does so subject to the correction and suggestion of the proprietor of the paper." When the ownership and economic affiliations of the newspapers opposed to President Roosevelt were tabulated, they fitted rather closely the line of division in the campaign contributions; and, if The Wall Street Journal was correct in associating opinion and news selection with proprietorship, there were some grounds for assuming that the rhetoricians of the press gave heed to the voices of the counting room.

Yet polls taken while the campaign was under way indicated that newspaper readers did not believe their own eyes or were impervious to the admonitions of their journalistic tutors. This indication, later confirmed by the election itself, led to the conclusion that newspapers had "lost their influence," and that other agencies of communication, especially the radio, had disrupted their empire over the popular mind. To some extent the conclusion was well founded. The credulity that accepted the printed word as a revelation of pure disinterestedness was doubtless diminishing. But other factors affected the influence exerted by the newspapers. It was not merely their support of the Republican candidate that alienated voters and augmented distrust; the manner of the editorial campaign also counted in the process of alienation and repudiation. Many editors were not content with analyzing and weighing arguments, with sober statements of policy, or with eloquent pleas for public sympathy. In the hysteria of the campaign their sense of fair play deteriorated. As a brash king had often weakened a strong monarchy, so intemperate editors weakened the empire of the press over national opinion.

§

Despite the clear indications revealed by preliminary polls, save that taken by The Literary Digest, the overwhelming nature of the Democratic victory at the election was a general surprise. It is true that the Institute of Public Opinion had recorded only three states as "sure for Landon" — Maine, Vermont, and New Hampshire, but it had admitted doubts as to some other states. So when the returns of the balloting gave only Maine and Vermont to the Republicans, even hard-headed politicians rubbed their scalps in amazement. Yet such was the triumph. Nothing like it had occurred in the long history of political campaigns since the victory of James Monroe in 1820, in the era of good feeling.

In popular terms, no doubt, the landslide was not so destructive. Although Roosevelt's plurality was eleven millions, in round numbers, the official poll showed that there were still nearly seventeen million Republicans left in the country — a far larger proportion of the voters than that recorded for Federalism in 1820 or for anything like Whiggery in 1836. According to any calculation, the figure was too substantial to warrant sending out the notices of a party funeral.

Nevertheless, political prognosticators, especially of the theoretical type, immediately began to speculate upon the probabilities of a new political alignment, implying the death or reconstruction of the Republican party. At last, they said, it seemed possible to have a "true" liberal or conservative party and a "true" radical party. But for this view there was little warrant in the immediate situation or the history of American politics. If logic suggested the sharp split, the realities of the popular process forbade it. The Democratic party had suffered defeats almost as drastic, in effect, as that just administered to Republicans, and yet had returned from forlorn hopes and years in the desert to hopes realized and the spoils of office. No foreclosure of history denied that possibility to the Republicans.

Any rational form of political calculation acknowledged that contingency. With Communists torn into factions, Socialists divided, Democrats at war with themselves, and Republicans ranging in type from Gerald P. Nye to Ogden Mills, two simple and unequivocal faiths for a single division, right and left, could not be formulated in words; nor were the economic interests and emotions as yet reducible to one positive set of antagonisms. Heedless orators and columnists were fond of saying that the nation could not exist half collectivist and half individualist, but, as Aristotle had pointed out more than two thousand years before, only some such an interpenetration of opposites could be called a society and stand anywhere, anytime.

A division on that line was improbable. The Republican platform and the orations of Governor Landon demonstrated the fact. Beneath words were configurations of economy and culture. As long as American society continued to display a wide diversity of interests, all interrelated, no political party could hope for a victory on an appeal to a single interest. An election map of the United States showing two states white and all the others red did not divulge the underlying substance of politics, and when Congress met the next year this truth became obvious to calculators busy with new projects for realignments. Political arithmetic was not limited to subtraction, division, and addition. If map students in party headquarters saw clear contours and sharp antagonisms, front soldiers in party trenches wrestled with mutiny and confusion.

What then was decided at the record-breaking election in which nearly forty-six million men and women expressed their judgments and the victorious candidate for the presidency commanded a plurality of more than eleven million voters? On that day a few items were certainly set down in the record and sealed with the seven seals of history. The image of power and proposed action presented by the Republican platform and candidate had been rejected by a staggering majority. The election did not repeat the performance of 1896, in which the Tiberius Gracchus of the agrarians, William Jennings Bryan, after a vigorous assault on "the money power," was decisively repudiated at the polls. Nor did it repeat the verdict of 1912. In that year, it is true, Woodrow Wilson denounced government by "the big bankers, the big manufacturers, the big masters of commerce, the heads of railroad corporations and of steamship corporations," as he characterized the foe, and was elected; but Woodrow Wilson had proposed no such program as that offered by the New Deal and he polled only a minority of the popular vote. And unlike Wilson, President Roosevelt was not steeped in the philosophy of Edmund Burke whom the fright of the French revolution had transformed into a Tory. Not even the defeated candidate on the Republican ticket had offered in 1936 the policies of 1896; on the contrary a comparison showed that his platform was more like the

Progressive tender of 1912 than the once orthodox creed of his party. However interpreted, the election of 1936 was no exact repetition of any episode in history; it represented a drift of events and thought flowing through the day into the morrow.

In other respects the outcome of the election was positive. To the Democrats, whose candidate had defied the power of "organized money," the responsibilities of the Federal Government were entrusted for another season. Upon the Democrats were also bestowed again the spoils of office. They had promised to go ahead along the lines already laid down in voluminous legislation and a huge majority of the voters had approved their pledge. On the issue set by the decisions of the Supreme Court against New Deal statutes the popular verdict was likewise emphatic; the barriers interposed by that high tribunal were to be vaulted, if necessary by constitutional amendment. This much, at least, seemed written in the record of 1936, but it was in the nature of history rather than visible prophecy. Just what definite propulsions to action, if any, were set in motion by the popular decision?

That question was not answerable out of knowledge on the morning after the election. President Roosevelt was re-elected. What would he do? What, in fact, could he do? Under the Constitution, he was not the Government of the United States. Though he could propose, urge, and press, he could not legislate at will. Swept into legislative power on the same popular tide was an immense majority of Democrats with wills, temperaments, and purposes of their own. In the Senate, seventy-six Democrats were to dominate a little group composed of sixteen Republicans and a few independents; in the House of Representatives the Democrats were to mass 331 members against eighty-nine Republicans and a handful of independents. If the Chief Executive mirrored the mind of a vast national majority, the legislators of his party mirrored the minds of 331 congressional districts and many states.

On analysis this enormous legislative bloc disclosed numerous internal variations. It included members from the Solid South who had little love for the New Deal and yet were entrenched as the heads of powerful committees; it embraced also other Democrats from the Solid South who had about as little affection for their regional colleagues as for the members of the Republican delegation — on many issues, less. With the Southern groups were associated under the banner of the Democratic party in Congress a few radicals from Northern labor constituencies and a far larger number of legislators picked by the political machines of great cities or the small-town bosses of rural regions. In a strict sense, no taut line divided the Democrats from the little assembly of Republicans, and their unwieldy aggregation was criss-crossed by deep antagonisms which were bound to erupt at every crucial shift in events. If, therefore, some pages were closed in the record of history by the great decision of 1936, no legible chart was delivered, revealing the avenues of advance into the hazy land of the future, near or distant.

CHAPTER VIII

The Execution of the Mandate

As if symbolizing the hurried spirit of the age, the inauguration of President Roosevelt to succeed himself occurred on January 20, instead of March 4, in accordance with the Twentieth Amendment to the Constitution shortening the time between the popular mandate and the beginning of official action. Certainly symbolic to his critics and opponents who believed in omens were the black clouds that lowered over the city of Washington all day and the sheets of rain that poured down, dimming the bright colors of banners and streamers designed for the pageant. But for these "accidents of history," the President was in no way responsible and they could be dismissed as meaningless. Far more sibylline were two features of the occasion which he arranged to express his own sense of the proprieties. Putting aside protests from citizens and associations pacifically inclined, he decided that a military parade, not a civilian pageant, should celebrate his return to power. And he also decided that he and his immediate entourage at the White House must review the marching men, with banners

339

and martial music, from a replica of the Hermitage, the home
of Andrew Jackson, the hero of New Orleans who had worn
boots and spurs in war and politics.

Although the outward signs of his installation were military, President Roosevelt's inaugural address pulsated with
peaceful professions. He opened with an emphasis on the
beneficent obligations of the State: "The need to find
through government the instrument of our united purpose to
solve for the individual the ever rising problems of a complex
civilization. Repeated attempts at their solution without
the aid of government had left us baffled and bewildered.
For, without that aid, we had been unable to create those
moral controls over the services of science which are necessary to make science a useful servant instead of a ruthless
master of mankind. To do this we knew that we must find
practical controls over blind economic forces and blindly
selfish men. We of the Republic sensed the truth that democratic government has innate capacity to protect its people
against disasters once considered inevitable — to solve problems once considered unsolvable. We would not admit that
we could not find a way to master economic epidemics just as,
after centuries of fatalistic suffering, we had found a way to
master epidemics of disease. We refused to leave the problems of our common welfare to be solved by the winds of
chance and the hurricanes of disaster." "Complex civilization . . . moral controls . . . services of science . . . master economic epidemics . . . fatalistic suffering . . . winds
of chance . . . hurricanes of disaster" — these were words
hard to discover in previous presidential addresses.

Long before January 20, 1937, a European philosopher,
Friedrich Meinecke, had found, in the eternal conflict between the ideal and the real, the tragedy of western civilization. Whether through reading or reflection President Roosevelt had come to a similar conclusion and in his address he
took account of the tragedy: "We are beginning to wipe out
the line that divides the practical from the ideal, and in so
doing we are fashioning an instrument of unimagined power

for the establishment of a morally better world." The times are changing. "For these reasons I am justified in believing that the greatest change we have witnessed has been the change in the moral climate of America. . . . Shall we pause now and turn our back upon the road that lies ahead ? . . . Timidity asks 'how difficult is the road ahead?'" The United States "can demonstrate that, under democratic methods of government, national wealth can be translated into a spreading volume of human comforts hitherto unknown — and the lowest standard of living can be raised far above the level of mere subsistence." In other words, the United States could have the material basis for a civilization shared by all; it need not rest upon slavery, servitude, or a vast body of laborers on or below the subsistence level. Its President was rejecting an argument buttressed by fifty centuries of history and disowning an explicit or tacit tradition as deep-rooted as the very idea of government and the main body of contemporary middle-class opinion.

Having thrown the weight of his intellectual and moral force on the side of resolving the tragic conflict between the ideal and the real, Roosevelt passed beyond generalities. He went on realistically and, judging by the phrases of mere thanksgiving so often uttered on such occasions, courageously, to specify the evils to be overcome. "In this nation I see tens of millions of its citizens — a substantial part of its whole population — who at this very moment are denied the greater part of what the very lowest standards of today call the necessities of life." At this point the President paused. His circle of hard-headed politicians preserved their inscrutable calm; chill winds blew gusts of rain hither and yon over the plaza in front of the Capitol; but he proceeded with his specifications: "I see millions of families trying to live on incomes so meagre that the pall of family disaster hangs over them day by day. I see millions whose daily lives in city and on farm continue under conditions labelled indecent by a so-called polite society half a century ago. I see millions denied education, recreation, and the opportunity to better their lot and the lot of their children. I see millions lacking the means to buy the products of farm and factory and by their poverty denying work and productiveness to many other millions. I see one-third of a nation ill-housed, ill-clad, ill-nourished." He also saw the other two-thirds of the nation : "In our seeking for economic and political progress as a nation, we all go up — or else we all go down — as one people."

This was not to say that a pessimist was addressing the nation : "It is not in despair that I paint you that picture. I paint it for you in hope, because the nation, seeing and understanding the injustice in it, proposes to paint it out. We are determined to make every American citizen the subject of his country's interest and concern, and we will never regard any faithful law-abiding group within our borders as superfluous. . . . If I know aught of the spirit and purpose of our nation, we will not listen to comfort, opportunism and timidity. We will carry on."

Yet across the plaza and a narrow street stood the Palace of Justice, under the clouds and in the rain. From its chamber had gone forth decrees proclaiming that vital measures of Roosevelt's first administration were forbidden by a higher power — the Constitution of the United States — whose cryptic meaning a majority of the Supreme Court could alone decipher. Since the Supreme Court had invalidated the main parts of a milder program, how could President Roosevelt expect to carry on, to achieve the larger promises ? His address contained no concrete answer, merely a premonition : "The Constitution of 1787 did not make our democracy impotent."

§

Fresh from the people, with the mandate in its hand, the Seventy-fifth Congress opened with enthusiasm. Among the first measures laid before it for consideration was the Guffey-Vinson bituminous coal bill to take the place of the Coal Act which had been declared null and void by the Supreme Court in 1935. The sickness that had long plagued the coal industry had not been cured by the judicial operation. By a consensus of expert opinion, some form of coördination and collective action was necessary to keep it alive, to say nothing of restoring it to health. Congress had tried to accomplish this purpose. The Supreme Court had intervened. Congress tried again. By April 12 it completed the passage of the new coal bill and the President's signature was soon affixed to this "little National Industrial Recovery Bill." The substitute law provided for public and private collaboration in matters of marketing, price control, and trade practices throughout the industry. In deference to the Supreme Court's rulings, Congress omitted the sections of the previous law pertaining to the determination of hours and wages, but it declared collective bargaining in labor relations to be a part of the public policy governing the administration of the law.

While the coal bill was on its way to passage, Congress began the study of several measures proposed on behalf of agriculture. In the campaign of 1936 the Democrats had assured farmers and planters that they would aid them despite the adverse decisions of the Supreme Court, and the Republican candidate, Governor Landon, had outbidden them in some respects for the support of this powerful interest. Now the response of Congress to the commitments was whole-hearted and found expression in a number of enactments. A sugar-quota law applied the principles of the dead Agricultural Adjustment Act to the sugar industry. It authorized the Secretary of Agriculture to determine the amount of sugar required by consumers in the United States, fixed the proportions to be allocated to foreign and domestic producers, empowered the Secretary to make allocations of quotas among domestic producers, made specific stipulations respecting the employment of labor, and provided benefit payments to farmers who complied with the terms of the law. Neither in intentions nor designs was there any pure laissez faire in this Act. Notwithstanding the pressures and objections of particular interests, the law brought within its scope exporters, importers, farmers, workers, and manufacturers engaged in the wide-reaching sugar industry.

Almost without opposition, certainly with no concerted Republican resistance, Congress amended and reënacted several provisions of the Agricultural Adjustment Act relative to marketing orders and agreements, especially in connection with the dairy industry. In destroying the Adjustment Act, Justice Roberts had said that agriculture belonged to the states. Bowing to his decree, Congress made grants to states for carrying out its "soil-conservation program"; the President called upon state governors to press for appropriate local legislation; and a majority of state legislatures responded favorably within a few months. To this circumlocution, Congress added a new Soil Conservation Act which was a kind of preliminary to a wider measure soon to follow.

Paying heed to the alarming growth of farm tenancy, reported by a special presidential commission, Congress made at least a feint in that direction. By the Farm Tenant Act, signed July 23, 1937, it gave to the Secretary of Agriculture the power to arrange long term loans to tenants, at three per cent interest, for the purchase of homesteads, and provided for initial appropriations. In the course of such transactions the Secretary could exercise a wide discretion in retiring submarginal land and rehabilitating run-down farms. More radical than the President in rural sympathies, Congress repassed, over his veto, a bill continuing low rates of interest on farm loans. In the House sixty-two Republicans voted for over-riding the President's objections and only seven voted against it, thus displaying an almost united front in favor of the agrarian proposal. In the meantime Secretary Wallace announced the most comprehensive agricultural program yet conceived in the United States — a program including an "ever normal granary" for the storage of five great non-perishable commodities. And action was promised on this proposal at the next session.

Amid the concern for agriculture, cities were remembered. Returning to the issue raised by municipal bankruptcies in many parts of the country, Congress passed the Municipal Debt Adjustment Act to replace the Bankruptcy Act declared void by the Supreme Court. Then the ill-housed, to whom the President referred in his inaugural address, were taken into consideration. On February 24, Senator Wagner of New York introduced a broad measure authorizing a frontal attack on the problem of bad housing. Although debate was long drawn out and some opposition came from members representing rural regions, especially conservative Democrats and Republicans, Senator Wagner's bill became a law on September 1. Not without reason was it called "the most important legislation of the session."

The Act set up the United States Housing Authority in the Department of the Interior and conferred upon it the power to issue within a fixed period $500,000,000 in securities, for the purpose of financing public agencies engaged in clearing slums, repairing buildings, and erecting new dwellings. At last taking cognizance of the fact that families in the low-wage levels really could not pay a sustaining rental for decent housing, Congress provided conditional subsidies to communities. It offered them annual grants in aid of low rents if they would make contributions equal to twenty per cent of the total. As a supplement in the same interest, it authorized federal subsidies running as high as forty per cent of the construction cost, subject to the stipulation that local authorities add twenty per cent. By this means, the author of the measure expected, construction would be stimulated and economic barriers to low-rental housing would be removed.

In the preamble the Housing Act announced a departure from traditional conceptions of federal responsibilities in matters of human well-being and a pledge of national concern for the living conditions of the people. It declared the policy of the United States to be the promotion of the general welfare by helping the states and their subdivisions to alleviate unemployment, to remedy unsafe and unsanitary housing conditions, and to overcome the acute shortage of decent, safe, and healthful dwellings for families of low income in rural and urban communities. From beginning to end the Act reflected the condition of the housing industry as a branch of capitalist enterprise. In the days of the golden glow thousands of investors had put billions of dollars into the real estate bonds which had financed the feverish construction boom, and in the days of its dissolution they had lost the major portion of their "savings." Many mortgage companies were proved to be little better than pillagers. The bankruptcy proceedings that followed the great smash of 1929 had been accompanied by speculation and peculation in which lawyers, receivers, referees, and harpies had thrived on pickings from the remnants. In such circumstances private investors were in no mood to hurl more billions, if they had the money, into an industry that had despoiled them and left behind a trail of chicanery and dishonesty added to folly. Whether by throwing public credit into the breach the Wagner Act could revive a decaying trade and accomplish, on any considerable scale, the promise of the preamble remained hidden in the general fate of all capitalist enterprises.

Other great measures, proposed or supported by the Roosevelt administration in fulfillment of the mandate, were blocked in Congress as the unwieldy body of Democrats broke up into snarling factions. Both parties had bound themselves in the campaign to extend the merit system in the rapidly expanding federal service. Instead of discharging this obligation, Congress raided the civil service and created more political jobs. Leonard D. White, who retired from membership on the Civil Service Commission, mildly described the operations of the legislators: "This record discloses a scandalous disregard of a solemn undertaking and a complete indifference to the plain mandate of the American people." Even the Housing Act, while making noble professions, exempted officers, attorneys, experts, and all positions paying over $1980 a year from the restrictions of the Civil Service Act. But in the summer of 1938 President Roosevelt offset this record by broad executive orders extending the merit system to practically all positions in the federal service not expressly exempted by law.

Dragged along for weeks and finally defeated was the President's plan for the reorganization and consolidation of the scattered and often conflicting agencies of the Federal Government. To this reform both parties had long paid lip service. On the basis of a special report from a Committee on Administrative Management, Roosevelt called upon Congress to enact legislation authorizing a realignment of federal administration in the interest of efficiency and economy. Thumbs were turned down on his project. A similar fate was meted out to the President's plan for the creation of seven regional agencies, akin to the Tennessee Valley Authority, for the purpose of developing the resources of seven great watersheds in the United States. With the Tennessee experiment already under fire and the electric power interests on guard against the project, Congress laid this proposal on the shelf.

§

In some measure, although not entirely, the futilities of the Congress fresh from the triumph of 1936 were due to a controversy over judicial reform, precipitated by the President. His inaugural address gave no hint of the method to be employed in releasing the executive and legislative departments from the bonds imposed upon them by the constitutional interpretations of the Supreme Court. Yet the conflicts of preceding months and the temper of the campaign made it almost certain that some proposal would emerge from administration circles after the delivery of the popular mandate.

Acquainted with Charles G. Haines' monumental treatise on judicial conflicts and with supplementary documentation, watchers of the political scene had practical grounds for supposing that the deadlock between the Political Departments of the Government on the one side and the Judicial Department on the other, in respect of primary policies, would be relieved by some process. They remembered, for instance, that the Republican party, with Lincoln at the head, had defied the ruling of the Supreme Court in the Dred Scott case, had refused to accept it, and had carried the day. They had in mind the way in which Democrats had later condemned the Supreme Court for its five-to-four decision in the Income Tax case and, though momentarily defeated, had seen victory achieved in the Sixteenth Amendment. John Marshall had been able to strike down an obscure provision of the Judiciary Act in Marbury versus Madison without evoking effective measures in rebuttal, but the Court had never succeeded in paralyzing a statute of major interest to any great political party without encountering a powerful recoil.

The whispering galleries of Washington between the election in November and the opening of Congress buzzed with discussions of the constitutional issue. In January, soon after the inaugural, a number of liberals, including Senator Norris, issued a call for a national conference to consider the issue and to concentrate opinion on a single plan for disposing of it. Of plans there were many; of opinions there were, perhaps, even more. Congress could follow a Republican precedent of Reconstruction days and by a simple enactment strip the Supreme Court of appellate jurisdiction over constitutional cases — a procedure once upheld by the Court itself. Congress could require a majority of six or seven Justices to invalidate a statute — a proposition obscured by juristic doubts.

From statutes, opinion swung to amendments. The thought was easy to entertain. But what kind of an amendment? Many had been devised. Sticklers for propriety proposed an amendment concretely enlarging or restating the power of Congress to deal with social and economic legislation. Scoffers replied that choosing effective phraseology would be difficult and that judges of the Supreme Court could quickly riddle the provision in their classic style, as they had already riddled many plain words in the law of the land. In a second projected amendment it was proposed that Congress be given power to over-ride an adverse judicial decision by an extraordinary majority, perhaps after a congressional election had intervened. Around and around these and other schemes, debate and oratory clacked and rattled without effecting a concentration of the talents seeking a way through the constitutional impasse.

Before the liberal conference could assemble, out of a blue sky, on February 5, 1937, came President Roosevelt's proposal for cutting the Gordian knot, accompanied by a bill couched in specific terms. In substance the scheme went beyond the Supreme Court and provided for the appointment of a new federal judge whenever an incumbent failed to resign or retire within six months after reaching the age of seventy. The number of judges so to be appointed was limited to fifty, of whom not more than six could be added to the Supreme Court.

In his covering message, the President referred to past changes in the number of Supreme Court judges; to the heavy burdens carried by the Court; to long and vexatious delays in litigation; to the clogging of administrative processes by injunctions or other forms of judicial intervention; to the phenomenon of a federal law constitutional in one district and invalid in another; to the fact that years often passed before such muddles were straightened out by final adjudication in Washington. Turning to the sanction of precedent, the President cited the Act of 1919, which required him to nominate a new district or circuit judge whenever he found one permanently incapacitated, and declared that no President should be asked to pass upon the ability or disability of a particular judge. "Modern complexities," he said, "call also for a constant infusion of new blood in the courts, just as it is needed in the executive functions of the government and in private business. . . . New facts become blurred through old glasses fitted, as it were, for the needs of another generation; older men, assuming that the scene is the same as it was in the past, cease to explore or inquire into the present or the future." The essential concepts of justice, he insisted, must be applied in the light of the needs and facts of an ever-changing world.

§

The President's message on his court plan stunned friends and foes. Apparently in drafting it he had not consulted or informed party leaders in Congress, or taken counsel with all the members of his official family. If he had, no inkling of the project had reached the gossip corridors of the capital in advance of his message. When the proposal was made known, it provoked feelings of wonder, resentment, and resistance. Republicans were quick in lining up their forces for opposition. Their own offering to the public at the last election had been rejected and they were searching for an opportunity to pound some general measure that touched no specific issues so recently decided by the popular verdict. This was their chance. It was now possible for them to condemn changes in the composition of the Supreme Court without approving the action of that tribunal in striking down laws which they abhorred. True to the party instinct, they made the most of the occasion, without obtruding their thin and battered ranks too obviously upon the public gaze. True also to political use and wont, they conveniently overlooked all their party had said and done in connection with the Dred Scott case and the first Legal Tender case. Gathering up the garments of righteousness, which Democrats had worn in 1857 and 1871, they clothed themselves in the apparel of pure theory.

The formulas of their argument were age-worn and simple. They had been recited by one party or another, as occasion permitted, since the establishment of the Federal Government, and they ran in this fashion. The Constitution ordains an independent judiciary. The Supreme Court consists of honorable and competent lawyers. In passing upon the validity of a statute, the judges, or a majority of them, perform an act as certain as calculations in physics or mathematics; they merely "square" the statute by the Constitution and, according to the reading of measurement, declare it correct or void. The act so performed involves no question of personal judgment, conscience, social preference, or economic predilection — nothing save the perfect and indisputable mandate and logic of law. When a statute is declared void, the Court merely expresses the will of the people set forth in the Constitution. It is, in short, the automatic and infallible (or almost infallible) executor of the people's will as against the erroneous judgment of Congress and the President. After the Court has invalidated a statute, the one and only procedure lawfully available to Congress, the President, and the people, if dissatisfied with the verdict, is to amend the Constitution by due process — a two-thirds vote in Congress and approval by three-fourths of the states.

Thus the argument moved from unequivocal axiom to unequivocal axiom and closed with the unanswerable demonstration. As long as the tacit assumptions of the major premise were unexplored and the sociology of the axioms was left entirely out of the reckoning, the conclusion was indisputable: Loyalty to the Constitution requires the indignant repudiation of President Roosevelt's proposal for reorganizing the federal judiciary.

On both the logomachy and the merits of the case, the President's own party was torn asunder. The chief committees and the general political management in Congress were largely in the hands of conservative Democrats from the South, although the numerical weight of the party was then in the North. On the whole the sociological jurisprudence of the Southern Democrats corresponded with fair exactness to that generally prevailing in the North about 1880. Apart from pleasure over cotton and tobacco legislation, the President's Southern colleagues, with a few exceptions, had been restive under his direction and had accepted many of his other measures without cordiality and often with strong distaste. Since an hour and wage bill, devised, among other things, to abolish the low differentials of the South, was then pending, these colleagues might well rejoice in the prospect of judicial annulment. It was not surprising, therefore, that their veteran leader, Senator Carter Glass, of Virginia, in a national broadcast, emptied the vials of his wrath upon the judiciary project, raked it from beginning to end with the fire of his powerful vituperation. Nor was it surprising that the Vice President, John N. Garner of Texas, deliberately left the Capitol for a vacation at home and did not return until he was able to administer the death blow to the statutory proposal, at least for the current session of Congress.

The liberal wing of the President's supporters was at first bewildered and then divided into factions. Many individuals within its fold, perhaps a majority, had hoped for a more fundamental treatment of the deadlock, on the assumption that a constitutional amendment could be adopted or that Congress could permanently alter the procedure of the Supreme Court by statutory enactment. Personal considerations, as usual, also entered into consideration ; and they were crystallized when Postmaster General Farley, Chairman of the Democratic National Committee, declaring that the votes for the bill were "in the bag," virtually ordered Senators who had ridden into power "on the President's coat tails" to obey orders from the White House. More than one wavering mind was apparently stiffened by what seemed to be a personal insult.

Whatever motives dominated quivering minds, in the end one of the most active Senators on the Democratic side, Burton K. Wheeler, announced his resolute opposition to the Court plan and condemned it in terms scarcely less withering than those called into play by Senator Glass. Of Mr. Wheeler's progressive orthodoxy there could be no question. He had taken his political fate by the forelock and joined the revolt of Senator Robert M. La Follette against both parties in 1924, when Franklin D. Roosevelt had supported John W. Davis, now a beacon of the Liberty League. For the opposition to the Court plan, Senator Wheeler was a godsend and he was taken into its fold with appreciation.

Of the other liberals who decided to support the Court plan

many were skeptical about the wisdom of the particular project but, confronting the necessity of choice, they cast their lot with the President. After all, they reasoned, it might be impossible to get an agreement in Congress upon any kind of amendment or to secure ratification by three-fourths of the states within a period of ten or fifteen years. Despite the brave arguments in favor of an amendment, there was no assurance of any gain in that direction. Perhaps the President, ingenious in interpreting popular dispositions, had correctly fixed the only practical line of advance against "the judicial oligarchy" that formed a majority of the Supreme Court. For these and other reasons, a number of "honest doubters" put aside irresolution and defended the bill to reorganize the judiciary.

Even with chances of defeat ahead, some liberals were happy to have an opportunity to debate before the whole country the issue presented by the steady advance of the federal judiciary upon the field of policy — an issue long discussed in the technical language of the law schools. Nowhere in the law journals could there be found in the austere language of jurisprudence competent support for the entire course which the Supreme Court had deliberately pursued for the preceding quarter of a century. To translate the language of adepts into the language of the street was the task assumed by the liberals who finally went over to the President's side in the conflict. Seldom if ever had they enjoyed such an opportunity to bridge the gap between erudition and popular impressions.

The division of the country on the issue presented curious contrasts with earlier conflicts. In the controversy over the judiciary that followed the Dred Scott decision in 1857, Respectability had been divided. Men of such talents and power as Abraham Lincoln and William H. Seward had led in rebuking the Court and had questioned its honor as well as its reasoning. During the debate of 1896 over the income tax decision and injunction procedures, Respectability had been mainly on the side of the angels, while criticism came from

"populists" and "anarchists," as they were called by sticklers for conformity. Now in 1937 Respectability was in
fierce discord. It is true that six New England college presidents deemed it necessary publicly to condemn the court
plan, and that the president of Princeton University went to
Washington in person to speak against it. It is true that
other eminent members of the élite openly aligned themselves
with the opposition. But talents, if not wealth, were ranged
in opposite camps. If the bulk of Excellence was antagonistic, the distinguished deans of law schools and the scholarly
students of constitutional history who favored the bill could
not be called populists and anarchists in the style of 1896. In
the lapse of time much water had run over the wheel.

As the contest advanced, the opposition adopted a definite
form of strategy. In the matter of maneuvering, on account
of numerical weakness or for less obvious reasons, the Republican management left sapping and mining mainly to the
Democratic insurgents. While quietly holding its own position, it chose to press Senator Wheeler to the front as the
strategist of the campaign rather than the titular Republican
leader, Senator McNary — who after all had voted for many
New Deal measures himself. Significantly absent now from
the Senate committee's hearings on the judiciary bill were
the "great constitutional lawyers" who the year before had
served the Liberty League in its disparagement of President
Roosevelt and all his works. Nowhere among the witnesses
that appeared before the committee was there a mighty
Joseph Choate, to declaim in the rhetoric of Webster against
"this assault on private property and the Constitution."
Eminent lawyers and distinguished citizens did file their
objections to the court bill, but none came forth from the
school of oratorical Supereminence to lodge his complaints in
person. Nor did those who protested against the Court plan
as a rule undertake to defend all the decisions of the Supreme Court that had precipitated the conflict.

Indeed one of the conspicuous features of the opposition
was the general admission that the Court had rendered

dubious or unwarranted opinions and had laid itself open to just criticism. A New England college president, in voicing his censure of the court bill, confessed that on the whole his view of the Constitution was that entertained by the dissenting minority. Senator Wheeler declared before the Senate committee that he had severely criticized some decisions of the Supreme Court, and he scorned the classic theory of judicial impeccability by advocating an amendment permitting Congress, by due process, to over-ride judicial vetoes contrary to its interpretation of the Constitution. In a speech upon the floor of the Senate, Joseph O'Mahoney, who ably seconded Senator Wheeler's attacks on the bill, declared positively that "the courts have upon occasion usurped legislative power, and that usurpation ought to be brought to an end. I have repeatedly denounced it. There can be no defense of it."

This was, of course, directly contrary to the classic doctrine that the federal courts only set forth the true meaning of the Constitution and could not possibly misinterpret it or usurp power. Nevertheless it is in the nature of politicians to accept aid even from a sworn enemy of their most precious propositions. If belief in the major axiom of judicial infallibility had been a test for membership in the opposition, the President's court bill would have quickly gone through Congress and commanded a far more general approval in the country. Agreement could have been reached on a concrete action amid differences of opinion over its meaning and consequences.

As usual in the discussion of great public questions, the contestants in the controversy over the judiciary "talked past one another," to use Karl Mannheim's phrase, for the sources of their difference in opinion did not lie entirely, if at all, in the theme of debate or the words employed in the argument. On their part, sponsors of the President's proposal declined to accept either the major axiom or the structure of the classic syllogism. They insisted on testing the purity of perfect theory by reference to historic practices.

They widened the frame of reference beyond logic to the borders of history and sociology. The Supreme Court should be independent? Has it ever been in fact wholly independent of the ideas and policies of the President and Senate that selected its members? The Supreme Court merely declares the law of the Constitution? Dissenting members of the Court, equally honorable, equally competent, have repeatedly maintained that the majority was simply reading its economic theories or predilections into the general language of the document. It is an unholy thing to change the number of federal judges for the purpose of influencing the course of constitutional interpretation? This had been done, more or less covertly — by Jefferson's Republicans, Jackson's Democrats, and Lincoln's Republicans. It is evil to think of the constitutional theories and social sympathies of possible nominees when making selections for the supreme bench? Have the President and Senate ever failed in practice to take these basic matters into account? When the Supreme Court declares a law invalid, the only way out of the impasse is a constitutional amendment? Other methods have been adopted in many cases and only once in a century and a half has Congress over-ridden an adverse decision by resorting to an amendment. Righteousness, patriotism, democracy, loyalty to the Constitution, knowledge, and logic, it has been said, are opposed to the judiciary bill. How can anyone be sure that he has sole possession of those virtues?

Taking into the reckoning the testimony and statements presented to the Senate committee for and against the bill, no monopoly of talents appeared on either side. The dean of the Columbia University Law School opposed it; the dean of the Yale Law School supported it. Against the opposition of the dean of the Michigan Law School was pitted the support of the dean of the Northwestern University Law School. For the bill, appeared the dean of the Notre Dame Law School; against it, the dean of the Fordham Law School. The dean of the New York University Law School filed stern objections ending in a prayer; the former dean of the Pennsylvania Law

School and head of the American Law Institute and the former dean of the Duke University Law School cast their influence on the side of the bill. Professor E. S. Corwin and Professor W. F. Dodd, both serious students of constitutional law and history, disagreed, the former supporting and the latter opposing the measure. Of more than passing interest was the fact that Charles Grove Haines, undoubtedly the greatest authority on judicial conflicts in American history, with the indefatigable researches of a lifetime at his command, went before the Senate committee to support the President's project for resolving the judicial conflict of 1937. Nor was it without significance that three or four outstanding masters of constitutional law, masters, as distinguished from advocates of causes, stood mute while the conflict was in progress. Above all things it was evident that a profound alteration in the climate of expert and general opinion had occurred since the great judiciary dispute of 1896.

When the Senate committee closed its hearings early in June, 1937, it decided by the narrow margin of one vote against the court bill. In its report the majority spared no words of excoriation. The summary denounced the proposed bill as a "needless, futile, and utterly dangerous abandonment of constitutional principle . . . without precedent and without justification." The bill, if enacted, would "subjugate the courts to the will of Congress and the President and thereby destroy the independence of the judiciary, the only certain shield of individual rights. . . . It points the way to the evasion of the Constitution and establishes the method whereby the people may be deprived of their right to pass upon all amendments of the fundamental law . . . a proposal that violates every sacred tradition of American democracy. Under the form of the Constitution it seeks to do that which is unconstitutional. . . . It is a measure which should be so emphatically rejected that its parallel will never again be presented to the free representatives of the free people of America." Furthermore, the bill was presented to Congress "in a most intricate form and for reasons that obscured its real purposes." In short, the President was proposing to evade the terms of the Constitution, subjugate the courts, deprive the people of their rights, violate every sacred tradition of American democracy; besides, he was guilty of deceit. Those were contemptuous words for seven Democrats to hurl at the leader of their party, the President of the United States.

§

Between February and June, while the debate was raging in Congress, in the press, over the radio, and before the Senate committee, no sound of complaint came from the Palace of Justice. It was a privilege of the Supreme Court to keep secret and sacred the conflicts of opinion, conviction, and temper which appeared at its inner council table. Rumors might escape through solid doors, but custom forbade authentication — at least until memoirs of the dead could safely be published. Custom likewise placed restraints on judicial participation in public disputes. Only once during the contest over the President's proposal was a voice heard from behind the veil. In response to an inquiry from Senator Wheeler, Chief Justice Hughes, with the approval of Justice Van Devanter and Justice Brandeis, wrote a letter declaring that the Supreme Court was "fully abreast of its work," thus directly denying one of President Roosevelt's main contentions that it could not carry its load; and the Chief Justice allowed the Senator to make this communication public. What the members of the Court thought of the court bill and of the national uproar over it was nowhere a matter of accessible record, but inferences from experience permitted a guess that mighty arguments were being carried on at the council table. Little more than a year had passed since Justice Stone warned his colleagues, in the Agricultural Adjustment case, that an abuse of power might destroy it, and the forecast of fulfillment now fell athwart the Palace of Justice. With the verdict of the November election behind them and the President's bill in front of them, the justices of the Supreme Court must have taken thought of the morrow.

What the justices would have done between February and June, 1937, had President Roosevelt quietly acquiesced in their previous decisions against his measures was not known, even to the justices themselves. Nor could it ever be known. History permitted no repetition of identical laboratory experiments in jurisprudence in different circumstances. The Court merely went ahead, entering its decisions and opinions upon the public record as the debate over the judiciary bill swept the forum. On March 29, by a five to four majority, the Court upheld the validity of a minimum wage law that came to it from the state of Washington. Less than a year before, the Court, by a five to four majority, the "same" Court, had declared void a similar measure from the state of New York. In the New York case, Justice Roberts had joined Justices Sutherland, Van Devanter, McReynolds, and Butler in holding that the state had no power under the Constitution to enact such legislation; while the Chief Justice had aligned himself with the dissenting Justices Stone, Brandeis, and Cardozo. In the Washington case, Justice Roberts was enrolled in the majority that sustained the minimum wage law.

To mere laymen this looked like a reversal of position but the Chief Justice, in his opinion, shrouded the transaction with the technicalities of the law, which spared his colleague the positive appearance of having changed his mind during the past ten months. But in so doing the Chief Justice did not spare the Court. In affirming the Washington statute, he declared without wincing that the contrary decision in the earlier District of Columbia case "should be, and it is, overruled." For some reason, despite the orthodox thesis, the Constitution which had not been amended in this respect was changed to mean something which it had not meant when President Roosevelt sent his court message to Congress in February. Had two plus two ceased to equal four?

A fortnight later, the Supreme Court, in another five to

four decision, upheld the Wagner Labor Relations Act designed to promote collective bargaining in industry. "Friends and Foes of Bench Change; Sweeping Progress within a Year," flamed the front page headlines of The New York Times announcing this new "victory" for the Roosevelt administration. Two years before, in the National Recovery case, the Court had held, in effect, that the regulation of industry, except where "direct effects" on interstate commerce are in evidence, belongs under the Constitution to the states. Now, in the Wagner case, it held that industries whose products enter into interstate commerce come specifically within the commerce powers of Congress. To the layman, this might have seemed to be a reversal of the position on the Recovery case; indeed, the four dissenting Justices of the Court thought it was and said as much. Yet in the refinements of judicial distinctions there was no reversal, merely a discrimination of substance and circumstance.

In vain did the minority declare that "almost anything — marriage, birth, death — may in some fashion affect commerce. . . . There must be no impairment of rights guaranteed. . . . The right to contract is fundamental and includes the privilege of selecting those with whom one is willing to assume contractual relations." The majority stood solid in upholding the constitutionality of the Labor Act and President Roosevelt revealed his jubilation in an open message to a friend. "It's been a pretty good day for all of us," he said. In truth it seemed a good day in general, for opponents of his court plan now said that the reorganization of the judiciary was wholly unnecessary, and supporters of the bill suspected that its efficacy was becoming obvious.

A third stroke came on May 24. On that day the Supreme Court held valid, by another five to four vote, the unemployment insurance tax provisions of the Social Security Act and an Alabama statute setting up a scheme of state insurance in coöperation with the Federal Government. To the inexpert mind this decision might also have seemed to be a direct reversal of the principles announced in the ruling of the Court against the Agricultural Adjustment Act. Like that measure, the Security Act laid a tax — not for revenue at all but for the purpose of inducing, indeed compelling, states to establish a certain program of insurance. In the Adjustment case, Justice Roberts had declared that agriculture was a matter reserved to the states. Was not insurance just as much a field reserved to the states? Even more, since promoting social insurance, in contrast to agriculture, was certainly not contemplated as a federal function in 1787. How could Congress constitutionally force states by punitive taxation to provide such insurance and yet not authorize the Secretary of Agriculture to enter into voluntary arrangements with farmers for crop adjustments? Had Chief Justice Hughes and Justice Roberts, who agreed in holding the Agricultural Adjustment Act unconstitutional, changed their minds? For these questions legal thought had good answers, if not real answers: namely, that the first case was no precedent for the second and that differences in facts warranted discriminations in the application of the Constitution.

Since the decisions and opinions of the Court in these cases seriously affected the general public, the inexpertness of laymen outweighed the panurgy of the legal fraternity in the formation of popular sentiments on the subject. Readers of newspapers, unskilled in the technology of the law, could readily assume from the morning headlines that the Court had reversed itself and surrendered. By many defenders of the President's court plan the new judicial rulings were read in this light, and on that ground some of them urged him to accept the substance of victory, drop or modify his project, and relax executive pressure on the judicial branch of the Government.

Opponents of the proposed Court reorganization now had mixed feelings. They still insisted upon defeating the court bill but differed as to reasons for the policy. Liberals in their ranks were inclined to approve the latest grist of constitutional law ground out by the Court and be content to let well enough alone. On the other hand, the conservative wing,

still determined in its antagonism to the bill, looked upon
the grist with displeasure. Could a Court that had sustained
minimum wage legislation, the Wagner Labor Act, and the
Social Security Act really serve as the indomitable protector
of free contract, private property, and the individual liberty
of possessors against the pressure of popular mandates? In
ditching President Roosevelt had the Court not surrendered
the very citadel of the constitutional stronghold which, after
all, formed the center of the contest over the bill for the reorganization of the judiciary? Thoughts of victory over the
Chief Executive were permeated by forebodings.

§

While the echoes of the Social Security decision were still
resounding, another flash broke into the surcharged atmosphere of Washington. Just as the Senate committee was
preparing to file its denunciation of the President's court
plan, Justice Van Devanter announced his coming withdrawal from the Supreme Court. For this action Congress
had recently prepared the way by passing a bill permitting
retirement on full salary. That measure and the announcement of the Justice had the superficial semblance of an economic bargain, though the semblance could be regarded as
deceptive. In any case Justice Van Devanter had been
among the consistent opponents of recent social and economic
legislation, and his return to private life gave President
Roosevelt an opportunity to select his first justice for the
supreme bench. That he would not choose a nominee with
the exact outlook of Justice Van Devanter was a foregone
conclusion. Despite the long-standing tradition that mere
honor and technical competence were sufficient qualifications
for a justice, it was reasonable to expect the choice of a man
under eighty years of age, belonging to a more recent generation, and in general sympathy with the constitutional outlook
of the Chief Executive of the Nation who was to appoint
him.

After the notice of Justice Van Devanter's retirement was made public, buzzing gossip was focused on his probable successor. Long lists of available and congenial candidates were canvassed by editors and commentators. For a while it was rumored that the President, compelled to reckon with opposition in the Senate, would make a recess appointment after the adjournment of Congress. Undoubtedly he was in a trying position and his perplexity was increased by the sudden death of Senator Joseph Robinson. The Senator, though conservative in attitude and affiliations, had been a loyal leader in the upper chamber; and it had been more or less taken for granted that his reward would be an appointment to the first vacancy in the Supreme Court. At the time of his death he was engaged in a struggle to engineer through the Senate a modified court plan which would permit the President to nominate two additional Justices instead of six. Now even that project was blocked. With the passing of Senator Robinson, Vice President Garner took charge of the legislative machine, aligned himself completely with the opposition, reduced the President's proposal to mere procedural changes, and killed the provisions for a reorganization of the Supreme Court. Stung by the repudiation at the hands of his own party and knowing that any nominee for the Court might be rejected by the Senate, President Roosevelt kept his counsel and bided his time.

At length, in a stroke of dramatic suddenness, apparently without the previous knowledge of his own secretaries, the President announced the selection of Senator Hugo Black to fill Justice Van Devanter's vacant post. The very name of Senator Black caused consternation among the conservatives of both parties, since he had been a vigorous and unwavering supporter of New Deal measures in Congress and outside. As the head of Senate investigations he had conducted inquiries into the mercantile marine, aviation, and utility lobbies. He had pushed the inquisitorial powers of the Senate to the limit — beyond the limit, his critics alleged — and he had been as zealous in sustaining what he considered the public interest as Justice Pierce Butler had been in the defense of special railway interests as a practitioner at the bar. Not without reason of its own did Respectability look upon Senator Black as an injudicious man, a prosecutor rather than a judge. Respectability was also aware that he had been supported in his candidacy for the Senate by the small farmers, share croppers, and industrial workers of Alabama against a combination of industrialists, business interests, and planters.

In the ordinary course of politics, the nomination of a man like Hugo Black outside the Senate, if another such person could have been found, would have brought about searching inquiries. The Senate committee on the judiciary would have made an investigation of his character and attainments, hearing critics as well as friends. A favorable report from the committee would have been subjected to the fire of a critical debate on the floor of the Senate. But, according to a long-established theory, Senators were supposed to be well acquainted with their colleagues through close association, and under this rule of courtesy the Senate committee dispensed with wide-open hearings on Senator Black's qualifications for the Supreme Court. When the nomination came before the Senate, however, the courtesy of the gentlemen's club was somewhat relaxed. There was an exchange of inelegant words on the floor; and insinuations that the candidate was or had been a member of the Ku Klux Klan were bandied about. Still the Klan issue was not pressed. The hints were discounted. Everyone acquainted with backstairs politics in Washington knew that, if affiliations with the Klan were to be thoroughly aired, a number of Senators might actually blush. Senator Black was readily confirmed.

For the moment the President rode the crest of the waves. He had forced the conservatives of both parties in the Senate, under their own rule of courtesy, to accept, from their economic point of view, the worst possible man for the Supreme Court. Their feelings were almost beyond expression. Editors who had castigated the President during the campaign of 1936 found a new occasion for lashing out at him. But as everything had been done with due constitutional formality, there seemed to be no way of evading the dénouement.

After taking the oath of office Justice Black sailed for a vacation in Europe. He had barely reached the other side of the ocean when a Pittsburgh newspaper, belonging to the chain dominated by Paul Block, an inveterate foe of the New Deal, sprang a press mine. It published serially a number of documents and facsimiles purporting to show that Mr. Black had been a member of the Ku Klux Klan, that he had received a life membership in that association, and that he had addressed his white-robed brethren in fulsome terms. For Catholics, Jews, Negroes, and the intelligentsia generally, the revelations were certainly upsetting, to put the matter mildly. And now that the Klan was ineffectual, if not dead, in Northern states, politicians could breathe more lightly and strike at the new Justice by joining in the wholesale indictment of the organization. Justice Black was accused of duplicity for failing to acknowledge his membership while his confirmation was under consideration in the Senate. He should resign ; he should be impeached, it was said by furious foes. Even his best friends were distracted. When reporters besieged the Justice abroad, he refused to conciliate them. When they raised questions in press conferences at the White House, the President declined to comment until Justice Black's return, but by the expression of his countenance gave occasion for the report that he felt embittered. Had he never thought to inquire about Mr. Black's membership in the Klan ?

On his return to the United States in September, Justice Black greeted a swarm of pressmen genially, refused to make any statement, and informed them that he would present his case to the nation over the radio. To newspapers already chafing over their failure to dominate the country in 1936, this was egregious. It was indeed a dismissal of their fiction that news was and could be reported objectively. It was also another vivid demonstration of the fact that the radio was a powerful rival of the press, perhaps now superior, as a means of reaching the public without incurring the perils of editorial emphasis or distortion.

Having waved the press aside, Justice Black, on the appointed night, laid his case before an audience estimated at fifty million people. He began by a homily on the evils of religious and racial intolerance. He pointed to his congressional record in the defense of civil liberties. Then, after a breath-taking pause, the Justice quietly confessed that he had once belonged to the Klan. But he had early dissociated himself from it, he asserted, and had paid no attention to any life membership card if presented to him. After referring again to his record in Washington and his services on the side of civil liberties, the Justice bade his auditors "Good night."

Either by accident or advertence, Roosevelt was at the moment on a prolonged tour across the continent. The pressure of engagements connected with the trip or a sense of circumspection may have suggested immediate silence on the whole issue of the Supreme Court, since no utterance on that subject could have allayed the excitement over the question of the Ku Klux Klan. A tremendous diversion of popular interests to some other theme was necessary to accomplish that end. Wittingly or not, the President made the diversion on October 5, the very day that Justice Black started his work on the bench, as a throng swarmed curiously around the Palace of Justice and through the corridors. On that day Roosevelt delivered at Chicago a belligerent speech against foreign disturbers of world peace and proclaimed a "strong foreign policy." By implication he denounced Japan, Italy, and Germany as dictatorial states threatening the peace and safety of mankind, and suggested a union of democratic nations in a "quarantine" against them. In a flash this address to mankind crowded "the Black affair" into an obscure place in the newspapers. One Roman holiday was substituted for another.

Since the possibility of a second world Armageddon for democracy was offered to thought, lively imaginations could hear the war drums throbbing in the distance. The effect was instantaneous. Emotions were channeled into other outlets. Powerful newspapers that had consumed a forest of trees in rebelling against the appointment of Justice Black now joined in a shout of commendation for the President's gesture of grandeur on the world stage. Even Colonel Frank Knox who, as the Republican candidate for Vice President in 1936, had almost invoked curses on his head, now praised his statesmanship in foreign affairs. Governor Landon, not to be outdone, pronounced his benediction. Fervent advocates of "collective action" against dictatorships quieted for the moment any feelings of rage they may have nursed against Justice Black and hailed the dawn of a new day in international relations. If a multitude of people shrank from the idea of another world war, President Roosevelt's Chicago speech certainly blanketed the sullen grumblings over the Black episode.

Undisturbed, according to outward signs, by the noise in the country, the Supreme Court received Justice Black into membership and went on its way. It dismissed protests lodged against his eligibility and turned to its regular business. Finding himself shifted to the minority by recent veerings in jurisprudence, Justice Sutherland resigned near the close of the year and his place was taken by Stanley Reed who, as Solicitor General, had argued before the Court in favor of sustaining the validity of New Deal legislation. So minded and so constituted, the Supreme Court, before its adjournment in the spring of 1938, rendered a number of decisions in line with legislative tendencies, with Justice Black frequently dissenting on the ground that too much caution governed the divagation.

The Court refused to allow power companies to stop federal loans made to municipalities for the purpose of building competing plants. Setting aside a long line of reasoning, it held that certain officials and other persons connected with state and local activities were subject to federal income taxes. Utility holding companies were instructed to register with the Securities and Exchange Commission and to disclose their financial operations as provided by law. On vital points of

authority, the Labor Relations Board was upheld; and the
Federal Power Commission was confirmed in the right to
extract information from utilities. A decision in a California
rate case indicated that the Supreme Court was putting behind it old theories of valuation for rate-making purposes and
preparing to accept the prudent investment theory of valuation. Most spectacular of all, however important, was the
action of the Court in reversing a previous decision ninety-
six years old; in 1938 it declared that federal courts must
apply state law, not their own law, in suits between citizens
of different states involving local matters. At the end of the
term only one major statute of the New Deal remained without some form of judicial sanction, namely, the Tennessee
Valley Act.

§

Although Roosevelt's plan for the reconstruction of the
Supreme Court was defeated, Congress did overhaul the
lower ranges of the federal judicial system by passing the
Judicial Procedure Reform Act before it adjourned in August,
1937. Somewhat obscured by the fog of that debate, the Act
nevertheless conceded and struck at many abuses with which
the President had tried to deal. It stopped judges in the inferior courts from passing upon constitutional questions in
litigation between private parties without giving the Government notice of such impending issues. By express terms
federal courts were required to notify the Attorney General
whenever the constitutionality of an act of Congress was
drawn in question before them, and the Government was
permitted to intervene as a party for the presentation of
evidence and argument on the matter of validity. Single
judges of lower courts were forbidden to issue injunctions on
constitutional grounds at their pleasure, as in the good old
days. Henceforward such actions were to be tried in courts
composed of three judges, including at least one circuit judge;
injunctions were to run for only sixty days; and appeals to
the Supreme Court were to be expedited. Indeed, all along

the line, the process of appeal to that high tribunal was accelerated in cases involving decisions against the Government on constitutional questions. The Reform Act was by no means sensational, but it did serve notice on judges and private litigants that the business of the Government was not to be held up, delayed, and befuddled by shrewd tactics pursued under constitutional theories.

Apparently the contest over the judiciary exhausted Congress. Through the hot summer it grumbled and fretted in recriminations, producing no other legislation of significance for the execution of the mandate delivered in the presidential election. The Republicans, reduced to less than one-fourth of the House and to fourteen in the Senate, could offer neither effective opposition nor constructive proposals. The Democratic factions, more impatient with one another than with the impotent Republican remnants, were unable to agree on a single major bill bearing on the economics of recovery or reform. Tired of the impasse, they adjourned and went home. So the first session dominated by the victors of 1936 came to a dreary end. The barriers raised by the Supreme Court had been beaten down; the way for law making had been opened; but the Democrats in Congress could not unite on a grand program of legislation in fulfillment of their opportunity and their mandate.

Despite the ill feelings fanned by the debate over the judiciary and against the counsel of many advisers, President Roosevelt called Congress back for a special session in November to consider three measures included in his own program under the mandate: a national hours and wages bill, a comprehensive scheme for agricultural adjustment, and a modification of the Housing Act with a view to stimulating private building. As soon as the Senators and Representatives gathered in Washington, the discontents associated with the struggle over the reorganization of the judiciary revived and were aggravated by the demand for additional labor legislation. And for several reasons, leadership in the opposition to such legislation came largely from the President's own party — to which the mandate of 1936 had been delivered by the voters.

For more than a century, Southern statesmen had fought the protective tariff as a device for exploiting the agriculture of their region in the interest of Northern manufacturers. That cause they had lost. Now even Democrats would not vote for a general and drastic reduction of the tariff, to say nothing of free trade. For the South the next best hope of economic advantage had been industrialization, and a wage scale far below the Northern rate had served as a magnet drawing capital, mills, and factories from the North. To the middle class of the South, therefore, a national wages law, even with lower rates for that section, meant a bar in the way of rapid industrialization — another historic defeat. Nor, in fact, was the business of adjusting conflicting claims among producers of cotton, tobacco, corn, rice, peanuts, and dairy products a simple proposition for "the great Democracy" which had carried forty-six states in 1936. While Republicans looked on with ill-concealed glee, faithful Democrats wrangled among themselves and Congress adjourned in December without disposing of a single problem raised by the President's instructions, except the matter of amending the Housing Act.

The difficulties encountered by the Democrats in exploring the mandate of the preceding election were increased by a decline in business, euphoniously called a "recession," which set in during the spring of 1937. A precipitous fall in stocks and industrial production marked the economic course through the summer and autumn, with no halt in sight. Whether it was a temporary drop or the signal for a deepening crisis made little difference in the psychology of the hour. However viewed, the recession was embarrassing and, indeed, alarming, to the administration.

Having proscribed many speculative practices in business and on the stock exchanges, Democrats had fancied that the capitalist system would run more smoothly and discharge more effectively its alleged function of providing prosperity.

While industry had been on the upward grade, President Roosevelt, not unnaturally, had attributed the good fortune to his own policies. "We planned it that way," he had said. Yet, despite his plans, provisions, and policies, production had slowed down rapidly, more railways had gone into bankruptcy, and the army of the unemployed had risen again to the ten million figure and beyond. Such facts could not be ignored and the opposition made the most of them by demanding a retreat from the New Deal. It called for a repeal of the high tax on the undistributed profits of corporations and the tax on capital gains, provided by the Revenue Act of 1936. Just as the Democrats had ascribed the troubles of 1933 to Republican policies, now the Republicans invited the country to look at the fruits of the Democratic mandate.

§

When Congress reassembled early in January, 1938, it received a mild and general message from the President. No startling suggestions for an extension of the New Deal program, no new proposals for tackling the recession, were contained in the executive document. Had President Roosevelt found in the mandate of 1936 no instructions to make radical alterations in the economic system inherited from the past? Like President Hoover in 1929, he called representatives of capital and labor to the White House. He consulted with Thomas Lamont of J. P. Morgan and Company, Owen D. Young of the General Electric Company, and John L. Lewis of the Committee for Industrial Organization. He sought their advice on policies and measures. Yet, if any major decisions came out of such conversations, none was made known to the public. From the White House conference Lamont emerged laughing, as well he might, while his associates looked dour, as well they might. The Lords of Creation and of Labor seemed as helpless as the President of the United States to set the economic Leviathan in motion.

Having taken counsel with big business and big labor, the

President summoned, through the Department of Commerce, a conference of little business men and women; and they almost made a riot. They scored nearly every feature of the New Deal and with a vengeance called for the establishment of laissez faire. Only with difficulty were they persuaded to adjourn and leave the formulation of their conclusions to an executive committee, which toned down their resolutions with the idea of making a program somewhat palatable, at least, to the administration. The two groaning mountains had produced one big laugh and two small mice.

During the season of "conferences," representatives of the administration mounted the platform to discuss the causes of the depression. For instance, Robert H. Jackson put the onus on monopolies and trusts and demanded sterner legislation against them. His addresses, fortified by speeches in similar vein from other members of the official family, seemed to indicate a return over the long road to a "trust-busting campaign." The way to recovery and prosperity might now be sought in a retreat, after all the ridicule, back to the days of horses, buggies, village smithies, and crossroads stores.

Yet the whole country did not seem to be enamored of the strategy. Trust-busting had been a recurring political diversion since the enactment of the Sherman Anti-Trust Act in 1890; and the charm of the results had scarcely been commensurate with the noise. Entertaining doubts on this score, Donald Richberg, formerly sponsor of the National Industrial Recovery Act, spoke genially and diffidently of coöperation with big business. But President Roosevelt countered by exclaiming at a press conference: "Why have any holding companies?" And in so doing, he gave a temporary shock to those pyramids of American economy. Although he later added that he did not mean to wage a wholesale war on all holding companies, his discourse increased the uncertainty and discomfort of leaders in high finance. One day, business was severely criticized; the next day, it was appeased. Such oscillations continued until near the middle of February when at a regular press conference the President lapsed into almost complete silence on the battle over business interests. That, at least, was a novel feature of the political scene.

If the President, pulled first one way and then the other by his advisers, was confused in his own mind in respect of the new depression and the concentration of corporate control in industry, Congress composed of 531 minds presented confusion confounded. The great machine for congressional control set up in the easy times of Joseph Cannon and Nelson Aldrich had been broken to pieces and no substitute had been devised. Democratic members of Congress who sought to lead their colleagues had no huge corporation favors at their command. They could use labor lobbies for limited purposes, but these pressure groups were not comprehensive enough to effect a general control and they were split into three factions — the independent railway unions, the American Federation of Labor, and the Committee for Industrial Organization. The principal cement for holding Democrats together was political patronage and that was mainly in executive hands. To get possession of it, leaders in the Senate and the House had to make terms with President Roosevelt or the main dispenser, Postmaster General Farley. In other words, no practical method was available for overcoming diversities of opinion and creating a self-contained unity in the legislative body. Individual members of Congress inclined to conciliate large economic interests were in constant peril of becoming entangled in the engagements between President Roosevelt, master of patronage, and the "economic royalists," as he designated opponents representing large affairs.

Although Roosevelt made concessions to "the little men" — the ardent "trust-busters" — in his administration and outside, his record showed that he did not completely share their view of American economy and the best method for putting it into efficient operation. On signing the National Industrial Recovery Bill in June, 1933, he had declared publicly: "History probably will record the National Industrial Recovery Act as the most important and far-reaching legislation ever enacted by the American Congress. It represents a supreme effort to stabilize for all time the many factors which make for the prosperity of the nation and the preservation of American standards. Its goal is the assurance of a reasonable profit to industry and living wages for labor with the elimination of the piratical methods and practices which have not only harassed honest business but also contributed to the ills of labor." In his annual message to Congress in January, 1937, he had expressed a similar conviction: "Sober second thought confirms most of us in the belief that the broad objectives of the National Recovery Act were sound. . . . The statute of N. R. A. has been outlawed. The problems have not. They are still with us." At the bottom of his mind, President Roosevelt had evidently decided that some kind of collective effort, not disruptive actions, furnished the fullest promise of success in setting economy in high speed.

In general, Congress was in a mood of hostility toward the corporate concentration which dominated large and strategic areas of economic enterprise and in this respect Republicans differed little, if any, from Democrats. As a matter of fact in the preceding campaign the Republicans had denounced monopolies and trusts more explicitly than had the Democrats and had called for drastic legislation to tear them apart and enforce competition. With such doctrines a majority of Democrats in both houses doubtless agreed. Though fifty years' experience had demonstrated that it was easier to condemn corporations and monopolies than to dissolve them or indeed put any brake on their growth, the politicians remained adamant in their opposition, at least for rhetorical purposes. Even so, a growing number of Senators and Representatives with progressive inclinations were becoming convinced that the favorite political sport of "baiting the trusts" was dangerous as well as obsolete, especially in the face of contracting capitalism and rising unemployment. Believing that capacity production could not be attained without the active participation of large corporate concerns, they were disposed to search for methods of coöperation rather than for weapons of destruction.

Recognizing the utility of caution in dealing with the central issue of the time, President Roosevelt surveyed the so-called monopoly problem from all sides, in a special message to Congress in April, 1938. In perhaps the most penetrating economic document ever drafted in the White House, the President reviewed the whole ground of concentration in corporate control and wealth and coupled the economic aspects of the situation with their significance for political democracy. He described and illustrated by figures the growing centralization of corporate power in the United States and showed that depressions had a tendency to accelerate rather than retard this movement. In the second section of his message the President dealt with the increasing centralization in financial control over industry, which made even more marked the unified character of American economy. Having presented a survey of the leading facts, Roosevelt came to "the choice before us." Under this head the importance of a thorough-going study was emphasized and a few broad suggestions were set forth: antitrust laws and procedures should be improved and strengthened, additional financial control invoked, the function of trade associations defined and clarified, patent laws amended, and taxation adjusted to the stimulation of competitive enterprise.

Although the President gave his monopoly message an antitrust cast, he spoke of that "approach" as "traditional," pointed out the need for a fundamental examination of the entire problem, and suggested to Congress ways and means of prosecuting that investigation. He warned "those who sincerely want to preserve the system of private enterprise for profit" that the inquiry was long overdue. To this warning he added a more portentous caveat: "No people, least of all a democratic people, will be content to go without work or to accept some standard of living which obviously and woefully falls short of their capacity to produce."

Nothing was more evident in the statistical returns of each day than the fact that American industry was operating at a level far below the level of capacity. It had been operating under that level even in 1928. It had thumped and dragged along near the bottom for four or five years. The revival of 1936 had been followed by another downward swoop and the precipitous drift was painfully obvious in the spring of 1938. In prosperous times President Roosevelt's reference to productive capacity might have passed as academic. In the circumstances it struck into a powerful and agitated stream of American thought.

In respect of politics, no less important than economics — parts of the same thing — President Roosevelt was also emphatic and monitory. Without mentioning the name of the author, he quoted a passage from that mighty Whig philosopher, Daniel Webster: "The freest government, if it could exist, would not be long acceptable if the tendency of the laws were to create a rapid accumulation of property in a few hands, and to render the great mass of the population dependent and penniless." That was a political axiom accepted by leading thinkers among the founders of the American republic, ranging from John Adams to Thomas Jefferson, from extreme right to extreme left. For many years, however, it had been neglected. Now Roosevelt placed it in juxtaposition with official figures showing the rapid accumulation of property in a few hands, as things stood in the fifth year of the New Deal, just after the hundred and fiftieth anniversary of the signing of the Constitution had been celebrated. Still he refrained from adding to his quotation from Webster the very next sentences of the original speech delivered in the Massachusetts convention of 1820: "In such a case [of accumulation and poverty], the popular power must break in upon the rights of property, or else the influence of property must limit and control the exercise of popular power. Universal suffrage, for example, could not long exist in a community where there was great inequality of property." Anyway it was suspected that the President had read and pondered the whole of Webster's thesis, especially as in an earlier paragraph of his message he referred to "unhappy events abroad" — the conquest of democracy by fascism.

Engrossed in their own concerns, members of Congress gave little heed to warnings from the White House. At the moment they were more inclined to spurn executive recommendations than to welcome them, except when it came to voting billions for pump priming and naval expansion. With a great display of oratory condemning dictatorships, the House of Representatives defeated the President's bill for the reorganization of administrative agencies. An anti-lynching bill was destroyed in the Senate by a filibuster of Southern members. In defiance of the President and in response to demands from private business, Congress overhauled certain features of the tax system. It modified the progressive surtax on the undistributed profits of corporations, imposed by the Revenue Act of 1936, and also moderated the tax on capital gains. While he criticized these actions in a public address, the President allowed the revenue bill of 1938 to become a law without his signature.

§

During the early days of the second regular session it looked as if the seventy-fifth Congress would waste its last period in idle bickerings but before the adjournment in the summer it reached agreements on a few fundamental proposals. The new Agricultural Adjustment Act of February, 1938, made relatively little disturbance in lobbies and committee rooms, for it included within its scope cotton, rice, and tobacco as well as wheat and corn, and thus effected a certain union of desires among the Democratic managers in Congress. In general lines the Act followed the prescriptions of the law which the Supreme Court had declared unconstitutional; namely, the assignment of production quotas to the producers of the enumerated crops and benefit payments for compliance with the terms of the allotments. Coupled with it were amendments of the Soil Conservation Act of 1936, stipulations respecting the division of payments between landlords and tenants, provisions assuring to consumers continuous and adequate supplies (an ever normal granary), the establishment of crop insurance for wheat growers, and declarations intended to encourage the formation of coöperative associations among agricultural producers. A number of staple commodities, such as dairy products, were not covered by the law and hence the chorus of agrarian approval was accompanied by discord, but the Act proclaimed again the resolve of farmers to follow capitalist methods and cut down production whenever surpluses threatened them with ruin.

No new National Industrial Recovery Act was passed to serve as a companion piece for the agrarian law. Instead, Congress enacted a bill for the investigation of the subject. It set up a temporary national economic committee composed of Senators, Representatives, and persons designated by the heads of certain executive establishments, and instructed this body to inquire into the causes of concentration in industry, the working of the existing price system, and the effect of government policies upon competition, unemployment, profits, and consumption. The committee was explicitly directed to make recommendations respecting the improvement of antitrust policy. So far its instructions seemed to imply a mere search for new "teeth" to be inserted in the antitrust legislation already on the books. An added phrase, however, implied that the committee might go beyond the consideration of historic remedies and make suggestions for the establishment of national standards for corporations engaged in interstate and foreign commerce. Here, at least, was a sign that the outcome of the inquiry might be more than a bill for the enforcement of the jungle law in competition.

The genuflections to agriculture and industry were accompanied by references to labor. Congress established a Maritime Labor Board charged with the duty of assisting in the formation, interpretation, and application of agreements between employers and employees in the shipping business — long a storm center of labor disputes. An act creating a Civil Air Authority provided for the development and enforcement of regulations relative to hours, wages, and working conditions in aviation. These special stipulations were supplemented by a general law, the Fair Labor Standards Act, popularly known as the National Wages and Hours Act, designed to apply throughout the country to industries engaged in commerce under federal jurisdiction. The Act looked forward to the establishment, by gradual stages, of a national minimum of forty cents an hour and a time schedule of forty hours a week by the end of seven years. Limited discriminations based on differences in cost of production were permitted but classifications founded on age and sex were forbidden, the latter provision meeting the ultra-feminist demand. The enforcement of the law was entrusted to an administrator in the Department of Labor and the administrator was empowered to make use of temporary committees for the several industries in arriving at immediate decisions and finally reaching the goal of the law.

The measures pushed through Congress during the endless disputes between "radicals" and "reactionaries" embraced three other acts of a general nature. A more elaborate Food, Drug, and Cosmetic Act was substituted for the famous Act of 1906. Authorization was given for a system of flood-control works extending from the Merrimack River to the lower Mississippi valley and westward to the basin of the Willamette. The work relief program was expanded to take care of an increase in the ranks of the unemployed and the "pump priming" process was renewed to cope with the depression. In all, approximately $3,750,000,000 was made available for these two purposes. General in importance, if local in geographical interest, was an act of Congress providing for an investigation of the Tennessee Valley Development, then in turmoil as the result of violent controversies among members of the Board, culminating in the removal of the chairman, Arthur Morgan. Whatever the upshot of the inquiry, it was bound to throw light on the power policy of the Roosevelt administration and give indications of national developments ahead. After Congress adjourned, the Treasury announced, on June 30, 1938, that the deficit for the last fiscal year was the smallest since 1931 and that the gross public debt stood at $37,165,000,000. Careful estimates made in July placed the deficit for the coming year at $4,000,000,000 in round numbers.

In this fashion the overwhelming mandate of 1938 was executed.

CHAPTER IX

Exploring Domestic Sources of Foreign Policies

DURING the tossing and pitching about that accompanied the search for an outlet from domestic difficulties, official and private investigators stumbled upon the sharp angles of foreign affairs. In some respects the outcome was a revolution in thinking about international relations, so called, for it had long been the fashion of American writers to treat foreign policies as a separate and distinct branch of politics. Such policies, according to their thesis, originate in the efforts of the Federal Government to deal with questions raised by the conduct of other governments and to apply, to emergencies of alien origin, historic maxims, for example, the Monroe Doctrine and the Open Door in China. As a matter of fact the official business of the United States known as "foreign" was by no means so distinct and separate from domestic transactions. In reality foreign policies and domestic policies for the United States, as for all other nations, were parts of the same thing and handled by

381

the same government. Policies classified as "foreign" had roots in ideas and interests prevailing within the political economies and cultures of the nations which maintained relations with one another, and scattered through history were illustrations of this axiom.

For nearly fifty years previous to the domestic crash of 1929, for instance, Americans had been told by influential politicians and naval officers that the prosperity of the United States depended, basically, on operations outside the country rather than on economic practices at home. Near the close of the nineteenth century, this thesis had been used to justify the American adventure in imperialism; that is to say, "surpluses" of agricultural produce and manufactures cannot be used by domestic consumers and profitable outlets must be found through colonial expansion, sea power, and diplomatic pressures abroad. Later, in the years of the golden glow, the American nation was informed by trusted instructors that markets for the goods which then clogged domestic commerce would be provided by the copious lending of money in all parts of the world — by "pump-priming" beyond the seas. When imperialist adventure and copious money-lending in all parts of the world failed to produce, in obvious reality, a continuing and expanding prosperity for the American people, other instructors who enjoyed public confidence revived the Victorian creed of international laissez faire — free trade, "lower trade barriers" — as the contrivance under which to work the miracle. At this point in time, however, that familiar device was being undermined by tough facts. The glut in the market which followed the economic breakdown of 1929 led even the most popular instructors of the people to doubt the possibility of escaping the domestic deadlock by foreign adventure, by colonial expansion, by selling pressures abroad, by copious money-lending, by free international capitalism, or even by the sea power.

Immersed in their economic tribulations for several years after 1929 Americans, in places high and low, reached the conclusion that the source of their trials lay somewhere else and began to search for origins at home. Representatives in Congress, through numerous official investigations, endeavored to find out just how the great economic misadventure had happened. They explored naval and shipping lobbies, foreign loans, branch factories, the advantages of empire in the Philippines, the munitions industry, aviation, the merchant marine, and other domestic enterprises, with an avidity seldom before displayed in the history of American unrest. And in their searchings they uncovered domestic sources of foreign policies more extensive and more powerful than had hitherto been imagined under the smooth and easy assumptions of inherited diplomatic formulas. To reports of official inquiries were added voluminous works by scholars, publicists, and other private investigators, who dealt with the processes by which the world war had come into being; with the settlement at Paris in which President Wilson had directly participated; and with the consequences of that vindictive experiment in pacification, economic settlement, and diplomacy. At the end, if inadvertantly, the conventional picture of world history and America's role in it was badly damaged and partly reconstructed with different lineaments.

§

By one of the curious occurrences with which history is crowded the first legislative investigation into the realities of foreign policy came as an apparent accident in domestic affairs, not as an outcome of agitations by peace societies. In fact, peace societies had rather consistently, if unwittingly, avoided the idea that foreign policy might have an intimate affiliation with economic interests at home and had largely confined themselves to preaching the word of good-will — though it so often seemed ineffective. On the whole, Respectability of every type, whether engaged in pursuing peace or the main chance, deplored congressional inquiries into the operations of private interests, even when related to matters of obvious public concern. But these traditions were given a singular twist in 1929 when President Hoover, with wide popular approval, sought to extend to naval auxiliaries the principle of limitation that had been applied to capital ships at the Washington conference. Immediately large shipbuilding interests were involved and, if it had not been for a strange incident, they might have successfully managed their lobbying behind the scenes. The strange incident was a suit at law brought by one William B. Shearer against shipbuilding corporations to collect his pay for propaganda which, he alleged, he had carried on for them at Geneva, where President Coolidge's attempt to reach a naval accord had been blocked.

For the shipbuilders the incident was inopportune. For President Hoover it was a clue and an occasion. Taking advantage of the partial revelation made by the mere filing of the suit, President Hoover excoriated propaganda designed "to create international distrust and hate," called upon the Attorney General "to consider what action we can take," and suggested that a Senate committee go "to the very bottom" of the business. It was a delicate matter. All except freshmen in international politics knew very well that the British navalists had been hardnecked at Geneva, that the British government would never rip into British interests through a persistent and comprehensive parliamentary inquest, and that the revelations of a Washington inquiry would be confined to American operations. Yet, if Hoover was not to be balked in his foreign policy, something had to be done to counter opposition at home. Accordingly the Senate by resolution instructed its committee on naval affairs or any subcommittee thereof to investigate the activities of William B. Shearer and the shipbuilding interests in connection with the Geneva naval conference. The inquiry was limited and a lukewarm Senator was placed at the head of it, but despite every care the investigation produced information of the first importance for the immediate issue, for naval policy, and for American foreign policy in its largest outlines.

The testimony and documents brought out by the Shearer

investigation, occupying almost seven hundred pages of print, uncovered a huge network of personalities, interests, and concerns engaged in making naval policy for the United States — and to that extent in making foreign policy. Eminent members of the shipbuilding industry, including Charles M. Schwab, appeared before the Senate subcommittee, underwent examinations none too severe, and yet told a story enlightening even to innocence. They had unquestionably furnished money to Shearer as their "observer" at Geneva. Of that they were sure.

On other points they were uncertain. They were vague as to his commission and could not remember many transactions of prime importance to themselves. Nevertheless they recalled that they had spent thousands of dollars on lobbying activities in connection with navy and merchant-marine promotion and had employed Shearer in their stealthy campaign. They admitted that the threads of the net spread far out into industries engaged in furnishing supplies to the navy and the merchant marine. The intimate relations between merchant-marine policy and naval policy they had thoroughly understood. They had treated the two interests as one interest and had spent money lavishly in bringing pressures upon Congress in favor of enormous appropriations for both kinds of shipbuilding. With this business, officials of the United States navy were vaguely associated by witnesses at the hearings, but the Senate committee refrained from bringing the principals in to deny or corroborate. Rumors of opposition between the Navy Department and the State Department were whispered, but apparently that subject was too mysterious for Senators to fathom or the public to consider.

Despite the restraints imposed on the inquiry, the hearings at Washington definitely showed that shipbuilding corporations had "orally" employed Shearer and had paid him substantial sums; that he had been notoriously engaged in anti-British propaganda at Geneva; that he had done his best to defeat arms limitation; that he had entertained naval officers and newspaper correspondents — all "for the navy and the merchant-marine." In performing these services Shearer had sent out literature discrediting American advocates of peace and had secured the insertion of his propaganda, under the guise of news, in such reputable papers as The New York Times. For the purpose of influencing federal actions, the shipping interests had organized a lobby in Washington, spent money freely, dispensed food and drink, maintained contacts with key persons — all in support of naval and merchant-marine bills pending in Congress. As a phase of nation-wide propaganda, articles had been prepared for publication in newspapers and magazines, lecturers had addressed patriotic societies and other civic organizations, the Hearst press had been enlisted, "experts" had been employed for activities undesignated, and speeches had been "doctored" up for the American Legion, chambers of commerce, and other agencies of power engaged in creating popular opinion and bringing pressures upon the representatives of the people in Congress.

Not less educational for the intellectual hinterland were the disclosures respecting the ideology employed to screen the profit-seeking instincts so interwoven with fateful foreign policies. In a pamphlet bearing the title, The Cloak of Benedict Arnold, Mr. Shearer had named names and classified advocates of peace and naval limitations. He did not exactly call them "traitors," but the implication needed no comment. Under Mr. Shearer's philosophy, "our country was betrayed by Charles Evans Hughes"; and Dr. Nicholas Murray Butler and Secretary Frank B. Kellogg were almost as wicked. Not all opponents, Mr. Shearer generously conceded, were communists or traitors; some had been merely deluded or misinformed — victims of foreign propaganda. They belonged among the "unrealistic idealists, the unsophisticated, and the gullible," to quote the epithets put forth by the Navy League in a release to the public. The true patriots, the sophisticated, the wise, the practical makers of naval policy and pertinent foreign policy were, it seemed, the great shipbuilders, their agents, and their editors ; and, if they made millions out of their activities, that was to be deemed just and incidental to the promotion of a noble cause.

According to the version of Mr. Shearer, the shipbuilders' agent, at the very heart of the opposition to naval and merchant-marine expansion was a deliberate conspiracy fomented by sinister foreign powers. "From October, 1914," he declared, "the weight of internationalism and communism was developed, the members of which, pacifists, defeatists, radicals of many hues and foreign agents, communists, I.W.W., and socialists, included in the merger, and a dozen or more organizations with impressive names designed to fool patriotic Americans and lend aid to the enemy. Associated with these agents and organizations of these anti-American bodies were statesmen, Senators, bankers, lawyers, actors, directors and writers, men and women of American birth who were used to fight the existing Government of the United States. . . . All names, records, checks from prominent people in this country, instructions from Moscow, speeches, theses, questionnaires, indeed the workings of the underground organization, working secretly through legal bodies in labor circles, in society, in professional groups, in the Army and Navy, in Congress, in the schools and colleges of the country, in banks and business concerns, among the farmers, in the motion picture industry, in fact, in nearly every walk of life — this information and authentic documentary proof of a colossal conspiracy against the United States were seized by federal officers and are in possession of the authorities."

If Mr. Shearer as the shipbuilders' agent was to be accepted as an authority, then patriotism was practically restricted to shipbuilders, professional patriots, and William Randolph Hearst. If, as he alleged, federal authorities had authentic proof of a great communist and pacifist conspiracy against the Government of the United States and yet pressed no prosecutions, those authorities made themselves parties to the conspiracy by refusing to arrest offenders and purge the official family. The thesis was too gargantuan for American credulity. It was such a tall tale that it could not elude the American sense of humor, although there was no Artemus Ward or Mr. Dooley to dress the story up in dialect for the newspapers. Naturally, in their raw forms, the confessions, assertions, allegations, and admissions of great shipbuilders and their magnificent retainer, W. B. Shearer, were enough to make people smile. And smiles changed to riotous laughter when the Senators brought out the fact that Shearer had once operated a night club, had been "taken" by the police in a liquor-dealing affair, and had failed to make an income tax return on the funds received from the shipbuilding interests. In such entanglements had grand naval policy and its accompanying foreign policy become enmeshed. Not even toplofty editors accustomed to belittle congressional inquiries as "fishing expeditions" and "scandal mongering" could accept such offscourings of shipbuilders' propaganda as "sound Americanism." The spectacle was not ennobling to contemplate, but it opened the way for more informed thought about foreign affairs.

With terrific force the disclosures of the Shearer investigation burst into the headlines of metropolitan papers, creating especial consternation in the East where certain business interests favored a naval compromise with Great Britain. The mentality displayed by the shipbuilders seemed infantile to such capitalists as were accustomed to subtler procedures in achieving results. For idealistic peace advocates the whole affair provided a basic education in realism. Long inured to the habit of regarding nations as legal and rational personalities capable of establishing international amity by written words, without reference to domestic interests, promoters of arms reduction and war outlawry were appalled when the lid was taken off the Geneva conference and they saw what lay beneath the pomp and ceremony of official circumstance. Henceforward workers for international concord and opponents of entanglements in foreign quarrels had to reckon with shipbuilders, naval bureaucrats, munitioneers, and wide-ranging supply concerns in calculating the interplay of forces and pressures. The problem of national security and good-will among the nations could never again stand forth in its old and simple form as a matter of Christian brotherhood or missionary zeal — at least to persons engaged in studying the practices involved in any theory of solution. Moreover the elementary lessons contained in the new arithmetic and philosophy of foreign relations gained wide popular currency through the firm action of President Hoover in supporting the Senate investigation and in placing the seal of his authority on publicity for the detailed analysis of the material interests functioning in the manufacture of foreign policy for which American citizens were to pay, fight, and die.

§

After the Shearer inquest had started and while the seamy story was being unfolded for public benefit, Hoover made ready for the London naval conference in circumstances more favorable than those surrounding the ill-fated Geneva affair. According to news reports, the Government issued notice to American "patriotic" organizations, such as the Daughters of the American Revolution now closely affiliated with army and navy bureaucrats, to watch their steps. According to the New York Evening Post it warned them that "their alleged connections with the anti-disarmament agencies will be ruthlessly investigated by the Department of Justice should they attempt to interfere with proceedings in London. All 'big navy' propaganda agencies in the United States are said to have been similarly warned. . . . To the shipbuilding interests which employed Shearer it has been intimated that President Hoover has legal power to withhold further contracts from private shipyards and that the President will not hesitate to exercise his power at the slightest sign of defeatist agitation. Finally, the United States navy itself has been reminded that the President is commander-in-chief and that his decision regarding future policy must

override the opinions of admirals." At last even Respectability was brought to book — contrary to ordinary use and
wont.

While the temperature created by the Shearer investigation was still rising, Hoover's delegates brought back from
the London conference the new naval treaty providing an
upper limit on the construction of auxiliary vessels until the
close of 1936. The document was far from satisfactory to the
American representatives at the conference. At best it was
a compromise. But it gave promise of holding down the
race in naval armaments for five years. Still sick from the
nausea of the world war, the peoples of Great Britain, Japan,
and the United States seemed to welcome a pause, even at
some inconvenience for Mr. Shearer's shipbuilders.

Nevertheless, in an atmosphere thick with the Shearer
scandal, the Navy League, largely founded and supported in
the beginning by munitions and supply interests, unleashed
its propaganda against the treaty. Perhaps smarting from
the exposure of his ingrained nature by the Senate revelations, the irrepressible Hearst sprang to the support of the
League's counter-activities. In his Washington Herald, it
was announced on July 7, 1930: "A smashing attack on the
London Naval Treaty was fired by the Navy League of the
United States yesterday on the eve of the special session
called by President Hoover to consider the Pact. Heretofore
the League, reflecting the viewpoint of the high command
of the American Navy, has withheld judgment on the
treaty. . . . The statement yesterday, however, issued by
Walter Bruce Howe, chairman of the board, ripped into the
treaty as jeopardizing American national security." Granting that this was true to form, the consequences were unusual. Hitherto the weight of Respectability had been on
the side of the Navy League. Now it was divided and the
Navy League, once able to dictate headlines and intimidate
private citizens, was an object of contumely in high places.
Its anatomy was uncovered — with additional results in the
form of public education respecting the manufacture of for-

eign policies for which the American people were to pay, fight, and die.

Thus the stage was being set for a dramatic contest in the Senate when the ratification of the London pact came before it for consideration. More scenery was opened to view by the hearings of the Senate committee on foreign relations in preparation for decision and action. In the course of the hearings, Senator David Reed of Pennsylvania subjected the admirals who resented ratification to a "grilling," exposed their hearts' desire for an unlimited sea power, even riddled their "expertness" in technical matters, and gave the nation an inside view of the naval bureaucracy. Despite the efforts of Senator Hiram Johnson to throw around the admirals the cloak of Hearst's inflammatory patriotism, Senator Reed dug and bored his way through the mystifications of naval ideology and showed the country the inner meaning of what they were fond of calling "adequate defense." In the end the treaty was approved and signed.

When the issue of naval construction came up later in Congress, the conflict was renewed. The Navy League again assumed its role as national instructor on foreign affairs and again berated President Hoover and his policies. It charged him with "exhibiting abysmal ignorance of why navies are maintained" and with knowingly serving British and Japanese interests "to the prejudice of analogous interests in the United States, although the responsibility of the President is primarily to and for the United States." In short the Navy League, serving as the mouthpiece for a small private organization and a faction in the official bureaucracy, came near to accusing the President of deliberate treason.

That was going far, in view of the recent testimony at the Shearer investigation. And, on behalf of the administration, a reply came in the House of Representatives from no less an authority than the chairman of the subcommittee on naval appropriations: "The issue right now becomes larger than the Navy League and resolves itself into whether or not the country shall have regard for actual naval needs and for the burdens of taxation that rest upon the people, as the President insists, or, ignoring national welfare, turn the Federal Treasury over to the exploitation of those who have personal ends to serve — navy yards and shipbuilders, aircraft and munition manufacturers — and to some extent officers who are blinded by personal interest in seeking their own ends." In the upper chamber, Senator Arthur Capper plunged into the fray and rebuked the Navy League for claiming to be a "patriotic" organization. "The country," he said, "should be grateful to President Hoover for having torn off its mask and shown it to us as the greedy commercial organization that it is — seeking to make excessive profits from the Government for steel and shipbuilding companies under the plea of superpatriotism."

For a moment prophecies were made that there was to be a congressional investigation of the underground relations between commercial interests and the naval bureaucracy in the manufacture of foreign policies. But, as if fearing the educative effect of such an inquiry upon the country, the leading participants on both sides patched up a kind of truce. Even so, Pandora's box had been torn open. In the recent history of American naval and foreign policies no President had asserted such an unqualified civilian supremacy over the Navy Department. If the public soon forgot it, the shipbuilding interests did not. In the campaign of 1932 representatives of those interests were readily enlisted against Hoover by Democratic campaign managers and their affections and hopes were transferred to Franklin D. Roosevelt who was advertised, and correctly, as "ship-minded." Although after the election of that year, the naval supply concerns received the largest golden stream from the Federal Treasury in all their history, the scars of the conflict waged under President Hoover remained in the record. If the shipbuilding concerns that financed Mr. Shearer's propaganda and later contributed to the Democratic campaign fund could gloat over bigger and better naval construction, that part of the public given to remembering in matters of domestic-foreign policy applied the knowledge they had acquired to the education of those who could endure the process.

§

Only a few days after the Shearer investigation closed, another Senate inquiry involving a phase of foreign policy was launched under the heading: "Independence of the Philippines." This also raised the question of sea power and its covering ideology in relation to the Pacific Ocean and Asia. It likewise brought out into broad daylight economic interests underlying the formulas of diplomacy and empire in the Orient. In striking contrast to the Shearer inquest, however, the examination of the Philippines situation encountered the strong and continuing opposition of President Hoover, the State Department, and the War Department, as well as of the Navy Department. Ranks once divided now merged, for the new inquest touched a network of interests and potentials far wider than any mild "limitation" of naval armaments advocated by pacifists. It promised to expose the morphology of Imperialism, America as a World Power, the White Man's Burden, and America's Coming of Age, so applauded in the martial days of William McKinley, John Hay, and Theodore Roosevelt.

The imperialists of 1898 had assured the country that trade would follow the flag and that outlets would be found for the "surpluses" of American farms and factories, but the test of experience had blasted the promise. Whatever industrial and commercial capitalists had got out of the excursion into the Philippines under the banners of war, American farmers were sure that they had got nothing; that they had, indeed, suffered severe losses from the competition of Philippine raw products in the American market. Frankly scorned by President Coolidge and treated with frosty tolerance by President Hoover, the agrarians were now resolutely bent on securing "farm relief" and they thought that the Philippines lay in the way. It was their insistence that forced the resolution for an investigation of the Philippines through the Senate, and when the hearings started their agents were present in full force.

On both sides noble sentiments respecting American outward politics were expressed to the listening Senators. Spokesmen for farmers and organized labor reminded them of the high ideals put forward when the Philippines were annexed and the insurgent revolt crushed by arms; of the pledges of independence repeatedly made by statesmen. The great principles of the Declaration of Independence were to be applied by granting full liberty to the Islands — and by erecting tariff barriers against their agricultural products.

On the other hand, agents of commercial and industrial interests placed their emphasis on "our moral obligations" in the premises, on "ethical grounds," and on "our responsibility" for defending "our" distant wards against predatory neighbors. Journalists and politicians who lifted their voices against the granting of independence to the Philippines gravely discussed the balance of power in the Pacific, the perils likely to arise from giving the natives of the Far East an example of emancipation, and the disturbing effects of experiments in democracy in that quarter of the globe. To some of them it seemed that the fate of the British Empire was at stake and that, if the United States should "scuttle and run," British and Dutch dominion in the East would be jeopardized. That state of affairs they contemplated with horror as directly involving American responsibility.

But underneath the lofty verbalism the substance of many things was visible. Speaking for the Farm Bureau Federation, Chester H. Gray presented a resolution of his organization reading as follows: "It is an idle gesture to place even high rates of duty on farm commodities and then allow such commodities or substitutes therefor to enter our markets, duty free, from our so-called colonies or dependencies. Therefore, we favor immediate independence for such dependencies." If that could not be allowed, the Federation demanded that the tariff duties on Philippine products be raised as high as those "applicable to similar products from foreign nations."

This statement was surely explicit enough. "Do not understand," Mr. Gray explained, "that the farmers of America approach this question wholly from the economic point of view. They are not forgetting the historic point of view or the humanitarian point of view," namely, the long-standing promises of independence contained in official statements scattered through the years from McKinley to Coolidge. The structure of their ideas and the structure of their interests coincided with impressive exactness. Arguments delivered by the anti-imperialists in 1900 without producing any noticeable effect on policy now seemed to have more weight with Senators of the United States.

Speaking before the committee for the American Federation of Labor, W. C. Hushing, its legislative representative, also advanced moral and economic reasons for granting independence to the Philippines. Since 1898 the Federation had consistently opposed "forcing our system of government upon an unwilling people." Later its members began to feel the pressure from commodities produced in the Islands and the competition of laborers who migrated to the United States. "The desire for cheap labor has acted like a cancer in American private and public life, destroying American ideals and preventing the development of a nation based on racial unity." A schedule taken from a publication issued by the Philippine-American Chamber of Commerce showed that the minimum daily wages of laborers in the Islands ranged from twenty cents a day for casual workers to $1.20 for mechanics. Special efforts had been made to induce Filipinos to enter the United States for the purpose of enjoying "the great prosperity existing there." Like organized agriculture, organized labor was willing to accept restrictions on imports and on immigrants, but it preferred complete independence for the Philippines. Thus two masterful interests, not to be minimized by Congress, were thrown on the side of "fulfilling the historic pledge."

To these arguments, commercial and financial concerns filed objections. They presented a case against the granting of independence — emphasizing grounds of moral responsibility. If the retention of the Islands was impossible, final adjustments should not be allowed to have an adverse effect upon their business, they contended; and four prime considerations — two of them connected with naval and military affairs — were offered in support of this claim. The erection of trade barriers between the Philippines and the United States would be "a blow at the American merchant marine." By reducing the import of coconut oil, it would strike at "a source of glycerin for the manufacture of explosives." The agrarian argument that Philippine raw materials competed with domestic products was not well founded, in their opinion; at all events business interests had as good a right to protection by the Government as the interests arrayed across the line.

With pertinent bluntness the president of the Philippine-American Chamber of Commerce declared: "Assuming for the purpose of the argument that our interests are selfish, I ask in what respect do they differ from the interests of the representatives of other organizations which have appeared before your committee?" The question was relevant and it brought forth a balance-sheet of interests in which the commercial and financial advantages of empire looked small.

In summarizing the parallel exhibits, Senator Hawes described the political upshot: "To put it on a selfish basis, if you please, 5,000,000 union [labor] men, represented by their national organizations; all the farm and dairy organizations in the United States; and, in so far as it could be given, the best sugar raisers of eleven states, the cane sugar industry of one state, and capital representing not millions, but two billions, as I understand it, of American money invested in Cuba, have all expressed their views. Put those things on a selfish basis. I hope this thing will be settled on a higher basis than that, but all those interests take a position exactly contrary to your own, on a selfish basis."

Similar economic measurements were introduced in the congressional debate on the issue of Philippine independence and an article from The Harvard Business Review, entitled A Balance Sheet of the Philippines, was spread upon the record. This article, by Rufus S. Tucker, an expert formerly in the Department of Commerce, maintained that the gain accruing to American citizens from Philippine trade was less than ten million dollars a year and that the cost of retaining the prevailing arrangements, even apart from naval expenditures, was many times the sum total of the private profits arising from commerce.

Exact weights could not be attached to the several specific interests aligned on opposite sides. Nor could the pressures of moral sentiments for and against independence be exactly gauged. What could be said with some assurance was that the combined votes of farmers and trade unions were not to be ignored by members of Congress. Things had changed since the great moral crusade of 1898 when "Americans were growing up" and America was assuming her place as "a world power." Against the stiff resistance of President Hoover, the State Department, and military and naval experts, Congress passed a bill offering independence to the Philippines. After Hoover vetoed the measure, the requisite two-thirds vote was marshaled to carry it over his protest.

When the Filipinos rejected the terms of the tender, Congress revised them and its modified bill became law with the signature of President Roosevelt in March, 1934. The new Act authorized the Filipinos to call a constitutional convention, draw up a plan of self-government, and pass upon the offer of liberty. Ten years after the fulfillment of the stipulations, American sovereignty was to be withdrawn. Pending the completion of the transaction, limitations were to be placed on certain imports and on immigration from the Islands. The question of a permanent naval base for the United States in the Philippines was left for later settlement. With such a matter of imperial strategy, neither farmers nor trade unions were much concerned, although the issues connected with that unsolved problem might be more fateful in terms of blood and treasure than anything they contemplated.

Whatever was to be the long-term effect of Philippine independence upon the shape of things to come in the Pacific Ocean, the debate over it had a profound influence upon domestic opinion. In 1898 the country had embarked upon a crusade to free Cuba and had unwittingly become involved in moral obligations in the Far East. There had been skeptics then — the anti-imperialists. But the election mandates of 1900, 1904, and 1908 had apparently, if not actually, set the seal of popular sanction upon the idea that America had "come of age" and must play a great role as a world power on the world stage in the concert of nations — for the sake of playing it, if for no other reason. The critics who had called the adventure "joining the greedy nations of Europe in a scramble for the spoils of empire" had been overborne and smothered. America became involved in the proceedings carried on by "the family of nations" — a family none too happy at the time and tragically disrupted after 1914. American sea power was to grow from naval base to naval base. Trade was to follow the flag. Outlets were to be found for the "surpluses" of American factories and farms. Such was the mirage in the good old days.

In 1933 the mirage had lost some of its charm. The outlets had not followed the flag. On the contrary, millions of farmers and trade unionists were protesting against the fruits of empire, calling them bitter and unbearable. Though the protestants may not have known or cared much about sea power, naval strategy, the concert of nations, or imperial obligations, they were positive that empire had not "paid" them and, by forcing independence upon the Philippines, they left American policy in the Far East and all its glittering phrases, such as the Open Door, hanging in a fog. By their action they also plunged naval and diplomatic bureaucrats into dismay and seemed to offer them no alternative save withdrawal upon the Alaska-Hawaii-Panama line; that is, withdrawal unless the allure of Woodrow Wilson's universal philanthropy could be employed to restore national morale for diplomatic, naval, and military excursions in Asia and Europe.

§

Before the effects of the congressional hearings and debates connected with commercial "expansion" in the Far East culminated in the offer of independence to the Philippines, the Senate committee on finance started an inquiry into another phase of empire — the sale of foreign bonds and securities in the United States. In what was lightly called the strategy of finance capitalism, territorial conquest was not always necessary to the gathering and accumulation of profits. Heavy investments in other countries — especially in "backward places" — brought returns, yielded influence over governments, and expanded trade, without the obtrusive use of the flag. If defaults led to punitive expeditions, protectorates, and annexations, State actions of that sort were mere means to larger ends.

Such was the theory of the finance empire. But the widespread defaults which followed the crash of 1929, particularly on Latin-American bonds, were followed by an upset in traditional strategy. They kindled popular indignation against domestic bankers rather than a frenzied demand for the employment of the army and navy in heroic efforts to collect from the defaulters. According to the strict logic of finance capitalism, American investors should have called for the extension of empire over the debtors and dollar diplomacy in the Caribbean had seemed to confirm that necessity. But going contrary to this line of logic American citizens insisted that American bankers be brought up on the public carpet and forced to tell how and why they had inflicted staggering losses upon "innocent investors."

It was this factual interest in the ways of American bankers, not a concern for dialectics, which dominated the finance committee of the Senate during its hearings, in the winter of 1931–32, on the sale of foreign bonds and securities in the United States. The hearings had not gone very far when they brought out evidence of an utter confusion in the minds of the bankers with respect to the benefits, significance, and consequences of their operations. Instead of making sure that the copious money-lending would redound to the economic advantage of the United States, they had been primarily absorbed in the pursuit of the main chance. Nevertheless their testimony demonstrated, if incidentally, that the promotion, flotation, and outcomes of foreign loans in the United States had a direct bearing upon the foreign policies and relations of the Federal Government.

From witnesses reluctant or voluble the Senate committee drew pieces of evidence which, when fitted together, presented a definite configuration. Collectively the fragments of testimony showed that finance capitalists, the State Department, and concession hunters operated according to a single economic hypothesis: It is the duty of the Government to promote foreign investments, concessions, and trade opportunities, in the routine course of foreign policy. Although the Senate committee could not get to the bottom of such matters as Bolivian loans and the Barco oil deal, it did discover Henry L. Stimson, the Secretary of State, acting as an intermediary in a manner neither dignified nor ceremonial. Disgruntled investors who held Bolivian bonds may not have appreciated the "diplomacy" of the transaction, but Senators and Representatives did. Readers of headlines caught glimpses of it. Editors all over the country must have been led to suspect the practical sense and fiduciary judgment of men in high official positions. Students of "foreign" affairs who were not asleep or engrossed in reciting their time-worn formulas must have been moved to reconsider some of their habitual assumptions. At all events the State Department as the attorney of private interests and the sea power as a debt-collecting agency lost some of their glamour as the public received a reëducation in the fine arts of banking, money lending, and huckstering.

§

Like the investigation of shipping and naval propaganda, the inquiry into empire-building in the Philippines, and the examination of witnesses in connection with the flotation of foreign securities in the United States, a long survey of the munitions industry commenced largely as a study of domestic affairs. For many years the American Legion and other organizations had been demanding that the profits be taken out of war, not merely to put a brake on belligerent propensities, ostensibly at least, but with a view to equalizing the sacrifices for war. A similar demand had arisen in Germany among war veterans, under the leadership of Ernst Roehm slain by Hitler in the purge of 1934; Roehm despised pacifism and saw in the limitation of profits cheaper, hence bigger and better, wars. On the other hand, genuine advocates of peace in and outside the American Legion regarded the profitable manufacture of armaments as a prolific source of international belligerency. They ascribed much of the friction and rivalry among nations to the pecuniary passions of manufacturers — "munitioneers" eager to sell their products anywhere, at any time, to any State or faction in a State, to friend or foe of their own country, to armies slaying even their own sons. Presumably, therefore, the argument ran, a reduction of profits will facilitate a curtailment of armaments and heighten the prospects for peace.

Thus many conflicting ideas could find refuge under the slogan: "Conscription of wealth and men." Even advocates of an immense army and navy for the United States and believers in "the inevitable war" found it useful for their purposes; if the populace could be marshaled against profiteering in munitions, it might be induced to approve larger military and naval plans for a total mobilization of men for war in Europe or Asia or both. Obviously no such mobilization was required for a mere defense of the United States and its adjoining sphere of interests. But for war on distant continents or in distant seas "universal service" was indispensable.

It was under pressure and with support from various directions, accordingly, that the Senate created a committee to study the munitions industry in April, 1934, with Senator Gerald P. Nye as chairman and Senators Barbour, Bone, Clark, George, Pope, and Vandenberg as colleagues. This is not to say that the project was warmly approved by the whole country. On the contrary the committee began to work in an atmosphere charged with doubts, sneers, and trepidations; accusations were even made that Senator Nye was mainly interested in turning the limelight on himself. Nevertheless, commanding a staff of competent investigators, among whom Stephen Rauschenbush was outstanding, the committee, for nearly three years, bored deeper and deeper into the ramifications of war industries, war finances, and war policies. And in opening up domestic operations, it detected corollaries in the conduct of foreign relations.

In the course of its proceedings, the Nye committee explored three special phases of the munitions industry and related activities: the structure and methods of the industry, military projects for total mobilization in the United States, and the economic background of the policies pursued just previous to America's entrance into the world war. Under each head, the committee produced pertinent papers from the files of munitions concerns, banking houses, and the State Department, and examined witnesses possessing special knowledge of transactions. In every direction the searches and presentations of the committee staff seemed to be thorough, except in respect of State Department archives. Although given access to the Department's collections of papers, the committee was limited as to the examination of witnesses and the publication of diplomatic documents. In the nature of things, the Department felt bound to protect the sensibilities of the powers associated with the United States in the world war by withholding certain transactions from public scrutiny. Consequently it was not exactly true to say, as was said at the time, that the Nye committee "went to the bottom" of munitions finance and diplomacy and gave out "all the facts in the case." Nevertheless its "revelations" were voluminous and long-hidden domestic sources of foreign policies were exposed to public view.

The evidence bearing on the structure and methods of the munitions industry, elicited by the committee, confirmed the knowledge of the subject already possessed by foreign experts and set forth in numerous European treatises. In this field of exposition the novelty lay in the American illustrations unearthed rather than in any additional practices discovered. But the total effect of the investigation was a demonstration that American munitions concerns had followed the patterns already established by European manufacturers of armaments in respect of "patriotism." American concerns had relentlessly pressed the sale of munitions to other countries wherever they could — not excluding potential enemies of the United States. They had opposed measures of pacification pursued by the State Department in Latin America and had fomented discords in the interest of sales. In the business of promotion some of them had bribed the buying agents of foreign governments or persons of influence with such governments. They had looked with disfavor upon all conferences designed to curtail armaments and had lobbied against the reduction of expenditures for munitions. American concerns had combined with foreign companies in pooling trade secrets, pushing the traffic, and distributing profits. In other words, the international character of the munitions business was once more demonstrated by a multitude of documents and witnesses. That the munitions concerns made enormous profits in supplying governments, especially in war time, was again proved by a wealth of evidence, and the practice of driving hard bargains with the Government of the United States in the midst of the world war was illustrated in detail.

During this phase of its inquiry, the Nye committee discovered that the official attitude of the War and Navy Departments in Washington did not differ fundamentally from that maintained by the military profession in European capitals. Army and navy officers favored the manufacture of munitions by private concerns, opposed the nationalization of the industry, and resisted the drastic limitation of private profits. They encouraged sales of munitions to foreign governments, on the ground, they alleged, that it kept the industry active, in constant practice, and hence in a better position to serve the needs of the United States in time of war. On such assumptions, war vessels of the United States had been moved around in foreign waters for the purpose of demonstrating the effectiveness of specific weapons and promoting sales to foreign governments. Army and navy officers, after retirement or resignation, had been given desirable berths in the munitions industry. Before the vision of officers in active service constantly loomed attractive opportunities in private enterprise. In such circumstances the spirit of coöperation prevailed. The Shearer investigation had unfolded a certain degree of affiliation between navy officers and propagandists engaged in discrediting arms limitation. By the Nye inquiry knowledge of such relations was greatly amplified, if still inadequately.

In their eagerness to secure an abundance of materials, army and navy officials had given little or no attention to the true costs of manufacture or to the gains accruing to private interests from munitions contracts. After even a limited inquiry into the matter, the Nye committee reported astounding profits in various forms of construction and supply services. It found out also that the Federal Government had little knowledge of these profits and no agencies for checking and controlling them. In one summary based on extensive investigation, the committee described the situation in respect of shipbuilding as follows: "The Navy has never examined the underlying costs or profits of the private builders. It makes no pretense of doing this. It has no staff for it. The figures studied by the Munitions Committee were all news to it. The Navy makes no attempt to examine the costs of the private companies to determine whether the profit limitation of 11.1 per cent in the Vinson-Trammell Act is enforced or evaded. That is left to the Treasury to do after three years, after a job is done." In the absence of accounting control, competition among bidders for naval construction seemed to be purely nominal. "If there were no conversations about bidding among them, there was telepathy. . . . In 1933 two shipbuilders knew and wrote down lists of the low bidders weeks in advance of the time the bids were opened. Mr. Bardo was one of them. Mr. Wilder was another" — two gentlemen who had employed the redoubtable Mr. Shearer in the campaign against naval reduction and in favor of ship construction.

Now, for the first time in American history, members of Congress in charge of military and naval affairs had before them exact patterns of the methods employed by munitions industries and the War and Navy Departments in drawing contracts and handling supplies. Furthermore, for the first time in American history, the War and Navy Departments were given a broad conspectus of the economics involved in their light-hearted transactions.

Under the glare of the evidence, testimony, papers, and figures brought out by the Nye committee, the heroic picture of many "Dollar-a-Year Patriots," so revered during American participation in the world war, shriveled into grotesques. Supply concerns which some of them "controlled" made exorbitant profits. "The committee finds, under the head of War Time Attitude of Shipbuilders, that the record of the present shipbuilding companies during the war, wherever examined, was close to being disgraceful. . . . They secured cost-plus contracts and added questionable charges to the costs. . . . They secured changes in contract dates to avoid war taxes. They bought from the Government, very cheaply, yards which had been built expensively at Government cost. In one case this was prearranged before the yard was built. One yard did not build necessary additions until it was threatened with being commandeered. Knowingly exorbitant claims were filed against the Government for cancellation. Huge bonuses were paid to officers. Profits were concealed as rentals. . . . The committee finds no assurance in the war-time history of these companies to lead it to believe that they would suddenly change their spots in case of another war." If, as argued by witnesses, large profits and high salaries were necessary to guarantee an adequate supply of war implements for the battle front, then the coloration of sacrificial patriotism was inappropriate for the heads of munitions concerns. In time of national stress, they had taken their pound of flesh — and far more.

From an examination of past practices, the Nye committee turned to plans for "the coming war." In more or less nebulous forms these schemes had been discussed since the close of the "war to end war." Before American soldiers were withdrawn from Europe, certain military officers and civilians had advocated the establishment of a large army based on universal liability to service — an army on the German and French model. Thwarted in this project, they did their best to attain their ends by the enlargement of the Regular Army, the closer unification of the National Guard, the establishment of training camps, and the wider introduction of military discipline into colleges and high schools. This increase in military effectives was supplemented by plans for mobilizing industries, labor, citizens, and relevant private agencies for a totalitarian war.

Army officers were eager. Industries, perhaps remembering the profitable experiences of the last war, were pleased to coöperate. But organized labor expressed misgivings. Advocates of civil liberty, recalling the "raids" instituted by the former Attorney General, A. Mitchell Palmer, proclaimed objections. The American Legion, while approving the plans, made some disturbance with a clamor about "taking profits out of war." Anyway the plans for a totalitarian mobilization had proceeded, were in process, and the Nye committee gave to the country a minute and accurate picture of just what was to be expected in the way of totalitarianism, Gleichgeschaltung, during "the coming war." For a nation that liked to think of itself as pacific, non-militaristic, and dedicated to liberty and democracy, the vision of its coming "day" was informing, to some extent shocking, in any event educative.

§

In the course of its inquiry the Nye committee discovered that "prior to our entry into the world war, a great deal of the sale, distribution, export, and also financing of arms and munitions of war was put into the hands of a few of our banking organizations." Under its instructions to investigate the whole range of munitions manufacture, distribution, import, export, sale, commerce, and promotion, the committee went into the financing of the munitions industries and the export business. It took up the study of such operations as they appeared just after the outbreak of the war in Europe in 1914 and traced the expansion of munitions and export banking down through the declaration of war on Germany by the United States. This procedure led into transactions of great financial establishments, especially the J. P. Morgan Company which had finally obtained a kind of monopoly over the purchases of the Allied Powers in the United States.

Inasmuch as the sale of munitions to belligerents and the granting of credits and loans to them involved pertinent policies of the United States Government, the inquiry advanced into a study of those policies in their development and of the relations of munitions-bankers to the Wilson administration. This was ticklish business. The exploration brought into consideration great personalities belonging to the period in question. It touched upon highly controversial issues and awakened slumbering passions. But the findings were of the utmost importance for the formulation of rules respecting neutrality and war trade in preparation for the possibility of another general war in Europe or Asia. And a by-product was a material revision of many historical judgments pertaining to the manner in which foreign policies were shaped.

This phase of the Nye inquiry opened with testimony and the analysis of documents bearing on the origin and expan-

sion of munitions financing after the outbreak of the war in
1914. To make clear the intimate relations between domestic
interests and foreign policies thus revealed, a somewhat
detailed recital of the committee's finding is necessary. On
August 3, the Rothschilds in Paris cabled the Morgan Company offering their services in aid of the French government
to the extent of at least a hundred million dollars, to be
devoted in part to "purchases of merchandise." To this
tender the Company replied that, owing to the uncertainties
of the moment, it was unable to take advantage of the offer
but it expressed the belief that in a little while such a transaction might be possible. August 8, 1914, Herman Harjes,
of the Morgan affiliate in Paris, cabled the Company in New
York, renewing the suggestion of a loan to the French government, though on a mere ten million dollar basis. In this
message more emphasis was laid upon the purchase of merchandise and the possible withdrawal of gold was minimized.
A small loan could be increased later. "Fear that if we do
not forestall others," ran the cable, "it is probable that such
houses as Kuhn, Loeb, and Company may try to do something for other nation."

According to the testimony of Thomas Lamont, "the
French government was then beginning to buy supplies in
the United States on a considerable scale, and they wanted
to have some ready cash available. That was the whole
thing." In terms of legal precedent, the proposed loan was
lawful, but the Morgan Company postponed decision and
cabled Paris that it was taking the question up with the
State Department in Washington. Three days later, Harjes
again cabled the Morgan Company from Paris, this time
proposing a possible twenty million dollar loan, perhaps
below par, at six per cent, to be entirely expended for goods
in the United States. Again the New York House delayed a
categorical answer and indicated a desire to observe strict
proprieties in dealing with the Government of the United
States.

Shortly after the Morgan Company lodged its inquiry

with the State Department, Secretary Bryan laid the problem before President Wilson, on August 10. He informed the President that the Company had asked "whether there would be any objection to their making a loan to the French government and also the Rothschilds — I suppose that this is intended for the French government." While the Secretary conceded that there were no legal obstacles in the way of such loans, he insisted that profound political and economic objections were involved. Loans would be taken by investors who sympathized with the respective belligerents and this would make more acute the divisions already existing in the country. "These expressions of sympathy are disturbing enough when they do not rest upon pecuniary interests — they would be still more disturbing if each group was pecuniarily interested in the success of the nation to whom its members had loaned money."

In time the divisions of public opinion might be sharpened by the money-lending influences. "The powerful financial interests which would be connected with these loans," Secretary Bryan reasoned, "would be tempted to use their influence through the newspapers to support the interests of the government to which they had loaned because the value of the security would be directly affected by the result of the war. We would thus find our newspapers violently arrayed on one side or the other, each paper supporting a financial group and pecuniary interests." With more precision no one could have described the forces of economic gravitation. "All of this influence," the Secretary continued, "would make it all the more difficult for us to maintain neutrality, as our action on various questions that would arise would affect one side or the other and powerful financial interests would be thrown into the balance" — a prophecy well fulfilled by subsequent events. Having presented his analysis, Secretary Bryan asked President Wilson: "Would the government not be justified in using its influence against the enlistment of the nation's dollars in a foreign war? The Morgans say that the money would be spent here, but the floating of these loans would absorb the loanable funds and might affect our ability to borrow."

Having consulted President Wilson and received his views, Secretary Bryan placed a "ban" on loans to belligerents in a letter to the Morgan Company on August 15, 1914: "In the judgment of this government, loans by American bankers to any foreign nation which is at war is inconsistent with the true spirit of neutrality." Complying immediately with this official dictum, the Morgan Company informed its Paris house that it could not negotiate the loan to the French government. Besides observing the formalities of the occasion, the Company accepted the idea that it was persona non grata at the White House. During his campaign for nomination and election, Wilson had been put to great trouble in disclaiming the "Morgan influences" connected with his sponsor, Colonel George Harvey, and perhaps the personal considerations still had weight in August, 1914. At all events, Thomas Lamont did not think that his banking house was regarded with special favor by the President of the United States.

After the Morgan proposal had broken down, the question of a loan to France passed to the care of the National City Bank, a friendly neighbor prepared to work in a coöperative spirit and to share its transactions with the Morgan Company. Public notice had been given that loans to belligerents were under an official ban, but agents of the National City Bank reopened the problem orally with the Secretary of State. Late in September, 1914, the French ambassador, M. Jusserand, presented France's case to Secretary Bryan and gained the impression that the official ban on loans would be reconsidered. On October 5 M. Jusserand informed Frank Vanderlip, president of the National City Bank, that, in his opinion, Secretary Bryan would not object to a lending arrangement with the French government.

Desiring a clear and direct confirmation from the State Department, a representative of the National City Bank called on Secretary Bryan and received from him oral advice to the effect that the proposed transaction had his consent. By October 18 M. Jusserand was convinced that the obstacles thrown in the way of money lending by the official declaration of August 15 had been definitely removed by the State Department. In making the private reversal of his public announcement, Secretary Bryan expressed to the National City agent "the wish that no advertisements of the forthcoming issue of French treasury bonds would be published in the press and he was assured that none would be."

Although doubly assured by oral promises coming directly from Secretary Bryan, the National City Bank, through a representative, took the question up again, on October 23, 1914, with Robert Lansing, then acting Secretary during the absence of Mr. Bryan. His oral statement the representative supplemented by a letter of that date. In the letter stress was laid on the stimulation of "the unprecedented and unusual buying that is now going on in this country by foreign governments and their nationals." But foreign credits were being depleted. "Lately we have been urged by manufacturers who are customers of the bank and in some cases by representatives of the foreign governments, to provide temporary credits for these purchases. . . . We strongly feel the necessity of aiding the situation by temporary credits of this sort, otherwise the buying power of these foreign purchasers will dry up and the business will go to Australia, Canada, Argentina, and elsewhere. . . . If we allow these purchases to go elsewhere we will have neglected our foreign trade at the time of our greatest need and greatest opportunity."

In fact the United States, at the moment, was suffering from a slump in business and, as bankers diagnosed the situation, credits to belligerents would help to relieve embarrassment all around. As Frank Vanderlip told the Nye committee in 1936, a newspaper dispatch in October, 1914, stated that "there were 100,000 steel men idle in the Pittsburgh district. That gives a picture of our industrial situation at that time. There was a large amount of idleness. There was great dullness in our industries, and there was every reason for us to stimulate those industries with an export business if we could." Other evidence of the depression lay in the fact that there had been a drop of about thirty per cent in the excess of exports over imports between June 30, 1913, and June 30, 1914. That an increase in war business, in lieu of other business, would help to lift profits and employment out of the trough was apparent to all informed observers and was a subject of general comment among negotiators.

On the evening after his conversation with the agent of the National City Bank, Mr. Lansing, as Acting Secretary, took up personally the question of money lending with President Wilson at the White House. As the result of their conversation, they worked out a formula which distinguished between "loans" to belligerents calling for bond issues and credits or arrangements for meeting debts incurred in the ordinary course of trade. The distinction was somewhat artificial but under this formula they agreed that certain obstacles, such as interference with an arrangement of credits or easy methods of exchange, should be removed. At the conclusion of their conference, President Wilson authorized Mr. Lansing to give these impressions "to such persons as were entitled to hear them, upon the express understanding that they were my own [Mr. Lansing's] impressions and that I had no authority to speak for the President or the government." The substance of this White House conversation Mr. Lansing conveyed to Willard Straight of the Morgan Company at the Metropolitan Club at 8 : 30 in the evening, October 24, 1914, and to R. L. Farnham of the National City Bank at the State Department on October 26. So the way was cleared for the flotation of French treasury obligations on November 4, 1914, and their distribution among banks in various parts of the country — the Morgan Company taking one-half the total amount and the du Pont Powder Company about half a million dollars' worth.

Thus the official ban publicly imposed on the Morgan Company by Secretary Bryan in respect of an earlier transaction was privately lifted by oral communications to bankers authorized by the President of the United States. The flood gates for the extension of credits were opened. In a short time credits grew to such proportions that President Wilson confronted the alternative of allowing them to be funded into term bonds sold to American investors or dealing with a drastic curtailment of foreign buying, if not a crash in domestic economy — that is, in "war prosperity."

Nominally Secretary Bryan's thesis stood as official. New York newspapers, it is true, announced in the middle of October, 1914, that there had been a "change of official attitude toward European loans" as "admitted in a high authoritative quarter," "on the highest authority." Yet the State Department gave out no official confirmation of this "news." On the contrary, in a letter to Senator William Stone on its money-lending policy, Secretary Bryan, over the protest of Mr. Lansing, declared on January 20, 1915, that his ruling of August 15, 1914, was still in effect. Not until March 31, 1915, was it officially and publicly stated that the Government had changed its ruling and had approved the extension of credits to belligerents while still maintaining the official ban on "loans" to belligerents. How this transformation had been effected was not made known to the public until January, 1936.

By the midsummer of 1915 the Allies had apparently stretched their short-term "credits" to the limit. At all events the British pound was slipping down. The British government and the Morgan Company either would not or could not sustain it, although the Company in fact sold sterling, thus depressing the exchange. If the pound continued to fall, British buying power would decline and American sellers would be in straits. Immediately the entourage of President Wilson began to close in. On August 14, 1915, Benjamin Strong, governor of the Federal Reserve Bank of New York, drew Colonel House's attention to the slipping sterling and to the influence "gradually growing stronger to curtail our export business." Three days later, J. B. Forgan, president of the First National Bank of Chicago, an American citizen of British birth, informed the vice-governor of the Federal Reserve Board that the Allies needed more than credits; they needed a loan. What would be the attitude of the Wilson administration? Copies of Mr. Forgan's letter reached William G. McAdoo, Secretary of the Treasury, and Robert Lansing, now in fact Secretary of State in place of William J. Bryan who had resigned. The Bryan ban on "loans" still stood, nominally at least. Should it be dropped? If so, why?

In a letter to President Wilson, Secretary McAdoo stated his views bluntly: "Our prosperity is dependent on our continued and enlarged foreign trade. To preserve that we must do everything we can to assist our customers to buy. . . . To maintain our prosperity we must finance it. Otherwise it may stop, and that would be disastrous." Secretary Lansing added his plea. He sent to the President a copy of Mr. Forgan's letter and declared unequivocally that "the large debts which result from purchases by belligerent governments require some method of funding these debts in this country."

Another hour of decision had arrived. The President of the United States was informed by his official advisers, on the basis of banking advice, that huge credits, such as he had orally approved in 1914, must now be funded into bonds sold publicly. American investors must furnish the money to pay American producers for American goods bought by the Allies. If this could not be done, the outcome would be, Secretary McAdoo declared, "disastrous."

Facing this hard dilemma, fateful for bankers, manufacturers, farmers, industrial workers, American boys who were to die in France, and all the families who were to suffer losses on the battlefields, President Wilson made his decision — that the rest of the Bryan ban should be swept away and the public flotation of term-bonds for the Allies duly sanctioned. Obliquely, as in the case of the credits in October, 1914, the President conveyed his decision on loans to Secretary Lansing on August 26, 1916: "My opinion in this matter, compendiously stated, is that we should say that 'parties [the

Government] would take no action either for or against such a transaction,' but that this should be orally conveyed, so far as we are concerned, and not put in writing. . . . Faithfully yours, W. W."

In October, 1914, Wilson's decision had been "orally" conveyed, but not as his decision, to those "entitled" to hear it, namely, a representative of the Morgan Company and a representative of the National City Bank. Now that his decision of August 26, 1915, had been orally conveyed to those entitled to hear it, the way was smoothed for bankers to issue all the bonds of belligerents that the borrowers could underpin with securities or American investors would buy either on their own motion or under the stimulus of manufacturers and bankers already entangled in war business. By the spring of 1917 the outstanding indebtedness of the Allied Powers in the United States amounted to about $2,700,000,000 — scattered widely among citizens, industries, banks, institutions, and especially concerns engaged in producing for and financing the Entente Allies. The pecuniary interests of a small group in New York had been extended to cover nearly every nook and cranny of American economy, carrying along implications for the making and enforcement of foreign policy.

Before the year 1916 closed, bankers were again having difficulty in upholding the pound sterling, despite their freedom in floating term-bonds for the Allies. In distributing loans, the Morgan Company was encountering "reluctance on the part of some institutions." Its inability to forecast British requirements and policies and to answer questions respecting the exigencies of exchange "was very disturbing to these bankers." In short, it was somewhat in the dark as to the intentions and capacities of British authorities; and in a cable to its London affiliate, the Company expressed the hope that the authorities would clarify the grave situation. "Perhaps they have," the cable ran, "some undisclosed resources that we are not aware of, but at the present rate of going they will soon exhaust all gold available or in transit and also available American securities, even going so far as to assume that we can possibly secure loans up to eighty per cent of the value of these securities."

In such circumstances, the Morgan Company urged the British government to mobilize more resources in support of the exchange and purchases in the United States, for British and French demand loans and floating paper had reached the straining point. What the British government could do by desperate effort remained unknown, but its hesitations and delays spread gloom among financiers in Britain and in the United States. The war boom had carried American agricultural and industrial production to a high point. Every part of the United States, important economic institutions, all classes were entangled in its inflated structure. A severe break in the exchange, a sharp curtailment of Allied buying, or a crash on the battle front would have brought a decided recession if not a panic. Informed financiers knew this. Government officials were likewise aware of it through their relations, direct or remote, with American bankers, if not as a result of their own observations. Appropriate foreign policies might be adopted.

To evidences of this situation drawn from various sources, the Nye committee added a summation presented to the State Department by Walter Hines Page on March 6, 1917, a month before the United States entered the war: "The financial inquiries made here reveal an international condition most alarming to the American financial and industrial outlook." Then followed a description of the strained position of the British government and a forecast of a material reduction in Anglo-French buying in American markets. "This will, of course, cause a panic in the United States. . . . This condition may soon come suddenly unless action is quickly taken to prevent it. France and England must have a large enough credit in the United States to prevent the collapse of world trade and of the whole European finance. If we should go to war with Germany the greatest help we could give the Allies would be such a credit. . . . All the money would be kept in our own country, trade would be continued and enlarged until the war ends, and after the war Europe would continue to buy food and would buy from us also an enormous supply of things to reëquip her peace industries. We should thus reap the profit of an uninterrupted, perhaps an enlarging trade over a number of years, and we should hold their securities in payment. . . . Perhaps our going to war is the only way in which our present prominent trade position can be maintained and a panic averted. The submarine has added the last item to the danger of a financial world crash."

The situation presented by Page's message on March 6, 1917, was verbally confirmed four months afterward by a letter from the British ambassador in Washington, Sir Cecil Spring-Rice, to Secretary Lansing, on July 1, 1917. In this letter the ambassador declared that the financial position of Great Britain was "of an urgent and critical character. . . . There is danger that the ability of His Majesty's Government to effect payments in America from today onward will be in jeopardy. . . . A collapse of the exchange will be no less disastrous than a great military reverse." It would throw commercial relations between the two countries "into complete disorder," including the cotton trade, "entailing the stoppage of the entire private export business from the United States." Nor was that the climax of the British plea. "Further, the basis of financial relations of all the Allies with the rest of the world will be removed, and a general collapse of credit and of all financial confidence will inevitably result." On such grounds the Allies were able to shift a huge burden to the United States Government after it had entered the war.

Yet in 1936 the Morgan Company's representatives sought to minimize the gravity of the impending crisis. They insisted that the British government was not at the end of its resources, that an economic crash was not necessarily impending between December, 1916, and April 6, 1917. Before the Nye committee they maintained the thesis that the

British had ample resources — gold, bonds, and stocks — which they could have employed as security for additional loans in the United States. Under this hypothesis, the British government had merely delayed mobilizing its securities during the period in question, for reasons none too clear. And there were grounds for accepting the Morgan thesis on this point of finance.

Acceptance, however, raised another dilemma. British citizens still possessed huge quantities of securities representing the ownership of enormous properties scattered throughout the whole world and, in consequence, control over commercial activities in other countries, especially in Latin America. The government of Great Britain could have commandeered these securities and sent them to the United States as pledges for additional loans. But it did not see fit to risk passing these guarantees of empire to American bankers and investors. In picturing itself as on the verge of collapse in July, 1917, it apparently falsified the picture — doubtless for the purpose of unloading as much of the burden as it could upon the Government of the United States.

By either facilitating or acquiescing in that operation, the Morgan Company was, wittingly or unwittingly, a party to the transaction. With its aid or silent consent, British authorities saved the equities of their empire, dumped upon the United States Treasury the responsibility for paying off huge Allied debts in this country, placed immense obligations for financing the Allies upon the Wilson administration, took back to Great Britain a large block of securities already pledged for American private loans, and shifted to the United States about four billion dollars' worth of British government paper that later went into default. This was banking — connected with war and foreign policy.

Such were the economic interests, pressures, stresses, and strains amid which the diplomacy of the Wilson administration was waged and its foreign policies were formulated. The American stake in the financial and military strength of the Entente Allies had swelled to enormous proportions after the

Bryan bans on credits and loans were lifted by President Wilson in response to the persistent requests of bankers. By the end of 1916 the government of Great Britain had a powerful weapon in its hands. If the Department of State had been intransigent in its protests against the high-handed manner in which the British government interfered with neutral rights and black-listed American merchants, a sharp contraction in buying could have brought a partial collapse of American economy, now geared to foreign transactions. The Secretary of the Treasury, the Secretary of State, and prominent advisers of the administration in Washington were fully conscious of this economic contingency. President Wilson was repeatedly told about the peril. Even German ministers were familiar with the prevailing conditions. Moreover President Wilson knew that the German government would renew the submarine warfare in case he could not or did not compel the Allies to relax the rigors of the iron blockade.

In the light of the documentation, the renewal of the German submarine campaign early in 1917 had inescapable implications for American economy and foreign policy. It might still be viewed as "an outrageous and immoral act of an autocratic power"; it might have been the revolting act that turned the balance of President Wilson's mind to war; but it did not stand alone as a cruel deed in a moral vacuum. Inevitably the submarine campaign made still more difficult the shipment of Anglo-French gold and securities to the United States in support of the exchange and the continued buying of American goods in enormous quantities. It increased the losses of goods at sea, adding strains to insurance. It weakened the military potential of the Allies and reciprocally their financial potential. If the Allies had made a sharp reduction in purchases, a terrific blow would have been struck at American prosperity. If the Allies had been defeated in the war or it had dragged on indefinitely, the losses in the United States would have been enormous in the best of bad circumstances. Temporarily the perilous state of economic affairs at home was relieved by the entry into the war abroad.

§

In sketching the domestic background of American foreign policy in its economic relations, the Nye committee did not ascribe President Wilson's war decision to "economic causation." It was not engaged in writing history. Under its mandate from the Senate to inquire into the adequacy or inadequacy of existing legislation for the control of traffic in munitions and implements of war, it was trying to discover the motives, interests, activities, methods, and conditions that favored such traffic and their repercussions on government policies. And the pertinence of the committee's findings was indubitable.

The Morgan Company, it is true, by its own publicity, insisted that it had been guilty of no legal improprieties and that the Nye revelations were merely sensational and unimportant. On the score of legal proprieties, it was successful in demonstrating the correctness of its procedure. The matter of "importance," however, remained in debate. With regard to this point, the Company argued, the country knew all along that the bans on credits and loans had been lifted, that an enormous trade in war supplies had sprung up, and that an economic entanglement in war destinies had come about. That was undoubtedly the case. But the country did not know, until the Nye inquest was completed, that bankers had hammered at the Wilson administration privately until they had broken down the ban on credits and then hammered at it again until they had destroyed the barrier against loans. Nor did the public know how President Wilson had made his decisions and caused them to be transmitted "orally" to privileged persons "entitled" to have the information. This was both sensational and important, if not to bankers, to everybody interested in pressure government, in foreign policy and the ways of making it, and in the practice of warfare.

In outcome the Nye committee's findings spread distrust of presidential discretion in handling foreign affairs and stimulated the popular interest that culminated in the neutrality legislation of 1935. They deepened, for a moment at least, the general resolve to avoid a repetition of such economic entanglements and "to stay out of the next war." They hastened the disintegration of ideology associated with President Wilson's "war for democracy," the League of Nations, and "close collaboration with the democratic powers of Europe."

Propaganda for that version of diplomacy had been conducted in the United States on a lofty plane of legal and abstract idealism. By disclosing the secret methods and the economic backgrounds — the interests, activities, and pressures — of the Wilson regime, the Nye committee injected realistic knowledge into the consideration of dynamic forces shaping foreign policies. Whatever the final verdict of that shadowy tribunal called "history" might be, the popular idea of Wilson as the pure idealist who went to war for the sole purpose of saving democracy was shattered beyond repair. Could "the universal philanthropy" of "the great moral crusade" launched in 1917 ever again present the same aspects to that part of the public which sought knowledge and did any thinking? Many imponderables had been let loose by the munitions investigation.

Nor was the contribution of the Nye inquiry to the economics of foreign policy as such to be treated as immaterial. The Morgan Company could point out that Americans had sold about seven billion dollars' worth of goods to the belligerents, with the aid of bankers' facilities; but simple arithmetic suggested that the war would cost the American people at least ten or twelve times this amount in the long run and that their former associates in the world war still owed ten or twelve defaulted billions on the final account. If imperialism did not furnish the outlets for the "surpluses" of American factories and farms, if armaments and war proved to be extravagantly expensive rather than profitable, could any foreign policy whatever dispose of the "surpluses" and keep American economy out of periodical collapses? The quest for an answer to that question was accelerated by the Nye investigation.

§

Another phase of domestic business brought under critical examination was the promotion of the navy and the merchant marine in relation to foreign affairs. If the generality of the people did not understand that the two sea arms were linked together and were clear and open manifestations of a foreign policy, key persons at the center of these interests were fully acquainted with the fact. In congressional hearings on the Geneva fiasco and on the London naval treaty, this acquaintance was plainly revealed. And by other inquiries it was made widely known that, in the midst of popular confusion and neglect, pertinent interests had formulated sea policies for civilians and landlubbers who sat in darkness.

"All navies," Admiral W. L. Rodgers informed a Senate committee, "relate to national policies. For many years the national platforms of both parties in this country have mentioned an adequate navy. They have not said 'adequate to what' so that the General Board [of the Navy], which has been charged since its inception with the general characteristics and size of the Navy, has been obliged to find out what the Navy is to be adequate to." In carrying out this assumed obligation, the Navy Board formulated the foreign policies to which the Navy must be related and, in effect, set the patterns for the performances of Congress in making naval and merchant marine appropriations and for the actions of the State Department in the conduct of foreign relations. For fifty years the country had been pouring millions of dollars into the Navy, without knowing why, and at last the Navy Board felt compelled to explain the hitherto mysterious transaction.

The program formulated for the country by the Navy Department was certainly as wide as the world. The Navy, it explained, should have sufficient strength to support the policies and commerce of the United States and "to guard its continental and overseas possessions." The Navy was under obligation also to exercise "ocean-wide economic pressure." It was "to make every effort, both ashore and afloat, at home and abroad, to assist the development of American interests, and especially the American merchant marine." Another responsibility assumed by the Navy Board was "to have always in mind that a system of outlying naval and commercial bases suitably distributed, developed, and defended is one of the most important elements of national strength."

Although the Navy Board, in formulating and continuing this policy, accepted the limitations imposed by naval treaties for the time being, it held fast to the center of its philosophy, namely, the sea-power doctrine of the Mahan school. By implication and by intent, the formula meant that the foreign policy of the United States was to follow the course of commercial expansion, supported by naval power, to develop a system of naval bases "suitably distributed," and to retain the "overseas" Philippines, with the corresponding obligations in the Asiatic sphere. In sum and substance, this was the straight imperialism of the British sea power, borrowed by Admiral Mahan and substituted for the older continental policy of the United States.

According to the true milk of the word, therefore, national greatness "depended" on sea power, and sea power meant overseas possessions, naval bases throughout the world, and a navy big enough "to keep the sea lanes open" in peace and war against all offenders. It was a sign that the nation "had grown up"; that little boys had become big men. For a time American "experts" in the subject had accepted a second place at sea — after Great Britain; but later they demanded supremacy. Indeed, logic required that. What, after all, was the use of having a navy inferior to any other? An inferior position, as the fate of Germany seemed to demonstrate, was about as bad as none.

As the scheme of thought and action was formulated by the Navy League, the American navy must be strong enough to impose its will on any power or combination of powers in the waters of Europe, Africa, and Asia. But the navy cost money and attached to the doctrine of the sea power was the plea that it "paid." It opened and kept open the lanes of commercial and territorial empire which furnished markets for goods and investment opportunities for capital. Trade followed the flag. Sea power was, in fine, the wonder-working Providence that assured the interminable outlets for the "surpluses" of American farms and factories. The glory of power and the pleasure of profits were thus wedded in a union of perfection.

The merchant-marine aspect of the sea power was fully developed in various congressional inquiries. When sifted and correlated, the rambling evidences on this point fitted neatly together under a simple hypothesis : A big navy is necessary to protect the merchant marine in all the waters of the world ; a merchant marine is necessary to the development of American commerce abroad ; merchant ships are to be armed in time of war and the number must be sufficient to supplement the increased navy. To a simple mind this amounted to a simple proposition : We must build more fighting ships to defend the merchant marine and more merchant ships to augment the power of the navy to defend the ships. Collaterally, the merchant marine was to assure bottoms for the transportation of American produce at reasonable rates in war and peace, to furnish the navy with trained sailors in time of stress, "to give steady employment to American working men in ships yards," and to afford business to the supply industries, therewith developing skill and plant for rapid expansion in all emergencies. Again powerful domestic interests were enlisted on the side of world-spanning "foreign policies," with a view to enlarging the oft-cited outlets for the "surpluses" of American farms and factories that swamped the domestic market and contributed to periodical crises in domestic economy.

When all was said and done, however, the maintenance of a merchant marine called for huge expenditures of public money and thus affected the prospects and profits of ship-building, supply, and operating concerns. As a result of the heritage left by the Wilson administration, it also involved the disposition of ships left on the hands of the Government at the close of the world war. Billions of dollars were at stake. During the Harding, Coolidge, and Hoover administrations, the pressure of ship lobbies had usually been effective in Congress and the sponsorship of the Navy Department constantly in evidence. The grant of lucrative payments for the carriage of mails made by the Jones-White Act of 1928 had induced a scramble for "mail contracts." The air was murky with agitation. One investigation after another, especially the Shearer inquiry of 1929, had uncovered the methods of ship lobbyists, and news of scandals in the Federal Shipping Board and the subsidized industry leaked into the corridors of the Capitol.

Stirred by rising expenditures, criticisms, and uncertainties, the Senate instructed a special committee, headed by Senator Hugo Black of Alabama, to investigate "air mail and ocean mail contracts." In accordance with use and wont, charges of politics, snooping, and muckraking were immediately lodged against the new Senate committee, and yet with relentless persistence it steered its way through the intricate history of the merchant marine in recent years. Another mountain of testimony and documents was heaped up for students, practitioners, and all citizens interested in the relations of merchant marine and foreign policy. Again the newspapers felt compelled to crown sensational revelations with tall headlines and that large public accustomed to deriving impressions from such sources was stirred to criticism of folly and waste.

In its quest for the "ultimate consumers" who received the Government's subsidies, the Senate committee plowed through a veritable mass of holding companies, subsidiaries, and collateral beneficiaries — an excursion bewildering even to adepts in the mysteries of contemporary finance. Although the story of the business was not completed, a number of chapters were established beyond cavil. Billions of dollars, for instance, had been poured into the bottomless hulks of the merchant marine during the world war and the following decade, and yet the United States had no "adequate merchant marine." In the construction of high class ships, the country lagged far behind the other great powers. If in the presentation of this contrast some real achievements were minimized, the general plight of the American marine was limned in the statistics of tonnage, in the classes of ships afloat, in the passengers carried, and in the mileage covered. "Although the United States ranks third in tonnage engaged in the international carrying trade, it ranks fourth as to speed, and last among the principal maritime countries in regard to the age of its ships."

A third-class ranking might have been accepted with some equanimity, had it not been for glimpses into shipping finance afforded by the Senate committee's investigation. For example, in 1923 a steamship company bought on liberal credit from the Federal Government at a price of $3,850,000 seven vessels that had cost the Government approximately $29,000,000. For carrying mail on these ships the Company received handsome payments from the Post Office Department. As a "service" supplementary to its operations, the Company organized a ten thousand dollar lighterage corporation. Besides paying large salaries to its officers, who were at the same time officers of the mail-contracting concern, the subsidiary garnered profits of more than a million dollars in five years. Grateful to its president for buying seven ships on credit for a low price, the shipping Company gave him over four hundred thousand dollars in commissions. Between 1924 and 1929, it made profits of nearly seven million dollars on ships bought from the Government, in part out of returns from the lucrative mail contracts won from that generous Government. Then, after a season of good luck, the Company defaulted on its payments to the Government for the ships and went on making payments to its president in appreciation of his services in buying the ships.

To the records of tangled finances, bonuses for officers, and high profits on little or no actual investments, the Senate committee added new chapters on the pressure politics played by the American Steamship Owners' Association and financed by a regular levy on the mail payments received by the companies from the Post Office Department. Money had been pried out of the Federal Treasury by lobbies and a fixed percentage of the money so gained had been spent to support the continuance of lobbies for the same purpose. With funds so collected, agents of the steamship interests prepared "news releases," formed contacts with editors, enlisted writers, hired radio broadcasters, bought popular orators, carried on "educational campaigns" to instruct the country in the patriotism of ship subsidies, maintained close relations with two mighty propagandists, William Randolph Hearst and Arthur Brisbane, and aided Congressmen who favored generous grants of public money to shipbuilders and operators. The "right" materials were supplied to a writer for The Saturday Evening Post. Successful efforts were made to win the support of General John J. Pershing. "Dope" was prepared for a high government official in the Post Office Department and then sent out as "news" through the American Press Association. An officer of an oil company that was also engaged in shipbuilding secured the publication of propaganda articles in a great popular magazine. Through all the ramifications ran the slimy trail of party politics; private interests greedy for appropriations from the Treasury could change their political spots like a chameleon and shift their affections from defeated Republicans to triumphant Democrats.

Magazines and journals notoriously affiliated through advertising with the shipping and importing business attempted to dismiss the findings of the Senate committee as "sensational and unimportant," and to charge it with "wrecking the great enterprise." But those members of Congress not dependent on the shipyard vote or on support from ship lobbyists were certainly "edified" by the investigation. Former sponsors of "big subsidies" suffered some loss of face and confidence. The reading public was once more jarred, momentarily at least, by frank testimony and confessions showing how private interests had burrowed into the Treasury. Their conduct had scarcely measured up to the lofty theory provided for popular instruction.

After all, the shipping propaganda had dwelt heavily and continuously on the merchant marine as an arm of the navy, an instrument of national defense, and a patriotic service. It might still be represented in such terms, but when the Senate committee got through with an exploration of practice, as against the beautiful theory, the shipping business was bereft before the country of that noble, sacrificial aspect which the lobbyists had insistently portrayed. Nor were hopes for American equality or superiority in mercantile shipping raised by the findings of fact. In the circumstances, Congress, without much display of enthusiasm, merely substituted direct grants from the Treasury for what had been euphemistically called "lucrative mail contracts." However considered, such sea power did not seem to "pay," and lust for it as a symbol of "national maturity" appeared to be diminishing, if congressional debates were to be regarded as reflecting public sentiment.

§

While the Shearer inquiries and the merchant-marine explorations were being carried on, a few admirals and experts in naval affairs began to suspect the gospel truth of the sea-power doctrine handed down by Admiral Mahan with the benediction of Theodore Roosevelt; and outside the naval circles independent thought was brought to bear upon it in articles and books. Questions were asked. How big a navy would be required to keep the sea lanes open to Europe if great sea powers at war decided to close them? If desirable from any point of view, in any interest, would it be possible for the United States to build a navy big enough to impose its will in the waters of Europe, Asia, or Africa? Would not a mere start on such a program encounter effective rivalry from sea powers whose strength was threatened? These were troublesome questions touching the technology of the vast ambition.

Other questions, involving national morale and practical economy, were also asked. Should the sacrificial patriotism of officers and men be enlisted in the promotion of profit-making propensities and the protection of investments everywhere in the world? Were officers and men to accept mere salaries and wages and to offer their lives in aid of commercial adventure? Was not the main function of the army and navy to defend the continental home of the American people and adjacent spheres of interest? Besides, did world sea supremacy "pay" as promised? The state of American agriculture after 1920 and of industry after 1929, the collapse of the Philippine "outlet," the scandals of ship lobbying, and the general disillusionment of the prolonged depression challenged, even mocked, experts in the theory of marine supremacy. The dream of commercial empire "sold" to the public in 1900 had burst, cracking the solid front of the sea-power specialists.

In a sensational broadcast to the country on May 8, 1935, Admiral William S. Sims repudiated, root and branch, the doctrine that it was the function of the American Navy to maintain freedom of the seas everywhere, to keep the sea lanes open for American profit-seekers in time of war. "The point of the whole business is this," he declared. "We cannot keep out of a war and at the same time enforce the freedom of the seas — that is, the freedom to make profits out of countries engaged in a death struggle. If a war arises, we must therefore choose between two courses: between great profits, with grave risks of war, on the one hand; or smaller profits and less risk, on the other. When I say 'we' I mean not only the traders themselves but all of us, for practically our whole population benefited by this wartime trade —

though we did not understand that we were inviting disaster
for ourselves and for the world. . . . We, as a people, must
come to understand that peace is priceless; that it is worth
any reasonable sacrifice of war profits; that a decent regard
for humanity must be placed ahead of gold. Therefore, let
every citizen who has the cause of honorable peace at heart
take this stand: Our trade as a neutral must be at the risk of
the traders; our army and navy must not be used to protect
this trade. It is a choice of profits or peace. Our country
must remain at peace." In his simple and cogent statement,
Admiral Sims pierced to the very center of the Mahan sea-
power doctrine — keeping the sea lanes open for trade profits
in peace and war.

But to what extent did Admiral Sims then speak for naval
officers at large as distinguished from the inner directors of
the naval bureaucracy and its supply interests? In a search
for an answer, the World Peace Foundation addressed three
questions to admirals and captains and received responses
from 130 of them. "Do you think the application of the plan
suggested by Admiral Sims would be politically possible in
time of war?" On this point naval opinion was divided
equally; four officers felt "that business acquisitiveness and
greed were more potent than patriotism." "If politically
possible, do you think the plan desirable in the interests of
the United States?" Fifty-two officers said "Yes" without
misgivings, thirty-six answered "No," and the others expressed doubts. "Are you in favor of the adoption of the
Sims plan as a policy tending to keep us out of war?" This
question cut to the core of naval thought and the upshot was
striking: "Sixty-two are for it, without reservation. Thirty-
nine are unqualifiedly against it." Admiral Herbert O. Dunn
took the position that "Sims' views, you will find, express the
idea of the Naval service . . . a majority of thoughtful
service opinion." Judging by this referendum, the Weltpolitik
of the Mahan school was dying, if not dead, as an active
principle of naval policy.

§

To the reports of congressional investigations and frank pronouncements of high officers were added the inquiries and findings of scholars and publicists engaged in exploring recent history and the roots of foreign policies. As a huge array of books, articles, and pamphlets demonstrated, a multitude of such seekers, armed with various instruments of research, struggled with might and main to discover just how the world, including under that symbol the United States, had come into the present passage. Applying their particular methods of authentication and analysis, historians examined the vast mass of documents released from secrecy by revolutions in Europe and by congressional inquiries in the United States and filled in, with increasing minuteness, the outlines of war origins in Europe and America. Publicists delved into recent history, compared theories and performances, and made special and general reports to persons accustomed to reading and thinking.

By 1927 the fortieth and final volume of Die Grosse Politik der Europäischen Cabinette — the immense pile of documents on war origins issued under the auspices of the German Foreign Office — had been completed and published. By that year the eleventh volume of British Documents on the Origins of the War had been placed in the hands of students, and the French were busy with their Documents Diplomatiques Français, the eleventh volume of which left the printers in 1936. Meanwhile the Russians were turning out papers, books, and articles giving the background of the mighty war as seen through the archives of the Tsarist regime. Into the main stream of new information flooded other papers, memoirs, and letters revealing details and generalities that had been closed to the ordinary soldiers and civilians who had played their part under the coverage of official ideologies emitted in justification of policies, actions, and war.

Written in many languages, frequently meaningless save when placed in juxtaposition with one another, often intricate and obscure even to the most highly trained adept, these thousands of papers and volumes made their way into libraries. Long before, Jacob Burckhardt had said that the opening of royal archives to historians would mark the doom of monarchies. Now these new archives, sifted, sorted, classified, analyzed, and pieced together by a host of scholars, marked the doom of all the simple explanations under which the world war had been launched, fought, and "settled." Practitioners, as usual, resenting the findings of the scholars, insisted that they knew better, and threw themselves athwart the streams of revelation; but, as Emerson had said, the State sketches in coarse outline the progress of thought. In time distillations of historical findings reached casual editors and readers, and even crept into the arcanum of the State Department where experts guarded the national mysteries.

Also in the wide open spaces of the United States reports on domestic sources of foreign policy circulated quietly but none the less potently. From library to library, from woman's club to woman's club, from university to university, from college to high school, from high school to grade school, from private study to editorial sanctum, seeped and crept the new knowledge of what diplomats, bankers, munitions makers, statesmen, and warriors had thought, planned, contemplated, fumbled, and done. Though imponderable, this knowledge dissolved the vision of diplomacy and war that had been officially supplied to the fighting, dying, and paying populace. Despite protests from monopolists of noble sentiments, it disrupted the grand fabric of official imagination; and men of practical affairs, protesting, explaining, and correcting, might not be able to restore for the coming generation the official picture of the grand foreign policies supplied to the war generation and its heirs. Once more the cruelty and justice of history were illustrated.

That all these investigations, searchings, and inquests exerted a material influence on the making of current foreign policy was attested by the commotion which greeted the neutrality legislation of 1935. Wise or foolish, according to the assumptions of philosophers and commentators, the neutrality legislation, coupled with the granting of independence to the Philippines, signified, at least temporarily, the steep decline of the imperialism sponsored by McKinley, Mahan, Lodge, Hay, and Theodore Roosevelt, and also punctured the universal philanthropy expounded by Woodrow Wilson. The failure of empire, sea power, foreign loans, munitions selling, and a war for democracy to bring permanent outlets for "surpluses" of farms and factories or peace to the earth was so glaring that the very plow boys and bond salesmen could grasp the fact. That lust for profits, facilitated in action by bankers, had accompanied the Wilson administration on what Walter Millis called the "road to war" was equally patent to the same personnel. Beyond dispute, the intellectual and moral setting for American policy in foreign relations had altered. The configurations of American thought, the posture of European and Asiatic nations, and the nature of "world economy" presented new aspects. Neither the imperial hopes of 1900 nor the philanthropic enthusiasm of 1917 nor the unbounded expectations of 1928 could be restored as sources of motivation for easy action by the President or State Department in shaping current policy. Some new mask might be needed for the face of war.

CHAPTER X

Shadows and Shapes of Foreign Policy

BY the numerous inquiries, official and private, into the experiences, interests, and ideas of recent and current history, inherited conceptions of world affairs were swiftly and extensively modified. Congressional inquests into the making of naval policies, the financing and results of heavy foreign loans, the management of the munitions business, the subsidizing of the merchant marine, and the fruits of empire as they had ripened in the Philippines helped to refashion the dream of America as a grown-up nation, with its trade ever expanding over land and sea, with its moral obligations in the four quarters of the earth mystically joined to its commercial enterprise, with its corresponding foreign policies. To more than one keeper of the auguries, what seemed to be the maturity of the preceding generation now took on the aspect of emotional adolescence. And people at large could no longer be easily satisfied by the facile doctrines of lending, pushing, subsidizing, shoving, and moralizing as guarantees of practical and ideal achievements anywhere, at home or abroad. New raw materials were thrust into the operation of

434

thinking and image-making. Over them hung the fateful question : What is all this worth ?

In whatever respect the foreign policies previously applied had affected domestic conditions, the deterioration of national economy after the application forced a reconsideration of the old tenets. Despite passionate desires and efforts, the Lords of Creation, operating under these policies, had been unable to stave off economic calamity ; they were also unable to get the machines over which they presided in motion again at anything like capacity rate. Though the State Department, the Navy Department, and the Marines were all co-operative and helpful in the enforcement of "national interests" in all parts of the earth, they could not accomplish that feat. Was it possible then that the widespread crisis in town and country could be attributed, in substantial measure, to the foreign policies that had been pursued by the Government of the United States, to the false hopes that they had raised ? Certainly neither the imperialism of 1900 nor the moral crusade of 1917 nor the feverish money lending of 1928 had led to the haven of prosperity and security. So what ?

§

In attempts to gather up the old fragments and to formulate new policy, the posture and conduct of other nations, of course, had to be taken into the reckoning. To some extent, it was highly probable, the policies of foreign governments were due to acts of commission and omission attributable to the Government of the United States. For example, the procedures of Germany, France, and Great Britain might have been different if America had joined the League of Nations; but how different, no one could say. Doubtless the outcome would have depended somewhat on the types of Americans sent to Geneva as participants in the affairs of the League. Surely proceedings there would have turned partly upon their instructions and also upon the power set up within the League. Judging by the history of American activities at

various arms and economic conferences, American membership in the League of Nations would have brought about few
drastic changes in international behavior. Going over the
League affair, however, was like quarrelling with history.

Apart from all that, European powers, since the close of the
world war, had been engaged in making adjustments in their
own style. Great Britain and France did nothing effective to
bring about the general reduction of armaments definitely
promised in the treaty of Versailles which imposed strict
limitations upon the vanquished. Nor did they strain themselves in efforts to aid the Weimar republic. After the German government had conclusively demonstrated that it
could wring no major concessions from them early in 1933,
the republic collapsed. Adolf Hitler and his party of National
Socialists seized sovereignty, set about rearmament, reoc-
cupied the Rhine zone, repudiated debts and reparations,
left the League of Nations, demanded a return of colonies,
called for a free hand in eastern Europe, persecuted Jews and
dissidents, grabbed Austria, shook the mailed fist under the
noses of Paris and London.

If such actions mainly involved the European powers,
other decisions in Germany had a distinct bearing upon trade
and diplomatic relations with the United States. In the
course of the transformation wrought by the Nazi administration, German economy was placed, to an amazing extent,
on a basis of national self-sufficiency now called "autarkie"
(autarchy). Whether this changed economy could be correctly classified as state capitalism as some alleged or as Bolshevism as others contended, it was certainly not the laissez
faire capitalism of the Cobden and Bright school and it was
unquestionably controlled by arbitrary executive decrees in
the manner of Bolshevism. Irrespective of the name given
this new Leviathan, autarchy fitted neither the money-lending proclivities of the Hoover tradition nor the free or "freer"
trade conceptions of the Roosevelt administration which
came to power shortly after the rise of Hitler to supremacy
in Berlin.

To the disturbance of "free enterprise" created by the Hitler regime were added tumults set in motion by Benito Mussolini, head of the fascist state established in Italy in 1922. Having pleased American capitalists and travelers at first by "suppressing communists" and "making trains run on time," Mussolini, at the outset of his dictatorial career, had aroused no economic alarms in Washington — any more than in Paris or London. Dr. Nicholas Murray Butler had praised his labors and policies in florid language. Thomas Lamont had visited him and the Morgans had floated a big loan for him in the United States. As Mussolini had come to terms with the Pope and at first let Jews alone, he had avoided setting the world against his system through religious and racial agitations.

But after consolidating his position at home and straining every nerve to build up his army and navy for war, which he extolled as a positive virtue in itself, Mussolini directed his energies abroad, to empire-building, like a Roman Caesar. He refused any longer to play a second political fiddle to Paris or London, or pay installments on the Italian war debt owed to Washington. He had grievances to air. By the peacemakers at Versailles in 1919, Italy had been deprived of spoils of victory, which had been promised when the Italian government, after bargaining two ways, joined the Entente Allies in the war. At that settlement the peacemakers had given the lion's share of Germany's colonial goods to Great Britain and France and had refused to enlarge the Italian empire in Africa.

Remembering this transaction, Mussolini flirted with discontented Germany, prepared the way for a Berlin-Rome axis, defied the League of Nations, looked after himself, in the historic way, by seizing the whole of Ethiopia, and joined Hitler in helping rebels in Spain to wage war on the lawfully-chosen republican government of Madrid. Earlier, in 1900, when the United States was administering the "water cure" to recalcitrant Filipinos and when Great Britain was "extending civilization" to the Boers, the Italian dictator's action would perhaps have excited less alarm in America, but a change in interests and attitudes had occurred during the intervening years. To a large number of Americans, in 1938, Mussolini's defiance of France and Great Britain seemed to be an affair of honor for the United States. It was, in fact, a defiance of the new morality, the Stimson doctrine, and the Good Neighbor idea.

Events in Russia likewise altered the world scene and its implications for America. For years the Government of the United States had refused to recognize the Soviet regime, largely on the ground that it had repudiated debts and in other ways outraged the ethics of the State Department. Deceived by biased press reports from Russia, the American people had daily expected the downfall of the Union of Socialist Republics. But expectations had not been realized. By efforts that seemed superhuman, the Russian government carried out a five year plan for industrialization and drafted a program in continuation. In terms of iron, steel, and factories, the achievement was monumental, at least as compared with the economic enterprise of the Tsarist regime.

After the suppression of Leon Trotsky and other self-dedicated makers of world revolution, Russia settled down to "socialism in one country" under the direction of Joseph Stalin, joined the League of Nations, and sought trade on a business basis. With the aid of experienced officers and foreign technicians, the Soviet government also built up and equipped a huge army in approved Western style and its representatives sitting in the conferences held by the family of nations could command, from colleagues similarly equipped, a certain respect for their remarks on matters of peace and international policy. Although, later, a crisis in Stalin's system raised suspicions as to the real strength behind the façade, by the year 1934 Russia had won a place in the concert of the great powers. For a time, her regime presented signs of permanence. Her economic and military strength appeared substantial. An alliance with France, as in the days of the Tsar, gave weight to Russian policy. With Japan growing daily more arbitrary and finally lunging into war against China, neither Great Britain nor France nor the United States could be entirely indifferent to the possibility of aid from Russia, East and West, however unpalatable the idea might be to private and public business conceived in the style of the nineteenth century.

Thought of Russia provoked more thought of Japan whence a violent shift in policies and measures had sent tremors to the banks of the Potomac, the Thames, the Seine, the Spree, and the Tiber. To some extent that shift might be ascribed to measures adopted by the United States, especially the Immigration Act of 1924. With some reluctance the Government of Japan had broken with Germany in 1914 and joined the democratic powers in their war on autocracy. Given the tradition of absolutism and the cult of emperor worship in Japan, the decision had been a wrench for the Elder Statesmen. Nevertheless it had been made, and the Japanese had been welcomed as noble comrades-in-arms by Americans, French, and British, if with some wry faces. As a Tokyo diplomat described the innovation: "We were invited to the very best parties given by the very best families in the West."

That was gratifying to Japanese pride and for several years after the war an active, if small, group of liberals in Japan exercised a genuine influence in directing the thought of the people and the government toward closer affiliation with Great Britain and the United States. While their task was arduous, they made considerable progress. Yet awkward incidents made their path harder, and whether the drift of economic and military forces in their own country could be overcome by that foreign policy was always dubious. At no time did the military interest, more provincial than the naval interest, surrender the hope of regaining supremacy and establishing an Oriental despotism in Japan and on the mainland of Asia.

At the moment when the Congress at Washington moved, in 1924, toward the enactment of the immigration bill positively excluding Japanese from the United States, the conflict of interests in Tokyo was trembling in the balance. In declaring that "grave consequences" would flow from the passage of the bill, the Japanese ambassador to America spoke with full knowledge of the contest in his native land. He did not mean, as the American yellow press insinuated, that war between the two countries would follow. He did mean that the open and specific exclusion of Japanese from the United States would enable the military party at home to whip up popular passion in favor of "Asia for the Asiatics," that is, Japanese supremacy in the Far East.

Frantically the Japanese government, then under liberal influences, sought to reach an adjustment with the United States that would save the pride of its own people. It was willing to accept the objective of exclusion if something like the "Gentlemen's Agreement" could be preserved instead of a flaunting congressional fiat to the world: No Japanese wanted. The State Department at Washington sought a middle way, but Congress would not follow its advice. Within a few days after the exclusion bill was signed, the liberal and democratic forces in Japan were started down hill to destruction by the "insult." Convinced by many educative experiences that western liberalism was a cloak for imperialist operations in the Orient, the military party in Tokyo set out to realize ends long in view — dominance over China and perhaps over Siberia to Lake Baikal. The seizure of Manchukuo in 1931 and the war of 1937 on the Nanking government were in perfect line with the logic of Japanese imperialism.

As Japanese despotism grew more belligerent in Asia, the "front" of the Western powers in relation to China, never solid or stable, showed a tendency to crumble. The policy of the United States had been pliable, if not sometimes surreptitious. American enthusiasm for the imperial adventure into the Philippines had not been universal; and now, under the pressure of agrarian interests and the disillusionment in respect of markets, it had simmered down toward the vanishing point. John Hay and William McKinley might have been willing to carve out and annex slices of China in the approved fashion followed by Tsarist Russia, Great Britain, France, and Imperial Germany, had they not known that such overt actions would make trouble for them in Congress. In the circumstances the best they could do was to adopt the formula of "the open door," supplied to them by a British representative, and make it appear as a generous homage to an all-around equality of trade. In reality it was, as Tyler Dennett said, "a form of intervention in China," though in popular understanding it merely looked like "a fair deal."

However understood in theory by the popular and missionary mind, the Open Door in China was in practice a cloak for imperialist intrigues. Nominally recognizing the territorial and administrative integrity of China, it formed a shield for constant interference in Oriental affairs by successive administrations in Washington and in other Western capitals. From start to finish, the "coöperating powers," while competing ruthlessly among themselves for favorable positions in China, showed a willingness to unite in keeping China weak. For example, they refused until 1930 to permit China to raise at will her own customs duties on imports. Had this boon, this right which China should have enjoyed as a sovereign power, been granted early in the twentieth century, the Chinese government might have secured revenues large enough to sustain an army of defense against all foreigners. In that case also it might have developed the domestic industries necessary to economic independence and military safety. This achievement would have meant a China strong enough to resist the encroachments of Japan. At the same time it would likewise have meant severe checks on the arbitrary and aggressive conduct of Western powers in Chinese waters and territory. By joining other powers in holding down Chinese tariffs, the United States had made its contribution to the weakness that yielded before militant Japan. Yet in spite of, to some extent on account of, alien interference, China steadily nourished the nationalist spirit which was inimical to the interests of foreigners accustomed to doing about as they pleased within her borders.

With China in transformation, Japanese power rising, and Great Britain caught in the web of European perils, the basis for a strong American policy in the Orient shrank rather than widened as time passed. Army and navy "games" might contemplate war in the Far Pacific, but it grew increasingly difficult to count upon popular zeal in the United States for that eventuality. Experience of more than half a century had disclosed no "ample outlets for the surpluses of American factories and farms" in that part of the world. Trade with China remained relatively trivial, notwithstanding the huge volume of wild talk about four hundred million potential customers. It was true that when the calculations of economic interest were put aside as unimpressive, the missionary interest and the traditional friendship of the United States for China could be invoked. Influential as these were, however, they lacked the unequivocal support required for effective diplomatic pressure on either China or Japan, to be backed up in final analysis by naval and military action. Some injury to American citizens, some deliberate insult, or some horrible outrage, might set the United States on fire, but by no stretch of knowledge or imagination could a rational argument be found, in practical considerations, for asserting American supremacy or rattling the sabre anywhere in the Orient. Preparations "adequate" to avenge some hypothetical affront, which might or might not occur, furnished no scheme of accountancy for the State Department and for army and navy appropriations by Congress.

§

With dissolvent effects, events at home and abroad — the cataclysm in domestic economy, the shrinkage of exports and imports, and the shift in the balance and conduct of the world powers — broke into all schools of thought concerned with American foreign policies. The oldest school, isolationism pure and simple, had originated in the administration of President Washington. It had contended that the United States could expand its trade in all parts of the world, avoid entangling alliances, and remain insulated against the endless wars in Europe. For all practical purposes this scheme of policy had been destroyed near the end of the nineteenth century when, under the leadership of William McKinley and John Hay, the isolationist creed of the early republic was abandoned and the United States Government set out on a course of imperialist conquest in the Far East and trade expansion everywhere under naval pressures.

In destroying the policy inaugurated under George Washington, the McKinley school did not, however, frankly and openly adopt the imperialist dogma in the British, French, and German style, although the deed implied the word. For this proceeding the McKinley administration felt that it lacked the support of the American nation. So it sought to combine the hazards of empire with continental security, and the correct characterization of this new policy was a bastard conception, Imperial Isolationism. With some justification its temporary vogue could be called "accidental." Taking advantage of popular enthusiasm for a movement to liberate Cuba from Spanish dominion, Theodore Roosevelt, Alfred Thayer Mahan, Henry Cabot Lodge, John Hay, Albert J. Beveridge, and other "war hawks" of 1898 turned the conflict into a war for the conquest and annexation of the Philippines and for the pursuit, they alleged, of commercial interests through the agency of the sea power. Taking advantage also of the fright induced by the bogy of Bryanism, free silver, and populist radicalism, the school of Imperial Isolation, it is true, secured the appearances of popular approval in the national election of 1900 and again in 1908. Yet as the course of events subsequently showed, the program of the school had not become a national creed rooted in the unshakeable affections of the whole people.

This was conclusively demonstrated in 1938 when Franklin D. Roosevelt's message asking for a super-navy authorization came before Congress. In the circumstances and by its very nature, the super-navy could be used, perhaps was intended by some sponsors to be used, in a new imperialist war in the Orient. But no sponsor rose in either chamber to defend it openly on that ground. In the House of Representatives, James W. Wadsworth, son-in-law of John Hay, and in the Senate Frederick Hale, a surviving member of the Old Guard, voted for the super-navy bill, but most of the Republican contingent was opposed to it in both branches of the national legislature, while Democrats expressly disowned all imperialist intentions, explicit or implicit, in the sea-power program.

Only in by-plays, insinuations, and occasional lines in reports, speeches, and press releases did any defenders of the super-navy bill, Democrats or Republicans, admit that hidden in it was what the minority of the House committee on naval affairs called "the British-Mahan sea power doctrine" — the main support of the imperialist creed. Nevertheless the super-navy bill passed both houses of Congress and everybody familiar with its terms and the circumstances of its adoption knew that, whatever the people in general thought about the transaction, experts in diplomacy and naval affairs were fully alive to its imperialist implications and utilities. If voters at large had little affinity for Imperial Isolationism, persons in key positions of power held fast to their imperialist emotions and ambitions. If bothered by events, they had not surrendered; their creed was still operative in shaping foreign policy.

Claiming to be intensely practical in their outlook, imperialists of the isolation persuasion operated on assumptions about the world, which were more or less systematic in form. They took for granted a high degree of world disorder, at least from time to time, and believed in taking pertinacious and prudent advantage of favorable opportunities for increasing trade, making loans, and pushing what they called national interests. They had toyed with Hague conferences, approved academic resolutions framed by peace advocates, and paid occasional homage to the peace sentiment, particularly, as Theodore Roosevelt remarked, when it was necessary to capture the votes of that "lunatic fringe." On the whole, however, theirs was a hard and presumably realistic view of international affairs — one which they regarded as sanctioned by human history as fact rather than by human aspiration as utopia. In their view of the universe the rivalry of imperial powers was a kind of natural law — an extension of the law of the struggle for existence within capitalist society itself. The rivalry, some imperialists conceded, might be mitigated by restraint or by limited collaboration; but competition for trade, investment opportunities, raw materials, protectorates, and prestige, they thought, would continue in the future as in the past.

According to their theory, American economy, having rounded out the continental domain and fairly completed the accumulation of capital goods for domestic uses, possessing surpluses, must widen beyond the seas in a contest with other great powers for acquisition of more profits and more capital through the disposition of the domestic surpluses and other activities. Briefly stated, an expanding foreign trade was a primary consideration of imperial isolationism. To assure success in this operation, it was the duty of the Government to utilize all the instrumentalities which rival imperial powers employed, such as tariffs, subsidies, and navies. Although this power-politics, Machtpolitik, as the German devotees named it, was not deemed as absolute by American imperial isolationists as it was by the German school of Weltmacht (world-power), it was persistent and pervasive among influential circles in America. The alternative among the German exponents was Untergang (downfall) and the American theory rather closely conformed to that rationalization and fear.

As practiced under Republican auspices during the golden glow, isolationism meant the vigorous pursuit of "national interests," identified with the support of tariffs, subsidies, and bounties at home, and appropriate use of diplomatic and naval power abroad. Earlier the promise of this policy had taken the form of ample outlets for the "surpluses" of American farms, factories, banks, and investors. Since experience, however, had brought disillusionment as to the "ample" part of the program, the phraseology was now somewhat modified, to run: "Upon these outlets abroad our prosperity depends." This being so, in the world as it actually is, pressures for the outlets must be maintained, with prudence, but persistently. Only such a policy can be followed in the world of nations as they are. Other policy is fantasy. It is possible to occupy a position as a creditor nation, to collect the war debts due the Government of the United States, and at the same time raise higher and higher the tariff barriers against the flow of manufactures and agricultural produce imported to discharge the interest on loans, to pay dividends on foreign investments, and to amortize maturing obligations. On these terms relations with other countries should be as friendly as possible and war might be safely renounced as an instrument of national policy, at least outside the Caribbean region.

In substance, this brand of isolationism was "dollar diplomacy," renewed under the more euphonious verbalism set forth by Charles E. Hughes when he was Secretary of State: "Foreign policies are not built upon abstractions. They are the result of practical conceptions of national interest arising from some immediate exigency or standing out vividly in historical perspective." Although the fruits garnered from the pursuit of this "national interest" early began to decay and drop away, it took awful reverses to shake the confidence of Respectability in that line of economic diplomacy. The reverses came with the calamities of the depression, with revolutions and loan repudiations in Europe, with upheavals and loan repudiations in South America, with the victory of imperialists in Germany, Italy, and Japan.

Scarcely less desolating, doubtless, was the impact of events upon the second school of American foreign policy — that of Collective Internationalism. At home and abroad it too encountered blow after blow. The effort of Henry L.

Stimson, as Secretary of State under President Hoover, to enlist French and British support against Japanese aggression in Manchukuo was an utter failure. Even with the support of President Franklin D. Roosevelt, the proposal that the United States adhere to the World Court, a foster child of the League of Nations, was rejected by the Senate. The withdrawal of Germany and Japan from the League, Mussolini's imperialist war against Ethiopia, the futility of the application of sanctions to Italy with the aid of President Roosevelt, the inability of the League to prevent "the little world war" in Spain — these and other occurrences made the stoutest hearts among the internationalists beat a little slower. By 1937 the morale of the League of Nations had disintegrated, for all practical purposes. Although Roosevelt's "quarantine" speech at Chicago in the autumn of that year gave the collectivists a temporary lift, the popular counterblast which greeted that address throughout the country had a tendency to explode their dreams.

Yet the image of the world on which the school of Collective Internationalism based its hopes persisted. In various respects this image represented a more realistic view of affairs than did the conception of Imperial Isolationism. It was in fact more recent in origins and more nearly in line with developments. The modern imperialist process had been started by European powers in the sixteenth century, in an age of wooden ships, and had stretched out over a three-hundred-year span of time, during which virgin continents and defenseless peoples had been exploited for the benefit of the rulers. Neither that history nor those circumstances could ever be duplicated exactly. The only imperialist hope worthy of "great politics" for the United States lay in the overthrow of the British empire and the substitution of an American empire for it, and no such prospect seemed enclosed in the contours of fate.

By contrast, Collective Internationalism was nearly up to date. It had assumed a positive configuration as late as 1919 when the League of Nations was established. As the American school of imperialists had taken advantage of an idealistic war against Cuba to impose the system of "expansion" upon the country, so the Collective Internationalists, under the leadership of President Wilson, had seized the occasion of a war that sprang largely out of imperialist rivalries to dream of imposing an idealistic scheme of permanent peace upon the world — after an imperialist settlement under military auspices at Paris. Their action, therefore, came later in time and had a closer relationship with the course of events during the midpassage.

The world image of which Collective Internationalism was a political and legal expression stemmed, in part, from the internationalism of the free trade system as conceived by Richard Cobden and John Bright in the age of Queen Victoria. The conception presupposed capitalism, especially industrial capitalism, as a final order for economic transactions, with, perhaps, modifications in the form of social legislation. It covered a number of subsidiary ideas : increasing world trade through the free exchange of commodities and raw materials ; a world market as a reality ; gold as the uniform medium of international exchange ; world-wide freedom of commerce for individuals and corporations without government intervention ; abolition or drastic reduction of tariff barriers between nations ; the free flow of capital, goods, and labor under the stimulus of the best returns ; automatic adjustments of exchange through the operation of the free price mechanism ; liberty for efficient competition without regard to national boundaries ; international division of labor, industries, and skills ; acceptance of world prices, as determined by efficient competition ; free and equal access to raw materials whether domestic or colonial ; the international liberty for developing investment opportunities.

In other words, this image contemplated the unification of the world for economic transactions according to certain rules to be collectively accepted by the participating States. It precluded or minimized unilateral economic action by governments, the management of currencies, and the insulation of domestic price and wage levels against the world price and wage levels attained by savage world competition. Governments might vary, though presumably capitalist democracies were preferable; cultures might be diverse; internal conflicts over economic interests, even civil wars, might occur; many types of civilization might exist along the scale from primitive African villages to the fashion center of France; but free transactions among the economic atoms of the whole world could be or should be maintained. "If only" this were done, the problem of outlets for national "surpluses" would be solved; the several peoples of the earth would be constantly employed at the enterprises for which they are best fitted; economic excuses for war would disappear; and an optimum or maximum economic satisfaction would prevail in the four quarters of the globe. Departures from the norms of this world utopia were to be explained in some measure by reference to "political psychiatry" or "nationalistic insanity."

Although this world conception was seldom set forth in completeness, fragments or huge sections of it were to be found in the flood of economic writings that issued from the intellectual workshops of professors, researchers, international experts, and peace societies. With modifications and vague fringes it was the basic frame for public policy upon which the Secretary of State, Cordell Hull, operated, while President Roosevelt vibrated between plans for establishing a "sound internal economy" and quarantines for aggressors. Most of the books by outstanding professors of politics and economics who dealt with "world" affairs — Alvin Hansen, Eugene Staley, Jacob Viner, Quincy Wright, James T. Shotwell, and Charles Fenwick, for example — took for granted the essential validity and realism of the world image, if with various qualifications; and the nature of their conclusions and contentions turned upon their preliminary assumption. As was said of another intellectual proceeding, they "got out of their major premise all they put into it."

From the polishing rooms of the philosophers who kept the

world image shining, their dicta, instructions, demands, and imperatives for policy crept into marketplaces, offices of exporters and importers, women's organizations, editorial sanctums and forums of public discussion, giving appropriate and automatic turns to locution respecting foreign affairs. With the formulas and mandates of this school, as of all the others, specialists in the business became so familiar that the moment the words "world economy" or "world trade" or "world society" appeared in literature or discourse, they could immediately foretell the conclusion — lower trade barriers — with a certainty of prediction like one in celestial mechanics.

Notwithstanding all their claims to the sanction of axiomatics, the world imagists encountered rough sledding. If historians asked them just when or where the world of realities conformed to the shape of the world image, they could be lightly dismissed as antiquarians. If an economist gave a different picture of things, as did Erich Zimmermann in his book on World Resources and Industries, he could be classified as a geographer. However, events which contemplation could not banish had a way of dealing perversely with the world conception. Though statesmen guilty of perpetrating these events might be called insane chauvinists, crazy nationalists, demagogues, and flouters of "sound economic principles," practitioners themselves everywhere worked against, rather than according to, the prescriptions of the world imagery. For instance, the original home of the grand dream, England, abandoned free trade, went back to protective tariffs even for agriculture, consolidated competing railways, set up a system of control over agriculture akin to that provided by the Agricultural Adjustment Act in the United States, forcibly fused public and private electrical concerns in a common grid, went in for government housing, and nationalized the coal industry — among many other departures from the "natural order." Everywhere nations sought to attain a high degree of self-sufficiency, in part by balancing agriculture and manufacturing, and employed collective regimentation of domestic enterprises as the instrument. Even in the United States, Secretary Hull, though endowed with large powers in making reciprocity treaties, could only effect minor changes in the high tariff wall erected during the Harding-Coolidge-Hoover regime; and the domestic economic regimentation introduced by the New Deal continued apace. A barrage of facts obscured the shining face of the world image.

For the third school of foreign policy, International Communism, the events of the midpassage were also disruptive. It too had a world view — one based on a specific interpretation of history. Like Collective Internationalism, this conception, formulated by Karl Marx and elaborated by V. I. Lenin, accepted capitalism as the actuating force of domestic and world economies; but it insisted that capitalism was subject to laws of development in time, of which imperialism was the latest expression. And it went further. According to the Communist theory, after imperialism had expanded to the ends of the earth, reached the limits of extension in a series of world wars, and arrived at the time-point of its own collapse, the industrial workers of the world, consolidated by the pressures of capitalism and embittered by the sufferings of peace and war, would seize power in every country and bring about the international unification and pacification of all toiling peoples, if with scant courtesy for all who toiled not.

Such was the theory. But facts did not exactly fit it. A few years after their triumph in Russia, amid the horrors of the world war and the political upheavals which followed, true believers in world brotherhood through world revolution were expelled from the Soviet republic or shot down at mass executions. Beyond the confines of Russia, the rise of fascism marked the destruction of many communist organizations. While all this was transpiring, the Russian government concentrated its energies on domestic affairs and on what was called "building socialism in one country." As a result communists everywhere split into two or more contending factions. Interest in the defense of Russia put a damper on interest in international communism or postponed the final triumph into an indefinite future, thus disintegrating it as a single force. And in the march of events it came about that the Communist party in the United States, affiliated with the party in Russia, eagerly supported Collective Internationalists in their campaign against the fascist foes of their world image and applauded the demands of imperialists for the use of sea power to coerce Japan — the long-standing foe of Russia.

During the turmoil of events that rendered older theories of foreign policy at least somewhat obsolete, a fourth school gradually emerged, without a neatly-fitting name. Like the other systems of ideology and utopia, it had roots in the past, but its conception of American interest and genius was both divergent and critical. At the center of its philosophy was the idea that through domestic measures, adopted by the democratic process, vast improvements could be and should be effected in American civilization, where at least one-third of the nation was ill-housed, ill-clothed, ill-nourished, and ill-educated; moreover, that this civilization could be defended in its continental home under prudent policies by small but appropriate military and naval establishments. Associated with the vision was the conviction that American democracy should not attempt to carry the Atlas load of the White Man's Burden in the form of imperialism all over the earth, or assume that it had the capacity, even with the best of good-will, to settle the difficult problems of European nations encrusted in the heritages of their long and sanguinary history. Its theories and sentiments were enclosed in such phrases as: let us keep out of the next world war; mind our own business; till our own garden; create the wealth; substitute abundance for scarcity; establish a sound and efficient domestic economy; make America a work of art.

Although owing to the lack of a precise name, this fourth school of foreign policy was often described as isolationist by critics, its defenders disowned the connotations of the kind of isolationist creed which had been sponsored by Henry Cabot

Lodge, Warren G. Harding, and Calvin Coolidge. They likewise refused to be battened down by the name "nationalist," with its chauvinist and militarist associations. They did not deprecate foreign trade as such; they merely insisted that the aim of such commerce should be to supplement the national resources and that in no form whatever could foreign trade, in the very nature of things, guarantee, by its own expansion, either prosperity or security for America. Surrendering shop-worn reliance upon imperialist pressures, money lending, and huckstering abroad, they turned to the efficient, humanistic use of national resources and technical skills as a means for making a civilization on this continent more just, more stable, and more beautiful than anything yet realized. Perhaps, in a world beset by clamant ideologies, the name "continental," or "American civilization," was most appropriate, if still inadequate, to characterize the thought of the fourth school of foreign policy.

The central economic thesis of this school probably came from the writings of the British economist, John A. Hobson. The primary force in the rivalry of nations for market outlets, he said, is the inefficient distribution of wealth at home — in other words, the enormous accumulations of capital that cannot find high profits in domestic expansion and must go abroad or burst. Associated with fierce international rivalry was domestic exploitation and ill-being. And the solution for the problem of attaining well-being or "prosperity," he argued, lies not in "the world market" but in domestic economy — in the wider distribution of wealth to sustain continuous and expanding buying power among the people.

Although this doctrine was grounded in a general economic conception, like the other theories of foreign policy, the school of American civilization did not contend that its creed was universally applicable; nor did it propose to employ any diplomatic or military engines to force the faith upon other countries. Its conception embraced a plural universe — a world composed of many nations, dependencies, protectorates, colonies, spheres of interest, degrees of industrialization, forms of government, patriotic and cultural ideologies. It was not concerned with efforts to run the steam roller of capitalism, democracy, communism, or any other "system" over the world. This act of universalization was not deemed possible nor, from the angle of national or human interest, desirable.

Evangelists might yearn to set up a world system and government on some religious credo, or democrats less theological might want to reproduce the capitalist system, American style, in all the world, with a police guard. On their part the continentalists who sought to formulate an American foreign policy relegated to the domain of utopias the denationalized idea of the world imagists whether it represented evangelism, the individualism of the capitalist persuasion, or the communism of the Trotzky direction. To the adherents of this school the world did not appear as a mere aggregation of individuals engaged in production and trade, but rather as an array of ever-changing political groupings, each with historical characteristics of its own. They rejected the imperialist doctrine of war "as the law of life" and deemed the Cobden-Bright, Wilson-Trotzky ideal of world pacifism to be an illusion beyond the purview of practice. They accepted the possibility of war for limited objectives, such as continental defense, and refused to accept war as an instrument of trade promotion, colonial expansion, or ideological world pacification.

In summary, they insisted that the real interests and needs of the United States did not exactly coincide with those of any other nation and that the geographical location and domestic situation of the country must and should give a different form and direction to the foreign policy of the Government. Experience, they argued, had demonstrated the failure of dollar diplomacy to attain its announced objective, that is, ample outlets for the "surpluses" of American factories and farms. The conception of world free trade, they contended, was really nothing more than a theory flung up for the British manufacturing classes in their peculiar and temporary position at the middle of the nineteenth century — a formula embedded in classical economics and repeated by rote in the speculations of American economists as if it were valid always and everywhere. Science and technology, they maintained, had slashed into the division of labor among nations, had universalized the use of machinery, had broken national monopolies of skills, had given greater economic independence to industrial societies, and had lessened the dependence of nations upon imports of manufactures and raw materials. They also contended that agreements for collective action recently proposed were old treaties of alliance in a new guise and would probably lead to war rather than to peace.

In rejecting as unreal and inapplicable to the United States the imperialist capitalism of the Lodge-Mahan fraternity, the free-trade theories of the Cobden-Wilson-Hull school, and the universal brotherhood of Marxism, members of the American civilization school did not repudiate international coöperation, conciliation, arbitration, collective action on definite matters of general interest, the tender of good offices to nations engaged in disputes, or necessarily association with a League of Nations constituted for other purposes than the perpetuation of historic wrongs. What they objected to was lecturing other nations, constantly stirring up, in effect, warlike emotions, and using the power of the United States to force any scheme of politics or economy on other peoples. They especially opposed, as distracting and dangerous to domestic life, the propagation of the idea that any mere foreign policy could in any material respect reduce the amount of degrading poverty in the United States, set American economy in full motion, or substantially add to the well-being of the American people. Foreign policy, they held, could easily be made the instrument to stifle domestic wrongs under a blanket of militarist chauvinism, perhaps disguised by the high-sounding title of world peace.

§

When it came to pressures for the realization of designs, each of the four schools of foreign policy had the support of particular interests to some extent, consciously or instinctively. Behind the World Imagists stood cotton growers of the South, cotton brokers, cotton handlers, railways and shipping concerns, and trading centers extensively dependent upon the cotton business. Exporting and importing merchants and bankers, oceanic shipping concerns, and whole armies of dealers, factors, and their employees naturally regarded any policy that increased the movement of commodities in international exchange as "good for business and good for the country." Corn, wheat, pork, and cattle producers in the West looked with a certain favor upon any procedure that promised larger outlets for their produce in foreign markets. Unlike the cotton growers, however, producers of other crops were subject to real and potential competition from imports of agricultural commodities and they clung to tariffs written in terms of their protection, while demanding bigger foreign outlets.

Imperial Isolationism, pure or mixed, to whatever degree modified in phraseology, was also approved by particular interests: by manufacturers demanding protection, manufacturers searching for foreign markets, bankers looking for investment opportunities abroad, traders and hucksters not content with their chances and gains at home. On this side also were enrolled, with shifts in politics, powerful forces in the army and naval bureaucracy and the supply interests which sold to military and naval establishments goods to the value of hundreds of millions annually. To be sure, the army and navy stood ready to support a war for democracy in the style of the world image, if officially proclaimed, but at bottom fighting men were suspicious of romance in these days, accustomed as they were to the business of getting naval bases, pushing trade, aiding in the collection of debts, and keeping order in backward places. Although many officers had no illusions about the dubious values of such operations, considered in any terms of national interest, agitations over "our commercial rights" in the ports of the seven seas always facilitated the passage of army and navy appropriation bills through Congress, and tended to vitalize the affinity between warriors and traders.

On the lists of the American Civilization school was likewise enrolled a motley collection of interests. With the formulators of its arguments, protected manufacturers went along a certain distance, that is, until problems affecting the domestic distribution of wealth were raised. Protected labor saw in the battle for "a national standard of life," insulated against European and Oriental competition, certain and immediate advantages. Discouraged about the prospects of market expansion abroad or producing especially for the domestic market, a multitude of agrarians found more hope for themselves in "parity with industry" and the "stabilization of agricultural production" than in the offerings of the world imagists. Opponents of war, assuming that it would be possible to keep the United States out of the next world conflict, took the ground that the more entanglements were created abroad, whether through world trade, imperial pressures, or underwriting world "democracies," the greater would be the likelihood of military and naval adventures in Europe and Asia. Since the world imagists generally assailed the ideology of fascism, American citizens of German and Italian fascist sympathies, though hostile to the aims of the American Civilization school, joined it in opposing collective action "on the side of the democracies."

Despite the torrent of spoken words and the oceans of ink used in supporting the four conceptions of foreign policy, it proved impossible to determine the long-term validity of any one. Nor was it easy, even in discussion, to keep each of the conceptions in its pristine purity, to insulate it entirely against the intrusion of fragments from the other conceptions. They were all vexed by internal logical troubles and by factual discrepancies. Nor was it possible, given the pressures of the conflicting interests involved, to marshal enough voters to assure the supremacy of any single policy in practice. As in all such cases, history to come would pass judgment on the competing conceptions. History would decide which of the four, if any at all, was to correspond most precisely with long-run practice.

§

That policy or no policy, stark faith in war itself or lust for it might overcome efforts to keep the United States aloof from the frenzies of Europe was intimated by a course of events running through the years. After the Hitler government in Germany set out on its line of sheer force, publicists, agitators, and editors began to hunt a slogan for the next war. Hamilton Fish Armstrong proposed one of the formulas: "We or They." According to this dictum the world is really ruled by ideas. Economic interests, imperial aggrandizement, efforts of ruling classes to save themselves do not count at all; or not much. Ideas make history. The democratic idea is challenged to mortal combat by the fascist idea. Germany, Italy, and Japan, if not broken by economic coercion or military might, will march to the enslavement of mankind. The United States will have to help Europe "solve" this "problem."

Reasoning of that kind appealed to innumerable minds in America especially among the idealists of the middle class. And strange as it seemed at first glance, communists of the Stalinist wing came to the support of the thesis that the democracies would have to coerce the fascist nations or overcome them by arms. In the early days of the Russian revolution, they had spoken contemptuously of "rotten bourgeois democracies"; German communists had voted with and fought on the side of Hitler's troopers against the Weimar republic. They had also sneered at ideas and magnified the power of material interests in peace and war. But they had learned a lesson from Hitler, and had received orders from Moscow to line up in a "united front" with democrats, mere democrats. Russia might need the aid of the United States in a coming world war, involving Japan. And, since Japan was now "the" enemy in American war games, communists were no longer to be so despised amid preparations for the approaching trial by battle.

Paralleling in time-development the four schools of foreign policy, with wide-reaching ramifications, though commanding no large vocal following, was the school of true believers in eternal war as a necessity of life — war as the independent and perpetual invariable of all human history, irrespective of systems, political and economic. This school, if a loose aggregation of thinkers could be so denominated, recognized, if it did not rejoice in, the ancient blood lust of man — the dark and convulsive urge to physical combat, which had manifested itself in endless wars, domestic and foreign, from the dawn of history, for one cause, or another cause, or for no cause at all — just an opportunity. How potent this dynamic was among Americans there was no way of knowing. That it quivered beneath the surface of things ready for an outbreak was evident in a multitude of incidents and articles from year to year — for example, in sadistic lynchings and in paeans praising battleships and great navies, composed for the populace.

But whether the mass of men, if decently employed in works of peace, would automatically leave loom or forge or plow and rush to war combat for its own sake or the sheer joy of blood-letting, could not be discovered by any available probe of psychology. Military history recorded that governments had never been able to recruit large standing armies with ease. Only by seizing loose-footed beggars, scouring prisons, snatching apprentices, kidnaping younger sons, knocking down and dragging off laggards, and buying the serfs of feudal lords, had they managed in earlier times to corral enough men for wars. Not until the adoption of conscription — the levée en masse — and the use of wholesale coercion had they succeeded in creating the monster armies of the modern world. And, as the Russian revolution of 1917 indicated, there were new perils of terrorism underneath such huge aggregations of men experienced in violence and slaughter.

In the United States, militarism as a regular way of life had never captivated the people. Nor were the army and the navy, recruited in respect of officers mainly from the civilian population, much given to the praise of war as war. They brought relentless pressure upon Congress for more and more money, materials, and men, it is true; and they sought to inoculate schools and colleges with "the martial spirit." But the majority of officers and men doubtless knew little and thought little about the psychology of the blood bath. The difficulty of holding reserve officers in the line of training and of getting enlisted men to reënlist on the expiration of their terms suggested a lack of professional interest and a dearth of hunger for the butcheries of the battlefield.

Even so, there were many men in the United States, military and civilian alike, who deemed war forever inevitable and who were propelled by passionate emotions to choose "the next enemy" and to bend propaganda toward war against that foe, when neither national peril nor national advantage was involved in the process. Moreover such men were always near centers of power where force was a factor. It could not be truly said, therefore, that the army and navy were mere pliant instruments of national policy and nothing more. On the contrary, the army and navy, by their very existence, form, and continuous expansion, expressed foreign as well as domestic policy, wittingly or not, and policy was continuously influenced, in some measure, by the historic, dark urge to war.

Belief in and enjoyment of the undersurging blood lust as a source of policy and action in foreign affairs were by no means confined to stray groups in the military profession and its associates in thought and emotion. Manifestations of the faith appeared in various forms. Gusts of the frenzy flamed out in violent language at assemblies of the very best people, lurked under disarming phrases, fluttered through ladies' smiles. "How they hate Roosevelt!" for instance, became a by-word accurately describing the fever that raged at clubs, garden parties, week-end excursions, in drawing rooms, Pullman cars, offices, and conferences of brokers, chambers of commerce, and manufacturers. Outbursts and retaliations from politicians, agrarians, labor leaders, and agitators at labor meetings exhibited the same kind of temper. Lynching parties, floggings, police beatings, third-degree procedures, sabotage, suppressions of minorities as in Jersey City ruled by Mayor Hague, all indicated that the veneer of civilization was thin enough in wide areas of society, that the restraints of civilization might burst under exceptional strain, unchaining civil or foreign war or both, in the fashion so often illustrated in history. Replete with meaning for the future was the swift decline in the great fear of huge military establishments which the founders of the republic, deeply learned in history and experience, entertained — against which they warned their own and coming generations.

Ascribing war to basic biological sources — to surges from the deeps of the irrational, shattering in action the whole web of civilization — exponents of "the next and inevitable war" made assertions that influenced the makers of policy. Had it not been for the rise of the irrational cult to great power in Europe under the guise of fascism, such alarmists might have been dismissed as a mere irritating minority in the United States; but events in the Old World gave point to their contentions in the New World and brought "war as the invariable" into discussions of American policy, domestic and foreign. Inasmuch as exponents of fascism assigned to women the primary function of bearing and rearing babies for war, inasmuch as the war urge and its consequences affected all society from top to bottom, the sweep of the war psychosis brought women and their role in civilization to the forefront of relevant discussions. What was the relation of women to this old, now re-exalted, phenomenon of war, conceived as the overwhelming dynamic of history?

On this point, generalizations were forthcoming, often with little regard for pertinent facts. And one of the easiest of the easy generalizations, indulged in by men and women alike, was to the effect that mothers hate war because it robs them of their sons; that wives shrink from war because it takes their husbands away from the home and the children; that unmarried women loathe its cruelties because they pity the wives and mothers or are in peril of lust and destruction in the war zones. But to these assumptions, history brought the penetrating light of long experience. Within its white glare, women were seen as war lords of the most intransigent type at points in historic time when they ruled States or sought to rule States. As queens they had been as ready for war as kings. Feudal ladies were personally familiar with battle and as quick as feudal lords to welcome advantages won by arms.

Moreover the immediate history of the world war offered to memory its sharp illustrations of the feminine tendency to go along with and goad men into the ways of war. Women like men, perhaps in greater numbers than men, judging from the roll calls of peace societies, had been registered as detesting war. But when the war came, women like men gave it their allegiance. Mothers, wives, sisters, and daughters rushed to the service of war — behind the trenches, as close to the front as they could get. They scorned "shirkers"; they urged males forward to the battle line. They shouted for funds in drives to finance the war. They made munitions. They drove trucks and planes. They "entertained" soldiers and washed their wounds, often taking war romantically as an escape from the rigors of the humdrum into the excitements of deadly peril. They wrote and delivered impassioned appeals to stimulate the war spirit, making use of the venerable argument that it was all for the defense of the nation, womanhood, and the home, irrespective of war origins and aims. Before and after the war, women served as auxiliaries in associations of every kind for the promotion of armaments, the extension of military control over education, and the increase of military and naval appropriations.

None the less, in the main, fighting was a man's business in history and women had been primarily engaged in the arts of peace, the making of civil society. From primitive times, when they introduced and developed the arts of the hearth and agriculture, down to the latest hour when they worked in factories, entered civil professions, managed modern homes, and took part in civic affairs, women's interests had been on the whole pacific. Their concern had been constructive and conservational, in the main, not destructive and explosive. Consequently, if the cult of the irrational, exalting man's fighting above humanity's peace, was to spread in America, as it had in Germany, Italy, and other parts of Europe, women's role was to be transformed with the overthrow of civilian supremacy in society. Was that contingency so remote in time as to seem bizarre? Handwritings on walls implied a negative answer.

§

The first pragmatic test of President Roosevelt's foreign policy came in connection with the World Economic Conference in London, called by the League of Nations in 1932. In accepting the invitation, President Hoover had asked Congress for an appropriation to pay the expenses of participation and had received a form of legislative sanction. American delegates were then chosen to serve on the organizing committee of the League Council and American representatives were dispatched to take part in the work of the expert committee charged with the duty of arranging the agenda for the coming conference. Although the political overturn of that year increased the uncertainty of the American line, preliminaries for the London conference were completed before the close of Hoover's term and Roosevelt agreed to carry out the obligations assumed by his predecessor. Furthermore during his campaign Roosevelt had hinted that he would broaden the scope of the conference by adding a consideration of intergovernmental debts and tariffs, which had been expressly excluded by the Hoover administration as a condition of acceptance. Though in conversations with the representatives of foreign countries, held in Washington shortly after his inauguration, Roosevelt avoided specifications too exact, he gave them the impression that his coöperation would be warm-hearted.

When the agenda drawn up by the preparatory committee came out, no special discernment was necessary to discover that its frame of reference enclosed the assumptions and program of the world imagists. It contained the regular phrases of that school — "the whole system of international finance," "the normal exchange of commodities," "an improvement in the world economic situation," "an international economic system," "world economy," "recovery of an economic system threatened by bankruptcy," "bringing world economy back to a more normal condition or, at any rate, to the situation that obtained a few years ago." The experts did not factually describe the system or order of world economy to which they repeatedly referred; nor did they say whether it was the system of 1928, or 1920, or 1914, which the phrase "a few years ago" implied. In effecting a compromise of conflicting ideas and interests, the framers of the agenda were cautious in giving specifications while making clear the corollaries of their logic.

Writing on the subject after the preparation of the agenda, Sir Walter Layton, who had been associated with the committee of experts, pointed out the contradiction between "an international financial system" and "economic nationalism" with its tariffs, subsidies, quotas, bounties, and other restrictions on free trade among the individuals of all nations. His image of the "system" to be established by the coming conference was fundamentally that of free private enterprise and free trade throughout the world — the dream in which Richard Cobden had reveled long before when England was in fact the workshop of the world.

That the Roosevelt administration would give some effect to the policy of the world imagists seemed fairly certain early in the spring of 1933 — before the World Conference assembled in June. In a public address, Secretary Hull sketched the outlines of his program. Concerning the center of his affections there could be little doubt. Mr. Hull had been an ardent champion of the domestic individualism set forth in President Wilson's New Freedom and a consistent believer in low tariffs, bordering on free trade as an ideal. If there were doubts, he dispelled them, by declaring: "The restoration of fair, friendly, and normal trade relations among nations at present would not only avoid serious economic, military, and political differences between countries in the future, but would go far toward composing those now existing." He condemned the "policy of economic isolation."

Nations were in profound economic distress. How were they to get out of it? Mr. Hull had his answer: "Business recovery must be preceded by the restoration of international finance and commerce, an alternative to which is a continuance of the unsound economic policies under the operation of which the entire world since 1929 has been in the throes of an unspeakable depression." Destiny pointed to American leadership in this work of reversal and restoration. America needed nothing special: "The interests of our government and our people seem so clearly to coincide with the interests of humanity." Here the whole case of the world imagists was proclaimed: the union of universal free trade on a gold basis with professions of humanity, if not of democracy. Two weeks later, in a message to mankind, Roosevelt seemed to confirm the faith by saying that the coming London conference "must establish order in place of the present chaos by a stabilization of currencies, by freeing the flow of world trade, and by international action to raise price levels." Therewith the hopes of the world imagists were buoyed.

Speaking as head of the American delegation, Secretary Hull recited his philosophy to the World Conference. He conceded that each country could by suitable steps, "to a moderate extent, restore conditions," but his accent was on the interdependence and interrelations of nations. He derided the "isolationist" for his failure to see "the international character" of the depression. The policy of self-containment, he insisted, "has demonstrated its inability to either avoid or arrest or cure the most destroying depression in all the annals of business." Mr. Hull shrank from asserting that free trade and a stabilization of the currency would positively bring the permanent prosperity of expanding outlets for "surpluses" and spoke of "a sane, practical middle course," but the upshot of Mr. Hull's theory in terms of practice was positive : Remove all excesses in the form of trade barriers; combined with "suitable" domestic measures, this will bring restoration, recovery, and advance.

In essence, Mr. Hull's creed had the predictive assurance of a formula in exact science : "Given a test tube containing an opaque liquid, add a given chemical substance, and the compound will assume a rosy hue." Emphasis on domestic production meant, in any case, he said, a lower standard of life for the American people ; adopt the practice of reducing trade barriers and America can have the substance of prosperity. Meanwhile, at home, the Government of the United States was doing exactly what Secretary Hull derided in London ; it was attempting "by boot-strap methods" to lift itself out of its troubles — with the Agricultural Adjustment Act and the National Industrial Recovery Act.

Just what happened at the London conference was not fully disclosed to the public. In accordance with custom, records were deposited in archives. It is certain, however, that dissensions early appeared. By mentioning war debts in his ceremonial address the British premier, Ramsay MacDonald, made trouble for the American delegation. If, as alleged, some agreement could have been reached on currency stabilization after the arrival of the Assistant Secretary of State, Raymond Moley, that project collapsed. Reports of a ten per cent horizontal reduction in import duties all around brought a squall instead of harmony. Whether Great Britain and the countries still on the gold standard would actually have agreed in a final test upon a specific tariff and currency program, based on the terms of the world imagists, remained among the unsolved mysteries of the world play. Beyond question, the efforts of the "gold bloc" countries to give precedence to monetary stabilization led to irritation in the conference and in Washington. There was reason for believing at the moment that the conference might last indefinitely without reaching any fundamental conclusions or disband as a result of internal conflicts arising from the diversity of national interests represented.

The knot that could not be untied by exchanges of propositions and opinions among the delegates was cut by a message from Roosevelt early in July, declaring that it would be "a catastrophe amounting to a world tragedy, if the great conference of nations . . . should allow itself to be diverted by the proposal of a purely artificial and temporary experiment affecting the monetary exchange of a few nations only." That would be to forget "the larger purposes" for which the assembly was originally called. Having paid his respects to the gold bloc countries, the President rejected in effect the agenda prepared by the experts of the conference and also the emphasis on mondial trade which Secretary Hull had so eloquently vindicated. "The sound internal economic system of a nation," continued the President, "is a greater factor in its well-being than the price of its currency in changing terms of the currencies of other nations." As far as the formula of lower trade barriers was involved in the London debate, that doctrine had recently been thrown overboard by congressional legislation : the National Industrial Recovery Act authorized the President to raise American customs duties if necessary to insulate against the whole world the new prices and wages to be brought about by measures adopted in the domestic interest.

Thus the onus for "breaking up" the conference seemed to fall largely upon the United States. But in none of the records made available to the public, nor in the nature of the national interests represented at London, was there the slightest evidence that any substantial part of the proposed agenda could have been realized. Although the Conference adjourned amid lame remarks that it might be reassembled, nothing of the kind was really expected or happened.

To all appearances President Roosevelt had made the great decision. Emphasis was to be placed upon a "sound internal economic system" as a greater factor in national well-being than monetary devices which merely promised to enlarge the outlets for American "surpluses." Adherence to this formula of independent economic action meant a fundamental shift in American foreign policy, with inferences for military and naval affairs. Incisively the President had cut away, in effect, the outlet theory of the imperialist school and the outlet doctrine of the world imagists. He had conceded the major contention of the American civilization school, namely, that the extent of foreign outlets as far as America is concerned is limited by the necessities of economy to a small percentage of the exportable production in the United States and that the principal hope for domestic well-being in America lies in developing to the utmost, by domestic policy, the materials, skills, and resources of the American nation. How deep-seated was the President's resolve, there was no way of determining in 1933, but signs suggested that at the moment he knew the nature of his choice and made it deliberately.

§

A few months after the London Economic Conference ended in confusion, President Roosevelt delivered another blow to another doctrine of foreign policy that had been sanctioned by the diplomacy of universal philanthropy under President Wilson and the diplomacy of aggressive national interest practiced by his successors. In keeping with its conception of the war for world democracy, the Wilson administration had publicly condemned the Soviet regime in Russia as contrary to the "free will and purpose" of the Russian people and had refused to recognize it. The Soviet government, the American Secretary of State had said, refused to pay its debts and carried on a propaganda for a world system opposed to the institutions of the United States. Under Republican auspices, the custom of reading moral lectures to the Russian government and refusing to recognize that sturdy defaulter had been continued. It had been all right for the United States to join in a war for revolutionizing the domestic institutions of Germany and Austria, but the not-unexpected counterblast was deemed invidious. Such had been the logical outcome of a foreign policy that involved mondial uniformity in political and economic institutions and placed upon the Government of the United States a burden of responsibility for realizing throughout the world this posited conception of universal propriety.

Ignoring, however, the notes and lectures accumulated in the State Department and, apparently, the private objections of Secretary Hull, President Roosevelt entered into personal communications with the Soviet government late in 1933. He sought and secured pledges that Russia would guarantee legal rights and religious liberty to Americans resident in that country and would abstain from all propaganda calculated to disturb the internal affairs of the United States. The question of the unpaid debts, apart from the elimination of Russia's claims for damages done during American occupation of Siberia in 1918–1920, was postponed for discussion in subsequent negotiations. Having reached an agreement on this basis, the United States and Soviet Russia reëstablished official relations in November, 1933 — to the consternation of professional foes of "alien influences."

In taking this step, Roosevelt abandoned the policy of reading moral lectures to Moscow, took cognizance of the world as diversity, and resumed the historic practice in force before the advent of the world-power school and the school of mondial philanthropy. No doubt practical considerations had some influence. Russia might be useful against Japanese aggression in the Far Pacific; and the prospects of enlarged trade, long dangled before American eyes by Russian propagandists, might be realized. But, aside from such matters, the abandonment of the Wilson-Harding-Coolidge-Hoover policy in respect of Russia seemed to indicate that the United States was returning to the policy of limited action —

attending mainly to its own affairs, recognizing de facto
governments without regard to their domestic forms and
policies, abstaining from ideological judgments on other
countries, and observing formalities in diplomatic intercourse. That might prove to be "impossible," as the new
mondialists contended, but it was being tried, at least
temporarily, by the Roosevelt administration.

With a firmness equally marked, Roosevelt renounced
the strong-arm program of dollar diplomacy in dealing with
American nations to the south. He had declared to Latin
America that his policy would be that of "the good neighbor." As a demonstration of his policy he withdrew the marines from Nicaragua in 1933. The following year he signed
with Cuba a treaty abolishing the principal features of the
Platt Amendment by which the imperialists of the McKinley
school had forced upon that "independent" country onerous
restrictions, including the right of the United States to intervene for the preservation of domestic order.

This Amendment had been a sore point with Cubans since
its inception, and had been regarded by Latin Americans
generally as proof that "the colossus of the North" really
intended to throw its sovereignty around the Caribbean
basin. Hence deliberate surrender of the control authorized
by the Amendment was more than an incident. It was a
generous renunciation — a pledge that the policy of armed
intervention was to be abandoned. In signing the treaty,
Roosevelt declared : "This Government will make it clear
that it not only opposes the policy of armed intervention but
that it renounces those rights of intervention and interference in Cuba which have been bestowed upon it by treaty."
From that time forward, it appeared, the pressure of the
United States upon Cuban affairs was to be economic and
diplomatic, not immediately military and naval. What might
happen in case of another real explosion in Latin America
was left to the future. For the moment dollar diplomacy and
the marines were pushed into the background of theory and
practice.

§

With such reformulations of policy in respect of Latin-American countries, Secretary Hull was evidently in complete sympathy. If irked by the short shrift that his President had made of the World Economic Conference and by the cavalier manner in which Roosevelt assumed responsibility for the resumption of relations with Russia, the Secretary of State nevertheless favored the release of naval pressures on nations to the south. He had long been an opponent of dollar diplomacy there; the South did not sell much cotton or tobacco to Mexico or South America. His temper was equable in ordinary negotiations. Yet in his quiet way he was invincible in pursuing objectives upon which his heart was set and those objectives included cutting down the protective tariff by any and every available process of law. Taking advantage of his influence as a former member of Congress, highly esteemed by his Democratic colleagues, the Secretary of State sought and obtained, on June 12, 1934, an amendment of the tariff act which allowed him to accomplish by his own operations some measure of his burning desire.

The new law — the Reciprocal Tariff Act — permitted the President, for a term of three years, to negotiate trade agreements with foreign countries and in so doing to increase or diminish by not more than fifty per cent the existing rates of duty. Such agreements, when duly consummated, were to go into effect without ratification by the Senate of the United States.

The business of negotiation was left to the State Department with the aid of a Trade Agreement Committee representing certain other branches of the Government. Briefly stated, the making of tariff legislation was by this maneuver transferred from Congress to Secretary Hull; and, through a gradual nation-by-nation process, he could, as far as that might be possible, effect a general reduction of the tariff without risking a frontal assault. Now the Secretary had an instrument for lowering trade barriers — and discovering whether the great powers represented at the London Economic Conference really could or would "restore the free flow of trade throughout the world."

When the term of the original Reciprocal Trade Act expired in 1937, Congress renewed it. By the end of that year Secretary Hull had consummated agreements with sixteen foreign countries, including Cuba, France, Canada, Belgium, Sweden, Brazil, Costa Rica, Haiti, and Honduras. Had the maneuver been a success? An exact statistical answer was then impossible despite extravagant claims and counter-claims. The criteria of judgment were furnished mainly by transactions with relatively small nations having peculiar economies. Excepting Canada, none of them entered into large-scale competition with the staple industries of the United States, and many enterprises in Canada were either branches of American concerns or generally represented investments of American capital. Furthermore in each case the reductions in rates were modest and frequently hedged about by quantitative restrictions on imports.

By that year, however, the Secretary had been unable or unwilling to effect agreements with such heavy competitors as Japan, Great Britain, or Germany. Prospects of an adjustment with Great Britain had been announced in Washington before the close of 1937, it is true, but that step was vigorously opposed in the United States by powerful interests and in London by British industrialists, especially by advocates of tariff preference within the Empire. Whether the British government would grant any substantial advantages to the United States in exchange for the appearances of closer political unity as against the Rome-Berlin-Tokyo bloc remained among the numerous uncertainties of the whole business. In the summer of 1938 when Hitler, after subjecting Austria to his dictatorship, threatened to take the German sector — the Sudeten — away from Czechoslovakia, Britain seemed ready to conclude the trade agreement with a view to European politics as well as to her own commerce; and before the year closed the treaty was duly signed.

In the limited circumstances the only basis of judgment on the effectiveness of the reciprocity policy — aside from Anglo-American political interests — appeared to be changes in the volume of trade between the United States and each particular country with which a reciprocity agreement had been reached. Perhaps no other criterion was available to economists. At all events one of the most distinguished experts in the subject, an economist in the State Department, Herbert Feis, employed it in reviewing "a year of the Canadian trade agreement" in the magazine Foreign Affairs for July, 1937. He concluded that "the trade in each direction continued to increase during 1936, the first year of the Agreement." Yet trade had been rising with the general upturn in commerce and production. Hence there was no absolute proof of anything in the mere continuance of the rise after the agreement had been concluded.

Certainly "more significant," as Mr. Feis said, was "the fact that during this year of world-wide commercial expansion the volume of trade between the two countries increased in greater ratio than did the volume of trade between either one of them and the rest of the world." Still this was no invincible proof of anything. Changes in the volume of trade between any two countries, over any period of time, had never mechanically corresponded to the changes in their trade with other nations, in normal conditions. And what were normal conditions? If, however, the large assumption was granted, namely that the disproportionate increase in volume of trade was due to the Reciprocal Agreement, another question arose: Did the economies of the contracting parties really benefit from the increased volume? Experts did not answer that question. Perhaps it was unanswerable. They merely assumed that an increase in the movement of goods was in itself a benefit to the people as a whole, as well as to the merchants, financiers, and factors of Canada and the United States, and represented in actuality material advances in the economic well-being of the respective countries. Adam Smith might have said that this was a fact, mysterious under the "invisible hand" of Providence but nevertheless a fact. American economists specializing in foreign trade commonly assumed it without the benefit of Providence.

To American producers little given to consulting the theories of the State Department, some fruits of the Canadian treaty presented strange aspects, however sound they might be in terms of mondial economy. For example, among the concessions granted to Canada, in exchange for concessions on her part, was a reduction in the American duty on cheese, and at that very moment American warehouses were bursting with millions of pounds of cheese for which the owners could find no outlet at all, domestic or foreign. In such circumstances the freer admission of Canadian cheese might be deemed by an inveterate theorist an act of sound economy, but to American cheese producers it certainly had the appearance of a vagary. In an age of general perversity, however, such microscopic items disappeared in the dream entertained by the supporters of reciprocal agreements for "freeing the flow of world trade." Even so, despite all the fanfare about overcoming the depression through foreign trade, at the end of Secretary Hull's three-year trial, American economy was rapidly running down in another slump and in the opening months of 1938 it was near the bottom reached under Hoover's management of affairs on other lines.

Whatever the future was to say about the invincible faith in a possible world of free and independent traders pursuing their acquisitive ways unchecked by national "politicians," the Senate of the United States, after voting for Secretary Hull's first Reciprocal Trade Bill in 1934, proceeded to vote down a measure designed to aid in mondial pacification. While the Secretary's personally conducted tour of tariff revision was in full progress, amid the applause of the world imagists, the project for taking the United States into the World Court came before the Senate for ratification, after a long delay. Immediately a throng of imperial isolationists and professional patriots descended upon wavering Senators. The Hearst press and Father Coughlin were especially vociferous in condemning the proposal. Although President Roosevelt, following the example of his predecessors, gave the scheme his personal blessing, he refrained from putting on full pressure. When the vote was taken in January, 1935, the World Court was rejected — an adverse outcome gratifying to imperial isolationists, discouraging to world imagists, and no consolation at all to the school of American civilization. It hastened the dissolution of faith in the League of Nations, already far advanced. It was also a collateral repudiation of reliance on collective action as a means of "keeping out of war." With reservations so extensive as to approach a cancellation of commitments, the World Court project actually meant little in terms of "entanglement"; nevertheless, not enough Democrats could be marshaled under the sign of Woodrow Wilson's crusade to carry the measure through the Senate.

§

Before the world imagists had recovered from the rejection of the World Court, they received a more direct and stunning blow from the Neutrality Resolution enacted in the same year, 1935. This measure was in large part an outcome of the munitions investigation and was thoroughly disliked by President Roosevelt and Secretary Hull. It had a wider background than that inquiry but the immediate impetus to action came from the revelations of the Nye committee. In express terms the Neutrality Act made it unlawful in time of war to export "arms, munitions, or implements of war" to belligerents abroad or to neutrals for the use of belligerents. It also authorized the President, when the security of the United States was in danger, to proclaim the fact and thereby place upon American citizens who traveled on the merchant vessels of belligerents full responsibility for all the risks, save under such executive rulings as might be issued. Coupled with the Johnson Act of the previous year, which cut off loans to governments in default on debts owed to the United States, the Neutrality Act struck at war booms in business such as had attended Woodrow Wilson on "the road to war." The ban was explicit and positive. Moreover it was mandatory ; that is, it was to go into effect automatically when the President found a state of war existing abroad. Discretion was allowed to the Executive in deciding whether any particular form of fighting constituted war, but when war was declared by a foreign power or the President "found" a state of war, the neutrality prohibitions became immediately applicable.

Although Roosevelt signed the Resolution, he resented the spirit and letter of the Neutrality Act and clung tenaciously to the idea of intervening in the controversies of Europe, despite the abstention and equality of treatment stipulated in the Act. His personal inclinations became open knowledge on the outbreak of war between Italy and Ethiopia soon after the passage of the law. He did find a state of war existing and he did bring the Act into force against the belligerents. In application the Act ran against Italy — one of the undemocratic powers ; for Ethiopia had no ships at sea, could borrow no money in the United States, and was in no position to buy munitions from American industries. Later in the year Roosevelt pledged the moral support of the United States to the policy of sanctions developed against Italy by the League of Nations, warned citizens against traveling on the ships of belligerents, in fact Italian ships, and discountenanced trade with belligerents in articles not covered by the embargo on munitions and implements of war. In other words, he made known to the world that, as far as he could, under the law, he would throw American influence on the side of the League's decision to penalize an aggressor. Obviously the Roosevelt administration intended to champion "democracies" against dictators in Europe.

Unmoved by Roosevelt's evident desire for a "free hand" in foreign affairs, Congress, in February, 1936, amended and continued the Neutrality Act. The mandatory embargo on the sale of munitions to belligerents was retained. The sale of the bonds, securities, and other obligations of belligerents was expressly forbidden within the jurisdiction of the United States; likewise prohibited were the making of loans and the granting of credits to belligerents. An exception was made of customary commercial credits and short-time obligations in aid of ordinary commerce, in case the President so decided, at his discretion. The transport of munitions on American vessels in war time was proscribed and American citizens were warned against traveling on the ships of belligerents. Remembering the Monroe Doctrine, Congress provided that the Act should not apply to any American republic at war with a non-American country, unless engaged in coöperating with a non-American state in such a conflict. Thus within a period of six months the national resolve against becoming entangled in foreign wars was strengthened, rather than diminished. The discussion which followed the first Neutrality Act had culminated in a tighter and more comprehensive measure.

The second Neutrality Act had been on the statute book only a few months when the outbreak of a civil war in Spain provided an acid test of President Roosevelt's foreign policy in respect of the conflict between democracies and dictatorships. By that time Mussolini had conquered Ethiopia and was ready for an excursion into Spanish affairs with the enthusiastic aid of Hitler. On this occasion, however, the Tory government in Great Britain, whose nationals had heavy investments in that part of Spain dominated by the rebel commander, General Franco, did not seem particularly interested in applying restraints to dictators occupied in a war on democracy. Of the circumstances, President Roosevelt took cognizance; and at his press conference in December, 1936, he suggested the extension of neutrality legislation to the civil war in Spain.

By some person in the administration — in the State Department or outside — a bill was drawn to give effect to his proposal. The bill so drafted was carried to Capitol Hill and jammed through Congress with little or no debate, early in 1937. In general terms the new Act imposed embargoes on both parties to civil conflicts deemed dangerous to the peace of the United States. In a haste so swift as to be unseemly President Roosevelt brushed aside the objections of the Spanish ambassador in Washington, Signor de los Rios, and barred the export of munitions to the Loyalist government no less than to the rebels.

From three points of view this was a strange procedure. As things stood in January, 1937, the civil war in Spain did not threaten the peace of the United States. Moreover the very essence of neutrality, as preached and practiced historically, forbade any legal change which adversely affected any belligerent after a war had started. Concerning the binding character of this principle there was no doubt anywhere among persons familiar with the law of neutrality, not even in the State Department. The embargo on munitions to Spain, imposed more than six months after the civil war had opened, was, therefore, a stark violation of a rule so rooted in history, law, and cautious policy.

Not only that; it transgressed the Treaty of Madrid consummated in 1902 between the United States and Spain and it was a slap straight in the face of the Madrid government. The Loyalist government had been and continued to be officially accepted in Washington as the lawful government of Spain. The belligerency of the insurgents had not been recognized. Under American theory and practice hitherto prevailing, the Madrid regime was entitled to buy munitions and supplies in the United States on the same terms as other foreign governments. But without notice or explanation the embargo applied by the Roosevelt administration deprived it of that right.

If Congress could be set down as consistent in its fierce resolve to stop all traffic in war materials, what could be said of the President's course? The Madrid government had come to power after a national election and was officially recognized in Washington as duly constituted. If it had the aid of Soviet Russia, it also had the open sympathy of the French ministry. Arrayed on the other side were avowed foes of democracy. The insurgent leader, General Franco, was an exponent of authoritarian government and he was notoriously assisted by the dictators of Italy and Germany. Without pretensions to secrecy, Hitler and Mussolini had dispatched soldiers to fight under General Franco's banner and had furnished aid, comfort, and supplies to his forces engaged in war on the Loyalist government. Here were the very dictators whom President Roosevelt repeatedly called enemies of democracy and foes of world peace. Yet by originating and signing the amendment to the Neutrality Act and then by putting it into immediate effect, he threw the support of the United States on the side of dictators and the professional warmongers of Europe. Even if the Madrid government had no merits whatsoever in his eyes, his action was a gratuitous favor to the Spanish rebels, to Hitler, and to Mussolini — a decided favor appreciated by the recipients, at the moment.

As the time approached for a renewal of the general Neutrality Act in 1937, the world imagists, encouraged, even led, by President Roosevelt and Secretary Hull, were well organized to riddle, if not defeat, it. Bent on having the power to determine American foreign policy themselves and to use that power in discriminating against parties to controversies abroad, according to their personal concepts of values, the President and the Secretary used their influence to secure modifications in the mandatory character of the existing neutrality legislation. Previous laws made the embargo on loans and munitions absolute as soon as the President had found a war of some magnitude raging to the peril of the United States. They did not permit him, at his own discretion, to extend or diminish the list of prohibited goods after he declared the embargo in effect. In 1937 this barrier to executive discretion was overthrown. The Act of that year continued and made mandatory the ban on loans and munitions; it empowered the President to place upon foreign belligerents responsibility for transporting goods bought in the United States — "the cash and carry" provision — and to stop the shipment on American vessels of "certain articles or materials in addition to arms, ammunition, and implements of war" whenever he proclaimed it necessary "to promote the security or preserve the peace of the United States or to protect the lives of citizens of the United States."

By this amendment, Congress completely reversed its previous rule that made mandatory and somewhat precise the list of goods to be embargoed in case the President found a war raging abroad. In substance, it permitted the President to add anything else to the list closed to American shippers, even after a war began and the embargo had been applied. Instead of reducing his control over foreign policies, as the Acts of 1935 and 1936 originally intended, the Neutrality law of 1937 enlarged his power to favor one side or the other in any foreign conflict that might arise. In other words, the advocates of mandatory neutrality — that is, of a definitive foreign policy — were decisively beaten. What Congress actually did, in the Neutrality Act of 1937, was to give the President large power over American economic resources in the conduct of his foreign policy along lines distinctly personal, thus adding control over commerce to his control over diplomacy, the navy, and the army.

Henceforward the President, if limited as to munitions and loans, could exercise sovereign powers in other respects without asking the consent of Congress. Executive discretion, such as President Wilson had enjoyed between 1914 and 1917, was, in effect, extended over all areas of American industry and agriculture involved in foreign commerce. In commenting on this measure, John Bassett Moore, the greatest American authority on international law and diplomacy, correctly characterized its upshot: "No one who wished unlimited power to make war could ask for more than the authority, in his own discretion, to impose and revoke, and to modify and adjust, embargoes on our foreign commerce. . . . To commit to the executive the power in his discretion to adopt and prosecute measures that naturally lead to war, is virtually to transfer to him the power to make war, so that the formal declaration by Congress of the existence of a state of war would be an essentially perfunctory act." To this fiasco the effort of Congress " to keep the country out of war" had led.

§

Shortly after the passage of the third Neutrality law, in the summer of 1937, came another test of the neutrality principle — when Japan plunged into a war on China without making formal declaration of hostilities. For months the conflict raged. Huge armies were set to fighting. Thousands of lives were destroyed. Yet neither belligerent officially admitted that it was making war. Perhaps an age of undeclared wars had arrived. At all events, Roosevelt did not "find" that a state of war existed and hence the mandatory ban on loans and munitions was not put into force.

While the President delayed action under the law, the practical value of neutrality agitation and legislation was reviewed. Some citizens demanded an immediate application of the existing Act to the war in China, without reference to the merits of the contestants. Others, in sympathy with China and hostile to Japan, explored the possibilities of application and reached the conclusion that delay in enforcement would redound to the benefit of China, owing to her heavy dependence on imports for self-defense. Rebuttal came in the form of a contention that an embargo would hit the Japanese government harder on account of its larger purchases in the United States. Little concerned with theoretic arguments, economic interests in the United States made hay while the sun shone, by selling implements and the accessories of war to both sides without reference to their deserts.

As in the summer and autumn of 1914, so in the summer and autumn of 1937, American industry slowed down and the United States entered a depression of uncertain nature and duration. With domestic buying power in process of contraction, trade with China and Japan, small as it was relatively, grew in significance for American capital, agriculture, and labor. As a heavy buyer of cotton, scrap iron, oil, and other materials, Japan could intensify the crisis in America by retaliating against a ban on munitions and loans. Consequently, to matters of sentiment were joined serious economic considerations in respect of an embargo. Reviewing American foreign policy, Newton D. Baker had insisted that bankers exerted little or no influence on President Wilson and that economic interests scarcely affected his policy at all between 1914 and 1917, and almost in the same breath he declared with equal assurance that in case of another war the passion for making profits on sales to belligerents would nullify neutrality legislation. The experience with it, as Japan's war on China proceeded, apparently confirmed Mr. Baker's judgment. The pecuniary advantages of trade with belligerents were not to be destroyed by the application of an embargo designed "to keep the country out of war."

While American producers, merchants, and shippers lent to Japan all the aid and comfort for which its government could pay, President Roosevelt and the State Department veered first one way and then another. They warned Americans in China to withdraw from the perils of war areas and announced that it was not the intention of the United States to maintain military forces permanently in China for the purpose of giving protection to American citizens who insisted on staying there for their personal advantage. When American business men in Shanghai cried out against this abandonment of "American rights," the State Department declared that military and naval protection would be assured as usual to citizens of the United States in China. Against this form of Realpolitik, peace societies raised the customary objections. Then the State Department put out assurances on the other side. With Great Britain and France taxed by events on the Rhine and in the Mediterranean, with their sympathies divided over the Sino-Japanese conflict, the State Department had to pursue a checkered course through the clash of ideas and interests in the United States. But on the whole it seemed inclined to maintain a show of neutrality, to abstain from open interference in the merits of the war then raging, and yet at the same time to give moral lectures to the three "trouble makers" — Japan, Italy, and Germany — two of whom it had in fact aided in their war on Spain and the other, in a war on China.

§

Whether considered on their merits or in relation to the interests of the United States, events in Asia and Europe were exhilarating for Americans who were eager to operate on the world stage. For nearly a hundred years subsequent to the establishment of the Constitution, the Government of the United States had abstained from taking an official and risky part in European and Asiatic controversies, but the rules of caution long followed had been discarded, save by a few Americans now called "old-fashioned" or "unpatriotic." After the advent of the Mahan-Lodge-Theodore Roosevelt school of actors on the world stage, the State Department and the President adopted the habit of bursting frequently and effusively into the limelight of publicity; intervening and lecturing here and there became a fashion; and publicity served as meat for Caesar. While rejecting the phraseology and symbols of this school, President Wilson had followed the practice in many ways and combined resplendent lectures to the world audience with various forms of positive action, including intervention in Mexico and in the world war. Now in bureaucratic circles it was considered a poor day when the State Department could make no startling statement of "grand policy"; and the newspapers, ever in quest of sensations, indeed living on sensations, fed the fires of official zeal.

While lecturing, tacking, lunging, and back-tracking in response to the winds of domestic opinion, the State Department informed the nations of the earth that in fact it had a world policy. Shortly after the opening of the crisis in China, the Secretary of State emitted an address to mankind, laying

down the proposition that serious hostilities anywhere, even
in a remote place, affected the interests, rights, and "obligations" of every country. On its part, Secretary Hull declared,
the United States advocated self-restraint, peace, and the
adjustment of controversies by peaceful methods, in a spirit
of mutual helpfulness and accommodation. "We advocate,"
he explained, "lowering or removing of excessive barriers in
international trade. We seek effective equality of commercial opportunity and we urge upon all nations application of
the principle of equality of treatment. We believe in limitation and reduction of armament."

Although the ink was barely dry on the official document
that embargoed trade with the Loyalist government of Spain
in violation of the Madrid treaty with Spain signed in 1902,
the Secretary of State thought it fitting to couple with his
formulation of world policy this statement: "Upholding the
principle of the sanctity of treaties, we believe in modification of provisions of treaties, when need therefor arises, by
orderly processes." Well aware that the preference of the
country ran heavily against entangling commitments, the
Secretary nevertheless ended on the note of collective action:
"We believe in coöperative effort by peaceful and practicable
means in support of the principles hereinbefore stated."

To this mondial manifesto, nearly all the nations of the
earth made favorable responses. The spirit of the replies was
characteristically reflected in the message from Albania to
Secretary Hull, expressing "the whole sympathy of the
Royal Government to the noble and well-wishing aims emanating from the statement in question in favor of the understanding of peoples, of the maintenance of peace, of the
increase of international solidarity, and of the betterment of
the world's economic situation." The government of the
German Reich found itself in complete accord with Secretary
Hull's lofty sentiments: "Its basic principle is, as is generally
known, directed toward the regulation of international relations by pacific agreement and hence coincides with the ideas
developed by the Secretary of State." The answer of

Mussolini was likewise sympathetic: "The Fascist government favors everything which may conduce to the pacification and economic reconstruction of the world." While asking for a full recognition of "the actual particular circumstances" in the Far East, the government of Japan expressed its "concurrence with the principles" contained in the Secretary's memorandum to the family of nations. Of such texture was the new diplomacy constituted.

Duly impressed no doubt by the unanimity of the nations, Roosevelt moved to the center of the world stage and in the impassioned speech delivered at Chicago on October 5, 1937, called for concerted action to quarantine and suppress disturbers of mondial harmony. His prologue described "the present reign of terror and international lawlessness," accompanied by ruthless bombing of men, women, and children without warning or justification. All civilization, he declared, was in peril of destruction: "Let no one imagine that America will escape, that it may expect mercy, that this Western Hemisphere will not be attacked." He then made pointed remarks about the disturbers of mankind. Without mentioning Japan, Germany, and Italy by name, he left no uncertainty as to the culprits. "The peace, the freedom, and the security of ninety per cent of the population of the world is being jeopardized by the remaining ten per cent." The answer? There must be a concerted effort of the peace-loving nations to restrain the marauders, and nations must seek "the removal of barriers against trade."

The Senate had repudiated the League of Nations and the World Court. Congressmen had expressed the resolve of their constituents to stay out of entanglements and wars. Nevertheless, defying both branches of the national legislature, the President, as Executive, called for direct and collective action against aggressors — for enforcing the gospel of world imagery. Instantaneously the world imagists exulted: "Roosevelt Abandons Isolation!" But other returns came in. Telegrams from members of Congress on vacation indicated disapproval in the "provinces." Opinion away from the Atlantic seaboard, as recorded by the poll-takers, was generally hostile to the terms of the Chicago address. Isolationists of all types again raised protests against entanglements. The school of American civilization repeated its formulas of antipathy for adventures likely to involve the country in another Armageddon. Instead of uniting the country, after the fashion of President Wilson's war message on April 6, 1917, the Chicago manifesto helped to divide it more acutely.

Stirred by Roosevelt's booming manifesto, the Assembly of the League of Nations, powerless to restrain offenders in Europe, showed signs of renewed life in dealing with the Far East. On the very next day it adopted a report urging League members to refrain from any action which might weaken China's powers of resistance and consider how far they could individually extend aid to China. The president of the Assembly invited the League members that had signed or adhered to the Nine-Power Treaty to initiate consultations. On the same day Secretary Hull issued a statement declaring that the action of Japan in China was contrary to the provisions of the Treaty and that the conclusions of the United States were "in general accord with those of the Assembly of the League of Nations."

A concrete outcome was a conference in Brussels attended by representatives of several interested nations, including Norman Davis, ambassador-at-large if not plenipotentiary, for the United States. The government of Great Britain was sympathetic but cautious and by no means united on any program. Badly burnt by previous experiences in Washington, British politicians wondered how far President Roosevelt would go or could go in backing up by force his Chicago pronouncement. Somewhat distraught by the suddenness and nature of the diversion, they cast out in two directions: they sent Anthony Eden to Brussels and a special agent to hold personal traffic with one of the three "disturbers of mankind," Adolf Hitler.

After many days of conversation the delegates at the

Brussels conference almost unanimously resolved that Japan had violated the Nine-Power Treaty and was to be viewed with disfavor by all right-thinking peoples. "Was it a bust?" a New York reporter asked Norman Davis on his return from the conversations. To this inquiry the Ambassador-at-large replied that it had been helpful to put the opinions of the pacific nations on record against Japanese aggression. Perhaps it had been. Still, the Chamberlain government in Great Britain soon freed Anthony Eden from his awkward position and made haste to effect a settlement with another disturber cited by Roosevelt at Chicago — namely, Benito Mussolini.

As a matter of fact there was little or no substance in the Nine-Power agreement. While it wore the guise of business, it was more evangelistic in spirit than calculative. The interest of the United States in Japanese trade was three or four times as great as its interest in Chinese trade, measured in terms of economic advantage. However conceived, the Treaty could not be enforced by the United States alone. Having what Theodore Roosevelt had called the Achilles heel in the Philippines, the Government at Washington was in no position to coerce Japan by single-handed diplomacy. With the whole-hearted aid of Great Britain, enforcement was possible, but the government of Great Britain had other perplexities to consider besides those in the Pacific. At the same time it suspected that the American State Department, no more than in John Hay's era, could enlist popular support for a naval adventure in the Chinese waters. Experience with the Philippines had been costly and disillusioning for the people of the United States. Why should they take on more troubles? Nor was the State Department at all sure of British intentions. In 1932, before the rise of Hitler in Germany and before Mussolini's imperial outburst in Ethiopia, Great Britain and France had trampled on Secretary Stimson's proposal for collective action designed to keep the door open in Manchuria. In 1937 Great Britain and France were exceedingly busy at home with their immediate neighbors. So for one reason or another the United States was left out on the limb, holding in hand the text of the Nine-Power Treaty, with the platonic blessing of other signatories and adherents. Such was the upshot of the Brussels conference called from the void by President Roosevelt's speech at Chicago.

§

For weeks after the delivery of the "quarantine" speech at Chicago in October, 1937, Roosevelt refrained from amplifications. To reporters who asked at private press conferences for additional comments, he returned curt and inane replies. For the time being it seemed that the economic crisis at home was enough to engross his attention. But appearances were deceptive and with a suddenness that flustered even his official family, he sent, on January 28, 1938, a special message to Congress calling for an enormous increase in armaments, including more battleships and cruisers, and for the enactment of a mobilization bill which, in effect, would prepare the way for a monster army. Although in one part of his message the President declared that the naval expansion, to cost about a billion dollars, was defensive in nature, in another part he reverted to the "quarantine" doctrine proclaimed at Chicago the preceding October. He made his recommendations "specifically and solely," he said, because the piling up of armaments in other countries involved a threat to "world peace and security." Taken in the sense of English as understood, these words meant that the new armament program, with its emphasis on battleships, cruisers, airplane carriers, and mobilization, was relevant to world policies — not merely to the defense of the American zone of interest in the western hemisphere. However, as a cry for more armaments had always appealed to powerful shipbuilding, munition, and supply interests, as well as to army and navy leagues, Roosevelt could expect the usual hymns of approval; and plans were made to pass the necessary bills through Congress with little friction and great dispatch.

A hymn of praise arose — from defenders of the League of Nations, from "peace" advocates committed to collective security, from the seaboard press, and from the Stalinite communists bent on using the United States for Russian purposes. It was also joined by W. B. Shearer, more than famous as a professional shipbuilding lobbyist. Delighted with the prospects, he appeared at the hearings of the House committee on naval affairs, not to argue a cause already accepted by the administration, but to rejoice over a victory won without labor. Shipbuilders had contributed funds for the election of Roosevelt and they were pleased with the results. They knew that he was a lover of the sea and that as he sat in his favorite rooms in the White House his eyes rested affectionately on his ship models and marine pictures.

There was, in fact, little work for the regular armament lobbyists to do. The President had outstripped their very imagination and would soon have the satisfaction of carrying one measure through Congress in a rush. Who, save men and women lacking in patriotism, could oppose a super-navy bill? The chances for a quick passage of the bill were all the more certain because Roosevelt, by executive interference, had recently blocked an attempt to carry through the House of Representatives a proposal advanced by Louis Ludlow to make the use of American armies abroad subject to a popular referendum. Great newspapers that had assailed him as a communist in 1936 or had supported him with a lukewarmness almost contemptuous, with The New York Times in the lead, now lauded him for his armament program and urged Congress to enact it into law.

Notwithstanding the favorable setting, the play, destined to success in the end, did not come off exactly as expected, nor as soon. That a large part of the country was against the "quarantine" doctrine and against all the entanglements in foreign intrigues, quarrels, and wars to which it might lead, was quickly demonstrated. This repugnance had been expressed to the White House and the State Department in a flood of letters protesting against the Chicago speech. It had been so strong that it had silenced the President temporarily and stopped further elucidation and frank advocacy of the doctrine. Now the opposition flared up anew against the armament program, with its quarantine implications and its mobilization features.

Even kindergartners in naval affairs knew that battleships such as proposed, with a large cruising radius, were for use in distant waters, rather than for defense in American waters. In his naval message the President himself emphasized the threat to "world" peace and security in justification of his demand upon Congress. About the same time unofficial spokesmen of the British government made it known that their coöperation could be relied upon in the Far East; and the participation of American cruisers in the celebration at the opening of the Singapore naval base suggested that coöperation for other than ceremonial purposes was not entirely beyond the range of probability.

The inveterate suspicion that the armament program at bottom was intended to implement the "quarantine" doctrine or interventionism in the Orient was strengthened by the paragraph in the President's message of January 28 calling for legislation to prevent "profiteering" and equalize the "burdens of war." That paragraph rewarmed the controversy over the army and navy plan for a totalitarian mobilization for war. As originally conceived, this plan provided for huge armies to be raised by conscription, the commandeering of agriculture and industry, the regimentation of labor, the taxation of profits, and government control over all organs of opinion. As a result of criticism from the outside and disputes in Congress, the original design had been whittled down. Even so, the President's demand for it confirmed popular belief that the proposal was simply a step to the drafting of huge armies for use abroad, to the suppression of trade union activities, and the destruction of civil liberties in general. Indeed the chief totalitarian provisions, except those controlling the press, were finally incorporated in a revised measure and reported favorably to the

House of Representatives by its committee on military affairs but, as the party managers were afraid of a national outburst, they let it die unheard and unmourned.

The President's appeal on January 28 for an enlarged navy, though finally heeded, likewise encountered fervent opposition. Immediately after his message was emitted, Senator William E. Borah and Senator Hiram Johnson asked pointed questions of the State Department and, when assured that no understandings existed with Great Britain in connection with the naval bill, continued to wonder. Was this a scheme to aid the British Empire in policing the earth? Was it a renewal of American imperialism in the Orient? Was it a prelude to another war for democracy? Such questions were annoying to advocates of mere "defense."

As soon as the President's naval bill reached the House committee on naval affairs, the public hearings developed into a thorough airing of the foreign policies implicit in the measure. General Johnson Hagood and General W. C. Rivers, who had combined a study of foreign affairs with devoted military service, pressed for a definition of the policy behind the call for battleships and challenged the contention that they were planned for the defense of the United States as distinguished from the defense of imperial interests and the quarantining of recalcitrant nations. As in the fight over judicial reorganization, the Republicans at first shrank from a party attack on the armament program, but individual Republicans took up the gage, under the leadership of Ralph O. Brewster of Maine. Hamilton Fish, a steadfast opponent of an imperialistic war, East or West, went before the House committee on naval affairs and denounced the naval bill as a plan for translating into actuality Roosevelt's idea of policing the world and shackling disturbers of peace everywhere.

Though the naval bill left the committee with a favorable report, it was accompanied by a minority dissent which condemned it as unnecessary for defense and as the offspring of the quarantine doctrine headed directly to entanglements in collective action. Before the bill passed, the large subject of sea power, imperialism, and protection for American traders in war zones was discussed critically and extensively. While the measure mustered an overwhelming party support, the opposition vote in the lower House was substantial and included, besides such leading Democrats as Maury Maverick, Caroline O'Day, Herman Kopplemann, and Harry C. Luckey, about two-thirds of the Republican membership.

In the Senate the bill was subjected to a still more searching analysis, under the greater freedom of Senate procedure. Long and carefully prepared addresses were delivered against it by Senators Nye, La Follette, Vandenberg, Borah, Clark, and King, strongly supported by colleagues on both sides of the party line. Day after day critics of the super-super-navy plan, as Senator Vandenberg called the project, attacked it from every angle, as if in concert, while members who were to vote for the bill absented themselves from the chamber, sat silent, or made minor interpolations. Not until May 3 was the roll called and the proposal approved, with twenty-eight Senators recorded against it. In other words, more than three months passed between the delivery of the President's message launching the program and completed action on it by Congress.

Finally achieved, the victory of the administration was not an unalloyed pleasure. Congress had withheld the swift and almost unanimous approval so customary in cases of military and naval expansion. Nor had the debates been limited to details. The entire foreign policy of the President and State Department had been drawn into consideration in Congress and outside. Searching questions had been asked by the opposition with persistent repetition. Was the naval expansion bill framed to implement the President's quarantine doctrine — the proposal for collective action against Germany, Italy, and Japan? Was it intended to strengthen the United States navy for operations in the Far East against Japan, in support of the McKinley-Mahan imperialism that had yielded no economic fruits comparable to the costs?

What subterranean negotiations were being carried on with Great Britain, in the style of Colonel House or Robert Lansing, with a view to "collaboration" in aid of "the democracies" and especially the British empire? If, as Admiral Leahy had testified, the navy was already strong enough to keep Japan out of this hemisphere, why was it necessary to add more ships to those afloat, under construction, and authorized? The House had passed on January 21, 1938, the largest peace-time naval bill in the history of the country, granting substantially every dollar for which the Department had asked. Why had the administration suddenly decided seven days later, without previous notice, that another huge increase was necessary? Since Admiral Leahy had confessed that he did not know the answer to this question, who did? Were the war scares reported in the press during the passage of the bill inspired by bureaucrats and munitioneers or did the cries of "Wolf, Wolf" mean something real this time?

On all these questions the debates in Congress and in the press were educative. If the President did entertain at the bottom of his heart a desire to mount the world stage, support collective action in Europe, and take a strong hand in the imperialist conflicts of the Orient, the Democrats who supported the super-navy bill, with few exceptions, indignantly registered their aversion for all such policies. Although the State Department continued to emit announcements which savored of the quarantine doctrine, most vocal Representatives and Senators disclaimed any sympathy with it. To settle all doubts on that score, Senator Walsh, in defending the bill, emphatically and even somewhat poetically, iterated and reiterated the contention that the super-navy was merely designed for the defense of America in this hemisphere, not for collective action in Europe or for imperialist adventures in the Orient. As if to clinch the argument he more than once pointed out obvious facts in the situation: the super-navy bill did not appropriate a single dollar; it did not make mandatory the building of a single ship; it did no more than "authorize, without time limit, the expansion of our naval strength" — an expansion that could not occur until, at some date in the future, if ever, Congress should appropriate the money for expansion. The bill, in short, its proponents affirmed, really marked no departure from isolationism and was a mere pious resolution that might or might not be carried into execution in the dim, distant future.

So it was written on the record that members of Congress, in sponsoring the naval expansion bill, expressly disavowed the very idea of collaborating with European democracies in a quarantine against Germany, Italy, and Japan and rejected all thought of waging another imperialist war in the Orient. If the President did not cherish the idea and the thought, then why, opponents asked, approve a naval program that might add two or three billions to the steadily mounting debt of the nation? It must have been with mixed feelings, therefore, that the President received the news of his naval victory in Congress.

Nor did the adventure end with the passage of the bill. Few citizens doubtless read the hundreds of pages that recorded the debate in committee hearings and congressional chambers. But some did, especially persons worried by the growing power of the navy and army in national politics. And in the records they read trenchant criticisms of "the British-Mahan sea power doctrine," of profiteering in munitions, of bankers' interventions in American foreign policy, of waste, poor bookkeeping and imperfect accounts in armament expenditures, of secret diplomacy, of imperialist tactics ranging from the use of the navy to protect Standard Oil shipments in war zones to the employment of armed forces in upholding "trade opportunities." President Roosevelt rode down the opposition to the naval expansion bill, but in the process the romantic version of armaments, armament interests, and armament bureaucracies was badly spattered. If, as stated in the Senate debates, the Government set its secret agents upon opponents of the naval expansion bill, to spy on them, and to report against them, even its undercover police activities could not stop the criticism — for the moment. Such tactics might be successful in the future, but the day had not yet arrived.

§

Although President Roosevelt pursued the policy of "the good neighbor" in the American regions to the south, that meant no lack of attention to practical interests in Cuba and other regions. Despite the swing of revolutions in Latin-American countries toward straight military dictatorships of the conservative order, sometimes called fascist, there were few occasions for the employment of Power Diplomacy or the marines. With members of Congress stunned by the conduct of the Lords of Creation in floating bond issues for Latin-American governments in the boom days, there was not much zeal for dollar diplomacy on Capitol Hill, for the use of troops or naval pressure to collect interest and installments on defaulted Bolivian or Peruvian bonds. Militant capitalism was discouraged for the time being at all events. Though heavy pressures were undoubtedly exerted especially in Mexico in connection with debts, the seizure of oil properties, and the expropriation of lands owned by citizens of the United States, they were not featured by open thundering or by displays of "the martial spirit" as in the days of Wilson's philanthropy and Harding's normalcy.

Hence exchanges of good-will on the Pan-American line could be made freely without encountering a serious test of revolutionary practice. When President Roosevelt and Secretary Hull went in person to the Inter-American conference for the maintenance of peace at Buenos Aires in December, 1936, they were greeted by lavish manifestations of hospitality. Roosevelt's eloquent oration on coöperation among democratic nations for neutrality and peace called forth hearty approval from the dictator of Argentina. Still, nothing tangible came out of the conference, except the discovery that there was a difference in policy between the bloc in Latin America oriented toward the League of Nations and the bloc of countries outside that sisterhood.

Unquestionably Latin Americans were happy to learn that the economic coercion which they had called "Yankee imperialism" in the old days was to be relaxed. They were also pleased to see the shield of the Monroe Doctrine furbished, if in storage, as it might be useful again. Momentarily they were in little danger from interference on the part of the great European powers in the style of Wilhelminic times, and yet they feared that the sick men of the Old World might recover.

Beyond that the ceremonial exuberation had little or no meaning. If partly united in condemning coercion by the Colossus of the North and in welcoming delays in the collection of debts, Latin-American states possessed little or no fundamental solidarity of interest — intellectual, moral, or economic. As Hubert Herring, certainly well-acquainted with the facts in the case, said, "Pan-American unity" was a "myth." In commenting on the Buenos Aires demonstration, "there is," he remarked, "no Pan-Americanism. There is no sense of American unity anywhere in the Americas. . . . Not only is there no sense of unity between Latin America and the United States, but there is little if any sense of unity among the Latin Americans themselves." The lack of realism in the picture of the world imagists was duplicated by the lack of realism in the picture of the regional imagists. Geographical propinquity and trade produced many common bonds, but no solidarity. Nor did the speeches and resolutions at the Lima conference in 1938 alter materially the diversity of interests.

The only peculiar feature in the situation was the frequent reference to ties of strength that might be created between dictators in Latin America and their brethren in Germany, Italy, Spain, and Japan. Attempts were made to evoke this fright in the United States, especially after a Brazilian dictator announced the formation of "a corporative state" in 1937. However, the specter had qualities of a scarecrow. There was not much likelihood that Latin-American dictators, usually of the formal military type, would actually welcome German or Italian intervention with their affairs. They wanted to rule in their own way, without instruction or interference from lords and masters. Neither by interest nor necessity were South American countries inclined to call in Hitler or Mussolini or Franco. Mussolini's dream might include dominance over Spain, but scarcely over the "once glorious Spanish Empire in the New World." For him, as for Hitler, naval bases in Latin America, if procurable, could only be liabilities. The navies of Great Britain and the United States blocked the way of any European despots who might seek to emulate Napoleon III and his ill-fated effort to establish an empire for Maximilian in Mexico.

Such being the topography of power, the peril of "a fascist Latin America" did not appear very substantial. Since the days of Simon Bolivar, the United States had managed to twist and turn along its way in dealing with a multitude of dictators in that region, and history, with curious features and novel ideologies, might continue along a similar course. The only event likely to make a general explosion would have been a communist upheaval in Mexico or elsewhere in Latin America, but that probability sank into the background as Stalinists and Trotskyists turned from bothering others to fighting among themselves.

§

To the very end, however, nothing in the course of events in either hemisphere could quench the insatiate desire of the Roosevelt administration to issue discourses on the virtues of peace-loving democracies and the wickedness of the three great disturbers of harmony — Japan, Italy, and Germany. However hard it tried, the State Department could not refrain from breaking into the newspapers every little while with some comment, homily, or innuendo indicating that it was driven by a Weltdrang as well as a Weltschmerz. Doubtless with the approval of President Roosevelt, his Commander-in-Chief, Admiral Leahy, in defending the super-navy bill before the naval affairs committee of the House, repeatedly linked the navies of the three world offenders as if the United States must prepare for a conflict with this combination. He even referred to their compact against communism in his eagerness to show their "solidarity." In a broadcast to the British commonwealth of nations, Secretary Ickes took advantage of the occasion to comment on the line-up of the bad against the good. Not to be outdone by admirals or the Secretary of the Interior, Harry Woodring, the Secretary of War, in May, 1938, after lamenting that heavy burdens for armaments had to be laid on suffering taxpayers, served notice on the world that the American army might fight another war for democracy. In keeping with expectations, Secretary Woodring's warning produced sharp criticism in Rome and Tokyo — criticism which doubtless confirmed him in his view that still larger armaments were required by the United States. He had said in 1934 that the army was ready to "take charge" of the country in case of a social crisis. Now it might combine with great fervor the two historic functions of the military.

On the effusions that poured out of offices in Washington, Joseph Kennedy, ambassador to Great Britain, made a pertinent comment at London in March, 1938, about as emphatically as a diplomat could. He expressed the hope "that the United States would solve its own problems if it stopped worrying about Europe," and he advised both America and Great Britain "to better their economic positions." Ending on a realistic note, the Ambassador said: "Nothing else will matter much — believe me." But Mr. Kennedy was an "amateur" diplomat. The tradition of keeping the mouth shut, the face inscrutable, and the powder dry had been definitely outlawed by the Roosevelt administration. With the ardent support of powerful economic and bureaucratic interests, with the rabid endorsement of belligerent elements in peace societies and the labor movement, it could, in fair confidence, count upon over-riding the opposition provided by mild-mannered liberals of the middle class and by agrarians in the Middle West. Although a little circumspection was required, as the contest over the super-navy bill indicated, incidents might remove the necessity for such caution: a major war in Europe would doubtless clear the way for another great crusade. When Secretary Hull complained that friends of the administration often misrepresented his attitude, he could take consolation in the fact that The Chicago Daily News and The Chicago Tribune supported him in "strong policies."

Even so, President Roosevelt and his Secretary of State were sensitive to public opinion and they could not fail to notice that the reports of popular polls and the consensus of editorial opinion showed the main body of the American people adamant in hostility to quixotic adventures intended to right the wrongs of the Old World, real or alleged. When Hitler's army pounced upon Austria and annexed that country to the German Reich in March, 1938, the Roosevelt administration, in common with the governments of France and Great Britain, bowed to that decree of violence. Later in the year, after Hitler had announced his intention to seize the Sudeten or German regions of Czechoslovakia, while France and Great Britain were striving to avoid a general war by introducing diplomatic regularities into his procedures, President Roosevelt wrote the Chancellor two letters in September, beseeching him, in the name of humanity, to restrain his eagerness and gain his ends by peaceful methods. Although these pleas, accompanied by disclaimers of obligations on the part of the United States, were warmly approved by the press, editorials and news from Washington confirmed the prevailing impression that the country was dead set against becoming involved in any European war arising out of old or new wrongs. It was one thing to regard Hitler and Mussolini as madmen at Munich, as the majority of the American people doubtless did, and it was another thing to maintain that the United States should pour out the blood of its sons in restraining the dictators after Great Britain, France, Russia, and the other powers of Europe had failed to unite against them in diplomacy and coercion. Profoundly moved as the nation was by the agonies of Europe and Asia, it seemed inclined to the view that the peoples of those continents, deeply experienced in their own histories and possessing special interests of their own, could and would order their destinies better without extraneous and incalculable interferences from the Western Hemisphere. Nevertheless the central drive of the Roosevelt administration was in the direction of intervention, as official declarations and armament measures indicated.

CHAPTER XI

Urban and Rural Labor in Evolving Economy

UNDERNEATH the stage on which the giant pageant of politics and business swirled and marched amid the pomp and circumstance of great affairs, labor kept on at tasks in town and country, as always in the long history of mankind. Nothing did or could change that necessity. Neither the delights that gleamed under the evanescence of the golden glow nor the detonations of the depression nor inquiries into the operations carried on by the Lords of Creation nor the tumults of popular elections nor the vicissitudes in the fortunes of leaders called statesmen nor the contests of court, executive, and legislature, nor all the bluster of war chieftains and pronouncements of diplomats across the borders of nations did or could alter that basis of industry, statecraft, and war. Whatever editors, columnists, elucidators, commentators, radio announcers, apologists, retainers, publicists, professors, and all the chorus of condemners and praisers felt moved to say, exclaim, or print, labor continued in town and country, supplying the goods and services upon which participants in the giant pageant depended daily for their very existence, without which they themselves would have been sent to field or shop to scrabble for their livelihood.

In every age, pagan and Christian alike, master minds had recognized the truth of the axiom that civilization, however low or high its superstructure of magnificence, rests upon labor and that its mutability turns upon the forms and processes of labor. More than three hundred years before the birth of Christ, Aristotle had said: "If every instrument could accomplish its own work, obeying or anticipating the will of others, like the statues of Daedalus or the tripods of Hephaestus, which, says the poet, 'of their own accord entered the assembly of the Gods'; if, in like manner, the shuttle would weave and the plectrum touch the lyre without a hand to guide them, chief workmen would not want servants nor masters slaves." But instruments did not produce articles of use without minds and hands to guide them; hence slaves and workmen were necessary to operate them and merchants to exchange commodities of use. "In the state which is best governed, citizens . . . must not lead the lives of mechanics or tradesmen, for such a life is ignoble and inimical to virtue. Neither must they be husbandmen, since leisure is necessary for the development of virtue and the performance of political duties." As to slaves, Aristotle thought that they were human and deserved some consideration and yet were mere servants of culture for others — for the strong and virtuous.

More than twenty centuries after the death of Aristotle, an American statesman, John C. Calhoun, strongly confirmed the judgment of the Ancient: "There never has yet existed a wealthy and civilized society in which one portion of the community did not, in point of fact, live on the labor of the other. Broad and general as is this assertion, it is fully borne out by history. This is not the proper occasion but, if it were, it would not be difficult to trace the various devices by which the wealth of all civilized communities has been so unequally divided. . . . The devices are almost innumerable, from the brute force and gross superstition of ancient times, to the subtle and artful fiscal contrivances of modern times. . . . It is useless to disguise the fact." The rule had ever applied, Calhoun maintained, and would ever apply to societies enjoying the benefits and blessings of civilization; and neither soft phrases nor words less shocking to beneficiaries than the old term "slave" could fundamentally alter the constitution of things human.

After the advent of Christianity, those idealists known as utopians had also made labor the center of their dreams and speculations but had sought to give to it both dignity and freedom. The Utopia of Sir Thomas More was based on labor in agriculture and the crafts; all men and women were instructed and exercised in agriculture; and besides every man had a trade to which he applied himself. "In a great city and in all the territory that lies around it, you can scarce find 500, either men or women, who, by their age and strength, are capable of labor, that are not engaged in it. . . . The slaves among them are only such as are condemned to that state of life for the commission of some crime, or, which is more common, such as their merchants find condemned to die in those parts to which they trade, whom they sometimes redeem at low rates; and in other places have them for nothing." This was labor in a dreamland and yet Sir Thomas More's utopians were the most highly civilized people that imagination had yet envisaged. Another famous utopian, of the nineteenth century, Karl Marx, saw in labor the source of the thought and energy which were to sweep all humanity into everlasting freedom and build a civilization shared by all. After Marx, William Morris, the princely esthete, whose works of mind and hand gave intense pleasure to idealists, in his News from Nowhere made labor an agreeable and beautiful manifestation of the noblest purposes in the human spirit. Perhaps in origin this utopianism was an expression of Christian ethics which deemed of one blood all mankind, exalted labor, and emphasized the eternal brotherhood of the great and the humble.

§

During the tensions of the midpassage, labor remained in town and country, at the tasks permissible or allotted, in the status which it had achieved, in its thought of its role in the social processes, and in the position of thought to which it was assigned by others; and it was both an active and a passive element in all that occurred. By measures public and private, designed to cope with the depression, labor was, of course, vitally affected. In their efforts to cut costs of production and make profits in spite of contracting markets, capitalists and managers scrapped old tools and methods, introduced new machines and processes devised by inventors and scientists, and stepped up industrial operations, thereby displacing industrial workers and often throwing additional strains on laborers engaged in mass production enterprises. In agriculture, the most conservative of the arts, as well as in machine industry, this subversive movement went forward with terrific speed. Illustrations of the havoc thus wrought were provided for public consideration by Paul Taylor in his Power Farming and Labor Displacement in the Cotton Belt. Theorists might argue whether this ruthless dynamism was the logic of technology, the drive of capitalism, or the outcome of human perversity; anyway, the rushing facts were realities in their span of time.

While private enterprise, doing as it liked with its own within the social constrictions, kept blasting at surviving features of the inherited "order," the Federal Government was helping to bolster up banks, railway companies, shipping concerns, farmers, and industrial corporations by loans, subsidies, and heavy purchases for public works, armaments, and other uses of State; that is, helping to underwrite enterprises which were constantly striving to cut costs and reap profits by the displacement of labor. With shifts in fact went modification in theory. The old conception of the automatic market, maintaining a just and efficient distribution of wealth through rents, profits, and wages, was disintegrating. The fundamental assumption of that theory was peppered with citations from reality — the crack of 1929, continuous unemployment on a large scale, government intervention, inflexible prices, contracting investments, and increasing concentration of corporate control. With these citations went a countervailing theory that an enlarged buying power for labor in town and country was absolutely indispensable to the high-level functioning of dynamic mass production. Since employers rarely increased wages on their own motion the color of economic justification was given, even by participants in the giant pageant, to legislation strengthening the bargaining power of labor for the purpose of enlarging buying power.

Into the dynamism of internal economy were injected ideas and forces emanating from revolutionary events abroad which impinged steadily and immediately upon the fortunes of American labor as well as upon the foreign policies of the United States. In Italy and Germany the free organizations of industrial and rural workers were suppressed by the apparatus of the State, supported by the middle classes. In Italy and Germany democracy was officially derided and the capacity of labor for self-government of any kind was officially denied. In Russia, where government was nominally carried on in the name of labor, assassinations, purges, and executions provoked more than suspicion that proletarian control in the Soviet Republic was growing weaker. News of these events filled columns of journals and magazines in the United States. American capitalists, politicians, and labor leaders were compelled to think again about the monitory experiences of the Old World in labor relations, as they had been made to think about them in the days of the French Revolution of 1848 and the Commune. Even the republic of letters and arts, despite many attempts, conscious or automatic, to provide insulation against the rude jars of practice, resounded with the searchings and arguments of the debate over labor relations beyond the seas, on its borders, and in its midst.

In all ages, indeed, the course of civilization had been marked by labor disturbances — the slave insurrections of antiquity, the peasants' revolts of the middle ages, the populist outbreak of Daniel Shays in the eighteenth century, and in the nineteenth century widespread revolts of industrial workers everywhere in western civilization. Could the history of labor be closed in the twentieth century by dictatorships of any kind, in the name of the middle classes or of the proletariat? Was the American ideal of free farmers and free mechanics, men and women endowed with equal suffrage, merely a transitory illusion? With the inherited system of economy running at a tempo far below its potential efficiency, with millions of men and women unemployed in town and country, with old crafts constantly disrupted by technological changes, could organized labor in the United States continue to function on traditional lines, merely, or at all? Were its responsibilities limited to bargaining with industrial employers over hours and wages? In these issues the mission or fate of the American labor movement was now defined. What was more, so all-embracing were the fortunes impending for the workers in factory, in mine, in office, and on the land, that all the apparatus of wealth, culture, and State resting upon labor became entangled in its destiny. Thus the labor problem stood at the center of American civilization in this latest age.

From the foundation of the American republic, acute thinkers had recognized the basic relation of labor on the land and in the shop to the forms and functions of government, and indeed to the very course of civilization. They had believed that the security of popular institutions depended upon the existence of free land. Jefferson had declared that when Americans were piled upon one another in cities they would go to eating one another as in the Old World, but he had no solution for the problem to be raised in coming years. His close friend, Madison, who also served as President of the republic, forecast a time when the great mass of people in America would have no property of any kind and prophesied that statesmanship would then be really tested. How and with what outcome, Madison did not venture to say. Later,

the humanistic wing of American democracy — led by
Horace Greeley, Elizabeth Cady Stanton, and Wendell
Phillips, for example — clearly understood the tendency to
separate labor from property, suspected that a crisis was
creeping over the country, and sought ways out of the
dilemma. Acquainted with ancient and contemporary political thought, including American speculations on that immemorial theme, Karl Marx, long a European correspondent of
Greeley's Tribune, declared the conflict thus comprehended
to be inevitable. In the Communist Manifesto published in
1848, he maintained that such struggles had ended in the
reconstruction of society *or* in the destruction of both contending parties. Nevertheless in his social philosophy, he
formulated a solution : With the spread of mechanical manufacturing, the class of industrial workers will be enlarged,
members of the middle classes will be driven down into the
proletarian ranks, and in the end the overwhelming majority
will take possession of and socialize private instruments of
production.

§

In the earlier analyses of the economic course a number of
tendencies were missed or at best dimly discerned. Nor did
the materialistic view of things always take into sufficient
reckoning the psychological forces of culture, taste, and
prestige influencing class inclinations. It was generally
thought in the nineteenth century that, with the expansion of
industry through machine processes, an ever-larger proportion of all industrial societies would be composed of industrial
workers living in cities. As a matter of fact, however, after a
long period of rapid growth, the number of industrial workers
in relation to the total population of the United States began
to decline. Automatic machinery and the rounding out of
giant construction projects contributed to the downward
tendency. Contrary to prophecy there was a relative increase
in the size of the middle class, defined as including merchants,
lawyers, doctors, teachers, government employees of the

upper range, service workers, writers, architects, painters, and other white-collar attendants upon economic processes. It was by the disintegration of freehold agriculture, rather than by the weakening of the middle class, that the proportion of landless, toolless, and homeless laborers was augmented. In the same agrarian shift the landlord class was enlarged and united by "natural" sympathies with the urban middle class rather than with workers in industry and propertyless laborers on the land.

The changing scene had been affected by the reduction of immigration. During the nineteenth century the flow of immigrants had contributed heavily to the ranks of industrial workers. And yet, curiously reversing the theory that capitalists could dictate all public policies, American trade unionists demanded limitations on immigration and, before the twentieth century had advanced far, were able, with collateral aids, to force restrictive legislation through the Congress of the United States. Bars were erected against foreign laborers willing to work in mill and factory for any wage or content to slave from sun to sun on the soil if they could only own a little patch of land however small or barren. When the laws were tightened by administrative measures after the economic crash of 1929, the stream of immigration from Europe dwindled to a trickle. Thus, largely through the efforts of American labor leaders, bans were placed on any proportionate increase in the number of industrial workers as compared with the size of the middle class. Whatever the causes, wherever the responsibilities lay, the fact was of deep significance to the course of American civilization. Dialectics reckoned with it. Realistic thought took note of it.

Within the ranks of the industrial workers so declining in relative strength of numbers, unemployment counteracted the natural trend toward unity and organization. In other words, the labor movement was weakened by the idleness of its members and of its potential recruits. With from seven to eleven million urban workers more or less unemployed — permanently, it was feared — and kept alive only by doles or mere makeshifts of one kind or another, the economic and political power of labor organization was reduced. In explanation of this situation the phrase "technological unemployment" attained a wide circulation, although the dictum rested on no investigation of facts both comprehensive and precise. Unquestionably machines had displaced multitudes of men and women from time to time. On the other hand new machine processes, with their almost infinite subdivisions, had given employment to workers in manufacturing plants, and increasingly to deft-fingered women.

But no system of accountancy offered a balance sheet. If there was no such thing as technological unemployment, as often alleged, there was indisputably a large amount of technology unemployed and millions of industrial workers were positively idle. Moreover the problem for labor organizers was complicated by the increasing use of women, mostly young, and children in the lighter machine industries. Labor officials could cut the competition of children by securing drastic child labor legislation in the progressive states, although the ratification of the national child labor amendment seemed to be impossible. They could attack the competition of women through minimum wage laws after the Supreme Court had sustained this type of enactment. And they could take women into their regular unions; women organizers had long struggled to bring this about in the interest of better living standards. But the swarms of adult men seeking a wage adequate for family care, of young women often burdened themselves with dependents, and of children helpless to exert effective pressure anywhere — all facing the terror of permanent unemployment — presented problems of organization which the most skillful union leaders were unable to solve. As members lost their jobs, they tended to drift out of the unions, whether dues were charged or not. When the contracting economy had no place for them, straight and simple unionism offered no immediate and evident advantages.

The process of organizing industrial workers and holding them in unions was further hampered by seasonal fluctuations in employment, intimately associated with many phases of the machine process. Since fluctuations were due in part to methods of advertising and marketing, their worst ravages could be prevented in some industries by longer-range planning, by deliberate coöperation between management and labor. Demonstrations to this effect were made in several industries, notably in the men's garment trade where the Amalgamated Clothing Workers and the heads of the industry clipped off the peaks and raised the valleys of unemployment by concerted efforts. Yet such arrangements were frequently offset by the spread of general unemployment, the introduction of displacing machines, and the turbulence of strikes. That control over seasonal fluctuations was possible on a larger scale could not be denied. That, if accomplished, it would diminish the adverse fortunes of many industrial workers was clear enough. But labor leaders could see in such control no material increase in the total volume of hour or day employment by the year; nor could they hope by that method to stem the trend toward the spread of labor-eliminating machinery.

In some respects the plight of workers ousted by the contraction of the market and the introduction of new machines recalled scenes in the early years of the industrial revolution, such as George Eliot described so vividly in Silas Marner. Plant after plant installed amazing inventions. As workers with hand tools and crude implements had been displaced in former times, so now even skilled technicians, experienced in operating complicated machines, were turned into the streets by the introduction of apparatus still more complicated or automatic. Often the discharged workers were so old that mastery of an unfamiliar trade was beyond their opportunity or capacity. Despite all the treatises on the economics of industry, despite the experiences of previous times, American labor leaders in 1938 were almost as much at sea over policies as were their forerunners a hundred years before. A dismissal wage might be secured to tide them over hunger for a while, but such concessions added no strength or assurance to a labor movement essentially concerned with a decent living standard and continuity of employment for the working class as a whole.

Nor did efforts to "stabilize" industry by "spreading" work among selected groups of employees add strength to labor organization. At the beginning of the depression, many employers tried to keep their labor forces together, sometimes at a material sacrifice, in expectation of a quick recovery and recurring need. In response to the desperate call to "spread the work," men and women still earning a livelihood undertook to share their wages with others. Although a larger proportion of workers won continuous wages by this process, in smaller amounts by the month or year, such earnings were below the standard of full employment and the operation afforded no aid to workers for whom even this limited assistance could not be provided. "The living wage" was frequently broken down, even for the employed. Wage earners lowered their own standard and shared their plight with their companions in the downward drift. Despite the fine spirit of sacrifice made manifest, "dividing work" generally meant extending disillusionment and diminishing the strength of labor.

Still another feature of the disintegration lay in multitudes of workers regarded as "unemployable" according to the rigorous requirements of new machine processes. High tension industry fed upon the strength of youth and shoved older men and women out into the streets to fend for themselves if they could. Minds and hands that might have been busy in handicrafts until near the close of life were often unable to keep up with the drive and speed of assembly lines or the stretched-out tasks at looms.

The number of such "unemployables" had been large in times of prosperity. The number grew with the collapse of prosperity. When the business curtailment of the depression came, the older workers were generally the first to be dropped by the wayside. Prolonged idleness diminished their powers. With no work to do for months or years, possessors of skills could easily forget their cunning, lose interest in work, and fall into a deep and shiftless discouragement. Men and women, even boys and girls, slid down the scale of stamina and ingenuity into or toward the abyss of unemployability. How many hit bottom was not officially reported. With all the statistical searching of the time, this mass of phenomena escaped a national survey. Undoubtedly the army of "economic derelicts" was large. Furthermore: it furnished the materials for demagogy, not for rational and effective labor organization. It might respond to romantic nostrums in the absence of sane remedies.

In some measure, usually overstated, the amount of unemployability, especially in the skilled trades, was due to craft-union policies. The strength of craft unionism had always depended to a large extent on the limitation of training and apprenticeship. Between sponsors of technical and vocational education, generally affiliated with employer interests, on the one side, and leaders in craft unions, on the other, there had always been friction if not violent antagonism. In their efforts to save something for their membership amid the devastating disruptions of the depression, craft leaders battled hard against the infiltration of new and cheaper workers by way of vocational schools and apprenticeship. Consequently, as industry rose slowly out of the trough, it sometimes found difficulty in discovering enough highly skilled workers to fill the new openings, among the six or eight million unemployed men and women who hung around on the outside. Compelled to consider the instant need of things, heads of craft unions placed limitations upon the rapid expansion of their own organizations and thus unwittingly enlarged unemployability — that menace to an all-embracing labor movement.

§

With the proportion of straight industrial workers declining, with widespread unemployment continuous, with efforts to stabilize seasonal fluctuations and spread work relatively ineffective in stemming the depression, with the army of unemployables large and perhaps increasing, the outlook for organized labor, compared with times called "normal," was gloomy in the extreme. As the years passed, it became increasingly evident that there was to be no steady march of industrial workers to the position of an overwhelming majority in the population. Within the ranks of labor, the strength of skilled craftsmen, relatively well-paid, fairly secure, and reasonably content with the shape of things present and to come, was clearly diminished. As long as private enterprise had earnings to share, the organizing of labor for bargaining purposes had been a task of relative ease. However, when in large areas earnings became non-existent, when whole sectors of economy depended for survival on money from the Federal Treasury, when the army of the unemployed and the unskilled swelled in size to mammoth proportions, the call to collective bargaining on old lines sounded more or less futile to the masses of the poor. At this conjuncture of realities, a crisis was reached in the labor movement; leaves were turned in the book of labor history; new methods were evolved. Those leaders accustomed to using their minds looked beyond the bargaining technique of the craft unions into complexities that could not be pierced by analysis according to any of their historic formulas.

To some extent, impossible to estimate and often exaggerated, the crisis in the labor movement was accelerated by practices which had grown up in unions long affiliated with the American Federation of Labor. Deriving their strength in part from their monopoly over employment within their respective crafts and from policies deemed advantageous to the crafts, labor leaders in certain fields had often found it possible to apply coercive measures to employers, members of their unions, and independent workers, even to enrich themselves in the process. In fact labor "rackets" appeared in nearly all the large cities and ranged from mere decrees imposed on employers and workers to brutality and murder.

Under the dictation of labor "czars," employers were compelled to hire more men than they needed or adopt operating methods for which there was not the slightest justification in economy or even in the welfare of employees. Heavy dues and special assessments were levied on members of unions and blackmail on employers. Destruction of life and property accompanied collections and terror reigned in whole trades. Workers were promised jobs in return for high initiation fees, given positions for a week or two, and then cast into the streets. A cafeteria "racket" in New York City brought $2,000,000 a year into the treasury of the labor bosses. Every now and then when gangsters shot things out among themselves or the Federal Government caught labor dictators who had failed to report their true "earnings," labor cases were aired in the courts and the broad ramifications of racketeering were revealed to the public at large.

On the basis of documentary evidence, Harold Seidman described the types and methods of such rackets under the heading, Labor Czars: a History of Labor Racketeering — a worthy companion of Max Lowenthal's important volume, The Investor Pays, both memorials of the age. According to Mr. Seidman, "miners, sailors, musicians, cloth shrinkers, furriers, shoe workers, waiters, cooks, barbers, janitors, window cleaners, milliners, laundrymen, and bakers have at one time or another come into the toils of the greedy labor leeches." In the building trades, the electrical trades, public markets, the restaurant business, and the motion picture business, such "czars" arose again and again in various parts of the country, spreading terror, and levying tribute. Sometimes they held power for years. At other times they were quickly discovered and prosecuted. Many were sent to prison. Many seemed to enjoy legal and political immunity despite the fact that their operations were well known. So far did the disturbances extend that legitimate unions suffered from the disreputable and criminal activities of the racketeers, unions were disrupted, and revolts broke out in the rank and file against domineering and dictatorial labor bosses, augmenting the industrial unrest that accompanied the course of the depression.

§

Immediately after the crack of 1929, William Green, speaking for the American Federation of Labor, expressed anxiety over the diminishing strength of his organization as its dues-paying members fell into the abyss of unemployment. Called into counsel with business leaders by President Hoover, he urged the maintenance of union wage scales to uphold buying power and keep the wheels of mass production turning. As such precepts failed to work and unemployment widened, Mr. Green warned President Hoover that he could not vouch for the passivity of labor if the strain was not relieved by some process. Representatives of the Railway Brotherhoods also protested against the wholesale dismissals made by managers in frantic efforts to pay dividends or to avoid bankruptcy.

Warnings and protests did not stay the course of economic disruption. On the other hand the tightening depression did not raise at once the volume of warnings and protests to unmanageable proportions. The Marxian prediction that a progressive impoverishment of labor would produce revolutionary action, rather than reform, failed to materialize. As a matter of fact, that calculation was not on the program of labor officials at all. Organized labor made no official break with the established rules for carrying on either political or economic transactions. It did not swing wholesale to socialism or independent action in 1932. Although Democratic, on the whole, in its sympathies, it was divided politically, and when the Roosevelt administration was first installed, the American Federation of Labor had no large program of action ready, despite its resolutions on the need for "planning" adopted at previous conventions. Like the Roosevelt administration, the Federation entered upon a career of improvisation.

In the various attacks upon the depression, the Federation

assumed no separate leadership but was satisfied with collaboration. When the demand was made for a federal, state, and local program of public works to set industry in motion and provide jobs for the unemployed, it attended conferences of business men and politicians and merely insisted upon its historic maxim — the eight hour day and the prevailing rate of wages on public enterprises. To secure the formal adoption of this prescription was generally a simple thing. Yet the victory was a minor gain for labor. The public works undertaken by government action consisted mainly of roads, bridges, dykes, dams, and similar types of construction in which machinery and unskilled labor were extensively used. The number of craft unionists set to work by such activities was small in comparison with the total volume of unemployment. When federal efforts to increase employment took the form of "work projects," other than heavy construction, organized labor was again able to force the adoption of a limited prevailing-rate-of-wages clause — for the meager number of hours allotted to men and women on the projects. Granting that it was carried against the protests of men bent on holding relief expenditures to the minimum, still the second victory for organized labor scarcely touched the fringe of the economic dislocation.

If public spending stimulated industry, perhaps kept it from a more general collapse, it left large bodies of industrial workers still bogged in the tragedy of unemployment. The appropriation of millions, even billions, for military and naval purposes, culminating in the super-navy program of 1938, did offer more opportunities to workers in the heavy industries, especially to skilled machinists, although the employment aspect of that bill was not impressive. Here also labor welcomed wages, without inquiring very thoroughly into the foreign policies or the war potentials involved. Labor might be given employment in using the war machines as well as in making them.

At best the armament business was limited and perilous. Carried forward at an increasing ratio, it might in time break the backs of taxpayers, culminate in war, and lead to the supremacy of the military over all labor as promised by the mobilization bill, reported to the House of Representatives by its military affairs committee in 1938. That prospect in the relations of labor to government and employment was not a happy one to contemplate. If, on the other hand, the armament program reached an end, a huge industry would be disrupted and labor would feel the consequences. That prospect was not encouraging either. While Marxists of the Stalinite direction supported the enlarged armament expenditures, with eyes on direct aid to Russia, some American labor leaders regarded the business with anxiety concerning the long outcome. John L. Lewis, for example, foresaw that labor might be buried under the ruins of the war monster. Whatever the secret wishes of individual labor leaders respecting foreign policies, there were no grounds here for jubilation by a labor movement.

When the Federal Government turned from "public works," as a means of moving industry, to direct efforts in stimulating private business through the National Recovery Act of 1933, organized labor received a kind of left-handed recognition. As originally drafted, the Act had been a pure business proposition conceived by the United States Chamber of Commerce; but in some curious maneuvering a labor clause was inserted in the bill — the now famous Section 7 *a*. How it got there was never fully explained to the public. When the recovery proposal came on the carpet, Congress had before it a bill prescribing a national thirty-hour week, designed to increase employment and enlarge buying power. The very sight of that measure, however, was alarming to business and to the Roosevelt administration. So the bill was scotched. Sponsors of the recovery measure then added to the original bill a section assuring to labor the right of collective bargaining under the new codes to be drawn up by industries. Just what was meant by the language of Section 7 *a* no one seemed to know, not even the President of the United States, though a placation of labor was presumably needed. Whether this was the true history of labor's appearance in the Recovery Act or not, efforts to enforce the Section in question brought labor into a somewhat novel relation to government, to industry, and to the vast body of hitherto unorganized workers in private enterprises large and small.

While industries were engaged in drawing up their codes of fair practices under the Recovery Act, representatives of organized labor participated, on a national scale, in the processes that involved wages, hours, and collective bargaining. As soon as steps were taken to put the codes, including labor provisions, into effect, in factories, stores, offices, and other establishments, leaders in unionism had to reckon with millions of workers who did not fit the old craft categories. Stirred by the drum beating that accompanied the concerted effort to bring about national recovery and invited to share in collective negotiations, industrial "misfits" by the hundreds of thousands acquired an interest in labor unionism which astounded most of all the American Federation accustomed to slow and tedious methods of organization. Thousands of the workers flocked to the unions long affiliated with the Federation. For others, perhaps the larger share, special organizations had to be provided.

Owing to the fact that miscellaneous workers were involved, the new organizations took on the tone, if not always the form, of industrial unions; that is, they were based as to membership on the nature of the commodity produced, such as rubber, cement, or automobiles, and included all the workers in each plant who helped in its making, as distinguished from unions based on special operations, or crafts, and split up in each plant along craft lines. Whatever the intention of the Federation when it sponsored Section 7 *a*, its decision helped to stimulate a flood of activities and agitations destined to shake the American labor world from center to circumference.

If the words "collective bargaining" seemed lucid as printed in the lines of the Recovery Act, practice under them was intricate and full of turmoil. At least five parties were drawn into the processes of enforcement throughout the country. Of labor organizations to carry on bargaining there were now in existence four distinct types: craft unions, which might number many separate bodies in a single plant; company unions, comprising all the workers in a plant, organized and controlled, more or less, by the management; industrial or vertical unions including workers of every type, independent of management, enjoying some degree of self-government, within the American Federation or outside; and the bodies of hitherto unorganized workers called upon by the law to bargain collectively. On the other side of the bargaining table were the employers, acting individually or collectively, who formulated their proposed wage and hour agreements. Framed in vague language, Section 7 *a* established no one stereotype of labor association for bargaining purposes and, in the circumstances, neither the federal agencies in charge nor the employers nor the labor organizers had any precise guidance. Perhaps an attempt to provide specifications would have defeated the adoption of the Section by Congress.

In the absence of clear guidance, labor actions under the law were chaotic, with federal officials, courts, and even President Roosevelt playing irregular parts in its application. Some employers, especially in the steel industry, resisted the enforcement of Section 7 *a* in their plants, in the courts, and in the forum of public opinion. Among the steel industries in general, company unions under the control of management practically monopolized labor relations and similar unions were organized in plants that hitherto had possessed no collective bargaining apparatus whatever. To meet the formalities of the Recovery Act, such corporate devices for keeping labor well in hand were altered in minor respects and declared to be in accord with "the new spirit."

Against independent unionism of any kind, the steel industry offered an almost solid front. Efforts by the Federation of Labor to organize the rubber industry also encountered resistance and collapsed. Attempts to introduce independent collective bargaining in the automobile industry precipitated sharp conflicts, involving management, the American Federation of Labor, independent industrial unions, and the Government. The upshot under Section 7 *a* was agitation and confusion. From its inception the automobile industry had been marked by seasonal and cyclical fluctuations, insecurity of employment, low annual earnings despite high daily wages in certain divisions, speed-up, espionage, and the rapid displacement of workers at an early age; but experiments in unionization under the auspices of the Recovery Act effected few material changes in the employment policies of the industry.

To some extent, certainly, the ineffectiveness of projects for the mass organization of industrial unions under Section 7 *a* was due to the policy pursued by the American Federation of Labor. The executive council of the Federation announced in 1934 that it would "encourage whatever form of organization seemed best suited to meet the situation and requirements of the mass production workers." Yet in practice the chief officer, William Green, insisted that organizers in the field must respect the rights and claims of craft unions already affiliated with the Federation. Strictly interpreted, his decree meant that when the workers in a plant were organized, they must be divided into as many separate unions as there were crafts represented in the concern, with the non-craft members as an appendix or the main body, according to the nature of the industry. Such was the theory. In practice, as organization proceeded under federal supervision, leaders of craft unions, in their struggle for increased membership, repeatedly clashed with leaders of industrial unionism. For the anticipated unity was thus substituted internal divisions among the workers themselves.

Collective bargaining under Section 7 *a* did not always mean, therefore, that a representative of labor sat down at the table with management and in conciliation arranged a schedule of hours and wages for all the grades and types of workers employed "in and around" the plant. On the contrary, it was frequently a multiple operation in which the heads of all the crafts represented in the industry participated; and if any one of the crafts was dissatisfied with the settlement, it might refuse to accept the proffered terms. Although a small minority, a single craft might order a strike after all the other labor bargainers had accepted the proposed contract. In fact jurisdictional warfare among unions themselves was a large part of the labor strife of the time.

Frequently managers of good-will, prepared to arrive at a general peace, were baffled by divisions within the ranks of labor. At the same time managers opposed to independent unions welcomed the opportunity to divide and rule and to represent all independent unionism as "utterly irresponsible." Nor could the most faithful supporters of organized labor deny the occasional truth of such charges. In the confusion so engendered, augmented by the use of espionage and intimidation on the part of many large employers, the public and the politicians found it hard to take their bearings. Nevertheless, under the National Industrial Recovery Act, the organization of labor was definitely stimulated, the membership of the American Federation rose from approximately 2,126,000 in 1933 to more than three million in 1935 — and then the Act was declared unconstitutional by the Supreme Court.

§

Notwithstanding the difficulties encountered under the federal intervention provided by Section 7 a, labor leaders were generally agreed that they must demand new legislation of a similar nature after the Supreme Court had invalidated the Recovery Act. They believed that it would strengthen their position as against company unions formed, guided, and dominated by employers, against managerial espionage, against the intervention of company and local police forces sometimes armed with machine guns and tear gas. In response to their arguments and to other considerations, partly political, Congress passed the Labor Relations Act, in 1935, to which was given the name of its leading champion, Senator Robert Wagner. The Wagner Act reasserted the principle of collective bargaining in industry, assured to labor the right to be represented by agents of its own choosing, and forbade employers to interfere with the freedom of organizing and holding elections in industry. The general task of supervising the enforcement of the law was entrusted to the National Labor Relations Board, endowed with power to hear complaints against violations of the Act, to investigate, to scrutinize elections within industries, to issue orders, and to defend cases appealed to the federal courts of proper jurisdiction. Immediately contested by employers, the Wagner Act was carried before the Supreme Court of the United States; and, shortly after Roosevelt had launched his campaign for the reorganization of the judiciary, it was sustained, in the spring of 1937. At last industrial workers had something that really looked like a "Magna Carta," offering federal intervention to guarantee their right to organize and hold elections for the determination of leadership and policy.

Although called by its foes "a radical departure" and "revolutionary," the Wagner Labor Act was, in fact, an extension of principles incorporated in older legislation, state and federal. The right of collective bargaining had long been recognized both by state and federal law and by practice. Again and again, disputes within unions over elections and control had been submitted to courts for adjudication. The Norris-La Guardia Anti-injunction Act of 1932, expanding the terms of the Clayton Act of 1916, had sought to protect organized labor against the free use of injunctions in labor disputes, against "yellow dog" contracts penalizing union members, and against other employer practices interfering with the formation and conduct of independent trade unions. These doctrines the Wagner Act elaborated by specifications. Reliance upon the courts for enforcement was now supplemented by the creation of a lay agency for administrative supervision — the National Labor Relations Board, appointed by the President by and with the advice and consent of the Senate.

While federal legislation in support of collective bargaining was by no means a novel feature of the depression, taken in connection with the circumstances of the depression it gave impetus to the labor movement. Workers in regions that had once been the scenes of union outlawry now had a larger sense of freedom — even in the coal and iron districts of Pennsylvania black with soot, livid with the memories of Homestead and 1892. "A man can talk in Homestead," wrote John A. Fitch, a close student of labor history, in February, 1936. The very managers who had been accustomed for twenty-five years to discharging men for joining a union now began to use a new labor language. The mood of the country seemed altered. "Times have changed," explained Mr. Fitch. "New laws are on the statute books, many of them of a character that could never have been anticipated. We've had a 7 *a* and now we have the Wagner law both of which in effect prohibit discharging men for joining unions. We are not lawbreakers. We go along with the government. . . . These laws and other things have created a great nation-wide sentiment about the right to collective bargaining and the idea that a working man has a right to join a union has gained widespread currency." With exuberance, some labor organizers inscribed on banners the words : "President Roosevelt wants you to join a union." Such was the spirit of the new day.

A "changed" attitude also seemed to characterize many great business executives. They, too, expressed a desire "to go along with the government." In the spring of 1933 they had hurried to Washington and urged the President to assume large powers in guiding the country out of the economic morass into which they had helped to lead it. If to many of them the "going along" meant clamping company unions upon their employees, while secretly resorting to industrial espionage, business leaders in general did not openly defy the government's officials as they had often defied labor organizers in times past. Some of them turned to the federal courts, to be sure, in the hope and expectation that the collective bargaining statutes would be declared unconstitutional; but they did not hire "finks" and "undercover men" for the express purpose of beating up and driving out of town representatives of the Department of Labor or agents of the various labor relations boards created under the Recovery Act and the Wagner Act. Usually the most antiunion manager, devoid of all respect for a labor delegate, had some respect for that part of the law which was represented by government officials and enforced in some measure at least. Even the hatred of vigilantes for labor leaders was not fierce enough to inspire the lynching of men and women who came as public representatives in the name of federal authority, to make inquiries, hold hearings, and supervise labor elections sanctioned by law.

Under the chairmanship of Joseph Warren Madden, the National Relations Board assumed one of the most difficult tasks ever undertaken by any agency of American government and, if the actions of federal courts in upholding its decisions formed criteria of judgment, it discharged its obligations with a judicial temper scarcely to be expected in the circumstances. It had not gone far, however, when it ran into a tempest of criticism. Of necessity, the Board was plunged into the controversy between craft unions and industrial unions and had to make rulings one way or the other on the basis of votes cast by the rank and file. Very soon the directors of the American Federation of Labor began to insist that their type of unionism was receiving "unfair" treatment from the Board and, besides assailing it in strong language, they demanded a revision of the Wagner Labor Relations Act. The Board was also attacked by employers; and conservative members of Congress, after demanding an investigation of its proceedings in vain, called for a drastic modification of the law under which it operated. Apparently disturbed by this conflict, Roosevelt ordered careful studies made of labor relations in England and Sweden, while defending the general course pursued by the Board in the enforcement of the law. As the time drew near for the convening of Congress in 1939, signs multiplied to the effect that an effort would be made to amend the Act.

In anticipation of the coming contest, the editors of the Fortune magazine, in the autumn of 1938, made a survey of the operations under the law and reached the conclusion that most of the proposed changes lay against collective bargaining itself. Usually the alterations suggested were not based on a temperate study of the law and the actual proceedings of the Board. Fortune's analysis of the controverted interunion cases dispelled the contention that the Committee for Industrial Organization had been favored over the American Federation of Labor. Warning the public against a rush to tear open the Wagner Labor Relations Act, the editors said: "The balance is a critical one. And nothing can so easily upset the balance as confusion concerning the motives and purposes involved."

§

Whether as a consequence of the new federal legislation or as another incident in a long stream of economic and intellectual tendencies, a terrific clash among labor leaders and within the ranks of industrial workers tore into the labor system and intensified the conflict of other interests in America. Labor leaders had not always seen eye to eye on organization and its objectives. There had been in times past many insurgent outbursts within the American labor movement and to one manifestation the newest upheaval was intimately related. After the Knights of Labor had been undermined and supplanted by the Federation of Labor, disputes had continued between the advocates of organization by crafts and the advocates of organization by specific industries — between craft unionism and industrial unionism. Owing to the very nature of certain industries where the output was the product of many hands, skilled and unskilled, such as mining and automobile manufacturing, the idea of one all-embracing union seemed to be fitting and was attractive to organizers and workers. But from the beginning industrial unionists experienced opposition when they sought to penetrate the entire labor movement, carrying into practice their ideal of the One Big Union.

Despite many historic reverses, they attempted it again on a large scale in the throes of the depression; and over this issue, in part, the labor movement was now ripped wide open. Craft unionists appealed to history in defense of their position and listed the failures of industrial unionism as contrasted with the successes of craft unionism. But the industrial unionists could not be silenced by history already made; they appealed to contemporary "facts," such as the non-craft character of mass production industries, the failure of craft unionists to organize more than a ninth or tenth of the industrial workers, and the inability of such limited unions to deal effectively with what John L. Lewis, head of the United Mine Workers, called "giant combinations of capital." Again political and industrial events were sharpening the struggle within the sphere of labor organization and giving it the quality of a life-and-death combat.

Between the rise of the American Federation of Labor near the close of the nineteenth century and the great depression, marked by the rush of labor to unionism after 1933, the two types of organizations had managed to adjust their disputes. For years, a large proportion of the Federation's members had belonged to unions primarily industrial in character, such as the United Mine Workers, composed of "all men employed in and around the coal mines, regardless of their skill or calling." Meanwhile mass production industries, such as the steel, rubber, automobile, and cement industries, had been occupying an ever larger share of national economy. Responding to new tendencies, the upswing of the Federation's membership after 1933 came in the industrial unions rather than in the craft organizations. Figures were confused but careful estimates gave the crafts a thirteen per cent increase in membership and the industrial unions a rise of more than one hundred per cent. At all events the balance of power within the Federation was moving from the old center.

Unmistakable evidences of the shift appeared at the San Francisco convention of the Federation in 1934. In response to a vociferous demand, the convention adopted a resolution approving "vertical," or industrial, unionism in basic industries and directing the executive council to charter unions among the automobile, aluminum, and cement workers, "and other mass production and miscellaneous industries." As a result of this decision industrial unionists expected a more active campaign on the part of Federation officials to organize the mass production workers. Their expectations were not fulfilled.

When the Federation's convention assembled at Atlantic City in the following year, 1935, its industrial-union bloc presented a series of resolutions calling for the establishment of more industrial unions in specified industries and for modifications in the constitution of national unions already in existence. In support of these propositions, John L. Lewis pointed out that, after twenty-five years of effort, the craft unionists had failed to organize the thirty-six million unorganized workers in the country and could not present a solid front to organized industry. On the other side, industrial unionism was decried as "an exotic importation of groups who do not believe in the American Federation of Labor." Many interests and personalities were involved and the debate was ferocious. The proposals of the industrial unionists were forcefully presented but, in the end, were rejected by a majority of about three to two.

Yet the victory for craft unionism at Atlantic City was not unmitigated. The opposition minority was large — and apparently growing. Uncompromising words were spoken. The executive committee of the Federation was charged with making "raids" on industrial unions and disrupting them by pulling out craftsmen for separate organizations; with blocking effective organizations in great industries, such as radio, rubber, steel, tin, and iron; and with gross neglect of organization work in the aluminum, cement, gas, coke, and other industries. It was accused of sabotaging the resolutions adopted at San Francisco and deliberately opposing the only type of unionism calculated to reach the huge body of unorganized workers. To the indictment equally curt replies were made; sponsors of craft unionism accused the leaders of industrial unionism of being agents of an alien and disruptive communism.

On its face the minority report presented at the Atlantic City Convention by Charles Howard of the Typographical Union seemed reasonable enough. It read: "We declare the time has arrived when common sense demands that the organization policies of the American Federation of Labor must be moulded to meet present day demands. In the great mass production industries and in those in which the workers are composite mechanics, specialized and engaged upon classes of work which do not fully qualify them for craft union membership, industrial organization is the only solution." But, mild as it was, the proposal warmed the memories of old conflicts over "one big union" and "revolutionary unionism." It defied the leadership of the craft executives well entrenched in official positions — the "bureaucrats" of the labor movement as they were called by the opposition. Thus a contest over organizing principles became an irrepressible contest for power — in the labor world and in the larger sphere of politics and culture where labor exerted decisive influences. This was no mere quarrel among kites and crows. It was a clash of powerful personalities, and, owing to the magnitude of the interests now at stake, the outcome of the struggle might well condition or determine fundamental phases of American civilization.

Outvoted at the Atlantic City convention, leaders of the industrial-union bloc held a meeting in Washington November 9, 1935, and there formed a Committee for Industrial Organization under the direction of John L. Lewis. The purpose of the Committee was "to encourage and promote the organization of workers in the mass production and unorganized industries of the nation and affiliation with the American Federation of Labor." In this declaration of purpose there was no revolutionary fire, no communism; there was not even a breach with the Federation. In effect it merely said that, since the Federation already embraced industrial unions and endorsed the formation of more industrial unions, the Committee proposed to perform the function which the executive committee of the Federation had failed to discharge.

Alarmed none the less by this aggressive organizing force, William Green warned the members of the Committee against factionalism in the labor ranks. In reply the Committee cited precedents for its action in the history of the Federation itself, denied any intention of raiding craft unions, and declared its desire to bring new unions into the Federation. At the same time it reaffirmed its resolve. John L. Lewis crisply informed William Green that rather than abandon the rights of thirty million workers his organization would leave the Federation if necessary to achieve this essential object of all organized labor. Claiming to be within the constitution and laws of the Federation to which its members belonged, the Committee took up the work of organization with an energy unexampled in the history of the American labor movement.

Fearing that the growth of industrial unions within the Federation might soon overwhelm by numerical strength the historic dominance enjoyed by the crafts, the executive council, in 1936, called upon the industrial unions of the Committee for Industrial Organization to defend themselves against a proposed order for their dissolution. Failing to receive a satisfactory answer the council "suspended" those unions — ten in all, with a membership of approximately a million workers. On the argument that only a convention of the Federation, not an executive body, could suspend unions, the council turned its back. It could see its fate without a diagram : if the rate of growth among industrial unions within the Federation continued, the craft unions would shortly be outvoted in the convention and on that day leaders of the industrial type would supplant the existing official hierarchy. Such seemed to be the tendency of events. At any rate the executive council decided to expel nearly one-third of the unionists from the Federation rather than countenance the struggle within the general organization. A wide cleavage was made in the American labor movement.

Hitherto when unions and labor leaders had been expelled from the Federation, the deed had been done rather quietly and the general public had paid little attention. In 1936, however, the heat engendered produced an explosion and, owing to the stresses and strains of the depression, the reverberations were felt throughout American economy. There was, in other words, a conjuncture of circumstance and personalities that could not be blotted out by an executive decree from the council of the Federation. Against the Federationists, such as William Green, Matthew Woll, John Frey, and William Hutchinson, seasoned and experienced, were now pitted John L. Lewis, David Dubinsky, Sidney Hillman, Philip Murray, Homer Martin, and other organizers, also strong in character and ingenious in negotiation. These opponents were not theoreticians or dialecticians of the type that had often been suppressed on the floor of the Federation's conventions. They were not Marxists arguing fine points up in the air. They were men of formidable strength with their feet on the ground. They represented unions already numerically powerful. They were social forces incarnate and dynamic. Their collision with the stalwarts of the Federation was no by-play. It was head on, and efforts at compromise failed to reduce the battle to a tea party.

§

The chairman of the Committee for Industrial Organization, John Llewellyn Lewis, was a veritable son of the

American industrial conflict. Born in Iowa in 1880, graduated from the public schools into coal mines, where his ancestors for generations had toiled, early drawn into unionizing efforts, rising rapidly as an organizer, Lewis became the head of the United Mine Workers in 1919. In that official position he wound his way through internecine strife, played the game of politics in the fold of the Republican party, used his big fists on more than one occasion, suppressed Red theorists, learned and practiced both the fierce and the subtle arts of negotiation and domination. Yet in the process he received an education in the higher learning of the most realistic sort. No one in a professor's chair or in any lofty position of government or business was able to give a calmer or more penetrating analysis of the structure and course of American economy — its manufacturing and mining industry, the transportation business, and the financing of corporate enterprise. Few, if any, among his contemporaries, had a keener appreciation of the perils in the way of labor organization or a wider comprehension of its role in civilization. While he could deliver orations on the platform and pound the table at conferences, he could keep his temper in the presence of a tumult when that was the better part of valor, or sit with the repose of a philosopher at a private discussion of things high and wide, asking questions quietly, venturing conjectures, suggesting qualifications, exploring probabilities, looking at all the angles of vision. Certainly with any Lord of Creation, Lewis could hold his own, when holding his own was an affair of knowledge, skill in argument, and tenacity of will.

That Lewis was more than a mere bargainer over hours and wages, that he had a broader view of politics and economics and culture, was demonstrated in a broadcast which he made on March 15, 1938. After summarizing the achievements of the Committee for Industrial Organization in respect of hours, wages, and civil rights, he discussed the state of the nation to whose fate that of labor was linked. He drew attention to the millions unemployed. "Their numbers," he said, "are steadily increasing, as the nation drifts with terrifying and deadly sureness to the never, never realm of financial bankruptcy, economic collapse, and human tragedy." He spoke of agriculture, banks, and business enterprises leaning upon the Government, subsidized by it. And what of intelligence and leadership in politics and economics? "In the months that have ensued neither industry nor government has come forth with constructive proposals designed to meet the problems of the depression. The federal Congress, lacking adequate or competent leadership, in continuous session for months past, has failed to devise or enact a single statute that would cause a glimmer of hope to penetrate the minds of millions of despairing Americans."

While Congress floundered around, the Politicos and the Lords of Creation fled from reason. "Meantime, cavilling and confusion prevail, and our statesmen and those carrying the responsibilities of the nation's manifold enterprises are reviling each other with an anger and bitterness that defiles, sears, and destroys. Meantime, the population suffers, and a creeping paralysis progressively impairs its functions. What is to be done? Reason calls for a change. More rational policies are indicated. America is menaced, not by a foreign foe that would storm its battlements, but by the more fearful enemy of domestic strife and savagery. It is time for Americans to coöperate. It is time for Americans to recognize each other's right of individual existence. It is time for capital to recognize labor's right to live and participate in the increased efficiency of industry and the bounties of our national resources. It is time for labor to recognize the right of capital to have a reasonable return upon its investment. It is time for statesmen to recognize their nation's peril and to decide to coöperate with labor and industry, to rationalize the nation's processes, and alleviate a nation's distress. Labor is willing to coöperate — now. Let the leaders of the nation's business step forward. Let the statesmen of the nation do the same. Let the council of reason and mutual toleration be convened. American leadership can accomplish this task, and in so doing will preserve its governmental structure and its democratic institutions." While he did not give a bill of specifications in that speech, Lewis made it plain that, in his judgment, an immense, rational, and coöperative effort was necessary to halt the creeping paralysis and set productive industry on its feet. That failing, trade unionism pure and simple could merely share the impending calamities.

Behind the force of his personality Lewis had the force of the United Mine Workers. He was the head of half a million men already organized and operating as a mass union, not as a congeries of craft unions. Its jurisdiction covered all workers laboring "in and around the mine." Its growth had been associated with one of the stormiest industries in the United States, beset by crises, cut-throat competition, price fluctuations, unemployment, and resistance to unionism. In his miner's post of observation, Lewis had seen his organization expand with the demands of the world war and contract in the post-war depression. He had witnessed the slight recovery and then the burst of 1929. But in good times and evil, he had fought to maintain miners' wages, to gain an inch here or a yard there for the mining population, and had gone through many a prolonged strike with that end in view. In attempts to effect unionization in "captive mines" owned by steel companies, he had secured contracts from those giants, while other organizers had tried in vain to unite steel workers. Rebellions against Lewis had broken out in the miners' ranks. Yet he had managed to ride every wave and he commanded greater loyalty and affection in 1936 than at any time in his tempestuous career. As head of the Mine Workers as well as the Committee for Industrial Organization, Lewis was no petty disturber of Federation peace.

In other respects and in his own right, Sidney Hillman, who was associated with Lewis in the Committee for Industrial Organization, was also a labor statesman. In his thinking he too had gone beyond trade unionism "pure and simple," and was both analytical and philosophical in his grasp of the social forces conditioning the labor movement. At the same time he was a positive genius as an organizer and an executive. In 1911 he had carried the United Garment Workers forward along the line of mass unionism and had effected with the management of great manufacturers, Hart, Schaffner, and Marx, an arrangement providing for an industrial board composed of employer and employee representatives authorized to make continuing adjustments under general terms. Three years later, Hillman became the head of the union which took the name of the Amalgamated Clothing Workers, and assumed direction of its fortunes — fortunes marked by an expansion of membership, a peculiar responsibility for industrial output, and a growth in social activities.

Throughout his career, Sidney Hillman had studied the men's clothing industry in which his union operated and had conceived unionism as a way of life, not merely as a pecuniary enterprise. The slogan "bread and roses," associated with the Amalgamated, if it sounded peculiar to business circles and garden clubs, expressed the union's desire for the good life. The son of a Lithuanian wool merchant, Hillman had come to the United States at the age of twenty and started work in a Chicago clothing factory at $7 a week. But he had lived at the Hull House and had taken advantage of its rare opportunities for training in languages, the arts, and social democracy.

When he entered upon unionizing activities, Hillman "shattered union precedents" and continued in that path. He insisted that unions should understand the state of industry, consider its problems of production and marketing, and seek to promote efficiency in its operations. Under his leadership the Amalgamated also assumed responsibility for the welfare of its members, even to the length of embarking upon housing projects. It undertook economic research, employed statisticians, often showed managers how to cut costs and maintain wage scales, and managed a bank of its own. Stranger still, it frequently came to the aid of embarrassed employers and lent them money from the union's treasury to form a bridge over hard times and keep up the rate of employment. By sheer force of intellect and moral courage, Hillman could accomplish results where others merely raged. He was a formidable member of the Committee for Industrial Organization, and the men's clothing workers formed a heavy supporting arch.

More akin to Hillman than to Lewis in social background, David Dubinsky represented still a third type of philosophy and energy. Polish in origin, with a childhood spent in the Ghetto of Brest-Litovsk behind him, Dubinsky had migrated to America at the age of nineteen and started on his American way as a low-paid worker in a clothing shop on the east side of New York. His career synchronized with the rise of sweatshop workers to a position of decency and self-respect through the organization of the International Ladies Garment Workers Union. As low-paid laborers, Jews had not found the doors of craft unions wide open for them. They had been compelled to develop their own organization and gain negotiating strength through their own solidarity. Although associated with the American Federation of Labor, the Garment Workers, in their struggle for a share in the benefits of civilization, had gone beyond mere wage and hour bargaining. Under the leadership of such indefatigable workers as Fannia Cohn, they had established an educational program, built summer camps, founded institutions for recreation, health, and mutual aid, and experimented with dramatics and art. Economic democracy they were seeking to enrich by social democracy. Trained in this school, a leader of this association, Dubinsky combined with hardheadedness in organizing activities an appreciation of the social and political implications connected with labor activities.

§

Men of such calibre as Lewis, Hillman, and Dubinsky were commanding forces. When they set out to organize, organization moved, backed by the miners and garment workers nearly a million strong. With unprecedented swiftness, the campaign swept into its train, through the strategy of the Committee for Industrial Organization, casual laborers, transport workers, white-collar employees ranging from clerks and stenographers to engineers, college professors, and journalists, and every type of worker in the mass production industries. Entering plants where company unions seemed entrenched, where in some cases independent unions had been crushed again and again, organizers carried stronghold after stronghold. In February, 1937, the Committee "breached the united front of the basic industries in winning a contract with the General Motors Corporation," hitherto an adroit and indomitable foe. Checkmated by Henry Ford, the Committee made encircling movements by applying propaganda and by invoking federal aid under the National Labor Relations Board which compelled him to present his claims for exemption to the agencies of the law.

In the course of its advance the Committee moved on "Big Steel," with Homestead, the old battleground, as a center of activity. There, more than forty years before, the secretary of the Carnegie Company had issued the employers' declaration of independence; now the new labor leaders proclaimed theirs. "The lords of steel. . . ." ran their manifesto, " have set up company unions. They have sent among us swarms of stool-pigeons. They have kept among us armies of company gunmen. Today we do solemnly declare our independence. We shall exercise our inalienable rights to organize into a great industrial union, banded together with all our fellow steel workers. In support of this declaration, we mutually pledge to each other our steadfast purposes as union men, our honor, and our very lives." The conflict had been revived. Seven men in it had just lost their lives.

When the reading of the declaration was finished, the crowd of auditors marched to the graves of the dead and there pledged themselves to the cause of labor. All through the steel districts flew the news and then it produced a national sensation. While the country was watching the outcome with anxiety, "Big Steel" came to terms with industrial unionism in March, 1937; but "Little Steel," personified in its spokesman, Tom Girdler of the Republic Steel Company, refused to sign on the dotted line and presented a solid front of resistance. For the moment the tide stood still, as the economic recession gave caution to the leaders on both sides of the line. Even so, at the close of that year the Committee for Industrial Organization boasted a membership of more than four million workers.

The rapid rush to industrial unionism was accompanied by new tactics, provoking and reflecting dissensions within the movement itself as well as outside. Included in the novel methods was the "sit-down" strike, evolved perhaps in imitation of contemporary labor innovations in France. Whatever the source of inspiration, the sit-down became epidemic for a time in the United States, spreading alarm and anger through middle class circles from coast to coast. It was especially virulent among industries in which company unions prevailed or where employers had refused to negotiate with independent organized labor. In industrial plants, hospitals, chain-stores, and other centers of work, men and women, boys and girls, stopped machines or other transactions and camped on the premises for the duration of the struggle. Instead of marching out and leaving their places to be filled by strike-breakers, they stood where they were, sat down, ate, and slept in the quarters of their employers. In many establishments strikers prepared for a siege by forming broom and dusting brigades to keep the rooms clean; they organized classes for instruction in various branches of learning, conducted by their better educated associates. In one store, religious services were held on a Sunday and prayers offered. Food and other supplies were passed through the lines by relatives and sympathizers and efforts of the police to dispossess the occupants jeopardized limbs or lives for everybody concerned.

To owners of property, their legal advisers, and guardians

of law and order, sit-down operations presented knotty problems. As the result of a long historic struggle, finding expression in legislation and judicial reasoning, certain rights in connection with labor organization and collective bargaining had been won, such as the right to form trade unions for the purpose of raising wages, to strike in relation to that purpose, and to picket, subject to specific and general limitations. None of these rights, however, had been exercised within the premises of employers. Nor was there any overt threat to property relations in the "vacation," occasionally used as a bargaining device, that is, in the sudden stoppage of work by remaining away from the place of employment. Sabotage in the form of breaking machines or putting sand in gear-boxes had been clearly an attack on property, unlawful from the beginning and later stigmatized as criminal. But the sit-down did not fit into established legal categories of any kind. Under the existing interpretation of law it was an illegal occupation of premises in defiance of the owners and in many places the police used tear gas and force to eject the occupants. In other places, where it was endured by owners and proved effective, its legality was not conceded. Since the sit-down strike was frequently a spontaneous combustion, even labor leaders shrank from assuming official responsibility for it, at least in such cases, although they sometimes took advantage of it to press for negotiations and terms. Some attempts were being made to formulate legal rights for workers who held "their places" when the epidemic died away almost as quickly as it had flared up.

§

Had it proceeded alone as a manifestation of labor unrest, the industrial-union movement might have immediately provoked a counter movement tightly solidified and able to use force against it without the formal restraints of law. But it did not proceed alone. Exponents of the "normal" countervailing opinion were shaken by doubts of their own virtue as a result of disclosures at congressional hearings paralleling this labor advance — disclosures which enlightened the public with respect to munitioneering, the manipulations of railways by banking cliques, and the employment of spies, private gunmen, fomenters of false labor troubles, and the assemblage of arsenals at plants by corporations high and low in the scale of Respectability. As these sordid features were unfolded at the congressional hearings, great metropolitan dailies carried vivid accounts for those who ran to read. Reporters began to fret over their diverse obligations to owners, publishers, editors, and the people at large, and to divulge secrets of their trade. Disputes between editors and publishers on the one side and the makers of so-called "objective news" on the other, the organization of the Newspaper Guild among journalists, and a strike against the Hearst press in Seattle with its anti-labor policy, contributed to the unsettling and churning of public opinion.

Into this ferment of facts and opinions, professional propagandists, known as public relations counselors, and, more openly, radio announcers flung their agitations. Seeing an opportunity to fish in troubled waters, many communists thrust their activities into industrial unionism. Their number was small in relation to the total membership of unions under the Committee for Industrial Organization; their doctrinal creed was disavowed by its leadership — to which communist proclivities could not be justly charged. But since communists were interested in promoting class conflicts or taking advantage of them, they pushed into the limelight and made disturbances incommensurate with their numerical strength. Their very presence in industrial unionism, however, furnished the pretext for opponents of that movement to brand it as "Red." Once more leaders in the work of labor organization were compelled, as they had been again and again in American history, to meet charges of revolutionary, alien radicalism while they pressed forward to improve labor conditions against hostile interests on the side of ownership and management.

Yet the communists themselves did not in truth present a united front toward the labor movement in America. Though capitalist ideologues and conservative craftsmen, lumping the communists all together, did their best to discredit the Committee for Industrial Organization as communist in intention and leadership, really the communists were as divided on principle and tactics as the labor movement itself. The division revolved around the issue of Stalin against Trotzky — communism within Russia, for the time being at least, as against world revolution and world communism in one vast conflagration and reconstruction.

This controversy added inflammatory elements to the strife between capital and labor in the United States. Despising the Stalinite wing of communism with the intensity of disillusionment following utter confidence in utopia, Trotzkyites took delight in pointing out and exaggerating the communistic element in the industrial unions. A small fraction themselves, they would have wielded slight influence had it not been for the energy of the general opposition riding full tilt against the Committee. Riding with it, they obtained for their testimony and for their "revelations" a degree of publicity that could not have been won otherwise. In this state of affairs their writings and agitations gave the press an opportunity to whip up resentment against the only form of unionism that, in the nature of mass production, could offer any method of accomplishing the wholesale organization of labor in the United States.

§

From one point of view, of course, the ebullition of labor unrest seemed to the worried upper classes like a volcanic eruption, without much rhyme or reason, offering no advantages even to labor. Strikers clashed with the police and state troopers. Heads were cracked and bodies broken. Men and women marching toward the industrial plants were shot down in their tracks. Sit-downers were ousted by gusts of poison gas. While dual unionism was splitting the workers into warring camps, stevedores, cooks, waiters, clerical workers, teachers, government employees, nurses, and doctors were making common cause with miners, automobile workers, actors, and reporters. On labor days, instead of the former united front on parade, there were now sometimes two fronts and two parades in many cities, with hooting and jeering on the side lines. Irresponsible strikers, not amenable to any union discipline, broke contracts signed by their representatives and business management. In their haste to avoid the impacts of industrial unionism, employers raced to make terms with the American Federation of Labor and praised where they had once damned. Leaders in the two divisions of labor sniped at one another amid the applause of their respective supporters and their common enemies. Then as a climax to all the uproar came the business recession of 1937. Men and women who had recently sat down in plants now sat down outside — in idleness — or marched on relief agencies and Works Progress officials with demands for "work or bread." With an impatience fanned by the conflict between the Committee for Industrial Organization and the management of "Little Steel," President Roosevelt exclaimed: "A plague on both your houses!"

If, in the circumstances, employers could view with pleasure the wide-open split of the American labor movement, politicians as the brokers and mediators in government were denied the privileges of such a complacent attitude. In 1936 organized labor had penetrated politics with unusual force. While the Lords of Creation were pouring hundreds of thousands of dollars into the Republican war chest, the Committee for Industrial Organization tossed more than half a million into the Democratic fund. Under the auspices of labor's Non-partisan League, sponsored for a time by both wings of the labor movement, Republicans and Democrats were pitted in a rivalry for "the labor vote." In the state of New York an independent organization calling itself the American Labor Party entered the field and threw its support to the Democratic side in national affairs, while insisting on separate representation in local affairs. The size of its vote was surprising, even a source of anxiety, to "the old-line politicos." In the autumn of 1937 the American Labor Party spurned the Democratic machine in New York City, backed Mayor Fiorello La Guardia, a nominal Republican, for re-election, and helped to rout Tammany Hall, blessed against such a fate by Postmaster General Farley. Repercussions were felt in all the industrial states already rent by labor agitations. John L. Lewis supported a labor candidate for governor in the Democratic primaries of Pennsylvania and, when this move was unsuccessful, cast about for another way to make the force of labor felt in the politics of that key state. As Democrats and Republicans girded themselves for coming congressional elections, the hopes of labor rose. Although the substantial gains made by the Republicans were interpreted by such outstanding friends of labor as Senator Burton K. Wheeler to mean a set-back, the future was still open.

Dependent in a considerable measure upon the labor vote in his struggle against the conservatives in his own party and against the possible revival of the Republican organization, President Roosevelt found himself in a dilemma. In an effort to hold things in balance, he sought to keep on good terms with both wings of the labor movement — the officials of the craftsmen and the officials of the industrial unionists. An offense to either side might swing it into the Republican camp. While he kept his channels of communication free, his Secretary of Labor, Frances Perkins, whose branch of government could be called in the circumstances a Department of Domestic Warfare, tried to confine the conflict within the bounds of negotiation. A representative of the Department attended the national labor conventions in 1938 to urge a compromise in the interests of unity, and Secretary Perkins continued to pursue the policy of conciliation.

All in vain, apparently. Committees appointed by the two labor organizations could not arrive at an agreement and politicians were equally helpless. It seemed as if no formula could permanently resolve the contradiction between craft unionism and industrial unionism. Craft unionism, embracing "the aristocracy" of high-paid labor and depending for existence upon a certain supremacy over skilled trades, was necessarily limited in its range and its possible membership. Reaching out for the whole body of workers, some thirty-six million strong, industrial unionism claimed to be "the democracy of labor." Asserting its claim to permanence, the Committee for Industrial Organization — without the coöperation of Dubinsky and the Ladies Garment Workers Union — changed itself into the Congress of Industrial Organizations at a convention held late in 1938, and adopted a regular constitution for the new association of industrial unions.

§

In keeping with the urbanization of economy which accompanied the apparently illimitable expansion of machine industry, the swift advance of industrial unionism, with its strikes, sit-downs, and social turmoil, almost monopolized the attention of that portion of society given to imagining itself the whole of society. Yet events no less crucial for that society were taking place in another division of labor — labor on the land. Tilling the soil had continued through all the ages of human history to bring forth some kind of livelihood whatever the varying fortunes of politics, industry, and commerce. As Miriam Beard pointed out, near the conclusion of her History of the Business Man, dealing with his role in more than forty centuries, "men suffered on the land but survived; while in the cities, they flourished — and faded." Craftsmen in the metropolis of Rome lost their occupations in the dying city; slaves once flogged to labor on the latifundia kept on tilling the earth as it slipped from the hands of their masters who were sinking into dissolution and death. Until the great modern illusion of urbanism, for its brief span, conquered thought, statesmen, poets, and agronomists had regarded the condition of agriculture — the distribution of the land among yeomen and the rewards of labor on the soil — as an indubitable barometer of social security and stability.

Once more, after the severe contraction of capitalism became indisputable even to its economists, and especially after the great débâcle of 1929 enfeebled the centers of industry and commerce, concern about agriculture, or rather about the buying power of those that labored in the earth, rose in the consideration of all who had capacity for consideration. This revival of concern found expression in the Agricultural Adjustment Act of 1933 and kindred legislation. But on the frank confession of the Secretary of Agriculture, federal activity affected primarily "the top third of the farmers in the country," that is, principally landowners great and small, in the upper ranges of well-being. If it saved a multitude from foreclosure and ruin, it conferred few benefits, often personal losses, on tenants, share-croppers, migratory workers, and field laborers, in the much-advertised effort to establish "parity between agriculture and industry."

In the midst of their deprivations the disinherited made their woes heard. They held meetings and protested. They organized unions and struck against the conditions of tenure and labor. At that point their activities were countered by acts of vigilante terrorism in rural regions, raising a noise that reached the White House. Late in 1936 President Roosevelt responded by creating a Committee on Tenancy authorized to inquire into the facts of the case and report remedial measures. With the caution of understatement he remarked: "The rapid increase of tenant farmers during the past half century is significant evidence that we have fallen far short of achieving the traditional American ideal of owner operated farms."

The findings of the President's Committee, expressed in mathematical language, described an economic tendency of sinister import not only for working families on the land but also for the upper circles of the American system. Comprehended in human terms, the naked facts depicted a widening area of servitude and misery. "For the past forty-five years," the Committee stated, "the entire period for which we have statistics on land tenure, there has been a continuous and marked decrease in the proportion of operating owners and an accompanying increase in the proportion of tenants. Tenancy has increased from twenty-five per cent of all farmers in 1880 to forty-two per cent in 1935." In the decade from 1920 to 1930 the number of tenant farms rose while the total number of operated farms actually fell. Estimated in terms of monetary value, forty-seven per cent of the land was tilled by tenants or wage laborers. In some of the states four-fifths of the equity in the land was in the hands of landlords and mortgage holders, and only one-fifth in the possession of operating farmers.

In this record of increasing economic degradation on the soil, there was just one little countervailing fact: the proportion of tenancy declined slightly between 1930 and 1935. Farm owning seemed to be on a rise, if a trivial rise. But Rupert Vance entertained doubts. It was true, he admitted, that in the sixteen states of the South a twelve per cent rise in owners had occurred in the period, to offset the growth of tenancy, but "the increase was entirely among white owners with small farms, and most of the gains were in rough upland areas of poor soil. Over one-fourth of the new owners' farms were located in the Appalachian counties of West Virginia, Kentucky, and Tennessee where between 1930 and 1935 many unemployed miners had returned to their submarginal farms. This development can scarcely be regarded as advancing the course of farm ownership. The loss of tenant farms occurred largely among the Negroes in the South." Degradation in the mining industry had driven workers back to soil from which they had fled in despair. The slight downward turn in the rising line of tenancy, on its face indicative of better things, in truth carried evidences of additional worse things.

Nor was the whole story told in the figures of tenancy.

In value, forty-seven per cent of the land of America was tilled by non-owners. Bad as it was, that did not complete the story. Nominal owners were saddled with mortgages, amounting to eleven per cent of the total value of their property. "The true ownership by farmers in the land they till," Vance went on to say, "has reached its lowest point in the Midwestern states of South Dakota, Iowa, and Illinois where it falls below thirty per cent. Next comes the Cotton Belt where the farm operators' equity ranges between thirty and forty per cent." Land, buildings, machinery, stock, and tools were mortgaged. On top of this pyramid stood short-term debts usually representing money borrowed to pay current expenses. In some states more than fifty per cent of the farmers — freeholders and tenants combined — had such outstanding obligations, often secured by liens on coming crops. The past, the present, and the future were bound by debt servitudes.

By statistical studies another cheerful American dream was shown to be deceptive. Armchair philosophers had fancied that tenancy marked a rung in the "ladder of progress" up which the stout young farm laborer climbed to ownership. In many cases he had no doubt made that climb. But the President's Committee on Tenancy dispelled the illusion as a general proposition. Its examination of the facts "indicated that in recent years movement from rung to rung has been predominantly in the direction of descent rather than ascent. It has also indicated an increasing tendency for the rungs of the ladder to become bars — forcing imprisonment in a fixed social status from which it is increasingly difficult to escape."

While the motion upward slowed down, collateral motion extended. Tenants wandered from farm to farm, from landlord to landlord, from region to region, on foot, in battered wagons, or in dilapidated automobiles, commonly dragging families with them, usually to conditions lower in the scale of living than those from which they had fled. In the spring of 1935 more than one-third of all the tenant farmers in the United States had occupied their present land merely for one year and in many areas the proportion exceeded fifty per cent. White tenants moved more frequently than colored tenants. Had it not been for laws binding debtors to their landlords, the amount of nomadism would have been still larger and the disintegration of communities and steady habits by locomotion would have been intensified; for settlement on the land did not always signify a poignant desire to be there — to pursue life, liberty, and happiness on the soil under any and all circumstances.

Between the growth of farm tenancy and the restless migration of tenants, on the one side, and the depletion of the soil, on the other, immediate relations were evident. Tenant occupancy of land did not last more than two years on the average. Having no long-term interest in the soil he tilled, and little or no capital, the tenant applied only those fertilizers calculated to yield a quick cash crop. "The shorter the operators' time on the farm, the higher the percentage of crop-land in corn tends to be, and consequently the higher the degree of erosion," reported the Iowa Experiment Station. At the same time the transient tenant had slight if any interest in improving the drainage system, the house, barns, or other structures on his temporary holding. From start to finish the tenant process worked for the wastage of the soil and the degradation of human life in all its aspects. Reciprocally, in its turn, soil depletion "contributed materially to the expansion of tenancy and the further impoverishment of tenants and croppers." In the domain of legal relations, state laws respecting the rights and obligations of landlords and tenants provided terms and conditions that made for an acceleration of the degradation. Considering for a moment merely the material features of the situation, the President's Committee reported that the proper use and conservation of the soil "require modification of our present system of land tenure." The bottom was sliding out from under the American dream, with "the degradation of the democratic dogma."

Correlated with increasing tenancy and ceaseless migration were unsanitary dwellings, ill health, biological deterioration, meager education, and the disruption of community ties. As the top soil washed out to sea, the physical and moral resources of human beings were also depleted. Stark in the figures, photographs, and reports stood this brutal reality. When to migratory tenants in this plight were added farm laborers and field "hands," the situation appeared even more tragic. In 1930 more than one-fourth of all persons "gainfully" employed in agriculture were casual farm wage-laborers; "hired men" who shared the life of the farm families were a diminishing group. Having no permanent abode, few comforts, deriving no immediate advantage from the conservation of anything, deprived of all benefits arising from insurance and unemployment legislation, farm laborers had even a shorter shrift than farm tenants. "The situation of the hand laborers in intensive agriculture is especially precarious," laconically remarked the President's Committee. That, at least, was not an overstatement. And the Committee concluded: "Approximately one farm family out of four occupies a position in the nation's social and economic structure that is precarious and should not be tolerated." This, also, was a modest deduction from the facts pertaining to tenants, croppers, laborers, families on submarginal land, families on holdings of inadequate size, owner-families hopelessly in debt, and young people stranded at the bottom of "the agricultural ladder."

Here was a field at least ready for agitation and agitation sprang up abundantly. Tenants, croppers, and laborers began to hold meetings and discuss their common problems. They formed local organizations. The Southern Tenant Farmers' Union was established and quickly reached out for membership and contacts with organized industrial workers. Calls went forth for modifications in land tenure, in the rights of tenants and croppers, in the laws of debt and indenture. Then this movement toward agricultural unionism evoked a counter-movement among landlords and the collateral property interests, industrial and agricultural. Families connected with union activities were evicted from their shacks;

the power of the police and county sheriffs was invoked;
vigilante groups fell upon "the agitators," irrespective of
their sex, inflicted violence upon them, shot some, drove
others into neighboring counties or states, called them "Reds"
— that last word of insult. Thus the frailty of the civil
liberties enjoyed by the landless and toolless was again and
again illustrated. Members of farm unions were blacklisted
or subjected to discrimination in the allotment of such opportunities as agriculture offered. Complaints soon reached
Washington. For a time they were little heeded by an administration engaged in subsidizing the "upper third" of agriculture; but eventually they awakened reverberations in the
Department of Agriculture and in the corridors of the
Capitol. The President's Committee on Tenancy took cognizance of the situation and Secretary Wallace went forth to
see with his own eyes the plight of those who cropped and
toiled in Southern fields.

Though tentative and conservative in the presence of
American folklore of property, the Committee on Tenancy
accepted the fact that the unlimited individual tenure provided in the Homestead Act of 1862 had been a complete
failure in large areas. Having made that confession, the Committee advocated the purchase and leasing of land by a
federal corporation, the limitation of re-sale to farmers by
provisions checking speculation, the reservation of certain
rights to the public, and a guarantee of soil conservation
against exploitation.

In other words, traditional freehold tenure under which
degradation had come about was to be restrained in the community and the national interest. Farming predominantly
commercial was to be supplemented by production for home
use, by coöperative enterprises, by the construction of camps
for migratory workers, by health services and education;
that is, public ownership, limited and conditional tenures,
and coöperative undertakings were called for — on an experimental footing.

Changes in state legislation affecting tenures and landlord-tenant relationships were also recommended. Restraints were to be placed on land speculation — a favorite outdoor sport in America for several centuries. More adequate safeguards for civil liberty were to be maintained. All in all, the report of the President's Committee, cautious as were all its terms, was a revolutionary document when placed beside the myth of the upstanding and independent American farmer and his family. A. R. Mann, provost of Cornell University, felt compelled to announce "strong reservations concerning the proposal for federal landlordism contained in the report."

§

At this point in time, in the midpassage, all comprehending thought, whether sophisticated or rude, took into account the obtrusive fact that the future of American society, including the form and process of government, was being conditioned by the vicissitudes, activities, and ideas of urban and rural labor; that the forms of culture to come turned upon the lot to be won by or assigned to labor. How profound was the antagonism or affinity between farmers as owners, debtors, tenants, or field hands on the one side, and labor in towns and mining communities on the other? How solid or fragile was the unity of that sector of society called "the middle class" which sought to be self-contained and so often came into conflict with labor, rural or urban? Was there anything more than the demagogue's machinations in the monotonous clashes between big business and little business, the "trust-busting" furor based upon the real or alleged opposition between the petty bourgeoisie and the plutocracy? Amid the swish and swash of contending groups, interests, and ideas, where lay the center of gravity, if there was one? Where was the controlling gyroscope for dominating and giving stability to the course of civilization?

To none of these questions were positive answers provided by the tumult of events. Efforts to unite farmers of various types with industrial workers continued unabated, but immediate results were limited and future outcomes were obscure. A party called "farmer-labor" surged to the top in the government of a great state — Minnesota. Across the border in Wisconsin the Progressives, under La Follette leadership, got possession of the government, mainly on appeals to farming and laboring groups, without assuming the Minnesota label. In the House of Representatives in 1938, five of the nine members from Minnesota were enrolled under the Farmer-Labor banner, with Paul J. Kvale and John T. Bernard capably leading. Of the Wisconsin representation, seven of the ten members were listed as Progressives and two of them certainly, Thomas Amlie and Harry Sautoff, were essentially farmer-labor in sympathies. In the Senate both members from Minnesota, Henrik Shipstead and Ernest Lundeen, belonged to the Farmer-Labor affiliation. In the main, however, Senators and Representatives from industrial constituencies, who manifested strong interest in labor, belonged to the Democratic party. In the chamber with the Progressive Senator from Wisconsin, Robert M. La Follette, for example, sat a Democratic Senator from that state, F. Ryan Duffy. In the Solid South, where conflicts were almost entirely confined to the Democratic party, Senators and Representatives of conservative bent were occasionally replaced by members more keenly alive to the agitations of tenants, croppers, field laborers, and industrial workers. From time to time blocs were formed in Congress to promote or oppose certain types of legislation, and bargains were driven between representatives from farming and industrial districts to create majorities for particular bills. But in these shifting configurations were few signs of permanence and unequivocal direction, and in the elections of 1938 labor and progressive forces suffered severe losses in many sections of the country.

Through the history of labor in town and country in the United States since the early years of the nineteenth century, its spokesmen and philosophers had vainly sought unity in some acceptable conception of economy. For a time near the middle of that century they thought they had found it in the homestead movement, which brought agrarians and even socialists into a common cause, and culminated in the enactment of the Homestead Act of 1862. By this process they hoped to guarantee holdings to farmers and permit industrial workers, suffering from low wages and unemployment, to escape from city tenements to free acres in the country. In fact, however, the Homestead law, viewed in the light of the buoyant hopes which inspired its original framers, proved to be almost a fraud upon farmers and industrial workers, as Fred A. Shannon and Paul W. Gates conclusively demonstrated on the basis of extended researches, the conclusions of which were published in The American Historical Review for July, 1936. Vast areas of land went to railway companies and speculators, sadly diminishing the areas of "free homesteads." And, whatever may have been the effect of free land on the lot of industrial workers in the East, it provided no "safety valve" for any huge number of them; nor did it overcome the evils of low wages and unemployment. This much was also established on the foundation of researches by Carter Goodrich and Sol Davison and incorporated in articles appearing in the Political Science Quarterly for June, 1935, and March, 1936. Allowing for divergencies of opinion on details of history, it was to be reported factually that the first immense effort to unite agrarians and industrial workers had attained an elusive success culminating in a default if not a complete failure.

Since the circumstances of 1850 could not be repeated in 1929 or 1938, what were the signs of a new unity? Psychological, as well as economic, differences were evident in thought and action. The memories, skills, and propensities of the handicrafts, which had kept artisans for countless centuries close to the life and ways of agriculture, had been diminished by the machine process. That was known to every one, but neither the philosophers of the labor movement nor the leaders in organization gave much thought to the agricultural end of the economic process. This was especially true of modern communistic thinkers. Marxism was essentially urban in origin and nature. Its heroes, Karl Marx and Friederich Engels, lived long in England and brought their ideological system to its perfection in a society highly industrialized, where agriculture had already lost its grip; and they both felt scorn for old-fashioned tillers of the land. Their disciples in the United States, likewise having little or no contact with the earth, conceived labor mainly in industrial terms, as they pored over Marxian texts in city tenements, apartments, and libraries. When they thought of labor in the country they thought principally of tenants, field hands, and casual workers — the weakest elements on the land; thus pity for the tillers of the soil exceeded interest in agriculture as the basis of all society.

On the other hand, workers in the earth, whether they were owners, tenants, or casual laborers, had, either from inheritance or experience, few affiliations with industrial workers, and were likewise mentally isolated. They often formed associations among themselves. They conducted milk strikes in the urban fashion. They blocked sheriffs trying to sell farms under foreclosure. They knew what it was to labor with bent backs and bruised hands. But the scheme of capitalism and its labor forms had unfamiliar, almost alien, features. Struggling along with a meager cash income or working for twenty-five or thirty dollars a month — and often less — farmers could not instinctively sympathize with industrial workers carrying on strikes to raise wages which seemed magnificent in comparison. Though with the cost of living in cities taken into account, urban wage-earners might still be about on the same economic level as the farmers, differences in ways of life naturally checked unanimity of understanding and hindered coöperation on any scale.

Even so, as conferences, agitations, pamphlets, and debates indicated, a growing consciousness of common interests marked the course of leadership among farmers and industrial workers. If the soil continued to erode and wash out to sea, if the standard of life on the land fell, if the buying

power of farmers sank, how would things fare with industrial workers engaged in producing goods and machinery for
use on farms ? The question was asked, again and again with
impressive repetition, by public officials, students of society,
and publicists. If, on the other hand, the wages of urban
workers declined, if unemployment for millions meant no
wages at all, where could labor on the land find markets for
its produce ? Farmers with the narrowest outlook could see,
when their attention was directed to the matter, how their
fate, to that extent at least, hung upon the state of industry,
on labor organization, on outcomes of collective bargaining.
As industry and agriculture contracted, as the web of a
mutual fate drew tighter around urban and rural workers,
thought followed, if haltingly and at a distance.

§

The renewal of agrarian unrest broke in upon the beati-
tudes while the golden glow was still shimmering. During
the dissolutions and detonations of the depression, its intrusion widened and its effects deepened; and then amid the
crashes in industry the agitations of urban labor were added
to the agitations of the agrarians. If not united by bonds of
immediate and palpable interest, labor in town and labor in
country were engaged in a common quest for a livelihood and
both disturbed the course of politics conducted in the traditional manner. Their quest for a living on modern levels also
brought discomfort to specific economic interests. For years
the possessors of great fortunes and the members of the
"middle class," so-called, had largely dominated, while they
directed, the transactions of politics and the currents of
thought; but they had often been in antagonism themselves, concealed or above board. Indeed no small part of the
political and social agitations culminating in party demonstrations had sprung from the struggle between "big business" and "little business," between "big men" and "little
men." In this contest the former had been denounced as

"economic royalists," and "trust-busting" campaigns had been waged against the masters of corporations, with agrarian and labor leaders often cheering on the side lines. Then as farm tenancy increased and industrial workers formed huge independent unions, fresh agitations jostled the classic politics of big business and little business and hinted at the desirability or necessity of unity against a common disturbance. With efforts to get American economy on a high production level baffled over a long stretch of years, these agitations assumed more serious aspects. Whether the struggle between the plutocracy and the middle class could be narrowly delimited and carried on indefinitely with the weapons and arguments evolved during the past fifty years became a question of social philosophy, historical interpretation, and time. If it could not be so delimited and continued endlessly without resolution, what forms were the future relations of the two groups to assume, especially in the presence of labor pressures in town and country? And in a showdown what position would labor take?

A mere analysis of the two groups from the standpoint of income yielded no categorical answer. The boundaries of neither were sharply defined, but one striking feature of the period consisted of efforts to disclose the composition and propensities of the respective interests. Though it is true that William J. Ghent and Thorstein Veblen had made such attempts earlier, their findings were only dimly remembered, if at all. So fresh inquiries were "timely." Lewis Corey's analyses, The Crisis of the Middle Class and The Decline of American Capitalism, for instance, applied the Marxian hypothesis and lent countenance to the idea that the country was headed toward a proletarian dictatorship. Alfred Bingham's statistical study in Insurgent America yielded contradictory evidence: the middle class, not that of the industrial workers, was increasing in relative proportions. Franklin Charles Palm's The Middle Classes Then and Now, while tending to confirm Bingham's conclusion, ended with no upshot in respect of policy or proximate tendency. Nor did

Ferdinand Lundberg's Sixty Families, an indictment of the plutocracy, throw much light on the problem of the coming relations between the middle class and the possessors of great wealth. Still, the fervid controversies aroused by such inquiries betrayed a public interest in the subject and the existence of a tension in popular psychology that might conceivably snap if no general economic relief came in sight.

The fact that the boundaries of the plutocracy and the middle class could not be precisely drawn did not mean that their centers of economic gravity and their general characteristics were beyond the grasp of understanding. Whether sixty or six hundred families constituted the dominant element in the plutocracy — a question much debated — was irrelevant. Researches substantiated the general proposition that less than one and one-half per cent of the nation's families at the top of the economic ladder in 1935–36 received a total income which equalled the combined income of forty-seven per cent of the families at the bottom. A high concentration of wealth was a reality, if not strictly measurable.

Nor could the exact number of families in the middle class be statistically determined. In composition it included lawyers, doctors, nurses, engineers, teachers, government employees running into the millions, army and navy officers, business men and women, small employers by the thousands, the police — local, state, and federal — members and officers of the national guard, editors, publishers, actors, artists, nearly all the professional entertainers, clerks, stenographers, and the white-collar careerists in general. According to an analysis by Donald S. Bridgman, published in The Yale Review in the autumn of 1938, the census returns of 1930 showed that "of all the men in gainful occupations 26% were in white-collar positions, professional, managerial, or clerical; 16% were in the skilled crafts; 15% were farm owners or tenants; 33% were semi-skilled or unskilled laborers, very largely in industry, and 10% were farm laborers. Of the gainfully employed women, 43% were in white-collar positions; 22% were household servants; 25% were semi-skilled and unskilled laborers in industry, and 8% were in agriculture, mainly as farm laborers. In the twenty years before 1930, the most rapidly increasing occupations had been in the white-collar group, principally those of the teacher, engineer, and clerk; the major decline had been in agriculture." If to the white-collar occupational groups were added the huge leisure class, women not gainfully employed, the total student body above the grade school level, and the millions of farming families enjoying a certain degree of prosperity, the combination doubtless outnumbered the strictly industrial workers, farm hands, and other blue, brown, and no-collar workers.

There was another consideration of prime importance. The division between members of the middle class and the handworkers in town and country was by no means completely economic. Indeed the income of skilled craftsmen was often far above that of many teachers, lawyers, or stenographers. Furthermore, in the struggle over the distribution of national income, thousands of white-collar employees flocked to trade unions, at least temporarily. In the characteristics of the middle class and its tendencies were psychological elements which did not perfectly correspond to the statistics of income or property; and these psychological features seemed to become more conspicuous as the depression deepened, the unionization of industrial workers advanced, and the unemployed showed some inclination to organize.

Hitherto native oracles had indignantly scoffed at the idea of "class" in the United States as "un-American." The absence of a fixed nobility at the top of the social ladder presumably made the term "middle class" inapplicable to a central grouping in the economic scene. A remarkable degree of mobility — from rail-splitter to President, from farm girl to candy queen — had given the signs of fluidity to American society that obscured the permanence of the gradations behind the screen of rising and falling particles or individuals. When, however, the organization of mass production workers by the millions got under way, evidences of a growing consciousness of identical interests appeared among elements of the middle class, tending to effect a closer solidarity within their own ranks.

An outward sign of this consciousness was to be seen in the changed usage of the term "middle class." For more than a century the British nobility and industrial workers had employed it freely as a phrase fairly exact or invidious. The French had long distinguished the bourgeoisie, as they called the middle class, from the remnants of the old aristocracy on the one side and the peasants and industrial workers on the other. In France the bourgeoisie had been regarded as "that portion of the community to which money is the primary condition and the primary instrument of life." Late in the nineteenth century Veblen had described pecuniary Americans as the "leisure class," dedicated to conspicuous waste and demonstrative thimblerig. Still later Sinclair Lewis had characterized its members as "Babbits," at first with a tone of ridicule and afterward with a positive affection, which helped to make them conscious of their position in society and then proud of their merits. The outburst of stories about life in "the raw" and the flood of proletarian novels accentuated the idea of opposites. In terms of sober scholarship, the publication of such frank treatises as Arthur Holcombe's The New Party Politics, in 1933, served as an index of tendency and a measure of advance toward unification. Fifty years earlier, Holcombe's book would have been as offensive to the American intelligentsia of the Hamilton Wright Mabie school as Marx's Communist Manifesto actually was to the Victorians of 1848. With time a psychological alteration had been effected.

This development in psychological imagery arrested the attention of Franklin Charles Palm who published his opinions on the subject in 1936. While declining to formulate any rigid definition of the term "middle class," he gave a certain approval to an older definition as the "not-so-rich and not-so-poor individuals between the proletariat-labor group and the wealthy capitalists and social aristocracy."

Yet Palm warned his readers against ascribing too much importance to the theory of income or the theory of derivation. He insisted that the members of the middle class must be thought of as possessing "subjective impulses." For instance, the true middle-class person "prizes education because he firmly believes that education is power and because he thinks it essential to democracy. He boasts of impartiality in politics and often observes a suicidal neutrality; but he is easily swayed by demagogues, for deep within him are biases and prejudices. He wishes to be known as a self-made man, capable, independent, self-reliant. . . . Profit has become the center of his thought and every action is in terms of that one purpose — to make money." In the past, money-making had been deemed an occupation on the way to a comfortable retirement; in the present, it had become a kind of continuous steeplechase, monopolizing energies, directing activities, and creating the values of culture.

While Lewis Corey, applying the Marxian theory, thought he saw the middle class diminished in numbers and force by the course of economy and furnishing some potential materials for the labor movement, other observers agreed with Palm in emphasizing the permanence of subjective consciousness and the growth of class awareness among the middle group. Unemployed industrial workers may have regarded themselves as covered by Franklin D. Roosevelt's phrase, "the forgotten man," but Herbert Hoover, pleading for a return of the Republicans to power, placed the forgotten man in the "great economic middle class." Noting the preponderance of cities in public affairs, Arthur Holcombe declared that "our new urbane politics will be middle-class politics" — less selfishly conceived than in previous times. Using income as his measurement, he claimed that, if one-half of the white-collar workers and one-fourth of the skilled workers stayed in the fold, the middle class "would surpass the proletariat in the adult population as a whole." Hewing to the median line of the Greek thinkers in antiquity, Hol-

combe concluded that "a State which is governed by the
middle class is not only safer than proletarian and bourgeois
class States, but the best State practically obtainable."
This was no surrender to the theory of middle-class defeat;
it was a declaration of faith and a call to liberal action.

Moreover, a study of small enterprises, conducted by the
Twentieth Century Fund and published in 1936, reported an
enormous area of economic activities still occupied by small
enterprisers, despite the concentration of wealth, demonstrating the tenacity with which members of the middle class
clung to their way of life and subjective purposes. Taking
up this line, Robert L. Duffus contended nearly ten years
after the crack of 1929 that there were no signs that the
middle class was being crushed. "We are still overwhelmingly a middle-class nation," he maintained. "It is harder
today to conceive of a solid proletarian lump in the United
States than it was a generation ago. We can, of course, conceive a proletariat — in fact President Roosevelt defined
one when he referred to the 'one third' which is ill-nourished,
ill-clothed, and ill-housed. This one-third would include the
worst-off portion of farm renters, share croppers, and laborers, the unskilled worker in every field, and no doubt many
clerical workers. The Negro, largely for historical reasons,
would contribute heavily to it. But it is doubtful if the
Mississippi field hand, the tenant farmer in Arkansas, the
migratory fruit picker in California, the 'mucker' on an
excavation job, the young clerk in Houston or New York,
the country school teacher whose rewards certainly place her
in the lowest third of the income groups, the textile operative, the Maine fisherman, have a sense of unity among
themselves merely because their incomes are low. The
routine of their lives, the geographical conditions which sur-
round them, and the local cultures in which they are embedded, forbid."

If the Wagner Labor Relations Act, the National Wages
and Hours Act, the heavy taxes on incomes in support of
social legislation, and the growth of organization among the

industrial workers all indicated that by some process labor in town and country was exerting pressure on members of the middle class, despite its disunity, the middle class was still motivated by the old subjective forces. "The upper-bracket owning classes can take care of themselves," exclaimed the editor of a small newspaper. "The unorganized middle class has no lobby, no special pleaders. It is largely the middle classes who pay the taxes, take out insurance, own their own homes, support the charities, and form the consuming public. When taxes go up they are the first to suffer. When prices go up their more inelastic incomes feel the hardest pinch. When monopolies expand their stores, shops, and little factories are gobbled up. And if inflation comes their savings are wiped out." Having put forward this thesis, by no means perfect in its economics, the same editor warned his readers that the middle class would not be trampled upon, that it would revolt before it succumbed to the tendency of things.

Other features in the drift of human relations fortified rather than uprooted the subjective interests that characterized the middle class. Although thousands from that general order affiliated with industrial unions, other thousands, forced downward in the wage scale or into unemployment, developed resentments against the more fortunate laborers and skilled workers. Even within the working class in the strict sense were cultural propensities over-reaching the limitations of the class line. The ability to buy furniture, radios, rugs, musical instruments, automobiles, and other signs of the middle standard on the installment plan, often with no payment down, awakened ambitions among rural and urban workers, which countered the acceptance of proletarian ways.

Still more significant, in this relation, was the curtailment of child labor state by state as the depression dragged on, the raising of the working age by legislation, and the enlargement of the school population. Boys and girls in the high schools were not taught merely the crafts of their parents, if any; they studied languages, literature, science, and the other branches of learning once deemed the peculiar possession of the middle and upper classes. The chances of satisfying the tastes thus awakened might be relatively declining; the subjective valuations were not thereby eradicated. Girls, hoping to leap the economic gulf by marriage, asserted the appropriate airs and manners. Wives of industrial workers, though often standing stanchly by their husbands in economic conflicts, naturally felt the pull of the middle-class ambitions exerted by their children.

Amusements, no less than education and refinements, flowed in the middle-class direction, especially the most popular: radio entertainments and the moving pictures. The sales "talks" that accompanied music, the news, jokes, and crooning over the radio stimulated wants not to be satisfied by the meager earnings of the ordinary worker. By the hour and day, wives listened to appeals to vanities and aspirations beyond the reach of the low wage level.

In endless profusion, the moving pictures portrayed the lives of the rich, the luxurious, the idle — their palaces, yachts, sports, manners, and morals. The delineation of plain labor on the screen offered no glamourous escape from the humdrum and appeared seldom in the repertoires of the blocked picture houses, seeking the patronage of the workers. To be sure, the portrayal of crime and racketeering did suggest outlets for sons and daughters of the proletariat into the world of high living, and moving-picture producers took advantage of the "appeal" — an appeal scarcely diminished by the hackneyed retribution that now and then sicklied over the primordial drive of the main argument. But as against the steady and remorseless flicker of middle-class valuations in script, costumes, and actions, the representation of crimes of crude passion seemed merely collateral or incidental. While millions might belong to industrial unions, the pressure of education and amusement worked against belief in the nobility of plain labor — against reliance upon the organization of labor as more than a negotiating convenience — and in favor of other valuations essentially middle class in origin and development.

For the fortification of their interests, deliberately or incidentally, members of the middle class were closely knit in innumerable organizations peculiarly their own : chambers of commerce, local, state, and national women's clubs, the Sons and Daughters of the American Revolution and other patriotic societies, trade associations, fraternal orders, teachers', lawyers', and doctors' associations, and kindred groups, with branches in every community and head offices in great cities. Whenever by direct action or through political pressure, industrial workers achieved some gain irritating to the middle class or rejected the middle-class idea of American values, reverberations followed in the form of resolutions, protests, and counter-measures. Despite the best occasional efforts to be "objective" in reporting, the metropolitan press by headline, position, selection, and emphasis in news presentation, was primarily middle class in attitudes.

That conspicuous organization in the domain of politics and police, the American Legion, together with its feminine auxiliaries, was likewise primarily middle class in official direction, notwithstanding the number of industrial workers among its members and among the veterans as a whole. Although it early berated war profiteers and plutocrats, the Legion grew more circumspect in statements, especially after securing the outright payment of the bonus in 1936; and its weight was, on the whole, against the independent organization of industrial workers, against sit-down strikes, and against all similar manifestations of labor power. While it sometimes frowned upon members who wore soldiers' uniforms in making anti-labor demonstrations, its code of public and private morals was middle class in materiality.

With mechanical regularity until 1938 the National Association of Manufacturers, at its annual conventions, repeated stereotyped doctrines. The manufacturers' economic science long consisted of formulas taken from the body of true faith evolved by classical or middle-class economics.

None of its committees investigated the actions of employers in hiring industrial spies, planting provocative agents in the midst of trade unions, setting working men against one another, importing thugs and ex-criminals as strike breakers. Not unnaturally, it was more concerned with racketeers in the labor movement, with making labor organizations responsible before the law, with preventing the growth of powerful bargaining organizations among industrial workers.

"The closed shop," ran its manifesto in 1937, "limits and prevents the free and full exercise by both employees and employers of their bargaining rights. . . . The practical problems of employment relations — the handling of complaints and grievances, and questions of wages, hours, and working conditions — can best be met by management dealing with its own employees in the light of the local plant and community conditions." Corporations might be national in scope and power; labor relations must be controlled by local management. In other words, at the end of eight years of depression, organized manufacturing in the United States had little more affection for independent trade unionism or its tactics than had the National Socialistic dictatorship in Germany. It was lack of power rather than of will that prevented it from laying down the national law on the subject.

But at its convention of 1938 the National Association of Manufacturers modified its former program in many respects. The faction that demanded forthright denunciations and assertions of doctrine in the historic style was overborne by the more liberal wing. The customary attacks on the New Deal were omitted, the usual criticisms of recent federal legislation were toned down, and an olive branch was offered to organized labor. In a program adopted without dissent, the Association called for a "united effort of industry, commerce, agriculture, and labor in coöperation with the Government." Instead of condemning the Labor Relations Act wholesale, it recognized that "employees who

wish to bargain collectively are entitled to do so, in whatever form they determine, through their own freely chosen
representatives and without intimidation or restraint from
any source." Through many lines of the program gleamed
the old animus of intransigence, but it was significant that
the Association felt it necessary in deference to facts and
opinions to move a little "leftward" toward the center of
the line.

That section of the middle class represented by little
business men and women was, on the whole, as rigid in its
hostility to industrial or any other kind of unionism as the
business men of larger affairs in the Manufacturers' Association. Perhaps more so. When the National Recovery
Administration was launched in 1933, little business men
did, it is true, coöperate with government agents in the
drafting and enforcement of fair practices codes. They
were as eager as their larger brethren to take advantage of
the opportunity to raise prices by collective action. In the
process they also accepted the collective bargaining Section
of the Recovery Act but that Section, loosely drawn, did not
outlaw the company or shop unions organized under the
auspices of the employers. Nor, in enforcement, did it compel employers to deal with independent unions wherever
they appeared. After the dissolution of the Recovery Administration under judicial decree, little business men in general
joined their colleagues in welcoming a return to the "imperfect competition" that had prevailed before the advent of
the experiment in collective recovery. A resurgence of
economic activity the following year brought a temporary
release of the tension.

After the recession of 1937 set in, little business men and
women were on pins and needles again, all the more on account of the rapid advance of industrial unionism and its
strike tactics in many centers. At a national conference
called by the Department of Commerce early the next year,
they freely expressed their sentiments and resentments in
resolutions which were later modified by their executive

committee for presentation to President Roosevelt. In the original resolutions they declared that "unwarranted and malicious attacks on business by administration representatives should be permanently stopped," and that "all forms of federal wage and hour regulation and legislation" should be resisted. Coming directly to the point of labor organization, the little conference demanded nothing less than a total repeal of the Wagner Labor Relations Act, and an investigation of the National Labor Relations Board, then under fire as unduly sympathetic to labor. It called for more curbs on monopolies and on government enterprises, and it went even beyond big business in demanding a total repeal of the undistributed profits tax and a curtailment of public expenditures. Having urged the Government to stay out of the labor relations field, the conference called on it to create an agency for the purpose of making loans "where financial institutions failed to function," that is, where little men and women failed to get credits at the banks. These expressions of middle-class valuations seemed illuminating for the hour and the tendencies.

Into the effervescence of subjective valuations were thrust the "lessons" of Italy and Germany. On the pretext of a communist danger, Mussolini had completely liquidated all independent trade unions and had penalized all independent labor politics. At the same time he had, beyond doubt, laid restraints on small private business and showed a special tenderness for great corporations. Would such "regimentation" be regarded in the United States as a small price to pay for the suppression or execution of labor leaders and the liquidation of "trade union domination"?

Still more instructive had been the "lesson" from industrialized Germany. There also the communist danger had been highly capitalized by Hitler and his party. Nevertheless it was obvious that, while putting down the communists with a strong hand, Hitler had been equally stringent in abolishing independent trade unions, in confiscating their funds, and in imprisoning or shooting labor leaders. The trade-union movement in Germany had been far stronger than in Italy. It embraced a larger proportion of the industrial and casual workers. It was powerfully organized and had large sums of money in its central and local treasuries. Yet independent unionism had been completely destroyed by the police and by the National Socialist storm troops, with only a little more shedding of blood than had accompanied some of the major strikes in the United States. Had this object lesson not been associated with the cruel treatment of Jews in Germany, it would doubtless have been more impressive as indicating the ultima ratio.

The simplicity of the formula was startling: Brand all labor unions, especially of the industrial type, as communist and, while making a social war on communists, suppress all labor organizations. It had been done. It could be done. Although such suggestions were probably depressing to tender minds in the middle class, the employment of spies and provocative agents by great corporations, the speed with which the business forces of any industrial center could be mobilized against "labor agitators," and the tenacity of the vigilante and Ku Klux tradition indicated the existence of volcanic forces beneath the white surface of law and order and the smooth flow of "democratic processes." "If Fascism ever menaces America," wrote an editor, "it will be because we have allowed the big pressure groups of society to squeeze the middle classes into revolt."

That the editor's middle class and the Lords of Creation, with whose fortunes, instincts, and methods it was so intimately affiliated, were possessed by no spirit of genial tolerance in the presence of labor agitations, urban or rural, became manifest in endless declarations and actions. In his volume, You Can't Do That, George Seldes gave a multitude of illustrations well authenticated, and added, for the benefit of those who cared to know more, a list of books, pamphlets, and documents occupying more than forty pages of fine print. Stark and staring before such intelligence as the nation commanded were the pages of testimony presented by informed witnesses to the Senate committee on education and labor, headed by Robert M. La Follette, instructed to investigate "violations of the rights of free speech and assembly and undue interference with the right of labor to organize and bargain collectively."

Indelible in the record were reports of third-degree tortures employed by police in violation of the law; arrests on trumped-up charges and no charges; police beatings in all parts of the country ending often in deaths that went unavenged; parties engaged in tarring and feathering economic dissidents; lynchings in North and South; the expulsion of critical professors and teachers; the Chicago "memorial day incident" at the Republic Steel Works; the use of spies, finks, gas, and bombs by reputable employers of labor; espionage and murder in the Harlan, Kentucky, mining regions; Mayor Hague's "little dictatorship" in Jersey City; the insistence of the Daughters of the American Revolution, members of the American Legion, the Liberty League, the National Civic Federation, chambers of commerce, shipping interests, Crusaders, Sentinels, Vigilantes, Paul Reveres, and other associations wearing the mantle of patriotism, on branding as dangerous citizens well-known persons of independent minds, ranging from Nicholas Murray Butler to Jane Addams, from Eleanor Roosevelt to William Allen White — all denoting violent reactions to labor agitations, to the advocacy of peace, or to the defense of the civil liberties offered in constitutional guaranties — advocacy or defense even when it expressed the most timid liberalism. What anything really challenging would produce could be easily imagined, by the imaginative.

The spirit of the times which prevailed in the military establishment of the United States Government, at least from 1928 to 1932, was given official form in its Army Training Manual No. 2000-25, issued for the instruction of officers and soldiers. Not content with its own function, the War Department entered the domain of civic education and among other things gave its verdict on democracy, for which presumably

soldiers had fought and died, and in the name of which, perhaps, a quarantine war was in preparation. In a single
paragraph it described democracy for the benefit of its men
in training: "Democracy: A government of the masses.
Authority derived through mass meeting or any other form
of 'direct' expression. Results in mobocracy. Attitude
toward property is communistic — negating property rights.
Attitude toward law is that the will of the majority shall
regulate, whether it be based upon deliberation or governed
by passion, prejudice, and impulse, without restraint or
regard to consequences. Results in demagogism, license,
agitation, discontent, anarchy." For five years this manual
of "instruction" was used officially by the War Department
— until protests from outraged citizens and members of
Congress led to its withdrawal. After that action a request
for a copy brought a reply that the Department had no copy
available; a three-hour search in the Congressional Library
unearthed none; everywhere in official circles, silence on the
subject reigned, when inquiries were made. Was the spirit
that animated military opinion on democracy dead?

Two years after the Manual was formally withdrawn,
doubts on that subject were allayed by Harry H. Woodring,
Assistant Secretary of War under Franklin D. Roosevelt.
In the Liberty Magazine, of January 6, 1934, Mr. Woodring
published an article on the Army, opening with the words:
"People who believe that the United States Army is not
ready and able to take charge of this nation in an emergency
simply do not know the facts. Our Army happens to be the
only branch of the Government which is *already organized
and available not only to defend our territory, but also to cope
with social and economic problems in an emergency*. [Mr.
Woodring's italics.] It is our secret insurance against chaos.
It is our 'ace in the hole' for peace as well as war." In this
vein he continued, to prove the point. The execution of the
Army's plans for industrial mobilization, he said, will "*accomplish in a large measure the purpose of those who have advocated
a 'universal draft' of property, money, and civilian labor*"

[Mr. Woodring's italics]. He went on: "It is my opinion that the Army *should* take over immediately some of the activities which are now being handled by some of the new executive agencies. Whether or not it is true, as many hold, that the C.C.C. camps are the forerunners of the great civilian labor armies of the future, I believe that this activity should be expanded and put under the control of the Army. . . . If the Army were so directed, it could organize the veterans of the world war, the C.C.C. men, and through them the administration of the emergency relief, into a system of economic storm troops that could support the Government's efforts to smash the depression. If the Army is not so directed, it will, as always, stand by and await orders."

"Let's speak frankly!" Mr. Woodring declared in large italic type; "*If this country should be threatened with foreign war, economic chaos, or social revolution, the Army has the training, the experience, the organization, and the men to support the Government and direct the country in the national interest.*"

Up until 1934 both law and innocence had supposed that it was the duty of the Army, when officially ordered, to wage foreign war or suppress domestic insurrection. They had not supposed that its obligation included a responsibility in case of "economic chaos" to "direct the country in the national interest." Evidently the War Department, under the New Deal, had made progress — of some kind — in a direction straight as a bullet's course.

When a deluge of telegrams and letters deprecating Mr. Woodring's manifesto in the Liberty magazine flowed into the White House, accompanied by demands for a removal or resignation, President Roosevelt called the author on the carpet. Shortly after the conference, Mr. Woodring gave out a statement to the effect that his words did not mean what they meant to anybody acquainted with the English language. The President did not ask him to retire. He did not resign. The oblivion common to a people that lived on the day's sensations passed over the episode. On the death

of Secretary Dern, President Roosevelt made Assistant
Secretary Woodring head of the War Department.

Against all such tendencies, protests were made continuously in press, pamphlets, books, meetings, and the courts of
law. The American Civil Liberties Union, directed by Roger
Baldwin and a group of determined colleagues, innumerable
associations concerned with the preservation of rights guaranteed by the Constitution of the United States and the
constitutions of the several states, innumerable individuals,
and members of Congress kept close watch on activities,
organizations, and officials connected with "red baiting," the
suppression of legal rights, and propaganda intended to
prepare the way for the day prophesied by Harry H. Woodring, President Roosevelt's Secretary of War.

Another sign of determined resistance to the arbitrary
spirit was the Southern Conference for Human Welfare held
at Birmingham, Alabama, in November, 1938, representing
agriculture, industry, labor, and social work. Every form of
effort designed to raise the standard of living in that region
and to assert the human values of society was discussed with
freedom and comprehensively. Tenant farmers, representatives of labor defense organizations, Negroes from various divisions of economy, employers, and specialists in housing,
relief, and taxation presented their cases without let or
hindrance. And at the close, provisions were made for a
permanent pooling of interests and for moving in a solid
phalanx upon the menaces to liberty and welfare everywhere
in the South.

If a crisis was to come, victory for tyranny would not be
easy or be won in a default. Many lawyers, including Frank
Walsh, Morris Ernst, and Arthur Garfield Hays, offered
their services to defend men and women in celebrated cases
involving freedom of press and speech; and even the
American Bar Association, spurred on perhaps by the formation of an independent legal society, the Lawyers' Guild,
announced in 1938 that it would give special attention to
civil liberty. From term to term the Supreme Court of the

United States handed down ringing decisions sustaining civil liberties, North, South, East, and West, in opinions worthy of a place beside the memorable arguments of Mansfield, Burke, Erskine, and Brougham, which featured the slow and toilsome advance of human rights in times past. It might so turn out that those who had been most severe in criticizing that tribunal's judgments in other causes would find it the last refuge against sheer force — if Secretary Woodring's "economic chaos" and "emergency" came, and dust gathered in the silent chamber of the United States Senate.

§

Given the numerical supremacy of the middle class, as the term was casually defined, over urban workers and rural laborers, given its subjective valuations and the lessons of Italy and Germany, limitations on the power of industrial unionism were apparent to all informed observers in the labor movement and outside. The tensibility of those circumscriptions could not be discovered by any method of scientific inquiry at hand. Efforts to test them by practice, if pushed too far, might produce the explosion faintly suggested by "A plague on both your houses." Anything like an exact prognosis was, therefore, out of the question. The amount of elasticity or good-will on both sides remained indeterminate if not indeterminable in both economics and politics. That astute, persistent, and viable statesmanship in the two domains might mitigate conflicts and keep them within the confines of debate and adjustment, apart from sporadic disorders, was probable. As Edmund Burke had said in the eighteenth century, greater changes may be effected gradually over a long period of time than by even the violence of revolution. But how much of this statesmanship was available?

Only one feature of the situation seemed fairly plain. If the prevailing system of economy could be kept running at a certain tempo, a major crisis could be avoided for the time;

that is, if production could be maintained on a level of output that would furnish employment for a large part of the industrial workers, provide revenues for supporting the unemployed on some scale of existence, and sustain the main body of the middle class, a disruptive tension could be indefinitely postponed. The size of the social and State apparatus at the command of the middle class seemed to demonstrate that proposition.

Could production be held on the requisite level and for how long? No one could settle that question. Only one aspect of the problem presented deterministic marks. For three hundred years the high productivity of American economy had been accompanied by the steady exhaustion of land and other natural resources either irreplaceable or replaceable at a high cost. A continuation of that process for another fifty or hundred years, as the engineers of a Mississippi Valley survey had reported, would lead to a wholesale impoverishment of the resources on which American economy had thrived. Only costly collective action coupled with incalculable inventive genius could prevent that impasse in the years immediately ahead. Was the collective action possible, the genius available? Not even the highest competence in the middle class could answer that question.

If domestic tension grew perilous and the productive economy slowed down too far, the explosion into a foreign war was always possible. There had been international frictions ever since the establishment of national States in Europe at the end of the middle ages. Such frictions had been somewhat mitigated in the nineteenth century while the resources of virgin continents were being exploited to feed Europe's pullulating millions, but with the closing of such economic frontiers everywhere the tensions seemed to be increasing. At all events, the statesmen of the leading powers of the world were lecturing and threatening one another, either in earnest or "for domestic consumption." "International" incidents were matters of almost daily occurrence.

War and costly preparations for war were at command. War would speed up industrial economy and once more provide employment. It would enable the Federal Government to put through its "mobilization bill," impose the discipline of martial law upon all recalcitrant persons, and, by "constitutional methods," suppress strikes and labor disturbances as effectively as Hitler or Mussolini had done under a different ideology. But what would a war do to American civilization as historically understood, even if victoriously waged? Or if it ended in defeat for the United States — a possibility, given the shifts and clashes among the great powers — what then? Neither event could be precisely prophesied, but both questions were vibrating in the minds of all Americans who employed intelligence in exploring the relations of urban and rural labor to grand policy.

In terms of civilization, the fortunes, the future, of America, what then did the activities, agitations, and organization of labor in town and country actually mean? To that quandary many solutions, more or less relevant, were proposed. Anthropologists and measurers of intelligence responded that a large proportion of Americans consisted of "morons" and little or nothing could be done about that "fact." In a similar vein practitioners replied that, on the whole, tenants, croppers, and field laborers were "lazy and shiftless"; that they had received their "just deserts"; that the plight of agriculture as mirrored in the report of the President's Committee was simply the outcome of human nature operating on the land; and that restless industrial workers possessing no craft or special skill got all or more than they deserved in the natural, that is, the current, run of things. A multitude of "misfits" had always existed in industry and agriculture and always would. On the basis of such interpretations, the upper third or fourth, or whatever it was, in industry and agriculture could and should proceed as in the past, relying upon the agencies of government for the protection of the fortunate position accorded to them by their merits. If not completely reassuring, this was comforting to the beneficiaries in the upper ranges.

Yet when it was conceded that the situation was due to the moronic, shiftless, and casual nature of labor in town and country, other quandaries remained. Were the white misfits to be deprived of the vote, as Negroes had been in large areas of the country? A strong movement in this direction took form in the North, with a nervous woman as its instigator. If not, how could the upper third or fourth, or whatever its size was, be indefinitely protected against the inroads of politicians and "demagogues" upon their apparently impregnable position? If not, how could prolonged agitation of the business be avoided? Assuming that the "misfit" men and women could be deprived of the suffrage extended to them during the early fevers of democracy in the United States or that the use of the ballot could be rather effectively nullified by a temporary or prolonged use of military power, what of the democratic ideals to which fervent appeals were made, for diplomatic and other purposes, against dictatorships in Europe and the Orient? If these vaunted ideals could be rendered harmless, or supplanted by other devices, there remained a final enigma not to be solved in terms of "just deserts for morons": Is mankind a maker or a victim of history?

§

Underneath the course of the great argument and the emotions that attended it was the drift of economic activities and physical facts upon which even the upper ranges depended for their rewards and security — against which the rhetoric of satisfaction or criticism could avail little. These facts were recorded in the reports of corporations and business concerns — industries and railways — and in the findings of engineers who surveyed the state and utilization of natural resources. Instead of the swift expansion in construction and capital goods industries, which had long furnished the élan of advancing capitalism, had come a

definite contraction; in that sense, the real capital of the
United States was declining, not rising. The mileage of
railways was shrinking; no huge demand for steel rails and
locomotives in the old style was anywhere in sight. Nor did
the "backward places" of the earth — Latin America, the
Orient, and Africa — to which imperialism had looked for
such expansion, present the familiar aspects of the nineteenth
century. Unemployment on a large scale continued persistently, with no substantial relief in sight. As capitalism
contracted, the depletion of crude natural resources upon
which industries had flourished and still depended went on,
if abated somewhat by the depression.

Both tenancy and freehold agriculture as historically practiced had led and were still leading to a depletion of vast
regions, the erosion of the soil, the destruction of fertility,
and the impoverishment of the land. If nothing effective
could be done in respect of rising tenancy, then physical
exhaustion would persist, perhaps at an accelerating speed.
If the standard of life on the land, the buying power of
farmers, sank, what of the industry, commerce, and professions upon which hung the fate of the upper ranges in cities
and towns, all the more now that the promises of imperialism
had been exploded by history as actuality?

CHAPTER XII

Sources and Forces of Entertainment

HEAVILY as the pall of the depression rested upon the country — perhaps partly on account of it — entertainment assumed functions of increasing significance for the tendencies of culture. Springing from biological and psychological characteristics common to humanity in all times, it perdured in this time and was adjusted to alterations in the economic conditions in which politics, business, and labor operated, by which they were nourished. Originally, and still in some measure, what Veblen called "a non-mechanical factor of culture," entertainment, was imbedded in the social heritage acquired from the pre-machine age. Primal in emotional sources, apparently as necessary to life as labor itself, entertainment was among the powerful forces that held society together, afforded diversion in the midst of its difficulties and burdens, and yet expressed its tensions and values too, contributing withal to the shaping of its evolution in gross and detail. When commercialized, entertainment could cut two ways: it could thrive like business enterprise on the social heritage; and, like business enterprise with which it

became increasingly associated, it could work disintegrations in the social heritage. Its twofold nature was not
overlooked in the drift of events.

§

Throughout the ages of civilization the amusements, spectacles, and ceremonies of the people had borne an intimate
relation to politics, economy, poverty, riches, labor, leisure,
the arts, tools, and intelligence of mankind. Among primitive
and rural peoples they were, in origins at least, more or less
spontaneous expressions of usages, ecstasies, and motor propensities connected with life and labor processes, such as
planting, sowing, harvesting, and with religious interpretations and rituals. Among such peoples diversions were communal, non-pecuniary, little affected if at all by importations,
and not devised for export or sale abroad. Processions in
propitiation of harvest gods and goddesses, for example, were
connected with economic activities indispensable to life, but
they were not designed to propitiate the god of the box office
or to serve the purposes of the State.

After the State had risen upon the foundations of communal life, its masters seized upon and used, for their purposes, amusements, spectacles, and entertainments, employing and adding to ancient rituals. State diversions were
connected with both domestic and outward relations. In
Sparta, for example, wrestling and horse racing served a
double purpose: they kept the ruling class and its animals
physically fit to maintain supremacy over helots and slaves
at home and to wage war abroad. In the days of Spartan
power, young people of the ruling families, boys and girls
alike, took part in athletic displays and pageants and the
laurel wreath was deemed a sufficient reward for demonstrations of strength and endurance. When a king's daughter,
Cynisca, who kept racing horses, won a victory at a spectacle, she received no purse of gold; the feat and the acclaim
were sufficient in themselves. Spartan youths were trained

in legends and music and dancing, intrinsically delightful. And yet, like such gymnastics as ball playing, dancing was directed toward the cultivation of martial vigor.

Likewise in the development of the Roman State from kingdom through the republic into empire, the character of amusements and entertainments followed the course of its civilization, until it reached a climax in the deadly gladiatorial contests. As Rome expanded, city mobs were spurred to militaristic hysteria by pageants of conquerors coming home with kings and queens chained to their chariots. Whether really essential to a militaristic polity or not, savage spectacles certainly accompanied the rise and flowering of that system. Generally associated with the fighting passion was sex sadism and this was fed by the tossing of Christian maidens to hungry lions in the circus.

Originating, it seems, in the ancient Etruscan custom of sacrificing slaves and prisoners on the tombs of great warriors, the gladiatorial spectacle became a favorite device of emperors, employed to illustrate their prowess and satisfy the growing mania of multitudes inured to cruel sights and sounds. Titus, it was said, ordered a continuous combat extending over one hundred days, and Trajan celebrated a triumph by the exhibition of ten thousand gladiators. The victims thrown into the arena were taken from prisoners of war, criminals, and slaves — men and women alike being driven into death grapples for the amusement of cheering and jeering throngs. Black lusts were drained to the dregs when human beings and wild beasts were pitted against each other for the pleasure of the Roman proletariat and the lords and ladies of the upper classes. A Marcus Aurelius might turn away from such spectacles to write state papers or to meditate upon the nature and sorrows of mankind, but the crowds that applauded and sustained the empire gloated over such displays of violence and judged successive rulers by the number and magnitude of the brutal shows which they staged for "the people." Such were the diversions of despotism at home while imperialistic wars were waged on the frontier — until the twin monstrosities perished and owls cried from out the palace of the Caesars.

Also intimately associated with the State were the amusements, spectacles, and entertainments of Japan under the Tokugawa shogunate. Athletic exercises for men and women, designed to keep bodies lithe for military purposes continued; but the supreme design of the Tokugawas was to subdue belligerent feudal lords to the discipline of the State and hold Japan insulated from conflicts with the outside world. To this polity diversions were subordinated, even when ancient rituals were retained or modified. The State desired concord at home and refrained from aggression abroad. Hence the fighting class had to be entertained in the interests of peace. Gladiatorial contests would have been out of line. It was rhapsodies over cherry blossoms and plum trees, over moon and mushroom, over fans and the holy mountain, Fujiyama, that were lifted to the height of cults. The ritual of the tea ceremony in an esthetic setting, made still more exquisite by poems, music, and specific apparel, was devised to soothe the nerves of feudal lords; while pilgrimages to view scenes of beauty and holy places supplied pleasure for peasants, serfs, and artisans. For the ends of State, under Tokugawa management, diversions took on pacific forms and lusty fighting men were restrained by the bonds of ceremony and esthetics. Though these bonds quickly gave way after the imperialist powers of the West blew open the gates of Japan and the Japanese State in its turn embarked on conquest, the diversions themselves did not immediately disappear. The tea ceremony became more and more the prerogative of women, but all the ceremonies lingered to give a "quaint" flavor to a civilization grown imperialist in ambition and taste.

If to Americans with little interest in history the records of entertainment in the past and of current practices inherited from distant times and countries seemed mere musty documents in the days of the golden glow, the development of fascism and communism and the rise in western civilization of the Nazi cult of "Blood" gave to the unhistoric-minded immediate and astounding examples of the relations which could exist between the State and diversions. Playing upon the instincts of wanton cruelty, Hitler turned his men loose on the Jews in a manner reminiscent of Roman holidays when Christians were the victims, without organizing this operation into a State pageant. He laid his heavy hands on every form of amusement. Mussolini and Stalin did the same. Giant parades and rituals, the tramp, tramp, tramp of men and women drilled in military manners, with modern lighting casting its exotic appeal, furnished spectacles that might have made a Claudius or a Nero green with envy. The theater, the film, athletics, and even ancient folkways were bent and twisted and subdued to the designs of a military State — a dictatorship — whatever avowed social and economic ends were associated with it. Down to the kindergarten in Germany and Italy were forced the militaristic rituals of amusement. Almost as soon as they could toddle, little boys were supplied with implements of war and their supple limbs and minds were trained to the configurations of war games. Huge masses of people, young and old, were goaded along the path to political and military aggression by the very diversions arranged for them, with the privilege of dying for the dictator as the crown and perfection of hysterical entertainment.

§

In the United States, with its democratic traditions and practices, with the historic subordination of the military arm of the Government to civilian leadership, with the State regarded as an instrument not an end, with the prevalence of pecuniary over political considerations, amusements, spectacles, and entertainments presented aspects appropriate to the milieu and the trend of affairs. Here too were survivals of diversions associated with ancient folkways, kept alive by aborigines, by white natives in farming regions, and by immigrants from rural communities abroad. But in the main, since the rise of cities, other forms of diversion had occupied the principal interest — that is, commercialized amusements, whatever their sources, substance, and appearances. Artificial entertainment, shaped with reference to the financial returns of managers and participants, occupied an ever-larger area of diversion, ranging from prize fights, with huge receipts for directors and fighters, to the gigantic spectacles manufactured by the moving-picture industry. Being essentially pecuniary in motive and thus depending directly upon the state of economy — prosperity or depression — the fortunes of commercial entertainment varied with the fortunes of the middle class, industrial workers, and farmers who supplied box office receipts. For the moment, at all events, the people of the United States showed few signs of devotion to drill-sergeant pleasures. Although standardized products spread, the regionalisms and polyglot population of the country still afforded variations. In the Far West, Indians could indulge in their ceremonies and go so far as to ridicule the white man's tin cans, archaeologists, and social workers. Throughout the nation Jews, Irish, Yankees, Italians, and Negroes could figure in the moving pictures, have theaters of their own, and be amused by themselves and one another. The subjection of them all to a Nordic, Roman, or Muscovite diagram would have been a difficult undertaking, notwithstanding susceptibilities to nostrums during the economic distress.

For a long time, the democratic manners, the comparative freedom, and the relative ease of life in the United States had found expression in corresponding diversions — often called trivial and vulgar by European commentators on American civilization. Though Europeans also had prize fights and music halls, critics of America were inclined to remember only the amusements provided for the upper classes at home, such as fox hunting and cricket, royal garden parties and pageants, and coronation shows. In the United States "everybody" took part in shows of some kind, if only in rollicking laughter over representations of human follies.

Americans were fond of parades, but they did not want parades all the time. They displayed marked propensities for violence in widely scattered, though numerous, cases, but they were neither attuned to the mass shock of the totalitarian violence, deliberately organized and buttressed by fear, nor to the inelastic class distinctions of England and continental countries.

More than once in their history Americans had been subdued to the imperialistic or militaristic psychosis, but they had always displayed resilient powers of release. A nation that had been almost one hundred per cent for war in 1917 could, twenty years later, cast a majority vote in a popular poll for the proposition that it had been a big mistake. When veterans of the world war held annual reunions, they listened, more or less dutifully, to speeches on preparedness and military virtues; but they were more interested in pranks than in anything else. After a week of reunion, they would disband amiably and ride home with their wives in their "old busses" to take up again their customary entertainments — poker playing, bridge, moving-picture shows, baseball games, back slapping, and joke cracking in barrooms and clubs. All this was in keeping with the physical ease corresponding to democratic liberties — a safety valve for distempers and, what is more, a certain pledge against the wholesale fanaticism required for the totalitarian State. If argument could not overcome a Caesar nourishing personal ambitions, people who preferred laughing at slap-stick comedies on the screen to goose-stepping for anybody or anything might conceivably be unable to take a dictator seriously enough to underwrite his schemes.

The old democratic practice of applauding, hissing, and talking back, so foreign to life in Power States, helped to keep alive the looseness and diversity of amusements that in turn nourished democratic sentiments. Since he was not watched by the police, a radio owner could simply turn off the boresome propagandist, crooner, story teller, politician, or announcer, without the risk of a police summons to answer for his conduct. When the people did not like an advertised moving picture they could stay at home or walk out of the theater. Though much given to bathos themselves upon occasion, they also had a flair for the absurd and were restless under any harping on one string. If they approved a film, they sent in "fan" letters voluntarily. If they disapproved, they could and often did deluge producers with protests, criticisms, and denunciations, write letters to the newspapers, and form organizations to strengthen their opposition. And the efforts of commercialized entertainers to catch pennies from every direction kept them alert to the endless turbulence of dissidence.

"To give the people what they want" was to swell box-office receipts; and evidently the people wanted, not one pattern of life, but many. Buying their pleasures in an open market, crowded with competitive offerings, they insisted on exercising the powers of choice vouchsafed to them by their impulses and the opportunities before them. Whether amid this swirling, buzzing diversity, definite and irreversible tendencies were leading toward social forms, higher or lower, or fundamentally different from prevailing customs, was a subject of unwearied speculation, culminating in no settled conclusions.

Nevertheless the very clarity with which the relation of the State to entertainment was brought out in imported films and plays, coupled perhaps with the contraction of American economy and the attendant agitations, excited a finer sensitiveness to the relations between so-called diversions on the one side and government and society on the other. The problem, well known to the historians of morals, came under wider discussion, both popular and philosophical; for even the most casual seeker after release in the United States was subjected to the impacts of scenes depicting armies, red, green, brown, blue, or black, with flags waving and bands leading them on the march. The goose-step of the mind might be vague and shadowy. The pictured goose-step on pavements and roads was visible and definitive.

If such was the upshot of entertainment dominated by a totalitarian State, where was the increasing commercialization of entertainment in the United States headed and what would be its forms and influences in the proximate future? So far the offerings were certainly varied. People were still free to choose and to buy. If the commercial entertainers were giving them "what they wanted," what did the purchases mean in terms of social tendencies? In searching for the lowest common denominators effective at the box offices, would entertainers more and more arouse "the beast that is within us," play upon fears and passions, resort to war propaganda, and portray women in approving attitudes? Or would they, by visual education, offer the people knowledge respecting the good life, the values of creative labor, and the issues of American economy, thus forwarding the quest for the maintenance at least of such civilization as had been developed out of ideals and practices? Since entertainment was now highly commercialized and concentrated, would it follow the practices of centralization so common in capitalist economy and induce regimentation under private auspices? Obviously such questions were far more fundamental than the thought of ordinary dramatic and theatrical criticism.

§

Cultural interests were given new forms of expression by the general introduction, in 1928, of the talking picture which, by rapid inroads upon the industry, soon captured the business. Talking-picture entertainers had to supplement acting by speech and the necessity of employing speech involved the use of words, that is, ideas of some kind. As a result the whole structure of the motion-picture play could be and indeed had to be reorganized. For the vast spectacles of the silent picture, costly to film, could be substituted in the talking pictures the simpler and more compact drama of life in home, club, resort, field, or office, in which mere conversations, orders, and repartee helped to carry the story.

Gesture and facial play had been the reliances of the silent picture — the pantomime. Now sound was geared to ideas, to emotions, and to their visible expressions. But ideas could be conventional, trivial, and commonplace — or creative, provocative, and powerful, whether on high planes or low. Suddenly, therefore, a pantomime industry faced new intellectual problems of some sort. At the same time audiences were brought into a changed relation to the cinema: they now had to use ears as well as eyes and were incited to talk back or at least think back. Thus the psychological aspects of the screen entertainment became more complicated.

As the talking-picture industry made strides in production and projection, the mechanical features were refined. Diction was watched. There were improvements in photography, in the manipulation of light, and in other technical matters, all of which enriched the flexibility, phantasy, power, and artistry of motion-picture entertainment. Color was even introduced though its cost hampered its general use. Taken in combination with various original and supplementary devices, the talking film transformed the motion-picture industry as the country groped its way from one depression to another.

Meanwhile the economic basis of the motion-picture industry underwent a revolution. As the devices employed in production and projection increased in number, intricacy, and cost, many sorts of industries engaged in manufacturing and processing were brought into close relations with the business. This was especially true of the electrical industries. Scenting potential profits in a growing enterprise, financiers showed an increasing interest in the cinema and applied to it the methods which had been so successful in railways, steel, and utilities — successful, that is, from the standpoint of bankers. At early stages in their development, production and distribution in the picture industry had taken corporate form; stocks had been issued and sold to the public; and in some cases bonds had been laid under the stocks. In the natural course, the securities of leading picture concerns were listed on the exchanges and the customary devices of Wall Street adopted in "churning" picture stocks in the market. While related industries and financiers were becoming more closely interlinked with the picture industry, producers and distributors, as their undertakings enlarged, often found it necessary to resort to bankers for credits, short-term loans, and other facilities. As a result, when the panic arrived in 1929, the chief producers and distributors were entangled in the corporate structures of general industry and in the banking and stock-exchange practices soon to be ventilated by Senate committees bent on discovering how large-scale business was actually conducted in the United States.

By 1937 the major portion of the commercial production and distribution in the cinema industry was controlled by corporations, usually with complex financial structures. Some were merely producers, neither owning nor operating theaters for projection. Others combined production, distribution, and exhibition, thus maintaining studios, selling agencies, and theaters. One concern was engaged in the processing of films and, if newspaper reports could be believed, its insiders were engaged in manipulating its stocks. The Universal Corporation, organized in Delaware, the home of high finance, was a holding company. Warner Brothers, one of the leading producers, operated a chain of exhibition theaters numbering about 445. In 1938 Loew's, Incorporated, with producing and distributing subsidiaries, had outstanding $13,604,000 in bonds, a subsidiary debt of nearly $17,000,000, subsidiary preferred stocks, preferred stocks, and 1,599,053 common shares of no par value.

Like most other industries, the motion-picture business was "over-expanded." On the basis of paid admissions, it was estimated by Standard Statistics, each available theater seat was occupied less than once daily and, in view of the fact that most houses gave two or more shows daily, the industry was operating at far less than capacity — at from twenty-five to fifty per cent capacity. It was under the terrific strain that marked the conduct of business in general

— a strain to get a larger share of the consumer's dollar by reaching deeper and deeper into primordial urges.

The grip of the interlocking corporate interests on the production of motion pictures was strengthened by their control over chains of theaters for exhibition and by the practice of "block booking." Under this practice independent exhibitors were offered sets of pictures and required to take all of them as a condition of receiving any, or at least were allowed favorable discounts on quantities. In other words, in order to secure films of undoubted quality and fascination, exhibitors were forced to accept a number of mediocre films, "the run of the works."

Against the requirement, loud grumblings went up to Washington from independent exhibitors and thus the "trust-busting" issue was introduced into the motion-picture business. The Federal Trade Commission conducted investigations, members of Congress threatened drastic legislation, and from year to year the controversy continued, with the customary denunciation of corporate control and the customary praise of "the little man." On each side of the quarrel a plausible case was presented, while the practice continued in spite of the orators. Irrespective of its merits or demerits, block booking marked a tendency to centralization and standardization, and it provided outlets for numerous motion pictures of the most mechanical type, characterized by no distinction in acting or themes. The best that could be said for it was that it helped to stabilize the picture business, as a business.

Studies of the film industry showed that the larger corporations were, on the whole, in a more secure position. Profits for all producers depended mainly on success in securing "stars" who caught popular fancy and lured millions of persons to box offices. With huge funds at their disposal, the great concerns could command higher managerial talent and more "stars" than could their smaller competitors. Minor establishments that relied on two or three luminaries for success might be hopelessly crippled by the loss of a single actor or actress, while the chief establishments could weather such a loss. But large or small, motion-picture corporations ran into troubles as the depression deepened throughout the country. Estimated box-office attendance fell from 3,660,000,000 in 1929 to 2,800,000,000 in 1933. A number of companies were pinched. Radio-Keith-Orpheum went into the hands of receivers in January, 1933. The Twentieth Century-Fox Film Corporation passed through "the financial wringer," exhibiting in the process a fantastic maze of inside manipulations that made some of its imaginary screen stories tame in comparison. Even the collapse of the Van Sweringen's railway empire, so extensively underwritten by the Morgan Company at public expense, was scarcely more bizarre than the "reorganization" of the Fox Film concern.

In the end, as far as there was any end to anything in 1938, the motion-picture industry was highly centralized in financial structure, despite the intense competition for stars and box-office receipts. Bankers and Lords of Creation from other industries were vitally concerned in its operations and fate. On the boards of motion-picture companies appeared persons whose primary interest was financial. A few actors and actresses of competence and talent might still organize companies and secure audiences at one or more "legitimate" theaters, but such an operation was out of the question in the motion-picture industry, with its hordes of distributing agents and chains of exhibition houses. However whimsical prima donnas might like to be in the cinema business, corporation directors and managers were in control of the situation, combining dominance in production with the selection of artists, plays, ideas, and features for presentation to the eighty or ninety million occupants of theater seats each week. Of course corporation managers and directors, engrossed in securing large financial returns, had to consider popular interests, tastes, and vagaries, and that was frequently a gamble. What they could be sure of was that nothing distasteful to corporate trustees and managers-in-general flickered constantly, if ever, on the silver screen. Depending upon the emotions of millions, their enterprise was precarious; but, having a certain power of choice, they could assure the supremacy of what Will Hays, the Picture Czar, called "escapist" presentations. The production of such pictures, he declared, was the legitimate function of the motion-picture industry; and the result was innumerable "beautiful bores."

§

Carrying a huge burden of fixed and contingent obligations, the motion-picture industry had to keep its mind on receipts from admissions. No audience, no profits; no profits, no films. Bound by this necessity, producers and playwrights were forced to bend their energies to making pictures acceptable to the populace. In so doing they were by no means blind to the difference between art and "the business that brought home the bacon." Actors, it is true, were permitted occasionally to indulge in "skits" on their trade or profession, or whatever it was, as in Boy Meets Girl and Once in a Lifetime. And in the seclusion of his elegant office near Wall Street, New York, one of the "top-flight" Hollywood executives, while twirling his Phi Beta Kappa key, could "discuss agreeably" with an interviewer "the gaucheries and vulgarities of the cinema, as a worldly bishop might discuss the regrettable but unavoidable flaws of revealed religion." Since success in the cinema, however, like success in preaching, was based upon the magnetism of appeals to the senses of the multitudes, the educated executive was as quick as a worldly bishop to recognize the role of the "unavoidable."

Of course popular films cost a great deal of money and bankers who advanced short-term credits on the basis of hopes were mindful of the risks. Hence there could be little room for bold experimentation. In the opinion of producers what the people most wanted to see was the sex appeal. Films on that theme, devoid of any social ideology, presumably could be sold in Nazi Germany, Fascist Italy, perhaps in Communist Russia, and in Japan, the land of the Sun Goddess; and Hollywood, like Secretary Hull in the State Department, gave prayerful attention to the foreign market. So "colossal" picture producers made the most of the sex theme. And to meet the universal demand of the sexes, men and women physically attractive were given fabulous salaries for film performances — some running into hundreds of thousands of dollars a year.

An unusual feature of the latest appeal was the flaunting of sex before little boys and girls who crowded the moving-picture houses day and night. Though in countries accustomed to sex slavery, nautch girls, sing-song girls, and geisha girls learned to participate in sex entertainment in their early years, never before in America had boys and girls ranging from six to ten years of age been permitted by the millions to witness daily displays of sex enticements approaching, as near as censorship would permit, to the climax itself. Just what effect "a century of progress" in that kind of education would have upon the morale of human relations and upon the institution of the family no one could say with knowledge but, given the lust for motion-picture profits, joined to the passions of sex, that form of "progress" was certainly rapid.

It was accelerated by the fact that the young persons who paid daily or weekly attendance upon their favorites in the picture theaters were also among the avid readers of the film magazines and tabloid papers in which the divorces, escapades, and scandals of the stars were explained in words as plain as the gestures, postures, and scripts of the cinema. On the screen, the stars lived and played in romantic settings. In Hollywood they lived, played, quarrelled, and made ready for divorces, remarriages, and redivorces, in mansions no less pretentious and gaudy — all befitting their incomes and the morality of the motion-picture industry, of which they were a part.

But the cinematic adults and "the universal infantiles" who everywhere streamed past the box offices, seemed to like magic and fun as well as biology, especially weird stories about the animal kingdom. Walt Disney's Mickey Mouse, for instance, swept through the country and around the world. Only when a Disney picture imputed some disrespect for royal authority did it meet a setback abroad. After the dictator of Yugoslavia banned one such break from the strictly neutral line, the producers of Mickey Mouse had a lesson to take to heart. Untold millions had laughed when Charlie Chaplin in City Lights swallowed a policeman's whistle and then "hiccoughed a high wheeze." Untold millions laughed also at animated cartoons, such as the Silly Symphonies with their dance motifs, at illusions created by painstaking drawing and photography. In the winter of 1937–1938 Snow White and the Seven Dwarfs, a modified version of the famous fairy tale, drew throngs to ticket booths.

Apparently, the perfect entertainment, apart from sex, was the perfect illusion snatched from a world of fantasy occupied by gnomes, talking animals, and dancing quadrupeds. When George Pal arrived from Europe in 1938 with "animated puppets," speculators in the domain of profits foretold new money-making triumphs. Puppets operated by strings had been popular for more than a thousand years. Puppets made in "movie animation studios" might last longer and awaken the glee of peoples for centuries to come. At least the success of Edgar Bergen's talking automaton, Charlie McCarthy, seemed to promise huge laughs and gate receipts for interminable years. Being permitted to say what human beings wanted to say but suppressed, Charlie McCarthy became everybody's prize scapegoat.

Judging by sales returns, historical romances were apparently third in the popular appeal. Like the puppets, they offered a retreat to the land of make-believe, by using exotic scenery and costume, by placing action in remote circumstances. According to estimates of film experts, Disraeli was the favorite picture in 1929 — a story of the Jew who long promoted Tory imperialism in Britain. In the following years, while the agonies of the world war were still in memory and before preparation for another world war had approached ecstasy, Erich Maria Remarque's All Quiet on the Western Front, an importation from Germany, was enthusiastically acclaimed; so was a picture about Abraham Lincoln, who led a great war to its conclusion. In 1931 a story of pioneering in Oklahoma, Edna Ferber's Cimarron, found high favor. Then came the full force of the financial crash, interrupting somewhat the flow of historical pictures since films of that type were expensive to produce. But as business took an upward turn, the historical romance rebounded. American democrats were entertained by kings and queens in a succession of historical pictures and still more historical plays were promised during an upturn in the recession of 1938.

Sex dramas, animated fantasies, and historical romances led in a bewildering variety of pictures but the total range was wide — from news reels depicting events and personalities in the four corners of the globe, to travel reels portraying labor, economy, topography, flora, and fauna in every part of the world. Industries, laboratories, operations in hospitals, eroding fields, slashed forests, flooding rivers, growing crops, wild life, functions of government, airplane flights, battleship launchings, and social work were filmed and exhibited in large theaters for the masses or to selected audiences. Only one note was lacking in the wholesale production and distribution of moving pictures: the note struck by the authors of the dissident fiction which bulked so large in the literature of the time. In the general motion-picture output, bare portrayals of labor conflicts or films showing the plight of a third of the nation were conspicuous by their absence.

Why was this so? Those given to an economic interpretation of events had one answer: the bankers, financiers, corporation trustees, stockholders, and managers for the huge and complicated motion-picture industry, with hundreds of millions at stake, for their own reasons, did not want the conflicts of labor and the misery of a third of the nation to be advertised to their millions of customers. Possibly, however, even participants in labor struggles and sharers of the misery did not themselves wish to see their hard and drab existence represented on the screen when they were seeking forgetfulness. Louis Adamic discovered that the proletariat did not read proletarian literature. Probably it did not want to work in factories and mines in the daytime and behold factories and mines at night in the theatre. It might be that the proletariat itself preferred the realm of fantasy and romance. One film showing a labor war between the Chicago police and strikers at the Republic Steel works could arouse national excitement, but a daily stream of such graphics might have cut down the sustaining box-office receipts.

Struck by the dearth of the labor note in the mass production of the moving-picture industry, a reporter sought an explanation from Rouben Mamoulian, a foreign-born artist, who had caught glimpses of American potentialities beyond the range of most natives inured to daily use and wont. The inquirer received an expert's answer. In High, Wide, and Handsome, Mr. Mamoulian had presented a saga of oil speculation. In Porgy and Bess, based on DuBose Heyward's novel, he had given a picture of servant life in the South, enlivened by the music of Gershwin. Knowing this record, the reporter suggested that the full-length saga of American labor awaited Mamoulian's creative energies — the saga covering the insurgency of the old Knights of Labor, the Molly Maguires, the leadership of the American Federation of Labor, the uprising of the I. W. W., the company union, and State intervention under the New Deal.

Mr. Mamoulian, in replying, contrasted the comparative freedom of music, writing, and painting with the limitations of a mass-production industry dependent entirely upon huge audiences for support. "The picture industry," he said, "is no different from the underwear business, for example. It is completely governed by the law of supply and demand." Many workers in the cinema did try to put as much into pictures as they could "get away with," and "imperceptibly the audience is being influenced to look for more and more in the films. Some day the screen public may be ready for your saga of labor." But the time had not come for it in 1929 or in 1938. Evidently it was not to be expected until a huge national audience was ready for it. Whether such an audience would ever be ready depended upon factors outside as well as within the picture industry.

§

Insistently as mass-production and commercialized entertainment penetrated the texture of society upon which government rests, its relation to the State received scant consideration until the vast rearmament program was authorized under the administration of Franklin D. Roosevelt. In other places and times, the State itself had maintained spectacles that regimented its subjects while undermining the morale upon which it depended in the long run. In the United States, on the other hand, the motion-picture entertainment seemed to lie wholly outside the sphere of government.

Yet, in part, the appearance was unreal. The industry was mainly corporate in form and the corporations which conducted it obtained their charters from state governments. In issuing stocks and bonds, picture companies came within the jurisdiction of the Securities and Exchange Commission in Washington. Concerns that stumbled upon evil days and underwent reorganization encountered congressional investigations and had to answer for their conduct before judges in charge of bankrupts. Under state boards of control, exhibitions were reviewed and censored. Campaign-fund collectors for political parties took cognizance of the industry's resources and in this respect the Democratic party, perhaps as the party in power, was especially favored in 1936. Rumors of legislation pertaining to antitrust practices and block-booking were bruited abroad. Far more germane to the course of civilization in America, however, was the relation of this form of mass entertainment and mass "education" to the ultima ratio of government, namely, armed force.

During American participation in the world war, the moving-picture industry had been the willing and abject servant of propaganda from Washington. After a brief season, while the war-sick nations were washing off the blood of the last conflict, the tension was relaxed. Then as politicians and warriors began to gird themselves for "strong foreign policies" and the anticipated consequences, the motion-picture industry came back into line. War pictures streamed from the studios at home and abroad for the American screen, notably The Singing Marine, Submarine D–1, Annapolis Salute, Navy Blue and Gold, Wings over Honolulu, Hold 'Em Navy, 23½ Hours Leave, Sweetheart of the Navy, You're in the Army Now (with none of the humor of the post-war comedy, You're in the Navy Now), The Road to Glory, Suzy, Professional Soldier, and Charge of the Light Brigade. British imperialism furnished two outstanding films: Lloyd's of London and Wee Willie Winkle. If Americans needed any cues in matters of production, they were aided by a British "saga in patriotism," The Big Parade of the British Navy, turned out by the British film industry in coöperation with the British Admiralty for release around the world in 1935.

To these sources of emotional incitement a few offsets were available. The production of Remarque's The Road Back showed the irreducible antithesis between trench habits and civilian habits; and They Gave Him a Gun suggested dangers lurking in the mere private possession of destructive weapons. An import from England, Things to Come, presented a phantasmagoria of awful events, and the French description of Carnival in Flanders ripped the tinsel and gilt from warfare.

Films inclined in the direction of peace were overwhelmed, however, after President Roosevelt's quarantine speech on October 5, 1937, and the launching of his super-navy program in January of the following year. The transition was not difficult, for the military and naval branches of the Government were willing coadjutors. Their position had been clearly revealed in the Army and Navy Register for April 10, 1937, in an article praising Wings over Honolulu, which called it "a story of naval aviation of some future war." Indebtedness for professional aid was acknowledged by the director of the film: "We are very grateful to the friendly and helpful spirit of the officers and crew of the *Ranger* and the air station. We are working hard to make Wings over Honolulu a picture of which the entire Navy can be proud. If this can be achieved, it will be because of the splendid coöperation of the Navy and the Navy people, officers, enlisted men, and some of their wives." Later in that year, when a superintendent of schools in a midwestern city objected to showing certain war films to the children under his care, naval reserve officers carried on a campaign of criticism against him. Such was the passion of the times.

After President Roosevelt announced his naval expansion policy on January 28, 1938, and encountered unexpected opposition in Congress and outside, his administration turned to the motion-picture industry for assistance in propaganda. Besides helping the newsreels in exploiting the Panay incident in the Japanese war on China, as a part of a campaign for new preparedness, the Roosevelt administration strengthened its coöperation with the picture industry. On April 13, 1938, Variety, an authentic voice of entertainment enterprise, was able to report "progress" in a dispatch from Hollywood: "The Government is showing a more friendly attitude toward pictures since the big naval appropriations, and a closer coöperation is pledged to pictures built around the military arms of service. . . . Washington now is trying to win over picture-goers to need of adequate defense and present the U. S. show of strength."

About the same time the syndicated moving-picture column of the International News Service explained this closer connection between Government and the industry in an illuminating sentence: "Perhaps the reason Hal Wallis obtained such ready permission for Warner Brothers is because Wings over the Navy is propaganda tied up with the recent

billion-dollar appropriation for added naval protection."
The President was determined to have his way and was eager
to see aid given to the production of films that would swing
the people over to his line of policy. For all practical purposes, the picture industry had become a servant of the
Roosevelt administration in respect of foreign, naval, and
military designs. The Secretary of War, Harry Woodring,
had said through the columns of the magazine, Liberty, that
the Army was ready to "take over the country" in time of
a domestic crisis. If the people could be convinced that no
military or naval appropriation could be unnecessary, the
way would be prepared for the ideology of things to come,
for any mask to cover the face of war.

Not content with making sure that the right "slant" was
given to moving pictures connected with its armament propaganda, the Roosevelt administration took care to keep out
counter-suggestions of a pacific nature. When Paramount
Pictures, apparently with the sympathetic "coöperation" of
the Government, was preparing Men with Wings, a saga
dramatizing the development of aviation, it arranged for the
heroine to deliver a vigorous denunciation of war; but,
according to reports of high authenticity, the Government
issued a ban against that speech in opposition to war. A
dispatch in The New York Times, May 28, 1938, declared:
"Government pressure on Paramount Pictures to eliminate
all pacifist preachment in Men with Wings has brought a
rewriting of the final twenty pages of dialogue." The following day, The Times' Hollywood correspondent, Douglas
Churchill, in an article, entitled Peace vs. Propaganda,
reported that "Paramount swaps principles for planes," and
described the way in which government pressure had forced
a reconstruction of the play's conclusion with a view to
eliminating the anti-war note. Commenting on the event,
Variety circumspectly remarked that "unofficial suggestions
from officials in Washington" had been responsible for the
redirection of Men with Wings in harmony with President
Roosevelt's armament policies and propaganda.

Although for a long time it was denied by federal authorities and film producers that they were deliberately united in any scheme of armament propaganda, facts belied the denial. It was a fact that film after film had been made with the coöperation of the armed forces of the United States. It was a fact that recognition of this coöperation was given in technical journals. It was a fact that a full page advertisement of Submarine D–1 in motion-picture trade journals paid tribute to the Navy Department, officers, and men in the submarine service "in grateful acknowledgement of inspiration and assistance." It was a fact that a journalist for the motion-picture industry openly boasted that the film, Wings over the Navy, was "propaganda tied up" with Roosevelt's agitation in support of naval expansion. It was a fact that the Government gave official sanction to coöperation with Warner Brothers in the production of this film. Thus, as a commentator on the facts remarked, the citizens who had to pay taxes for wars and shed blood in them also paid for war-propaganda in the form of "entertainment." An Aeschylus could scarcely have done justice to the scene.

Experience had demonstrated that motion-picture producers and directors were masters of the propaganda technique and knew how to condition popular reflexes for any war that politicians might decide upon in Washington. In 1918, while America was making the world safe for democracy, Cecil B. De Mille, an authority on the screen, had bluntly described the art: "I consider the development of the motion picture . . . into a conspicuously vital factor for the dissemination of governmental propaganda . . . to be most important. . . . And so, Pride of Patriotism — Grim Determination to Win the War — Calm Decision to support every measure of the Government unreservedly to that end, is finally — through nightly and daily iteration — instilled with telling force, into the breast of the spectator — a spectator taken from every class of American." Even before the United States entered the world conflict war films had pointed out "the enemy" and intensified the passions to which President Wilson appealed when he decided to take the country into the combat at arms.

In a republic whose Constitution provided for civilian supremacy over armed force, that vigilance which is the price of liberty took into account the trend of events. Every popular poll showed that the overwhelming majority of the American people wanted to stay out of all imperialist adventures and wars on other continents, although ready to defend America itself to the last ditch. Reflecting this positive public opinion, the National Council for the Prevention of War established a motion-picture department, under the direction of Albert Benham, formerly of Hollywood, studied the film offerings that bore on war and peace, kept close watch on the connections between the Government and the picture industry, and issued bulletins on this traffic. If the Naval Intelligence service of the Government, as alleged in the Senate, investigated and shadowed such observers and critics, politics had not yet reached the point in the American scene where either the War Department or the Navy Department could round up and shoot opponents of super-expenditures for the army and navy bureaucracy.

Within the industry itself and among reporters and critics associated with it were also watchers of events. Right on the spot where "the hope of heaven" burned brightest, Welford Beaton wrote in The Hollywood Spectator: "Each morning the newspapers demonstrate afresh that, of all His creations, Man is the one of whom God must be most ashamed. . . . In our own country today are children being reared in luxury on the profits their parents make by selling Japan war material which murders Chinese children. And we call ourselves civilized! . . . Nations have become the playthings of maniacs their unwise people blindly follow. A great theme for a great motion picture, but we have no producer with brains enough to see it or guts enough to make it." To one of the two or three true artists that the picture industry had produced in the course of its long life, Mr. Beaton turned with the plea: "Shoulder arms, Charlie Chaplin!

The World needs your Little Man now as it never needed him before."

The news had been whispered that Charlie Chaplin was working on an anti-war picture. But it did not appear. From every "practical" angle, the production of such a film seemed impossible. Costs would be enormous. No "hearty coöperation" from the Government of the United States would be forthcoming — twenty years after the end of the war to end war. If produced independently, distribution could scarcely break through the grip of the corporate industry upon chain theaters and block-booking. Sales abroad — to Germany and Italy, Spain and Japan at least — would be out of the question; nor could Soviet Russia, thirsting for American aid against Japan, be expected to import this film. Even its exhibition in the United States might bring about retaliations curtailing the export of other American films. Time and circumstance seemed prohibitive. Anyway government propaganda held this sector of entertainment.

§

It was one of the ironies of American entertainment that the picture industry could produce no film for wide domestic distribution if it was unpleasing to Hitler and Mussolini. Under the economic theory of "the more foreign trade the better for the country," according to which Secretary Hull proceeded with his so-called reciprocity treaties, the great American film producers received a substantial percentage of their total income from other lands. With foreign governments limiting American exports by "quota" legislation and other restraining devices, with the industry materially dependent upon receipts from foreign sources, with censors abroad scrutinizing every inch of film, American producers would lose huge profits, might be thrown into bankruptcy, by offending in the slightest degree any dictator in Europe. The President of the United States could exert a positive force in the production of war films; foreign dictators could exert a telling influence against democratic films and against films of peace. The most frenzied promoters of the armament race throughout the world had access to American armament films to illustrate "the imperious necessity of the case."

The situation was neatly illustrated by the fate of Sinclair Lewis' It Can't Happen Here, a novel dealing with fascist tactics, methods, and spirit and representing the American democratic spirit in strong resistance to the cruelties, lies, and enormities of such despotisms. In all the years of depression and turmoil, no novel written in the United States portrayed more dynamically the ideals of democracy pitted against the tyranny of the demagogic dictator. Moreover the writer's name and fame had already commanded immense audiences — readers and "picture fans" in America and Europe.

Soon after publication came an announcement that a screen version was "in the works" at Hollywood. Months passed. No film emerged. Questions were asked. Gossip said that agents of Hitler and Mussolini had clamped the iron censorship on the picture. Producers denied the allegation. At all events the anti-fascist film was not produced. From the American people was withheld the privilege of seeing a great national ideal in conflict with fascism personified on the screen. Instead they were offered the "entertainment" of naval and military films. No longer could it be said that the State had no relation to the commercialized amusements of America. What that meant for 1950 or 1960 no one could foretell precisely, but guesses could be made — and all realists made them, if the world imagists looked the other way. Mussolini had shouted that democracy was a "farce" and "a mask for capitalism." History yet to come would test the validity of the thesis.

In the present, behind the smooth front of corporate and official control, restlessness existed among the writers, editors, actors, and actresses who were necessary to the profitable conduct of the motion-picture business. This ferment had been manifested in the agitation over the efforts to unionize the industry, especially after the appearance of the Committee for Industrial Organization in Hollywood. It found tumultuous expression in 1937 when the popular slap-stick comedian, Hal Roach, a member of the Liberty League, attempted a kind of coup d'état among producers by bringing to the seat of the industry Vittorio Mussolini, the son of the dictator, fresh from his bombing exploits in Ethiopia. Expecting a fanfare of favorable publicity, Mr. Roach encountered a revolt.

On receiving advance news of the young Mussolini's coming, the Hollywood Anti-Nazi League released counter-publicity, stirred up local trade unions, won the support of important stars, and held the threat of a general strike over producers. When the conquering Vittorio appeared on the scene with his host, he met stony glares. Parties organized for his entertainment were suddenly called off; he was publicly snubbed by famous stars; beauties did not dance with him. Screaming circulars quoted his statement that bombing natives in Ethiopia had been "exceptionally good fun." Later it was explained that Vittorio's actual words had been "molto divertente" and should have been translated as "highly diverting," not as "exceptionally good fun." But Hollywood was not troubled about philology and it turned "the social heat on him" until he literally fled from the place, slipped back across the continent, and quietly sailed away for his father's land. The "international incident" was symptomatic. It revealed underlying tensions in the entertainment industry itself. Certainly that; perhaps nothing more.

§

Shortly after the successful commercialization of the sound picture, the newsreel entered the market as a standard feature of exhibitions and entertainments and was soon associated, like armament films, with great politics. Unlike motion-picture plays, the newsreel was free from official censorship, resembling the newspapers in that respect. Operating under such general titles as The Talk of the World, The

Eyes and Ears of the World, and The March of Time, it was often called the "educational branch of the theatrical motion picture." But it was, in fact, a medium for supplying sensational news; and newsreel photographers, in the manner of reporters, went into the field in constant search for "hot stuff." In reality, the picture reporters were forced to undertake far more daring adventures, to incur the risk of battle and sudden death, for they had to go into action with their cameras at the very center of scenes to be snapped. They were compelled to keep up a stream of "thrilling novelties" to prevent their goods from becoming a drug on the market. Since they could not be present at every "stirring" episode that occurred, they had to supplement fortunate "catches of hot news" by the deliberate selection of stated occasions that could be known and prepared for in advance. And it happened that a large proportion of such occasions was "official," that is, governmental in nature.

Although on dull days newsreel photographers in the United States had to be satisfied with reporting bathing beauties, carnival queens, and tennis players, they frequently had political events to film: the launching of battleships and cruisers, naval displays, military parades, army maneuvers, new bombing planes taking off, and bigger tanks going into action. When mere instrumentalities of violence paled at home, actual scenes of wars abroad could be employed to "tone up audiences." When pictures of death, destruction, and suffering on the battlefields of China began to arrive after the summer of 1937, at least one newsreel concern employed them to promulgate the doctrine that American "rights" were being endangered after the fashion of 1914–1917, with the implication that another war for the defense of American rights would become the necessary and proper thing.

That some producers of newsreels were fully conscious of just what they were doing was indicated by an arrangement for a private "preview" in Washington of a film dealing with China, attended by the Chinese ambassador, members of his staff, and officers of the United States Government, including cabinet members. To appear as mere reporters of news, "impartially transmitted," the producers invited Secretary Daniel Roper and Senator Bennett Champ Clark to make addresses to the prospective audiences through the sound track. While on the surface the balance was apparently even, in fact it was the jeopardy to American business interests in China that received the emphasis. Even so, when the film was exhibited in Washington, the public listened to Secretary Roper's appeal with stony silence and gave hearty applause to Senator Clark's plea for staying out of war.

After the films showing the bombing of the American gunboat, Panay, by Japanese airmen had reached the United States, official facilities were tendered to expedite the exhibition of the pictures. To use the language of The New York Times' picture expert: "Aroused by the bombing of the Panay and compelled to crystallize quickly the nation's foreign policy under pressure of disputed incidents . . . President Roosevelt asked the motion-picture industry to show the public exactly what happened to the little American gunboat on the Yangtze." The industry eagerly complied with the request and supplied announcers who made flamboyant speeches calculated to lash popular emotions into frenzy. After reviewing newspaper editorials and newsreel narrations, Walter Winchell reached the conclusion that editorial writers "refused to get hysterical," but "the newsreel narrators put on the big jingo act — noticeable to those over soldiering age." And yet, despite the furious efforts of narrators to whip up the war spirit, theater-goers in general looked at this newsreel and heard the announcement without going into hysterics. From the military point of view, the "big scare" was an almost total loss. Had American citizens at large read in the newspapers that the Panay was in a war zone convoying Standard Oil tankers? In any case, the outcome of the exhibition was a disappointment to the Roosevelt administration, especially to the State Department, if its press releases on foreign policies gave the correct version of its attitude.

Whether the newsreel was a device for education, sheer entertainment, whatever that might be, or propaganda, it became the stormy petrel of Czar Hays' quiet sea of escape. When newsreels of Mussolini's swank troops or Hitler's thumping goose-steppers were shown, friends and foes of the dictators sometimes cracked heads and smashed seats. Shouts of anger attended the showing of a newsreel made in Connecticut in which New London boys appeared as German Storm Troopers engaged in persecuting Jews. Foreseeing fights in theaters, Ohio censors banned this film as detrimental to public morals; it was also kept out of the "Aryan" districts of New York City and similar regions in parts of the West. College boys at Princeton and Amherst hooted and boycotted the Hearst Metrotone News. In fact opposition to his exhibitions became so widespread that producers found it expedient to drop the name of Hearst from the title. Minneapolis audiences broke up in factional fury over pictures of an industrial conflict in that city. The fan mail that poured into the managerial and editorial offices of newsreel companies, following hoots and cat-calls at exhibitions, warned them that their patrons would not quietly accept the fiction that newsreels merely gave "the news that's fit to print." In respect of newspapers that illusion had about disappeared and it was too late for newsreel editors to succeed with pretensions to such "objectivity."

Although no comprehensive survey was made of the newsreel contents over a period of time, the accent in reportage was unmistakable. Acts of violence, whether public or private, "made news" for pictures as well as papers and one impression readily gained from the reels was that violence ruled the world. If actual violence was not enough to fill the screen, preparations for violence on a large scale supplied any deficit. Where the pictures themselves lacked an appeal to hysteria, as in the case of the Panay affair, announcers tried to furnish the stimulating force by vehement words and roaring vociferation. Of course no one claimed that newsreels covered all civilization, including acts of kindness, wisdom, and virtue. But with the regular motion pictures concentrating so heavily on crime and the biology of sex and the news films crowded with scenes of crime and war, the emphasis was on the side of destruction, passion, and brutality.

§

What relation did the technics, art, and emphasis of the moving-picture industry bear to the maintenance and development of society, especially a republican and democratic society? That question rose above all minor points of criticism and appreciation and it could only be answered, if at all, with reference to the characteristics of such a society as set forth by men and women competent to speak through experience and knowledge. High on the list was knowledge of the forms and functions of society and government and the issues arising in their time unfolding. "A free, virtuous, and enlightened people," James Monroe had said more than a century before, "must know well the great principles and causes on which their happiness depends." No less fundamental, equally requisite was virtue, above all in the sense of devotion to the public good as distinguished from the overweening pursuit of private gain or the irresponsible enjoyment of personal passions. In the third place, it had long been an axiom of political observers that while a State resting on force, buttressed by a hierarchy of power, lay and ecclesiastical, and fortified by awe-inspiring ceremonials, might, at least for a time, dispense with virtue, this quality of the human spirit was the active, indispensable requirement of a republic. Also embedded in the necessities of such a society was the supremacy of civilian agencies over that immense interest which had helped to lay all the States of antiquity in ruin, namely, the military interest. And underlying all this were habits of moderation, respect for human rights, prudent conduct of private affairs, without which no society could long endure on a civilian basis.

Accepting as valid the axiom that virtue is an absolute as
well as a relative value, Will Hays, shortly after he retired
from the Harding administration to serve as the czar of
morals in the motion-picture industry, issued his declaration
of faith: "We must have toward that sacred thing, the mind
of a child, toward that clean and virgin thing, that unmarked
slate — we must have toward that the same sense of responsibility, the same care about the impressions made upon it,
that the best teacher or the best clergyman, the most inspired
teacher of youth would have." Without taking this lofty
sentiment as an eleventh commandment, it could be said
that everyone who thought about the moving-picture industry in relation to society agreed with Mr. Hays that it did
and might have a profound influence on the sustaining
morale of American habits and institutions.

Whether Mr. Hays intended that teachers should take his
dictum as an unequivocal command or not, they did manifest a persistent and continuing interest in the influence of
motion pictures on the children whom they were training for
life in American society and citizenship in the republic. In
efforts to get at the elusive nature of this influence they
devoted attention, of necessity, to the content or emphasis
of the pictures, as distinguished from the nominal theme.
Through the Committee on Educational Research, formed
under the auspices of the Payne Fund, with W. W. Charters
of Ohio State University as chairman, a group of teachers
and specialists made extensive inquiries into the components,
or ingredients, of motion pictures for four years, 1929–1932,
with a view to arriving at some consensus of opinion respecting their influences upon youth. One survey, made in this
connection by Dr. Edgar Dale of Ohio State University,
covered fifteen hundred pictures for the years 1920, 1925, and
1930 and the results were incorporated in The Content of
Motion Pictures.

During those three years, according to Dr. Dale's classification, the "love theme" led all the others; crime ranked
second with a rating only two per cent lower in 1930; sex

as biology came third in 1920 and 1925; comedy stood fourth in 1920 and 1925 and third in 1930, showing signs of increase as the economic depression deepened. War was at first sixth in position, but its status showed signs of rising as the world's rearmaments expanded; after 1930, especially under the stimulus of President Roosevelt's naval and military policy, and with the coöperation of the army and navy, the war theme mounted swiftly, events in Spain and China presumably giving it warrant in the factual substance of contemporary history. So low in the statistical scale were pictures of constructive significance for American democracy that they could be easily overlooked. The heroes of the films, in an impressive measure, were "great lovers," portrayers of biological urges, parasites, criminals, gangsters, and warriors engaged, under law, in killing, burning, and destroying.

In respect of background, the big cities, particularly New York and Paris, were utilized for scenes of wealth and power. These were varied by pictures of splendor in the palaces of princes, from Europe to India, with special attention to sleeping quarters. According to reports on forty pictures showing residences, studied in detail, sixty-nine per cent of the accent was upon life among the rich and only four per cent upon the simple annals of the poor. Most of the actors were young men ranging in age from twenty to thirty, while the actresses on the average were still more youthful; for heroes, the age limit was about fifty-six; for heroines, about thirty-five. A villain might be in his sixties and the vixen in the late fifties, but no hero or heroine was that old. Among the economic occupations represented in 115 pictures, commercial business led the list. About half the women and a few of the men had no known lawful occupations. Little girl actors, effusively advertised, were, as a rule, smartly gowned and coiffed in Hollywood vogues, though toward the end of 1938 youngsters were being drilled for tougher roles. According to one student of the pictures, three-fourths of the output of forty pictures examined made a feature of intimate clothing. The

pajama fashion originated by Gloria Swanson continued in
vogue, with bathing suits of scant proportions sharply competing, and the "strip tease" gaining.

Only lines from Juvenal describing the diversions of decaying Rome were applicable to the facts in the case. Among
1500 pictures examined, Edgar Dale found that only a small
percentage treated love as romance, as enduring personal
happiness, as possessing deep social importance. The kiss, so
profusely and obtrusively exhibited, lost most of its meaning
save as a gesture of biology. Some producers seemed to
delight in the innuendo of the promiscuous; but whether it
was also preferred by audiences only the admissions could
indicate. With love so depicted, crime was closely associated.
Every gangster had his "Moll" and interest in crime itself
was fanned by manifestations of sex. Criminals were rarely
caught and punished in the films. Nor were the subtler forms
of retribution often graphically or artistically treated; where
punishment did follow crime, that was usually the end of the
matter.

In studying 115 pictures in detail, the Payne Fund researchers found that the heroes were responsible for 13 murders, the villains and villainesses for 30. In all, 54 murders
were committed; there were 59 cases of felonious assault,
17 hold-ups, 21 kidnapings, and numerous other crimes. The
total number of deaths by violence was 71. In short, in 115
pictures, 406 crimes were actually committed and 43 additional ones were attempted, making a total of 449 crimes in
115 pictures, or nearly four crimes per picture. Inasmuch as
there were about thirty million admissions of boys and girls
under twenty-one years of age to the moving-picture houses
every week, such detailed specifications, however discounted
and interpreted, was certainly pertinent to the maintenance
of the American republic and the basic institutions of American society.

The findings and conclusions reported by the surveys
under the auspices of the Payne Fund, coupled with criticism
from other sources, produced more than a flurry in the mo-

tion-picture industry, with its eyes ever on the box office and public relations. Disturbed by the growing revolt, representatives of the industry cast about for some David to destroy Goliath and found in Raymond Moley, former member of President Roosevelt's brain trust, the appropriate person for the mission. His reply was made in a slender volume entitled Are We Movie Made? published in 1938. Although an expert investigator himself, Moley chose to base the burden of his argument upon a book on Art and Jurisprudence by Mortimer Adler, a professor in Chicago University, passionately engaged in teaching the doctrines of Thomas Aquinas to midwestern Protestants. With little difficulty Moley, aided by Adler, tore up the thesis that science could demonstrate a "causal" connection between representations of crime and anti-social acts on the screen and specific instances of crime and anti-social acts in everyday life. Having done this, Moley treated as unimportant the informed judgment of teachers and other investigators actually in daily contact with children subjected to motion-picture influences; and substituted his judgment, tinctured by cautious qualifications, to the effect that on the whole, by and large, in general, the moving pictures were good for the public, that teachers should stick to their last, and "that each should attend to the perfection of his own business."

No doubt, conclusions on the dispute were largely matters of personal opinion in respect of everyday experience and knowledge; and all the controversy about the "science" of the business simmered down to issues of common sense. It required no elaborate statistical calculations and correlations to convince bystanders that the probabilities were on the side of those who maintained that the strong emphasis in the moving pictures on crime, sex, violence, racketeering, and high living was not conducive to the development and preservation of those virtues essential to the health of a democratic republic.

Most pictures that were well patronized had to have a "kick"; in other words, they had to violate the conventions

of rational and prudent behavior. In supplying these sur-
prises, demonstrations of delinquency, open passion, and
overt cruelty were commonly employed. In an age of bank
crashes and defaulting bonds, intrigue and blackmail were
more likely to be portrayed on the screen than devotion to
fiduciary trust and to the tender consideration of others —
perhaps unwittingly a portrayal of democratic culture as its
course was then being shaped. No doubt there was creative
intelligence in America, coöperation for the common good,
and heroism as social action; but such aspects of society
necessary to its continuance and vital to its improvement
received relatively little attention from directors of the regular motion-picture industry. For Horatius at the bridge was
substituted the gangster preying upon society; for morality,
a-morality; for the ethics of religion, incalculable mysteries.
If "morality" was drawn upon for inspiration, it was generally to reveal the "horrors" of race suicide, labor conflicts,
bolshevism, socialism, and all forms of radicalism in contrast
with the "heroics" of patriotism depicted as subservience to
the valuations of the pecuniary Respectability.

With physical passions and energies so glaringly emphasized, the theory of the motion picture as a release, as an
escape into a world of phantasy, as a pleasing antidote to
the monotony and hardships of life was clearly defective, at
least as applied by a vast number of commercial films. Far
from offering sedatives to audiences, such films suggested
stimulation to overt action in line with the portrayals of the
screen. This aspect of the business was analyzed and set
forth by Herbert Blumer in his volume on Movies and Conduct. After a long study of the subject, Blumer came to the
conclusion that the moving pictures are not "merely a device
for surcease." For many patrons of the business, Blumer
decided, they were "authentic portrayals of life" from which
were derived patterns of behavior, incitement to conduct,
ideas of reality, and "content for a vigorous life of imagination." In other words, day and night, the motion pictures
were arousing in millions of boys and girls, men and women,

impulses to actions of passion and violence that defied the moralities necessary to the rational conduct of affairs in society. Resting his case on this ground Blumer stated his summary: "Because motion pictures are educational in this sense, they may conflict with other educational institutions. . . . This is likely to be true chiefly among those with least education and sophisticated experience."

Confirmation of this general finding came from the Newspaper Guild, the national organization of reporters and other newspaper workers. Among the various participants in American life, men and women of the press were not especially addicted to sentimentality and petty moralities. On the whole, among the intellectuals of the country, they were the most realistic in experience and thought. But in 1937 even the Newspaper Guild was moved to protest against the films that touched upon the reportorial occupation. It complained that seventeen pictures produced that year vilified reporters and made workers in the business appear indecent; that five pictures treated them as innocuous persons playing no useful role in society; and that only two pictures presented them as having intelligence and character. It called special attention to the film They Won't Forget, in which a columnist was made to be a home wrecker, and to Back in Circulation, which showed a reporter so devoid of humanity that he could whimsically send a woman to execution or as lightly secure her acquittal. Rumors circulated to the effect that Hearst and other employers close to Hollywood were thus secretly waging war upon their reporters and employees in response to the organization work so successfully carried on by the Guild but, entirely apart from this allegation, it was evident that many newspaper workers were as indignant against the films as some intransigent members associated with the Legion of Decency.

§

To indict the whole picture industry was as foolish as to indict a nation, and yet there was so much social dynamite exploding before millions day and night on the screen that protests and counter-actions came from every quarter of responsibility in the United States. If some objections developed from the overwrought imaginations of puritans, Protestant and Catholic, by no means all sprang from that source. In fact, as early as 1922, leaders in the picture industry had become so alarmed by the back-fire that they had organized the Motion Picture Producers and Exhibitors of America, Incorporated, with Will H. Hays, President Harding's Postmaster General and the former manipulator of Republican campaign funds at the head, with the official title of czar of the business and the functions of a water boy. This agency of the industry continued to analyze complaints, consult with objectors, arrange for "previews" before religious societies and women's clubs, and form committees of advice and counsel. Meanwhile the National Board of Review, a private organization established in 1909, operated directly and through local committees as a voluntary agency of criticism and approval. To such private agencies were added official boards of censorship in a number of the states, which imposed various restraints upon the scenes, actions, and lines of pictures before exhibition to the public.

Still protests mounted. By 1934 a Catholic association, the Legion of Decency, had entered the fray with a national campaign that frightened the leaders of the industry and led to the imposition of limits approved by Catholic authorities. Inasmuch as the Catholic hierarchy was engaged in the pursuit of its own ideals and interests, had great economic stakes in all parts of the country, and was connected with a complex of economic and political interests in all parts of the world, its control in practice went far beyond mere matters of faith and morals, into spheres where political contests raged. Nor was its control merely confined to moral suasion. According to Elizabeth Yeaman, in The New Republic of October 5, 1938, it induced film executives, "ninety-nine per cent Jewish," to employ at a high salary Joseph I. Breen, a Catholic of Irish descent, to act as its dictator-censor for the moving-picture industry. So with the censorship exercised through threats of exclusion and retaliation by Hitler and Mussolini was associated the iron discipline of the greatest authoritarian church on earth. Against this combination, Protestants sometimes fumed and chafed, but they were unable to affect it in any material respect. In the circumstances the prospects of libertarian democracy receiving any consideration at the hands of the moving-picture industry were not flattering; in fact amounted to something near zero.

Within the picture industry itself, individual directors and actors subjected their products to more critical examination and sought to improve the artistic quality and intellectual standards of their films. Within and outside the studios, some playwrights and players displayed a strong sense of integrity and an interest in the currents of lay opinion that ran through the years. Out of pressures from audiences and criticism, out of genuine artistic impulses, and out of a sincere desire to end the tyranny of biology and the rawness of crime, came many productions of undoubted, if limited, quality. Among them was The Story of Pasteur, of the indomitable French scientist dedicated to the idea of serving humanity through the elimination of disease. Another was The Life of Émile Zola, portraying the great French humanist who valiantly challenged class intolerance and racial bigotry at the time of the Dreyfus affair. Pearl Buck's The Good Earth, a picture of fundamental life and economy in China, conformed to canons of universal value and artistry. If these were products of criticism, then the industry was not lacking in sensitiveness. At the same time idealistic and independent playwrights, directors, actors and actresses were passing severe judgments on their own trade — in letters, articles, and books — under the very eyes of producers and reviewers.

From other angles appraisal and criticism fell upon the motion-picture industry. Teachers and leaders in organized education encouraged the production of films that were informative in character — dealing with inventions, nature, travel, manufactures, discoveries, and the useful activities of normal social living. They urged local houses to exhibit pictures that could be approved for children and to enlarge their offerings of pictures appealing to adult intelligence and aspiration. From year to year various associations of teachers carried on studies and issued analyses and lists of pictures deemed appropriate for use in the schools. In 1938, for example, the National Council of Teachers of English issued a Handbook in Moving-Picture Evaluation, prepared by Helen Rand and Richard Lewis, with the "advice and counsel" of Edgar Dale and Sarah McLean Mullen, specialists in the content of film productions. In communities scattered over all the country, parents and teachers, in regular and special associations, brought the picture output under review and swelled the volume of criticism and appraisal that rolled over the directors, actors, producers, and exhibitors. Going beyond criticism to constructive action, two hundred distinguished educators, artists, civic workers, playwrights, and politicians, disturbed by the growth of intolerance and reaction, organized in 1938 Films for Democracy to produce pictures dealing with the pressing issues of the time in the spirit of humanistic democracy.

The Federal Government itself supplied contradictions to its war propaganda by producing for public use a large number of films showing its scientific and humane enterprises, from the work of the Coast Guard saving lives in storms at sea to the labors of the Bureau of Mines rescuing miners from underground disasters. Flood control, for example, was portrayed in The River, fighting fires on the public domain in Forest Fire, and agricultural extension in Helping Negroes to Become Better Farmers and Homemakers. Since government undertakings touched most phases of American life in their physical settings, motion pictures of public officials in the discharge of their duties covered a wide range of economy and culture. To the large store of federal films, teachers and leaders interested in the future of American democracy could turn for concrete information respecting democracy at work and for inspiriting scenes of public service.

§

In the contest for popular interest, enthusiasm, and patronage, the moving-picture industry pressed hard upon the regular theater, affecting the forms of drama offered and the talents of dramatic artists, if in ways difficult to grasp and measure. Conflict was, no doubt, in accord with the line of experience in the past open to comparison. After the art of the theater in ancient Rome had developed to a fine point through a mixture of Greek learning and principles with Roman originalities, it confronted, despite imperial favors, the growing rivalry of spectacles in amphitheaters and "the maddening excitement of the circus." At length, as A. W. Ward, the British dramatist, described the outcome, "the art of acting had sunk into pandering to the lewd or frivolous itch of the eye and ear; its professors had, in the words of a most judicious modern historian, become 'a danger to the peace of householders, as well as to the peace of the streets.'" The majestic lines of the great dramatists were heard no more, the appeal to the mind and to humane sensibilities died away, and finally the theater crumbled with the circus into ruins as Roman society itself dissolved into fragments.

That a deep gulf separated the moving picture from the drama on the stage was universally admitted even after the talking film succeeded the silent film. Actors in the theater could, if they would, give expression to subtler involutions of thought, to complex ideas of life and destiny, to judgments explicable only in terms of tone and gesture immediately conveyed to auditors. The theater brought actors and audience into direct contact, both creating and stimulating psychological relations essential to the supreme illusions of drama. These distinguishing characteristics of the theater were not and could not be duplicated by the moving-picture industry, with its mechanical devices, its commercial restraints, its performances in the glare of freakish lights, in the presence of technicians and roustabouts, all so obtrusively artificial. Nor was the theater absolutely bound through the box office to the lowest common denominators in America, Europe, and Asia; it could appeal to selected groups in cities and sustain on the boards for years a single play which no motion-picture corporations could afford even to produce on account of its limited audience or which, if produced, would have quickly dropped into the oblivion accorded to the greatest of films.

So attractive was the opportunity offered by the theater for the expression of ideas and the subtler skills of artistry that many film actors, despite alluring salaries, chafed at their routine, deadened by performances in mere studios, before mechanical apparatus, piecemeal, to photographers and stage hands. The inspiring essentials of drama — character, personality, and nuances — were difficult, if not impossible, to preserve in such circumstances. From year to year theatrical journals and reviews reported the discontents of writers, actors, craftsmen, and directors in Hollywood who were not satisfied intellectually and emotionally, though bound physically by the charm of their earnings. Some of them actually turned away from mechanics and luxury, real or potential, to assume the obligations and enjoy the compensations of the stage.

But the transition was not always happy or successful for, in returning to the theater, prodigal sons and daughters were likely to carry the tattoo of the cinema; and experienced dramatic critics were quick to discern the signs of the mechanical studio. When, for example, Alfred Lunt and Lynn Fontanne undertook to interpret Greek legends on the stage, J. Brooks Atkinson, critic for The New York Times, remarked that they might as well have stayed in Hollywood. Their performance, he declared, was clearly "show business" — a "suave and crackling performance of a bawdy jest," admittedly, but a mixture of classical brawling, intrigue, and gossip for the sheer purposes of masquerade. Although such was not the outcome of all translations from the screen studio to the stage, even of other adventures by Lunt and Fontanne, the difficulties involved in movement from the one medium to the other served to widen and deepen the gulf that separated them.

While huge financial corporations with expensive mechanical devices at their command, newly invented, used the moving picture to effect a transformation in historic entertainment, the theater kept its roots in the past, though responding to the spirit of changing times. Its wellsprings of inspiration and ideas, its sources of economic support, its wide range of experimentation in the subtler arts of thought and acting remained substantially unaffected by the revolution that overtook entertainment by the cinema, even if its use of light reduced the use of paint. Groups in small towns and in great cities, moved by dramatic urges as in the most ancient days of the human race, could test their impulses behind the footlights, at a financial hazard exceedingly trivial in comparison with the outlays for Hollywood spectacles. An individual producer could employ an unknown playwright, assemble a few players, and assume risks beyond the daring of huge picture corporations. After all, playwrights and actors, with rare exceptions, had been forced from time immemorial to endure the buffets of pecuniary misfortune; neither prosperity under President Coolidge nor the second depression under President Roosevelt made much difference in that respect.

The motion picture moved along a straight path from highly centralized workshops, under corporate trustees, to the multitude of consumers who took what they got, whether they liked it or not. On the other hand, the theater, large and small, professional and amateur, regular and irregular, chose to twist and turn in town and country. Whereas seven or eight great corporations virtually dominated the commercial picture business, innumerable small theater proprietors had a fairly free hand in controlling stage performances. No little group of playwrights and actors could rent a huge Hollywood plant even for a few weeks, but it could engage a vacant theater, or even a barn, for an experiment. Owing to the relatively small pecuniary commitments of the single theater, mere playwrights and foot-loose actors with the dramatic sense and talents could work up from the bottom, from the ranks of the nameless and unknown, to failure or success on the stage. To use a hackneyed phrase, by no means irrelevant for the times, the theater was far more democratic in sources of inspiration and control than the motion picture. It offered more elbow room. It was more hospitable to the expression of popular opinions. It helped to form stereotypes as well as to impose them. Protected by constitutional guarantees of free press and free speech, the theater permitted a freer ventilation of ideas and interests in the discussion of all great and petty themes of the age.

So constituted, the theater in relation to the moving-picture industry stood somewhat in the position of the farmer, artisan, and small business man as against corporate enterprise in the field of economy and of politics. It possessed a certain degree of economic independence. It allowed a high degree of movement, if only from failure to failure, as in the case of grocers, bakers, and vegetable gardeners. Players could set themselves up in business about as easily as a garage mechanic could establish a wayside gasoline station. Indeed all over the country, barns and small auditoriums were converted into theaters in which local groups or strolling players entertained farmers, villagers, and "the summer people." Individually often unimportant, in mass the multitude of independent theaters and playing groups signified the will to a free public expression of taste in drama, as against the centralizing and standardizing tendencies of the film corporation. Beside the commercial theater there could be the art theater. Although remnants of chain theaters survived the competition of the screen, the theatrical business, in the main, was still "a little business." Its unmechanical whimsies, its reliance upon the strange processes that throw up talent in one year or one decade and mediocrity in the next, made it unattractive to most financiers. The moving-picture business was hazardous enough, but the theater defied all hopes of steady mass production and calculable profits. In remaining precarious, however, like life, it permitted more life.

§

Those branches of theatrical enterprise which were essentially, if not predominantly, commercial in control continued in their historic role, with an eye to box-office receipts. Yet they too underwent some changes with the vicissitudes of the time. As the masses were swept into the moving-picture houses, the old ten, twenty, and thirty cent melodrama, for all practical purposes, disappeared and the heyday of pure vaudeville was also ended. When the country was plunged into the depths of the economic depression, theaters, like the banks, were often closed if not thrown into the hands of trustees or receivers. Having lost the ten, twenty, and thirty cent patronage and pinched by the steep decline in employment, strictly commercial theaters became more dependent upon the classes, that is, the middle and moneyed classes. In response to market exactions, the eternal triangle, the bedroom play, and commonplace though sometimes titillating scenes from small lives were endlessly reiterated, with minor fluctuations as the economic depression tightened, relaxed, and intensified.

As a matter of course also the regular theater kept on presenting crime and mystery plays as well as the eternal triangle, often importing them from England, the original home of the redoubtable Sherlock Holmes. In 1932, when the graph of the business indices dipped almost to the bottom, Edgar Wallace's Criminal at Large, a story of frenzied murder, "enjoyed" a long run in New York to crowded houses. Regional and special aspects of American civilization, always a source of dramatic inspiration, received their customary consideration. Taking a series of Negro legends as a basis, Marc Connelly produced Green Pastures, a vision of heaven, with God presiding, in which religion, philosophy, and the comedy of life were treated with gentleness and sincerity in a medley of folk fantasies. Besides commanding an immense popularity, the play won the Pulitzer prize for the year 1930. As to what it signified critics did not agree but they were united in proclaiming it "a work of art." Life in a little midwestern community flared up before the footlights for a brief season in Torch Song, with characters "pleasantly imagined." Business, reporting, crime, and profanity blazed out during the days of the "bull" market of 1928 in two newspaper dramas: The Front Page and Gentlemen of the Press. With representations of mystery, localism, and particular enterprises ran the usual "revivals," ranging from Shakespeare to Molière, from Ibsen to Bernard Shaw, indicating a continuity of interest in history and in the thought of undoubted Old Masters of the dramatic art.

Although women appeared in the triangle as ever, they received a peculiar treatment on the stage in the age when Nazism was denouncing feminism as a phase of "Jewish liberalism" not to be tolerated. In the play written by Clare Booth and captioned The Women, an all-woman caste of forty actors depicted a set of "city slickers" as a futile crowd, futile even in the home; their chatter was the chatter of the "smart set"; they were devoid of friendship for one another and satirical even in references to maternity; if there was a heroine, she was the economically independent woman who might be called a feminist.

Audiences packed the house night after night to see this play in New York — an outstanding "comedy hit" as its manager boasted. Men laughed and laughed. Was the interpretation of women in this drama a mere portrayal of frustrated and quarrelsome creatures belonging to the bourgeoisie, defeated and befuddled in a realm of conspicuous waste? Or was it a symbol of a sex about to be subjected to the function of rearing soldiers under a fascist ideology? These questions were asked — and found no categorical answer — even in the reply made by the playwright to the prohibition ordered by the British censor when her drama was sent to England for review and possible production. The reason put forward by the censor for his action was the speech against maternity in which one of the women had in-dulged; that much was illuminating. While The Women was still very popular in New York, arrangements were made to send it on the road as "the nearest thing to an old time carnival on a tour of one night stands in which he [the manager] had ever been implicated."

In Susan and God, Rachel Crothers gave woman another interpretation, with Gertrude Lawrence as its spokesman. She challenged the spirit of war and hatred exemplified in violent political movements and in such a drama of despair as Hemingway's Death in the Afternoon. With "death stalking the earth, death in the morning and evening and night, on land, in the sea, and in the air," it seemed to Rachel Crothers that evil rather than good was dominant on the earth through the folly and indolence of people — men and women alike. Her Susan, accepting God as a symbol of the good, was just an average person, observing and taking part in the affairs of the hour and day. "Personally," said Miss Crothers, "I believe all that Susan says, though not quite as she says it, and I'm with her when she declares 'It's the only thing that will stop war,' but I am afraid her 'bright and shining army which can't be stopped and is marching gloriously on' will have to march very fast indeed now and recruit many new soldiers, or it will be overtaken by the hideous one which is on our heels." Besides attracting theater-goers night after night, the drama of Susan and God won the Theater Club's award as the "outstanding play" for the season of 1938.

§

If many theater-goers did not want to see on the stage, night after night, the visible and outward signs of political and economic conflicts daily reported in the headlines of news-papers, playwrights and actors could not entirely evade the spirit of the times, the drum beats of the economic depression, the reverberations of the New Deal, uprisings among debt-burdened farmers and tenants, or the conflicts of labor that produced the Committee for Industrial Organization. The truth is that dramatists and performers were frequently immersed in the surge of opinions and emotions which accompanied the making of history, great and small, in the United States, itself a part of world history. Workers in the dramatic arts, no less than the Lords of Creation, were certainly alert to the detonations, dissolutions, and bewilderments that followed the wild days in Wall Street in the late autumn of 1929. And it was a proof of elasticity and vitality that the American theater could present, in many cases with notable success, convulsive episodes, realistic scenes, and intellectual clashes, illustrating and, in some measure, comprehending the main clusters of events. Perhaps never before in the history of the American theater were so many and such varieties of crucial political, economic, and cultural experiences presented on the stage within so short a span of years. Whatever the verdict of critics, especially concerned with "art for art's own sake," on this profusion of "social dramas," the very profusion itself was indicative of ideas and moods commingling in the central tendencies in American life.

Was it merely a unique flare-up in history for example, the affair of Sacco and Vanzetti, two "social rebels" put to death in Massachusetts on charges of robbery and murder, which provoked outcries and riots from Boston around the world? In a message to the legislature, the governor of Massachusetts urged that body to relieve future governors of the "difficulties which were forced upon him in 1927 by zealous defenders of persons convicted of first-degree murder" and to consider revisions of the law pertaining to appeals, exceptions, and motions for new trials in capital cases — the exact points of law against which many cogent objections had been lodged during the long contest over the trial of the two defendants. The very year following the execution of the accused, Maxwell Anderson and Harold Hickerson seized upon the raw materials of the trial, the agitations, and the outcome, and wrote for the stage their Gods of the Lightning — a play of harsh and powerful realism. J. Brooks Atkinson, a dramatic critic who kept his head in storms, calmly remarked of the play as acted: "The authors had told their story so forcefully and the actors played with such simple fervor that the effect was cruelly disturbing in the theater. As special pleading, Gods of the Lightning was one of the most effective plays ever produced." From the box-office point of view it was not a "smashing success," but at all events there it was in the repertory of the year 1928 as dramatic idea in action. Within a similar category, involving the administration of justice, came John Wexley's They Shall Not Die, a representation of the Scottsboro case, in which a group of Negro boys on trial for their lives were the center of another national agitation.

While banks were bursting in 1933, depositors were holding their breath, and the New Deal was being inaugurated amid party uproar, Maxwell Anderson launched his political play, Both Your Houses, to which the Pulitzer Prize was awarded. Far more penetrating, more understanding in its grasp of politics and business than The Gilded Age, written by Mark Twain and Charles Dudley Warner in the period of "Grantism," Anderson's drama of Washington in the period of New Dealism spared neither business nor politics, while taking account of idealistic forces operating under the mantle of intrigue. In its personnel appeared the hard-headed manager of machine politics and the young "progressive" from the hinterland bent on "serving the people." The tragic conflict between the real and the ideal, which had torn western thought since the dawn of Greek civilization — and beyond — was brought down to cases in the national capital of the United States. The very texture of "practical affairs" was dissected — that everlasting contest between good and evil that had marked the whole course of world history. Playgoers seethed in politics and acquainted with Washington lost the illusion of illusion as they followed the movement of the play, and Both Your Houses was acclaimed as "the most conspicuous success" of the year.

The following year, 1934, Elmer Rice, whose Street Scene had excited both New York and Chicago a short time before, gave theater-goers an acid test of Fascism and Communism, then the sources of physical riots and verbal battles in various parts of the earth. On the burning of the Reichstag in Germany and the trial of the accused as a basis, Rice built, in Judgment Day, a drama of clashing ideologies and fighting ideologists. Witnesses were divided over its ideas and merits, and critics differed in their opinions, with some reference to predilections, of course, but chroniclers of the theater felt compelled to set it down in the records as among the events of the season. Rice's second play, Between Two Worlds, was another attempt to dramatize the conflict of social philosophies — this time on an ocean liner — literally between two worlds. Its lukewarm reception discouraged the author and he withdrew for a time from the theatrical world, but only for a time.

While the mirage of recovery seemed to lie ahead, despite signs of an approaching recession, the authors of You Can't Take It with You put on, in 1937, the good-natured musical farce, I'd Rather Be Right, and won that year's Pulitzer prize. In this skit on national politics, the ideas and actions of President Roosevelt were the target, but the arrows were tipped with humor; the art of balancing the budget was treated jocosely; and the conflicts between the executive and judicial departments of the government were made amusing. In the process the "dignity of government" was reduced to the level of a "romp." Everybody was happy in confusion. Democracy, despite the plight of its economy, had no ground for fearing disaster. The jolly George M. Cohan, who impersonated the President, resolved the budget dilemma in a "skitting, waggling dance." An effort was made to treat unemployment as a matter of fun by having a labor chorus sing:

> We work all day
> For the PWA.
> Let the market crash,
> We collect our cash.

We sing as we work,
And we work as we sing,
Skit-skat Beety-o!
Skit-skat Beety-o!
Labor is the thing, my lads,
Labor is the thing.

Whether the comedy had animus or not, Liberty Leaguers, smarting under the defeat of 1936, found satisfaction in beholding the victor ridiculed. And so sharp indeed were some of the barbs that timid bourgeois, forgetting the thrusts of "Mr. Dooley" at an earlier Roosevelt, wrote letters to the press in protest against this musical "harlequinade," lest it be popularly deemed lese majesty — against the American form of government.

As the lines between advocates of collective security and advocates of abstention from foreign quarrels tightened, the Theater Guild offered to the public Sidney Howard's The Ghost of Yankee Doodle. In this play "liberal" men and women appeared as Yankee Doodle resuscitated and rushing to a new war for democracy in foreign lands. Its time was set "eighteen months after the commencement of the next world war." Its "hero" was an aviator who placed himself at the disposition of France despite the sinking of an American ship by a French submarine. Its upshot seemed to be a commentary on the folly of mankind and on Americans as prize sentimentalists. "You make that one out! I can't," grumbled the critical Jean Nathan, "unless the mumbling and gargling of the actors played havoc with the playwright's intention. . . . One thing is obvious. The play in its entirety indicates anew that the place for playwrights who have been spending most of their time in Hollywood is still Hollywood. . . . Howard evidently believes that a pregnant play of ideas is to be achieved through a painstaking restatement of the platitudes of the late Herbert Croly [Progressive Republican] indignantly crossed with those of young Mr. Corliss Lamont [Communist] and periodically interrupted

with a wistful quotation from Ruskin or Milton." Whether
in this case the critic was "just," whatever justice might
mean, the play itself held up to play-goers' view a number of
ideas that might help to burn the world if European nations
made repetitions in history.

The uncertainty, alarm, horror, and indignation associated
with the very thought of another world war for anything —
democracy, commerce, fascism, communism, or any other
symbol or image — found expression in Robert Emmet
Sherwood's Idiot's Delight, a title that carried the author's
own interpretation. In the course of the play, the thesis was
advanced that intelligent men and women do not want war,
that they abhor war, and that conscience and self-interest
alike spurn this ancient heritage. Why then does war come?
Characters in the play gave their various answers : capitalism,
munitioneers, and nationalism. Neither the agonized cry
nor the ready answer could enclose all history and solve the
problem, and yet so great was the success of the play in the
United States and at the capital that it caught the attention
of England and was taken to London in the spring of 1938,
to be given in a country furiously engaged in rearmament, apparently against its own will, in sheer desperation.

In conception and lines, Idiot's Delight was so effective
that it evoked debates far and wide. Critics who shared the
view that war is madness spared no praise. Adverse commentators employed all the well-known arguments that had
been heard in parliaments and public assemblies since the
eighteenth century, especially the formula that war for
"defense" is supreme heroism. No student of war had ever
been able to draw the exact line between defense and aggression. Professors who had climbed mountains of documents
and memoirs still quarrelled over the "guilt" of the last world
war, without reaching consensus of decision. In fact, the
author of Idiot's Delight and his critics, unable like all
mortals to "explain" history, left the mystery veiled. Only
one thing was certain in the play : the blame for war could
not all be laid upon women.

The theme of war, always thrusting itself up in domestic affairs, as if incompetence, fear, and evasion could not have it otherwise, formed the burden of the argument in Paul Green's Johnny Johnson, a play of 1936, voiced by a veteran of the world war engaged in trying to allay the new war fever. With the aid of modern stage settings, the ex-soldier sought to bring the idea of peace to life. Eschewing the tumult and rattle of What Price Glory and other exhibitions of battle and sudden death, even in his trench scene Paul Green relied upon the subtler arts of bewilderment and inquiry. Does anybody know what this is all about? How do we get in? How do we get out? What is the upshot for plain people scurrying along streets and around corners? No clear answers were forthcoming. Folly was apparent, but perplexity colored the scenes and the lines. Lloyd George had said that the great powers had "stumbled" into the world war in 1914, and perhaps that was the just word. The playwright seemed to suspect as much in reference to war in general. Though far from a major favorite, Johnny Johnson had its special vogue.

Into the lines and tunes of musical shows also crept notes from the conflicts in economics and politics. Among other playwrights George S. Kaufman, Moss Hart, and Morrie Ryskind bent their talents, singly or in combinations, to the art of depicting politics, not too seriously or at least not too blatantly. While President Hoover was wearing himself out with efforts at "recovery," amid the slurs of Democratic criticism, and making little headway, Kaufman and Ryskind, aided by the musical geniuses, the two Gershwins, Ira and George, satirized the political show in a glittering slapstick circus entitled Of Thee I Sing. Friends and foes of the administration alike laughed, and the committee of Columbia University bestowed the Pulitzer prize upon the authors. In the years when wiseacres were suggesting that President Roosevelt was really the Kerensky of the political crisis, Let 'Em Eat Cake was offered as a kind of sequel to Of Thee I Sing. After the New Deal had made great progress — into the depression of 1937, Ed Wynn took the center of the musical comedy stage with Hooray for What, in which four playwrights had collaborated, for which Agnes de Mille had arranged a dance satirizing the hero as warrior. Without any reference at all to music, many citizens were saying off Broadway: For what indeed? The great referendum of 1936 had not answered the question. Neither did musical jibes at collective security, war, the administrative alphabet, or handing out political jobs. But they lightened the gloom and eased the tension between "economic royalists" and the "dictatorship" in Washington.

For those who thought politics, and probably history, senseless, Kaufman and Hart provided consolation and pleasure in You Can't Take It with You. In lines that must have fascinated persons who attributed the troubles of the times to "lack of confidence," old Grandfather Sycamore suggested to the befuddled world that "life is pretty simple if you just relax." To members of the audience whose heads were still above the financial waters, the prescription doubtless seemed excellent; perhaps no others had passed through the box office to the auditorium. Yet there was something heartless in the suggestion. After seeing the play, a sociologist had the temerity to contend that "when Rome burns, the least a playwright can do is to say that he is sorry." The comment, however, was scarcely pertinent; nor was the play itself to people outside the theater, who had nothing to take away with them when the judgment day came. If the theme was a trifle irreverent to economic royalists, it afforded no comfort to the millions that had not entered the Economy of Abundance. Anyway Hollywood thought it a good gamble for the screen and borrowed it from the regular theater.

As a rule the plays which struck into the main current of American life were concerned with urban ideas and conduct, but the most successful drama, in terms of the long run, touched upon the sickness of agrarian economy. That was Tobacco Road, a dramatization of Erskine Caldwell's novel of life among the Southern lowly — not the dynamic lowly, but people crumbling into dust. Politicians and agitators, Huey Long and union organizers were making the nation conscious of bottom poor and Caldwell thrust the problem, if with no issue, into the face of theater-goers. He made no concessions to melodrama to sustain the interest. Virtue did not conquer vice, nor did the heroic triumph over the villainous. To all appearances the denizens of Tobacco Road were immersed in a tragedy of poverty and ignorance far beyond their control or the possibilities of escape — hungry Americans, hungry. Did their plight strike chords of defeatism in popular consciousness and so attract the large audiences, one after the other, on and on through the years? Was this the explanation of the popular appeal? Did audiences really know why they liked this story? Critics found difficulty in answering the question, as the play ran through the months and the years — from 1934, on and on — far outstripping in success the dramas of urban realism and revolt. In some cities expurgation was demanded, but New York City took the play straight. Long after Gods of the Lightning was forgotten by casual visitors of theaters, Tobacco Road was being played day and night, a kind of mystery, yet maybe a challenge.

Taking up another phase of the tragedy emerging from the agrarian dissolution in America — the life of casual laborers on large ranches, of lonely, wandering men and derelict women — John Steinbeck dramatized his novel Of Mice and Men for the season of 1937. Told in the powerful simplicity that characterized the story of the Prodigal Son, this tale of two men journeying in search of work, finding work, caught in the iron grip of things, tender in their humanness, finally brought to a frightful climax, had held readers of the printed page in its spell. On the stage it translated itself to pit and gallery and wrung response from even old and weary critics. In every scene and nearly every line it portrayed with throbbing life actualities reflected in statistical tables of the Department of Agriculture, in the report of President Roosevelt's Committee on Farm Tenancy, and in Paul Taylor's monumental studies of migratory labor on the land. The grandest dream of one of the men was to have just a little land of his own, a rabbit, some chickens — something to care for and love. For a moment it seemed as if the earth hunger of fifty centuries, the human hunger of all time, was epitomized in living symbols. Did all the defeated hopes merely suggest faults in the law of land tenure? Or something primordial? Was any other upshot to this tragedy possible? Since economists had not answered these questions, the novelist and the actors were within their rights in leaving the issue of labor on the land staring quizzically from the stage.

§

After the economic collapse of 1929, playwrights, actors, and theaters were carried into an unprecedented relation with the Federal Government. Far-seeing leaders among the makers of the American Republic, with William Dunlap in the advance guard, had called for a national theater to serve as an instrument for the inculcation of republican ideas, manners, and morals. But the early republic let this opportunity slip by and with the passing of John Quincy Adams the idea of associating government constructively with the arts was only kept alive by a stray advocate here and there, such as Julia Marlowe and Kenneth Macgowan. After the Jacksonian uprising little was heard of the "elegant arts" as instruments of public policy, and the theater was left to private interests.

Like most private enterprises, the theater had made fortunes for a few and kept the main body of entrepreneurs and actors in a precarious state, with poverty always just around the corner for the lesser lights of the stage. Long before stocks hit bottom in 1932, the theater, like agriculture, was in the throes of a crisis. The industry was "overexpanded"; there were too many theaters for the effective demands of box offices. Like the railways, the stage was suffering from competition — in this case from the moving-picture industry.

Clever playwrights and actors were lured away by the giant corporations at Hollywood, with huge sums of money as the bait; the cinema was draining off theater-goers; the demand was falling; and famous houses were already going dark when the night came in 1929.

For the theater, as for holding companies, railways, and construction industries, the economic débâcle was devastating as it widened through the years. Great producers went into bankruptcy. Theaters were sold at auction. Lights went out in cities all over the country. Thousands of actors, thousands of men and women who had lived by writing and playing, were turned into the streets with the makers of automobiles, cement, and shoes. In the friendly spirit that had always characterized the profession, their colleagues who remained in employment raised funds, gave benefits, and shared their wealth. But in time the burden passed beyond the limits of private philanthropy.

When at length the Roosevelt administration faced the total economic situation squarely, it confronted the theater. By general consent the country was opposed to the dole, for it kept recipients in idleness and tended to degrade the national morale, while producing no wealth whatsoever. This point of view Roosevelt expressed in a message to Congress and in 1935 the Works Progress Administration was established to create and provide projects that would give employment, occupy beneficiaries at tasks for which they had some experience and competence, and tide them over "until private industry could take up the slack." Among the divisions of this Administration was the Federal Theater Project. The undertaking was at best experimental and delicate but it was carried out with skill and circumspection under the supervision of Hallie Flanagan and her associates.

Of necessity under the continuous pressure of politics, the Theater Project steered its course with ingenuity, pleasing in the process neither the extreme Right nor the extreme Left, but allowing a substantial margin of freedom, befitting the variety of interests in America. It attempted and attained

a notable success in reinstating poetry in the drama, using
T. S. Eliot's poetic narrative, Murder in the Cathedral, as
this experiment. It was the patron for a dramatic version of
Sinclair Lewis' It Can't Happen Here, after this play had
been suppressed or rejected by Hollywood, following a protest
from places where it had happened. In harmony with more
democratic conceptions, the Federal Theater Project organized a number of companies to present It Can't Happen Here
in all sections of the country, and "for the first time in the
history of the American theater, the curtain rose simultaneously on twenty-one stages in eighteen cities from the Atlantic to the Pacific, presenting twenty-one different versions
of a new play by a distinguished American author." With
propriety, it was presented in Washington, the capital of
the nation, where decisions significant for the future of
democracy were being made from year to year. While irate
citizens were flinging charges of dictatorship at President
Roosevelt, throngs of theater-goers all over the country were
watching in this play a conflict between power and freedom,
on the stage, under federal patronage.

By remarkable unanimity of opinion The Living Newspaper — in a strict sense the creation of the Federal Project — was accorded the honor of being a "lasting contribution" to American drama. Under government auspices a
number of researchers, reporters, and writers dramatized
the leading issues of the time and presented, by means of
actors on the stage, events and personalities that made headlines for the daily press. Into this Living Newspaper were
introduced, for example, the question of agricultural relief:
Triple-A Plowed Under; a résumé of the news: Highlights of
1935; labor disputes and the law: Injunction Granted; and
public utilities: Power. These plays were crowned by a more
difficult undertaking: One Third of the Nation — the housing
issue with its elements of fire hazards, disease, and crime-
breeding tenements, against a background of rack-renting.
When the Federal Theater Project announced a dramatization of the theme for an opening in February, 1936, the

advance sale was so large that bookings were made for the following May. Finally George Bernard Shaw became sufficiently interested in the American federal theater by 1938 to grant it the right to produce his plays; he cut his royalties to the low figure established by the Project, and his dramas were widely performed. Eugene O'Neill consented to a similar arrangement.

The limited funds allocated to the various federal projects helped to restore the primal elements of ideas and character interpretation to the American theater, so long confused and overlaid by the expensive operations of scenic painters, costumers, mechanical inventors, and allied artists and craftsmen. Under the financial limitations of the Federal Project administration, complicated and costly scenery was out of the question, and so was elaborate costuming. Besides, all parts of the country called for the privilege of seeing the plays produced by the Project, and its companies could not carry around with them cars full of scenic properties. To be sure some setting was necessary, and so managers turned to the lighting effects developed by the motion picture. Light was relatively cheap and almost infinite in flexibility and variability. Where special results were required or were appropriate, it was employed, as the director explained, "to emphasize the living bodies of the actors." At the same time, with its limited funds, the Project was able to employ at its peak in 1937 approximately 12,700 workers who had been in or on the edges of poverty and despair.

According to reports for that year, nearly ninety-five per cent of the Government productions were written by American playwrights. The Project operated in twenty-eight states, as well as the District of Columbia. It sought to stimulate interest in the theater in communities, "sixty per cent of whose adults and children have never before seen living comedy and drama." The coöperation of local organizations, clubs, societies, and civic associations was solicited and, it was hoped, the foundations of permanent activities were laid in all regions of the country. Experiments in

Atlanta and Savannah, for instance, were taken over by local organizations as regular civic enterprises. Plays were given in villages that had never seen actors on the stage, in Civilian Conservation Camps, in orphanages, hospitals, prisons, veterans' homes, schools, and colleges, ranging from the Dakotas to the Mississippi delta, from Maine to Seattle. More than twenty-two million people, it was estimated in 1937, had witnessed performances under the auspices of the Federal Project, and thousands of local communities, hitherto beyond the theater belt, had been brought into some acquaintance with playwriting and acting.

About all the activities of the Federal Theater Project, as about all the devices of the New Deal, criticism foamed. Commentators, passing judgments born of their particular frames of experiential and intellectual reference, often scoffed at the federal plays, rating them as deficient in construction and poor in performance. Why waste money on "bum writers" and "ham actors"? it was freely asked. This question could be answered as quickly and easily as the other question: "Why shouldn't the poor and unemployed everywhere be allowed to starve?" Such questions involved, of course, matters of taste and insight by no means as exact as problems in Euclid. If only the plays approved by Jean Nathan, for instance, were admitted to the stage, would there be any reservoir of theatrical resources from which to derive the best? And what in fact would be the best?

When fitted into the larger context of cultural history and cultural resources, the Federal Theater Project's operations suggested a connotation far wider than that of particular theatrical criticism, namely, the obligation of the Government toward the arts as source and force in social life. However considered, the Federal Theater Project was more than a spasmodic event in American history. The organization and administration of the project, notwithstanding the shortcomings, criticisms, and failures, were among the extraordinary upthrows of the economic crisis. Whether for good or ill, whether for the enrichment or impoverishment of the cultural resources upon which society, industry, and government depend for existence, whether permanent or impermanent in influence, judgment would be rendered, as in all cases, by history as actuality yet to come, not merely by the verdicts of contemporary critics, dramatic or social.

§

While full judgment waited on time, the legislature of California took up the idea of public responsibility and coöperation in relation to the drama by designating the Pasadena Playhouse as an official State Theater. For several years The Playhouse had been functioning. Summer after summer it had held a Drama Festival built on some particular theme. In 1937 the subject was the Great Southwest, the historic unfolding of which was enacted gravely and with reference to authentic characters and events. This festival opened with an English version of Gerhart Hauptmann's poetic play of the Spanish conquest, Der Weisse Heiland, under the English title of Montezuma, but critics called the performance "passionless and lifeless" and attributed its pallor largely to the German playwright's lack of clarity in interpreting that series of historic events. Nor did the attempt to portray the rise and fall of the Catholic conquest of California fare better in the criticism; the result was described as a "Chamber of Commerce entertainment, with white velvet charro costumes, bespangled china poblanas, and the singing and dancing which belonged to neither Old California nor Mexico." In short, the effort was dismissed as merely a "civic pageant," not true drama. A third play, however, Night over Taos, by Maxwell Anderson, originally produced by the Group Theater in New York in 1932, was ardently defended as "a production which in poignancy, power, and moving force is worthy to be set alongside some of the most thrilling experiences in the contemporary theater." A second European, Franz Werfel, was drawn upon for a fourth play, Juarez and Maximilian, but the poetic fire of its printed lines burned low in the spoken lines. In the American play, The Girl of the Golden West, a natural quality of acting was regained, only to be lost again in The Rose of the Rancho. Then "significance" returned with the closing bill, Miner's Gold, the story of quick wealth won in the Southland seeking social recognition in San Francisco — a tale carrying the theatrical series to the period of the twentieth century.

That the Federal Theater Project was not limited in influence to its own operations received confirmation from many quarters. To the International Ladies Garment Workers Union, for instance, it furnished aid to the Union's musical skit, Pins and Needles, which became a Broadway success and then was taken on a national tour. As employment rose with the progress of recovery in 1936, actors from the Project returned by the hundreds to the regular theater and many playwrights found outlets for talent in private fields. Definite borrowings of techniques were made from federal projects, as in the case of Kaufman and Hart's The Fabulous Invalid, a defense of the living theater.

Meanwhile, two young "graduates" from the federal theater, Orson Welles and John Houseman, organized the Mercury Theater in New York and opened with Julius Caesar in modern dress, to a highly interested audience in the theatrical metropolis of the country. Making use of modern lighting and sound devices, they accented the play itself, quickened its speed of action, and intensified its passion. So appealing was the contemporary implication of Julius Caesar presented in this style that the audience clamored for other "great plays of the past presented in the modern way," for other "classical plays excitingly produced." Once more the illusion of permanence amid the illusion of change was conveyed to theater-goers. With dictatorship weighing heavily on the public mind and bulking large in the daily press, with refugees from its persecutions daily walking down the gang planks of steamers docked in this New World, as in the early days of the republic, Americans again hurried to the theater to behold "resistance to tyranny," to see the resurgence and challenge of Caesarism embodied in personalities and events on the stage.

When The Cradle Will Rock — an operetta by Marc Blitzstein dealing with a steel magnate's war on trade unionism — was banned by the Federal Theater Project, following an indignant outburst among some of the taxpayers, Welles and Houseman took over the production on their own responsibility. In performance as well as theme, it was unquestionably radical. As for technique, it adapted a method developed by Clifford Odets. All the actors were seated in the audience and only the musician remained on the stage to play accompaniments at the piano. From their seats in the audience actors sang their lines, including martial hymns of labor, thus transforming the illusion of "play acting" into the appearances of a militant labor meeting.

A forerunner of the Mercury group was the Theater Union which enjoyed a four-year career, from 1933 to 1937, on the outskirts of Broadway, specializing in the struggles of labor in the modern world, with occasional thrusts at the menace of war. Eight plays were produced during its brief existence. It opened with Peace on Earth, more argumentative than dramatic, in the opinion of austere critics. It followed with Stevedore, Sailors at Cattaro, Black Pit, Mother, Bitter Steam, Let Freedom Ring, and Marching Song, the titles of which proclaimed the themes. With a view to attracting "the mass of the people," otherwise diverted to the moving pictures, admission charges were fixed at low figures. To make possible cheap admissions, costly scenery was eliminated in favor of the irreducible minimum. Although in time an unbalanced budget halted these leftist producers in their mass appeal, the production of John Howard Lawson's Marching Song was so well received that it finally reached the main theatrical district of Manhattan.

Less definitely located in the spectrum of political colors, the Group Theater opened a more successful career with Paul Green's The House of Connelly, in 1931, and managed to win the plaudits of the metropolitan press as well as full houses for a number of its performances. Among other things, the Group pioneered with plays in which actors were placed among the members of the audience and the theater was transformed from stage to gallery into a single meeting. So attractive was the novelty to novelty-loving New Yorkers that middle-aged dowagers of the middle class, who normally supplied a large part of all theater patronage, seemed to enjoy active participation in labor meetings, as drama, with revolutionary fire and action sweeping through to a conclusion. Although, naturally, the Pulitzer prize was bestowed upon the Victorian romance, The Old Maid, enthusiastic audiences, including many maiden ladies, clapped lustily at Clifford Odets' series of labor plays : Awake and Sing, Waiting for Lefty, Till the Day I Die. The politics of the nation might not be going left, or anywhere on its way, but Clifford Odets demonstrated that there was an audience for drama built upon the conflicts of the industrial world, reported in newspapers and uncovered by the Senate committee inquiring into civil liberties under the direction of Robert M. La Follette.

"These young people are succeeding in doing what they set out to do," wrote Winifred Smith in The Survey. "Instead of turning back to sentimental versions of our forefathers' conflicts — whether with a foreign enemy, as in Valley Forge, or with their own traditional inhibitions and conventions, as in The Old Maid . . . these strong, fresh talents are living the life around them, probing its tragic depths, pointing out its inherent contradictions and its painful injustices, and making theater-goers wince with the realization that, for all our boasted high standards of living in America, our day is one of the cruelest eras in human civilization." But she quoted a declaration of Virginia Wolff in another connection to point a moral in this relation : "This force of theirs, this smouldering heat which breaks the crust now and then and licks the surface with a hot and fearless flame, is about to break through and melt us together, so that life will be richer and . . . society will pool its possessions instead of segregating them, and . . . all this is going to happen inevitably." Having made this positive assertion relative to the midpassage, the writer concluded her opinion with the question: "What more can the theater contribute to our common life?"

In some cases a playwright could get a hearing at the Group Theater in the byway and a commission from a producer more centrally located at the same time, showing that the division between art and pecuniary considerations was not as sharp as cynics sometimes asserted. In a single year Robert Ardrey's Casey Jones was announced for the Group Theater, and How to Get Tough about It for the Martin Beck Theater. According to rumor the latter was really a propaganda play revolving around a steel strike, cement workers, and the "socially unassorted." To the gossip the playwright replied that it was nothing of the kind; that it refuted, or attempted to refute, the theory that the meek shall inherit the earth and to raise the issue whether anybody with ideals can make headway in the tough world. To leave that query unanswered was possible to meditation, but words and action, even in drama, did make an answer in fact, if only provisionally and tentatively.

The vitality of the sociological group was again illustrated in 1938 by the organization of the Playwrights' Company composed of men with "wisdom and experience," not "fledglings." Under its auspices were immediately produced two successful plays: Knickerbocker Holiday and Abe Lincoln in Illinois. Once more the power of collective effort was demonstrated. It was on the basis of group experiences that the American Theater Council was formed in 1937 for the purpose of criticizing manuscripts and inducing a greater flow of high-grade plays for the country.

§

With bold experimentation shaking the traditions of playwrights and productions, what was taking place in that much acclaimed source of dramatic expression — the world of schools and colleges? With what themes was it concerned? What creative imagination did it foster or display? It was a poor institution of learning indeed that did not "do something in dramatics." After all, Eugene O'Neill had studied at Harvard and Princeton, Maxwell Anderson at the University of North Dakota and Leland Stanford; and Archibald MacLeish at Yale and Harvard. Turning from inspiration purely academic, Stephens College in Missouri called Maude Adams to give instruction to girls in dramatic expression. Undoubtedly there were relations, if often tenuous, between the schools and the stage. Playwrights and actors did not burst into full power without encountering some educational experiences, somewhere.

But judging by the collegiate plays produced on campuses and frequently outside, the formal world of dramatic education was little affected by either the regular theater or the course of national affairs. In the year 1937 the fifty-year-old Mask and Wig Club of Pennsylvania University presented Fifty-Fifty, a bit of fluff, as light as air, the mimicry of women by an all-man cast attaining the acme of masculine interpretation. At the center of the banter was Mimi, a gypsy, a child-woman of Hawaii, who persuaded her father to modernize the tribe by adopting fifty trailer gadgets tendered by her salesman-lover; and so equipped with modernity, the gypsies glided to a new habitat in the fiftieth state — to the delight of old graduates in the audience. Afterwards the student players slipped away to their dancing. The flight from substance was almost complete. But in 1938 the Club took a sociological turn in All Around the Town, a satire on celebrated features of contemporary civilization, ranging from night clubs to dictators and radio broadcasting.

From the Workshop at Yale, with its superb theatrical equipment, a group of six persons organized as the Eastern Collegiate Players, came forth with two one-act plays, Gift of Gold and The Bride Wore Red Pyjamas, written for motion-picture devotees. The leader of this group lamented that audiences "had been sitting through the same old

Westerns, domestic dramas, and gangster operas for years without a whimper," and concluded: "We know that we were quieter than most of these and perhaps a little shorter." When the Collegiate Players submitted their plays to the judgment of girls at Smith College, they received a verdict that the "little venture would set the American theater back fifty or sixty years" — a judgment that might lack in historicity more than it did in emphasis. Despite the adverse conclusion of the Smith girls, the Players gave 427 performances on tour, conceding at the end that while their show was "nothing to make an audience stand up and cheer, it was one that they would listen to, laugh at a little, and even applaud now and then." Pleased with this achievement, the group planned to adjust its sketches to the average motion-picture patron and ignore any high-hatted minority likely to be present.

To celebrate the forty-ninth anniversary of dramatics at Princeton, the Triangle Club chose to "put on" a musical comedy in 1937, called Fol-de-rol, fashioned on the frivolity of the English Restoration period at the end of the seventeenth century. With this play the Club, carrying twenty-five dancers, toured the East, Middle West, and South during the holiday season. Everywhere it was greeted by Princeton alumni, their families, and friends, with a cordiality which implied that no intellectual interruption had come in the Princeton tradition through the flight of years. While the Princeton boys were going back to the English Restoration for inspiration, girls at Barnard clung to the Greek drama, as they understood it, impersonated horses in chariot races, and tried to be Pan or Dionysus. In such fashions were illustrated the advantages of collegiate training in the classic sources of dramatic inspiration and in the art of histrionic expression.

§

In the strange times of the midpassage, entertainment by radio expanded with the pressures of mass production, as in-

ventions and improvements in devices flowed out of laboratories and workshops; and it responded to those forces, financial, intellectual, and moral, which affected other forms of
diversion and communication. As in the case of the moving-
picture industry, broadcasting on a national scale tended to
come within the control of relatively few corporations possessing large capital and equipment; and these corporations
in turn became entangled with banking on the one side and
with supply interests, especially the electrical industries, on
the other. They borrowed money; their stocks were sold on
the exchange or over the counter; capitalists with funds to
invest could buy into them and exercise the rights of stockholders in determining the policies of management and the
selection of broadcast themes. Like the moving-picture
industry, the radio industry was engaged in mass production.
Dependent almost entirely upon advertisers for their revenues
and profits, national broadcasting concerns had to reach out
for the millions, for the lowest common denominators, ignoring in the main "the select few, the élite, the precious."
Under such pecuniary drives, entertainment over the air
went wider and deeper throughout American society than
any other type of amusement, diversion, or suggestion.

Through the installation of the radio in private homes and
hotels, in offices and shops, in schools and other institutions,
in motor cars and trains, on tractors and plows, the market
for receivers became almost universal in America. Special
devices furnishing "free-wind" power enabled rural homes in
regions not yet electrified to have the radio; farmers' wives in
their kitchens could listen to an all-day program indoors
while their husbands in the fields could get the same out of
doors. As they toured for fares in the cities, taxicab drivers
could divert themselves with their dials. For the leisure class,
radios were designed to fit lounging chairs and coffee tables.

While tonal quality of reception was being improved, the
keyboards for tuning in were being made as "easy to read as
a ruler." In a split-second, the owner of the "refined" radio
could get the station he desired merely by pressing the button

marked with the call letters. And on the basis of sales after January, 1937, business leaders looked forward in August to 9,000,000 buyers of these perfected instruments for that single year. August forecasts ran the figure for radio sets of all kinds in the homes up to 26,000,000 and added 5,000,000 for autos. On that basis radio manufacturing proceeded.

Through radio enterprise, including the radio-phonograph combination, the broadcasting business reached comparable proportions. The number of broadcasting stations mounted to 674 as of October, 1937. Cincinnati acquired a million-dollar station, built according to modern architectural taste and containing an auditorium seating 600 persons, twelve studios, a music library, and twenty-eight offices for the administrators. The Rockefellers provided New York with Radio City, in which the National Broadcasting Company settled permanently, occupying palatial quarters high in the sky.

Seeing that the radio was becoming a powerful competitor for advertising and in the distribution of news, proprietors of newspapers reached out for control and by the end of 1936 at least 168, or about twenty-six per cent of the commercial radio stations, were under the dominance of newspapers or their affiliates. In 1938 promoters were so enthusiastic that a project for a broadcast newspaper — Nation — was actually on their docket. Inventors were trying to perfect a method for producing from the radio news a kind of continuous news-paper automatically printed on receiving machines installed in homes, by the bedside if desired.

As the demand rose for "features" to be broadcast, supply concerns were created to furnish stations with any kind of verbal or tonal commodity on a minute's notice and in whole-sale lots. One of the high stakes in this branch of the industry was held by amusement specialists known as Tin Pan Alley, domiciled in New York City. In 1937 it was equipped to turn out daily wares for hundreds of stations about as fast as manufacturers could roll out cars or lipsticks. It also fur-nished highly-paid song writers to the moving-picture pro-

ducers of the land. "Constant bustle" kept the offices at
white heat. According to a reporter who surveyed an establishment, "a movie outfit wants a specified number of ballads
on specified themes before a specified date. A radio band
leader needs a new swing tune for a definitely scheduled
program. A soprano orders a theme song. The publisher
himself must have a dreamy waltz to balance a new catalog.
As deadlines approach for melody orders, song teams work
straight through lunch and dinner and, if necessary, far into
the night." Tin Pan Alley, in short, was as hysterical as the
mad market which it served.

Knowing that they had a competitor in the radio, and yet
unable to prevent its expansion, adventurous moving-picture
producers decided to benefit from the supply business at least.
Well acquainted with the fact that "what is given away in
millions of homes cannot be sold for an admission price,"
they formed alliances with commercial sponsors of radio
broadcasts in 1937 and sold the talent of their studios in the
market of the air. In Your Hollywood Parade a manufacturer of cigarettes brought the stars of the Warner Brothers
to the national assembly of radio listeners. But this experiment provoked more questions of a pecuniary nature : Would
the people now prefer to "listen in" at home beside their sets
instead of going to the movie houses to look ? Or would they
be incited by what they heard at home to pass through the
box offices on their way to see as well as hear ?

Perhaps such questions were to be answered by television,
bringing more pecuniary dilemmas to the radio and movie
industries alike. With intense concentration, inventors
worked to make this device technically effective and com-
mercially marketable. Although the date of that achievement could not be fixed, the thought of American entertainment and instruction was energized by faith in the impending event. It was contended by critics of the microphone
that its "cold, mute" aloofness could never make a Henry
Irving or an Ellen Terry out of any actor or actress, nor
a Patrick Henry or a Daniel Webster out of any politician,

however magnetic voices might be in themselves. But if television was to be perfected the dynamic personalities of actors, politicians, and other public figures could be made visible to their audiences, and in some measure more alive. While the subtlest forces uniting speaker and auditor in warm relations could not be induced even by television, sight blended with sound promised to raise the temperature of American amusement, diversion, and discussion in the home.

Program by program the interests and passions of the throbbing universe were enlisted in the service of the radio. Lonely women in isolated cottages could be entranced every day, if they wished, by the crooning of the "women's sweet-heart" — not as of old a troubadour hymning heroics but a paid hack chanting of You, You, You — or they could pick up items touching the conduct of their households and the management of their children if they so desired. Farmers at their chores in barns or fields could get weather reports, prices of crops, baseball scores, or the joking of Amos 'n' Andy. In country or town, persons to whom good music was an esthetic delight could tune in on symphony concerts put on the air by the leading orchestras of the nation, varied by grand opera distributed from its great center in New York City.

Even into the music programs, however, were injected the rush and roar of a factory-like enterprise. "The idea seems to be," complained one customer, "to give at least eight or nine items, with the result that the performers are breath-less, while the condition of the listener is one of complete exhaustion. Instead of cutting programs in half so that every-thing can move along in an orderly manner, the pace is so feverish that the final chords of one number have hardly faded when the announcer is back again detailing the next item." Time was costly and not a moment was to be lost.

The factory taint attached to symphony concerts and operas was made especially obtrusive by the introduction of advertising. Such music was expensive to broadcast. Only the biggest advertisers, the "financial angels," could afford to sponsor it, and for sponsorship the pound of flesh was taken. Before concerts opened, auditors were put in a frame of mind for musical appreciation by the announcement of the soap, perfume, or gadget that was paying the bill. During pauses, announcers kept audiences aware of the commodity that was serving as patron saint. And at the end, when enchanting strains were sinking into memory, came the renewed tender of the sponsoring soap, perfume, or gadget. So music was charged with the blares of the marketplace. This had definite drawbacks, but radio listeners in America accepted them, though not without complaint. Perhaps they were more willing to take advertising with their music than to pay for it themselves through an annual tax on radio sets.

Carrying music, story telling for young and old, sporting events, comic skits, news reporting, prize fight announcements, and similar diversions, broadcasting programs were pitched to the general level of the vast audience. It seemed that almost everybody who had anything to say and nearly every idea bidding for popular allegiance had a hearing. Minorities protested that they were not accorded their due proportion of space and the necessity of paying for it was a handicap to them. Yet among the items, amounting to more than seven thousand daily in 1937, few interests that attracted any considerable proportion of the population eluded review in one form or another.

And here and there in the democracy of the profusion serious efforts were made to introduce and apply intelligence and artistry. After he had discovered that delicacies of tone as well as stridency could be transmitted, the great conductor, Leopold Stokowski, consented to broadcast symphony concerts. For months he had worked directly with radio engineers on the problem of refining transmission, and after making his first successful demonstration he continued to labor at the task of perfecting the mechanical device. Such efforts in behalf of culture were rewarded by popular appreciation; and quick to make use of anything that "paid its way," owners of broadcasting stations saved "time" for the best that musicians could produce. Toscanini and Paderewski became as popular in the air as they had been on the platform.

Yielding to the demand for manifestations of intelligence amid the great noise, broadcasting companies allotted some room, often grudgingly, to poetry, drama, book reviewing, education, information tests, and the discussions of public questions, apart from the arguments of politicians. Thus Shakespeare's Twelfth Night eventually competed for popularity with Mae West's sex appeal. In 1937 Archibald McLeish's dramatic poem, The Fall of the City, a tragedy of dictator worship, went over the air in reply to the orations of contemporary dictators who shouted to democrats in America through the microphone. Under the auspices of the Town Hall of the Air in New York City, the chief issues of the days were debated by speakers of competence, subject to the criticisms of hecklers.

As to the effect of all this uproar upon the multitude of listeners, estimates were more difficult to formulate than in the case of the moving pictures, and the best of calculations remained little more than guesses. Amid all the din, however, one thing could not be refuted : contemplation, meditation, and quiet reading were made increasingly difficult for men and women throughout the country. If a father or mother wished to do a little thinking or to read a book, the children might insist on having noise. Children had, it is true, always indulged in clatter of their own making, limited somewhat by their physical strength, but now canned rumbles, thumps, and rattles poured out of radio sets, unremittingly and ceaselessly. Even adults, formerly accustomed to read in silent rooms, acquired the habit of sitting with books open on their knees, if open at all, while the radio blared or crooned its rival attractions. At home or abroad, in hotels and streets, at bars and on railway trains, and in taxicabs, the everlasting cacophony went on day and night. It was not surprising, then, that James Rowland Angell, former president of Yale University, after serving as an adviser to a national broadcasting concern, confessed somewhat disconsolately that education, even in the most diluted form, was a kind of waif in the radio storm.

§

Everything considered, attempts to measure, appraise, and evaluate the influence and promise of the radio, especially in relation to democracy, brought few positive results. Unmistakably, in totalitarian countries, where the radio was a censored government monopoly, it was an instrument of sheer authority for enslaving the minds of auditors, crushing opposition, and producing a rigid uniformity of thought and feeling. In the United States on the contrary, where the business was in private hands and to a large extent competitive, broadcasters relied almost entirely upon advertisers for leadership. Only great corporations, with immense resources, could afford to pay for expensive programs. Would business concerns, therefore, enmesh all actors, musicians, orators, producers, announcers, crooners, educators, and commentators in their scheme of values and proprieties? Would such concentration reënforce economic conservatism, strengthen vulgarity, and drive the American mind to an undemocratic Right? If so, and business enterprise could not of its own motion find a way out of the dilemma of unemployment and mass poverty, would the radio merely make more explosive the snap of the tension when it came? Such questions inevitably made the issue of free speech over the radio a prime consideration, and in so doing brought the Federal Government, representing all classes and interests, into the discussion of the radio's future.

Indeed there was no way for owners of broadcasting stations to keep the Government out of the scene. By its very mechanical nature, radio broadcasting could not be left solely to "free enterprise." The number of wave lengths for transmission was limited and too many stations in a given area would lead to mutual interference and destruction. Only a small number could operate successfully in the United States and the radio industry composed of competing interests could not, or did not, police itself. So control by the Federal Government was invoked, the number and location of stations compatible with efficient service was determined, and no station was allowed to proceed without a federal license. Otherwise there would have been utter chaos. To administer the "order" thus established in the air, the Federal Communications Commission was created and given power to license private concerns on the basis of "public convenience and necessity." For a time the Commission left some of the radio spectrum, or series of wave lengths, in individual hands free from licensing and control, but in 1937 it assumed supervision over practically the entire range.

With the adoption and extension of federal supervision, all the old conflicts of economics and politics reached this field of interest. When Frank R. McNinch was appointed chairman of the Communications Commission by President Roosevelt in 1937, he laid the cards frankly on the table. Was the radio industry a public utility, a kind of monopoly subject to specific types of regulation? Or was it a competitive industry, holding down prices while, in the higgling of the market, advertisers paid the bills? Did not the high charges made by some companies and the concentration of control over chains in the hands of relatively few concerns indicate that the radio was following the trend of corporate centralization in general?

Since neither the Government nor the American people could arrive at a conclusion on the merits of trust-busting and regulation in other industries, how was any major decision possible in respect of the radio? If private monopoly was intolerable, what would happen if the radio became a government monopoly? Broadcasting companies, it was alleged, had censored their programs and speakers, or at all events had exerted selective pressures on them. But how could the existing freedom of speech, such as it was, be preserved if the Federal Government assumed direct charge or operated the industry, as in Great Britain, through a government corporation? Around these questions revolved a prolix debate. If the industry was to continue, permanent evasion of such issues was impossible.

A neat question, touching this problem, involved the form and support of radio programs to be transmitted to neighboring Latin America — a matter which seemed to many citizens and officials to become exigent after European dictators, hostile to democracy, began supplying their propaganda, even in the guise of music, to the nations south of the United States. What, then, could be offered by the United States as a democratic offset and as a means of awakening sympathy among peoples who had not experienced democracy? What, precisely, was this democracy to be explained over the air? Were Amos 'n' Andy, bedtime stories, symphony concerts, and kitchen recipes adequate to the occasion, or was something else needed to convince the people beyond the Rio Grande that the democratic way was the best of all ways? In just what terms was American civilization to be described as the grand contrast to the culture of fascism? Since exaggeration comparable to the extravagances of European utterances was demanded as an offset to such propaganda, exactly what kind of exaggeration would most effectively serve that purpose?

CHAPTER XIII

Mainsprings and Ranges of Letters

No less than the makers of entertainment, the makers of letters worked in the substances and styles of the age. The business of America is business. . . . High plateau of permanent prosperity. . . . Another downward slide in agricultural prices. . . . The spectre of poverty vanishing. . . . Foreclosure of farm mortgages. . . . Republican policies. . . . Hawley-Smoot tariff bill. . . . Crash in Wall Street. . . . Reassurances from Washington. . . . Millions of tons of top soil washing out to sea. . . . Stocks. . . . Bonds. . . . Brilliant opening of the opera season. . . . Hollywood Hit. . . . Colossal. . . . Stupendous. . . . Crime. . . . Stocks. . . . Bonds. . . . Unemployment mounts. . . . Hilariously funny. . . . Stocks. . . . Bonds. . . . Bread lines. . . . Sweepstakes. . . . Millions idle. . . . Bankruptcies. . . . Army Maneuvers. . . . Election. . . . . Save rugged individualism. . . . Roosevelt promises an adequate navy. . . . Crop control plan endorsed. . . . More millions idle. . . . Suicide. . . . Save liberty. . . . Bank crashes. . . . Dancing lessons at reduced prices. . . .

653

Schools close doors. . . . Bank holidays. . . . New Deal inaugurated. . . . N.R.A. . . . A.A.A. . . . C.C.C. . . . P.W.A. . . . C.W.A. . . . Abundant life. . . . Signs of recovery. . . . Supreme Court blocks New Deal. . . . Foul breath of Moscow. . . . Twelve million idle. . . . Roosevelt carries forty-six states. . . . New hit from Hollywood. . . . Ill-fed, ill-nourished, ill-housed. . . . Roosevelt's plan for revamping judiciary. . . . The Constitution in danger. . . . Communism. . . . The Constitution in danger. . . . Learn swing. . . . War rages in Spain. . . . Kidnapers busy. . . . Big Apple. . . . Sit-down strikes. . . . War in China. . . . Recession. . . . Idleness rises. . . . Syphilis must be stamped out. . . . Birth control goes forward. . . . Debts. . . . Deficits. . . . Vigilantes. . . . Business strikes. . . . More railway bankruptcies. . . . Super-navy. . . . Civil liberties. . . . National defense. . . . Depression. . . . Trade agreements. . . . Catholic protests against films deemed favorable to Loyalist Spain. . . . Quarantines. . . . House votes billion for navy. . . . Whither? Why? Whither? Why?

Ears could not muffle the detonations nor could eyes misread the headlines that daily recorded shocks and agonies, diversions and pleasures. The coldest of hearts were not chill enough to congeal the distempers and resentments surging up in the course of personal and social transactions. Where life was, there was the clamorous insistence of personalities and events. To live was to know — at least something of contemporary fears, hopes, appeals, sufferings, frenzies, escapes, evaluations, decisions, and aspirations. To think as well as to know was to employ some wisdom related to the elements of the situation. To feel and to wonder were to join the quest for an interpretation of the ways pursued by fortune.

Mingled in the minds of writers with impressions received from immediate events were memory and knowledge of the literary traditions in America built up in times past by masters and apprentices and kept alive by the elders of the

craft still living. For the precious and the genteel, making
the best of both worlds, matrices had been left, for example,
by such exponents of the reputable as Hamilton Wright
Mabie, Richard Watson Gilder, and Josiah Gilbert Holland.
For the larger public, Mark Twain had written prose and
Walt Whitman and Vachel Lindsay had written poetry, in a
distinctly democratic way, sometimes in joyful acceptance of
American life, sometimes reiterating plaints against the
lawyers and money-lenders as old as the laments of Daniel
Shays.

A third tradition, set by unquestioned masters dead and
living, was that of positive dissidence, the inability to accept the American scene. Throughout the course of imaginative literature in America, and particularly since the
Second Revolution of 1861–1865, the accent of criticism had
been acute. One of the chief mainsprings had been dislike
of the plutocracy which burst upon the stage in full panoply
during the gilded age, a displeasure burnt into the novels of
Edith Wharton, Winston Churchill, and to a considerable
extent of Henry James, all of whom were ranked by their
contemporaries as literary artists of high order. The values
upon which their criticisms rested had been fundamentally
middle class in imputation and the source of their revolt had
been essentially nostalgia for the past, real or romantic.
Sharing in a degree the same distaste for the plutocracy,
another dissident school of novelists, represented by William
Dean Howells, Edward Bellamy, Jack London, and Upton
Sinclair, had as its standard of criticism an idealized future
rather than a past — a future neither plutocratic nor middle
class but socialistic in its theory and practice.

Unable to submit unreservedly to any one of the four
fairly definite types of social valuation, another group of
writers had given the country a tradition of literary insurgency without permanently fixing the locus of their exasperation or indicating the end of their desires. In 1928 Eugene
O'Neill, whose work had awakened great expectancy, still
seemed unable to break the bonds that confined his genius

within the terms of personal struggles and frustration. Robert Frost and Carl Sandburg in poetry, and Sherwood Anderson in prose, voiced emotions that had turned and veered but had no precise terminus. After leaving the American Mercury, Henry L. Mencken remained in a fine fury against the Philistines, fairly bursting his afflatus in a crusade that finally brought him up short in the political camp of Alfred M. Landon. Memories of Frank Norris, David Graham Phillips, and Robert W. Chambers — the mighty Galahads of the joust against corruptionists and plutocrats — lingered as fuel for more vexations of spirit. Neither The Octopus nor The Deluge nor Cardigan was entirely forgotten by the writers who pondered on theme and appeal. With Sinclair Lewis' Main Street and Babbitt continuing in wide circulation, the petty bourgeois was getting a drubbing as severe as that administered to the plutocrat — when the thunder of 1929 announced the opening of frantic days. Nowhere in this heritage of dissident form, style, and interest was there a sign that sheer optimism might soon gloss over the antipathies of times passed and passing.

According to Lewis Mumford, "everyone who grew up" in the period immediately preceding the crash of 1929 "had a conscious or unconscious debt to Van Wyck Brooks." And what was this debt? It was a bill owed to Brooks for his peculiar brand of biting criticism respecting American society, coupled with his keen appreciation of its potentialities for improvement. "Long before the modern movement had begun in American literature, in 1908," said Mumford, "when David Graham Phillips was a promising writer and Mr. Theodore Dreiser was a neglected 'genius' and Mr. Mencken was exercising his European scholarship and his knowledge of Nietzsche, before Mr. Frost had published 'A Boy's Will' or Vachel Lindsay had preached his Gospels of beauty, in a day when the Woodberrys and Barrett Wendells loftily shuddered at Whitman, and the American past was the sort of thing that nice people didn't mention in public, except in relation to George Washington or the Puri-

tan fathers — in these days Mr. Brooks was the first to announce that we had still to discover the body of our country
and had still to use its earth and its sky and the experience
that lay between them in the creation of American art and
thought. Mr. Brooks, throughout this whole period, was
perhaps the only critic who both saw the importance of using
our American sources, and the equal necessity . . . of holding
our own expression in literature up to the highest standard.
The school that was interested in standards and values forgot
America and, within their narrow university walls, had no
commerce with its life; the school that was interested in
American life, and dilated on the esthetics of the comic
supplement or the exquisite style of the Advertisement, had
no values; but Mr. Brooks was the first of our critics, since
Emerson's time, to have both, and to keep both equally in
view."

In short, a critical strain had characterized strong currents
of literature previous to the economic crisis of 1929 — dissatisfaction with the pecuniary culture produced by the enormous
growth and power of the plutocracy and its Philistine imi-
tations. The vulgarisms of conspicuous waste, satirized by
Veblen at the turn of the century in The Theory of the
Leisure Class, had continued to try the spirit of those who
worked in imaginative letters. If, as always, censure had
been accompanied by belief in some ideal, clear or vague,
attained but lost or not yet attained, attainable or perhaps
half inevitable, still the censure was unmistakable, sometimes humorous, often bitter.

Unwilling to endure the stresses and ugliness in the
American scene, more than one novelist had fled from the
New World to more congenial cultures in the Old World.
In his Portrait of the American as Artist, published in 1930,
Matthew Josephson dealt sympathetically with American
writers who went beyond the sea to their Holy Grail in
England, France, or Italy. For a brief moment at that time
an iridescent apparition seemed to be suspended over Mos-
cow.

If such had been the state of the literary arts in the years before the great depression, if criticism of American economy and culture had long been the insistent motif, what was to be expected after the deluge that followed the general breakdown of 1929? In the late nineteenth century the plutocrat, his ladies, and his politicians had been a theme of literature. Now investigation after investigation and bankruptcy after bankruptcy were unfolding more evidences of their mutuality in interest and operation — revealing some Lords of Creation as betrayers of fiduciary trust and in a few cases even as plain criminals. Finally a President of the United States, popularly applauded, was threatening to drive the money changers from the temple. Were writers to take account of the typhonic events, the fear of social dissolution, the dreams of a reorganized society? Were novelists and poets to rewarm their tradition, their heritage of realism, censure, humor, irony, hope for a better world? Or was America to close its literature? Writing certainly did not cease. What writers, then, what books, what imagery or symbolism, captured esteem and commanded loyalty?

§

A survey of the Best Books of the Decade from 1926 to 1935, made by A. D. Dickinson, covering the years of the golden glow and the black depression, disclosed the intellectual and moral evaluations of the reading public. The survey was based upon 102 sources of information, including library book lists, review digests, group and "expert" classifications, booksellers' selections for the White House, anthologies, and other compilations. Out of such data, more or less statistical, the surveyor arrived at certain conclusions respecting the "best" books of the period, using the term to mean "selected by a consensus of expert opinion as most worthy the attention of intelligent American readers." On this basis Dickinson compiled lists of "favorite authors" and "best books" of the ten years in the several divisions of intellectual interest, general and special. It could be said, of course, that the expert opinion so registered was principally middle class in source; even so, the appraisals expressed the concerns and dominant ideas of the largest reading and writing class amid the upswing and crash of American economy, revolutions and wars abroad, and overturns in domestic politics. Whoever sought to meditate upon American culture thus possessed a group of impressive materials in books widely distributed and elaborately praised in the current years.

At the top of the list of Dickinson's twenty-five "favorite authors" for the years 1926–1935 stood, in order, James Truslow Adams, Willa Cather, Pearl Buck, and Ellen Glasgow — one historical and political writer and three novelists. Mr. Adams' *New England in the Republic, 1776–1850*, published in 1926, had been acclaimed both for scholarship and for grace of style. His subsequent writings on current questions were marked by devotion to the historic ideal of individualism, the advocacy of mild reforms, criticism of the New Deal, and defense of the general principles espoused by the Republican party. He had by no means accepted all the policies pursued by the Lords of Creation, but in the political division his fundamental allegiance lay on their side. Of the novelists, Willa Cather had avoided the stresses and strains represented by unemployment, bankruptcy, defaults, and growing labor unrest and found refuge in preciosities of language, devotion to beauty in itself, and solace in the mystic reaches of the soul; Pearl Buck up to this point had directed her sympathies toward the primordials of life and culture in far-off China; Ellen Glasgow, while personally sensitive to the pending and impending conflicts in America and keenly receptive to the idea of change as necessity, had skirted around the volcanic center of contemporary events in her fiction. Nor was it without social implications that the zestful poet, Carl Sandburg, who had known toil and sweat as a casual laborer and had written of the world he knew, stood at the bottom of Dickinson's list of the twenty-five "favorites."

In the schedule of "fifty best books," evaluated by the survey, the five standing first were Mark Sullivan's Our Times, Douglas Southall Freeman's Robert E. Lee, Pearl Buck's Good Earth, Willa Cather's Death Comes for the Archbishop, and Thornton Wilder's Bridge of San Luis Rey. There was the cream of the years in the judgment of the market. Parrington's Main Currents in American Thought ranked thirty-seventh and Stuart Chase's Men and Machines, forty-fourth. Heading the eight "best books on philosophy, psychology, ethics, and religion" was Will Durant's chatty Story of Philosophy; ranking fourth in this category was Walter Lippmann's genial Preface to Morals; and a place at the bottom was assigned to Bertrand Russell's erudite Philosophy, with less than half the "points" of evaluation given to the work at the head of the roll. In the field of the "social sciences," the Encyclopaedia of the Social Sciences rated first, Chase's Men and Machines second, and Lewis Corey's Decline of American Capitalism next to the last of twenty-five books. Helen Gardner's Art through the Ages crowned the pyramid of "the ten best books on art and music."

In the three years which followed the decade covered by Dickinson's survey nothing occurred in the literary market to alter the general verdict of his statistical returns. No new "favorite" author burst upon the scene with an interpretation of life and values essentially different from that presented by the established favorites. No new "best" book offered either a revulsion or revolution in feelings. At the top, among the best-sellers, favorites, and bests, were Van Wyck Brooks and Margaret Mitchell. They too wrote of past times and dealt with memories. Departing from the caustic analysis and the social framework that had marked his earlier work, Brooks now described The Flowering of New England as he saw it, looking backward in 1936 — spoke of Hawthorne, Emerson, and their friends, of apple blossoms, of splashing rivulets, of the fragrant honeysuckle. With such exultation was this sweetness and light hailed by reviewers and readers that stray objections were buried in the oblivion which could so easily be accorded to doubters in America. The Brooks triumph was almost Roman in its magnificence: eager buyers grasped at edition after edition and the author was crowned with the laurels of the Academy.

Although likewise historical in time-setting, Margaret Mitchell's Gone with the Wind was more rugged in its rhetoric and more resonant with the clatter of the contemporary palace and plaza. While it dealt with the moldering tragedy of the civil war, it vibrated with mighty passions — blind, confident, greedy, heroic, futile. Through its pages pressed ardent youth seeking adventure under arms, slaves, soldiers at war and afterwards, the women of their circles, politicians, and speculators. Rhett Butler, a star performer, might have been a contemporary Lord of Creation battening on war trade, with the trader's contempt for the country gentleman's heroics. Bright colors were offset by black soot. In the trail of the perfume came stench. Nevertheless the characters and events were of times long passed and, if the thought was of necessity contemporary, it was softened and blurred by the illusion of shadowy perspective. So clothed in the appearances of distance, if intelligible to a society still in conflict, Gone with the Wind made a national sensation and sold more than a million copies in the years of the great economic plague.

§

But such surveys of "the favorites" and "the best" by no means encompassed the vast range of American letters; nor did they cover the incomparable richness and diversity of themes and modulations. As a matter of fact, during the radiance of the golden glow and the tempests of the depression, with rushing vitality imaginative writers reached out further and went deeper for materials than in any previous epoch in American literary development. When the market for material goods narrowed and publishers complained of declining sales, dynamic writing seemed to be stimulated, not quenched. If there ever had been an Augustan age in American letters it certainly had not come to a close in falling energies and decaying intellectual powers. Although stocks were in the doldrums and trade remained dull, publishers' desks were heaped high with manuscripts and, discard as they did by the thousands, the volume of their publication continued to be enormous.

For the several forms of media to which writers resorted all human interests and manifestations of life in all kinds of places and circumstances were utilized as content. Authors turned their microscopes on every nook and cranny of geography — regions, cities, towns, villages, lonely farms, plains, mountains, deserts, bayous, lakes, and seas — North, South, East, and West. This they did with such thoroughness that if all other records were destroyed and novels alone survived, students in some distant age could reconstruct from the pages of fiction alone the human geography of the United States in the age of Coolidge, Hoover, and Roosevelt. Every phase of the family, for instance, and in its varied connections was explored and described — love, the eternal triangle, relations legal and economic, parent and child, conflict of generations, and lines of heredity, in all social settings from the idle rich to the idle poor. Classes and races, their characteristics, their cultures, and their clashes were also themes as immediate materials or as illustrations of broader facets of the everlastingly human. All types of persons were pressed into the service of literary artistry: politicians, economic dynasts, labor leaders, industrial workers, farm laborers, brahmins, puritans, cavaliers, feminine careerists, and all the rest. The focus of inquiry was brought to bear on multitudes of "the plain people"; on the ferments among their several orders. Descending to the ultimate unit, the individual, resourceful writers meticulously dissected and described single persons variously circumstanced, making their way in American society, struggling for a living, seeking compensations for suffering, hunting for some gyroscopic principle that would give steadiness and assurance amid the welter, the hopeless discontent, and despairing hope of the times. And although convenience for thinking about the sum of imaginative literature required classification as to theme and emphasis, any classification was bound to be more or less false, so interwoven were the strands of life which ran through the classes of literature.

While many writers still insisted that their function was to sing into the sky if they wanted to or "describe things as they actually were," some of their fellow travelers were conscious of the philosophic implications raised by their very language and saw something to be gained by considering them, if dimly and without gaining any absolute certainty. Among writers, literary critics, editors, and publishers proceeded a vigorous discussion of controlling philosophies for selection and emphasis in imaginative letters and of the writer's role in society. This interrogation and sifting of opinions brought into letters all the currents of thought that had run through philosophy, theology, politics, economics, and historiography for centuries. On every side the Socratic elenchus was freely applied to cherished convictions and enthusiastic ambitions. As imaginative literature was swept nearer to the vortex of great politics and economics, so it was more interpenetrated by the thought, majestic and mean, that had been generated in other manifestations of culture.

Apart from idea, substance, and philosophy, imaginative letters were characterized by great energies, penetrating and searching interest, indefatigable studies first and second hand, indubitable force and literary skill, and a sensitivity to the action and spirit of the time. No longer regnant were the simple hopes of Horatio Alger or the polished refinements of Hamilton Wright Mabie; none was able to "translate the stubbornness of fortune into so quiet and so sweet a style." What was equally significant for the nature and future of American culture was the wide distribution of skills and powers throughout the country. No metropolis or region monopolized them. The intellectual and moral forces for sustained writing seemed to burst out spontaneously in city, town, village, farmstead, desert, and valley, as if some protean urge had shaken the whole nation.

"Contact with life" — with the vernacular, perduring or ever renewed — was the clue to the new writing. In no corner of the literary world did writers wholly withdraw from this vitalizing relationship to copy old masters, refine, whittle, and polish inherited models, to play with convention and tradition in a spirit of literary affectation. Even when they resorted to what was recklessly and often falsely called "escapist" fiction, they did not shine entirely by reflected light.

After all, human nature underlay and survived the fortunes of States, politics, industries, institutions, and academies — pomp and circumstance of every kind — and continued to exhibit its facets and propensities, however colored and deflected by current events. It never wearied of romantic love, the characteristic that so sharply distinguished the family impulse in Western civilization from the categorical regimen of the Orient. Nor did it ever cease to thirst for adventure, for mystery, for the primitive from which it sprang, for the wit and humor that enlivened the commonplaces of life from the cradle through the bridal chamber to the grave. Despite its narrowness and meanness, human nature never failed to display, upon occasions great and small, qualities of character that gave an elevation and dignity to life, even to its trivialities.

In the face of many warnings from philosophers, annotators, and dust sifters, mankind, with or without benefit of clergy, insisted on conceiving history as tragedy, as divine comedy, as progress toward a golden day, or as melodrama, with heroes, heroines, and villains. And respecting the truth of things as they actually had been or were, such conceptions of life, for all any one knew, might be nearer reality than the most solemn treatise composed for personal satisfaction or the classroom or the parlor table. Graphs could reveal variations in American culture, but the breath of life could not be blown into digits, curves, and cubes. To be sure, no writer of fiction brought the whole of that culture into an artistically composite unity. Nor did anybody else. On the American continent there was no tight frame of aristocracy, middle class, and toiling mass, such as had engaged the genius of Byron, Thackeray, George Eliot, and Dickens in England. "The Great American Novel" was not achieved in this epoch of the midpassage — doubtless lay beyond the powers of any genius — but many important and powerful novels were written as the solemn ways of Mr. Coolidge's age merged into the kinematics of the New Deal.

Responding to the multiformity of human experience, imaginative literature ranged from top to bottom, from bottom to top, from the center to the circumference of things. Carrying little or no baggage of pedantry, it could penetrate more swiftly to the heart of human situations and baldly tell truths too shocking for incorporation in the grave pages of sociology or psychology. Whether considered as entertainment or inspiration, it rose above and far outstripped the motion picture, eternally striving to become the agency of the lowest common denominator. It was more plastic, freer in the choice of emphases, less standardized. For many reasons, its influences also ran far beyond those of the stage, notwithstanding the creative liberty and subtle nuances peculiar to the living play; indeed play after play was dramatized from a successful novel. Nor did the formal history, with few women in its pages and fewer romances, compete with imaginative literature in delineating the many-sided manifestations of human nature in action. Over the greatest of State papers and the most accurate statistical tables hung an air of abstractness. In imaginative literature the meaning of such papers and tables could be made as full-blooded as life.

This is not to say that when the plummet reached the depths in all waters that no dregs were stirred and that no writers took advantage of the occasion to exhibit or commercialize wanton prurience. As in every age when preceding order and precious forms had been rudely dislocated by historical events, the pendulum of anarchy had swung far away. That had been true, for instance, in the literature of the English restoration which followed the stern system of Puritanism. Yet when everything was in flux and history was being made at great cost to what had seemed to be eternal institutions, it was difficult, in fact impossible, to determine in every case just where a novel that attempted to depict life as actually lived by men, women, and children of all classes, at all levels of human nature, fell in any scheme of classification separating the prurient in motive from the truth-telling passion of science and art.

No criteria of judgment conceived in terms of mere literary art enabled critics to obtain an unquestionable consensus of informed opinion on the fifty or five hundred books, poems, stories, or essays to be deemed most worthy of admission to the temple of fame. Despite some evident gradations of force in style and substance, any selections from the profuse literary offering, whether for library lists or for historical records, had to be more or less arbitrary and could only serve the purpose of illustrating the variety of ideas and interests represented by imaginative letters. A pretension to a categorical judgment of pure literary merits was bound to be hollow and to be greeted by a torrent of warrantable protests.

§

To the short story the Americans continued to resort like ducks to water. Wedged in between bizarre announcements of manufacturers' commodities for sale, in the magazines, it often seemed a mere appendage to advertisements. Yet a few magazines managed to supply stories without such accessories. Even loaded with advertising appeals to the upper income groups, the New Yorker encouraged a peculiar approach to this form of literature, characterized by whimsy; it was illustrated in Leane Zugsmith's series of stories, Home Is Where You Hang Your Childhood, eventually issued as a separate collection. Without numerous advertising pages, the magazine, Story, transplanted from Majorca to the

United States during this period, manifested a primary interest in snapshot tales as works of art. In 1934 it discovered one of the most original of short-story writers, William Saroyan, who entered its pages with The Daring Young Man on the Flying Trapeze and was soon well launched on his creative career with the coöperation of Mencken's American Mercury.

Saroyan's first little tale dealt with a poverty-stricken writer sleeping fitfully, rising to seek work for sustenance, suffering the pangs of defeat and hunger, dropping back upon his bed for the long sleep but, in the interval of waking, humming the song about a daring young man on a flying trapeze: "a trapeze to God, or to nothing, a flying trapeze to some sort of eternity; and he prayed objectively for strength to make the flight with grace." That the young man succeeded in doing. Grasped in his hand was a one-cent piece which he had found and as he lapsed into his final slumber, he regretted that he had not given it to a child, for a child could buy so many things with a penny.

For a few cents Americans by the thousands were buying the sheets of music about the daring young man and as this music came over the air through the microphone and out of the phonographs, Americans literally by the millions began to sing and whistle in the wind, on their individual trapezes, to God or to nothing, with the daring young man. Thoroughly established on his own course, Saroyan developed the short story as a deft combination of running commentary on life and parable, sinking toward the depths for his subject matter and attaining heights. When Modern Books issued a collection of his stories in 1937, it maintained that Saroyan possessed "a vision as lucid and honest as Whitman's or Rousseau's and clarity akin to the spirit of the early writer-thinkers of the East."

Among the new manipulators of the miniature tale, none was more adventuresome than Erskine Caldwell of Georgia, a Prometheus unbound, using his fire to scorch mankind with accounts of its cruelty, helplessness, ignorance, poverty, and the general inhumanity of man to man. His stories were about people on the soil principally. With the accuracy of his vignettes in detail, the doughtiest Southern defender of regional virtues did not quarrel à toute outrance; but when Caldwell, after using such titles as Kneel to the Rising Sun and The People's Choice, called a collection of his lurid tales, Southways, he was taken to task for implying that such traits and situations as he described were peculiar to the South. Jonathan Daniels, a leading critic of the section himself, also objected to Caldwell's growing inclination to pity his subjects and declared, in effect, that he was exceeding his function as a literary artist in putting his heart into the plight of the wretches whose stories he told. But Daniels was not running away from truth for he said that growing hunger was the great problem of the South.

All Southern localities were made to talk about themselves through the short story. William Faulkner, of Mississippi, undertook to construct a city in that region, Jefferson, with six novels and three volumes of little tales. Among his short stories was a collection entitled The Unvanquished and readers who expected to find only heroes so honored in fiction were surprised to meet Old Granny, a heroine, indomitable though a slave.

In the center of the agrarian middle west, many short-story writers called attention to their region through this medium. Formerly, as Wallace Stegner said in The Saturday Review in connection with Josephine Herbst's novels, westerners had enjoyed "lampooning the culture clubs which sought sordid realism with bated breath and buzzed with indignation when they found it." Now verities were piling up in western fiction and even the cultured were consenting to know the worst as well as the best about their communities. One of the most granitic among the new writers of the short tale was Wallace Stegner himself whom some exuberant critics ranked with Edith Wharton for his ability to tell a story as unvarnished as Ethan Frome.

Taking politics for a gay ride, Katharine Dayton treated

the subject in comic skits which ran in issue after issue of The Saturday Evening Post. In one of these tales, Mrs. Republican, a comfortable person who loved her quiet old house, twitted Mrs. Democrat about the "dirt" which had become so vexing. She had to keep putting up new tariffs, she said, because the old ones simply would get covered with smoot. When the Tiger Cat brushed its tail against her knees, Mrs. Republican exclaimed genially: "Goodness!" In her quiet old house she could easily forget the Vare machine in Philadelphia.

Foreign politics was a theme chosen by Thomas Wolfe, determined for once to subdue his volubility and make his point emphatic. Ancient wisdom had declared that "nothing is too small to mirror the Buddha" and putting much into little was surely a fine art. To accomplish that feat, Thomas Wolfe had more to compress than any of his writing colleagues. But in 1937 the author of the monumental Look Homeward Angel, a novel of North Carolinians, confined his turbulent emotions and brought a terrific surge of political and social ideas to a focus in a brief story called I Have a Thing to Tell You — his opinion of the totalitarian State in Germany.

In respect of domestic problems, the short story was a vehicle for trenchant statements of positions. For instance the difficulties which second and third generations of immigrants faced in trying to adapt themselves to a new and a democratic civilization were discussed in the form of narratives dealing with their situation and their ways of handling it. Irish adolescents in Chicago stood out in bold relief in the writings of James T. Farrell; to seventeen stories about them he gave the title, Can All This Grandeur Perish? The painful efforts of Jewish students in the great cities to master the intricacies of the English language formed the core of Leonard Q. Ross' merry tales of Hyman Kaplan. Old and new Americans disporting at Coney Island, the people's great playground, were the substance of Robert M. Coates' short story, The Fury, which won an O. Henry award in 1937.

That many of the short stories were more than fugitive leaflets was evidenced in the numerous collections published by the writers themselves and in collections assembled by watchful editors. For example, among the authors' own collections, sometimes grouped under the caption of a leading story, were Stephen Benét's The Devil and Daniel Webster; Dorothy Canfield Fisher's Fables for Parents; Charles C. Dobie's San Francisco Tales; Vincent Sheean's Pieces of a Fan; and Wallace Stegner's Remembering Laughter. With the assistance of Elinor Clark, Horace Gregory collected and published in 1937 a series of leftist brevities entitled New Letters in America. Annually Edward J. O'Brien issued a volume of The Best Short Stories, selected on his principles of excellence, theoretically formal, practically rightist in upshot. And yet, if nothing was too small to mirror the Buddha, neither the short story nor the museum of vignettes satisfied writers and readers who grasped at the fullness of life.

§

Without diminishing the favor accorded to the short story, the "full-bodied" novel continued in vogue and on its larger canvas appeared the shapes and colors of widely assorted social arrangements among the men, women, and children composing American society. At a time when sociologists and hygienists on college campuses were trying to impress upon youth the meaning of the family as a prime social institution, novelists were basing works on the family as they saw it or understood it during the years when millions of families were going to pieces in the high winds of the panic. Gladys Hasty Carroll kept the dignity of life and the worthiness of labor on the land surviving despite business conditions, As the Earth Turns. Ruth Suckow contributed more pictures of The Folks in Iowa; LeRoy MacLeod invited comparisons with farming families in Indiana, in The Crowded Hill. Trilogies and even longer spans of family chronicles were written as interest in what was happening to lines of heredity, as time unfolded, supplied stimulus for such inquiries. New England clans were the substance of Inez Haynes Irwin's pleasant Family Circle and Samuel Rogers' Dusk at the Grove — the latter a tale of degeneration.

A Southern family was followed from The Forge and the Store to Unfinished Cathedral by T. S. Stribling, to its culmination in an atmosphere of commercialized religion, with Muscle Shoals, the Ku Klux Klan, and the Scottsboro boys figuring prominently in its setting. Passing beyond ordinary secular affairs, in These Bars of Flesh, Stribling ridiculed higher education so remorselessly that John Erskine, reviewing the book amid memories of his own professorial days, refused to take it seriously and preferred merely to enjoy it. It was in Stribling's neighborhood, not far away, that Edward Turpin of Mississippi traced four generations of Negroes rising out of their slave past. Marjorie Kinnan Rawlings put families from the Florida scrub lands on the literary map with South Moon Under and The Yearling. In 1938 Laura Krey described the renewal of a planting family in Texas after its trials in the civil war, under the title, . . . And Tell of Time. The struggle of a family to become merely rich in a capitalist society and the proneness of women to waste their affections on futilities, in vain at that, was the content of a trilogy proposed by Josephine Herbst and executed in part with Pity Is Not Enough and The Executioner Waits.

One of the most horrendous family novels was Maria Sandoz's story of her own group in the sandhills of Nebraska. Her father, Old Jules, had been born in Switzerland and studied medicine there in his youth. But he came to the new world and went west to farm. With the ferocity of a lion, he persisted in subduing a cattle region to crop bearing and in the course of his career he struck down everything that stood in his way. His very wives quailed and died in his company but he found new women ready to try living with him. Here was man wrestling with the soil in a terrifying fury, in a strange spot of the earth where nature had incalculable ways herself, the contest between human will and nature's course forming a phase of this cyclopean drama of family life in the High Plains.

Second and third generations of immigrants figured in several of the long chronicles : in Meyer Levin's narrative of The Old Bunch, which pursued the fate of nineteen Jewish boys and girls of Chicago freed from sweatshop servitude to adventure in the professions and in politics, to racketeer, gamble, or succumb to parasitism and inertia; in William Carlos Williams' study of middle-class immigrants in Manhattan, White Mule; and in Daniel Fuchs' Jewish group portraiture, Summer in Williamsburg. Using materials on family life to develop the theme of character in slow maturing, Vardis Fisher produced a tetralogy; after declaring that Passions Spin the Plot, he argued that No Villain Need Be. In Roots in the Sky, Sidney Meller placed in juxtaposition the Jewish elders of a community trying to uphold the Talmudic code and their offspring endeavoring to adjust themselves to the contemporary age and place.

The flow of the love story never faltered. But through the changing experiences of these years, it ran into strange channels as it coursed through the trivial and the tragic, from frustration to the triumph of fulfillment, from the intimately personal to the social implication. After eight years of silence, the boy terror of the post-war years who had once emitted tales of flaming youth, F. Scott Fitzgerald, broke out with a story of disintegrating marriage, Tender Is the Night, a recital that displayed more consciousness of milieux. In this so-called "era of business and professional women," Elizabeth Corbett related the life of one, After Five O'Clock. What they experienced in careering Allis McKay discussed in Woman about Town. Women Live Too Long thought Vina Delmar. But Dorothy Canfield Fisher, in The Deepening Stream, permitted a woman born in the gay nineties to live even through the awful experience of the world war and yet arrive at a sense of personal fulfillment. Rose Feld chose a Young Man of Fifty as a study in emotion. Djuna Barnes, unwilling to think of the love life short of a compound of

French, English, and American impacts, framed a novel on that model, Nightwood, for which T. S. Eliot prepared an introduction.

Whether Ernest Hemingway's To Have and Have Not belonged in the category of love stories or social interpretation was a matter of hot debate among literary critics. At all events, when he interrupted his long silence, Hemingway recounted a story of animal vitality resisting enervation, of a man's passionate devotion to his family driving him into a desperate struggle for their existence and his own, to defeat and death. Although many commentators airily dismissed this novel as "leftist" and others charged it with being "hard-boiled" and "indecent," Elliot Paul gave it eloquent and discriminating praise in The Saturday Review. Wherever it belonged in any scheme of classification, it was no simple exploration of subjective propensities. Disturbed as a novelist and a citizen by the amount and nature of fiction representing human beings sinking beneath a sea of trouble, Ellen Glasgow wrote Vein of Iron, a story of dignity maintained under the stress of genuine hardships. Though it was an offset, it was no apology.

As the Freudian fever ebbed, the novel of introspection became less conspicuous, and "extrovert," socially alert fiction achieved more prominence. After publishing in 1933 his mammoth Anthony Adverse, a treatise in psychoanalysis combined with lush adventure and romance, Hervey Allen took a rest. In 1938 he was less subjective and less ambitious; in his comparatively short novel, Action at Aquila, he simply revived the warrior, the least introspective of mortals, as a hero displaying his prowess in civil war.

Back in 1929, while authors of the problem novel in the newer spirit were merely cleaning their typewriters and preparing to write, Sinclair Lewis brought into bas relief a rich man from the automobile world, Dodsworth, engaged in a quest for culture at the heels of a hectic and imperious wife. The applause that greeted the performance was loud but not prolonged. Within a few months mild lampoons were being submerged in tougher fiction and by 1930 a more clearly directed realism than Lewis had yet commanded was pressing into the novel. In that year Charles Norris in The Seed brought this method to bear on birth control; Cornelia James Cannon, in Heirs, on the assimilation of aliens; Julia Ellsworth Ford, in Consequence, on the opium trade; Mary Heaton Vorse, in Strike, on the labor struggle; Gertrude Shelby and Samuel Stoney in Po' Buckra, and Gilmore Millen, in Sweet Man, on the race conflict; Upton Sinclair, in Mountain City, on the role of money and in Little Steel on the conflict of capital and labor; Edwin Seaver, in The Company, on business organization; John Tunis, in American Girl, on the exploitation of the tennis champion. Choosing a broader plot, Irving Fineman undertook, in This Pure Young Man, a critique on the whole of contemporary civilization. In a highly charged Mothers' Cry, Helen Carlisle fairly shrieked for recognition of basic maternal needs.

Racial affiliations, trials and tribulations, peculiar characteristics and modes of meeting life — the minority issue within a political democracy — furnished substance for long stories as for short. From the perspective of the white race, Oliver LaFarge in Laughing Boy and Florence E. McClinchery in Joe Pete, like several other writers, gave their versions of the American Indian. But steadily the Indians were learning to be articulate about themselves. The same was true of the Negro race; it had other interpreters and its own. Based on her personal experiences in modern plantation management, Julia Peterkin wrote sympathetic character studies of South Carolina Negroes. Katharine Hamill, in Swamp Shadow, a novel of the Mississippi low lands, and Zora Neale Thurston, in Their Eyes Were Watching God, a tale of Floridans, also dealt with the Negro character struggling to make terms with life in America.

The insecurity of the Jews on the world stage had repercussions in American literature, although in practice their persecutors were kept within some bounds of decency by democratic politics in the United States. Before Hitler commenced his "Aryan" purge, as early as 1929 when the skies seemed almost azure for most races in America, Robert Nathan made the Jew in a Gentile world the theme of his novel, There Is Another Heaven. In the year of Hitler's rise to mastery over the Germans, Irving Fineman in Hear Ye, Sons warned his readers of a spreading racial conflict involving the Jews — the conflict so serio-comically treated in Lewis Browne's How Odd of God.

Like families and races, individuals as types had their days in the literary court. Men of untamed temper were the subjects of W. R. Burnet's Iron Man and The Giant Swing. Man tamed to labor interested William Wister Haines, author of Slim, an electric lineman, and Archie Binns, whose Lightship described men willing to guard sea lanes for navigators. Men tamed by inner checks called puritanic served as theme for the philosophic scholar, George Santayana, whose The Last Puritan presented a victim of new times caught in a devouring pool of spiritual ruin. Another type of Puritan, the Boston Brahmin, was genially satirized by John P. Marquand in The Late George Apley. It seemed, therefore, that the Gentile in a nation of Jews, Negroes, Indians, and peoples of many other races and nationalities was also getting his due, more or less.

Occupational characteristics, so superficially listed in census returns, stared out of the pages of fiction. In her own way Willa Cather had brought the musician into fiction. Now James Cain did the same thing but in an entirely different fashion. His Serenade, like The Postman Always Rings Twice, belonged to the "hard-boiled" class. Its singer was swept through American-Mexican relations, politics, and brothels, through commercial battles over music in Hollywood, through controversies over the merits of mechanical reproductions of music, through grand opera in New York and back to Mexico where a tragic fate awaited his beloved Mexican woman and deep sorrow came to her lover. Certainly this was no book to be read and enjoyed by patrons of chamber music. That could also be said of Paul Horgan's

The Fault of Angels, a satire on the musical set in a small western town, which received a Harper prize.

As the search light of imaginative letters swung on its axis, its glare was cast upon the politicians. W. R. Burnett in 1936 personified one as King Cole. The political battles between Yankees and Irish, Republicans and Democrats, corruptionists and purists, all in Boston, were the theme of Joseph Dineen's Ward Eight. Under a title peculiarly apt, What People Said, W. L. White ventilated small-town and small-time politics and crooked finance in the middle west, utilizing first-hand facts and intimate experience in a manner that cut beneath the camouflage of conventions. Persons familiar with American politics could visualize through his word pictures smoke-filled rooms with brass cuspidors shining and "the boys" fixing things up. To the surprise of her wide public accustomed to her simple tales of adventure, Mary Roberts Rinehart mingled politics with the story of a woman in The State vs. Elinor Norton.

In a study of The Liberals, which Granville Hicks, close student of the literary tradition in America, called "one of the most exciting novels of our time," the hopes and difficulties of that tribe were set forth by John Hyde Preston out of knowledge and with penetrating consideration. Going backward in time Janet Ayer Fairbank caught up in Rich Man Poor Man the saga of the Progressive revolt under Theodore Roosevelt and traced its evolution through the fortunes of Hendricks Smith, son of a great capitalist, a Harvard graduate, who snapped off from his family pretensions, cast in his lot with the rebels of his day, and worried his way with a suffragette wife through the world war into the golden glow.

Careening both vertically and horizontally through human society, historical novels brought remote times and places into competition with the here and the now for the diversion of readers. Novels of wars, revolutionary and civil, came from the presses with an insistent regularity which implied that neither Hemingway's Farewell to Arms nor Mary Lee's farewell to martial futility in It's a Great War, had exhausted the interest in death and destruction. If, as often alleged, American democracy was basically pacific, its writers produced no great novel of peace as such to offset blood-curdling stories of war passions.

The historical novel was of course an expression of contemporary ideas and interests read into the past. In two novels of the South the vigor of two points of view was illustrated: the nostalgic, in Stark Young's yearning for a past deemed exquisite, River House, written in 1929, followed by So Red the Rose; and, in 1934, the critical, in William Faulkner's story of the decaying old order, called The Sound and the Fury. Honoré Willsie Morrow ended her Lincoln trilogy with The Last Full Measure. Blair Niles plotted a series of historical novels dealing with Latin America and executed a part of the plan in narratives of Guatemalans and Peruvians with fidelity to source materials and a sympathy nourished by experiences among descendants of the peoples whom she described. Combining meticulous research with flights of fancy, Kenneth Roberts, in Northwest Passage, carried a host of readers through frontier intrigues and wars during years before the American revolution, with Major Robert Rogers, the Indian fighter, as the central figure. Reaching back into the seventeenth century, Esther Forbes related tales of colonial Massachusetts, including in her repertory Indian wars and witches and summing it all up under the name Paradise. Gertrude Atherton enlarged upon her novels of statecraft, which had taken early American republicanism and the age of Pericles as their substance, to cover the time of Caesar Augustus and rendered her own verdict — Peacock.

In an age when everybody and everything furnished grist to the literary mill, it was inevitable no doubt that the makers of polite and imaginative letters themselves should be made to stand forth in their settings. Applying her biting analysis to the writers, Dawn Powell, in Turn, Magic Wheel, held up to ridicule the literary circle in New York, its hub of the universe. But with a gentleness as light as a perfume-laden breeze in springtime, Robert Nathan wafted his humor into

Winter in April — in 1938, at that point in the midpassage. His central figure, Henry Pennifer, had reached the top rung of the ladder as a critic, a member of the Academy, a Pulitzer prize winner, emeritus editor of the University Quarterly. What more could a man of letters ask in this world ? The days of Pennifer's years were now pleasantly passed writing on small matters, attending meetings of the Academy where new candidates were discussed, idling hours away over domestic details. The man of letters as artist was well-housed, well-fed, and well-clothed. He lived in an appropriate section of the city. Any disciple of Richard Watson Gilder would have been charmed with the delicacy of these features common to the correct literary way.

But Robert Nathan did not forget spring clouds. Into the thin, mellow light of the literary set, of which Pennifer was an ornament, fell dark shadows from the outside. Old Stuart Orrin, who had been a literary editor and a discoverer of talents in former days, encountered Pennifer at a cocktail party and complained that "the old boys" were writing the same kind of books year after year. Aware that something was actually happening in letters, Pennifer replied, "Not the new ones," and remarked that the new books seemed different to him. Enlivened by the rejoinder, Orrin thanked God for the new books and, warming up, rejoiced that "pretty writing" had gone out of style, that the new books smelled of life. Also into the pale light another shadow fell — Nadia Balakov, whose father and mother had been murdered in the Bolshevik revolution, whose prayers went up for old Russia, the Russia before the revolution. And yet another shadow : a German youth driven from home by the cruelties and dishonors of the Nazi revolution, an accomplished linguist and musician ; aflame with the zeal of a great hope, he cast aside literary pleasantries to fight for the Loyalist government on the sodden fields of Spain — in the year of grace, 1938. It did seem indeed that something was happening to polite letters and the literary set.

§

Poets likewise ranged the wide realm of fact, ideas, and judgments in a world manifesting signs of degeneration and reconstruction. Never was so much poetry published in America in so short a span as during the midpassage. The year 1933 alone produced sixty impressive titles as testimony to the activity of poets. Willa Cather was still reveling in April Twilight. Ruth St. Denis was still dreaming of her mystic dances in Lotus Light. In Innocent Summer, Frances Frost, like Robert Frost, her father, was finding peace for the soul far away from troubled cities in singing of nature and tradition. But Cale Young Rice sniffed High Perils and Ezra Pound in The Fifth Decade of Cantos lashed harder at his obsession, economic materialism. If Allen Tate remained in the realm of "super-reality" while composing The Mediterranean, Mark Van Doren confessed deep concern for earthly character and made the affirmations of a town and country gentleman, with respect to values, in The Last Look. Louise Bogan sought to unite the concrete substance of things with concern for the metaphysical in The Sleeping Fury. With his distinctive modernist idiom, Horace Gregory sounded the call for No Retreat. The sharpening conflict put a keener edge on Stephen Vincent Benét's poetry; in the Burning City, a collection of his poems, he expressed his passionate revulsion against tyranny — against war, fascism, madness of all varieties, stupidity, and degeneracy.

Only Robinson Jeffers seemed to be content with complete frustration, seeing no escape from humanity's incapacities and violence even in death; Such Counsels As You Gave Me followed Give Your Heart to the Hawks — both statements of the tortured poetic soul in a world infinitely hideous. If the world would become communist, Muriel Rukeyser, like Isidor Schneider and the older comrades generally, thought she would like it very well; her USI, for instance, using items in the daily press as reportage of abuses to be removed, offered a social revolution as the way to clean the Augean stables. That it might be possible to return to the old

American dream in memory at least, to the great westward movement, Helene Magaret implied in The Great Horse. The disillusioning present was the burden of Josephine W. Johnson's Year's End. But if quotability was the test of poetry, Ogden Nash led all the rest in skill. His verse was freer than Whitman's had been — as free as conversational chaos. His satire was contemporary and catholic in its appreciations; his wide-ranging observations on the little and the big — first families, bankers, consciences clean and foul, ditherers, divorcees, politicians, night club revelers, bounders, simplicities with complexities all under the heading, I'm a Stranger Here Myself — exactly fitted the moods of countless fellow creatures.

The great democracy scattered out over the continent, which travelers prefigured in snapshots general and particular, Carl Sandburg commemorated in a long poem bearing the cryptic heading, The People Yes. High and low, far and wide, over plains, amid factories, farms, dust bowls, across mountain ranges, rivers, and lakes, among all unemployments and occupations, professions, jobs, skills, and no skills, this poet wandered, listening to words spoken in trains, in lobbies, filling stations, streets, barns, offices, and shops. Then he reported — the voices, aphorisms, sayings, hopes, and cynicisms of the multitudes. In line after line of his poem fluttered inanities, without evident meaning, or at least with no more meaning than was put into the rattle, clatter, and clack of kitchen, barn, and parlor chattering, whether at noon or at midnight. But through the texture of the poems gleamed flashes of great and homely wisdom — axioms enduring, wrought of strong life, casual comment revealing unbeatable men and women, penetrating observations far beyond the notice of "big shots" at mahogany desks or lecterns or microphones. Corrosive sublimate dripped, page after page, upon formalities, conventionalities, "stuffed shirt fronts," the high proprieties of the high.

Below figures set down in the ledgers and the words in his book, no balance was struck by Sandburg; perhaps, none could be struck just then, by any poet, had he wished to do so. Yet some things were writ very large:

> Stocks are property, yes.
> Bonds are property, yes.
> Machines, land, buildings are property, yes.
> A job is property,
> no, nix, nah, nah.

At the moment one clear command rang out:

> First class passengers, keep your seats.
> Second class passengers, get out and walk.
> Third class passengers, get out and shove.

Even so, the people were reaching out "for lights beyond the prison of the five senses, for keepsakes lasting beyond any hunger or death."

> The people know the salt of the sea
> and the strength of the winds
> lashing the corners of the earth.
> The people take the earth
> as a tomb of rest and a cradle of hope.
> Who else speaks for the Family of Man?
>
> In darkness with a great bundle of grief
> the people march.
> In the night, and overhead a shovel of stars for
> keeps, the people march:
>   Where to?   What next?

By any test this was more philosophic than the report of the learned men who fabricated a history of Everyman in three words:

> Born,
> troubled,
> died.

Travelers with imaginations, not in Altruria — an imaginary land — but in America as it was, encircled the country, penetrated the crowded streets of cities and the byways of rural regions, and made elaborate reports on what they saw and heard in the language of ordinary discourse. John Spivak looked for people ready to mount the barricades and discovered people merely eager for jobs or bread. Out of impressions gathered on prolonged journeys, out of interviews with "folks" of all sorts and conditions, and out of correspondence, serious, gay, and distempered, Louis Adamic assembled in 1938 a mountainous mass of materials in a rambling fashion, though with some method in madness, and crowned it with the title, My America — a document of prime importance for watchers of underlying surges and tendencies, especially in the North. In an Odyssey all his own, Jonathan Daniels took in the South as far west as the Mississippi, with little excursions beyond, talked with the very best people and the very worst people, discussed matters economical, political, and sociological with writers, philosophers, planters, tenant union leaders, lawyers, and seemingly everybody else. At the end of his wanderings, he summed up his discoveries, snapshots, and verdicts in a single volume, A Southerner Discovers the South, causing his readers to wonder in just what realm lay the "solid South" so celebrated in the legends of politics. Compared with a Don Quixote on an odyssey was Bradford Smith's American Quest published in 1938 — an attempt in a transcontinental journey to find the American soul.

§

Framed in the democratic tradition and flavored with dissidence were numerous biographies recounting the personal experiences of individuals. Distinguished by great labor and supported by scholarly paraphernalia, they differed from the stout volumes produced by family gardeners and from the works of professional historians deemed "scientific" by members of that gild. Although Henry Pringle's life of Theodore Roosevelt passed the standard tests of the historical profession, it presented no wooden image of righteousness, entire and intact. Harvey O'Connor's tale of Andrew D. Mellon and his millions, based on documentation and laden with citations, worked much havoc with the memorials of that titan in finance and politics from Pittsburgh, called by a friend "the greatest Secretary of the Treasury since Hamilton." Criticized as "unfair," nevertheless O'Connor's biography told truth so irrefragable that even Lords of Creation had to give heed much as they might despise it.

In a similar manner O'Connor dealt with The Guggenheims : the Making of an American Dynasty, monarchs of copper who climbed from peddling to great riches, to the patronage of learning and art, sheathing as with a cloth of gold the smudges of the conflicts that had raged around mine and smelter. It was also upon prodigious research in newspapers, letters, and other documents that Ferdinand Lundberg built his volume on the Imperial Hearst, master of a vast journalistic and industrial corpus, crumbling at the borders and rotting at the center ; and his broader treatise on the dynasts, Sixty Families — with their riches, their philanthropies, their newspapers and magazines, their universities, and their politics. Giant figures from the muck-raking age ascended from the grave in The Autobiography of Lincoln Steffens.

Turning upon actors in the American scene a mind trained in the subtleties of French letters and hitherto devoted to such great European characters as Rousseau and Zola, Matthew Josephson drew full length portraits in The Robber Barons of the gilded age. Here were knights of the bags, not of the crags, the great American capitalists of 1861–1901, revived in 1934. Josephson later enlarged his gallery by a volume on their political retainers, The Politicos, who served as negotiators between business and government during the years when the lyrical "Give us what we want and let us alone" rang to the sky in the morning of youth. Although heavily documented and written in historical form, these books brightened the pages of current congressional investigations by resurrecting rugged personalities whose works had spanned the continent and erected an economic tradition. This division of literature Oscar Davis entered in 1938 with the story of The Big Four — Collis P. Huntington, Leland Stanford, Mark Hopkins, and Charles Crocker, all lusty figures among the barons of old America.

§

Although the makers of polite letters were not likely to admit it and critics were often inclined to overlook it, there was meaning for the matters they discussed in the literature of humor. That too was germane to the interpenetration of opposites pointed out by Bernard DeVoto in his appraisal of proletarian fiction. Moreover in both form and flavor it was distinctly American. In Europe, humor was often mordant and, like politics, bore the stamp of antagonisms almost irreducible. This had long been so — in the scarifying wrath of Dean Swift, the sardonic blasts of Maximilian Harden, and the appalling lines of Daumier. In America, however, humor had generally been homely, earthly, gushing, relatively tolerant — "childish and silly," falling short of wit, said critics given to comparisons.

Humor had rippled into every domain of culture, economy, and politics, as a softening and moderating influence. Many a time in the worst days of the civil war, for example, when men before him, all nominally on his side, were quaking with anger and on the edge of using their fists, Abraham Lincoln had relieved their tension merely by "telling a story." His "yarns" were often artless enough, as simple as fables from Aesop, and possibly irritating to men who were "hell-bent" on having things just their way, but the interlude provided an armistice, eased off passions, and made listeners forget their petty differences, like children diverted by a wise and patient mother. "Why so hot, little man?" The question was frequently an antidote useful to both sides of innumerable conflicts — an antidote conducive to rational adjustment.

The question, for instance, controlled the humor of Clarence Day. From his original Crow's Nest, a watch-tower of his own creation, Day surveyed a wide landscape, occupied by human beings given to curious antics resembling those of the animal kingdom. In After All he described a world "peopled with egocentric men, gracious women, and his favorite barnyard and jungle animals which he used in fables outlining the small absurdities of the human species." With a whimsical air of detachment, he viewed little mortals, strutting about cocksure, imagining themselves most sophisticated when they were most naïve. His laughter even played around the solemnity of that major psychological and sociological obsession — family relations — in sketches of his father and mother, showing the trivial bickerings as well as the permanent formalities of life in a circle distinctly middle class in manners and values.

While Clarence Day joked at simian ways among humans, Don Marquis made a very good philosopher out of a cockroach. The conduct of Milt Gross's Feitelbaum family, unlike the Marxian conception of "bourgeois family relations," was as funny as any of the antics in Clarence Day's domestic circle. Seeing the absurd, amazing, and ludicrous at every point, acres of diamonds glistening, Ring Lardner, Robert Benchley, and James Thurber embroidered letters with sparkles of their own witticisms, during the sternness of Calvin Coolidge's administration, the gloom of the Hoover depression, and the fitful variations of the New Deal.

It was with poetic justice, when Ogden Nash, Milt Gross, Robert Benchley, and Wolcott Gibbs were making merry with the human race, that Negroes began to laugh at themselves and the "superior" whites. They were winning headway against heavy odds in politics and economics and through powerful figures, such as Langston Hughes and Walter White, were demonstrating their capacity for survival in the welter of defeat and hope called civilization. Able to see the ridiculous and grotesque within the tragic, Jessie Fauset, in her Comedy American Style, described the wreck and ruin of lives produced by a colored woman, nearly white, who devoted herself with a tigress's energy to the mission of carrying her family over the line into the white camp. Incidentally Miss Fauset drew jewelled pictures of life among middle-class Negroes and, with humor aforethought, foibles and follies among the whites, including the most futile among them, with whom "aspiring" Negroes so passionately desired to associate themselves. Perhaps in a strict sense Miss Fauset's book belonged neither to comedy nor tragedy but to that mysterious realm where amusement and sorrow melt into a supreme unity. In any case its readers who wept over the absurdities of Negroes must have laughed over the antics of Nordics deemed so worthy of imitation.

§

However excellent the "best" and "favorite" books, however meritorious the volumes written in the democratic tradition or in the spirit of regional or personal exploration, they did not entrance all workers in the field of imaginative letters, nor indeed the entire appraising and reading public. In the midpassage came something like a definite break in the flow of the literary tradition. This new dissidence was not directly concerned with vulgarians of the plutocracy, with monopolists and corruptionists who figured in the muck-raking school of Lincoln Steffens' age. No disciple of Edith Wharton dealt so remorselessly with the clashing habits and customs of the "seasoned" and the "new-rich" classes, both suffering from resentments. That old type of writing by masters no longer commanded the spirit of genius. The new rejection was not that of prudent and cultured merchants crushed by the weight and behavior of upstart plutocrats. Nor was the protest exactly that formulated by William Dean Howells and Edward Bellamy. On the contrary, it was largely an outcry in the name of the disinherited, sometimes called by the outlandish name of "the proletariat." It looked in the direction of the working class, sought to voice its tragedies, and in animus, if not positive upshot, to impress upon readers the message that something drastic should or will be done to redeem the disinherited, by the will of the disinherited if in no other way.

Grinding poverty, it is true, had never been absent from the American land despite its fabulous resources and growing democracy. From early times slaves, indentured servants, casual laborers, and farm hands had lived near or at the minimum of subsistence. Apart, however, from the slaves who were mere chattels bought and sold as such, the proportion of the propertyless had once been small in America as compared with that in Europe and Asia. Moreover the dream of endless opportunity to acquire comfort and security had served in America as a check on the drift of spirit toward the beggary or turbulence of urban "mobs," so familiar to the eighteenth century that they filled the mind of Americans, such as Thomas Jefferson and Benjamin Franklin, with horror. Yet the dream of comfort and security in the historic style was now growing paler. No optimism could be so innocent as to obscure the fact of a contracting economy, unemployed millions, and expanding degradation. Even if there had been no connection with European life and its events, even if Americans had been isolated like the denizens of the lost Atlantis, some sense of this reality would no doubt have been awakened in America and it would have expressed itself in some literary fashion, unless all vitality had departed from the people.

Of course America was not completely isolated and, whether so intended or not, many of the volumes that came from the presses had in fact a "foreign flavor." Often the authors of such works were more concerned with the thought and tactics of Marx and Lenin than with the thought and tactics of Tom Paine and Walt Whitman. Yet, despite the fragments or the whole frame of Marxism which gleamed through much of the new literature, the sources of artistic creation in American letters of the distinctly labor tendency lay by no means wholly within that rigid and alien scheme of ideology. Most, if not all, the writers of this direction were American born and reared, more or less familiar with the great literary tradition of the United States. It was not known, perhaps the writers themselves did not know or care, whether their themes, their plots, the involutions of their sentences, or the dénouements were true to the political line drawn by Moscow. The mere fact that a literary design was hailed or abused as proletarian or Marxian meant little and settled nothing, save for appraisers who were insensitive to signs of universality within national particularities. All that could safely be said, then, about the underlying animus of "proletarian literature" was that it pictured the life of the underprivileged of America, caught the irony of the discrepancy between noble theory and poor practice, and let the rays of hope play through the mists, openly or by implication. So conceived, this literature, whether imbued with a foreign flavor or not, was at home in the United States, and as much as Cooper's tales, influenced by Scott's, it could be called indigenous.

However widely they differed over form, style, and upshot, radical writers agreed on certain things. First of all, they believed that life in America, as elsewhere, was pinioned to the nature and fate of the politico-economic system and its conflicts — in other words, to great history as distinguished from family squabbles and village commonplaces. They were conscious of the plight of labor in town and country, of its miseries, struggles, and oppressive fortunes. For ethical or esthetic reasons, or both, they could not or did not close their minds and hearts to this situation. Whether they saw redemption for the disinherited in Marxism or American agrarianism or no salvation at all, they undertook to describe, photograph, and give voice to industrial workers, miners, tenants, share croppers, field hands, and the drifting nomads of the dustbowl and seasonal agriculture. An American literary tradition was thus revitalized with social insight and criticism.

The plutocracy might still treasure its town houses, country places, and yachts, the middle class might still cherish its peculiar securities of property and income, precarious as everything seemed in the economic panic, but dissident writers insisted on thrusting into general thought the specific thought of other values. As Huey Long raged about poverty and under-privilege in the Senate until he was shot down, as the La Follette committee calmly investigating violations of civil liberties received publicity on the first pages of the newspapers for its findings about labor spies, poison gas, factory gunmen, and police beating or killing strikers — all in the service of "the best people," as a presidential committee on farm tenancy traced the steady degradation of labor on the land, innumerable men and women writers resolved that some readers of literature must hear about people who never figured in society columns or adventuresome romance, people who merely toiled and plodded, suffered in silence, protested, questioned, struck back, or aroused the interest of politicians in Washington. Many economists knew that in the long run the permanence of the banquet table itself depended upon transactions outside, and creative artists in letters also had an inkling of this truism.

§

The result was that not a year passed without the appearance in the book marts of one or more novels which concentrated on life and labor in field or factory, in shack or tenement, in regular employment or out of luck. Jews without money, on the East Side of New York City, almost in a ghetto, rose to public view in the pages of Michael Gold. Up from the deep South came the wretched figures of Erskine Caldwell's Tobacco Road. Out of the Far West Robert Cantwell brought the desperate war between laborers and middle-class vigilantes at Centralia in The Land of Plenty. Southern workers were seen migrating from the mountains into the mill towns, in Fielding Burke's (Olive Dargan's) Call Home the Heart and A Stone Came Rolling and in Grace Lumpkin's To Make My Bread, only to be caught in the trammels of exploitation and the necessity of taking up the weapon of the strike in efforts to secure a livelihood. Straight communism was prescribed for white and black share croppers in Grace Lumpkin's A Sign for Cain. From the moving belts and human clashes of the automobile industry in Detroit, James Steele, in a story of The Conveyor, carried an American citizen, surprised to discover that he was just a laborer, to the minds of readers who bought fiction. One must go back to Dickens, a reader declared, to get such vivid reports on labor conditions as Albert Halper delivered in The Foundry; but Halper's Union Square gave vent to laborers' emotions, in a fashion unknown in the Dickens' era, as agitators shouted their solutions to a motley crowd of workers, peddlers, artists, and mere strollers of the streets. The irony of Normalcy and the New Deal alike, Catharine Brody portrayed under the heading, Nobody Starves.

Who, among the many writers of the dissident school — the school of a great continuing and reworking literary tradition — most artistically blended distinction of style with precision of material and propriety of philosophy? This was a subject of argument among the partisans and critics who regarded themselves as "disinterested" reviewers. Proletarian writers, so-called, might praise one another or abuse one another, according to their notions of artistry and the correct political line; in that case, they erected standards for their own dissent. But when the great metropolitan reviews, such as The Saturday Review of Literature, Books of the Herald-Tribune, and The Book Review of The New York Times, granted large spreads of space and considerable cordiality of treatment to members of the newest school of revolt, this was proof of a stronger kind that some of the protestants represented a force of theme and a manner of manipulation meaningful in and for America. Granting that the judgments of the journals of opinion were not infallible, nevertheless they were evidences that Americans were facing the bright glare of social documents without wearing heavily smoked glasses.

§

Symptomatic of the newest upheaval was John Chamberlain's Farewell to Reform, published in 1932, while President Hoover was twisting and fretting in the White House. The title was oracular and the subtitle was definitive: "Being a history of the rise, life, and decay of the progressive mind in America." With an inclusory glance, Chamberlain surveyed the teeming years that followed "the nineties" of the preceding century — their vast economic changes, the protests of the old dissenters, trustbusters, and muckrakers, the fiction of this protest, the lower-middle-class character of "progressive" nonconformity, and the failure of the "liberal" technique. Then, with an air of finality, he buried all that. It had not been without insight and merit, the young critic confessed, but its plaints and its efforts to dissolve the battlements of plutocracy had been in vain: the census returns of modern corporations showed the inanity of its hopes and the ineptitude of its methods.

After the funeral speech, what of the future? Chamberlain faced that question and made replies. Russia "with no six per cents to pay investors" will put a clamp on capitalist expansion. The uncovering of new markets in distant places or in new gadgets offers no promise. Fascism? Yes, it may intervene, but not forever, "for Fascism implies the development of the labor-syndicate idea; and it would be only a question of opportunity before the syndicates attempted their own march to power." What of labor on the land, a continent washing out to sea, the physical base of civilization disintegrating beneath the "labor-syndicates"? Into that final question even the daring Chamberlain did not go. Perhaps, in drawing the curtain of oblivion over progressivism and its works he had done enough for one young man. At all events, he had correctly described the intellectual cleavage that separated "the great tradition" of letters from the thought of the current years.

In illustrating the rupture between the old and the new, John Chamberlain contrasted John Dos Passos with Frank Norris and the juxtaposition was effective. Dos Passos was born in 1896, the exciting year of populism, Bryan, and the crown-of-thorns speech; moreover, he was born in Chicago where the "revolutionary" Democrats assembled to challenge Mark Hanna and gold. Graduated from Harvard while the world war was raging, he served in an ambulance corps under the Red Cross in 1917–1919, spent seasons of searching and appraising in Washington, London, Paris, and Madrid, and was apparently fascinated by the mighty upheaval in Russia. In the buzzing years of normalcy he began publishing and kept on writing in the rosy prospects of the golden glow. His play, The Garbage Man, issued while President Coolidge occupied the throne of contentment, was symptomatic of unrest beneath the seats of the mighty.

Beginning in 1930, while the Lords of Creation were caught in their own melée, Dos Passos published three studies of the American scene, the like of which had never before appeared in American print: The 42nd Parallel, Nineteen Nineteen, and The Big Money, all combined, revamped, and published in 1937 under the title U. S. A. Like a Kansas cyclone that gathers up men, women, children, houses, barns, shops, factories, machines, dry goods, and chickens in a swirl of dust and wind, Dos Passos tore through the years from the close of the nineteenth century and across the continent, scooping into his omnibus events, personalities, scenes, conversations, maladies, stews, aspirations, and follies. Whatever verdict sciolists or philologists might render on this feat, it proclaimed an underlying, persistent, and irresistible rejection of complacency — a dynamic, typhonic, devastating rejection. Such satire might perish from the earth. It might not. Juvenal survived even the Empire.

To whatever category of ideology Dos Passos' U. S. A. belonged, it was certainly not fiction to be enfolded by the adjective "genteel." Here was no soft story opening with a stately mansion in a setting of graceful elms or fragrant magnolia blossoms and finishing at the bridal chamber. Its fibre was hard and its range was as wide as the total economy of American society. Starting with the Spanish-American

War, it raced on through the fruition of imperialist expansion. The reader was introduced at the outset to the symbol of foreign adventure — General Miles, dressed in a gaudy uniform, mounted on a spirited charger to head the great military parade in the national capital, at the verge of the closing nineteenth century, during the administration of President McKinley. General Miles was not long erect, however, for the spirited horse threw the rider in the dust of the capital, suggesting an anagoge. Leaving the President and his successors to rustle papers in their office, the narrative then crashed through time to the point where the utility magnate, Samuel Insull, incarnation of great capitalism, at his trial in Chicago for defrauding investors, confessed that he had made a petty error of ten millions in his accounting, was pronounced "not guilty" by a jury of his peers, and went into retirement on a pension, smiling through his tears.

In the involutions and evolutions of U. S. A., the tale of the promised land of youth led on, under the caption of "Mary French," to a group of workers wrestling with they scarcely knew what; on to stranded young people hitch-hiking across the continent, uprooted, while Pullman airplanes roared through the skies above them. In bas relief stood out a typical lad who had been indoctrinated at school with the patriotic ideas of U. S. A. as a fairy realm of opportunity, home-owning, survival of the fittest, and the speed indicative of prowess and courage. He had listened to radio crooners, in the excellent age of the machine, whispering of girls, girls, girls, and he had seen platinum blonds coaxing boys from the screens in motion-picture houses. He had read about millions of dollars chalked up on boards at the Exchange and of big executives with three telephones on their desks, always ringing amid the roar of business enterprise. Misfortune had overtaken the lad, however, not fortune, and, in the closing scene of U. S. A., he is the Vagabond waiting beside the speeding traffic, hungry and footsore, hoping only to thumb his way "a hundred miles down the road."

In the interstices of U. S. A. were newsreels, camera shots, fragments from headlines, blinding word pictures of daily scenes, and stories of life, common and uncommon. The eternal man-woman problem gleamed and sputtered through the pages in all the different settings for its never-to-be-attained solution, though not alone — always with its place in the economic scale. In impetuous yet not altogether disorderly array, were crowded politicians, editors, financiers, gamblers, stocks, bonds, "furreners," detective agencies, livery stables, Manila Bay, automobiles, "the Roosevelt boys," cold wind blowing, Andrew Carnegie extolling the advantages of the higher learning, locomotive firemen, large men fond of whiskey, Eugene Debs in Woodrow Wilson's jail, an infidel believing in Darwin and natural selection, the world war with all its blah, blah, boom, boom, munitioneers cutting melons, Dr. Wilson a man of standing who talked correct English, morgues, reek of lime and death, Y. M. C. A., Mr. Harding praying to God, United States Steel, martial law, strikes, mine explosion, Lindbergh the aviator, Russia, Trotsky, Stalin, Hearst in a black frock coat and a ten-gallon hat, big smash in stocks, down, down, down, prosperity near, "real values unharmed," Roosevelt administration, companies, corporations, J. Pierpont Morgan, and Owen D. Young. On and on passed the pageant to its end — youth thumbing its way down the road — somewhere, nowhere.

If to possessors of the orthodox frame of social reference — profits, progress, and prosperity — the brain storm seemed sheer madness or awful effrontery, it had justification in the historical record, with a multitude of things unmentioned. This version of the U. S. A. might not be wholly true and permanent. But what was wholly true and permanent? Who in high places, with the most efficient research secretaries at hand, could answer that question?

Whether to be praised or condemned, Dos Passos' apparently impressionistic, yet closely-knit portrayal of years and scenes had lofty sanction. Long before it was published,

Herbert Hoover had given some warrant to every passage. Speaking before the Federated Engineering Societies in 1920, Mr. Hoover had said:

"Our economic system [despite its accomplishments] . . . presents a series of human and social difficulties to the solution of which we are groping."

(Dos Passos illustrated them.)

"The congestion of population is producing subnormal conditions of life."

(Dos Passos documented them.)

"The vast repetitive operations are dulling the human mind."

(Dos Passos described results.)

"The intermittency of employment due to the bad co-ordination of industry, the great waves of unemployment in the ebb and flow of economic tides, the ever present industrial conflicts by strike and lockout, produce infinite wastes and great suffering."

(Dos Passos lifted the lid of the seething cauldron covered by this politico-economic generalization.)

"Our business enterprises have become so large and complex that the old pleasant relationship between employer and worker has, to a great extent, disappeared."

(Dos Passos made pointed references to the new, unpleasant relationships.)

"The aggregation of great wealth with its power to economic domination presents social and economic ills which we are constantly struggling to remedy."

(Dos Passos incorporated these ills in battered and torn personalities.)

§

Also in the forms of poetry the scheme of things entire was drawn into the reckonings of the midpassage. Swinging around a wide circle of urbanism and ruralism, Archibald MacLeish sought to wrest from the totality its guarded meaning. Son of Yale University, graduate of the Harvard

Law School, destined by birth and education for the circle of genteel comfort, MacLeish had been plunged into the world war and thrown back from that chaos shocked and pensive. Presumably he might have joined Richard Whitney at the Stock Exchange, but he turned to letters instead. Tentatively, it seems, he groped his way through unfolding experience, recording his adventures in verse and play, growing steadily in strength and precision. New Found Land was published in 1930; Conquistador, which won the Pulitzer poetry prize, in 1932; and Frescoes for Mr. Rockefeller's City, depicting crassness and beauty, in 1933.

Then in 1937, MacLeish's saga, The Fall of the City — a tale of the dictator's coming and of masses prostrating themselves in the presence of the false, if fair, god — was recited to the public over the radio. This theme was "the pitiful, blind, foredefeated, subhuman, yet all-too-human, bowing of a people before an invading Conqueror, whose actual hollowness is disguised by heavy clanking armor." As the Conqueror lifted his visor a Voice cried:

> The Helmet is hollow!
> The metal is empty! The armor is empty! I tell you
> There's no one at all there; there's only the metal;
> The barrel of metal: the bundle of armor. It's empty!
> The push of a stiff pole at the nipple would topple it.
> They don't see! They lie on the paving. They lie in the
> Burnt spears: the ashes of arrows. They lie there. . . .
> They don't see or they won't see. They are silent. . . .

That was a startling literary event: the actor at the microphone, speaking unprinted lines, emphasizing, giving color and compulsion to words and sentences, an unseen audience at night listening, following, awaiting the climax, transported by the author's moving narrative and the spell of the intonations. And perhaps strangest of all was the fact that MacLeish was an associate editor of Fortune, the new magazine sold at a price which only the rich could pay.

The following year, 1938, MacLeish chose still another medium: a combination of photographic pictures and verse, entitled Land of the Free. From the pictures stared, in livid shapes, personalities and situations recorded in the statistics of labor and tenancy : a coal miner's daughter on an old iron cot, wandering fruit pickers, share croppers, the Republic Steel riot, police wielding clubs against unarmed workers, men and women falling in heaps, trade union organizers beaten over the head by agents of law and order, farmers evicted from homes by dust storms, hovels called homes collapsing into tatters, hard-favored heirs and heiresses of ignorance, misfortune, and neglect, children bending their backs over gruelling toil, thin-lipped, squint-eyed, or pop-eyed men and women stranded in the march of progress to success.

Margaret Bourke-White, Dorothea Lange, Arthur Rothstein, Russell Lee, and others supplied the photographs of life in the land of the free. MacLeish furnished the words — simple, questioning words; inadequate only because human inventiveness had never found a language capable of expressing such human feeling, human sorrow, human wonder. Although literary experts inquired whether the poet had really captured the mood of dying hopes, bloody tragedy, confusion, and pulsing fear, there could be no doubt that he had conveyed the contrasts between the "ill-housed, ill-clad, ill-nourished" of President Roosevelt's second inaugural and the American dream of freedom, abundance, and victory.

Wondering fathers, mothers, and children found voice in the poet's voice:

Maybe the proposition is self-evident.

Maybe we were endowed by our creator
With certain inalienable rights, including
The right to assemble in peace and petition.

Maybe.

But try it in South Chicago Memorial Day
With the mick police on the prairie in front of the factory
Gunning you down from behind and for what?
  For liberty?

Between photographs of strikers and police at the Republic
Steel Company's plant in South Chicago and of a prostrate
laborer vainly trying to protect his skull from a rain of blows,
MacLeish questioned the promise of nature and nature's
God incorporated in the Declaration of Independence:

> Maybe God Almighty wrote it out;
> We could shoot off our mouths where we pleased
> and with what and no Thank-yous.

> But try it at River Rouge with the Ford militia.
> Try it if Mister Ford's opinions are otherwise.
> Try it and see where you land with your back broken.

What answer had the poet for the question that came
hurtling through the pictures of people, land, and factories?
No smooth and certain spring into freedom. Perhaps the
disinherited had some resolution for the dilemma? Probably
not. Neither did the poet, who may have double-distilled
the quintessence of the hour and occasion better than statisticians and dialectitians:

> We wonder if the liberty is done:
> The dreaming is finished
> We can't say
> We aren't sure. . . .
> Or if there's something different men can dream . . .
> Or if there's something different men can mean by Liberty,
> We wonder . . .
> We don't know
> We're asking. . . .

While MacLeish left his characters wondering and asking,
Paul Engle supplied a definite answer to the big question.
In one of his earlier poems, The Troubadour of Eze, Engle
had avowed implicit faith in the American way:

> Here to my town has the world's
>   great power come over
> The torn, dream-furrowed ocean,
>   and now waits
> A stronger form that the New
>   World alone
> Can give to its old and proud
>   nobility.

But in 1936, in Break the Heart's Anger, Paul Engle cast off the spell and avowed himself a disciple of Lenin. Having scrutinized America, England, Germany, and Russia, he could find no praise for democracy; nor for fascism. The riddle of the universe, in his opinion, had been solved by Lenin, if not by Russia.

Often the titles of poems themselves betrayed the underlying points of reference: as for instance Maxwell Bodenheim's To a Revolutionary Girl; Kenneth Fearing's No Credit; Robert Gessner's Cross of Flame; Langston Hughes' Ballad of Lenin and Sharecroppers; Joseph Kalar's Worker Uprooted; Alfred Kreymborg's American Jeremiad; Norman MacLeod's Coal Strike; Harry Alan Potamkin's Haymarket; and Muriel Rukeyser's City of Monuments. Coming from a Utah Canyon to the great city of New York, its ways throbbing, its thought shaken by disturbing events, its people in tumult, Phyllis M'Ginley burst into a Carol with Variations:

> Sing hosanna, sing Noël.
> Sing the gunner and the shell.
> Sing the candle, sing the lamp,
> Sing the Concentration Camp.
> Sing the season born anew,
> Sing of exile for the Jew,
> Wreathe the world with evergreen.
> Praise the cunning submarine.
> Sing the barbed and bitter wire,
> Poison gas and liquid fire,
> Bullet, bomb and hand grenade,
> And the heart of man, afraid.
> Christ is come, the Light hath risen,
> All our foes are safe in prison,
> And the Christmastide begets
> Seven million bayonets.

§

Positive as to the frame of social reference were the novels of James T. Farrell: Studs Lonigan, Gas-House McGinty,

and A World I Never Made. Any controversy about that
he himself dismissed in A Note on Literary Criticism, characterized by Edmund Wilson as "One of the few intelligent
discussions of literature from the Marxist point of view which
have yet been written by Americans." In A World I Never
Made, published in 1936, Farrell centered his story in
Chicago during the year 1911, and gave another picture of a
working class family of Irish origins, struggling in the jungle
of economic scarcity and uncertainty.

The hero of the occasion, if a defeated driver of an express
wagon could be called such, was Jim O'Neill, who knew a
little Shakespeare, married a gay lass, and in her company
slid down hill into endless toil, poverty, and wrangling,
relieved by rare bits of good luck. Their home? Peeling wall
paper, drab red bricks, noise of trains, smell, smoke, and dust.
The bedroom? "The worst in the whole place. Jim glanced
around, junk all over, the dresser in the corner piled with
it, rags, clothes, junk, and the table on the left with a slab
of grocery box in place of one leg; it, too, was piled and
littered with every damn thing in the house." Here lay Lizz,
his wife, "smiling weakly at him, her face round, full, un-
washed, her mouth weak, her eyes dark, a soiled rag under her
chin, her hair uncombed" — bringing another child into the
world that already had too many. In the weary round and
round of toiling and moiling came one stroke of dubious
fortune — a thousand dollars in cash as damages for an
injury to their little boy, run over by a wagon!

Woven into the life of a single family were the lives of
relatives — some begirt by the bands of wage-earning, others
mounting to the rim of the middle class — salesmen, hack
lawyers, politicians of large hopes and small accomplishments. Threading his way through the scene was a little
lumber man with the psychology of a Napoleon in business.
"Well, Peg," boasted Lorry Robinson, "things will pick up.
The possibilities in this country are endless. America is going
to be the richest nation in all history. Why, we've got everything here. Peg, you should see some of my lumber lands.

Resources? They are beyond calculation. We are coming into an age that is bound to be the wealthiest the human race has ever known. Times are a little tight now. I know most of my money is tied up, and I've had to put up every cent I could raise as collateral for loans I needed to swing some of my deals out west. But that's only temporary. . . . The business system is catching its wind again now. Don't you worry." In time, said this little king of big business in dreams, he would divorce his wife and marry Peg — a wastrel and bounder, on her way in the great rich America, now burdened with casualties but certain to be the wealthiest country the human race had ever known. In its fashion, that too was an American dream, not true at the moment all around, but prized and nourished.

Seeping into the minds of little men dreaming of great riches through salesmanship was the animus which Farrell treated as "spiritual success." Is there sales resistance on the ground that times are hard and business is poor? "The power of wishing and concentration is a mighty force that no man can beat. Jesus said that faith can move mountains. And it can! Al, if you wish for something and concentrate on it wholly and completely with strong faith in your wish, there is nothing on God's earth that can stop you! Absolutely nothing! The power of the wish is the mightiest of powers. It is the true kernel of wisdom in the teaching of Jesus. That's what he meant by faith."

It was all well and good to believe in God, the Holy Trinity, and the hereafter, but the business man's paradise was to come on earth. The concentrated wish would bring it. No doubt about it. Only the week before, the wishing shoe salesman had sold a big order "to old Guggins of the High Class Shoe Emporium" in Kokomo. "Before I called on him I sent out a thought-wish that would go through the cosmos and connect up with his psyche." When the salesman entered Guggins' store on his errand of wish-fulfillment, he greeted the crusty codger: "And, say, you're looking fine, young and peppy, just like a college boy." Result? "Well, Al, to make a long story short, he bought three cases of shoes off me. And you know, he still doesn't know how he was sold." Faith, confidence, wish-concentration, they would move mountains, break down sales resistance, master the panic, and make everybody rich, except possibly salesmen who did not have the right line of talk and ought to be digging ditches.

In and out through Farrell's narrative, too, ran threads of politics, the real politics of corralling voters with favors, electing the right boys, playing the game with men of money, holding the jobs, democratic and Democratic politics. "Any workingman who votes for the Republicans," exclaimed the express-wagon driver, "is a damn fool!" It was the right thing to hold a trade union card, strike, wreck wagons, "and punch the living Jesus out of every damn scab who tries to drive one." A mild Socialist of the Debs school protested that "sabotage and violence will never get you anywhere. The bosses like that. They can put the cops on you then, and the newspapers say you're anarchists." That may be "but you Socialists will never get anywhere. . . . You Socialists are lunatics."

Times were hard for Jim O'Neill, but "I'll make my kids something better." Jim was not going to crack his brains about socialism. He would depend upon his own fists and do his own fighting — against scabs who tried to cut wages and take his job. There was, however, a small hope in politics: "Maybe if we get the Democrats in Washington next year they'll give the people some things." Well, Farrell might have added, Woodrow Wilson was elected and he gave labor Samuel Gompers' "magna charta" and the eight hour day for trainmen — and a little later war and the sedition act. Debs got somewhere — that is, in the Atlanta penitentiary, where he stayed until President Harding and Attorney General Daugherty let him out. But Farrell was writing of 1911 and at that time Al thought that by 1931 "everybody in America who's worth his salt ought to be rich." In massing his materials Farrell relied on force, not grace but, as Ralph

Thompson said in reviewing for The New York Times his No Star Is Lost, "merely graceful writers come by the dozen."

§

While Dos Passos and Farrell centered their thought mainly upon the realm of urban industry, Erskine Caldwell crashed into the world of letters with descriptions of labor on the land. Before President Roosevelt's committee on farm tenancy had made its statistical report, Caldwell had made reports in human terms: Tobacco Road and God's Little Acre. Life might be hard for industrial workers near the bottom of the industrial jungle in Chicago, but it was degrading even to idiocy at the bottom of the tenant and share-cropping region. Beside the hunger and futility of Caldwell's Jeeter family, the junk and wastage of Farrell's O'Neill family took on the colors of paradise. In driving sentences, telegraphic in brevity, Caldwell described men, women, children, houses, fields, misery, deformity, imbecility, dirt, and turnips in that never, never land where even animal life could scarcely struggle for existence against adversity, starved soil, incapacity, and misfortune. Delicate sensibilities were not spared. No red roses were added for decoration. The strongest of stomachs could hardly bear the sight. The meanest of realists could not believe their eyes. It was a nauseous dose that Caldwell served his readers. But he would be heard and he was heard. Where readers failed, theatergoers saw, for Tobacco Road, in its dramatized form, was enacted steadily in New York City for years, while the New Deal of beneficent planning rose, flourished, and declined. How was that to be explained in a land that placed Willa Cather's Death Comes to the Archbishop near the top of the best books?

Widening his arc beyond Tobacco Road, Caldwell united barren farm land with a mill in God's Little Acre — a novel which Jonathan Daniels pronounced "one of the finest studies of the Southern poor white that has ever come into our literature" and certain to "lift the noses of the sensitive." On Tobacco Road, where hope and aspiration had been quenched, just hungers remained; but in God's little acre, joining mill and farm, human life, while still sordid, manifested vigor, a restless searching for better ways, a few aims, humor, touches of heroism, the sanguine expectancy of labor reaching out for something. An old man digging for gold and a direct-action radical simply would not be crushed, though they got nowhere in the going.

While noble males of the species tossed around in futility, the females, in the stress and strain, sought a way to security and happiness in the labor of their hands. "The men who worked in the mill looked tired and worn, but the girls were in love with the looms and the spindles and the flying lint. The wild-eyed girls on the inside of the ivy-walled mill looked like potted plants in bloom. Up and down the Valley lay the company towns and the ivy-walled cotton mills and the firmbodied girls with eyes like morning glories, and the men stood on the hot streets looking at each other while they spat their lungs into the deep yellow dust of Carolina." For the older women life was hard enough, cruel enough, but the girls ever anew brought to it the surge of young blood and desire. The treadmill was swiftly turning, broken intermittently by industrial conflict, and then ever turning again; the determinism of biology and of work with things was clear in the picture; if there was any wrath, it was God's wrath; if injustice, it lay in the very nature of the drama. At all events Caldwell kept his frame of reference hidden under the procession and struggle of human creatures.

§

Cutting deeper into the pungency of experience in the world of labor than did Dos Passos and making a wider sweep around economy than James T. Farrell, Jack Conroy in 1933 incorporated his impressions in a saga of toil, The Disinherited. The central figure of this saga was the son of a miner; his associates were the husbands, wives, sons, and daughters of laboring families in mines, mills, and shops and on the land — in town and country. The scene opened in a mining camp dominated by a dump, "like an Old World cathedral towering over peasants' huts." Father did his long daily stint in the mines, when there was work or strikes did not intervene. Brother Dan went into the mines when he was only twelve, despite the child labor law.

While Mother was frying salt pork one day, Jimmy Kerns came with shadows on his face to say — but Mother snatched the words from his mouth: "Tell me, Jimmy! Is it Tom? . . . Then it's Dan." They brought the boy home, all broken and crushed, a sickening sight, to writhe in agony and die. Then Tim took his place. Not long afterward Father was carried home, maimed and bruised by a cave-in, also to die; and "The Methodist choir sang 'Jesus, Lover of My Soul'" at his funeral. Mother took on the double burden and slaved at the wash tub and over the ironing board to keep the family together, day by day losing in the struggle as she grew older and feebler.

As soon as Larry, the Ulysses of the saga, was strong enough to work, he became a laborer in a car repair shop and soon was caught in a vortex of events in that fourth dimension called time. Strike — America enters the war — an "agitator" shouts that it is a capitalist war and is beaten into pulp by an angry mob bent on "the war for democracy" — "Five men for a steel mill. Must be husky" — work in a rubber factory steaming with gas and stench — wage cuts, strikes — scabs, fights, defeat — a gassed soldier coughing on a park bench — trek to the great automobile town — hard, driven labor on the assembly line — Hoover prosperity dawns — rush, rush — crash in Wall Street — the conveyor belt slows down and stops — men out of work — men and women in old cars driving, hunting, growing weaker and poorer, children bawling — "No men wanted" — Hoover-towns of tin and old boards rise on the edges of cities — a job here for a day or two — a job there, for a day or two — a "chance" to lay pavements — "Hey, there, you're drinking out of the 'Niggers' cup'" — what of it for Nordics in the same plight? — down and out — home to Mother in a leaky miner's shack, a pot of greens on the stove, seasoned by a bit of lard — "That'll be fine. . . . Been a long time since we've had any good old wild greens" — odd jobs, odd jobs — "the steam shovel does the work of 500 miners" — "Father always wanted me to be a lawyer or doctor" — hungry men and women in St. Louis march on city hall demanding relief, police throw tear bombs, a gigantic Negro catches the bombs and hurls them back, authorities grant demands (moral suasion or force?) — odd jobs, odd jobs, no place fit to live in — children blue with cold — and on and on — Bosses "lookin' for beef today."

Around, everywhere, women — mothers, aunts, cousins, sisters — yes, and Bonny Fern, a farmer's daughter who looks down on miners' "brats." Gleams of life and beauty for a brief season of youth — marriage, children, shacks for homes — more children — strikes — rags, bones, and hanks of hair — bent backs, leathery skins, watery eyes, rheumatism — hungry kids wide-eyed — one room, two rooms, three rooms, with rickety furniture — bawdy houses on the edges of town — American family life, well, there it is — why have romances, marry, and make the grand start, down hill? — Bonny Fern, yes, she's still beautiful and losing her pride while father is sliding lower, to a sheriff's sale — labor agitations — workers arise! — ideologies and agrarian crises, why not talk American? — Sale day comes to the bankrupt father — farmers and workers gather in old man Fern's door yard — a rope with a noose is hung over a limb — auctioneer, sheriff, and state police (all swank, with guns unloosed) — what am I bid? — one low bid — a few cents, for the furniture — none dares to raise it — one low bid — a few cents — for the farm — none dares to raise that — old man Fern, by due process of law and order, repossesses his home — Bonny still appealing — But, no, Larry has seen family life — it's not for him — into the old car with two labor philosophers and organizers, Ulysses rides away to the west. Why West? No answer. There you are, said Jack Conroy, in effect; it's real; take it or leave it.

Taking it, Sinclair Lewis, in It Can't Happen Here, gave a fascist upshot of the class climax, in which a raucous demagogue, Buzz Windrip, assailing the rich and using their money, hacked his way through democratic restraints and suppressed in violence the voices of wonder and protest expressed in the literature of dissidence. And Lewis drew both plot and figures from the actualities of American life. Possessors of good things in the United States, as well as revolutionary workers, had spoken of the need for "a man on horseback." Neither wanted, of course, exactly what was likely to come, but force was the essence of desire. Senator Huey Long was an embodiment of fury; until overcome by an assassin, he spread genuine terror in politics. He could dine with the rich, heap up treasures for himself on earth, and flatter and feed the poor; yet he could be ruthless enough whenever it pleased him to cut either way in the social scale. Steeped in American experience — tingling with the force of vigilantes and lynchers — It Can't Happen Here, if not, as critics claimed, a supreme work of art, had the substance and air of verisimilitude. Too hot for the moving-picture industry catering to the German and Italian trade, Lewis' story was kept off the screen. It eventually reached theater-goers, as we have said, but only through the enterprise of an actors' project under the Works Progress Administration in Washington. That too was minatory.

§

Defying easy classification, yet certainly outside the domain of the "best," the democratically general, and the sharp-cut "proletarian," were writers of grave disposition who concerned themselves with the ironies, wastes, and frauds in American society, without visibly attempting to bring them into any fixed mold of social ideology, unless perchance a conception of chaos could be deemed a mold. Indeed an overpowering sense of futility, enveloping the small as well as the great, had in times past smitten strong minds, versed in old wisdom and deeply experienced. "He that increaseth knowledge," said the preacher in the Bible, "increaseth sorrow." While carrying the burdens of the Roman empire, Marcus Aurelius had fretted over the vanity of vanities. Centuries later in Germany, on the eve of Hitler's rise to sovereignty, Theodor Lessing, gifted with many tongues, western and oriental, and learned in the philosophies and the arts, reached the conclusion that history-writing was merely an exercise of the art of putting sense into the senseless. The idea that man is simply a faux pas had long burdened Old World thought.

In America, land of "liberty and opportunity," however, the conception of life as chaos, as meaningless, had not flowered into the cogency of literature before the collapse of Mr. Coolidge's prosperity. Afterward, as the economic depression dragged its ugly length through the years, writers began to strike bass notes of futility — for labor, for Lords of Creation, and for their emulators lower in the scale of incomes.

Henry James, no doubt, had once believed nearly everything in the United States to be poor, thin, and too "bourgeois" for the delicacy of his nature. Edith Wharton had expressed this view of the plutocracy while finding some solace in the seasoned families of America. The new futility, however, did not stem from their tastes and notions of the good life. It offered no escape, either to the once "mellow culture" of Italy, France, and England or to a classless utopia by the proletarian route of revolution.

Absorbed in the idea of a "lost generation" hiding away in Europe, Elliot Paul, in Concert Pitch, engraved a story about a group of such frustrated persons in musical Paris, representatives of the post-war cults, insecure and overwrought, fluttering about and indecisive "like a tangle of uprooted plants floating pointlessly on a sullen sea." It was not because these feckless persons were expatriates that futility had swamped them; they were doomed by their own resentments, incompetence, malice, and constitutional inability to face life, their discords attaining "concert pitch." And with what hope of redemption? None, visible, apparently, on Paul's horizon.

Shortly after Lords of Creation had tried to explain to the Senate committee on banking and finance just how the formation of holding companies and the issue of watered stocks and bonds had enriched American economy, Kay Boyle, likewise an American living in Europe, "le doute incarné," as George Sand said of Byron, depicted in My Next Bride the stature and psychology of Antony Lister, son of a New York financier, searching for the art of life — in France. This wandering youth, who had no stomach for his father's office, dabbled, played, wondered, and thought, a little hither and yon, scattering his money, toying with women, stumbling through a narrowing alley to his doom. One day he was seen carrying Henry Adams' The Degradation of the Democratic Dogma under his arm. Another day he put a strange question to Victoria John, an American girl scratching for a livelihood among the wastrels of Paris: "Have you ever read a man named MacLeish? I've never read anyone like him. I've a book of his for you if you'll have it tomorrow afternoon." Here and there little plaintive notes were piped: "Le Poète, doit-il reconnaître l'Empire de l'Age Mécanique?" Should he indeed? If so or not, why and what upshot? No answer. Antony was no good for business, inept in everything else, blundering around, uttering hollow sounds with dim meaning, only a wraith of reality.

And how had Antony Lister got that way? Kay Boyle gave her explanation in Antony's own words. "Where I went to school," he said, "the conversation was the most elegant you could find for the price. The boys used to talk about how many cocktails their mothers served at home in the evening and to how many people, and how many bridge tables they had. There weren't any black people being hung in the

South, the Supreme Court was the highest, the supremest. Buddha had never sat quiet, year after year, reflecting. Nothing was sacred enough to kneel to, not even a mountain, nor an element like the wind, or the rain, nor an astral body."

In that emptiness Antony had spent his boyhood. In his young manhood he could lay hold of nothing that satisfied his spirit. He vaguely thought "that the rich and the poor were not the issue; it had to be something better than that or else he might as well be dead. If you had no money at all you were finished, but also if you had money it was possible you were finished too. Rich or poor, everyone was stabbing everyone else with hate, stabbing in envy and in terror." No light in any direction. "The whole universe on a honeymoon of horror, wedded to their daggers, stabbing their way from one betrayal to the next. Even your own family and friends eager to do it to you."

In this torment, the addled youth confessed: "I am weak, too weak to take up a weapon and go into the orgy, unless I turned it upon myself. . . ." To this outburst, Victoria, deeply longing for America, the land of her birth, replied with equal futility: "You don't have to. You can always get on a boat and leave the country. You can always keep on going." So it might seem to a dreaming girl, as it had seemed to the knights of endless industrial progress in the United States — keep on going and going and going. While the going was good, no question need be asked; when it slowed down or stopped, no answers for any questions. At least Antony could find none: "I can't go far enough. Nobody can. Wherever I am, just looking out of the holes in my skull is enough to scare me. I'm scared of what's happening to everyone and I can't do anything to change it."

Nor, indeed, could Victoria herself, despite the apparent optimism of keeping the faith in her own words: "It's no use, Antony, I know how little use it is. There are two kinds of people in the world, there are the rich and the poor, and if you're the poor you're finished from the first, even though you don't see it right away. You can make a little struggle, very brief, and after a while you begin to see. You see they've got you down and they certainly aren't going to let you up again. It wouldn't be clever at all. Once you got up and were still young enough you might tell what you had seen down there." This came from Victoria's heart, for she was poor and just hanging on to the rim of existence. Antony could not see the situation in the simple terms of rich and poor, although he knew riches and beheld poverty, but he agreed with Victoria about the slight possibility of avoiding the envy and terror of things.

In the middle of futility, Antony had to go back to New York where he had a father called Horace. From this center of the business empire in the machine age, he cabled his wife, Fontana, a kind of sensuous shadow into whose toils he had fallen in Paris: "Wall Street narrow as the bier. . . . Horace believes in the future of gold, silver, copper, steel, and other metals. . . . They've put bars on all the windows because so many people committed it this year now it seems more like a prison than last. . . Nijinsky should have stayed sane long enough to create the dance I see myself doing in wreaths, garlands, festoons of stock quotations on white ticker ribbons. . . . I walk all night after parties or when there're not any. . . . I am not gold, silver, or copper, I am something waiting to be set to music. . . . Mozart forgot me in his eighth year . . . hummed me over between Don Juan and the Magic Flute and forgot me going up stairs to bed in Salzburg. . . . Anaconda Copper, Cerro de Pasco, Seaboard Oil are passwords for departure. . . . New York explodes inside me every time I step out the door. . . . I can't do it. . . . I can't do it. . . . I can't do it. . . . Have you seen a girl called Victoria John she's trapped in ancient Greece." A few days later, Fontana and Victoria, while riding through the streets of Paris, opened up the Paris-American newspaper and read: "Prominent Young Club Man Cuts Veins in Father's Office," and a subtitle: "Antony Lister Takes Own Life. Wall Street Losses Rumored." Fontana turned to her companion and said: "Don't cry. Antony said you never cried." Tears themselves were futile.

If the son of a rich man who had been educated in the most elegant conversation that money could buy could find in the end no impulse or reason for going on, the promise of things was different for Emma Troy, a woman who had made money in the manufacture of "triple-whipped mayonnaise" and set out in a rush to break into "the American aristocracy" at home. Her story Hamilton Basso told under the title, In Their Own Image, published right in the middle of the New Deal, during the feverish quest for "recovery" of things past. Emma was no daughter of the rich. She had worked her way into the business of making mayonnaise and on the crest of success had sold out her establishment to a kind of holding company for a huge pile of income-bearing paper. Spangled with gold, she took her son and daughter, Freddie and Virginia, to Aiken, South Carolina, where many possessors of great wealth spent their winter months in the pursuits of the leisured.

Like the courtiers who danced at the balls of Louis XVI, the "winter set" had created a ritual of inutilities, if with no Most Christian Majesty to serve as the center. Around and around this "round of pleasures," Basso carried Emma, Freddie, and Virginia Troy in their effort to "break into the ranks." Unlike Edith Wharton he did not set the newcomers off as mere vulgarians against the culture of seasoned wealth which through long years had sloughed off the barbarism of manual labor and "the odor of trade." No such purpose or illusion shone through his pages. For Basso, these holders of liquid claims to America's wealth were not merely "new people" annoying to the ordered and aromatic world of established families. Nor were they mere grinders of the faces of the poor. They rose to no such zenith of force. In sum and substance, in relation to going concerns, they were simply useless and, incidentally, wasters. While Basso did not say this so baldly, the cold irony of his story — sayings and doings in Aiken — could leave no other impression.

He made no point of tragedy, comedy, farce, or fraud. His characters spoke and acted for themselves, where they were — in Aiken, for a winter round of pleasures.

There were no happy endings for the mayonnaise family or at least no realization of ambitions. Though the son Freddie was married off, the achievement turned out to be a mess. Virginia, the daughter, having inherited, perhaps, some healthy memories from Emma's days in the mayonnaise kitchen, managed to elude the snare her mother set to capture an impecunious Italian count. And Emma found no prince for herself. As fortune went badly with her climbing, she attached herself to the lower rungs of the social ladder by marrying an advertising man who laughed at publicity and public relations as heartily as he did at the ritual of the Aiken set.

While describing its ineptitudes, Basso allowed the set to hear the rumble of an industrial conflict; but that was, to all appearances, an accident of geography and time. It happened that there was a mill town not far away from the scene of the ritual and that a strike occurred during the season. The rich heard of it and were a bit discomfited. Indeed a boy of artistic proclivities was seen prowling around the homes of the rich, carrying an easel and brush, and was shot as a suspicious character. Neither the strike nor the shooting affair, however, had any evident connection with the mayonnaise family or the doings and sayings in the Aiken crowd.

Never before in American fiction had families of great riches been treated in just such a fashion. In Basso's pages they appeared not as mere vulgarians, or exploiters, or ogres of any kind. They were simply purposeless, useless, futile, in respect of the economy that sustained them. Though inwardly hearty and vivacious, they seemed to be turning yellow, like autumn leaves about to fall. They might drop to earth. They might flutter in the breeze a long time. Basso left them hanging there.

With a similar surgery John O'Hara carved at the system in Hollywood, cutting off the celluloid mask and exposing its

inner life, tormented and retching. In Hope of Heaven he
framed the dream, the romance, and the ravages of reality.
An examination of the precious "studio atmosphere" seemed
to discover "no more hope in it than there was in Appointment in Samarra, no more heaven there than there was in
Butterfield 8." That meant exactly none at all. In the
glittering land of fancy, despite Shirley Temple and all the
rest, boundless deceit, passion, and intrigue boiled over in one
compact spot. Undeniably that was a harsh judgment and
it must have been disagreeable for Deacon Will Hays, Czar
of the Movies, and his committees of ladies. Yet it had an
outside homology in revelations of the methods employed by
some financial magnates in the motion-picture industry —
financing being an euphonious term that could cover betrayal
of trust, inside deals, and the duping of "investors." Besides,
Deacon Hays himself, the very chief of the motion-picture
captains, had displayed an amazing virtuosity, in matters
fiduciary, as he explained to a Senate committee in describing
his relations to Harry Sinclair and the oil scandals while he
had been arch financier of the Republican campaign fund.
O'Hara's literary conception of the Hollywood scene was,
therefore, not wholly out of line with the once orthodox conception of the politico-economic scene over which the Czar of
the "industry" presided with such aplomb.

In another place — not Paris or Aiken or Hollywood —
just Tenth Street in New York — Edna St. Vincent Millay
in the medium of verse presented a few mortals from the busy
city holding a Conversation at Midnight, that is, setting
forth their interests, ideas, hopes, fears, and ambitions, in
1937, while business, recently at the crest, was slithering
downward in its course. Among these mortals gathered after
dinner around good whiskey and wine were a man of affairs
listed as a stockbroker, a communist poet, a painter, a story
writer, an advertising expert, a Roman Catholic priest, and
a kind of Olympian host who combined amiability with general agnosticism. For hours the conversation splashed,
flashed, and bubbled along like a brook, meandering and

getting nowhere. Yet in the splashing and flashing, lights illuminated all facets of American culture — ranging from sports, business, sex, music, and the arts, to religion and politics. The kaleidoscope of American civilization was turned over and over, producing fragments of figures, but no figures. Neither art nor letters nor religion could stop and possess the stream of talk. Giving it up as hopeless, the priest went away early; in such a group he could not command. The advertising man spoke of love as the great need of troubled times, without evoking ardent responses. The artist seemed merely wistful.

At one point, however, the conversation at midnight simmered down to a broad and irreducible antithesis. The stockbroker as capitalist and the poet as communist faced each other and spat fire. From his home in Palo Alto, Herbert Hoover had shouted to the man in the White House whole paragraphs and speeches which could be summarized in a few words: "Regimentation, regimentation. Give us freedom." Perhaps the stockbroker had heard them. Perhaps he just felt like Hoover for similar reasons. At all events he cried out:

Oh, God, why live, to breathe a prescribed and rational air!
    — All free
Opinion, all interchange of vigorous thought, suffocated
By the poisonous motor-exhaust of motor minds!
Passion regimented; curiosity regimented; endeavour regimented;
Culture, and grace, and all the things I cared for
Equally divided among the mob, and sauced to their taste!
This is the time for the proud to take his pride by the hilt
And slit his bowels with it; this is the time for the individual,
    for me,
To lock himself in his room . . . and get it over with.

This was the cue for the communist who answered in a fierce tu quoque:

You, an individual? — you, you regimented mouse?
You Harvard Club, Union Club, white tie for the opera,
    black tie for the theatre,

Trouser legs a little wider this year, sir,
I would suggest dark blue instead of black, sir,
Pumps are no longer worn, sir,
Mah-Johngg, cross-word, anagram, backgammon, whist,
    bridge, auction, contract, regimented mouse!
Why, you're so accustomed to being flanked to right and left
    by people just like yourself
That if they ever *should* step aside you wouldn't stand up!

. . .

You, an individual?
You salad for luncheon, soup for dinner,
Maine for summer, Florida for winter,
Wife-pampering dog-worshipper!

Where was the synthesis, the resolution of the contradiction? The conversation at midnight did not bring it forth.
The priest had not produced it. The advertising man's love
offered no single wonder-working providence. The host
could tender only the uncertainty of liberalism: both fascism
and communism were intolerable to the human spirit; liberalism might play the eclectic role, pick, elide, combine. But
liberalism seemed to get nowhere. Even so, where were
fascism and communism getting, in terms of precious human
values? Uncertainty prevailed:

Let us abdicate now; let us disintegrate quietly here, con-
    vivially imbibing
The pleasanter poisons.

Although Sinclair Lewis probably did not intend to place
his novel of Prodigal Parents in the class of futilitarian literature, he certainly cast the children of a prosperous business
man, Frederick William Cornplow, and his wife, into the pit
of wastrels, while mixing sex vaporings and communist
fumes in a curious concoction. To be sure, Cornplow was
mighty enough, in Lewis' pages, but his offspring were silly
and hopeless and then as ever the future belonged to youth.
In final analysis, Lewis' panegyric on Cornplow in itself
raised a question: Did the boast spring from fear or assur-

ance? "Cornplow," he said, "is the eternal bourgeois, the Middle Class, whom the Bolsheviks hate and imitate, whom the English love and deprecate, and who is most of the population worth considering in France and Germany and these United States; when he changes his mind that crisis is weightier than Waterloo or Thermopylae." Possibly, but the sweeping assertion boomed with the oratory of the advertising agent and was far beyond the reach of demonstration. In the Congress of these United States, where eternal bourgeois were at the time ostensibly busy making laws, they were also digging their own graves apparently in preparation for burial under a mountain of debts, deficits, inflation, and armaments. Perhaps they would change their minds, if they could, and prove that it could happen here, but if that crisis was to be weightier than Waterloo or Thermopylae it might settle just as much as those historic battles settled for the long movement of civilization. It was possible that warriors and priests would outlive the Cornplows.

§

Continuous insistence that the genteel tradition had become a hollow farce, that democracy of the political tradition was not enough, that fundamental changes in economic and social usage must come, were now coming, coupled with the repeated allegations of futility, introduced a heat almost revolutionary into literary reviewing, appraising, and discussing. The sit-down strike, metaphorically speaking, broke into editorial sanctums, publishers' teas, and assemblies for considering the state of beautiful letters.

The bearers of dissident reports devoid of glad tidings had often known at first hand the experiences of which they wrote — long hours at rattling machines, tedious hours digging in mines, strikes, battles with police, the search for work, riding the rods, clashes with "scabs" and "finks." Their novels rang with an authenticity and an assurance that could not be called artificial on any score and this may have been a factor in winning the reception which was accorded to so many of them in the reviews. At all events, though, in the main, literary criticism, as of old, revolved around the pivot of persistent concern with form and symmetry, style and rhythm, finish and grace, with emphasis on pure, rather than practical, artistry, the dissidents were accorded full hearings beside the "favorites" and the "best." No editors in fact clung so tenaciously to the genteel tradition as to reject completely the men and the women who wrote vivid reports and sizzling tales of life and struggle at the lowest levels of economic subsistence. Literary militancy "made" the front pages of reviews and drew serious consideration from the leading critics of the country.

During his tenure of office as editor of the Saturday Review of Literature, Henry Seidel Canby, though by no means captivated by the proletarian appeal as such, greeted the novels of that school with fair appreciation when they demonstrated literary power and skill. Perhaps more comprehensively, his immediate successor, Bernard DeVoto, continued this appreciation with criticism. Indeed the hospitality of literary critics to the new writers of fiction and poetry was itself symptomatic of a catholicity in spirit extending beyond that manifest in the marketplace and the counting house. Despite some intemperate appraisals and violent encounters, the character of the great literary debate was on the whole a tribute to the quality of American culture and meaningful for its future. Americans were not to Laugh and Lie Down, as Robert Cantwell had phrased it, passively.

In volumes, essays, and little magazines, the Marxists kept harping on a problem more easily stated than solved: "Since the writer is perforce a product of time, place, and social milieu and cannot stand entirely outside his own experience, cannot acquire by any means an Olympian detachment from earthly affairs, how can he avoid giving expression to acquired values and, if he can not escape that necessity, what values shall he choose?" That was a tough nut for Marxists to crack as well as for all writers and critics; and nobody cracked it — to universal satisfaction. One thing was patent at least: the time had passed when young persons could set out upon literary careers equipped merely with Samuel Smiles, Matthew Arnold, and a few of the classics as models of substance and style.

In fact no writers even in the era of high American prosperity had done just that. Before Mr. Coolidge left his office as President of the United States, V. F. Calverton had brought to literary criticism the wide pattern of sociological interest, in a treatise called The Newer Spirit. This was followed by a sociological interpretation of American literature since the civil war set forth by Granville Hicks, a close student of the subject, under the caption of The Great Tradition. With full historical warrant, Hicks declared that ours has been a critical literature, critical of greed, cowardice, and meanness. Then he put this question to his countrymen: How can authors refuse to strike at the sources of the evils they have so constantly attacked? When they choose to go to the roots of things, he insisted they must take the communist line: they must give their support to the class that is able to overthrow capitalism. Pondering longer on the American tradition, Hicks declared in 1938 I Like America; he hoped it would improve its ways, however.

If to youth unmindful of long history the application of the sociological method to literature looked like an original achievement, historians of literary criticism found in it confirmation of a common-sense view long held by masters of literature. Voltaire certainly had written on life, manners, thought, and cruelties under the old regime of the eighteenth century, no matter how many hours he had spent on polishing his sentences. At the opening of the nineteenth century, Madame de Staël had lucidly applied the sociological critique in a treatise On Literature Considered in Relation to Social Institutions. In the Victorian age, John Morley had said in his inimitable way: "Poetry, and not only poetry, but every other channel of emotional expression and aesthetic culture, confessedly moves with the general march of the human mind, and art is only the transformation into ideal and imaginative shapes of a predominant system and philosophy of life." Minor writers could be consigned without disrespect to the region of the literature of taste, graces, stray variations of shade and color. But "the loftier masters, though their technical power and originality, their beauty of form, strength of flight, music and variousness of rhythm, are full of interest and instruction, yet, besides these precious gifts, come to us with the size and quality of great historic forces, for they represent the hope and energies, the dreams and the consummation, of the human intelligence in its most enormous movements." This view Edith Wharton sustained out of her own experience and power as a writer — as one of the masters. The patient study of style was no vain literary pursuit; the born-poet could scarcely evolve Alexandrine verse out of his inner consciousness in New York or Kansas; but it was certain, as the New Deal moved toward its finish, that American literature was becoming concerned with "human intelligence in its most enormous movements." Perchance the hour of great politics was drawing nearer.

The discussion of the literary movement took various forms. In part it was an affair of the writers in prose and poetry themselves bent on examining their own intentions and obligations. In 1937 a throng assembled in New York in their second Writers' Congress to talk about the direction of the literary movement and its relation to society, as members of P. E. N. had been doing in national and international assemblies for some time. The discussion revealed a wide diversity of opinion and judgment about the function of the writer, and participants soon found that the direction of the dissident movement was not to be perfectly straight, narrow, and well-lighted for everybody who took part in it. Marxists made speeches characterized by the fixed idea that literature in America as in Russia must exhibit correctness of doctrine and soundness of verbalism but they differed acutely over the nature of that correctness and soundness. Inasmuch as all Marxists had rejected the Pope, inasmuch as the Russian dictator, Stalin, was too distraught with many other matters to settle the quarrels of Grub Street in New York, who among the Marxists was in fact anointed, consecrated, and authorized to approve or excommunicate? While Marxists wrangled over the correct line, other authors at the Writers' Congress asserted the right to describe what they saw and knew of labor, poverty, and disenchantment without reference to prescriptions authoritative in the temple of the orthodox. It was a lively meeting of dissident minds, observed by crowded galleries.

During the sessions Malcolm Cowley, literary editor of the New Republic, author and poet, retaining memories of a youthful expatriation in Paris, laid stress on the power of revolutionary conceptions in kindling and feeding the fire of creative energy. On the other hand, Edwin Seaver, critic and novelist, warned his colleagues against subservience to shibboleths and dogmas. John Crowe Ransom, agrarian, poet, critic, professor at Vanderbilt University, later transferred to Kenyon College, took the floor to scourge the "amateurs" who appeared to dominate the literary field, and contended that critics must be trained — presumably in the seats of learning by professor-philosophers; this left in a haze the familiar problem: Who is to train the trainers? Other speakers kept bringing back into the argument the force of varied experiences, inner fire, and grand conceptions of life whatever they might be. In the end, the Writers' Congress adjourned without agreements defined in thirty-nine articles of faith, or more or less, and without a manifesto, despite the number of members who came with neat prescriptions in their heads or in their pockets. Naturally, therefore, after the congress was over, a spirited controversy took place in the press over the meaning and the upshot of the literary assembly. One aspect seemed positive, namely, emphasis on the substance of letters.

To this sociological analysis of literature, Kenneth Burke of the dissident school and a participant in the Writers' Congress added a critique entitled Attitudes toward History.

By history, Burke meant the substance of economy, life, and labor, actuality, and culture, rather than the fragments of totality carved out by professors of history obsessed merely by warriors and politicians. It was his contention that the writer interprets life, that is, history, according to his experience with it, and assumes an attitude either of acceptance or rejection of the forms which life displays. The essence of life being permanence amid change, the writer will be, with respect to that essence, passive or disturbed, content or malcontent, sentimentally satisfied or maladjusted and overwrought. Applying this dictum to American literature, Burke inquired whether American writers had at last accepted American life or were still fleeing from its issues and conflicts even by making them despicable. Thus the problem of the determinism or indeterminism in "objective relations" was thrust by Burke into the obscure realm of subjective moods. In his discussion of American literature as history and in his analysis of contemporary writing, Burke seemed to call for the recognition of life in America as theme worthy of the highest intelligence, to demand hard work in penetrating to its substance, and to make imperative the literary master's affection for the competent forms and shades of expression.

Over the tempest raised by disputes about pure proletarian literature, as distinguished from dissident literature in general, broke a torrent of discussion among readers of fiction, poetry, and criticism. The escaping steam was sometimes called the vaporing of little minds learned neither in Marxism nor in letters, and indeed there was some justice in the allegation, for much nonsense was written on the subject by little persons who could scarcely write at all.

After carrying on a searching inquiry, Louis Adamic declared that the proletarian authors were either non-proletarian in origin or ceased to be proletarians when they entered the white-collar career of letters. In the second place, he contended, on the authority of Trotsky, that a real proletarian literature was impossible under capitalism, for the actual workers were too busy "making a living, fretting, agonizing, scheming, and struggling to seize power" and, however energetic, could not find the leisure required for writing. Under a well-functioning communist state to follow capitalism, the proletariat would cease to exist and, in that happy order of things, art would simply be human art. Humanity would be emancipated from bondage to things and class. Whether the literature of revolt was written by the proletariat or not, another question remained: Did the workers in town or country read it?

The answer to this query Adamic sought by traveling far and wide over the country and interviewing the kinds of men and women described in the so-called proletarian literature. On the basis of his journeying and inquisition, he reported that the influence of such literature on the working class was negligible; in fact, nil. Workers in factory and field did not care to read about themselves — about the men, women, and children of the disinherited. They read few novels and fewer books of a general character. Now and then industrial workers bought the Liberty magazine, True Stories, Wild West Tales, or Screen Romance, if they ventured beyond the sensational newspapers, tabloids, comic strips, and picture magazines. "Ninety-nine and one-half per cent" of the American workers, Adamic concluded, in 1934, "seem to me to be practically beyond the reach of radical printed propaganda or serious, honest writing of any sort. This, to my deep regret, is the brutal truth of the situation, and anyone who does not realize it . . . is, I think, ipso facto, open to the suspicion that he is not qualified to write about the American proletariat." Exceptions to the rule, remarkable exceptions, Adamic did find here and there, but they merely served to bring out forcefully the main conclusion of his survey. The following year, in America Faces the Barricades, John L. Spivak made a confirming report: "I am convinced that the American worker does not want to overthrow the government. All he wants is food." The plight of the people was grievous. What are you going to do about it? Spivak set down as his answer: "I don't know."

To the further confusion of the Marxians, Robert Herrick, an elder statesman of American letters, contributed a trenchant inquiry. If, as the Marxists believe, all social movements and class actions are determined in the very nature of things, why the laudation of proletarian virtues and why the moral indignation over capitalist "vices"? If Marxism is the science of prediction, as precise as the science of physics, why all the righteous heat over the way to the predicted end? One does not quarrel with water running down hill on its inexorable course. If the movement of history is determined, it is determined for all classes. And yet, Herrick said, he could not remember "a single instance" in which this logic was applied by intransigent writers to show that the employer was under the same bondage to the capitalist system as the workers were. According to the strict logic of Marxism, both should be represented as caught in a mechanical trap, but Herrick could not detect in proletarian literature a single case "where the top dog is presented not with sympathy but with a definite awareness that he too is moved by a terrifying necessity along predetermined lines of least resistance — the bosses, the executives, the impersonal boards of directors, all without exception bound to the same coil of necessity through fear, shame, desire, habit." In short, Herrick held, the proletarian school was lacking in perception and failing to apply its own dogma of determinism. If some of its expositors were right, if Marxism was merely a portrayal of mechanical economy and iron prediction, then Herrick could be deemed more Marxist than the writers who suffused description and revolt with sentiment and evaluation. But could literature be reduced to physics and still be literature?

Going persistently on his own way, Edmund Wilson directed his thought with increasing effectiveness to the issue that had engaged the hot concern of the writers' congress, and indeed of all workers in the domain of letters, namely, the substance of literature amid its forms and accidents. Having graduated from regular services on the New York Evening Sun, Vanity Fair, and The New Republic, Wilson tried to pierce further beneath the surface of volumes, chapters, paragraphs, and sentences in search of the controlling conceptions that accounted for authors' selections, omissions, and emphases. Whether he dealt with single authors, as with Edith Wharton in an appraisal written for The New Republic after her death was announced, or with a group, as in his volume on Triple Thinkers, Wilson never lost sight of the heart of the business: Under what overarching conception of things has this configuration in letters taken shape? It was no accident then when he turned to an examination of the historical development of socialism from the French revolution through the partnership of Marx and Engels, in his unresting exploration of the forces conditioning or determining the substance of "polite" letters.

In this literary tournament, Bernard DeVoto, critic, essayist, and novelist, likewise jousted. What was the meaning for American civilization — for the trajectory of the future — to be found in all the literature called proletarian? DeVoto made an answer: "Class literature, the literature of any class whatever, quite apart from its esthetic function which may in part at least affect all classes, must serve at least one of two functions. First and most important, there is the function of heightening and unifying the sentiments of the class which it represents. It may confirm or increase their group-consciousness, step up their solidarity, make stronger their sense of power and injury and communion, and create, propagate, and enliven those vital myths, beliefs, ideals, aims, dogmas, slogans, personifications, purposes, and sanctions which are at once the bonds that hold the class together and the energy that makes action possible. Second, there is the interclass function. Literature may be an agency of attack on other classes or of conversion among them. It may assist disintegration, weakening the other classes by making them pity or fear the class it represents, giving them a sense of shame or guilt or futility, hammering at their doubts with ridicule or horror or terror. Or it may proselytize among them, converting the essentially religious symbols of its own myths into symbols acceptable among the religions it invades, and carrying the position by outflanking it with visions of the greater glory to come — or the equivalent in the eschatology of the period. These functions are usually quite distinct. Only rarely and only in great literature will they coalesce. A work of genius may well fuse them together, achieving symbols that are both incandescent for its own class and immediately authoritative for other classes."

This terse summary by DeVoto, covering the class substance of literature and artistic appraisal, certainly had direct application to Marxian forms, efforts, and propensities. Whether it applied also to the whole body of letters displaying economic and political awareness was another, and broader, issue. Nor did DeVoto's judgment on this point take into account the measurement of literary influences on secular history — on the makers of that history. If in time to come American history as actuality should be simplified down to an acute conflict between the owners of property on the one side and the non-owners on the other side — as James Madison and Daniel Webster had feared it might be — then the proletarian literature could be described by distant historians as at least foreshadowing, if not in any manner shaping, the course of things to come.

But there was no way, in any "science," Marxian or otherwise, despite much bold asserting, of knowing in the days of the golden glow and the New Deal whether this conflict, in bald and simple forms, would come to pass. Nor, if it was to come to pass, was there any science for predicting the hour, the circumstances, or the immediate outcome. Judging by European experience and by hints and signs in the United States, Sinclair Lewis could have been right in the verdict rendered by It Can't Happen Here. Although the unquenchable hope of Marxists looked far beyond fascism, wars, revolts, and suppressions to the final day of the spring into freedom, an air of remoteness and uncertainty hung over that assurance. If for the long time, or all time, the course of history was to run against the disinherited, the makers of proletarian letters might well have wished that they had stayed within the confused and blurring lines of "the united front." Neither friend nor foe, however, could lift in 1928 or in 1938 the curtain on that realm of possibilities.

The whole philosophic problem thus posed in Europe as in America was analyzed and clarified in Karl Mannheim's Ideology and Utopia, translated into English in 1937. Class interests and ideas, he affirmed, do appear in society, but they do not lie insulated, side by side, like eggs in a basket. In times of peace and relative well-being, transfusions, modifications, disintegrations occur and, even when tension sharpens the insular character of ideas and interests, no absolute cleavages take place. It was so in respect of any literature that touched life at all, especially the literature of economic and political consciousness. Like realistic writings in sociology and politics, realistic literature dealt with actualities of life and labor, gave voice to peoples and interests, thrust upon the first class passengers, who rode, some knowledge of the second class, that walked, and of the third class, that pushed the wagon — to repeat Carl Sandburg's imagery.

However rough and untraveled the road ahead, the literature of dissidence certainly gave suggestions respecting the way. It expressed and echoed the swelling sentiments that swept every state in the Union in 1936 and shook both the powers and the convictions of those Bourbons who spoke of "restoration." The prose and verse of economic and political sensitiveness were not read by the millions, but they were read and discussed by some men and women, boys and girls, who would help to make history in 1950, 1960, 1970.

§

Like the literature of imagination and literary criticism, with which it was inevitably associated, the newspaper press reflected the tendencies of the time — its mechanics, its centralization, its economies, its moralities, and its ironies. While Berle and Means reported the intensifying concentration of corporate control over national wealth, statisticians of newspaper ownership and circulation traced the rise of dailies correctly called "chain" and recorded the death and consolidation of papers. In 1928 the "chains" dominated 280 daily newspapers. In 1933 they held 361 dailies in thrall, with a circulation of "13,244,574 or 37.4 per cent of the total daily issuance and 11,044,646 or 45.9 per cent of the Sunday," to use the figures of Alfred M. Lee, in his volume on The Daily Newspaper in America.

Mergers and suspensions marked the course of this development. In the decade between 1924 and 1934, "a net decline of 136 units" occurred in the daily and Sunday field. Under the expert editorship of Walter Lippmann, the New York Morning World weakened and died. Hearst was compelled to bury his New York American for want of sustenance. Competitors consolidated until cities of the smaller rank were sometimes "served with news" under the auspices of single concerns. Perhaps the climax was reached when Republican and Democratic sheets in one city rolled from presses under common ownership, with malice toward none, charity for all, and counting house receipts augmented. Although country weeklies and small town dailies continued to flourish, the circulation of urban and suburban papers in rural regions expanded rapidly, with improved roads, the perfection of high-speed trucks, and the advancement of rural free delivery by automobile.

In some measure this centralization was the outcome of ambition and avarice. In some measure it responded to mechanics and economics. Efforts to achieve more rapid printing — ordinary, color, and rotogravure — led to the construction of machines more complicated and expensive. A single plant opened by the New York Daily News in 1930 cost ten million dollars. When other equipment, services, and devices were added to mere plant, capital and current out-

lays mounted. According to reports, the Philadelphia Inquirer was sold in 1930 for eighteen million dollars.

Without world news services, the most expensive plant was
worthless and the cost of these services rose with the area and
intensity of coverage. The outlay of the Associated Press
alone nearly tripled between 1917 and 1931. When wire-
photo reporting was added to telegraph, radio, and telephone
reporting, a new element of expense was introduced. Competition for circulation, on which advertising revenues rested,
led to the increasing employment of special writers for sports,
the arts, the sciences, radio, education, the theater, cosmetics,
lingerie, and accessories, the motion-picture kingdom, wars,
foreign affairs, and every other phase of public interest; and
all this raised the cost of newspaper production. To meet
these and similar charges, ever larger receipts were required,
merely to keep alive, apart from making profits.

In such circumstances metropolitan journalism became a
business that could be carried on effectively only by great
capitalists or great corporations. The day when a brilliant
journalist, such as Horace Greeley, could borrow a little
money or buy a cheap machine on credit and set out on a
career of intellectual leadership had passed. Convinced by
tradition that the press was still a power, families that had
made fortunes in industry and commerce put some of their
millions into journalism. They bought up newspapers or
bought into them and, as more or less silent owners or partners, added the weight of industrial capital to that of the
publishing capital invested in presses, plants, and services.
The extent to which newspapers were actually owned by
capitalists outside the "profession" could not be determined
by any available figures, but there seemed to be few great
dailies built up entirely out of their own earnings, without the
aid of stock and bond issues or bank loans. In other words,
journalism became a branch of business enterprise, controlled
by its necessities, penetrated by its spirit, interlocked with
its fortunes. Editors and readers sank into the background.
Subsidized newspapers could be run at a loss. The capitalist

with his immense resources, supported by advertisers, could alone cope with the costs of publication and supply the multitude with the diversified news, special articles, photo-gravures, comic strips, and cartoons necessary to meet mass demands.

Coupled with the high capitalization of the publishing in-dustry was a tendency toward uniformity of cultural, politi-cal, and economic opinion. In the course of this development the open "crusading" journalism of the type launched in the late nineteenth century by Hearst and Pulitzer declined toward the vanishing point. In their early days they had berated the American plutocracy without mercy, campaigned against trusts and monopolies, and demanded heavy taxation on incomes and inheritances. Pulitzer, however, was now dead and his morning New York World had gone with him to its tomb. His St. Louis Post Dispatch went over to Alfred Landon, the Republican candidate in 1936, and to big pot-tage. As Hearst grew richer and his interests extended, he shed his old radicalism, actually surpassed Tories in his de-fense of primitive capitalism, and as he aged he turned his lingering energy to Hollywood, art treasures, and efforts to conserve his decaying estate.

In big journalism, crusading now came to an end. Ap-parently it did not "pay," especially as the picture news-papers carried off readers, or rather "lookers," who could not stand the strain of construing sentences. Even the Scripps-Howard chain of papers, which had flirted with labor and trust-busting, went over to the Right on all major issues, leaving behind merely the faint incense of diluted sentimen-tality. Nowhere in the land was a great editor left to battle heroically "for the plain people," in the style of the youthful Hearst or Pulitzer. Only cartoonists ingenious at their craft could now say things by insinuation that once could have been put into double-column leaders. And their number and skill were striking features of the age.

Coöperating with artists of the ordinary comic strip in creating totalitarian imagery on a national scale were the columnists whose effusions flowed across the continent in rising volume. Highest among them, with reference to the number of newspapers served or to circulation claimed, were O. O. McIntyre, "Dorothy Dix," and Dale Carnegie. The first, until his death in 1938, supplied the middle class in the small towns and cities of the hinterland with gossip about life in New York City — the land of dreams for fresh-water automobile salesmen, little executives, realtors, morticians, aspiring wives, and restless girls. The second, "Dorothy Dix," touched a universal chord, by giving advice to the love-sick and the love-lorn of both sexes. The third, Dale Carnegie, provided instruction on such matters of business enterprise as how to turn garage mechanics into sales orators or lift harassed insurance agents into company presidents. By these three columnists, the popular hunger for the trivia of metropolitan gossip, for the experiences of sex, and for the acquisition of riches was cleverly served, while the newspapers gathered in pecuniary rewards.

To that other great lust of Americans — politics — a small army of columnists avidly catered. For a long time Arthur Brisbane, the employee of Hearst, led them all in the number of estimated readers and emoluments, but Brisbane died in 1936 and his name dropped quickly into devouring oblivion. Pitching his thought to the level occupied by such persons as the officers of the National Manufacturers Association, executives of Morgan and other banks, aspiring enterprisers of the middle west and beyond to the Golden Gate, and women of the well-to-do clubs in search of moral and economic security, Walter Lippmann, who had previously attained fame as a liberal, reached a lofty peak as the intellectual purist among the columnists. While his star was glittering in the heavens, Dorothy Thompson, specializing in fascism and communism after years spent as a newspaper reporter in Germany where the two systems clashed so savagely, played upon the emotion of fear and the flair for horror and violence as she ostensibly engaged in discussing American public questions and politics. Among their rivals and associates, Drew Pearson and Robert S. Allen, in a joint syndicate, and Boake Carter, acting alone, were alleged to reach more readers and command more minds, though there was no way of proving the claim; nor did this trio seem to enlist as much affection as the others among the intelligentsia of the upper income brackets, for they were not always tenderly faithful to the honorifics of such circles.

Clearly, there was a diversity of talents and audiences in the syndicate field. Yet the most popular columnists, including the sportive Westbrook Pegler, agreed as a rule on one thing: they preached an economic orthodoxy which the highest pontifex in the United States Chamber of Commerce could usually scan with pleasure and approval. Such deviations as they occasionally allowed themselves could readily be taken as that homage which regularity pays to liberty. It was, therefore, strictly fitting that Dorothy Thompson should receive an honorary degree from Columbia University at the June commencement of 1938. Among the columnists of large following only Heywood Broun kept up a running fire on the left and certainly no university made him a Doctor of Humane Letters. Only incidentally could the First Lady, Eleanor Roosevelt, as a columnist, be called a strict defender of the New Deal.

During the turmoil of the panic and persisting business depression, when new social doctrines were advanced in the country, the popular columnists contributed to the maintenance of uniformity in opinion. Nearly all of them came out openly for the Republican candidate in 1936, laying bare the secret wishes of their accredited Olympian impartiality; and their services were even employed by Democratic publishers not too much enamored of the New Deal. Lukewarm editors, unable or unwilling to attack the Democratic machine or to flout the fixed ideas of their readers, were wont to balance such Democratic editorials as they chose to write by one or more "columns" on the opposite side of the political battle. This operation satisfied their covert desires while giving the semblances of catholicity in free journalism.

Whatever the motives, the syndication of columns throughout the country helped to stifle diversities of opinion, at least in the press, and tended to spread the uniformity of conservatism even among potential dissenters, at least as far as the influence of newspapers extended. In other words, syndicated columns made for a greater degree of standardization or totalitarianism in the materials editors chose to publish and in journalism as an industry; and the uniformity on the whole reflected a belief in the illusion of permanence.

The actual influence of the columnists, students of journalism sought to estimate but all the relevant facts were not available, and the undertaking was impossible. No instruments of precise measurement were at hand. Promoters of columnism claimed enormous circulations for their clients, but how many newspaper buyers and subscribers read the columnists? Only guesses could be made. Sample surveys showed that the readers of one distinguished columnist voted against his creed in the election of 1936. Similar surveys of another gave opposite results. There was some significance, perhaps, to the fact that with a few exceptions the columnists were fiercely opposed to the reëlection of President Roosevelt, and were thus in accord with the bulk of the metropolitan press. Yet what significance? Though speculative fancy might presume to say, science could not. If there had been no political columnists in 1936, President Roosevelt might have polled more votes or, for aught any one really knew, fewer votes. So slight was exact knowledge of the influence exerted by ideas, tempers, and thought upon the minds of the millions. About all that could be said on the basis of precise information was that there were many columnists, that most of them were against the New Deal, that they made money out of their industry.

The suggestion was even broached that the conservatism of the columnists, added to that of editors in general, helped to intensify the criticism of newspapers that came from the Center and the Left. Certainly this criticism heated the dispute over the vague idea phrased as the "freedom of the press." The debate became especially hot when President Roosevelt made a drive against child labor in formulating the newspaper code under the National Industrial Recovery Act of 1933 and in pressing other measures directed to the same end. Since newspapers were among the largest employers of children, especially newsboys, their earnings were immediately affected by efforts to raise the age limits of employment, and their reaction was generally hostile. In resisting the elimination of child labor, several newspaper proprietors and distributors raised the cry that the freedom of the press was endangered. Some of their colleagues in the industry, it is true, disagreed. "Alone among the industries," the New York Daily News remarked, ". . . the newspapers insist on the retention of child labor, in the form of newsboys and carriers working before dawn or after dark." But the chief force of the press was thrown against President Roosevelt's proposal. Newspaper representatives were able to put limits on the code provisions touching child labor and even then complained loudly against what they were pleased to regard as attacks on their independence and freedom.

The opposition of the press to restrictions on the use of newsboys before dawn and after dark was not appreciably diminished by criticisms and arguments advanced by the opponents of child labor. Editors commented on the sad plight of boys in search of employment, and were fond of saying that "some of our finest citizens have made their start in life through selling newspapers." Against this optimism was placed the evidence of Warden Lewis E. Lawes, of Sing Sing Prison : "Recently I had a census taken here in Sing Sing to determine the number of inmates who had sold newspapers in their youth. The examination showed that of the 2,300 men, over 69% had done so. Most of our population is drawn from the metropolitan district, and Sing Sing receives over 70% of all felons sentenced in this state." Newspaper proprietors and distributors continued to insist, however, on the right to make use of child labor and to rest their case on "freedom of the press." A. M. Lee was speaking by the record when he said : "Not a little of the unpopularity of the Roosevelt regime with the daily newspaper industry arose from its stand on child labor."

In some measure the acrimony connected with this argument sprang from popular confusion respecting the meaning of the phrase "freedom of the press." Judging by criticisms directed against newspapers, it seemed to be generally taken for granted that freedom of the press meant impartiality of the press; and newspaper proprietors were charged with suppressing and distorting news and deliberately maligning personalities and causes. That such complaints were often well founded could not be gainsaid. George Seldes, in his Freedom of the Press, gave chapter and verse for a damning indictment. Nevertheless, in the tumult of discussion, misapprehension was evident, for it was not true, as critics often intimated, that the Constitution of the United States guaranteed the impartiality or fairness of the press. The Constitution merely forbade Congress to make any law respecting the freedom of the press and state constitutions left proprietors free to print what they pleased subject to the law of libel and slander. In short, owners of papers could handle their industry in their own way. They had a constitutional right to suppress and distort news and even to malign and they exercised it to a degree that undoubtedly augmented popular disgust with the press — a disgust exhibited in the election of 1936 when the advice and appeals of the majority of the great metropolitan newspapers were spurned by millions of their readers.

For the popular impression that freedom of the press necessarily implied impartiality of the press, newspaper publishers were partly responsible. While asserting the generally conceded right to pursue a partisan editorial policy, several proprietors of distinction made pretensions to neutrality in their news reporting. They used such phrases as "objective news columns" or "all the news that's fit to print," to assure readers that they did not suppress or distort the news itself, whatever they did in their editorial columns. In other words, they themselves seemed to assume that freedom of the press implied impartiality of the press — or at least of the news — and in so doing they called forth from readers and critics innumerable demonstrations of their partiality.

In truth the ideal of a completely "objective" report on any complicated series of events was an impossible ideal. Necessarily, if not at all by intention, the slogan "all the news that's fit to print" was repeatedly violated. At best the maxim was merely a vague aspiration beyond the reach of the finest resolves. Although such ideals and aspirations were noble in conception and efforts to realize them gave distinction to a few newspapers throughout the country, no publisher managed to scale Olympus.

The very circumstances of newsgathering — the immaturity of many reporters, the rush, the confusion, the limitation of space — conspired against the attainment of "objectivity" and all-around "fairness." A comparison of reports on any single series of events, such as a strike or a mass meeting, published by two or more papers dedicated to reporting in the fulness of the truth was sure to disclose the inadequacy and the falsity of the claim to objectivity. The amount of space assigned to the series varied. The different positions given to the report — first page or sixteenth page— represented estimates of news, that is of "importance" — in other words, subjective determinations of values. The attached headlines signified interpretation, if not an obvious animus. Besides, it was a matter of common knowledge among reporters that each paper had its "general policies" and that, in selecting, condensing, and emphasizing news for telegraphic or telephonic dispatch, these general policies acted as a broad psychological control. It was likewise a matter of common knowledge that in the everlasting search for the sensational, headline writers were prone to seize upon pungent phrases or items, tear them from their context, and give to news reports a "turn" or "slant" which was distorting or suppressive in nature, whatever the intention.

An illustration makes concrete the fallacy of the claim to

objectivity or to reporting all the news that's fit to print. On March 6, 1938, an anti-war rally was held in New York City. It was organized by a small group of citizens opposed to the super-navy bill then pending — a group including liberals and a few Socialists. The meeting was addressed by several speakers, among them General William C. Rivers and Norman Thomas. The following day the meeting was reported by The New York Times to the extent of about three-fourths of a column. The report stated that the meeting had been held under the auspices of a new organization of "Socialists and other liberals." It gave extracts from the address by Senator Robert M. La Follette and then added that "among those who spoke were Homer Martin, president of the United Auto Workers of America; Norman Thomas, Socialist leader; Major General W. C. Rivers, retired, and Bertram Wolfe, writer." And the report was published on page ten, while the rumor that President Roosevelt would soon give the country a "lecture" on phosphates was assigned to the front page with appropriate headlines. By what criterion of "objectivity" was all the space given to Senator La Follette and none to General Rivers? Or the tenth page given to an anti-war mass meeting and the first page to a rumored discourse on phosphates so useful for war purposes?

Evidently not all the news "fit" to print was printed in this case; nor, indeed, did the exigencies of space permit that feat. Given the limited space and an effort to report all the speeches, by what process of selecting a few words from each could a perfectly "balanced" and "objective" report of the whole have been achieved? Only by publishing all the speeches in full, exactly as delivered, could any paper give an objective account of the discourses, and that was practically out of the question.

The fallacy of the "objective" theory of news reporting was also illustrated by comparisons of the "stories" printed on the super-navy issue by two papers of high quality. For example, on March 7, 1938, a dissenting minority, led by Congressman Ralph O. Brewster of the naval affairs committee in the House of Representatives, issued a report against the huge navy bill approved by the majority of that committee. The New York Times and The New York Herald Tribune made first page news of the report, the former with small headlines, the latter with big headlines. Both published extracts from the report, but different extracts. Committed by general policy to the principle of collaboration with Great Britain and collective security, The Times placed its emphasis almost entirely on the foreign policy statements of the Brewster report and said little about the technical objections to the navy bill advanced by the minority. The Herald Tribune, on the other hand, a "big navy advocate" and an opponent of President Roosevelt, used as its extracts from the report sections almost entirely technical, that is, designed to show that the authorizations of battleships and other craft already on the statute books made the new bill unnecessary for efficient defence. How could two "objective accounts" of the same "event" be so different, if the two great newspapers concerned were actually controlled by the iron law of objectivity and not by publishing policies?

The conclusions indicated by such illustrations were sustained by Leo C. Rosten's survey of the Washington correspondents made under the auspices of the Social Science Research Council. Eighty-six per cent of those correspondents believed that comparatively few papers gave significant accounts of our "basic economic conflicts." Forty-eight per cent did not believe that newspapers were equally fair to "big business" and "labor," while forty-three per cent held the opposite view and the remainder were undecided. Fifty-five per cent agreed that their reports had sometimes been played down, cut, or killed for reasons of policy followed by their publishers. Sixty per cent of the correspondents said that their orders were "to be objective," but that they knew how their respective papers wanted their stories "to be played."

While such evidence destroyed the "objective" myth, it

also indicated a wide-spread desire for "fair" reporting, and the greatest of the newspapers did give to labor and minorities more space than had been customary in the history of the American press. Unfortunately, however, from the standpoint of a "fair" hearing, the omission of single items could offset all the passages that were printed, as every attorney acquainted with the rules and effects of evidence knew very well.

Discussions of newspaper policies in the matter of objectivity served many purposes. They made American newspapers look like the white hope of humanity in comparison with the enslaved and "reptile press" of totalitarian states. At the same time critical analyses put American readers on their guard against the extravagant pretensions of the press to complete fairness and neutrality. Criticism induced skepticism, sometimes great contempt, and acted as a check on the excesses of the press. Even boys and girls in high schools developed keen eyes for "propaganda" in the form of alleged news. Reporters who presided over the auguries of newsgathering and reporting often laughed up their sleeves, sometimes sardonically. The success of the Newspaper Guild in acquiring members and the action of the Guild in joining the Committee for Industrial Organization were straws in the wind. Whatever proprietors, managers, and editors might say or claim, working newspaper men and women evidently knew that the political science of Calvin Coolidge's age, at least, had passed. Warned against making false pretensions and subjected to close scrutiny, proprietors with a sense of public responsibility and private honor seemed to redouble their efforts, year by year, to attain a higher and higher degree of fair and balanced news reporting. In the situation there were elements of encouragement to citizens of a patient and tolerant spirit.

Among the magazines only a few decided tendencies could be observed. Chief among these, perhaps, was the widening reception given to The Readers Digest, in pocket or purse size, by means of which men and women amid the hurry of things could get synoptic glimpses of the outstanding articles in the whole array of magazines. More original was the Coronet. By the range and diversity of its materials and the size of its reading public, it demonstrated that the cultural desert was not as large as critics of philistinism had apparently imagined. Another tendency was the unabashed shift of older magazines to the Right. The Atlantic Monthly went over resolutely to the creed of the National Manufacturers Association and shortly afterward seemed to be engaged in distributing the propaganda of oil interests adversely affected by the policies of the Mexican government. Its former editor crowned a long life of literary endeavor by making a trip to Spain and publishing a laudatory account of General Franco's beneficent rule, for the edification of the American public.

Most striking of all was the quest of magazine editors for sightseers as distinguished from readers. On the principle that what the eyes see must be interesting and thought provoking, a new magazine brazenly called Look, filled with gripping pictures, often ingeniously selected, was launched and soon boasted of more than a million lookers as buyers. The old magazine Life was taken over by the owners of Time, filled almost entirely with pictures, and floated to success on a tide of prosperity. Competing with Look and Life in profusion of pictures and yet slightly, not dangerously, radical, another newcomer, Ken, set out to jostle minor conventions and showed some skill in the undertaking. No longer was it necessary for buyers of magazines to be wholly literate. Painted tabloids reached parlor tables.

Meanwhile the vogue set by the dazzle of Time, founded in the age of normalcy, affected nearly all weeklies of large circulation. To be brisk, curt, concise, telegraphic, and bright became the verbal mode of the hour. To print nothing that would take more than ten or fifteen minutes to read became almost a ruling fashion. Even so complicated a matter as the collapse of American railways could be summarized and disposed of presumably in a few "crystal-clear" paragraphs for readers who had but ten minutes to spare from their looking.

Yet one event in the great magazine world, apart from the editorial achievements of the Yale Review, the Virginia Quarterly, and the Southern Review, ran clearly counter to the degradation of the democratic dogma. That was the establishment and success of Fortune under the auspices of the men who published Time and Life. Issued as a monthly, with an expensive format, to sell at ten dollars a year, Fortune was designed directly for the rich, and yet it printed solid and bold articles on highly controversial issues, such as housing, munitions profiteering, labor, and other aspects of capitalism. Its articles were packed with information, characterized on the whole by a rare degree of objectivity, and written in a vein of gravity and concern, notable instances being the discussions of housing and the munitions business. Its policy was penetrated by critical thought and marked by courage. Acutely conscious of the various schemes of reference under which selections of fact and types of interpretation could be made, the editors of Fortune sought to avoid the naïve and attain the comprehensive. Though their surveys were shorter and less heavily documented than those of the old North American Review or the British quarterlies, and therefore not so limited to select audiences, they displayed a freedom from neat formulas and a reach of thought that were unusual to the rich who cared to read the fact-burdened pages.

Popular magazines for women seemed to prefer the deadly dominance of the commonplace. Owned and managed almost exclusively by men, as commercial enterprises, the journals "for women" automatically registered men's ideas of the audience to which the appeal was directed, and their enormous circulations implied that the managers correctly gauged the women to whom they supplied month by month fashion plates, fashion articles, society gossip, tepid fiction, bloodless sentimentality, Cinderellas, Fairy Princes, directions for the use of cosmetics, advertisements of the "allure."

Just as Godey's Lady's Book, even while Sarah Hale was editing it, stuck tightly to domestic sweetness through the military struggles and calamities of a civil war, so the popular women's magazines of the great depression largely adhered to beauty hints and baby-tending during the course of economic and moral disintegration.

A survey of the five women's magazines with huge national circulations, made by Elizabeth Bancroft Schlesinger in 1933, inventoried the stock in trade. "During the six-month period, the five periodicals offered no major articles on power control, immigration, farm problems, economic planning, child welfare, education, the labor movement, taxation, or international affairs. Peace and governmental economy were honored with one article each." Of the thirty-two articles featured by The Ladies Home Journal, "four dealt with the political, economic, or international situation. . . . Among the remaining twenty-eight features, women were introduced to the engaging spectacle of Alice Roosevelt Longworth tripping lightly along the flowery path; in four articles Billy Sunday stormed his way along the Sawdust Trail." In view of the fact that these five journals could reasonably claim thirty-six million readers, the index to feminine taste was suggestive, to say the least. Were millions of women really that indifferent to the forces sapping away the sub-structure of their world? Or was journalism so conceived for women no more representative of women's minds than journalism in general was indicative of all minds?

In the winter of 1937–1938, when magazines were losing circulation and questing for security, The Ladies Home Journal, under the editorship of Bruce Gould and Beatrice Blackmer Gould, changed its tactics, on the assumption that women could be "aroused" to take an interest in public affairs if the Journal awakened among them a consciousness of great issues. Leaving out of account, for practical purposes, the customary interest of women in public affairs, like most of women's preceptors in colleges and universities, the Journal, as if about to inaugurate that relation, sought from women over the country replies to questionnaires respecting their opinions on such matters as marriage and divorce, birth control, the war on venereal diseases launched by the federal bureau of public health, and, more cautiously, on economic and political measures. Encouraged by the replies they received, the editors launched their series, but the titles and contexts of the articles under the new policy showed no radical departures from the earlier policies described by Elizabeth Schlesinger. Women had been and still were interested in public affairs and took part in public affairs, but evidently they had to look elsewhere for enlightenment concerning the major issues of State.

§

Surveys of newspapers and magazines engrossed in the current, the immediate, and hence the superficial, argued for the proposition that the country would have been intellectually impoverished and regimented had it not been for the searching inquisitiveness and daring individualism of workers in the field of imaginative letters. Newspapers played up the sensational and transitory for the delectation of the millions in the fashion set by motion pictures and radio broadcasting. With a few noteworthy exceptions, the magazines catered in a similar way to the same audience. On the other hand writers of imaginative literature, appealing to large yet selected groups capable of sustained intellectual effort for at least a few hours at a time, had more freedom in selection and emphasis than editors and publishers had. Perhaps in the long evolution of civilization what mattered was the thinking of those who did some thinking rather than the lucubrations of those who did no thinking at all.

At all events in the wider latitude granted to them, under the American system of liberty, the makers of letters, less controlled by the technique of medium, by mass production, by corporate interests, and by government intervention, explored and covered all phases of culture in the United

States and with an energy and verve of style that betokened, on the whole, a vigorous mental and literary power. Taken collectively, the letters of the period were marked by a penetration and a thrusting force that signified a growth rather than a diminution of insight and creative intelligence. Even the crudeness that characterized many works was the crudeness of a search for life rather than a sign of decaying talents.

The condition of American letters was thus in brilliant contrast with the degeneration which characterized Roman letters, for instance, in the fourth and fifth centuries of the Christian era, after the passage of Augustan grandeur, as traced by Samuel Dill with broad knowledge in his Roman Society in the Last Century of the Western Empire. In the letters of that period betraying the declining culture, Dill found "conventionality and tradition, slowly but surely fading from lack of fresh impulse and inspiration . . . bald and scrappy gossip. . . . The idolatry of mere literary form combined with poverty of ideas, the enthusiastic worship of great models without a breath of the spirit that gave them enduring charm. . . . Vanity and literary affectation. . . . [Incapacity to speak] in a simple, straightforward style. . . . Sterility and failure of original power. . . . The higher intellect of Rome seems to have been overtaken by a paralysis, and incapable of making any further advance. . . . Erudition without critical judgment, finesse of style, without purity of taste, took the place of originality and enthusiasm for ideas. . . . Civilization became everyday more stereotyped and materialized."

No such pallor of death spread over American letters in the days of the midpassage.

CHAPTER XIV

Esthetic Affirmations

WORDS alone did not, could not, suffice for the assertion of values and ideas; in objects of art and in human gestures, the spirit of men and women also proclaimed experiences and judgments on striving and practice. Discussing the difference between the media of words and paint, Thomas Benton, outstanding American painter, laid down this principle in the magazine, Common Sense: "To begin with, I am puzzled about the instruments and materials used in thinking. What bothers me most about thinking is that it has to be done with words. . . . You get to dealing with relations — and not with relations between what is apprehensible to your senses, like a painter with his colors and his shapes, or a chemist with the matter performing in his test tubes, but with linguistic descriptions of things. A thought takes form in a word pattern — another thought in another pattern. They meet. Out of their conjunction can come the most unexpected progeny imaginable, which, if your mind is active, mature like lightning and run all over the place. To keep from going crazy you have the job of gather-

745

ing in all these verbal brats and putting some order in the confusion of their conflicting pretenses to meaning. You have, generally, to kill a lot which are unmanageable. For killing off your hopeless brats and getting the rest of them lined up, you have that tricky instrument, *logic*. . . .

"I am deeply suspicious about this business of logic. I know that in the art of painting what makes an assemblage of represented things coherent, what sets up sequential relations between them, also distorts them. I know that representations of things of the real world cannot be put into any kind of logical design, in which one part follows from and is linked with another, without being modified, without having some of their aspects subordinated to others, without stressing or squelching parts, without finally losing exactitude of representation. This does not bother me with painting, for painting does not aim primarily at accuracy of statement, as Truth, but aims — if I may risk it — at a value called *Beauty*, at an organization of materials and symbols which by their nature and through their associations produce sensuous and emotional satisfactions."

In this "illogical" medium, esthetic affirmations were made which contained their own judgments. If illogical in the verbal sense, they too expressed values and ideas. Indeed the very cult of non-objectivity, pursuing its quest for the formless, for an "irreducible and sometimes inscrutable Absolute" was itself an evaluation — a rejection of "reality" on some basis of values. At the institution in Chicago, for the promotion of abstract and non-objective art, supported by the Solomon R. Guggenheim Foundation, attempts were made to approach the "Upper Reaches to which the Soul aspires" — The Nirvana, the No Thing perhaps of the ancient East — and examples of this retreat from the known and the flight to the unknown were assembled for the inspiration of students. The body of this collection was the work of a Russian, Vassily Kandinsky, and of a German, Rudolph Bauer, both of whom had experienced the collapse of monarchical realities but adhered to absolutism in the form of esthetic affirmation with "playful imaginations."

For non-objectivity as pursued by the cult, the Baroness Hilla Rebay von Ehrenweisen, long an adviser in art for Mr. Guggenheim, was curator and chief spokesman, and the latest Know Nothing movement in America lighted fires from her flambeau. This is not to say that "purely abstract" art had not already been produced in America. In fact by 1937 when this gallery and school were opened in Chicago, there was a considerable amount of non-objective art in important places in America. Augustus Vincent Tack in 1930 had painted a series of panels in this mood for the library of the Phillips Memorial Gallery in Washington, D. C., and his work had been called by an enthusiastic critic one of "the most notable artistic achievements of the present day." It was an expression of emotions, it seemed, "which each individual must interpret according to his own spiritual understanding."

But all the abstractionists, native and foreign, did not go so far toward aloofness from the known and the visible. Some of them maintained that their products did not represent a flight from life but, on the contrary, the great reality itself. These heretical exponents admitted that their art was abstract but they declared that it suggested "joy and esthetic motion" amid the gloom of tragedy and frustration. Their forms, they said, "were not ghostly-pure-spirit-suspended" nor designed to "freeze a sublime non-intellectuality." They recognized that "after all an artist must live some super-worldly existence to create super-worldly art and few did." Explaining their divergence from the pure superworldly view and insisting upon their memory of life, they argued that their output resembled rather the "semi-abstraction of an Einstein and carried generative force."

For its mystical imputations, Sheldon Cheney gave the palm to Oriental art "above that of any other continent," in his review of A World History of Art published in 1938, praising the Far Eastern testimonial to experiences beyond rational analysis and disapproving the humanistic, intellectualized western art of modern times. But however intellectualized the modern western art might be, it had to deal with abstraction as idea if it had the vigor of beauty and meaning. For instance, the most chaotic surrealist picture was built on the abstract idea of chaos in contradistinction to the idea of dynamic symmetry governing the precisely ordered flower arrangement in an Oriental art form. Life as confusion. Life as a divine system. Both abstractions. In non-objective lines, rhythm could be conveyed no less than with the movement of figures. Sculptured human beings with abstract heads, with no faces, were fully capable of expressing personality — the personality of posture and gesture, for the face is not always the measure of distinction in the case of man, woman, or child. Sargent was able to convey it in a hand or an arm.

Enveloped in the controversy over meaning and beauty, the impulse to paint, draw, and carve worked its will in America during these latest years in the time of man. To combat madness in art, as she called it, Mrs. Frank Granger Logan, Chicago art patron, rallied around her a corps of other art patrons and devotees at the shrine of the conventional and agitated for "sanity in art." Censoriousness was thus not confined to the nations ruled by dictators. "The academic painter, even the least inspired," she maintained, "will be found to have constructed his picture on a better pattern than the most exalted modern."

Near to the earth and often of the earth earthy the main body of artists worked to interpret what they felt and saw as life, experience, struggle, and ideal. In their media, in oils and water colors, in bronze, wood, stone, marble, and alabaster, in song, in compositions for musical instruments, with dancing feet and arm gesturing, in steel, glass, and prefabricated materials, they spoke their minds about human nature, human behavior, and human purposes in society. When they had commissions to fill, they often filled them according to specifications deemed desirable by their patrons.

But sometimes they took the matter into their own keeping or deviated from the sketches submitted. Now and then the public grumbled and riots even occurred on occasion, attended at one such an affair by the slashing of a portrait. Often the public knew nothing about the origin of a mural's composition and emphasis, but it learned about one artist's willfulness when his work was ordered removed by his patron, after it had gone upon the wall.

§

In the golden glow and on through its lingering memory as hope of recovery, painters decorated the walls of public and private buildings — of city and state edifices, of banks and private clubs, of railway stations and department stores, of dwellings and colleges — with compositions glorifying commerce and industry or the pleasures they brought in their train. Smooth portraits were painted for the well-to-do who, of course, wanted to look handsome in their pictures. Busts of public officials and leading politicians multiplied at the hands of sculptors and were placed in imposing positions; in the halls of fame effigies of the famous multiplied. Congress appropriated large sums of money to Gutzon Borglum for carving the faces of four Presidents on a mountain cliff.

"The sword on the event" remained a favorite theme in war memorials and equestrian statues, but Harvard University ventured a trifle beyond it by commissioning the American Old Master, John Singer Sargent, to place on the wall of its Widener Library, after the world war and shortly before his death, a mural depicting peace springing from the body of the soldier dead. For the Elks' Memorial in Chicago Eugene Savage in 1930 painted two enormous murals on the same theme: The Armistice and Paths of Peace. With notable fidelity, however, to local military history and heroes, state capitols clung to battle scenes.

Economic institutions entered the stream of mural consciousness with commissions for works of art commemorating commerce and industry. The Merchandise Market of Chicago invited Jules Guerin to produce for it a gleaming portrayal of The Markets of the World; for the Kaufman store in Pittsburgh, Boardman Robinson was invited to paint the movement of commerce from the days of the Persians and Arabs and his product received a gold medal from the Architectural League of New York. The Groos Bank in San Antonio was adorned by Paul R. Cook with events in banking. A new Edison structure in Los Angeles glorified power with the esthetic aid of Hugo Ballin. To lighten the severity of its plant which made grinding wheels and machines, the Norton Manufacturing Company of Worcester, Massachusetts, in 1929, when Tyrian rays were purpling the business heaven, ordered for its administration building a series of murals by Arthur Covey "to bring to the senses of the workman the nobility of his task, and to express, through the high appeal of art, the spirit of the organization which recognizes primarily the human element." That glowing year when news was attractive, John W. Norton was commissioned to depict its dissemination for the building occupied by the Chicago Daily News. That year also the new building in New York acquired by the brokerage firm of Lee, Higginson, and Company, promoters of Krueger's financial adventures, was dressed up in a series of murals by Griffith Bailey Coale, who utilized a "novel and interesting painting process" to represent a Pageantry of the History of Commerce by Sea.

Devotion to habitat governed innumerable selections of artists and themes. In this connection California's self-esteem exceeded any flight of fancy in which her real estate offices could indulge. What was said to be "the largest set of murals ever put on canvas" became the proud possession of the Los Angeles Public Library; for their completion in 1933 the artist, Dean Cornwall, had worked five years recounting the history of the city and the state. Throughout the nation it was generally assumed that history was identical with "Progress of Man" and art affirmations were made in that spirit far and wide, with captions reciting the epic quality of man's struggle through the ages always upward and onward.

While pride in national progress was exultant in painting, rapture soared to the empyrean at the touch of an "inspired" composer of music. In 1928 the Musical America prize was awarded to Ernest Bloch's "America" played simultaneously by the five leading symphony orchestras of the United States, the conductors of which had served as the judges in the contest made up of ninety-two competitors. Six movements formed the elements of this composition, built on a historical conception, the first movement bringing America to the year 1620, the last hymning the future. In the interval the melodies of the civil war were introduced. The conclusion was a swelling anthem to America — the Epic Rhapsody. In this period also, women of the clubs opened their programs for great occasions with a hymn entitled "America the Beautiful."

Strong as was the motif of progress in painting and music, it did not monopolize esthetic interests any more than big business embraced all economic activities. In the midst of what seemed to be firm unity, esthetic affirmations were made in diversities almost as numerous as the kinds of commodities turned out by machine industries. Among the diversities were included thrusts at the confidence of optimism, paralleling the rejections palpable in letters and the fact-finding energies of researchers and investigators.

On the subject and emotion of religion, esthetic affirmation ran the gamut from the most rigid fundamentalism to free questing for the spiritual essence. No writer comprehensively described this artistic movement, but its vitality was displayed throughout the nation. In 1928 Sister Mary Stanisia of Chicago painted Christ among the Doctors for St. Luke's Cathedral in St. Paul. He Hath Sent Me to Heal was the message inscribed in a mural by William De Leftwich Dodge for the Virginia Baptist Hospital at Lynchburg. For a Negro congregation not far from New York City aspiring to the ownership of a mural, Ruth Krylenko, a Russian-American, painted Christ as the workingman and advocate of brotherhood. As for religious music, Ernest Bloch, a loyal Zionist, composed a new musical service for the Reformed Synagogue in New York City, grounded on a laborious study of Jewish history. Under the patronage of the Warner Brothers, Hugo Ballin, in 1929, painted episodes in Jewish history for Temple B'nai B'rith in Los Angeles.

And as the zest for murals spread over the nation, paganism as well as religious conformity was unrolled in classical allegories; for instance, in Arizona, where land and sky are so little broken in their intimacy by intervening forests, the Legend of the Earth and Sun was revived for the Arizona Biltmore Hotel at Phoenix. The vogue for pagan themes was intensified by the popularity of archaeological and geological excavations, and to this stream of influence anthropology and the theory of evolution contributed their incitements. In the Field Museum at Chicago, as an illustration, Charles R. Knight placed in 1928 seven murals dealing with prehistoric life as unfolded by the studies of scientists — the first of a projected series of twenty-eight pictures. At Pomona College in California, according to José Clemente Orozco's own explanation of what he had done, Prometheus was given high place upon a conspicuous wall as the bearer of fire to humanity. Less ambitious, the Country Club at Detroit accepted a Zodiac of Sports by a more conventional painter as a ceiling adornment.

Geared to the idea that opportunity was waiting for artists without number to demonstrate their talents, art schools enlarged in size and expanded their instruction. That faith seemed not to weaken even when Wall Street was dolorous, for 1933 events in the art world included the initiation of mural instruction at the School of the Boston Museum of Fine Arts and the organization of a Guild of Fresco Painters in New York. While the season of expansive luxury was still open, discussion of the possibilities for "a great American art" resounded over tea cups and in academies. Art "activity" flourished, its energies illustrated in countless exhibits of painting and sculpture, in the launching of new magazines devoted to art, in the quantity and character of the books on art which moved in a steady procession to the marketplace, and in huge sections of newspapers assigned to the news and criticism of art events. Certainly there was an art movement in America during the golden glow, and its dominant characteristic was the serenity of assurance rather than the dynamism of a tumultuous creative urge. The nerves of artists, patrons, and critics were not seriously ruffled by any grave presentiment of things to come.

A clue to the nature of this art movement was given by Henry Ladd of Columbia University in his concise volume entitled With Eyes of the Past. Deeply troubled as far back as 1928 by the common habit of forgetting that great art is something perennially fresh and alive, the author discussed the art movement of the hour as a phase of the general spirit of the times. "Appreciation of art today is believed to be a necessary part of culture," he said. "The conviction is so universally held that a large part of our educative machinery has been turned to the production of artistic capacity. Periodicals devoted to art have increased their circulation; museums throughout the country have enlarged their endowments and suffered the indignities of publicity for the glory of the cause. Even department stores have exploited the glamour in modern art or the precarious splendor of the antique with, one sees, tangible profit. There has come upon society an enormous will to believe in art which has encouraged a maximum attitude with a minimum learning to evoke enthusiasm and confound taste.

"The awe which has thus been generated has reached immeasurable proportions; it has thrown about the fine arts a cloud of mystification, a sentimental and false reverence, which tends to isolate them from their normal province of enjoyment. Even our conscienceless and incomprehensible youth have become seduced into a low seriousness about higher things which enjoys none of the sharp observation, the humor, the liberty that characterize the more real aspects of their shocking young lives. The general disintegration of inherited illusions about life has not cracked the shining faith in art. This faith, indeed, has for a good many individuals so confused the direction of their natural inclinations as to have very nearly inhibited the possibility of esthetic pleasure."

That was one kind of faith, though not the only one, however dominant. Another sprang from an intuitive feeling that a material civilization was not in itself sufficient for the human spirit; and thus a quest for more satisfaction continued — a quest, in fact, as old as history. In a civilization filled with machines, smoky with fumes from factory chimneys, so motor with activity that it seemed to be always running away from itself, and yet having a rich cultural heritage, complete peace of spirit was impossible; and discontent with the hard features of this civilization turned increasingly to the thought of tapping esthetic sources. For many years Lewis Mumford had been sounding alarms, expressing objections to mechanization as an end rather than a means of life. Yet annoyed as he was by popular complacency with mechanical activities and products as such, Mumford was himself torn by contradictions in the course of his development; he had a deep appreciation of the handicraft arts while arguing that art must reflect contemporaneity, and he encountered perplexities in his search for a way of combining the art of living with the exigencies of machine production.

§

In truth, American artists had never accepted universally the mechanics and democracy of American life. Many workers in the plastic arts, like workers in imaginative literature, had fled from the worship of the dynamo, declaring that the economy of American life was incompatible with creative art. Shaking the dust of the "plutocratic democracy," as they called it, off their feet, they had pursued and continued to pursue the beautiful in distant lands where, in "seasoned cultures," they assumed, adjustments to the commonplace could be avoided and untrammeled sensitivity could be their happy lot. Near the middle of the nineteenth century the sculptor-poet, W. W. Story — after a trip abroad from the land which his distinguished father, as lawyer and a justice of the United States Supreme Court, had found ample for his great talents in law and government — settled in the Anglo-American colony in Rome, there to be enveloped in the classical tradition and become so saturated with it that he could dedicate his arid ecstasy to immortalizing Cleopatra in marble and verse.

Struck by the flight of young Americans from their own scene and its interpretation in the mid-nineteenth century, an Englishman ejaculated: "Whatever the American men of genius are, they are not young gods making a new world!" Certainly not. With few exceptions they were hovering, like "moon calves" chewing their cuds, around ruins of a time long passed and losing themselves in its legends. They were imitative, not creative. And as late as 1929 the "passionate pilgrims" were still imbued with the idea that older civilizations had the shrines at whose altars the neophyte could find lasting peace. Meeting in Europe an exotic and enchanting variety of customs, sights, and values, they assumed that foreign societies were stable and that as long as they remained expatriates they would not have to endure the changeful progress of American life, the boastful self-assertions of American industrialists, the "vulgarity" of American masses, the noisy machines of a nation dedicated to business, and the general mediocrity of a "frontier folk."

In his Portrait of the Artist as American, written during the reign of Babbittry, if published in 1930, Matthew Josephson, loyal disciple of Jean Jacques Rousseau, defended the retreat of Henry James and other dissident geniuses to an older civilization "where some quantum of individual liberty is still to be enjoyed — or even to regions of a primitive culture where liberty is embraced to the exclusion of all other advantages." In fact, several American artists, including literary artists, so revered the distant past that they could even "go primitive." "We're the *disinherited* of art!" Josephson made the "wrecked painter" exclaim like a Henry James. "We're condemned to be superficial! We're excluded from the magic circle! The soil of American perception is a poor little barren artificial deposit. Yes! We're wedded to imperfection! An American to excel has just ten times as much to learn as a European! We lack the deeper sense. We have neither taste nor force. How should we have them? Our crude and garish climate, our silent past, our deafening present, the constant pressure about us of unlovely conditions, are as void of all that nourishes and prompts and inspires the artist as my sad heart is in saying so! We poor aspirants must live in perpetual exile!"

Democratically inclined American tourists who encountered the émigrés in their dear little dark little corner of Paris or in the "smart sets" of Rome were astonished at the degree of hostility the fugitives entertained for everything American, almost to the point of being dehumanized. Few expatriates could express good words for democracy in the United States and with such democracy as existed in Europe they were little concerned, if at all. On the contrary with assured complacency they harked back in their minds to "the finished ages" or eventually joined the deriders of democracy in the style made so vocal and final in Moscow. If non-political in mentality, they could easily slip into the habit of disapproving "everything distasteful to their souls" which so characterized the post-war years.

This long indulgence in exoticism was made possible for the expatriates, as it had once been for many of their European masters, by the prosperity of business enterprise, while it lasted. In the wake of merchants, traders, and concession-seekers, the artists of Europe had been going to the four corners of the earth to feast their eyes and gratify their feelings in experiences with the unknown. Gauguin had escaped from France to pleasure in the South Seas. "The little customs officer, Henri Rousseau, spent his life recapturing in fantasy the memories of his one Mexican trip. Matisse added the Near East to his domain, and a Persian or an Arab would understand his art and its relation to their culture. But the flight into exoticism met with success only as long as there were new cultures and countries to provide new material. The Futurists of Italy under Marinetti decided to face instead of flee from the machine. They deified it and made it part of their programme. The Cubists had moved in the same direction, deliberately choosing geometric patterns and reducing even the human form to the essential forms of machine parts."

After the upsurge and decline of the Cubists, a younger generation, victims of the war, disillusioned, frightened, confused, rebellious, sometimes brutal, displayed the chaos of their minds and the agony of their nerves in the canvases they painted and in the objects which they carved. For a time young American émigrés basked in that atmosphere. But a day arrived when they had to scurry home for two reasons: the reduction in that "quantum of liberty" which had been attracting non-conformists from the art circles of America and the devaluation of the American dollar or its total disappearance from their pockets.

"Dear old Europe" was ceasing to be a haven for malcontents. After the Russian, Italian, and German dictators achieved totalitarianism in economic and political supremacy, they glorified their power by commanding artists to serve the dictatorships. Writers as well as painters, sculptors, designers, and even craftsmen were compelled to conform beyond any compulsion which their kind had ever experienced in America, from its yeomen and patrician to its industrial years. Elasticity in esthetic pleasure was coming to an end in Europe. If the revolution was possible of acceptance by native artists it was scarcely to be borne by many outlanders.

Up to this revolution European artists in misfortune, economic or spiritual, like the Americans, had been able to wander freely to distant places of patronage. Far back in history, Greeks had followed in the wake of the city-building and city-decorating Alexander the Great; afterwards they had gone to Rome, their next conqueror, if sometimes as slaves bought to celebrate power by their skills. From Italy, artists had gone to Spain, and from Central Europe to France and England, seeking adventure, work, and appreciation. And since the eighteenth century when Benjamin West, the American colonial, reached the proud position of a court painter under George III, wandering artists from America had been entrusted with the portraiture of monarchs, members of the nobility or business magnates, and the very pope himself.

Now, however, most monarchs were tumbled from their thrones and that patronage had almost disappeared. Lords and ladies, instead of seeking the publicity of portraiture, were more inclined to withdraw from the public gaze in a desire for safety first. In Russia even the bourgeois were ruled out as subjects of art unless for purposes of derision. Finally Hitler and his advisers fiercely censored artistic expression, removed at will finished canvases and statues from German galleries, began to demolish synagogues, and set up canons of taste they deemed strictly fitting for the insurgency of brawny men under arms. Even the Orient was, for practical purposes, closed to foreign artists after the outbreak of Japanese fascism in the course of aggression in China. Wandering might be directed to the South Seas still, but not to all of them. The quest for excitement, work, appreciation, and pleasure in distant places seemed to be as a tale which was told. In this situation returning Americans substituted apologies for their former condemnation of the American culture. That prized "quantum of liberty" was mainly in their homeland, they discovered to their great surprise. Moreover, to the newest civilization, from the "seasoned cultures," exiles, voluntary and involuntary, turned for an asylum.

§

Partly through support given by the returned natives and by exiles coming in a new wave from Europe, but more especially through enthusiasms at home, a different art atmosphere was created in America and an approach was made to the making of a finer civilization in the United States. Over the outcome of this quest, pessimists were dubious as ever and optimists hopeful as ever. The music critic, W. J. Henderson, refused to see signs and symbols of genuine esthetic feeling in America upon which to build great art. Music, he said, had its roots in national lyricism, rhythm, martial zest, religious majesty, and a patrician economy — all lacking in the new world and incapable of transplantation. "It is one of the auspicious signs of the times," he admitted, "that efforts in the direction of improvements are numerous. Some are assuredly good; some are at least questionable. Radio broadcasts of artistic music in schools should produce results. The organization of thousands of high school bands may or may not be laudable. Tell me what those high school bands are playing and I can tell you whether they are raising or lowering the standard of taste among the young. Tell me what your children are singing and I can determine even more. If they are discovering their sense of beauty through the daily practice of 'Smoke in Your Eyes,' I do not believe they are journeying toward the stars."

To such doubts, Roy Harris, among others, replied: "Why limit our expectations to the mighty Beethoven?" And in view of the conditions on the trans-Atlantic continent in 1937, he added: "I imagine all the great masters would welcome a vacation from Europe these days." Anyway, he said, "music reflects the spirit of the social environment from which it arises. It passes from one generation, one nation, one century to another, always seeking the social fermentation in which it thrives. . . . Music is no more a dead art today than we ourselves are dead people. And American music is in a particularly provident spot. We have been growing up in just the same cycle of development in which Germany and Russia matured. We have gone through the first period of musical culture: that of importing our musicians and our music. We have gone through the second period: that of developing our own musicians, who are supreme in interpreting the music of other nations (with the possible exception of conductors). We are entering the third period, wherein the quantity and quality of our musicians and our audiences demand a new native music, conceived in the mood and tempo of our time." Coming back to America from a European sojourn in the summer of 1937, Serge Koussevitsky, conductor of the Boston Symphony, announced that "European composers simply have nothing to say. Our American composers are consistently better artists." Presumably this was a contention that art was no longer a monopoly of older civilizations, that new energies were astir on this side of the Atlantic.

In fact they were, and around all the arts now swirled critical inquiries and affirmations respecting their nature and their relation to the society in which they had their being and flourished. As Ruskin had hammered into the heads of the English, art was closely connected with the crafts, with the whole state of society, and the great art of sincerity and genius had sprung from this relationship. Re-emphasized in America by the debate over the arts, Ruskin's axiom was applied in making discoveries in the New World, and "America the beautiful" was given a thorough investigation. Very soon the inquiry got as near to the bottom as Erskine Caldwell's Tobacco Road. The long popularity of this drama in the art center of the country — a drama enacted in sheer dust, without so much as a blade of grass visible in the background of human life — gave notice that emotions were stirred by revelations of degradation in "the land of plenty — by abstractions in the concrete." Against these emotions all artists could not be entirely insulated. Nor could they be kept "pure"; that is, entirely shut off from the other categorical declarations made by artists in imaginative letters and by thinkers and practitioners in economics, politics, and social reconstruction.

As the debate over the arts expanded, penetrating deeper and deeper into the social milieu, objective and subjective, upsurges of esthetic feeling from below enriched the discussion. Though Hull House and Greenwich House, like other social settlements in the major cities, had early explored sources of artistic expression among the industrial workers and given opportunities for explicit demonstrations in settlement studios, men and women who had climbed to the top of the business or artistic ladder had generally supposed that men and women at the bottom were devoid of sensitivity to "the finer things" reserved for the elect. But times were changing, and all over the United States, especially after the coming of the federal art projects, artists from urban quarters and from rural regions helped to correct this point of view.

Another factor contributing to the extension of the debate on esthetics was the wider social use of the camera, which had been steadily improved in the matter of mechanics, especially light controls. Through the skilled manipulation of the camera by Margaret Bourke-White, Russell Lee, and other experts, following the path blazed by Stieglitz and his disciples, photography was turned from depicting unwrinkled faces and the machine to examining life and work among all sorts and conditions of people. Thus the imaginations of the artistically inclined were enlivened by photographic vistas of the polyglot population and the democratic task. To countless Americans who had now "Seen Their Faces," the desire for more beauty in American life became mingled with the desire for a better organization of labor and a wider distribution of its fruits.

The esthetic quest was merging with the social quest. "Aesthetic enjoyment and artistic creation are anticipations in our civilization of what the Good Life would really be," declared Irwin Edman, writing on The World, the Arts and the Artist in 1928, from his chair in Columbia University. "Such happiness as is present among our contemporaries is the happiness of those who are doing work that is itself delightful to them and enjoying things that are themselves a delight. . . . The image of a perfect society is not that of aesthetes in a museum but of artists at their work. The function of the arts in civilization at present is largely that of a dilettante escape for the observer, a truant absorption for the artist. In a rationally ordered society all work would have the quality of art, all enjoyment would have the immediate and glamourous character of aesthetic appreciation." That was not to disown the dynamo and revert to handicrafts. It was to say that democrats, even in the age of machine industry, must enjoy esthetic experiences if their labor and living were to be satisfying. The words "art," "democracy," and "culture" became more commonly associated.

To the members of the American Association of University Women, Lura Beam, director of their newly-planned art education, explained in 1936 the significance of the program in terms of this tendency. "Art is a statement of the interaction of the individual and society," she said in introducing the subject, at the annual convention. Then she proceeded to show that "in seven years the old channels of introspection have opened again in painting and new directions and content appear. The Chinese influences come via painters of the Pacific Northwest and the exposition of the European situation by Russian, German, and Austrian émigrés. Around Fourteenth Street (New York) and partly by way of Mexico an assertive minority paints only three panels — the bankers, the strike, and the breadline. These brushes paint mines, machinery, railroads, science, oppression, propaganda; no madonna unless she upholds a malnourished child, no cross unless it is marked 'opium of the people.' For art is the synthesis of a time. . . . The artist is thus the pioneer in the interpretation of the individual and society. . . . He resists the mold, the mold presses on him, the mold is stronger. Man resists, absorbs, adapts, becomes average. Or, at the two extremes, he wrecks himself in refusal, or he pioneers against environment and makes new patterns. This residue of the struggle between the natural man and the inevitable environment is personality." Logically of course a democratic society should give the freest play to personality.

A similar point of view was elaborated by Philip N. Yountz associated with the popular art movement at The People's Institute and at this moment with the federal art project, in his foreword to the book on art by Ladd. "Books about art," he brusquely asserted, "are a dangerous form of literature because they are apt to be misused by educated but unintelligent Philistines as a substitute for art itself. Just as the pedant comes to look on book knowledge instead of venturing to have thoughts of his own, so many readers fancy they are studying art when they are actually studying about art. . . . The path to independent judgment in the appreciation of painting begins with a knowledge of the best critical thinking of the past, though it does not by any means stop there. With this background and much study of pictures themselves, one may soon begin to hold his head erect, daring to praise what is meritorious though perhaps unpopular and to scorn what is cheap and imitative. Such independents are the real allies of the artist. It is their discrimination and intelligence that inspire him to exert his best efforts and it is from them that he receives his most valued approval."

The doctrine that art must free itself from the dogmas of the schools and refresh itself by contact with life at work was supported by Thomas Craven in his treatise on Modern Art. Though some of the modernists felt that Craven was a renegade, a commentator in The Nation rejoiced: "Craven has anatomized the new man and the new movements with a penetration hitherto unmatched by any historian or critic of our time. He strips their solemn pretentiousness from the abstractionists, the surrealists, the snob artists, the Bohemian cults which make art out of other art in a world where the fresh impulses of life never penetrate. If his ultimate appraisal of the achievements of modernism gives small comfort to the radicals, it gives even less to the traditionalists, whose painting 'has ceased to become work and has become genteel behavior.' . . . One feels that the author has gazed with profound dismay upon the Gallic aping and posturing of American painters these many years. The situation has

called for strong language, and he has mastered all his resources of invective, sarcasm, and contempt in order to sting
his readers into a sharp awareness of a sad, sad spectacle."
In short, an American art form, if it arrived, would come as a
result of absorbing old art forms and transfusing them with
the spirit of indigenous experiences, as great Italian art had
come.

In the gilded age, the public at large had not entered
extensively into the dispute over art values, but now even
the making of everyday commodities for the market involved
heated arguments. As long as prosperity flamed and flared
in industrial economy, designers by the thousands were
employed to render articles of use more attractive, articles ranging from kitchen utensils, tableware and bathtubs
through fabrics to automobiles and trains. From the distant
day when primitive woman had given form to the pots in use
at the hearth to the latest hour, objects of utility had both
expressed and invoked esthetic pleasure. But they had not
done so uniformly. Commercial demands, induced by hectic
hunts for markets, had interrupted theory and practice in
their unified course and relegated designers to the task of promoting the sales of gadgets which constituted larger and
larger areas of industrial output; that is, designers were
required to stylize products in terms of the competitive
market and a quick turn-over of commodities. Necessarily
this practice often ran contrary to the rule — a law of beauty
— that the best of design is that which attains the highest
functional perfection. Since the new mass production was
more closely related to purses than to art, to salesmanship
than to utility, protests arose against the ready acceptance
of the mere glitter and glamour expressed in stream-lined and
polished objects and that form of commercial art was subjected to criticism from various angles.

Facing more responsibility, a great engineering school, the
Massachusetts Institute of Technology, began to fall into
line with the critical trend. In advance of its 1938 Alumni
Day, the chairman of the committee, John E. Burchard,

announced in the press that a leading feature would be a symposium on the "influence of science and engineering on modern art." Two schools of thought, he said, would be considered : "The first and more conventional point of view of the older group of artists is that which holds that science, engineering, and the machine are tools of art, and, so far as esthetics is concerned, exist only to provide new facilities for the arts. The second point of view, the philosophy of the younger school of industrial designers, is that the artist is the prism through which the rays of esthetic potentiality engendered by the machine are focused. Under this conception the artist seeks to use the machine and its products in undistorted form merely to direct the natural workings of the machine into the logical forms which mean beauty." In connection with the symposium, an exhibit of modern industrial arts was projected to "include only those products of science and engineering which, either because of the influence of the industrial designer or as a natural result of thorough-going and sincere application of science and engineering, are in themselves beautiful."

The discussion of beauty and art widened out to the schools of philosophy which now contributed thought about the very nature of the esthetic sense, its sources, and manifestations. Works on esthetic theory, as distinguished from treatises on artistic practice, began to be prominent in publishers' lists, and arguments were heard from all the schools of speculation : the absolutists, the formalists, the empiricists, the universalists, the institutionalists, the pragmatists, and the geneticists, to vary somewhat the broad distinctions sketched by Katherine Gilbert in her Studies of Recent Aesthetics. On behalf of the absolutists, art was defined as a concern with the One Big Reality — a spiritual world, beyond appearances, eternally true and good ; and criteria of esthetic judgments as imperative as the ex cathedra pronouncements of the pope were provided for orthodox believers. The phrases of the old and endless debate on art for art's sake were rolled over again, with variations and minor additions.

Voices were also heard, speaking "an American language." It was a characteristic sign of the times that John Dewey, dean of American philosophers, came to regard the issue of art as so important that he brought his profound learning and his sensitive humanism to bear upon it in a volume on Art as Experience. Rejecting absolutism in esthetics as in philosophy, refuting the isolation of the formalists and specialists, Dewey related art to ways of social life, to forms of government and economy, to democracy, thus revitalizing a tradition to which Tolstoi, Ruskin, and William Morris had given force. Art and the artist Dewey placed in their political and social context. That was to say : The artist is a person, with a mind influenced by values and interests arising out of society ; art is a language or form of communication ; it is an endlessly creative function ; it expresses conceptions of life, such as freedom, equality, tyranny, servitude, war, or power. Having a social setting and rooted in universal human values, art finds in the freedom, tolerance, mobility, and respect for labor, which characterize a democratic society, conditions favorable to inspiration and expression. In an argument for years overdue, Dewey contended that great art cannot be brought into being merely by having museums filled with loot gathered by war or money or simply by meticulous study of forms peculiar to old societies ; it must be indigenous, expressing phases of humanity in the strivings of the place and the time. Thus Dewey drew art into the main stream of American history and philosophy, broke through the restraints of class, and gave esthetics an organic connection with the humanistic aspiration of society.

America was sufficiently sophisticated now for important and impressive symposia, one of which was arranged by the Baltimore Museum of Art in the spring of 1938 to discuss the naturalistic movement in art led by Courbet. The participants traced out the ramifications of the naturalistic movement in science, literature, music, and the graphic arts of today. The Johns Hopkins Press published the whole debate.

§

It was during this ferment of taste, experience, and opinion, this contest of emotions, ideas, and interests, that the Federal Government, in common with state and municipal governments, undertook the deliberate and conscious patronage of the arts and in the process encouraged a popular art movement of extraordinary proportions. Artists and the wide public were now united as they had never been before in America. Art was becoming public art in a new sense. In the long history of mankind, art had presented many aspects. Primitive art had expressed communal organization and purpose; for brief periods and in given places the individualism of the bourgeois, with their hostility for State and Church, had expressed itself in art; monumental art had generally been an affair of State or Church, or both, of aristocratic institutions hierarchal in form, evoking passionate loyalties and lifting their devotees in their noblest moments to causes and dreams larger and more enduring than themselves. Now, through the patronage of the arts by the government of the United States, art was again to be a public affair, but emphasizing in form, color, and line the esthetic affirmations of a democratic society wrestling with profound social disturbances, yet dreaming dreams of a greater dignity for man.

By the subject set for treatment and by the master-apprentice relationship which the undertaking required, American democracy was now directed to the production of social art. The subject was the American Scene in all its aspects and this gave free rein to popular experiences as sources and attitudes for art. In employing professional artists who no longer had other patrons, the Federal Government instructed them to commune with the people at large — the fountain-head of democratic government. Literally millions of people were thus invited to see beautiful things for the first time, and what is more, to try their skill at drawing, painting, modelling, and the other forms of artistic expression with no other object in view than expressing themselves with relation to the American scene. Through such a contact with popular art, even academic art was energized. Moreover what had hitherto been only a revolt against philistinism and preciosity deepened in the understanding of art as social meaning.

But this development, in truth, represented continuity rather than sudden innovation. A long line of precedents lay behind it in the erection of public buildings, public memorials, and government commissions to sculptors and muralists. An elaborate program of federal construction had in fact already been started in the national capital in the age of normalcy. Chief Justice Taft had set his heart upon and helped to plan a gigantic temple for the Supreme Court. Herbert Hoover, while Secretary of Commerce, had started a monument to business enterprise, — an enormous palace to house the expanding activities of his Department. Authorizations or projects also covered separate buildings for the Departments of Labor, Justice, Agriculture, Interior, the Post Office, and the National Archives. And as unemployment rose to the point of national frightfulness, the execution of these designs was pushed forward to provide work for the idle. Excitement was added to excavating and erecting by decisions respecting the location of these buildings, as L'Enfant's grand plan of the nation's capital was now being given a wider fulfillment. For the architecture of the structures, as well as their location, congressional approval had to be secured; and politics, as in all things congressional, played its part in determining appearances.

The result was far from pleasurable to all the people. The miles and miles of columns supporting nothing and the tiers upon tiers of steps leading up to Greek or Egyptian portals in the age of elevators were condemned as mere "archaeological architecture" by critics who preferred the symbols of contemporaneity and the conveniences of function. Hostility was not only vocal but well organized by 1936 when John Russell Pope, who had designed the shelter for the National Archives and other Washington buildings, proposed to honor

Thomas Jefferson with a Pantheon. Many citizens had experienced no enchantment as they stood before the pseudo-Greek temple in the dim recesses of which "Honest Abe," the rail-splitter born in a log cabin, had been made to pose in a manner suggesting a Zeus or an Apollo, instead of a man of the people as he truly was. It was more appropriate, they insisted, to have the mortal simplicities, the directness and responsibilities of democratic statecraft in America symbolized in the memorials of the national capital.

Among the severest critics was Joseph Hudnut, Dean of the Harvard Graduate School of Design and formerly associated with the Columbia School of Architecture. Writing on the Twilight of the Gods for Magazine of Art, the journal of the Federation of Arts, Dean Hudnut said in 1937: "I am aware that symbolism and romance are inescapable elements in architecture. They are highly desirable elements also, provided one does not pay too dearly for them. The price of Washington is colossal. To attain a 'perfect harmony' of classical form, to create a stupendous symbol of the power and permanence of the Federal Authority, to satisfy a romantic sensibility towards that quality of form which was established by the Early Republic (as if scale and magnitude had nothing to do with the quality of form!), we deprive the Federal City not only of that sense of a heroic past which is the true source of dignity in cities but also of that organic order (itself a kind of history) which is a condition of power in all the great traditions of architecture."

While the Dean was arguing in the sober terms of his profession that this architectural style did not fit the spirit or function of American government, Robert Littell and Harold Stuermer, in Today, a weekly journal of opinion, were declaring journalistically that the style made "Washington seem like a museum of caution and paralysis." They strenuously objected to the failure of the New Deal to take advantage of its opportunity to "reflect its own beliefs in stone, and affirm in its architecture the determination that government shall not be a cold, impersonal pile of rules and red tape, but a close friend of the people and a bold leader out of mediocrity and confusion." Names applied to conventional public speakers, particularly "stuffed shirts," were commandeered to describe this conventional building. With historical injustice it was also called "Hooverism." But as it continued to find favor under President Roosevelt, critics said it represented the trade agreements so dear to Cordell Hull, the Secretary of State: while America was exporting industrial and apartment architecture, she was importing public architecture. What was the real balance?

To some extent an offset to imports was obtained in the decorations. When in 1934 the Procurement Division of the Department of the Treasury, to which the task of securing murals and statues was assigned, entered upon its responsibility, it was widely agreed that art in America "underwent its most eventful year of the past two decades." Enthusiasts called the esthetic affirmations made under this regime the greatest artistic events in three centuries of American art. Unquestionably the zest of the Federal Government for visual interpretations of its role was marking a revolution in its leadership with respect to design and decoration. In 1937, for example, Boardman Robinson finished eighteen mural panels covering 1025 square feet in the Department of Justice.

Organized in December, 1933, the Public Works of Art Project was financed by a grant from the Civil Works Administrator to the Treasury Department and over its fortunes Edward Bruce was called to preside. At the capital and out over the country where federal buildings were being erected, embellishments proceeded to take form under this Project. Artists were employed at craftsmen's wages. At the capital, they were selected and supervised directly by the Treasury; in the sixteen regions into which the Project was divided, regional committees and sub-committees were charged with this responsibility. In 1935 the Painting and Sculpture Section of the Procurement Division of the United States Treasury Department, organized in 1934, consolidated and extended this national enterprise and announced competitions for mural assignments.

Edward Bruce, who was given such power over art in America, was both a financier and a painter. Among his own productions was a mural executed in 1931 for the San Francisco Stock Exchange and hung over the mantel in its Board room — a picture of the local business district with the Golden Gate just beyond. In 1933 Bruce went to England with Cordell Hull, as a delegate to the London Conference; and during its sessions, on the initiative of the Secretary of State, an exhibit of his art was held in London. Known on both sides of the Atlantic, an experienced painter in sympathy with the New Deal, Edward Bruce pressed not only for results but for creditable results in the art projects under his administration. In some instances he had to yield to sentimentality when he preferred vitality, but on the whole his supervision of painting and sculpture under federal auspices was deemed so competent by professional artists that the Architectural League of New York awarded him its Friedsam Medal in 1937 for his "outstanding achievement" and Harvard gave him an honorary degree.

As for fortunate artists who won important commissions to decorate the capital, on the whole they too deserved medals in that they responded to their opportunity for communicating with the people through visible forms in a spirit of public service such as had actuated great artists in other times and places. "Exactly as it would be absurd to imagine a Giotto or a Piero making his mural illustrations unintelligible to the peasant who came to them with faith, so it would have been absurd for Reginald Marsh to have made his murals in the Post Office Department at Washington unintelligible to the man in the street or for Henry Varnum Poor to make his panels in the Department of Justice meaningless to a clerk in the building."

If such was the theory, practice did not always signify genius in communication. The monstrous figures, male and female, which sat before the portal of the Supreme Court

temple were notable mainly for their ponderosity. Nor was
communication of other sorts always acceptable to the public
for whom it was intended, as Rockwell Kent discovered after
impressing his political conceptions upon a mural for the Post
Office Department; when some one deciphered an inscrip-
tion within his composition, his leftist tendency was called
to public attention and the matter was ordered corrected.
But critical interpretations of Justice by Henry Varnum
Poor seemed to provoke no bitter protest against their
validity, and among the quantities of paintings and statues
completed for Washington in these years a substantial
number of the esthetic affirmations were technically competent and alive with social statement, freely expressed.

Out of want, unrest, and fear a general Federal Art
Project took form in 1935 as a measure of relief, its periphery
extending to work in all the arts and crafts whether utilized
for the embellishment of buildings or not. As the construction of private buildings came to a halt, architects were
thrown out of a livelihood. As funds for museums shrank
and private collectors began to convert their Old Masters
into cash and curtail patronage, painters and sculptors lost
their means of support. As mills closed, designers of fabrics
and other commodities walked the streets with no employment in sight. As magazines lost subscriptions and publishers their market for books, writers and illustrators, editors
and critics were checkmated in their careers. How were the
numerous orchestras to survive and the musicians generally?
By the thousands, artists of all kinds faced destitution and
were compelled to ask for public relief.

For the precipitous let-down in art commissions, the nation
was no better prepared than it was for the collapse on the
Stock Exchange. In respect of art casualties, however, statistics were less satisfactory, since art could not be measured
numerically like declining stocks and defaulted bonds.
The fact that several thousand artists, in a population of
130,000,000 people, were deprived, in 1933, of ways to earn
their living, if set beside the fact that millions of industrial

workers were out of jobs, might have been dismissed by mere statisticians as a meager item in the social reckoning. That it became a large item in this accounting was due to the deep-rooted convictions of influential Americans with reference to the role of art in civilization and to a keen recognition of the plight into which artists had fallen.

"During boom years architects, particularly in the larger offices, became imbued with the psychology of their clients," avowed Talbot Faulkner Hamlin, a member of the American Institute of Architects, in August, 1933. "All the Hooverian dogmas of individualism, salesmanship, profit-making, were swallowed unquestionably," he went on to say. "Architectural magazines were full of articles on the money-making side of the profession; the architect was often a promoter and a business man rather than a designer. As he became immersed in financial schemes and details, his professional position weakened; the architect was merely one of several cogs in the machine of corporate and individual profit chasing. Then came the falling off in investment building between 1928 and 1929 and the stock market crash; and one after another the great hotels and office buildings paraded into bankruptcy and foreclosure. The profit chasers sought other fields; the architect was forgotten. He learned bitterly of the gratitude of wealth, and all his grandiose promotion schemes vanished. Out of it all he found he had won only small pay, worry, and a loss of professional prestige."

In 1932 architects were reported as having less than one-seventh of the work they had in 1928. The crumbs that fell from Dives' table grew scantier and scantier and yet graduate recruits from schools of architecture continued every year to enter the scramble for such crumbs as there were. Elaborate corporations employing designers, organizers, and managers of great buildings waited a while for orders that did not arrive and then steadily reduced their forces or drew the curtains and locked the doors. Lesser business establishments engaged in designing small homes fared a little better and hoped for a public housing program to provide them with work; but that program also lagged, leaving minor alterations or repairs in tenements and shops or houses the mainstay of such concerns. Even the smaller firms had to face the competition of architects out of work as the total income from architectural enterprise slumped in 1932 to a fifth of the 1928 figure. If many men and women hitherto employed in architectural labors could make adjustments, many others could not.

"Some have turned artists or interior decorators," Hamlin reported. "One makes decorative maps. One, with a musical avocation, plays the piano for a radio circuit. Another is a taxi driver. And many have gone into commission selling — that last chaotic field which modern finance and industry have developed to absorb those technologically and otherwise unemployed — and hawk over the country everything from pencils to life insurance." But like the scholar who, after his dismissal from a leading university for having opposed America's entrance into the world war, tried unsuccessfully to sell washing machines for his daily bread, architects did not find it possible to transform themselves immediately into high-powered traveling salesmen, handling just any kind of goods.

As helpfully as their own situation permitted, members of the profession aided one another in the crisis, "perhaps the worst that has overtaken a similar body." They opened an Emergency Work Bureau in New York City, for example, and secured some commissions for the applicants, such as traffic surveys for the State Housing Board, participation in the Columbia University Energy Survey for the United States, and model-making and measurement drawings for museums. However, the fees they charged, though far below the architect's customary rewards, were often contested and the workers on relief tasks hurt themselves and the profession by accepting such slight returns for their labor.

The very styles of architecture which did materialize during the general prostration indicated "symptoms, at heart, of exhaustion and despair," in the opinion of Hamlin. Architects "played safe," the "joyless conservatism" of Hoover's Department of Commerce building in Washington illustrating that timidity and ennui. In 1933, at the World's Fair in Chicago, structures "almost without architectural meaning," devoid of the "great architectural problems of plan, material, use and proportion," betrayed, according to Hamlin, a similar feeling of "insecurity and doubt, in the actual terror of destitution which these last years had brought to the architects especially."

By 1935 the number of unemployed musicians, painters, sculptors, architects, writers, playwrights, actors, and dancers had grown to such an extent that the country faced the possibility of an utter collapse in the art movement. With professional artists roaming the streets hunting for work, what prospect could students training for a livelihood in the arts see ahead when they left the "threshold of life"? If America could not support artists, it was surely poverty-stricken in things of the spirit as well as of the purse. To the forefront came a fundamental question of civilization itself: Are the arts to be viewed merely as luxuries to be lopped off when the economic machine is in trouble?

The very hope of "recovery," not to mention "progress," was involved in the question, since industry itself depended upon the preservation and development of skills in the arts of design. For at least fifty years American business men had recognized this dependence, and international competition had made it clearer to them with every passing year. To stimulate the home market, artistic skills were equally imperative and yet the risk of hopeless deterioration in skills was apparently imminent. Deeper down in psychological sources lay the peril of dissolution that threatened aspiration and the creative spirit so intimately associated with the arts, humble and great, and so important as sustaining forces in the growth and preservation of society itself.

For the awakening of public interest in the state of the arts, the Bohemians of the prosperous age were only slightly, if at all, responsible; they had often fled to places more

delightful to their eyes than the American scene or had con-
gregated in the alleys and corners at home for idle "conversation at midnight." The awakening came from two sources,
apart from the obvious income needs which were mainly
responsible : one, the more or less quiet and steady leadership
of men and women who had given privileged segments of
the population the advantages of concert-hearing and choral-
singing, museum-visiting, the enjoyment of and training in
the arts; the other, the folk art which had weathered the
hazards of time and furnished a basis on which to build
public art. The merging of these two streams of interest and
action created a New Horizon in Art, as Holger Cahill expressed it. And toward the challenging illumination of the
new horizon, the American democracy blazed its way, experimentally.

With extreme pleasure Eduard Lindeman, from the van-
tage-point of his long social work, hailed this movement "out
from the alleys of Bohemia and onto the highways." But it
was not merely from the alleys of Bohemia that artists
marched toward the assumption of public obligations. In the
ateliers of established artists still receiving commissions, men
and women caught the vision of a democracy in dire cultural
and economic distress and they moved from their secure
positions along the path to be marked "the American way,"
carrying others with them toward a collective effort to meet
the menace of an artistic collapse. Indeed so many Americans rejected the idea that the arts could be neglected or
lopped off when the economic machine was in trouble that
federal, state, and local governments were induced to assert
leadership in saving and promoting the arts by administrative and financial measures. Had there been no appreciative
public behind them, even Aeschylus, Bach, and Michelangelo
could not have demonstrated their genius, as Maxwell
Anderson averred.

The new measures did not, however, signify the very
beginning in the relation of the American State and the arts,
as many protestants seemed to suppose. For more than a

hundred years in the United States, governments had given commissions to artists in connection with public buildings and memorials; there had been "political" artists and architects since the first days of the republic. Again and again politicians had projected great public works, buildings, parks, and monuments with a view to giving "fat jobs" to political contractors and designers associated with them, as well as to serve interests of utility and esthetics. Often indeed considerations of profit had outweighed public interests of any kind. And in such circumstances artistic beneficiaries had accepted the fruits of politics as "natural" and "proper." When the idea that planned public works should "take up the slack" in employment during slumps in industry came into vogue early in the twentieth century, and was generally approved, few citizens regarded the commissions that went to artists as a form of "contemptible relief."

But no such expedients were adequate to handle the economic dislocations of the arts in 1933 and the following years, any more than the privations of industry and agriculture. Artists, no less than home owners and industrial workers, were human beings, and government actions directed against the economic reverses, unless deliberately partial, also had to take them into account. Were artists and the rest of the unemployed to be given doles and allowed to lose their skills, to sink into lethargy and despair? That question President Roosevelt faced definitely in January, 1935, and in his annual message to Congress he declared that "continued dependence upon relief induces a spiritual and moral disintegration fundamentally destructive to the national fibre." For haphazard relief and scattered public-works undertakings, he proposed to substitute "selected and planned" projects which would provide general employment at such useful undertakings as would afford "permanent improvement in living conditions" or create "future wealth for the nation."

Accepting this program as sound in conception, Congress gave appropriate authorizations; the Works Progress Ad-

ministration was set up under the direction of Harry Hopkins; and in August, 1935, the Federal Art Project was
organized as a division of that Administration. Arrangements were made for the employment of musicians, actors,
writers, painters, sculptors, architects, etchers, frescoists, and
photographers; and at the peak of the load thousands of
persons were engaged in public arts projects. Conceived as
emergency measures for the occupation of the unemployed
and the maintenance of skills and attitudes, these projects
developed into a cultural movement and received such strong
commendation that a permanent federal bureau for the promotion of the arts in America was proposed in Congress in
1938 and widely sponsored in the country.

To Jacob Baker, a believer in experimentation and liberal
in his tastes, Harry Hopkins entrusted the general supervision of all the relief projects for artists, actors, writers, and
musicians. As his aides Baker chose Holger Cahill, an authority on folk art, an outstanding museum technician and
art critic, to direct work in painting, sculpture, and the
crafts; Nikolai Sokoloff, organizer, and for many years director of the Cleveland orchestra, to head music projects; Hallie
Flanagan, in private life Mrs. Philip H. Davis, director of
the Experimental Theater at Vassar College, to manage the
theater project; and Henry Alsberg, an editorial writer for
the New York Evening Post and a foreign correspondent
for liberal magazines, to take care of the writers project.
When Mr. Baker left the government service on his own
motion in 1936, Mr. Hopkins selected for his position Mrs.
Ellen S. Woodward, of Mississippi, who was then in charge
of the women's division of the Emergency Relief Administration. Associated with the federal relief program from the
beginning, Mrs. Woodward had previously been a member
of the state legislature and executive secretary of the Mississippi State Board of Development.

By May, 1937, $46,000,000 had been spent on the arts
through the Works Progress Administration, an amount in
excess of the government subsidy in any other nation for the

maintenance and promotion of art in its various branches. France in 1937, for example, was spending only $6,000,000.

The federal enterprise was not to be appraised, however, solely in terms of expenditure, absolute or comparative. Despite the lavish outlays for art training, museums, and galleries, despite achievements of a high order, Americans had done relatively little, under either private or public auspices, to stimulate universal interest in the arts and deepen esthetic experience among the broad masses of the people in cities and rural regions. Estimates placed the number of men, women, and children in the United States who had never had the pleasure of seeing or studying original works of art, deemed great, at a figure as high as ninety per cent. This calculation included thousands of teachers charged with elevating the tastes of the young.

Though music of a sort was "as indigenous as corn-on-the-cob, jazz, breakfast food, and comic strips," though song rolled from the slate mines of Vermont where Welsh quarrymen were employed and from the coal mines of Pennsylvania where miners of other origins still sang the songs of their ancestors, though Negroes swayed and lilted as in plantation days, though the radio carried grand compositions to more homes over the land, still there were millions of Americans who had heard only chants or hymns and Americans without number who knew only the crudest rhythmic forms or the "canned music" of the radio. Only in the most backward places of the earth were there people who knew as little of esthetic pleasure as multitudes in great areas of the United States — in "the drought lands of the Dakotas, in the Corn Belt of Nebraska, in the hay valleys of New England, in the culturally isolated settlements of the Ozarks and parts of the Carolinas, on the tobacco roads of Georgia, and even in some sections of Greater New York, Chicago, San Francisco, and Los Angeles." But at last the American democracy was to explore this form of its great unknown — to pioneer on new lines.

The spirit guiding the enlargement of artistic expression

was set forth by Holger Cahill in an exposition of working doctrines. "The organization of the Federal Art Project," he said, "has proceeded on the principle that it is not the solitary genius but a sound general movement which maintains art as a vital, functioning part of any cultural scheme. Art is not a matter of rare, occasional masterpieces. The emphasis upon masterpieces is a nineteenth-century phenomenon. It is primarily a collector's idea and has little relation to an art movement. When one goes through the galleries of Europe which preserve, in spite of war, fire, flood, and other destructive forces, an amazing quantity of works from the past, one is struck by the extraordinary amount of work which was produced in great periods. During the early part of the twentieth century it is said that some forty thousand artists were at work in Paris. It is doubtful if history will remember more than a dozen or two of these, but it is probable that if the great number of artists had not been working, very few of these two dozen would have been stimulated to creative endeavor; in a genuine art movement, a great reservoir of art is created in many forms, both major and minor. . . . If American art is to continue, the talents of the younger generation of artists must not only be encouraged but must be given an opportunity to develop." In that mood and with that same faith, his colleagues in the Federal Art Project directed their respective enterprises. Dr. Sokoloff reminded the public that "training for the participation in music" is as desirable as training for performing music and "remedies a weakness which has long been recognized in America's musical life, the decline of the amateur."

To take care of all the artists in need and make a social return to the supporting nation at the same time was the combined problem and ideal for the administrators in charge of this public works program. Of course every person on the list of projects was not a genius or even technically very competent. Nevertheless all of them had been identified in some way with the profession of art. And their tasks were assigned as far as possible according to their disciplines and talents. For example, more than half of the artists were directed to photography, to making posters, designing stage-sets for the federal theater projects, and to other activities in applied art. Some were sent out over the country to manage art galleries and art centers, opened in town after town where good pictures and sculpture had never been seen before, even by the teachers in the schools. In fact 600 new art centers were established in churches, settlements, and schools, in many cases with financial aid from cities and private citizens. In these centers local residents were invited to hear lectures given by the government teachers, to see the exhibits, and if they so desired to attend classes in painting, sculpture, etching, photography, music, the drama, writing, and other branches of art. Hitherto relatively little thought had been given in the United States to community expression in artistic forms but within an incredibly short time a million persons, old, middle-aged, and young, were enrolled for the study of art in centers under public auspices.

Especially manageable and appealing to the whole country was the Music Project which found employment for several thousand musicians, set up laboratories for the encourage-ment and training of composers, organized musical programs, stimulated local participation by communities, and carried music into hospitals and other institutions. In the congested quarters of great cities and in far-scattered and isolated com-munities throughout the United States, concerts were given, young and old were invited to participate and try their talents, local groups were formed to assure a continuity of interest and services, and the love of rhythm was enriched by a finer experience. Within a few months 4000 works by 1400 native composers were rendered, many mediocre, some positively bad, others called "distinguished" by competent critics. Scarcely a state was untouched by this novel enter-prise in public leadership and private coöperation. In 1938 more than 6000 musicians participated in the national music week organized by the Music Project; programs were exe-cuted in forty-two states by symphony and concert orches-

tras, bands, opera and choral groups. By that time the
number of attendances recorded at musical events held under
the auspices of the Project had risen to more than 85,000,000
and coöperative arrangements had been perfected with innumerable established musical organizations. Singing societies began to hold inter-community festivals. Indoors and
out-of-doors America was brought within the spell of un-
canned rhythmic sound.

§

Severe critics of the Roosevelt administration decried all
such activity as "boon doggling," as a departure from the
fixed principles of American government. On the merits of
particular performances experts in esthetics could differ radically. But unquestionably federal responsibility for the promotion of science, letters, and the arts had the sanction even
of supreme authorities among the founders of the republic.
In his first annual address to the first Congress of the United
States, President Washington himself had declared that
"there is nothing which can better deserve your patronage
than the promotion of science and literature." Speaking of
the national university which he wished to see founded, he
said : "I have greatly wished to see a plan adopted, by which
the arts, sciences, and belles-lettres could be taught in their
fullest extent, thereby embracing *all* the advantages of European tuition." In commenting on his Farewell Address to
the nation, in after years, Washington expressed regret that
he had omitted references to education and particularly to
the establishment of a national university "where the youth
from all parts of the United States might receive the polish
of erudition in the arts, sciences, and belles-lettres." Such
views he was moved to announce, doubtless, by his concern
about the development of civilization in America and the
attacks directed by Europeans against the "thinness" of
culture in the New World.

In the very convention that drafted the Constitution of
the United States, indeed, the issue of social refinements had

come up for consideration. James Madison proposed that Congress be empowered to establish a university and Charles Pinckney that it be authorized to found seminaries "for the promotion of literature and the arts and sciences." It was not the so-called "practical arts" alone that the statesmen of the eighteenth century had in mind as objects of solicitude. Their intention was correctly re-expressed long afterward by John Quincy Adams when, as President, he recommended to Congress the enactment of laws "promoting the improvement of agriculture, commerce, and manufactures, the cultivation and encouragement of the mechanic and of the elegant arts, the advancement of literature, and the progress of the sciences, ornamental and profound."

It is clear, therefore, that the concern with and appreciation of arts and letters represented by the Federal Art Project had sanction in the most reputable American theory respecting relations between the State and the arts, although amid circumstances far different in nature. Had statecraft undertaken to foster and guide esthetics in the age of Washington, the patrician culture of the eighteenth century might have been reinforced on American soil. Had statecraft assumed that function in the age of John Quincy Adams, commercial culture might have become dominant, almost beyond challenge. Now in the twentieth century with political democracy triumphant, statecraft, in reaching out to esthetics, reflected the democratic spirit engaged in an effort to conquer the crisis in thought and economy, and was in a position to make arts and letters powerful assets in the balance sheet of national wealth.

At all events by 1935 the President, the Congress, and private citizens intensely regardful of culture in America had become cognizant of artistic resources to be conserved and strengthened, of risks inherent in allowing them to waste and decay. Together they assumed the obligation to foster such neglected talent as the nation possessed and give it a chance to develop by use, supplementing, not supplanting, private endeavors. And why should the idea have received so much criticism? No artist of the highest academic standing had ever been unwilling to accept an attractive government commission in the years of the golden glow, whatever its political origin or utility. Only in the recession was contumely attached to the public patronage of the arts. Perhaps it was not in the arts that the roots of the controversy lay but in conceptions respecting the economy in which the esthetic collapse had occurred.

When once the decision was made by the Roosevelt administration to provide employment for artists as well as for industrialists, contractors, and industrial workers, it soon became explicit that the thought of contemporary democrats and the thought of the early republicans were alike in that both diverged from the thought of old monarchies in one fundamental characteristic. There was no court in the United States to be served and flattered by genius. Talent, unless it still retreated from the American scene, had to work in and with the common life of America. And it was concern with this life that, from the beginning of the republic, had sustained the ideal of an advancing civilization in America, now to be carried forward in part by the encouragement of art.

§

Not until the Federal Art Project collected the materials did Americans begin to appreciate the extent and nature of their esthetic resources. Beneath the imported academic art, most of which "the people" either never saw or did not understand, in American regionalism the art of the people survived. As an editorial in the magazine Fortune rightly declared in June, 1937, "one thing every sophomore knows about the tradition of American art is that there isn't any. . . . It rests on no peasant handicrafts, no popular taste, no anonymous workmanship. It arrived ready-made from Europe. And the best of it arrived on the *Ile de France* within the last decade in a case marked 'Picasso: use no hooks.'"

From the misinformation given by their preceptors and their attitude toward art, sophomores derived their assumptions in part. Nor did popular writers on American culture have a wide and intimate knowledge of folk art upon which to base their treatises. They, too, often imagined that Americans had little or no taste, inherent or inherited. They paid tribute to craft and peasant taste in Europe and Asia but they were inclined to scorn every species of rustic expression in their homeland as "pioneer" and "frontier" bungling, thereby missing the imaginative resources of an American culture and in consequence the conscious and ingrained traditional feeling that America could actually do important things in the arts.

In fact it was not until the Federal Art Project explored underlying tastes and attempts at their expression, from the seventeenth-century furniture of the people, their silver, pewter, textiles, coverlets, toys, glass, ceramics, embroideries, clothes, woodcarvings, ships, houses, drawings, wall decorations, portraiture, and water colors, for example, to things produced in the twentieth century, that Americans got the slightest notion of the continental resources in artistic matters. The Federal Government's Index of American Design was an immense educational enterprise.

Other nations had long been devoted to their own popular art, had collected specimens for their museums, had enjoyed the fructifying force of the inspiration which professional artists had derived from studying achievements of the unprofessional, had acclaimed their sense of beauty as their distinction, and had received the laurels of outlanders in recognition of their cultural greatness. On the other hand, Americans had been inclined to relegate their folk art, when they encountered it inadvertently, to the realm of the merely "quaint." But this infantile esthetic attitude was educated to more sophistication when in twenty-five states the workers on federal projects, in the spirit of sensitive archaeologists and not of simple antiquarians, explored the people's esthetic affirmations on this vast continental mainland. Off the highways, in the byways, these microscopic searchers found that "homespun art" was not a mere anachronism, that handicrafts still flourished, and that skilled manipulators of materials in many "back regions" had means for surviving the depression that industrial and white-collar workers did not possess.

Impressed by the discoveries and interpretations in the Index of American Design, museums grew more hospitable to folk art. And not only that; they saw in it new values. Painters and sculptors likewise were invigorated by the quality of the near at hand; by contact with sincere and unsophisticated work. Constance Rourke, through her experience with the editing of the Index, found, for example, that "painters staring for the first time at seventeenth and eighteenth century New Mexican painting on wood have been humbled by the devotion of these unknown artists who served a discipline as old as Catholic Spain."

With respect to folk art as a whole in America, the discipline, it might be added, ran back through the aborigines to the very beginning of all art when the appreciation of beauty was associated with the most elementary production of commodities for everyday use at the hearth and in the field. It represented an eternally human insistence upon attractions for the eye, a will to express self in meditation and work imaginatively; and when such art was now assembled and re-emphasized, it quickly became recognized as a social asset. Thus the magazine Fortune, reviewing the Index to American Design, made that comprehension articulate. "Men cutting weather vanes out of iron and blowing goblets out of glass and shaping plates from clay," it avowed, "did not cease to exercise their sense of form and color merely because the oil painters had quit or run away to Italy or stopped drinking. Women sewing quilts and stitching samplers continued to use their eyes and their imaginations. Wood carvers and furniture makers went right on concerning themselves with the lines of their figureheads (for their seagoing vessels) and the just proportions of their cabinets. The popular arts, the practical arts, the arts which always must exist in a living society, whether the artists find them or not, survived and were vigorous."

Among the artists who did find them was Charles Sheeler, one of the earliest disciples of modernism to do it. Born in Philadelphia, his own background was urban. His art education had been pursued both in the United States and in Europe but it did not leave him creatively paralyzed. On his return from a third trip to Europe, he drew closer to folk art in America, to a study of form as function, spending much of his time in Bucks County, Pennsylvania, where the fine old barns elicited his enthusiasm. He studied intensively the art of the Shakers too and became steeped in the idea that "every force has its form." Deliberately looking for the real beneath the meretricious, he discovered the American heritage, assimilated it, and gave to his painting of barns, boats, flowers, and human beings not only a high plastic quality but an integrity suggesting the spirit of the original handicraftsmen, the vitality and beauty of flora, and the vigor of healthy life.

What was true of handicrafts as an American art affirmation was also true of music, as the units of the Federal Music Project discovered. These units collected or recorded "the early music of Mexico and Texas — on the plains and the border, Acadian and Creole songs in Louisiana, African melodies sung by the Negroes of the Mississippi bayous, the folk songs of the Southern mountaineers, white and Negro spirituals from the Carolinas, settlers' songs and songs of Indian origin from Oklahoma, early Spanish songs from California, liturgical music from the California missions, songs sung by the Penitentes of New Mexico, music brought into Mexico in the time of the conquistadors." Though federal workers were not the original explorers of this heritage, they widened the investigation. Symphonies based on the songs of the mountain people of North Carolina had been composed in the music department of the university of Chapel Hill. Carl Sandburg had published his American

Songbag. The two Lomaxes, father and son, had wandered among the people and issued volumes of the songs they had heard among cowboys and fieldhands, among Negroes in the cotton fields and Negroes in jail. But the Federal Music Project helped to call the attention of the entire country to the wealth and meaning of the music heritage and to shake academicians out of their routines.

In the merging of the academic and the non-academic, Charles Seeger, teacher, lecturer, assistant to the director of the Federal Music Project, seemed to find enclosed the promise of a creatively significant popular music. Writing for Magazine of Art, he said: "Unquestionably, the musical soul of America is in its folk music, not in its academic music; and only in its popular music to the extent popular music has borrowed, stolen, and manhandled folk music materials. On the other hand, the gestures, the nervous energy, the characteristic flair of America — industrialized, sophisticated, learned America — is in its academic and popular, not in its folk music. It is quite as necessary to have an outside as well as an inside. And quite desirable to have both! But they should not fight with each other; for there is every reason to believe each has something the other needs for its well-being and for the well-being of the country. Great musics in the past have been formed out of just such interplay of diversity and integration as can be seen now in American music. There is some reason to believe it is happening again.

"Both the wide diversity and the rapid integration are desirable factors in American music. Diversity without integration, in so large a unit as America, would mean chaos, and might well fit into a state of social, economic, and political anarchy. Integration without diversity spells standardization and regimentation, and would fit only too well with the totalitarianism of fascism. A balance, or complementary of the two, points to the preservation and further evolution of democratic social organization. Actually, this is, I believe, what is happening in American music today."

Along this exploratory line, the Writers Project likewise

carried on an extensive search for folk lore in tales and legends. It promoted studies of the ethnic groups in the United States, surveyed American archives, explored old buildings, and scanned faded photographs, maps, and charts — with the aim of discovering neglected treasures and presenting comprehensive data relative to deep-lying cultural patterns.

That all the arts projects were not merely antiquarian in aim was demonstrated by the response which men, women, and children made to the Government's invitation to paint, model, carve, etch, dance, act on the stage, tell stories, write, design, and photograph. Their eagerness to take advantage of the opportunities offered them proved that reservoirs of creative energies, hitherto unutilized, existed in all parts of the country. Out of them might flow the esthetic interests necessary to the vigorous nourishment of the arts and, for aught any one knew, an occasional genius might in time again illuminate the heavens.

Summaries, even skillfully made, could give no adequate insight into the strength and depth of this national movement. A single clue may be afforded by a single illustration taken from the Painters Project in Chicago. The regional director of that enterprise under federal auspices was Mrs. Increase Robinson, herself a painter, who had long been helping young artists, mainly from the middle west, to carry on their creative work, and educating Chicago in the process. In various ways she had befriended and encouraged such talented young persons as Aaron Bohred, Grant Wood, Francis Chapin, Davenport Griffin, and David McCosh.

Accordingly, Mrs. Robinson brought to her task both abilities and wide experience when she became a government art official; and under her direction the Chicago project produced in 1936 seventy-five murals, "placed or had in process thirty large sculptures and woodcarvings; put up a 114-foot plaster frieze in the new Kish Hall of the Field Museum of Natural History; prepared dioramas for visual education; and produced 40,000 posters for health and safety

campaigns." Comparing its exhibit in 1937 with the current
exhibit at the Chicago Art Institute, critics accustomed to
reporting the products of the academies pronounced it
worthy of more than grudging recognition. It was said that
the "best young painting" in the middle west was being
done by workers on the Federal Project. The democratic
aspect of this federal patronage, as directed by Mrs. Robinson, was reflected in its interracial catholicity. Many nationalities were listed among the painters and sculptors whom
critics were watching. Their very names indicated the
liberalism of the federal policy, for they included such as
these: Viviano, Britton, Breinin, Michalov, Stenvall, Murray, Bennett, Millman, Jacobson, and Siporin. In all the
projects, men and women of the Negro race were given
access to the working tools of art; their products were
exhibited with the rest and were acknowledged in a spirit
free from racial antipathies.

In California, a similar development took place. Linked
with the Federal Art Project this most-western section of
the nation proved its power to create distinguished objects
surpassing the preciosities of philistinism. In a combination of "faith, freedom, and discipline," its mosaicists
achieved decorations commanding the attention of art lovers
and critics of the most defiant types, much credit for which
belonged to William Gaskin, the San Francisco government
supervisor. In this form of art several women did notable
work as in fact they did wherever the opportunity was given
them. The hospitality shown by the Berkeley Art Gallery
was responsible for California's record, in part.

As for sculpture, its comparative expense gave less leeway
on the whole to the encouragement of that art medium. Its
dependence on building was another factor holding it back.
But as federal and private housing crept forward, little by
little, sculpture did the same. In some of the housing projects, innovative work was done in carved murals; symbolic
statues were made to typify the life and labor of the older
residents; and frolicsome animals were sculptured to amuse

the children. Through their opportunity to apply modern conceptions of taste and new techniques, artists were led to subdue freakishness in the interests of sincere workmanship. In some cases the residents were permitted to pass judgments on designs in advance of their execution.

An important phase of federal action lay in the effect of the arts projects upon impressionable childhood during the years ranging from extreme youth to maturing adolescence, in school and outside. Whatever promise American life held was to flower out of the rising generation but millions of that oncoming population were being cast adrift with nothing substantial to employ their active bodies and restless minds. No doubt it seemed foolish to many globe-trotting adults, accustomed to think of art as something completed — the adult product of Old Masters never young, that American children should be given wholesale opportunities at public expense to paint, model, and carve. Having felt awe or weariness in the galleries of other civilizations, many such tourists shouted vociferous condemnation in which they were joined by the weary at home. But other Americans both felt and thought differently. Some of them were disturbed by the social menaces, such as delinquency and crime, which mentally undernourished children, victims in part of the economic casualty, could so easily enlarge. Analytical artists, wise in their knowledge that "eyes on the world" turn there in very infancy and that a peculiar charm of art may represent a childishly direct selection of values, urged that the arts projects be opened wide to youth. Countless children were made happy by this arrangement and an extraordinary demonstration of their power to express themselves resulted from the opportunities provided for them.

Federal projects so extensive, designed to reach all parts of the country and give occupation to old and young by the hundreds of thousands, constituted an art movement that called for an army of competent painters, sculptors, musicians, and craftsmen to inspire and direct. More than technical mastery was needed, of course. Sympathy, insight, and comprehension of the possibilities at stake were likewise imperative. If the movement was to gather great force and acquire the strength of permanence, long and persistent discipline was required.

Yet all the arts projects had an air of improvisation and impermanence. The experiment was an experiment. In part, if not mainly, it had been regarded by the general public at the beginning as a mere makeshift, a form of relief. Skeptics accustomed to concentrate on what they called pure art and to think of esthetics merely in terms of their own tastes jeered at the enterprise, at the paints, daubs, and horrors often — perhaps generally — produced under its auspices. Yet those who studied it closely and in its intimate social setting concluded with remarkable unanimity that immense cultural potentialities might lie in this art movement, might come out of it — and be expressed in some form of permanent patronage of public art. On the other hand, a return of prosperity might lead to the abandonment of the whole Art Project and a restoration of all artists to the private market; or, if American economy continued to deteriorate, artists might be put to digging ditches or marching in military ranks. Nowhere was the nature of the midpassage better exemplified.

After three years of experimentation in the arts under federal auspices, with intense local coöperation, no immediate appraisal could be made on a comprehensive scale; nor could the heavy curtain shutting off the future of American art be lifted. Judgments were numerous; indeed multitudinous. As usual those who knew the least about the vast aggregation of activities were likely to be sternest in scorn and condemnation.

Offsetting the criticism, though by no means fully disposing of it, were citations of indisputable achievements in detail and general verdicts from authorities commanding public respect. For example, it was announced in 1938 that the commission to paint the murals for the New York Public Library, which gossip had once assigned to Whistler or

Sargent, had finally gone to a young worker in the Federal Art Project, Edward Laning, whose mural for Ellis Island, The Role of the Immigrant in the Industrial Development of America, was felt to be worthy of this succession. After referring to the work submitted to the City of New York by artists engaged on the Federal Project, I. N. Phelps Stokes, president of the Municipal Art Commission so long identified with matters of taste in the metropolis, declared in his report for that year: "There was a time when many artists, as well as the Art Commission, feared that the depression would go down in history as a period characterized by the large production of poor work in painting and sculpture, whereas the best-informed authorities now agree that it will be remembered rather as a period of renaissance."

§

The arrival of immortal American genius was not assured beyond a doubt. But since the sources of genius in the arts lay and had always lain in sensitivity to life and thought about its meaning, the movement of artists in America toward that fountain of inspiration and vitality was at least an encouragement to those who longed for its coming. The general feeling that "Europe was not a success" revived the eighteenth-century hope that America might be a success. The Idea of Progress reverted to its original humanism so often travestied by recent mechanicians. Now there was more meditation and discussion of potentialities in the western hemisphere; more independence of spirit and aim. Thus the "milk and water" painting of a Puvis de Chavannes, the pride of Boston when it was placed in her imposing public library, and the swarms of allegorical "lady Justices and Liberties in classical robes," inherited from the neo-classicists and widely distributed, were reappraised as "sentimental," "lugubrious," and "academic" by a generation disillusioned with respect to make-believe and yet sturdy in its faith in life. The vernacular surging up into art was in part protest and in part fresh esthetic energy.

This tendency was invigorated by Mexican artists so near the border of the United States, affirming their knowledge and taste. In their concern with the indigenous, the Mexicans seemed to be effective exponents of the contemporary revolt against sheer imitation. On their return from a visit to Moscow, whither they had gone to see sights and dream dreams keyed to their own recent revolution, several Mexican artists issued a manifesto declaring: "Our fundamental esthetic goal is to socialize expression and tend to obliterate totally individualism, which is bourgeois. We repudiate the so-called easel painting and all the art of ultra-intellectual circles because it is aristocratic and we glorify the expression of Monumental Art, because it is public expression."

Among the manifestants was Diego Rivera and, though his revolutionary ardor was unmistakable, the spell of his creative art brought him commissions in the United States even from capitalist sources. Catching warmth from warmth, both the San Francisco Chamber of Commerce and Radio City in New York, a Rockefeller enterprise, invited Rivera to paint murals for their walls. For the former, Rivera made concessions in his composition. Apparently he hoped to make none for the latter but when a portrait of Lenin stood forth at the center of his scheme the mural was ordered to be taken down. Even friendly critics in some cases thought this painting was melodramatic.

Another Mexican invited to paint in the United States was David Alfaro Siqueiros, also a signer of the Mexican manifesto. Though he sometimes used the modern blow torch as tool and cement as material for individual experiment, Siqueiros was collectivist in both his ideals and his art practice. While American muralists were to encounter the labor issue as trade unionists demanded the right to do the actual work from designs, Siqueiros and his group of coöperating artists did their own work together, in the style of old Italian frescoists. Siqueiros thought in terms of public art.

In the fervor for emancipation from Europe, Orozco joyfully proclaimed himself a "painter of the new world" and exulted in the very skyscraper as a first step toward Monumental Art in the new world. It was not surprising, then, that Orozco also found patrons above the Rio Grande. For example, he placed a mural on a wall of Pomona College in California and another on a wall at Dartmouth College in New Hampshire. Perhaps few, if any, sightseers or parents of students knew just what the painter was trying to say in his forms and colors, but he declared, as we have indicated, that the Pomona mural depicted Prometheus giving fire to mankind. His Dartmouth mural was not so mythological in theme or so primitive in treatment. It was described as a synthesis of life in America, as life flowing in a fairly straight line from Indian aboriginal sacrifices before the gods of war to modern prostration before machines of war directed by politicos, with education lurking in the environs as something uncannily related to this main purpose of life.

From the Mexican school, while its vitality was strong and its commissions numerous on both sides of the national border, American artists derived a new excitement which affected their own esthetic affirmations, inducing more concentration on the immediate and the known in the social scene. Both in painting and in sculpture this influence was revealed. For instance Boardman Robinson, prepared for the Mexican challenge by his own long concern with the substance of the common life, now revealed his qualified acceptance of Mexican tendencies in a mural painted for a great department store in Pittsburgh; and Leo Katz, working on the theme of Light, moved close to the type of expression evolved among the Mexicans in a mural he executed for the Century of Progress Exposition in Chicago.

A much older Mayan-Mexican bent was to be noted in American sculpture: in its monumental character, however small the figure, in the growing inclination to cut directly into stone instead of modeling through the medium of clay, in the simplification and sturdiness of form, in the architectural quality of the work, in the group compositions, among other signs and symbols. But did sculptors in America merely look to Mayan art for novelties? Or did it invigorate their thought about what they were doing and carry them deeper into consciousness of their affirmations? Doubters even denied this influence but the prominent New York art critic, Emily Genauer, was positive about it. To the skeptics she put these questions: "Have the sculptors incorporated in their own work the monotony of Egyptian figures? Have their sculptures the gravity and stoicism of Chinese things? And are they not more monumental than the little African Negro fetishes from which the sculptors did, doubtless, learn much of the investiture of stiff, angular form with dramatic force?"

§

Decried by the traditionalists and feared by the anti-chauvinists as inconsistent with internationalism, the American Scene was the assignment for all the artists connected with the federal projects. What, then, was the American scene? The Mexicans had been painting their scene as they saw it. What would Americans say through their own techniques? In Magazine of Art, Alfred Frankenstein made his answer: "It is not merely a matter of subject. Thousands of American artists have been painting the American landscape, American architecture, and the American people for generations past, but without remotely approximating this thing called the American scene. What distinguishes the American scene group — Benton, Curry, Wood, Marsh, Hopper, Burchfield, to name only a few — is a highly complex attitude toward the subject, an attitude compounded of romantic emotion and realistic delineation, of a desire to expose the plain, unvarnished facts of American life plus a strong, even sentimental love for the facts that finally emerge. It is primarily, but not exclusively, a phenomenon of the middle west, where the natural landscape is comparatively unspectacular and offers the artist little challenge.

People have been 'exposing' Main Street for lo, these many years, but you can't 'expose' the Yosemite Valley. The American scene thus depicted is basically the human scene. . . . It is an art of people and what they do and the places they live in, not an art of mountains, clouds or the sea." So Breugel, Rembrandt, and Van Gogh, among others, had yielded to their own artistic impulses at other times, in other places, and allied themselves with the fundamental human scene.

For the instruction of directors and directed, Harry Hopkins, relief administrator, laid down just one rule — no indecency. If this curbed the output of nude women, it was no damper on the depiction of "human beings in the dignity of their labor, in the poignancy of their response, the intimation of all they had missed, and that which they have had, their ambitions, contentments, and desires, their full completeness and their lack of completeness," as a defender summed up the work that was being done. All the currents of ideas and interests that worked their way to Letters found articulation in this medium without words.

Just as writers moved from the periphery of life toward its vortex, so artists, for whom the general public was now patron, brought into their thought and its expression the primordials of life and labor. In ancient Egypt, labor had been represented in art as slave toil, which it was in fact. In mediaeval art, labor had often been represented as grotesque with a mingled respect and ridicule. Now in America, labor was made to appear in every style which the American experience had produced — from slave to free, to disinherited. An emancipated Negress in the middle west was painted as if "saying it" with her broom, implying that liberty was not synonymous with paradise.

Bereft of a livelihood in a big city, where could a man go for succor? Several artists in the federal relief project asked that question with oils. The dustbowl — was that the answer? Joseph Vavak's watercolor of a Dust Storm was full argument against it. Pictures in large numbers showed aridity to be no friend of man or beast; the very horses and mules were seen decaying. A Sheeler barn among the comfortable Pennsylvanians was work of art no doubt, in its plastic vitality, but a barn in a dust storm was a barn battling with nature and the elements, giving poor shelter to man and beast, not a pliable thing wholly within the craftsmanship of man. Was not that affirmation also art? Winds and fires, historic enemies of frail mankind, engaged the brushes of many artists, with rain as a variant. In the prints of Japan, gentle rain was one of the characteristic features. But rain in some of the new American painting, notably in Paul Meltsner's, was a cruel thing — a bearer of terror and ruin.

Human life stranded, though temporarily in a Civilian Conservation Camp, was the theme of a young portraitist, David McCosh, himself an artist on relief. What was the lad in transient encampment seeing on his horizon as he gazed off into space? Touching as it did the necessities of life, the work of artists on relief was often drab — as drab as life for the broad masses in America, as pitiable as the little Main Streets of the continent that now stood out in oils still more crudely than they had done in the novel of Sinclair Lewis. Was it then a tragedy for the artist to be an artist of and for the people?

Apparently that "enfant terrible," Paul Cadmus of New York, did not find it so. The sailors in port having a "hot time" with their girls were painted with laughter as wild as nature in her primordial force. Making his affirmations in a concern with the lowly as fierce as that of Caldwell or Hemingway, Cadmus accomplished an overwhelming plasticity of form positively terrifying in its power. Naturally the naval bureaucracy and its patriotic affiliates were appalled by Cadmus' canvases and unwilling to display them prominently, though Cadmus joined in competitive contests.

Joylessness, in vivid contrast, ruled the derelicts who gathered in the All Night Mission, at Bar and Grill, in Siesta, as Eli Jacobi saw them. Though he was called "the

Hogarth of the Bowery," that title seemed more appropriate to Cadmus with respect to a painter's mood. Jacobi made use of the woodcut. Anatole Shulkin of New Jersey was impressed by mob psychology and by the heavy muscles which could come into play when its lawlessness was released; and in the Need for Law, he gave vent to this emotional observation in a mural for the main entrance lobby of the Courthouse in Morristown. Just who were the lawless was an interesting suggestion for New Jersey at this moment in its history.

The need for wise leadership was the affirmation of Mitchell Siporin of Illinois, whose mind was charged with memories of the Haymarket Riot. Leadership he depicted in a series of murals, and his technique was affected by the Mexican artists though he greatly modified their color and forms. Siporin saw "a potential fresco in every poem of Sandburg." The People Yes. And Vachel Lindsay's call to the native genius to complete its soul was like a master's voice:

> Record it for the grandson of your son
> A city is not builded in a day;
> Our little town cannot complete her soul
> Till countless generations pass away.

The young generation on relief, if Siporin had his way, would not wait for more generations to pass away. He called to his own for action, in murals symbolizing the leadership exerted by three western singers of the good life, Lindsay, Sandburg, and Masters; by the political activists, Lincoln and Altgeld; and by Jane Addams, the social democrat.

The utilization of reason was implied. And Jack Levine of Massachusetts was concerned with that theme. Avoiding the wrath of a Daumier at its neglect and the raucous laughter of a Hogarth at human folly, Levine resorted to the devastating wit which only pure reason could command, entitling one of his canvases Feast of Pure Reason and another, Conference.

As the amount of landscape produced by workers on federal projects seemed to affirm the continuity of hunger and love for the land, even where the land was shown to be abused beyond repair, so the amount of portraiture demonstrated the persistence of interest in personality, in spite of the strong emphasis on environment.

All in all, the men and women on relief who were given the chance to state what was on their minds and hearts with respect to the American scene in forms other than words presented remarkable testaments of meditation, criticism, and faith as popular documents offered in return for public patronage. Whatever academicians might think and say with regard to mastery of form, color, rhythm, gesture, and composition, however strictly such affirmations might be relegated to the realm of mere reportage, or sociology, tasteless as many of them were, the broad interpretations of life and scene under the freedom of federal auspices were amazing and vitalizing contributions to a new art movement in America.

§

Moreover the federal encouragement of art affirmations, if only as an experiment in the relief of the hungry, seemed to incite similar and livelier assertions in circles more secure. At any rate, whatever the cause, artistic fervor was not deadened but intensified, and in the intensification new elements of imaginative preferences were evident. Take the matter of portraiture. In discussing this branch of art in connection with a discriminative exhibit of historic illustrations which he had arranged for the Pennsylvania Museum of Art at Philadelphia, E. M. Benson declared: "The lack of fine portraiture in our time is partially the result of a conflict between the artist's social and aesthetic convictions. This accounts for the fact that, with few exceptions, the Lionello d'Estes of the twentieth century have gone unrecorded by our best artists. . . . Although portraiture is not the burning preoccupation of most artists of our day, there is a strong undercurrent of interest in portraiture, mainly among those artists who draw their inspiration from the social scene. . . . The kind of forthright portraiture which this has engendered is a far cry from the commissioned portrait of yesteryear. It is doubtful, therefore, whether the breach between the artist and his erstwhile patrician sitter will ever be healed. What will probably happen — it has been happening since the French Revolution — is that the 'cabinet' or easel portrait will become more and more honest and personal, though not necessarily more subjective; and that this will be accompanied by more formal, although no less sincere, civic portraiture contained in public murals and incorporated into architectural units. Portraiture in photography and the film, because it can be shared by everyone, will, by its concreteness and nearness to life, probably remain the most popular form of portraiture."

Irreverently Peggy Bacon implied that better heads would be acceptable for portraiture. In her rollicking but subtle analyses of available subjects for portraiture, she said "Off with Their Heads," drew specimens to substantiate her decree, and in companionate verses told why this would be wise. In a mood all his own, Peter Blume, young surrealist, growing older, found the face and symbol of Mussolini enough to emphasize at one time. In a picture of the Italian scene, which agitated all the critics, he represented the dictator as a kind of gargoylic Jack-in-the-Box shooting out in front of a sun-colored background painted so skillfully as to make the master of the new Roman Empire, in his foreground of poverty and superstition, all the more sinister.

Few professional artists or critics enjoying private patronage were wholly indifferent to the kind of work done by artists enjoying federal patronage. It is true that some remained irreconcilable in their hostility to "unknown" men and women who dared to affirm their right to speak their minds in the vernacular. But artists of unquestioned standing visited the shabby warehouses and other crude studios, in East Erie Street, Chicago, for instance, shabby because the government economized on rent, and attended the public exhibits of this popular art movement to see what was being produced, to observe the skills made manifest, and to meditate on the conditions of esthetic expression and the reactions. When the Design Laboratory in New York, one of the units of the Federal Art Project, which had been developed under the administration of Mrs. Audrey McMahon, regional director, was unable to continue, owing to the dearth of federal funds, it was adopted by the Technical School of the Federation of Architects, Engineers, Chemists, and Technicians, who considered it too valuable to be closed.

In landscape painting even by artists of the academies changes induced by the intense concern with the whole American scene were particularly striking. In the romantic nineteenth century, pretty scenes of peace and plenty on a continent of virgin soil had stirred the esthetic emotion of Americans. In the early years of the twentieth century the forest splendor of America, in spring, summer, autumn and winter, fascinated artists and buyers. But a new mood toward the physical universe in this age of scarcity seemed to take possession of many artists operating under private as well as public auspices. In their portrayal of burnt forest areas, blighted fields, eroded plantations, dust storms, and humanity in retreat from the elements, they appeared to be asking how it came about that man had so mistreated a nature which had offered him friendship in forms of virgin soil, forests, and other resources beyond comparison. While surveys of natural resources were piling up on the desks of engineers and politicians, pictures were multiplying in studios and exhibits as declamations of esthetic thought about the very earth on which American civilization rested. Among these commentaries one of the starkest was offered by Arthur Emptage, national executive secretary of the American Artists Congress — a melancholy scene labeled Work for Scarecrows — displayed in 1938 at his "one-man" show.

Into pictures of still life the more critical affirmations penetrated. A mere basket of potatoes on a bare board was used in one case as a symbol of riches. If the influence of the garden clubs, an outstanding form of women's quest for beauty, was visible in the wealth of floral offerings, the tributes did not always appear now as conventional horns of plenty; the very flowers, at the hands of Charles Sheeler and Georgia O'Keefe, asserted the life principle. Sheeler attained the quality of plastic art in his painting of flowers. In other cases orderly flower arrangements, derived to some extent from Oriental manipulation, stood out against chaotic still-life arrangements, as a re-affirmation of symmetry amid the imbalance prevalent in economy.

Into the style of the age Thomas Benton brought an imagination which Sinclair Lewis described as displaying in paint the humor of a Mark Twain. Benton portrayed frontier scenes on canvas as jocosely as Roughing It did in print and small-town folk amused him enormously. In the temper of the mature Twain, he also fumed over the sufferings and follies of the American people. The Negro share-cropper forced to destroy the cotton which nourished life awakened Benton's infinite pity. To the timeless universal of romantic love he responded with a sensitiveness beyond class or race in a painting sent to Paris in 1938 in connection with an exhibit of American art. The economic calamity, marked by the dissolution of old hopes and faiths and the ferment of ideas as yet chaotic in form, supplied him with materials for endless social representation, as the rush of prosperity had done in earlier days. In murals of indisputable force he depicted the disorder, the confusion, the interplay of optimism and defeat.

Though called a communist by upholders of the genteel tradition, Benton testified in his autobiography published in 1938 that he had no easy solution for the dilemma. "The philosophy that most appeals to me," he confessed, "is that relatively illogical and unsystematic body of comments called Pragmatism. . . . I am convinced that experimentalism is tomorrow's philosophy. I say this because of its flexibility . . . and because it seems to me better attuned to the actualities of emerging scientific invention and of human psychology than any other." Midpassage might well be inscribed as the caption for his thought.

Although for many critics Benton was the one great American painter of these years, he did not accept a sheer nativist creed in art. With a few of his colleagues, he disclaimed fidelity to either national or international dogmas. If through his comparative "objectivity" gleamed an enduring interest in the common ways of labor and life, no artist understood better than he that the distinction between the general and the particular, the universal and the local, could not be drawn in absolute terms.

As in the case of Thomas Benton, so in the case of William Gropper, subtlety and versatility baffled critics bent on stuffing all artists into neat pigeon holes to the left or the right. Like Benton, he too was intensely interested in ordinary life and action, whether he was painting a bar room or a rural landscape for the Schenley Products Company or a town scene in winter time for the Post Office at Freeport, New York, or a water color of "Senators" for the market. With an air of equity, he interwove interpretations with colors. Writing on this quality of Gropper's work, Ernest Brace, an artist appraising another artist's achievements, said with tense brevity: "William Gropper's painting is unequivocally effective. Whether he paints the agile mouth of a senator or the thin, tight lips of a judge, prisoners being marched off to execution or the prostrate victims of an air raid, the briefest glance tells the story. And yet, as with all significant stories, there is much more than plot. It is impossible to turn away without going deeper into the picture, savoring the details of gesture and setting and color and movement which are as closely knit into the picture as a whole as the separate lines of a dramatic climax. Gropper's purpose seems as inseparable from his painting as the pigment."

While men, especially those in charge of purchasing paintings for museums, usually, as Lura Beam phrased it, turned instinctively "toward the male directness, the stout fist, the sword upon the event," constantly renewed in battles, Georgia O'Keefe opposed to that affirmation a feminine point of view. Technically skilled, inclined to symbolism beyond most artists of this day, she had "spent a long time painting lilies, petunias, and those cup-like flowers which have the odd capacity of enlarging to the bowl of the universe. After that she painted heroic sections of flowers which expanded visibly before your eyes. Impossible to tell if they were Jacks-in-the-pulpit or cathedrals or pattern and texture or the tremendous affirmation of male strength. Later, the painting of the little New Mexican churches and of the cross in the desert stood for the sad permanence of religion. The picture of the skull and flowers above the mesas says without words that over and beyond the death wish, life still comes out of death." To the power of her work, museums yielded little by little and in the spring of 1938 the college of William and Mary awarded her the honor of a degree as Doctor of Fine Arts.

Concern with the contemporary age appeared in new contests held by museums and patrons. For a competition set by the Museum of Modern Art in New York, with the Post-war World as the theme, sixty-five artists submitted canvases. Georgia O'Keefe sent in a vision of Manhattan; Henry Varnum Poor expressed himself on the conflict between the arts and the crafts; Hugo Gellert painted capitalism as he saw it on its last line of defense; Benjamin Kopman interpreted militarism metaphysically; and Ben Shan, a pupil of Rivera, recalled the Passion of Sacco and Vanzetti. When the Town Hall Club in Manhattan sought a theme for the bar at the cocktail hour, Luis Mora provided a mural of old New York; for a generation that was celebrating the repeal of the Eighteenth Amendment the affirmation was enlivening.

As artists drew closer to the people and so to life, their fancies were stirred by the potentialities in the print, long known as "the poor man's art." In the days of Jacksonian democracy it had flourished as an effective medium for depicting types, races, and social scenes in America. Stage coaches and pack horses had scattered prints from metropolitan centers to log cabins on the frontier and to miners' shacks in the most distant mountains. After Currier and Ives developed color lithography to a high point, another surge of popular interest almost transformed the print into a national institution. But during the gilded age, with its passion for the ostentatious and the "genteel," and especially with improvements in photography and engraving, this democratic form of art declined in esteem. Importations of prints from Japan accelerated the process; an average American who wanted to decorate a home inexpensively found great pleasure in a Japanese reproduction — pleasure unspoiled by the knowledge that frequently the subject of the picture was prostitution or sex slavery, surrounded in the Far East for the upper classes by the glamour of costume and setting. Only the best of American etchings could meet this competition in the marketplace.

But as technical advances were made in methods of reproduction, as American democracy was again stirred by social conflict, the print, using the term in a generic sense, once more came into its own through a diversity of media: wood cut, linoleum cut, lithography plain and colored, etching, lithotint, and aquatint. Again, as in the uprush of Jacksonian democracy, artists concentrated upon the portrayal, for print purposes, of types, races, industrial, and social scenes. A few titles picked at random illustrate the range of depiction: Early Irrigation Methods in Colorado; New York Harbor, Mine Accident, Machinery, Fish Day, The Flies at Minsky's, Women's House of Detention, In the Park, All Night Mission, Landscape, Dock Scene, Flowers, Unemployed Office, Confusion at 40, Idle Governor. Most of the documents and papers collected by librarians and historians could be illustrated, supplemented, and made living, if not livid, by documentary prints.

To the renewed emphasis on the print, the Federal Art

Project, with its interest in democratic art, gave encourage-ment and patronage. Reporting on this phase of federal promotion, Holger Cahill unfurled his flag for the print: "As might be expected from its history in this country, the print is extremely sensitive to the contemporary environ-ment, and is an art rich in social content. It would almost be possible to reconstruct a social history of our period from the prints produced on the Federal Art Project. The prints give a fresh and vital interpretation of life as it is lived in America today, and give first evidence of new directions. Every aspect of the American scene is reflected, the cities with their medley of architectural styles, skyscrapers, bridges, interiors, gaso-line tanks, factories, subways, railways, airplanes, harbors, farms, cabins, wheat fields, mountains, mines, sports, politics, racial and social types, the whole kaleidoscope of American life." Harry Sternberg's pictures of coal regions were an awful commentary on culture in the American scene.

On the other hand at an American contemporary painting exhibit held at the Whitney Museum and the Museum of Modern Art in New York late in 1937, art, as if accompany-ing the decline in fervor for the New Deal, seemed to have turned back to conservatism. Discussing this particular collection, Edward Alden Jewell said in his regular column of art criticism in The New York Times: "The Whitney show supplements and reinforces the experience at Carnegie this year, from which one emerged satisfied that the artists of today, considered as an aggregate, have gone in for a wassail of sheer painting, with the world, so to speak, well lost. And again it becomes urgent to add that life has not been be-trayed, but rather that a vehement distinction is drawn be-tween the everyday business of living and the holiday transcendence of art."

§

Like the fervor for murals depicting the common life, the ardor for the ballet was a notable feature of these years. Swing had succeeded jazz, it is true; men and women, frantic to jive and shag, were bestowing positive worship upon band and orchestra leaders capable of inciting them to jangling muscular agitation; enormous swing festivals were held in great open spaces such as the beaches near New York; and a language all its own grew up as a means of communion among the itching, shaking, quaking "jitterbugs."

Such an anarchic trend might seem unfriendly to the intellectualized ballet, but in this land of paradoxes the group dance also became a vogue. In essence the ballet was akin to the fresco and the favor granted the one was a favor granted the other form of art. Though solo dancers and rollicking acrobatic musical comediennes still had opportunities for exhibitionism, especially through the patronage of Hollywood, though preciosity, showmanship, and art for art's sake or no art at all, all aloof from social import, still characterized much dancing, five thousand of the ten thousand dance schools in the United States had included the ballet as part of their training by 1937. Ballet groups were organized on college campuses. Museums of art invited the choreographers to dance in their halls amid painting and sculpture. The New School for Social Research in New York added the study of dancing to its economics, psychology, and politics. And the Federal Government gave assistance to ballet groups as a sign of its modernism.

For the ballet, team work was imperative. It was a collectivist undertaking. All its members had important parts to play in interpreting its theme and the monumental character of its art form was claimed to afford the highest creative opportunity to dancers. In the language of a spokesman of the "American Ballet" organized in 1933 by George Balanchine, formerly connected with the Russian ballet, "no slick formulas can be used here. Few, if any, tricks and novelties are of use. Here depth rather than superficiality is sought after; it is a field of research and study rather than one of exploitation and flashy appeal. Here it is the dancer's task to study, sometimes at great personal expense, all that the past has been able to hand down in the way of forms and traditions, and then slowly but bravely to choose, prepare, and build up a personal credo."

For three years the American Ballet functioned under the aegis of the Metropolitan Opera Association, but in the spring of 1938, Balanchine severed official connection on the ground that "the tradition of the ballet at the Metropolitan is bad ballet." Condemning its standards in particulars, he explained that for his first ballet planned for Aïda he had delved into documents in a serious effort to make his troupe's frescoes as lifelike as Egyptian life itself, only to find his audiences, especially the dowagers in them, unappreciative of what he was trying to do. The upshot as far as those audiences were involved was an effort of the Metropolitan to build up its own ballet.

Behind the abrupt change illustrated by Balanchine's action lay a long chain of innovations precursory in nature. Even in Tsarist Russia Michel Fokine, exponent of impressionism in the dance, had recast the decadent ballet of the court system — which Catherine de Medici had fostered centuries ago. By verbal argument and by physical demonstrations he had made the art of the ballet a dramatic play, adjusted to modernism in thought, using action to represent new situations. His fire lighted fires elsewhere as the revolutionary spirit gained momentum. Afterward other imaginative Russians, experimenting with the ballet, tried out the art in the American scene, first at the Metropolitan Opera House. Now Balanchine, an exile from revolutionary Russia, was endeavoring to carry on the ballet in a setting of interests and ideas less devastating than Sovietism to an institution inherited, though with mutations, from the old regime.

By this time the ballet had become domesticated in America in places far beyond the stage of the Opera House, partly under the leadership of Isadora Duncan who had herself revolted against "the dark age" of stage dancing, reverted to the Greek classics for dramatic inspiration, and changed a conventional diversion into an intellectualized medium of interpretation. Drawing inspiration from Pavlowa in part, Ruth St. Denis, Duncan's American successor in the intellectualized dance, acquired a new élan in a spiritual revolt that found satisfaction in the mysteries of the Orient. More quietly but none the less effectively at the Neighborhood Playhouse in New York, Irene and Alice Lewisohn carried on their school of the dance as theater — the essence of the ballet — and to their creative enterprise students and observers had recourse for instruction and inspiration.

For the ballet in Russia music had been a requisite feature; but as this art took firmer root in the United States, it began to separate itself from so much reliance upon accompaniment and to make its form of expression a medium of pure interpretation. Additional impetus was given to the ballet, with or without music, by the visits of Kurt Jooss and his group who performed such vivid compositions as The Green Table, an anti-war ballet, and themes of old Vienna, their home city. From the Orient came other inspirations. Uday Shankar and his Indian mystics with sword dances and other exotic pantomimes suggested methods, if not themes, to Americans. The Japanese dancer, Nimura, in a successful tour, displayed to them feudal patterns, foreign to the American way, and yet suggestive of creative patterns, saying American things.

Under these various influences company after company was organized by Americans to perform the ballet, all breaking with conventions, all attempting to give through the dance impressionistic interpretations of life in action and as idea. Though an old art, old as civilization, group dancing took warmth under the stimulus of the local environment and seized upon its potentialities for commenting on events and civilization. In the golden glow, a comic ballet, directed by Trudi Schoop, made audiences laugh from coast to coast by its composition, Blonde Maris. More sober themes and forms followed, as the economic crisis diminished occasions for laughter, until gravity grew more exigent in the ballet and issues chosen from social and political conflicts became prominent themes for interpretation.

Having departments for the study of the drama, colleges added departments for this branch of drama. Bennington, the newest woman's college in New England, won high distinction for its patronage of the ballet, and festivals were annually held on its campus for the exhibition of the art. Vassar encouraged this dancing as well as experiments in its dramatic workshop, and when the Federal Theater Project had acquired momentum it subsidized the director of the Vassar ballet, Tamiris, whose composition, How Long, Brethren, was a campus sensation carried further afield as part of a program handled under federal patronage. Teachers College at Columbia University and New York University called upon the Bennington dancers for instruction; and on the Pacific coast six or seven colleges in the San Francisco district, not remote from Hollywood, took to this collectivistic dance art really remote from Hollywood's. Under federal auspices a National Youth Administration dance group was organized in San Francisco and its performances were witnessed by large public audiences. In a cycle arranged by Lenore Peters Job, for this group of young persons, a strong democratic motif was chosen, Women Walk Free. A dance unit under the Works Progress Administration was also formed in Chicago to provide expression for artists who had been formerly limited to other art projects.

Women were certainly dancing freely and, as in fiction, they were expressing their intuitive judgments, their comments on life, their criticisms and their dreams without other let and hindrance than the consent of the public to attend their ballets. But this left plenty of room for men in the ballet. Ted Shawn and his companions, all men, devoted themselves to the collective dance form. Mixed groups also worked together to comment on life through the agency of gesture with arms, heads, and feet. Often the touring companies carried no music with them, thus making all attention concentrate on the ideas they were trying to convey. As in the case of the murals, voices of highly irritated people protested at this "arty nonsense," sometimes calling it an "insult to art"; but voices of other people also approved it, as the box offices demonstrated.

Dance theaters invited the public to participate in America's "new art." One was established by the New York Young Men's Hebrew Association and opened with the announcement that "all dancers and groups who feel qualified to give a recital are invited to apply for the use of the recital hall in accordance with conditions which will be sent upon request. The qualifications of each artist will be rigidly scrutinized before the use of the recital hall is granted, since the Dance Theatre considers it almost as important to discourage mediocrity in the dance recital as to encourage first-rate ability."

In keeping with their sensitivity to group rhythm, Negroes searched this medium for an expression of their racial experiences and social views. So the Negro ballet became an interesting feature in the panorama of pantomime in America where the people had a right to say what they wished to say and were permitted to enjoy release. At Hampton Institute, the art was seriously promoted and the Creative Dance Group from that institution gave demonstrations of its talent in New York and other cities, North and South, and at Bryn Mawr. "The itchin' heels" of the race, directed by Negroes familiar with the work at Bennington, now moved together in the ballet to express, through forms technically disciplined, the folk dances and rituals of colored people, their labor themes and spiritual aspirations. Under the guidance of a man from another race, Eugene von Grona, a German, the American Negro Ballet sought to give group dancing a still more theatrical unity. One of its first performances was an interpretation of the story and music from Stravinsky's Fire Bird — a strange undertaking and achievement for artists whose ancestors far from remote had toiled in the cotton fields and rice swamps of the South.

Among the ballet groups which received the highest tributes from watching critics were those for which Hanya Holm, Martha Graham, Tamiris, Doris Humphrey, and Charles Weidman served as choreographers. With remarkable uniformity the themes employed by them were germane to the economic and social vortex. As in the case of artists engaged in public painting and sculpture, they were forced both by their own impulsion and by the exactions of public understanding to identify their work with the experiences of others. Employing modernism in the art form, they also employed modernism in the theme form. Hanya Holm had come from Germany but she developed the ballet at Bennington and in her double experience with life she produced a composition called Trend which ended on the motif of faith in the constructive power of humanity amid decadence and cataclysm. Using music especially scored for this ballet and percussion instruments of contemporary popularity, the ballet leader dealt with the "meaninglessness of forms of living when they are perpetuated as empty shells after their usefulness has been exhausted, and the inevitable resurgence of new forms of vital function out of the inherent powers of re-creation which belong to man by his very nature." In this fashion John Martin, expert on the dance, explained the pantomime to the readers of The New York Times. At Bennington also, Anna Sokolow, trained under the Lewisohns, created a dance, entitled Facade — Esposizione Italiana, an exposition of dictatorial absolutism.

Supported by their own company Doris Humphrey and Charles Weidman traveled far and wide, giving ballet programs to audiences diverse in social composition — in one instance to the annual convention of University Women. Humphrey broke traditions with My Red Fires, among other compositions. Weidman, a humorist in this medium, staged dances for the political skit I'd Rather Be Right and danced The Happy Hypocrite elsewhere. In the summer of 1937, Shawn and his all-men ballet group danced to the accompaniment of the Berkshire Symphony Orchestra at a Massachusetts festival, including in their repertoire a "labor symphony, tribal themes, play, folk and art motifs." As if recognizing the universal in the particular, Agnes de Mille organized an Anglo-American group with interchangeable ballets. As the dance movement reached the ballet stage, the dance film was produced and as a consequence this form of artistry was more widely enjoyed, in fact nationalized in its appeal.

Especially engrossed in the American scene and with leftist sympathies was Martha Graham. Her composition, Primitive Mysteries, had for its basis her reverie about the American aborigines. She also took account of incoming Europeans and of pioneering in Frontier; she was concerned with the current threat of war and its implications in Chronicle; in Theatre Piece she gave her interpretation of the world as it is and in New Dance she offered the world as it might be. Accepting America as her center of thought and action, she proclaimed in American Document her feeling for time, place, perils, and prospects of survival. This is "the most important extended dance created by a living American," said a commentator in The Nation, "and if there has been another in any time more important, there is no record of it."

§

Architecture, like all the other arts, illustrated the conflicts and tendencies of the midpassage. Especially linked to the functional, whatever its vagaries — connected, that is, with industrial processes, office requirements, living, public enterprises, the theater, the museum, the library, and the school — it was associated with the forms and fortunes of all these institutions. In the days of the golden glow, while the boom was on and capitalists were rushing ahead with construction to take up the lag created by the world war, architects were overwhelmed by commissions in private enterprise. Then, after private patronage went into a steep decline and government projects were planned to give employment to technicians, construction companies, and labor, architects were called upon to design structures which were, of necessity, conceived rather in the spirit and terms of the public service.

Projected in the days of brilliant prospects, the mathematical architecture of Radio City, designed by Raymond Hood, Harvey Corbett, and Associates, swept upward to the skies amid the detonations and crashes of the economic depression and worked havoc with real estate interests in all the neighboring parts of Manhattan. Perhaps it was the last monumental structure of its kind to be built in America — an expression of the wealth and power of one man, bent, like a Pharaoh, upon securing immortality in stone and mass. To fill its vacant spaces the City of New York was combed for tenants and special inducements were offered to encourage them to cancel their existing leases and find shelter in the city within the city. As the sections were completed, their capacious areas were filled by a multitude of business and social interests; and the immense pile became more and more the mechanical center of an urban culture — the center for radio broadcasting, advertising displays, concerts, moving pictures, art exhibitions, musical comedies, dancing contests, and every type of excitement. Its monolithic walls pointing to the heavens, its gorgeous, if not garish, auditoriums, its gardens, its open-air pool, its shops, offices, and entertainments all conspired to draw interests and events within its magic compound.

When the huge thing was nearly completed, indeed while it was part way up, professional architects engaged in spirited debates over the merits of its design. Did it have a "soul"? The question was asked and remained unanswered. Was it pure mathematics, solid geometry for instance? It was — almost. As it grew, even its own designers made changes and were disturbed by uncertainties. One professional architect, commenting in the American Year Book, called Lee Lawrie's model for the main entrance "noble" and "beautiful." It fitted, he said, "the ponderous pile above it, whose very size makes it noble," and it helped "marvelously to atone for what otherwise might have been a bit too stark and brutal." In general the words employed to characterize the pile and its details were "superb," "imposing," "startling," "garish," "monstrous," "colossal," "enormous project in permanent advertising." No one seemed to speak of it as "frozen music" or as "Christian." If anything it was Babylonian in its majesty and pagan in its spiritual assertions. At all events it was among the wonders of the world and as symbolic as the removal of Rivera's mural from its walls.

Two of the world fairs built in this period, in animus at least, fitted the conception of Radio City. The exposition called Century of Progress, opened in Chicago in 1933, just as the economic depression reached its deeps, was an apotheosis of mechanistic science, machinery, advertising, selling, and promoting. At first the architectural press spoke of "the great influence" the exposition would have upon "the art of the future." Later Harry F. Cunningham, professor in the University of Nebraska, came to an opposite conclusion in his annual review for the American Year Book: "The opinion is about unanimous now that the influence will indeed be great, but it will be a negative influence — a sort of 'Keeley cure,'" presumably administered to drunkards. If justified, this prophecy was given little heed, for the enormous exposition, erected for the New York City celebration of 1939, under the administration of Grover Whalen, the supreme salesman and advertising agent of the metropolis, displayed in similar, if more subdued, forms, the fireworks spirit of the great mechanical show at Chicago. In necessary revolt against the colossal and obtrusive with which it could not compete, the administration of the fair for San Francisco in 1939 turned for designs to the symbolism of old cultures — Spanish-American, Mayan, the exotic, the soft, elusive, pre-machine.

When architects, along with the Lords of Creation, rushed to Washington in 1933 for financial aid, they encountered strange pretensions and in some cases a changed spirit. Even when the real intention of the Government was to invent "fat contracts" for favorite builders, the ostensible ends and uses were not private advantage in the form of rents, profits, and gains by the year but public and collective — official buildings, housing projects, and resettlement undertakings.

Architects of factories, private office buildings, and apartments had to consider the rental value of every corner, turn, and square foot. Architects employed on public work were not so closely restricted by pecuniary considerations and there acquired, despite red tape, a considerable freedom of imagination and design.

Recognizing at last, if reluctantly, that private enterprise really could not house the bottom third of the nation in habitations worthy of humanity and befitting the resources and skills of the country, politicians and architects set to work on projects for rebuilding large sections of great cities and providing homes for millions of people. So great was the pressure of contractors, building material producers, labor, and social reformers upon governments, federal and local, that a wide area for the exercise of architectural talent in a different mood was now opened out. On public housing projects, to be sure, architects had to watch every detail with a view to cutting costs, but the controlling motive was to give as much light, convenience, and beauty as possible within the limits — not as little as the traffic would bear.

Although with the extension of public functions calling for the coöperation of architects, opportunity was theoretically opened for remarkable patterns of dwellings, postoffices, and other buildings made possible by the new potentialities of materials for supplying light, air, functional utility, and esthetic pleasure, practically the exigencies of politics, the pressures of local customs and building interests, and the demand for speed hampered the spirit of innovation. It was relatively easy for speed of design to match the rush of political pressures, whenever it was a mere matter of collecting stones and mortar, brick and cement, or timbers and nails for the construction of buildings on lines inherited from the centuries; but the problem of expressing beautifully the functional spirit with the wealth of new materials could not be quickly solved at brief conferences among politicians, business men, and architects.

That was a problem calling for great skill and long patience, in combining the sense for comfort, convenience, and beauty with a mastery of the amazing materials which invention and manufacturing enterprise had furnished to the modern market. It was indeed bewildering in its nature. Mere lists of the materials, ranging widely in substance and flexibility, filled bulky volumes, with steel and glass among the simplest and plastics among the most diverse and wonderful. Mastering them and bending them to dreams of use and beauty required time, perseverance, and genius.

Modifying and elaborating the conceptions which Frank Lloyd Wright had worked into architecture, Richard J. Neutra, operating independently and in his own way, emphasized the time element in architectural forms, pointed out the difference between the methods of financing classical building and modern building, and made explicit the consequences of the change from slave to free labor in the construction process — all the while putting up houses, schools, and other buildings as demonstrations of the possibilities of modernism in architecture. In a discussion of the altered psychological attitude in the appreciation of architectural designs, Neutra said: "The most momentous tasks of the architecture of the near future are clearly not individually cherished issues of luxurious waste or extravagant purchasing power of exalted personages, but communal and housing problems. The last 'third of the nation' is being added to the consumers' list. Apart from all considerations of societal morale, the character of industrial production automatically aims in this very direction.

"However, even in the pre-industrial ages down from Swiss lake dwellers to Slovakian and Japanese villagers, building work followed standards, at least regionally accepted as valid. Such standardization was the cause of pleasing and convincing harmonious uniformity in each communal district. In contrast, spasmodic individualism turned our cities into a milling multiform turmoil, where no reliable taste would develop as perhaps it did in classic times, with centuries of frank architectural repetitions and indifference to mere fashion in building.

"Playfulness, biologically legitimate, becomes unbearable license when the Arabian minarets of Hollywood apartment courts rise beside the false shingle roofs of 'English Cottage' real estate offices, and the restaurant structure across the street takes the shape of a brown derby. A responsible new tradition must be built up for the integration of present-day facts and it cannot indulge in the arbitrary picking up of quaint tid-bits. We can follow but one path, that path which true contemporaries of all ages have chosen by necessity: base our creative efforts on the best technical means and standards accessible to us at our historical moment; not live voluntarily below the level of our historical age! Infants appear sweet when they crawl on the floor and use baby talk; adults who rightly adore them look nevertheless awkward and even alarming if they try to imitate them.

"The present stage of technological advance, of informality in living, of growing scarcity of underpaid labor and domestic help, of hygienic cleanliness, of appreciation for natural and open air health factors, of communal responsibility — all this can only be practically and esthetically digested, assimilated, evaluated, integrated, by frank efforts in truly contemporary design, which is witnessed by a growing volume of such building work throughout the world."

How could opportunity be furnished for that kind of architectural designing, provided architects were disposed to shake off tradition and to transform dreams into reality? Evidently alterations would be required in the ideas and methods of productive economy; and the selling pressures behind the amazing new fabrications would have to be channeled into the simpler operations required by the integrated efforts of truly contemporary designing. But this outcome was not altogether fanciful. Colleges and other institutions were beginning to call for competitive designs and permitting the modernists to enter the contests. So strong became the interest in the functional and the rational, in the best sense of the terms, that Harvard University made room in its Department of Architecture for Walter Gropius, the former director of the New Bauhaus at Dessau, Germany; and a New Bauhaus was established at Chicago under Laszlo Moholy-Nagly, one of his associates. In these institutions, it was announced, the traditions of the École des Beaux Arts, formerly so dominant in American architectural thought, would be frankly challenged, and the usual professional curriculum supplemented by the study of bio-technics, biology, psychology, philosophy, literature, art, and economics. According to many appearances, collective architecture was to play an increasing role and the profession was to assume heavier responsibilities to the public which it served.

§

Thus within the broad domain of esthetics, amid its orders and confusions, appeared signs of a consolidation in cultural affirmations, as indeed in the social and political world — the signs of a concentration of talents such as had featured the ages called great. Workers in art were reaching for a deeper social rootage. Philosophers and politicians were coming closer to the view that life without art is a poor thing, even impossible, that esthetic forces are among the sustaining energies of every society, large or small.

Nothing save the reconciliation of science and art seemed necessary to complete the tendencies toward such a concentration of talents, and even this inclination was manifest in the land. In his lectures on the fine arts, significantly entitled Scientific Method in Aesthetics, published in 1928, Thomas Munro had made a plea for a philosophy of life embracing both science and art. "Any conception of human behavior," he said, "which omits the writing of poems and systems of philosophy, the playing of violins and the carving of statues, the attempt to appraise these things in logical and intelligible words; or any psychology, which fails to take account of them, is too narrow to deserve the name. It is this

narrow-mindedness in some natural scientists which gives
continued strength to the mystic and idealist, with their talk
of a 'subjective' world, and of realities and values which
cannot be reduced to material terms. A philosophy based on
such distorted science will rightly appear one-sided and de-
meaning to those gifted with more sensitive intuitions. While
it fails to correct itself, it will be distrusted; it will need supplementing at the hands of religious, metaphysical, and poetic
imagination. But a total world-view thus built of maladjusted and conflicting parts can never be fully rational. It
remains for science itself to broaden its outlook. Without
abandoning its experimental approach, or its conception of
the physical basis of things, it can go on to adapt that approach to a more sympathetic study of what Santayana has
called their 'ideal fulfillments.' . . .

"That science aims at control of nature, including human
nature, does not imply that it must also aim at universal
mechanization. For insuring the necessities and comforts of
life, large-scale mechanical production is an effective means,
and science has therefore developed it. For attaining ideal
values, radically different means may be necessary, and intelligent control will then consist in their discovery and application. . . .

"If aesthetics discovers limits beyond which life cannot be
made systematic without destroying elements of value within
it, then intelligent control will consist in holding system
within those limits, and in stimulating variety, surprise, and
unanalyzed feeling outside of them. As in government, the
attaining of genuine freedom can be the chief aim of scientific planning. Control through applied aesthetics can aim,
likewise, not at directing the courses of intuitive impulse, but
at freeing it to seek its own paths of adventure and growth,
by harmonizing unwanted conflicts, and dissolving the
routine mechanical habit."

CHAPTER XV
Science in the Widening Outlook

WORKING in a field of research essentially limitless, taking for their domain all things open to observation and testing, driven by the dynamic of the analytical quest, and claiming liberty of inquiry as an indispensable condition of achievement, scientists, in forging ahead, responded to the impacts and demands of the enveloping world. No more than business enterprise, politics, letters, or art could science operate in a vacuum, be free from the impingement of the forces that buffeted the thought and action of the age. In all times scientists, at least in the course of applications, had sought answers to questions thrust upon them by the given conditions of society, by the state of mankind. At no time had they been born, reared, and sustained in work within the four walls of their research chambers. They had come to their undertakings from various spheres of social life, bringing with them presuppositions and postulates formulated outside or on the periphery of their dominion; and they had lived, while pursuing their investigations, in the lay world with its exigencies, interests, and modes of thinking. The relations of their learning to society were to be called, for want of a more exact word, "organic" in nature, and could not be severed even in theory. Everything that happened, then, during the years of the midpassage, had a bearing, immediate, imminent, or infinitesimal, upon science — upon its substance, its method, and its spirit. Replying to notices of change, while continuing its inquiries, in some measure science itself was transformed.

Proudly but with justification, the Science News Letter could exclaim, with simple, and therefore supreme, eloquence, that the frontier of science "extends from the interior of the atom to the furtherest reaches of astronomical space." More-over it embraced time, for it took within its view tools of the late ice age unearthed in Colorado, shattered thrones in ancient Guatemala, music and art sixty centuries old in Tepe Gwara, Mesopotamia, "the world's oldest city," and a Babylonian mathematical treatise hitherto ascribed to the Greeks. Beyond human time lay geologic time. In 1937 ex-cavators discovered the fossil bones of a "hippopotamus-sized mammal that lived in Colorado forty-five million years ago when the Rocky Mountains were a flat grassland."

Stirred to practical research by experiences in the eco-nomic calamity, scientists sought new substances and con-trived new devices for manufacture or for cutting "the costs of labor." When the Government of the United States was wrestling with unemployment, whether technological or not, and seeking the conservation and "wise use" of material resources, scientists were drawn into surveying, planning, and applied action or called upon to consider their relation to all these activities. Finding the potentials of their knowl-edge and power hampered in application, frontier thinkers among the scientists began to wonder about the forces in civilization that prevented the full fruition of their mastery. As they drove the keen edge of their analysis deeper and deeper into the nature of things, all the while reporting technical findings in a profusion of details, they transformed the "appearance" of "reality" and found themselves plunged into the central problems of philosophy, letters, and art, while making their own contributions to the "understanding" of the issues underlying all thought and conduct.

§

The achievements of the scientific spirit were traceable, in part, in the summaries of events and achievements put forth from year to year by Science Service in Washington. In 1928 it announced the death of Doctor Hideyo Noguchi of the Rockefeller Institute as event, but associated with the occurrence was the memory of the man who had accepted the perils of his exploration into yellow fever — a martyr to research struck down by the disease he was studying. This same year came the report that the Bell Telephone Laboratories had developed a loud speaker with three hundred times the volume of any existing instrument and also the news that photographs had been transmitted by radio across the continent. In 1929 a medley of events hinted at the diversity of scientific interest: the Iowa State College recorded the production of a chemical compound, evolved from corn cobs, three hundred times as sweet as sugar; Yale University broke the ground for a two-million-dollar Institute of Human Relations; Madame Curie subjected herself to gaping crowds in the United States to secure a "gift" of radium; and the success of the new eleven-inch gun "surprise ships" of Germany were proclaimed to the naval world.

In 1930, while President Hoover was confronting the issue of "recovery," scientists went on developing their specialties. Pluto, the ninth planet of the solar system, was discovered. Improved radio beacons promised to make it possible for passenger and bombing planes to land safely in fog or darkness. An "artificial lung" was invented and put immediately into life-saving service. The United States Patent Office issued 49,599 patents and accepted 117,790 applications. Plans were made for the Golden Gate Bridge at San Francisco, with the longest center suspension span in the world.

Astronomers reached the conclusion that interstellar space, instead of being transparent, was filled with diffuse materials absorbing light. A great dispute over the nature of cosmic rays became a sensation; a worker in the California Institute of Technology suggested that possibly the whole universe would in the timeless future fade into a mere nothing save radiation. In 1931 medical research disclosed the fact that a flea could transmit typhus fever, and that new methods had been devised for treating bacteria — an aid in the quest for the causes of diseases. Beside the little was placed the big: the Akron, the largest airship in the world, was commissioned and launched on its fate, to raise new speculations over communications and armaments.

The years immediately following witnessed advances in the conquest of yellow and typhus fevers, the discovery of the neutron, the determination of the properties of "heavy water," record stratosphere flights, the commercial extraction of bromine from sea water, the spanning of the Pacific Ocean by a commercial airline, the unearthing of new evidence confirming the view that human beings lived in America at least ten thousand years before the birth of Christ, the completion of the Boulder Dam, and the shipment of the two-hundred-inch glass disk to Pasadena for polishing, in preparation for the installation of the world's largest telescope. In 1937 "the biggest human skull ever found was unearthed among Indian remains in Virginia. . . . Two new interstellar gases, neutral potassium and calcium, were discovered. . . . Plant cancers, usually caused by germs, were experimentally induced with chemicals. . . . Seventy compounds closely related to life-sustaining chlorophyll were prepared synthetically. . . . The earth's age was checked by studies of radioactive potassium. . . . Scheduled transpacific air travel was established. . . . Two new adrenal gland hormones were discovered. . . . Calcium was successfully used to calm excited patients and banish their hallucinations."

Creative powers within the American civilization were certainly not exhausted. In that judgment of competence represented by Nobel prizes, ten American scientists won first mention amid the golden glow and the shadows: in physics, A. H. Compton, Carl D. Anderson, and Clinton J. Davisson; in chemistry, Irving Langmuir and H. C. Urey; in physiology and medicine, Karl Landsteiner, Thomas H. Morgan, G. R. Minot, W. F. Murphy, and G. H. Whipple. But the list of individuals singled out for honors by no means completed the roll of talents. The truth is that there was an element of injustice in it, as recipients of Nobel prizes were the quickest to concede, for each advance in science rested upon the labors of a multitude and was, in some measure, the next step rendered inevitable by a concentration of efforts on posited problems. Consequently an element of fortuity as well as of genius entered into the "natural selection" of individuals destined to make the culminating experiments and calculations. Nor could it be claimed at the time that the disclosures chosen for decoration were to be the most significant when considered in terms of the morrow. Recognizing the somewhat anonymous nature of the general advance, Science Service discontinued the practice of associating names with specific achievements in its annual summaries.

§

In the main, the advance of invention was along lines of mechanical improvement. No revolutionary device such as the automobile or airplane emerged from laboratory or workshop. Though business men in general hoped that a novel instrument or gadget, to be made by the millions, would lift industry out of the depression, no magician produced it. The opposite occurred: more striking than inventions to occupy labor was the perfection of machines "to save labor." At the end of seven years of depression, it was estimated that the industrial equipment of the country could produce a far larger output than in 1928 with a much smaller force of industrial workers, so rapid was the improvement in the machinery and techniques of production. Incorrigible optimists might continue to say that every new machine "gave employment" and that "technological unemployment" was a fallacy. On the face of things facts did not seem to support the theory. At all events, one effect of the depression was clearly a greater concentration on the cutting of costs by labor-saving devices and an immense display of inventive skills in the creation of automatic machinery.

Although no machine, such as the moving-picture apparatus or the automobile, came out of the laboratory or workshop to furnish employment to millions, many revolutionary devices of the opposite type were in the offing or in process of testing. Month by month the mechanical cotton picker, long an object of inventive inquiry, was improved. If applied to cotton culture along prevailing lines of capitalist enterprise, it would mean the annihilation of the semi-primitive features of that industry, making obsolete the small cotton farm with its mules, plows, and field hands. Efficient application would call for the huge plantation, plowed and tilled by tractors, and cropped by the new machine, producing cotton at a cost so low that American producers could undersell even the drivers of the fellaheen on the banks of the Nile. If this should happen, what would become of the millions of whites and Negroes in the cotton belt already hanging on the weak lifeline of marginal subsistence? Were they to be employed in manufacturing mechanical pickers or to be sustained by a benevolent government? The inventors of the machine themselves trembled at the thought of their Frankenstein monster. And yet to the mechanical picker was added the mechanical "chopper" that might complete the ruin of hand labor on cotton lands, and then a reaper for cutting sugar cane that threatened disaster for more field hands.

Other inventions were less fear-provoking. Devices for the air-conditioning of factories, offices, and houses in summer and winter were brought to a high state of efficiency, with results somewhat incongruous. If members of the privileged class could ride from air-conditioned offices in automobiles to air-conditioned homes, industrial workers and white-collar employees enjoying ideal temperatures in shop and office might find the air of their houses unendurable and even injurious by contrast. Nor did the polar auditoriums of moving-picture palaces in summertime go very well with sweltering streets and stewing slums. Nevertheless, if comfort was one of the marks of civilization, the expansion of air-conditioning devices indicated an upward movement — as had the air-warmed palaces of Roman Britain. Combined with the more efficient placing of machines in plants and the adaptation of lighting facilities to specific processes and operations, they offered ameliorations in the circumstances in which industrial work was carried on. That improvements in the housing of machines might eventually affect the housing of human beings or at least suggest something to industrial managers in search of higher efficiency was among the probabilities of the time.

More relevant than air-conditioning to the problem of human housing was the development of the prefabricated house. Models that seemed to represent the acme of perfection in terms of economy, comfort, and convenience were created by designers. The wide use of special materials, such as rustless steel, chromium, aluminum, and plastics, was forecast by actual demonstrations of potentials. Artistic skill in varying forms and colors within the limits of fixed measurements bourgeoned in laboratory and atelier as functional principles were substituted for loyalty to traditions. Practical tests proved the wastefulness of historic designing, carpentry, and masonry and illustrated the specific economies to be obtained by large-scale production. Yet none of the concerns experimenting in these lines succeeded in the establishment of a vast industry. All were handicapped in their efforts at mass production by vested interests in local real estate, contracting, and building and by encrusted custom. Extraordinary possibilities were certainly embodied in the prefabricated house, but whether private or public enterprise could release them still remained problematical. Did human powers measure up to undoubted human needs? The answer to that question did not lie in design or engineering.

Greater success attended the manufacture of a movable house, known as the automobile trailer. Content at first with turning out a mere box on wheels to be driven to mountain or seashore by summer campers, designers and manufacturers in this field seemed to be catering merely to amusement and recreation. Indeed this phase of the business remained an essential interest. But from elementary beginnings, the industry advanced in the direction of technical perfection and expanding utility. By the use of light metal and plastics, by the installation in compact form of the latest household devices, manufacturers were able to make trailers that exceeded at least the comforts of Pullman cars and yet could be sold at prices within the reach of hundreds of thousands.

Attached to automobiles, these movable homes could be drawn anywhere and established for any length of time. Owners with small incomes could spend winters in the South and summers in the North, perhaps supplementing their resources by local earnings. Municipalities provided trailer camps and supplied them with water, lighting, and sanitary facilities. To be sure, problems in health, education, and social living accompanied the rolling caravans; nevertheless, within ten years a diversion had developed into a substantial enterprise, with far-reaching implications. Classical economists had long posited the ideal mobility of capital and labor. Perhaps one-tenth or more of the population could soon forsake landlords and rents, take to wheels and migrate on an hour's notice.

To that part of the people not moving around in trains, airplanes, and automobiles, inventors promised to bring motion by the improvement of the television apparatus. From year to year advances were announced from laboratories at home and abroad, until by 1938 the main technical problems had been solved. All that remained was the perfection of picture reproduction and the design of a machine that could be sold at a price within the reach of moderate purses. In

1937 a coaxial cable for carrying television messages was put into operation between New York and Philadelphia and television tubes were placed on the market. Already the transmission of photographs and facsimiles had reached a commercial stage and was affecting newspaper reporting and business intercourse. In 1928 photographs were sent successfully from Oakland, California, to Schenectady, New York, by radio. In 1938 such transmissions were everyday affairs.

By that time it was demonstrated that pictures, articles, documents, and even whole pages of newspapers could be sent to all parts of the country, through the air. The hour for a national daily seemed ripe, therefore, since the same general news, features, and advertising could be instantaneously reproduced in every city and the varieties of local news and advertising easily added. Technology had done its work. The adventurous publisher was awaited. Opponents of standardization as an evil in itself seemed on the verge of their last ditch.

Meanwhile the transformation of substances and the creation of new products acquired an accelerated pace. The manufacture of plastics for infinite uses and of artificial fabrics from cellulose released whole industries from dependence on crude raw materials over which economists and diplomats had long been haggling. Cellophane now enveloped almost everything vendible — from plucked chickens to cigars and "boiled shirts"; verily women's dresses were made of it. Synthetic substances hard enough to bore holes in stones or strong enough to resist fire rolled out of laboratories and mills. For innumerable purposes wood and other materials were discarded and bakelite substituted. Synthetic rubber appeared, if in the mirage stage; though the chemical problem was largely solved, costs remained insurmountable for practical purposes. The manufacture of gasoline from coal was demonstrated as a physical fact, but the costs of labor and materials still made it prohibitive as an economic proposition. If silken garments could be devised from "surplus" milk and bath tubs from cornstalks, old channels of world commerce might dry up and the ancient struggle for the ownership of the earth and its resources might be mitigated. When all fantasies were discounted, the theory that there was a natural division of labor among regions and nations according to climate and resources was certainly a distorted view of reality. Another fifty years as revolutionary as the past ten might almost complete the destruction of that picture of the earth and its material determinants on which traditional economies, governments, and national and international policies all rested.

To the drive of universities, special institutes, and commercial laboratories in the industrial sphere was joined a new dynamic — an effort to stimulate agriculture by the scientific use of materials and resources hitherto neglected. Recognizing the difficulties that impeded the flow of agricultural produce to profitable uses, industrial leaders and the managers of experiment stations brought the energies of science to bear on the development of new crops and new commodities to be manufactured from them.

Especially sensational were experiments and achievements in agrobiology, notably "tray agriculture." By successful operations it was established that plants, such as tomato vines, would literally grow like magic in shallow trays of water, if carefully fed exact amounts of balanced chemicals, and would bear so prolifically as to make even "progressive agriculture" look like a primitive art. As usual, claims and counter-claims were filed. O. W. Wilcox, in ABC of Agrobiology, prophesied enormous potentials: perhaps a state no larger than Nebraska could produce all the foodstuffs needed by the 130,000,000 people inhabiting the United States. In the name of practice, farmers called all this forecasting visionary. Nevertheless some of the billions spent on armaments, if directed to agrobiology, might bring ten or fifteen per cent of the dream into execution. Problems were set. Lines of advance were laid down. Even methods for transporting highly perishable milk over long distances and keeping it fresh for weeks were perfected and awaited only the skills of practice to carry them into general use.

§

If proud of their intellectual achievements, many scientists felt humiliated as they observed the various applications of their discoveries and inventions. In the innocent days of the Victorian age, they had shared the impulsive optimism that hailed each device and machine as another sign of "progress." In those times there had been, no doubt, a few critics who scoffed at "cheap and nasty" things made by the machine and bemoaned the huge slums that appeared everywhere in the wake of inventions. Yet in the main, until the disaster of 1929 and the universal preparation for "the next war," scientists could shout down the pessimists. They could point to general gains, setting credits against debits. When such a balance sheet proved ineffective in curbing criticism, they could take refuge in the contention that bigger and better things were really ahead despite "temporary" or "transitional" shortcomings. Or they could lay the blame for the abuse of science and invention on human nature, disclaim their own responsibility, and refuse to debate the merits of progress in bombing planes for war and in poison gas for industrial conflicts. But after ten years of depression and disintegration, in which both the intellectual methods and material achievements of science were heavily involved, the temperature of optimism fell and the delights of willful escape diminished.

In a strict sense, no doubt, scientists had an alibi. The nature of their work called for the spirit of absolute neutrality in the matter of arguments over uses and values. The chemist, for example, as chemist, was not at all concerned during any of his chemical experiments as to whether his discovery was to be employed in healing the sick or blowing bank safes. His business, as chemist, was to find out by analysis the nature, composition, and combinations of substances. To that quest the possible utilization of his findings was irrelevant and preoccupation with human issues would have been disconcerting to his scientific investigation. Moreover there was nothing whatever in the knowledge or methods of science that enabled scientists to speak with any special authority on the subject of uses and values. Nothing in the explorations of chemistry or physics dictated their human applications. In the presence of that issue, scientists, however profound their learning in physics or chemistry, had to rely upon morals, mores, and ethical judgments common to the general mass of the people. The Nobel prize winner might differ from the garage mechanic over the desirability of a war on Japan, let us say, but no laboratory experiments enabled him to prove that his verdict was "better" or more in accord with "truth." A master of physics, engaged in expounding economics, was not necessarily wiser than a labor organizer or a more perspicacious interpreter of history than a poet.

Despite the spirit of neutrality reigning within their circle, scientists did not work in a void. Among the problems that attracted their attention, some carried more unneutral implications than others. In the domain of physiology and medicine, including their physical and chemical aspects, positive problems of human welfare could scarcely be escaped, save in the field of pure research. The state of human beings suffering from typhus or yellow fever, for instance, had to be examined and one evident part of inquiry along such lines was a comparison with, or a creation of, a different state, known as health or well-being. A particular scientist might be interested in extending the ravages of typhus for use in "the coming war," but this was not the main problem suggested in practice by investigations of its nature.

The spirit of scientists was also activist. For the prosecution of researches, funds and laboratories were necessary. Stoppages in income for dwellers in ivory towers arrested interest and certainly awakened some curiosity in respect of causes. Outside the chambers of pure research were the practitioners of science — engineers, industrial chemists, the huge body of technologists. Their possibilities of activism, to say nothing of a living, depended upon the rate and curve of industrial production. When their beautiful machines slowed down or came to a dead stop they were inclined to ask for a reason. The question might not be scientific in form, but it was a "natural" one. Besides facing problems of operation blocked by business recession, technologists faced problems of increasing productivity, of putting new inventions and discoveries into use. Why make them, only to have them perish? In reality, therefore, it was impossible to insulate scientists and their researches completely from life and work in general.

§

How can the magnificent discoveries of science be put to the most efficient and most desirable human uses? The query was not new but the intensity of interest now engendered in the problem gave promise of exploration and action. Among physicians, recognition of the challenge led to searches for answers and for ways and means of practice. After all, doctors from time immemorial had come into the closest contact with humanity and its needs. An engineer making cigarettes in Durham, North Carolina, saw few of his "ultimate consumers" and thought little about them, but all practicing physicians, seeing their patients, had to consider their science in terms of its everpresent human outcomes. Furthermore professional ethics, as theory at least, forbade them to apply purely economic canons to relationships with patients and to turn the helpless out of doors in the manner of the managing technician under the necessities of a business slump. Doctors were bound by a historic oath and a system of moral conduct supposed to control the application of their knowledge. Perhaps, having taken over the healing arts of primitive women and ancient midwives, modern physicians, men as well as women, had inherited some of the sacrificial spirit displayed by mothers from time immemorial.

Whatever the sources of their inspiration, within the science or outside, physicians took leadership in the quest for the utmost beneficial use of discoveries and inventions in their domain. In 1927, when the golden glow was almost at its height, the Committee on the Costs of Medical Care was organized under the direction of Dr. Ray Lyman Wilbur, funds amounting to more than a million dollars were granted by foundations, and an investigation was begun into every nook and cranny of public and private health. The general field was broken down into minute subdivisions and competent specialists were engaged to explore them without fear or favor. At the end of five years the Committee produced the most comprehensive survey of illness and of facilities for coping with it ever made in the United States — indeed a monument in the long history of medicine. Fact statements, painstaking and precise, were supplemented by conclusions with reference to proposed actions in perfecting medical services throughout the country. Although there was some dissent in the Committee, the majority agreed upon recommendations which were called, and rightly, "revolutionary" for the United States, in their demands and implications.

The conclusions so startling to Americans unfamiliar with health insurance in Great Britain and Europe could be summarized under five heads. Medical services should be grouped around hospitals, that is, community institutions. Public and private health services should be made "available to the entire population according to its needs." The costs of medical services should be put on a group-payment basis through insurance, taxation, or both. The function of studying, evaluating, and coördinating medical services belongs to every state and community; for the policy of haphazard drift must be substituted the policy of collective planning and action. After a criticism of medical education so exclusively concentrated on scientific techniques, so neglectful of the social aspects of costs and practice came the fifth conclusion: medical education should be broadened by laying stress upon the prevention of illness and upon the social obligations of the profession. Sustained by an immense array of special studies, statistics, and expert testimony, the final report of the Committee in 1932 shook physicians in general, and laymen as well, out of their complacency and started a nation-wide discussion of sickness and healing that seemed to gather momentum as time passed.

Support for the collective action suggested by the Committee was augmented by subsequent studies. For instance, a house-to-house inquiry conducted by the Federal Public Health Service in the winter of 1935–36 brought out the generalization that, on an average winter day, six million men, women, and children were unable to work, attend school, or pursue other usual activities on account of illness, injury, or gross physical impairment resulting from disease or accident. Forty-two per cent of these unfortunates were afflicted with chronic diseases. The amount of illness in the United States was appalling in its magnitude.

This illness, moreover, bore a relation to economic status. By a wide sampling study, the Service reached the verdict that about sixty-five per cent of the sick persons belonged to families with an annual income of less than $1500, and that eighty per cent were in families having incomes below $2000. The duration of illness was longer in the low-income group and the extent of medical services received by victims of illness varied roughly according to income schedules. The illusion that "hospitals were open to everyone" was completely dispelled by the realities of the situation : over sixty-five million people lived in communities of ten thousand or less, or in rural areas, with no immediate hospital facilities, and eighteen million lived in counties where there were no hospitals of any kind. On the one side, millions of people sick. On the other side, facilities available, doctors and nurses idle for lack of paying clients.

Such were indubitable facts, and yet they did not dictate an unequivocal policy of social or public medicine. As in all debates over policy to be adopted, the outcome depended on preliminary assumptions or major premises, involving an interpretation of civilization and its course. Since industry, society, and general welfare depended upon sound bodies and sound minds, from that point of view the United States presented alarming aspects. On this matter doctors agreed. Moreover civilization depended, if to an immeasurable extent, upon individual intelligence and the sense of personal responsibility. On this truth too there was a general agreement. It was likewise established that a certain correlation existed between income and illness.

But at this point opinion broke into factionalism. Critics of social medicine presented itemized expenditures by the very people who lacked appropriate medical and dental aid : millions for patent medicines, millions for radios, millions for movies, millions for lipsticks and other cosmetics, millions for gin that gave drinkers stomach disorders, millions for numbers rackets, millions for prize fight tickets, millions for sweepstakes and race-track gambling. From such facts it was reasoned that people who would rather lose money on numbers rackets than spend it for medical services deserved slight consideration at the hands of government and no consideration at the hands of taxpayers asked to meet the medical bills. Why should radios be bought out of meager incomes and medical service be supplied free or below cost?

If the conventions of the American Medical Association faithfully represented its membership, doctors were on the whole against any material changes in historic practices. At its assembly in 1934 the Association strongly condemned both voluntary and compulsory health insurance. Physicians who organized or served voluntary associations for the maintenance of medical services on the basis of fixed annual or monthly fees from the members were assailed for "unethical and unprofessional conduct" and occasionally haled into court under statutes put on the law books in the name and interest of the medical profession.

Yet as the agitation proceeded, there appeared to be a decided increase in the number of physicians eager to see the fullest possible use of their science and sympathetic with the collective approach to the solution of the problem. At the convention of the American Medical Association in 1937 the New York delegation presented a set of resolutions indicating that the profession in the Empire state was moving rapidly in the direction of what was loosely called "social medicine." The adoption of the resolutions, materially altered by amendments though they were, betrayed at least some drift in medical thought since the declaration of positive immobility three years before. About the same time the opening of a clinic by the Group Health Association in Washington to a large number of federal employees raised the issue of associational medicine in the very center of government circles and precipitated a legal contest as well as an emotional outburst.

The literature on social medicine produced during the ten years' debate contained all the familiar phrases and assumptions underlying the contemporary discussion of economics: individualism and communism, self-help and community responsibility, American way and progress, greatest country in the world, unfinished business, planning and autonomism. Practice displayed similar contradictions: private hospitals and public hospitals, high charges and charity, public health services in bewildering variety and private practice in the old style, group doctors and individual doctors, doctors concentrating on the main chance and doctors generously giving time and money to social medicine, collectivism emergent in public agencies and associational clinics, and rugged individualism good and bad.

By the year 1938 the drift of discussion and practice had deposited in the thought of the country the idea of compulsory health insurance for the lower income groups, along the lines of British legislation. Bills were drafted and introduced. Debate was started. If precedent in the rise and development of legislative action in other matters still had force, then the United States was on the way to supplementing the old practices by state medicine of some type, added to, rather than completely supplanting, the historic freedom of private practice. A Congress that had hesitated to attack the evils of quack remedies and their carriers of advertising would doubtless balk at enacting a national health law, but a powerful movement of thought and energies was headed in the direction of a social medicine that would give fuller release to the dammed-up and frustrated forces of medical science, curative and preventive. At the New York State Constitutional Convention during the summer of 1938 a proposal authorizing the legislature to establish health insurance was approved, submitted to the voters, and adopted.

§

Like scientists engaged in medical practice, engineers were concerned with applications bearing directly on human interests and conduct. It was true that they did not always have before them as an immediate end the specific and somewhat determinable welfare of determinate individuals; nevertheless their researches and applications were constantly directed, more or less, to human uses, constructive or destructive. They were not, however, complete masters in their own household. If a corporation raised money by selling stock to the public and ordered an engineer to build and operate a plant that merely duplicated an existing plant for the output of which no market could be obtained, it was ostensibly the engineer's business to build and operate the superfluous establishment, not to reason why or why not. If a lumber company ordered whole counties denuded of timber and left barren as eroding wreckage, it was apparently the engineer's function to denude and let nature take her course. If politicians decided upon a foreign war, for whatever reason assigned, engineers were expected to take orders, produce, and apply engines, chemicals, and gases ever more frightful and destructive. Neither individual welfare nor social welfare in the large was the controlling conception in the engineering profession as such. As long as its members found employment, in the bright days of alleged general prosperity under the auspices of President Coolidge, repairing ravages of the world war, overcoming the housing shortage, and building plants to meet demands created in part by copious lending to impecunious foreign borrowers, members of the profession could look upon their work and pronounce it good.

Yet, from older days in the rise of engineering, some engineers, such as Nikola Tesla and Charles P. Steinmetz, often called dreamers, had been impressed by the contrasts between engineering knowledge of matter and force and engineering practice considered in terms of human welfare; between potentials and achievements; between operating postulates and possible postulates. During the closing years of the golden glow, under the leadership of Herbert Hoover as Secretary of Commerce, engineers had piled up mountainous evidence of waste in designs, in production, in the use of materials in private industries; and the existence of even greater wastes had been noted in discreet hints. Out of their inquiries had come proposals and, to some extent, actions coöperative in nature, under the auspices of the Federal Government, with the special aid of the Bureau of Standards in Washington.

By that time the "science of management," associated with the name of Frederick Winslow Taylor, had broadened its interest beyond the immediate relations of industrial workers to materials, beyond the plant itself, and was taking into account various elements of industry, education, and social living that made for the efficiency and, correlatively, for the happiness and welfare of workers outside the shop. Speaking in 1931 at a Senate hearing on the establishment of an economic council, the director of the Taylor Society, H. S. Person, traced the growth of managerial interest and added: "I think I perceive, in the history of the extension of this principle and technique of control in ever wider areas of managerial responsibility, the compulsion, in order to conserve stabilization accomplished in any lesser area, to reach out and stabilize the influencing environment."

Shortly after the publication of a symposium on civilization, Whither Mankind, in 1928, a group of prominent engineers in New York City, taking the volume as a kind of provocation to their profession, issued an answer formulated by leaders in science and technology, entitled Toward Civilization. In their own volume, to use the language of the editor, technicians "recognize their responsibility for the future of humanity, see in the materials at hand the promise of great advances for mankind, and are already seriously considering the drift of things and the nature of the readjustments necessary for a better future." Somewhat later the American Engineering Council created a committee "on the balance of economic forces," with Ralph E. Flanders, former president of the National Machine Tool Builders' Association, as chairman, and the committee went into complex problems of balancing technology in operation against consumer requirements, controlling money and credit in relation to industrial processes, increasing human well-being through progress in industry, and adapting public works to public needs.

While the economic crisis was at its crest in 1933, a committee selected by the Society of Industrial Engineers submitted a report on the Economic Significance of Technological Progress, together with a memorandum on Technocracy which had made such a sensation during preceding months. Among other things, the committee concluded: "The advent of the new mode of production alters the position of labor and management in industry. Productivity of labor is determined more and more by the nature of technological process and equipment employed and less by physical strength and trade skill. Hence, compensation for work stands in no relation to old piece rates and time rates. Failure to recognize this fact has resulted in the increasing intensification of work and in deterioration of earning capacity. . . . We are suffering not from technological unemployment, but from the unemployment of technology. The inadequate purchasing capacity of the majority of the population restricts the market necessary for the full utilization of the existing means of production. Unregulated competition led to the duplication of productive capacities of the past."

Inquiries conducted by engineering committees were supplemented by individual investigations into the reasons for the antithesis between technology half-defeated and technology employed at high power. For meetings of societies and for technical journals, specialists engaged in these investigations, for example, Walter Rautenstrauch, Bassett Jones, David Cushman Coyle, and Walter Polakov, prepared statistics, graphs, and demonstrations bearing on the problem of bringing technical resources into the fullest possible use. By the papers and books on such widening inquiries vigorous controversies were started and strong currents of opinion bearing on the issue were set in motion. When in 1938 the National Economic and Social Planning Association surveyed courses on economic and social planning, economic policy, industrial policy, resources planning, and community planning offered by American institutions of learning, it discovered that a widely scattered, apparently spontaneous, and yet fairly general, concern with the utilization and rationalization of material and technical resources had arisen in these intellectual centers of the nation.

In one field, that of public works and conservation, the engineers of the period made substantial contributions to thought about the underlying purposes of technology and the fuller use of its potentials, though the initiative seldom came from purely engineering circles. The source of inspiration was rather that small group of persons within the Roosevelt administration who were considering the breakdown in economy in terms of national areas and long-time planning. At all events, under the auspices of the National Planning Board, later called the National Resources Board, and other agencies of the Federal Government, numerous special studies were made which increased the public knowledge of natural resources, called attention to the science of efficient use, and proposed the integration of public works on a large scale. The conservation of natural resources was, of course, an established principle, but features of novelty appeared in the efforts to obtain complete pictures of the total situation, to discern the direction of tendencies, and to devise the positive measures of constructive action required by the all-round application of engineering rationality. While it could not be correctly said that perfection was attained in the conclusions based on such surveys, the researches and formulations marked a widening of engineering thought far beyond the borders of planning and operating individual plants — toward the periphery of technical potentials.

Among the documents so prepared were reports on the watershed of the Mississippi River; on maladjustments in the use of land resources in the United States; on forest resources, problems, and policy; on soil erosion, soil conservation, and flood control; on wind erosion areas and control practices; on the use of "little waters" in relation to the land; and on public works planning. Another engineering inquiry was devoted to the study of the influence of inventions on the development of society, the cultural readjustments required by technological change, and the probable effects of new industrial devices already in process of creation. In response to a request from President Roosevelt a group of distinguished scientists, including Karl Compton of the Massachusetts Institute of Technology and Robert A. Millikan of the California Institute, presented to the country an imposing list of technical problems awaiting solution and the collateral issues involved in the human uses of material and scientific resources. Besides presenting an eloquent essay on the contributions of science to civilization, their reports went into specifications respecting latent powers awaiting release and achievements yet to be accomplished.

Both the findings and the recommendations of the federal committees and agencies revealed a broad range of interest. Nothing pertinent to the problems set was too small for examination. No measure of national policy indicated by engineering rationality was too large for exploration and conclusion. Called upon to study soil conservation, for example, the National Resources Committee went into microscopic details. On the basis of minute investigations it estimated that the annual soil loss included approximately sixteen million tons of nitrogen, thirty-six million tons of potash, fifty-three million tons of calcium, sixteen million tons of magnesium, and three hundred twenty-two million tons of organic materials. It found that crops and pastures consumed from one-fourth to one-half of the total amount and that the remainder was lost by erosion. Patient observation at one point in the state of New York showed that the run-off of rain water from a given area of corn land was nearly seven times as much as the run-off from the same area of meadow land. Ingenious calculations of rainfall in different parts of the country over a period of centuries revealed variations from year to year and cycle to cycle, but relatively slight changes in the long trends. On the basis of these and similar studies, federal authorities worked out conservation and flood-control legislation involving nation-wide coöperation among federal, state, and local agencies and individual farmers and concerns. New statutes were placed on the books and hard work was begun without the sound of drums and trumpets, those boisterous instruments deemed indispensable by politicians and warriors.

Another indication of the tendencies in technical thinking was the six-year plan for public works published by the National Resources Committee in 1936. Originally, public works, such as river and harbor improvements, had been generally regarded as the rightful spoils of politics. Engineers had planned and directed the execution of particular projects as ordered by Congress in "pork barrel" legislation. Somewhat later came the idea that public undertakings should be used to provide work for idle contractors and unemployed workmen in times of business depression — "to take up the slack." Through a combination of petty politics, local greed, and the frustrations of crisis, many works of undoubted utility had been constructed. At the same time millions of dollars had been wasted, despite engineering excellence in detail, and the relation of such works to the total economy of land, forests, and water had been neglected.

This dark jungle of engineering performances the Resources Committee illuminated by inquiry and exploratory thought. Besides making recommendations on the construction of dams, irrigation plants, levees, and other control projects, it proposed a coördination of hitherto unrelated policies and projects with reference to "the promotion of public safety, public health, the public convenience and comfort, and the establishment of high living standards." Coming down to blueprints, it worked out precise methods of procedure pertaining to public and private interests and definite calculations respecting the apportionment of costs with relevance to general and local benefits.

The application of the engineering mind to the study and solution of problems involving the beneficial use of technology on a national scale, freed from immediate time and market limitations, was accompanied by an increase in the number of engineers employed on public projects. Although government services had always attracted engineers, especially civil and military engineers, the major portion of technical graduates had gone into private enterprise. The largest pecuniary rewards lay in that division of economy. Only there could an engineer hope to rise, perhaps through the channel of management or promotion, into the exclusive circle of the high income recipients. There, too, was greater freedom from red tape.

Lured by dazzling prizes, engineers became consultants for great corporations and undertook to defend specific economic policies as well as purely engineering projects. So strong had this tendency become that it was often difficult for a federal, state, or municipal agency to find competent technicians who could hold a fair balance between public and private interests. Distinguished professors in engineering schools steadily supplemented their salaries by serving private concerns and were often accounted valuable "educators" in proportion to the magnificence of their clients. Given the material circumstances, this development had the characteristics of inevitability.

But during the years that followed the crash of 1929, graduates of engineering schools tramped city streets and rural roads with the proletariat looking for work. In the overwhelming rush of business enterprise upon the Federal Government for assistance, the "need for public works to give employment" was constantly emphasized by leaders in private enterprise — by contractors, cement makers, and capitalists who found the investment opportunities of business closing rather than opening. On this occasion they were stayed by no goblin of communism or collectivism. So appropriations for public works multiplied. Scientific planning for forestry, land use, water control, highway construction, and power developments eventuated in actions that employed thousands of engineers in the public service. The regulation of utilities and other forms of private enterprise called for engineering competence on the government side as well as the private side.

In this changing scene, engineers skilled in the "public relations" of their profession came into demand. And no scientific mind could be long at work in the middle ground between collectivism and individualism without acquiring characteristics foreign to the consultant of the old type who accepted the formulas of classical economics as akin to, if not identical with, the formulas of physics or mathematics. Into the professional societies now filtered a growing number of engineers employed in the public service or in closer contact with that service and its requirements than the old-style members. Technical institutes took note of emerging educational requirements and courses in social economy edged their way into schedules loaded with physics, chemistry, calculus, and bacteriology. How far the trend would go could not be discovered by consulting a table of logarithms, but the direction was clear enough.

In the long run, the explorations of individual engineers and the great studies of land, water, and other resources in relation to beneficial uses would presumably influence all technical thought. The elements of physics and mathematics remained the same. Chemical combinations remained unchanged. But the first-hand contacts of engineering minds with nation-wide efforts to control materials and forces for humane ends, to make wholesale adjustments to the inexorable ways of nature, to provide employment for capital and labor, to bring governments, corporations, and individuals into effective combinations for the general welfare — all served to push out the borders of scientific thought. Fresh problems of research and application for physicists, chemists, biologists, and engineers were formulated, suggesting fruitful projects of inquiry along functional lines. Whether the mandate of the times and circumstances was considered as a mere matter of creating employment for members of the profession or a mighty call for the full use of technological potentials, germinal ideas exfoliated in scientific thought, even in the laboratory and the drafting room.

Influences were reciprocal. Engineering surveys and inventions crashed against government, business, and historic practices. A political economy that was still based upon the handicraft philosophy of Adam Smith, despite all trimmings, qualifications, and adaptations, was badly shaken by engineering assertions and achievements. Committed to a respect for facts and to the use of the rational method in all procedures, the very spirit of technology ran counter to the myths, symbols, and habitual assumptions so regnant in the domain of law, politics, and economic speculation. An engine constructed according to physical theory either worked or it did not work. If it did not, the theory was revised or the engine was scrapped as a failure, for flat contradictions between theory and practice were unendurable in the scientific world. When Harold Loeb and his engineering associates indicated by the calculations summarized in The Chart of Plenty that the production of wealth, as a physical fact, could be immensely increased in the United States by applied engineering rationality, perhaps doubled, politicians and economists showed signs of cutting loose from the theory that capitalism was automatically efficient and of inquiring into the problem of bringing realities more in line with potentials.

Judging by experience it seemed probable that the growing recognition of the fructifying relations between science and culture in general would prove to be correlatively stimulating. For example, it had been forcefully demonstrated that war and preparations for war had called forth new scientific energies in response to different demands and had promoted scientific knowledge and achievements. Again, on the other side, the contrivance of new building materials by engineers had precipitated a reconsideration of acquired architectural theories. Could not national demands in the interests of human welfare as great as those expressed in war also act as a persuasive incitement to scientific exploration on a scale more vast than ever experienced? Inasmuch as science, long confined largely to the study of form or matter and force or energy, was now reaching out more actively into the study of function with the aid of a different logic and mathematics, the probability of an affirmative answer was all the more promising.

§

At all events, facing, like capitalists with idle plants and industrial workers without employment, the undeniable fact of tremendous powers going to waste, enormous resources of nature and skill unapplied, with scarcity and suffering oppressing the nation, scientists and engineers not entirely subdued to laboratory routine saw in the crisis a summons to action akin to that prevailing in the medical profession. That their interest might diminish with another outburst of prosperity was possible; that it would completely disappear was improbable, for economists were giving the antithesis between performance and potential an increasing consideration. For instance, meticulous studies carried out by the Brookings Institution, published in America's Capacity to Produce, indicated to popular surprise that even in the years of alleged prosperity machine industry had been running far below its capacity considered in narrow terms and, despite criticisms directed against it, the essential proposition of the Brookings report was incontrovertible.

Translating its findings into monetary terms, the Brookings Institution estimated that "this increased productivity would have approximated fifteen billion dollars. Such an increase in the national income would have permitted enlarging the budgets of fifteen million families to the extent of $1000 each, adding goods and services to an amount of $765 (on a 1929 price level) to every family having an income of $2500 or less in that year, producing $608 worth of additional well-being for every family up to the $5000 level, raising the incomes of 16.4 million families whose incomes were less than $2000 up to that level, increasing all family incomes below the $3500 level, by forty-two per cent, adding $545 to the income of every family of two or more persons, or giving $125 to every man, woman and child in the country." To this statistical presentation of unrealized powers, the Brookings Institution attached a document on America's Capacity to Consume which indicated the extent of the human needs unfilled by applied science and industry. About one-fifth of the families in 1929, the great season of prosperity, had incomes of less than $1000 a year, while "nearly twenty million families, or seventy-one per cent, had incomes less than $2500."

Such reports on frustration increased the skepticism already entertained by inquiring scientists of high standing in their special fields. In dedicating a new building of the Mellon Institute in 1937, Irving Langmuir could say in the customary language of optimism : "Our greatest hope for future well-being and prosperity lies in further applications of science." But Alexis Carrel, in his book on Man, the Unknown, fairly cried out in the spirit of criticism : "The enormous advance gained by the sciences of inanimate matter over those of living things is one of the greatest catastrophes ever suffered by humanity. The environment born of our intelligence and our inventions is adjusted neither to our stature nor to our shape. . . . The groups and the nations in which industrial civilization has attained its highest development are precisely those which are becoming weaker and whose return to barbarism is the most rapid. But they do not realize it. They are without protection against the hostile surroundings that science has built about them." Nor could Raymond Fosdick, one of the presiding geniuses of the Rockefeller group that had done so much for natural science, enjoy the comfort of an unshakeable faith; so he posed the issue: "Is man to be the master of the civilization he has created or is he to be its victim? . . . Will this intricate machinery which he has built up and this vast body of knowledge which he has appropriated be the servant of the race, or will it be a Frankenstein monster that will slay its own maker?"

While the resounding threats of Fascism were echoing across the ocean, Edwin Grant Conklin, distinguished for his achievements in biology, as president of the American Association for the Advancement of Science in 1937, chose to discuss the theme, Science and Ethics. He conceded that many scientific specialists dismissed ethics as a matter of no concern to them, and then reminded his colleagues that "free thought, free speech and free criticism are the life of science"; that "these freedoms are stifled in certain great nations 'with a cruelty more intense than anything western civilization has known in four hundred years.'" What have scientists done to win and maintain these liberties? "In spite of a few notable exceptions," Conklin answered, "it must be confessed that scientists did not win the freedom which they have generally enjoyed, and they have not been conspicuous in defending this freedom when it has been threatened." Asserting that every program for human welfare of necessity includes both science and ethics, Conklin pleaded for their union in scientific thought and action. And he made an emphatic appeal for the cause of freedom and responsibility. "We, who are the inheritors of the tradition of liberty of thought, speech, and press, and who believe that freedom and responsibility are essential to all progress, should use our utmost influence to see that intellectual freedom shall not perish from the earth." In this spirit the Association established a series of conferences on Science and Society devoted to exploring the relations of scientific knowledge and activities to the problems and interests of humanity.

Looking upon technology from the outside and yet a careful student of its social repercussions, Lewis Mumford explored in many directions the cultural roots and implications of scientific work. After patient and penetrating researches in history and practice, he set forth his conclusions in two large volumes: Technics and Civilization, published in 1934, and The Culture of Cities, in 1938. Running down through long centuries, he traced the conditions of mind and economy favorable to science and technology and then demonstrated the reciprocal influences of the two worlds in a manner that belied the isolation of science and scientists from cultural forces and obligations. As to the future, it offered, Mumford thought, tensions and dilemmas rather than soothing confidence: "In the development of the neutral valueless world of science, and in the advance of the adaptive, instrumental functions of the machine, we have left to the untutored egoisms of mankind the control of the gigantic powers and engines technics has conjured into existence. In advancing too swiftly and heedlessly along the line of mechanical improvement we have failed to assimilate the machine and to co-ordinate it with human capacities and human needs; and by our social backwardness and our blind confidence that problems occasioned by the machine could be solved purely by mechanical means, we have outreached ourselves. When one subtracts from the manifest blessings of the machine the entire amount of energy and mind and time and resources devoted to the preparation for war — to say nothing of the residual burdens of past wars — one realizes the net gain is dismayingly small, and with the advance of still more efficient means of inflicting death is becoming steadily smaller."

Out of his search for answers to the questions in his mind, Mumford came to this conclusion: "We are now entering a phase of dissociation between capitalism and technics; and we begin to see with Thorstein Veblen that their respective interests, so far from being identical, are often at war, and that the human gains of technics have been forfeited by perversion in the interests of pecuniary economy." Instead of ascribing, in the popular style, all the special advances in productivity to capitalism, Mumford insisted that many of those gains were "in reality due to quite different agents — collective thought, coöperative action, and the general habits of order — virtues that have no necessary connection with capitalistic enterprise." Without surrendering to the cheerful dream that Nature or God or the Machine would automatically open paths out of contemporary frustrations, Mumford detected signs that the organic, the ethical, and the esthetic were beginning to dominate the material and forecast a wide reconstruction, rural and urban, which would unite with the efficiency of the mechanical industry the excellence and the delight of wholesome living and working.

§

Notwithstanding the wealth of volumes, journals, reports, and technical papers produced in the course of scientific research, relatively little material was offered pertaining to the nature of scientific methods and thought in relation to other forms of activity and speculation. In accordance with the mandates of their interest, scientists usually concentrated upon a firmer and finer analysis of things called matter and force. If the proceedings of the several scientific societies formed any basis of judgment, the minutiae of specific knowledge increased almost in a geometrical ratio. Nothing organic or inorganic seemed to be left untouched, as instruments for analysis, observation, and measurement were multiplied and refined. "Fields" regarded as highly specialized fifteen or twenty years previously were broken into smaller areas, as unfolding scientific inquiry marked off realms yet uncon-quered. Although for a time the economic depression dimin-ished the funds available for research and placed some check on the flow of new workers into the domain of science, it placed no discernible impediment in the way of scientific zeal or the output of reports. For that situation, democratic liberty was responsible in part.

Here and there, however, in the publications which emerged from the scientific world were testaments to shifting interest and suggestions of new affirmations akin to those appearing in letters, esthetics, and social thought. Among the signs of the time was the evident decline of concern with the kind of metaphysical physics which Jeans, Eddington, and Whitehead had supplied from England and Robert Millikan had popularized in the United States during the cheerful days of prosperity. At all events, no scientists now wrote big books in their vein or captivated popular fancies with similar assumptions. This is not to say that their works left no indelible impressions on forms of scientific and speculative thought; but rather that something had happened as the edge of analysis was applied to the higher reports on the nature of nature.

Among scientists as well as laymen developed a suspicion, if nothing more, that these physicists, masterful in their own domains, had read their own theological predilections into the appearances of the realities with which they dealt. The suspicion was deepened when theologians and even evangel-ists could seize upon the indeterminism of "the new physics" and employ it in fervid arguments for freedom of the will, if not for the whole scheme of innocence, fall, and redemption. To be sure, Jeans, Eddington, Whitehead, and Millikan were not responsible for the uses made of their declarations, but their successors in physics seemed to grow more cautious. Perhaps psychological inquiries into epistemology, that is, the relation of the knower to the things presumably de-scribed, suggested warnings if not open skepticism.

Apart from metaphysical conceptions applied to it, the

work of physicists exerted a profound and continuing influence on all thought, philosophical and social. "It is, it appears, characteristic of the past thirty years or more," explained Alfred Cohn, in his work cited below, "that, in an unusual degree, a growing knowledge has instilled the belief, founded on deeper insight into natural processes than was possible to Locke and his successors, that there exists a vast difference between appearance and reality. I refer, of course, to the fact that atoms, as we are told, and consequently all matter, which they compose, consists to a small extent only of so-called 'solid' substance; this 'too, too solid flesh' is, in fact, far from being as solid as has been supposed. The appearance of things is indeed vastly different from reality. The realization of this discovery has had, as one can easily be persuaded, far-reaching consequences, both in physical theory and in the philosophy which reviews these theories and their underlying data critically."

Just what picture of nature scientists would finally acclaim, with unanimity, as having appearance corresponding to the reality, however, remained uncertain. At one period in the nineteenth century they had employed the imagery of the mechanical model: the physical world was a mechanism and it could be described in the non-mathematical language employed, for instance, in a simple description of a steam engine. A few among them still clung to this terminology and hoped that, after the new physics had settled down, the simple terms of mechanism would be again sufficient. Others expressed doubts as to its adequacy. In an essay on Modern Concepts in Physics and Their Relation to Chemistry, Irving Langmuir took his place among the skeptics. "We have no guarantee whatever," he concluded, "that nature is so constructed that it can be adequately described in terms of mechanical or electrical models; it is much more probable that our most fundamental relationships can only be expressed mathematically, if at all." The conditional phrase, "if at all," was arresting. That was, indeed, the query which rose on all sides among searchers for the connections between reality and appearance, between the nature of the world and visions of it, whether scientific, artistic, historical, literary, or theological.

Although no scientist now wrote a huge volume in the manner of Jeans and Eddington in mediation between scientific method and thought on the one side and lay method and thought on the other, Alfred Cohn, in a lecture entitled The Difference between Science and Art in Their Relation to Nature, incorporated with other essays, in his Medicine, Science and Art, published in 1931, projected adumbrations of the form which such mediation might assume in coming years. Trained in medicine, a specialist in cardio-vascular diseases, a member of the Rockefeller Institute for Medical Research, equipped with European experience and languages, Cohn was in a strategic position to describe the nature of scientific work and its relations to the rest of life and thought.

Science, he said, in language fairly intelligible to laymen, "is that effort which men keep making to understand deeply events in this world and in the universe and the method of their occurrence," and it proceeds by analysis, observation, classification, meticulous description, and interpretation. The definition was broad: "Not long since, the study of nature was confined to the non-sentient world, the world outside the perceiving mind of man. But times change. . . . A new and vigorous assault is in progress, destined perhaps to illuminate, maybe to annihilate, the old doctrine which separated mind and body. . . . Critical philosophers are again beginning to concern themselves [with] that world of the mind which seems to lie outside of and actually to escape the will but which, nevertheless, is accessible to experience and appears in fact to be that part of the mental apparatus in which experience, often completely forgotten in our waking hours, is stored. . . . This function of the whole human organism is also a phase of nature."

While scientists in general go forward with analysis and description into details, the most powerful intellects among them, Cohn contended, have another object: "To make statements about the world, and as few of them as possible, the proof of their value being that they be genuinely descriptive and permit the deepest possible insight into its processes." This is exactly what Harvey, Newton, Clerk-Maxwell, and Einstein, for example, actually did. Any layman could understand that, even one who saw no connection between the indeterminism of physics and the free will of theology. School children could read in their elementary texts that "every mass tends towards every other mass with a force varying directly as the product of the masses and inversely as the square of their distances apart." That was a majestic generalization about an almost infinite number of particularities in "as few words as possible." It could be grasped by any mind able to comprehend the ancient rule : "The squares of the two containing sides joined together are equal to the square of the hypotenuse."

More significant in adumbrating coming forms of scientific interest were Cohn's conclusions respecting the nature of the scientist and the scientific method. The conception of complete objectivity, of a mind entirely empty of concerns and presumptions, he dismissed without hesitation : "We no longer believe that the eye of any beholder is disinterested. Nor, as a matter of fact, can I learn that this was ever believed to be true." In examining the history of great scientific discoveries, Cohn took cognizance of meditation, inspiration, and intuition, as well as knowledge and experience. Archimedes, according to tradition, observing the water of his bath overflowing as he stepped into it, suddenly solved a long-pondered problem and was so excited by the flash of insight that he ran home without his clothes, shouting "I have found it! I have found it!" Similar incidents illustrating the scientific method Cohn derived from the lives of Harvey, Kepler, and Newton : "Their solutions were, in the present sense, all intuitions — the nucleus of their thought had slowly been maturing, had long been dormant, had been the continuous irritant that left them no peace, until an arrangement in some simple order dawned upon them. Harvey, in describing his discovery that the blood in animals circulates, confessed, 'I frequently and seriously bethought me, and long revolved in my mind'; and in the end declared triumphantly, 'I began to think whether there might not be a motion, as it were, in a circle.'"

This instrument of science, called for convenience intuition for want of a better word, Cohn defined as "the function by which, as the result of experience, usually extensive and often profound, I know with incredible swiftness, within the time of a lightning flash, what inference I must draw in an argument or what action I must take in a difficult situation. I have used the phrase 'experience usually extensive and often profound.' Because I have experience of this sort, though I need not be conscious of its possession, I can in argument or a situation arrive at a conclusion far in advance either of one inexperienced or of one not previously interested in a related problem. I arrive at the result I need quickly; I telescope, as I say, with the speed of lightning, the thought perhaps of years which engrosses ponderously the energy and the time of other men. . . . Of the process itself I can say little. The function is not one of the conscious reason. Indeed, the conscious reason cannot force it into activity. This much can be said: the extra-conscious activity requires the painful preparation which is the function of the mind in its conscious period."

What Cohn actually did in his report on the nature of science, therefore, was to bring scientists into that stream of social and psychological realism so long a force in general thought. Without condemning, he eschewed mysticism, related the scientist to his medium of experience, and sought the roots and nature of that "inspiration" or "intuition" to be found in great science and art. Independently, sociologists had reached the conclusion that the mentality of each normal human person is encircled by "a social frame of memory," is not a tabula rasa, an empty sensitive plate, at any time, in acts of observation, procedure, and thought. The problem of genius or hero or leader in science, Cohn left unsolved, just where sociologists had left it in their domain, after giving positive intimations of its elements. But by stating the problem and by tracing the differences and similarities of science and art, he gave recognition to the steadily accumulating impingements of social environment upon science and to the intimate relations of science and art.

In essence Cohn's testament was an indication of a movement toward the unification of the many divisions of human interest long sundered by petty minds unable to wrestle with it and by generous minds unwilling to face it or paralyzed by its ramifications. If the movement was to continue, there were grounds for the expectation that all the arts and sciences would be enriched by interchanges and brought more intimately into the services of the life and society that nourished them.

From another angle of vision, that of the mathematician, Alfred Cohn's summation of trends in science was confirmed — by Tobias Dantzig in his Aspects of Science, published in 1936. Physical science, he reported, has abandoned "the naïve realism of the classical period. . . . It has recognized the anthropomorphic origin and nature of human knowledge. Be it determinism or rationality, empiricism or the mathematical method, it has recognized that man is the measure of all things, and that there is no other measure." The efforts of scientists to rationalize all nature and all history have failed. Attempts to supplant, to support, or to demonstrate the validity of religion by the scientific method have likewise come to naught. Even the ideas indispensable to scientific thought, such as inductive inference, space, duration, motion, derive their validity from neither logic nor experience; they are rooted in race sublimations and are "tinged with collective predilections." Scientific theories are linked with action; they take meaning from action, and they are revised as action proceeds. Science as such knows no single absolute. Nothing in "these amazing electrons" dictates action. The sources of action lie in mankind and, by collective predilections, the sphere of action is created and enlarged. Therein science works. Only therein can science work. If Dantzig's report was correct, the separation of physical science from the texture of all human thought, interest, and action was not even theoretically possible.

At bottom, then, the experiences classed under the head of science did not differ in any absolute manner from experiences in other so-called domains of human interest. Its votaries were disturbed by "outside" events, shared the hopes and frustrations common to mankind, and responded in some fashion to the insistent demands of practice. The idea that they were a peculiar group working without any assumption or preconceptions respecting the nature of things and thought, on the basis of "demonstrated" and "indefeasible" facts, steadily lost prestige as inquiries into the character and background of scientific methods, activities, and generalizations proceeded. No unbridgeable chasm, for instance, separated the scientist from the artist in methods of work and intellectual operations. The forces of culture penetrated, it was recognized, the laboratory of the physicist as well as the closet of the politician, and conditioned thought and conclusions there prevailing. Nor did scientists, any more than anybody else, escape unscathed the gravamen of the tragic conflict between the ideal and the real that had tormented great spirits for centuries and had inspired momentous actions designed to draw them closer together.

CHAPTER XVI

Frames of Social Thought

As in physical nature the flash of lightning always pre-
cedes the roll of thunder, so in human affairs the
flame of thought has always gone before a transformation in the social arrangements of mankind. In
Machiavelli, it presaged the triumph of the National State
over the ruins of feudalism and the disruption of the Church
Universal; in Montesquieu and Rousseau, the overthrow of
absolutism; in Adam Smith and Ricardo, the flowering of
capitalism; in Mary Wollstonecraft, the dissolution of the
patriarchal regime; in Marx and Engels, the upswing of the
world-wide proletarian movement; in Sorel, Pareto, and
Mosca, the uprush of fascism. Was there such a flash in
the United States during the tumults of the midpassage, and,
if so, what was presaged?

§

As in previous years, the function of writing voluminous
and systematic works on government, economy, society, and
social destiny was assigned mainly to professors in the

academies, or to men and women trained in the academies, although newspapers in expressing contempt for an idea found endless satisfaction in caricaturing it as a professor with a mortarboard on his head and a scholar's gown hanging from his shoulders.

This allocation of erudite thinking to the academies did not mean, however, that the professors had a monopoly on thought or that they excogitated their premises and syllogisms wholly within ivory towers. As in other times thought was expressed in the homely sayings of the people-at-large, in articles, essays, manifestos, editorials, belles lettres, and works of plastic art. If at first glance such classification as to origins seemed to mark a division of thought distinct enough to require wholly separate expositions, more deliberation suggested a pause. In fact great treatises on philosophy couched in language far beyond the reach of peasants and artisans had always rested more or less and continued to rest more or less on the broad base of maxims or axioms representing the common-sense experiences of ordinary humanity. Even natural science, as E. W. Hobson explained in his Domain of Natural Science, sprang from the observations of primitive peoples and, in its development, revolved around common-sense assumptions and "animal faiths," despite flights into the realm of higher physics and metaphysics. Franklin Giddings' sociological axiom, "consciousness of kind," expressed in another form the old saying, "Birds of a feather flock together." Nor could the hardest-headed practitioner in economic affairs, without renown as a thinker, maintain that he had no idea of what he was doing — no idea gathered up in association with his fellows, fellows having their background among the people.

Whenever a great system of thought, called philosophy, got down into the dusty way of life as a dynamic force — and such systems often had — the intrusion and drive were due, certainly in part, to the fact that the system, in essentials, expressed or was translated into current proverbs and maxims sometimes of hoary age. Thus, for instance, in his recondite philosophy of history, Hegel assumed, like farmers and housewives, the existence of God and the manifestations of God's will in human affairs. Farmers and housewives also had known something about conflicts and contradictions in life though they had not formulated a dialectical coverage. In transmuting Hegel's dialectics and applying it to practical politics, Karl Marx reduced it in the Communist Manifesto to terms intelligible to the proletariat of all lands.

Indeed thought in every age had seemed to flow in a kind of cycle, out of current proverbs into erudite coverage and back again into common sayings. The process was illustrated in 1931 when Albert H. Wiggin, head of the Chase National Bank, engaged in instructing a Senate Committee at Washington, based his philosophy of finance on the maxim of "let us alone," therewith merely repeating a "truism" of the marketplace that had formerly got into the heavy pages of Adam Smith and David Ricardo and out again into the marts of trade.

In the effulgence of the golden glow, the most general system of American thought, upon which professors and nearly everybody else drew for inspiration, was that of smooth and ready acceptance of the prevailing order, from which Satan and nearly all evil had been effectively banished. Its central conception was that the United States of America was a pretty good place, just as constituted. Its special interests were comfort, convenience, pecuniary advancement, emulatory display, salesmanship, unbroken progress in the straight utilitarian direction, and efficiency, with education as a preparation for the realization and enjoyment of such interests. Its philosophy was on the whole "matter-of-fact" and pragmatic. Our world will go on very much this way forever; and if disturbances should arise, we can "recover" the past again by doing more of the same thing we had been doing. There will be no more devastating jars to the American social order, no more wars, revolutions, cataclysms, and national tragedies.

Even after the glow had faded, faith in this system continued to be general and was compressed into neat linguistic forms such as: return to prosperity, recovery, restoration, bigger and better, bad luck today, better luck tomorrow, stage a big come-back, and the good old way. So soothing and pervasive was the creed that clergymen, as a whole, seemed inclined to preach fewer fierce sermons on man as a sinful creature, a wicked beast, and to spend more time in denouncing "Reds" than in condemning the "works of the devil." Under the popular system of thought, man had become "a pretty good fellow," and would continue to be as long as he followed his acquisitive nose assiduously enough.

While all went well with the best of systems, neither business men nor politicians nor practitioners of any type paid much attention to the logic-chopping and hair-splitting of professors occupied in refining the maxims of Adam Smith, Ricardo, Boehm-Bawerk, and John Bates Clark. Occasionally the irate alumni of a university rejoiced in the expulsion of a professor who got too far off the beaten track but they bothered their heads little, if at all, about furious disputes over marginal utility or the relation of competition to the survival of the fittest, or fine distinctions between production and consumption. The situation changed, however, after the depression spread desolation all around. Then economic and political practitioners began to search feverishly for explanations of the plight into which they had fallen and to wonder how they could get out of it. Then the keepers of the higher learning were remembered and the function of systematic thinking received more consideration than had been the case in the days of automatic prosperity.

§

While the economic stringency struck at the financial resources of the educational system from the universities to the elementary schools, the influence of the academies on American life increased rather than diminished during the midpassage. There were a number of reasons for this expansion of influence. One was the larger proportion of college graduates in positions of public and private power, partly owing to the lavish support which had been given to the higher learning and the rush of young people to its seats. Presidents Coolidge, Hoover, and Franklin D. Roosevelt were all college graduates: Coolidge from Amherst; Hoover from Leland Stanford; and Roosevelt from Harvard. Not only that. Seven of the ten members of Roosevelt's Cabinet were college graduates: Cordell Hull held a degree from Cumberland University Law School; Homer Cummings from Yale; Claude A. Swanson from Randolph-Macon; Henry A. Wallace from Iowa State College; Daniel Roper from Trinity College, now called Duke University; Harold Ickes from Chicago University; Frances Perkins from Mount Holyoke. Only three members of the Cabinet were outside the category: Henry Morgenthau had spent a brief season at Cornell; James A. Farley and Harry Woodring, according to Who's Who, had come up through the university of hard knocks. Among the Lords of Creation deemed masters in the world of business enterprise, as we have seen, a large majority were college graduates, the New England institutions providing the major portion of the leadership. Evidently the days of log-cabin Presidents and office-boy wizards of finance had come to a close. Even among village bankers, members of town councils, and state legislators, as well as clerks and minor office holders, the proportion of college-trained men and women was phenomenal.

While the thought cultivated in the higher academies percolated through graduates into business and government, the universities and colleges were taking possession of the whole public school system as well as private schools. Prohibitions on child labor had lengthened the school years for more boys and girls, and the curtailment of employment opportunities in the depression had served to stretch out the education of young persons in high schools and colleges. By subsidizing thousands of students through the agency of the Youth Administration, headed by Aubrey Williams, the Federal Government enabled them to advance further in education. The intensified competition in the race for teaching positions, even in elementary schools, gave superiority to men and women who held the higher degrees. No longer was it easily possible for boys and girls just out of elementary schools or high schools to find places within the system as teachers. Thus the influence of the higher learning penetrated the entire process of popular education.

College graduates who did not go into teaching were now more inclined than formerly toward political action as a type of personal career or toward official public service. When opportunities in private business contracted, the once belittled "government job" did not seem so contemptible and, besides, improvements in the personnel administration of government, coupled with a growing interest in public welfare, made the civil service more attractive than ever to ambitious youth. Through one channel or another, therefore, the spirit and learning of the academies were insinuated into all divisions of public administration.

Into business as well as teaching and government, the influences of the academies reached with ever-increasing force. Since most of the Lords of Creation had been college men, in some instances their minds reverted to their old preceptors when the best of all possible worlds about which they had heard so much on campuses was badly damaged by events in the marketplace. To be sure they did not always remember the names of the dons under whom they had been trained; when a graduate of Harvard, class of 1906, was asked to name some professors who had made an impression upon him in his college days, he could recall only the distinguished Professor Taussig as "Professor Towsig." But the memories of others were better. Besides, business men of the larger establishments had long been accustomed to have at beck and call college-trained accountants, engineers, and other specialists to tell them what they wanted to know and hear. A few corporations employed "economic advisers" from the academies and a prominent financial house put upon its staff a teacher of finance to instruct it in the theory of money.

Consequently, when the alarms of the business crisis pierced their air-conditioned rooms, any of them in search of thought could press a button to summon his philosophic and literary consultant. It was in keeping with the state of things, accordingly, for Albert H. Wiggin of the Chase National Bank, to give as a handout, to the press and a Senate committee groping in darkness, a one-page summary of right thinking in the shape of a succinct formulation of classical economics by Benjamin Anderson, once of Missouri, now the "economic adviser" of the Chase Bank.

When the Liberty League was organized to "sell" the philosophy of big business to the voters, it took counsel with a few friendly professors and their disciples in the profession of law, as well as public relations experts. At its successive conventions and in preparing its literature of thought and propaganda, the National Manufacturers Association likewise drew upon text books and academicians whenever necessary to confirm established convictions. In a strict sense, of course, this procedure was not an innovation, for the covering of interest by ideology had been a common custom in ages past. The divine right of kings had its Filmer and Bossuet. In 1852 the theological, economic, anthropological, and sociological demonstration that chattel slavery was the best possible system in the circumstances was perfected in a treatise frankly called the Pro-Slavery Argument, composed by Thomas R. Dew of the University of Virginia, professor of history, metaphysical, natural, and national law, government, and political economy. Whether the elaboration of manufacturing theory in 1935 or 1937 meant that the demonstration of manufacturing practice was insufficiently convincing to the generality of people, or that manufacturers were in a fair way to become philosophers could not be determined on the basis of any data lending themselves to tabulation. It did seem to indicate, however, that business interests were not entirely content with their inherited wrappers of thought.

Even more imperative than in private business was systematic thought when planning and action in government were involved. After all, private business had no legislative and executive unity; it was a congeries of particular interests requiring limited if exact knowledge respecting particular enterprises; and, if one or more great corporations went into bankruptcy, the episode was not necessarily ruinous to the nation. On the other hand, government embraced all interests, economic and cultural; persistent thought about it had to be comprehensive, systematic, and informed by immense knowledge, unless government was to fail and bring other institutions down with it. This fact had been recognized during the eighteenth-century crisis with which the Constitution of the United States was designed to deal; and it was fortunate for the country that the chief architect of that frame of social thought, James Madison, trained at Princeton, was an assiduous student of history and government and a systematic thinker as well. Madison was as indispensable to the convention that framed the Constitution as were the hard-headed men of practice associated with him in the undertaking.

It was more than a coincidence that in the great crisis of 1929 in commerce, economy, banking, and finance, analogous in many respects to the breakdown of 1786, systematic thinkers trained in universities were again drawn upon for counsel and public service. They had, of course, not been entirely neglected in times immediately preceding. For instance, the Industrial Commission, charged with investigating economic conditions in 1898, had made extensive use of college men in the course of its inquiry, especially of Professor Jeremiah Whipple Jenks of Cornell University; and to Professor Jenks was committed the task of writing its report on Industrial Combinations and Prices.

This precedent President Hoover was following when, in September, 1929, he called upon a research committee com-

posed of professors, "to examine and report upon recent
social trends in the United States with a view to providing
such a review as might supply a basis for the formulation of
large national policies looking to the next phase in the nation's development." Through the agency of numerous experts the Committee made exhausting if not exhaustive
researches and reported changes in every department of
American life during the preceding decade or beyond. One
thing it declared indispensable: "Willingness and determination to undertake important integral changes in the reorganization of social life, including the economic and the
political orders, rather than the pursuance of a policy of
drift." It is true that in his brief foreword to the Committee's
report, finished in October, 1932, President Hoover displayed
no great enthusiasm over the findings of the Committee,
but by that time three years of business casualties had indicated rather conclusively that profound changes were in fact
taking place in American economy and society.

When Franklin D. Roosevelt took the reins of government he made wholesale use of professors as counselors and
administrators. During his first campaign and after his
inauguration, he was surrounded by a group of personal
advisers from universities, which included Raymond Moley,
Felix Frankfurter, Rexford Tugwell, and Adolf Berle, popularly known as the "Brain Trust." Three of the group,
Moley, Tugwell, and Berle, were given official positions in the
Roosevelt administration for periods short or long; and many
other officials were drawn from university circles, for example,
M. L. Wilson in agriculture; O. M. Sprague and Jacob Viner
in finance; Thurman W. Arnold in enforcement of antitrust
laws; and James Landis in the securities and exchange commission. Indeed the use of professors became so general that
it was made a target for ridicule and attack by political and
business critics, and so contemptuous became the derision of
the "brain trust" by the opposition that a member of the
Cabinet shot back: "With what part of his anatomy should
a man think?"

Nevertheless, when the Republicans prepared to drive the Roosevelt administration out of power in 1936, newspapers reported that they too had assembled something like a brain trust, including Professor Thomas N. Carver of Harvard and Professor Edwin W. Kemmerer of Princeton, to advise the directors of the campaign. The following year when Republican managers began again to search for an explanation of their misfortunes and for an avenue to victory, they created a large council of advisers headed by Dr. Glenn Frank, who had recently been president of the University of Wisconsin — until the Progressives ousted him. It seemed, therefore, that it was not the professor as such but the style of his thought that excited praise or derision — according to circumstances and predilections. At any rate, wherever comprehensive knowledge and systematic thinking were regarded as useful, consultation with the possessors of brains was considered appropriate, and perhaps advantageous. Thought was elusive and troublesome and yet practitioners, high and low, apparently could not get along without it — or with it. In America it could scarcely be said of scholars as was said of Lavoisier when he was sent to the guillotine: "La Republique n'a pas besoin de savants."

Given the intimate and varied relations of professors in the academies, and of the students they trained, to the education of the nation from the primary school upward and to the conduct of practical affairs, inquirers into the nature and future of civilization in America had to ask what the professors were studying and teaching and thinking that had a bearing on American society in gross and in detail. Under what frames or schemes of social thought were they operating as teachers, advisers, and writers? Where did they stand in the conflict of ideas and interests, in the clash of tendencies and systems? Did they avoid issues or face them in the full light of their knowledge as courageous seers? Did they regard themselves as belonging to a privileged gild entitled to go its own way without reference to the fate of society? Did they favor particular interests or seek overarching hypotheses of values under which adjustments, reconciliations, and elisions might be made in theory and practice? To what extent was the appearance of schools and controversies among professors due to personal or institutional emulation in the competition for prestige? In what direction and in what manner were they prosecuting their researches in economics, political science, sociology, education, philosophy, and history? In what systematic and comprehensive treatises were they revealing their thought and the fruits of their investigations?

§

As befitted a country that esteemed itself eminently "practical," writers and teachers who dealt with economic matters stood first on the roll of popular consideration; and in books, papers, essays, journals, and proceedings the thinking of economists was fairly well revealed. Unlike members of the encyclopaedia group in the old regime of France, they did not have to write in a manner that required the public to distinguish between what they said and what they really thought. On the whole, so far as they were given to comprehensive schemes of theory, economists adhered rather closely to the classical heritage of laissez faire received from Adam Smith and Richard Ricardo, though in forms refined and polished by many hands in the intervening years. Despite the agitations of labor in town and country, the dislocating effects of inventions, the development of administered prices, the depletion of natural resources, recurring wars, and preparations for wars, no radical departures from accepted doctrine came to dominate the academies, considered collectively. Neither the optimism of the golden glow nor the afflictions of the business and social depression altered in any fundamental respect the perdurance of this general cast of thought in academic cogitations.

Indeed in 1931 right in the middle of the great disequilibrium, it was presented to the public by the president of the Chase National Bank in the form of a summary by Doctor

Benjamin Anderson, adviser of that institution. Taking for granted, without mention, his assumptions respecting the nature of man and the permanence, for practical purposes, of "the natural order," Anderson plunged into his thesis: "In general it is not the function of government under the capitalist system to produce or perform economic services. The actual direction of industry, the decision whether more wheat shall be planted and less corn, or more shoes shall be produced and less hats, is not made by the State, or by collective society, but is left to the choice of independent producers. These independent producers make their decisions with reference to the state of the market. The up-and-down movements of prices and wages determine whether more or less of a given thing shall be produced. . . . Under this system of free, private enterprise, with free movement of labor and capital from industry to industry, the tendency is for an automatic balance to be maintained and for goods and services to be supplied in right proportions. A social order is created, a social coöperation is worked out, largely unconscious and largely automatic under the play of the impersonal forces of market prices and wages. . . . The ability to understand the highly intricate economic life of today, the ability to see through it and to see the different parts in relation to one another, to coördinate wants and efforts, to distribute resources properly among conflicting claimants — this ability does not exist." Hence Anderson concluded that any effort to use economic theory effectively "in the actual regulation of economic life," in the way of social planning and control, "is an impossibility." In short, individuals, government, and society stood in the presence of an unconscious, largely automatic, self-adjusting system, akin to the mechanism of nature. Nothing constructive on a national scale could be done about it. It was too elemental.

Persistently as the classical doctrine hovered in the foreground or background of economic thought, it nevertheless encountered, even in academic groves, some neglect and dissent. No economist furbished it up in a grand re-statement that brought forth universal acclaim. Judging by the character of monographs and treatises turned out, there were several "schools" of economists at work and many economists were more interested in particular economic activities than in any comprehensive theory about their common nature or their overarching "laws." Rather than refine and recast syllogisms, scholars of this inclination preferred to study and describe particular economic institutions, such as banks, railways, corporations, public utilities, and trade unions, and for this reason were loosely called "institutionalists."

In some measure the tendency to institutionalism was due to discontent with classical theory, to a belief that the creed did not correspond to the facts in the case, that it assumed an economic man, a static order of society, and a "normal equilibrium" which did not exist anywhere, that it neglected change and development in society, that it minimized the influence of institutional loyalties on human conduct. To this extent, institutional economics acted as a dissolving force on economic orthodoxy and boded ill for the kind of thick-and-thin defense which capitalists were likely to expect in academies supported by endowments or taxes on property.

Whatever the explanation of their dissent or their proclivities, the institutionalists were by no means united on a platform of their own. Those who chose merely to study and describe a single institutional set-up, such as banking or transportation, could evade almost entirely the necessity of thought and the imputation of heterodoxy by sticking close to surface and reputable facts. Economists who did this were institutionalists in the strictest sense of the term. If, however, an economist went below the surface of reputable facts into underlying facts, for example those registered in law suits and legislative investigations, he encountered practices out of conformity with the canons of reputability and, by describing them or checking theory against them, was almost sure to collide with the advertised moral canons of the business community. If, perchance, an institutionalist thought persistently about the relation of any single branch of economic activity to the rest of society or considered the probable upshot of any special development, such as corporate concentration, he incurred the ethical hazard of committing himself to some theory or interpretation of all economy and its evolution.

So, to speak broadly, there were two schools of institutionalists: the strictly and narrowly descriptive who ventured no large interpretations; and the more thoughtful who accepted as their general guide either classical theory or some competing scheme of doctrine. A few institutionalists combined the function of description with that of interpretation, but this involved an occupational hazard perilous to academic calm. Apart from fine distinctions, what the institutionalists really did was to establish on a factual basis the integrated, national, and collective character of American economy without providing a corresponding theory for the guidance of practice.

With the institutionalists were sometimes bracketed the economists who devoted themselves to "quantitative analysis" and the preparation of graphs showing the fluctuations of production, prices, wages, and other elements of economy in time movement. Although the quantifiers stood on their own ground, the results of their researches, plotted in rises and declines, strengthened an institutionalist conviction that the normalcy or equilibrium of orthodox economics was somewhat mythical in nature. Coupled in spirit with such inquirers were economists who investigated and described what Americans were fond of calling "trends," that is, "lines of development" in selected institutions or practices. As early inquiries in geology, chemistry, biology, and ecology prepared the way for Darwin's synthesis, so the labors of the institutionalists, quantifiers, and trendists might be opening the road for a general reconstruction of covering theory.

Ranking high among the volumes and special studies produced by the institutional school was The Modern Corporation and Private Property, published in 1932, by Adolf Berle and Gardiner Means, both of whom later entered the service of the Federal Government. Their work was an elaborate description of corporate structures and operations. It showed that control over about thirty-eight per cent of all business wealth in the United States, apart from banking, was concentrated in the hands of two hundred immense corporations. After attempting to estimate, as far as the records would permit, the number of stockholders in these concerns, Berle and Means gave special consideration, on the basis of legal and other factual materials, to the managerial methods employed by the directors and heads of corporations.

The upshot was a demonstration that corporations were dominated, as a rule, by trustees who held only a small proportion of the stock, and that the multitude of nominal "owners" had little influence on the management of "their own property." Through loose charters of incorporation, secured in such states as Delaware, through the separation of "voting stock" from common stock, through voting trusts, and other legal devices, not mentioned in Adam Smith or Ricardo, a relatively small number of men, assisted or ruled by bankers, had a fairly free hand in managing the two hundred corporations, diverting surpluses, appropriating salaries to officers, and giving bonuses to members of the managerial personnel. In the light of this upshot the automatic distribution of wealth through the price mechanism did not seem to be quite perfect, unless the corporation trustees were to be regarded as automatons when they appropriated bonuses to their associates and themselves.

Having described the structure of corporate industry, Berle and Means compared it with the use and wont of property on which the assumptions of classical theory rested. The early manufacturer or business man owned real property, as distinguished from paper claims to property. He resided near his material possessions and generally carried direct responsibility in management. In those simple days the issue of paper was ordinarily for the purpose of extending operations, to acquire or construct real property, not merely to buy stock in other property, perhaps at a high price. That is, under the old system, moral responsibility generally went with ownership; under the new system, the multitudinous owners of corporations had little or no responsibility for management, labor, or anything else. Since highly profitable operations could be effected by merely combining or buying into existing corporations, entirely apart from any increase in plant or the production of wealth, a large section of business enterprise bore no relation to the function which justified its existence, even in classical theory, namely, the increase of real capital and the production of real wealth in the form of goods and services. This general picture of enterprise had been elaborated by Veblen long before; but not until Berle and Means published their treatise was the extent of the factitious element in business even dimly appreciated by those interested in such matters.

The study of the modern corporation was supplemented later by Liquid Claims to Wealth, by Adolf Berle and Victoria Pederson, published in 1934. This work, also factual and statistical, traced the historical development of the proportion which the paper expression of wealth bore to real wealth. In other words, here was a picture of a "trend." On the basis of elaborate evidence the authors showed that the proportion of liquid claims to real national wealth rose from about sixteen per cent in 1880 to around forty per cent in 1930, and that the jump between 1912 and 1930 had been almost equal to the rise from the foundation of America to the year 1880. In a brief term of years about one-sixth of the national wealth had shifted from the hands of responsible owners into the hands of corporate managerial or manipulating groups; another half a century, at the same rate, would see all real property blanketed by paper claims of one kind or another. In this development, Berle and Pederson found a "reorientation of life," of all moral relations connected with management, economy, responsibility, labor, thrift, and prudence. The direct ownership of real property accompanied by personal management had meant independence, liberty, and responsibility. Ownership through the possession of liquid claims — such as stocks, bonds, and bank deposits — meant dependence, inter-dependence, and a different kind of moral responsibility, if society itself was to endure.

In a minute study of price variations, made for the Department of Agriculture and published as a government document, Gardiner Means dealt with inflexible or managed prices and compared them with prices in areas where corporate control did not exist or had a slight effect on price variations — agriculture, for example. In part, Means declared, the inflexibility was due to monopoly elements, including control of patents. In part it came from the overhead costs and fixed charges of corporate structure and management. Whatever the source, stiff prices existed in large areas of economic enterprise, put a drag on rapid adjustments, and served as an economic drain on those areas where competitive flexibility prevailed, more or less. Here also was a picture of economic practice that did not correspond exactly with the configuration on which classical theory rested.

From the Brookings Institution in Washington, D. C., issued reports likewise descriptive in character, bearing such self-explanatory titles as America's Capacity to Produce, America's Capacity to Consume, and The Formation of Capital. These works, too, were institutional in approach and factual in supporting evidence. The first showed that even in the golden glow, in the year 1929, the productive plant of the United States was running at approximately eighty-one per cent of its capacity. Here was another statistical picture that did not precisely conform to the classical imagery, under which each enterpriser made the best and fullest use of his capital in the circumstances and the combined result of all operations was an almost peak output of national wealth.

The second Brookings study in institutional economics, dealing with America's capacity to consume, indicated that the American people were not fully supplied with the houses, consumers' goods, and services required for a high general standard of living. In other words, American business was not held down to a low level of capacity merely because the people had practically everything they needed; because the domestic market was saturated. Then what was the trouble? A statistical study of the distribution of income in the United States in 1929 indicated "that 0.1 per cent of the families at the top received practically as much as forty-two per cent of the families at the bottom of the scale." Although available figures did not permit perfect exactness by any means, the Brookings conclusions, if extensively discounted, showed a serious disparity in the buying power that went to the few and the buying power that went to the many.

If these conclusions did not invalidate the contention of classical economics that the distribution of wealth in capitalist economy roughly approximates deserts and justice, they did raise a question respecting the efficiency of that distribution, that is, its power to keep business enterprise producing at or near the capacity point. Mass production required a correlative mass buying power and in actual operation business enterprise did not seem to be furnishing it. This was another discrepancy between theory and practice and aroused some curiosity among those Americans whose reading was not confined to romances.

The third Brookings investigation, into the formation of capital, brought out still another discrepancy. According to classical theory, savings were necessary to the constant increase of capital and went into plant extensions which furnished employment and augmented the production of wealth, at least in the main and quite beneficently. Looking at the facts in the case, the Brookings Institution found that, between 1927 and 1929, the major portion of "surplus savings" went not into the construction of new wealth-producing plants but into refunding operations and into bidding up the prices of already existing liquid claims to wealth — stocks and bonds.

This also seemed to confirm earlier suspicions. About thirty years before the Brookings discovery, Veblen had concluded, on a factual basis less extensive, that a large share of capitalist operations had nothing whatever to do with the production of real wealth. In truth too, as Ida Tarbell's work on the Standard Oil Company indicated, a number of business men, not educated in the universities, had come to suspect the validity of the theory, taught by John Bates Clark, at Columbia University, that all economic activities, apart from the consumption of goods, were "productive" in character.

Somewhat in the vein of the Brookings inquiry into America's capacity to produce, although on different lines, was the study conducted by Harold Loeb and associates, including a number of engineers, which eventuated in the publication entitled The Chart of Plenty. The Brookings investigators took existing plant capacity as the area of their inquiry. Loeb and his associates extended the area to cover also natural resources and technological potentials in American economy. They sought to find out what and how much America could produce if all skills, machines, processes, and resources were brought into full and efficient operation. As a result of their researches they reached the conclusion that this full and efficient operation could provide every American family with goods and services to the annual value of approximately $5000. Although the Loeb philosophy and findings were sometimes confused with Technocracy, which made a popular furor about the time of the great economic crash, they stood on an independent footing.

Whether The Chart of Plenty really belonged in the domain of institutional economics was, however, a subject of dispute. In a strict sense it did not. It belonged rather in the sphere of engineering rationality. Dealing with what was technologically possible, it left more or less out of account what was sociologically possible. Not without some reason, therefore, did professional economists regard it as "utopian." At the same time there was significance for economic theory in the fact that managers of industries could produce twice as much wealth if they could get a free hand to operate at capacity speed.

Perhaps the best notable example of institutional economics in its most comprehensive form was Adolf Berle's memorandum on "Investigation of Business Organizations and Practices" prepared in the summer of 1938 for the federal committee engaged on the inquiry into monopolies, published in Plan Age for September of that year. In this document appeared the realism of Berle's approach to the subject, the meditative character of his analysis, and the constructive nature of his thought about policy. Early in this paper Berle warned the committee against taking for granted the easy assumptions of the marketplace — the folk lore of capitalism — such as the preconceptions that small business is necessarily competitive, that small business is necessarily humane, that the efficiency of a business bears a positive relation to size, that the highly praised productivity of industry does in fact meet the "legitimate claims" made against it by labor, consumers, and investors.

To this warning Berle added a caution against the common assumption that the relation of government to business is merely incidental to industrial processes. In a few pages as dispassionate as a telephone book, he cited illustrations: direct government subsidies, for instance, to aviation and the merchant marine; indirect subsidies — low mail rates to newspapers; government purchases; special privileges — patents, copyrights, and licenses; tariffs; protection against price fluctuations; collateral subsidies — to the automobile industry through highway construction; public relief to take care of industry's unemployed in unprofitable seasons; direct loans; credits and banking facilities; regulation of rates; privileges to organized labor.

Knowing very well that no investigation of such a complicated problem could get anywhere merely by heaping up miscellaneous facts, that general objectives should be set in the beginning, that every specific problem has intimate relations with culture in its wide ranges, Berle proposed that the federal committee test economic organization by the following criteria : " (*a*) Does it provide an adequate supply of goods as tested by the normal market ? As tested by the apparent need ? (*b*) Does it provide a maximum number of people with an opportunity to make a living under this process — a life under this process — conceived as conditions under which people can live, maintain families, expect to continue in the economic system, and end this side of the relief line or poorhouse ? (*c*) Does it accomplish this process with due regard for the liberty and self-government of the individual ?" The idea that an industry was to be judged by its dividends to stockholders and not also by the number of its unemployed workers on relief, Berle rejected as not pertinent to national policy. Taking the constructive line, he analyzed control by methods of incorporation, by competition, by capital financing, by taxation, by patent legislation, by regulation, by private monopoly, by quasi-public ownership, and by public ownership and public production. Devastating to the insulated and closed dogmatism of the communist and classical schools, Berle's memorandum brought the consideration of economics down to earth and related it to going practices, reasonable human expectations, and explicit possibilities.

§

While the classical economists, the institutionalists, the quantifiers, and the trendists, as a rule, kept within a frame of thought that implied no drastic modifications in forms and ownership of property, other schools of economic opinion contemplated alterations more or less fundamental. As a matter of course, the Marxians continued and expanded their exploration and critique along the lines of their presuppositions. The transformation of economy in Russia, Italy, and Germany by acts of state power and the collectivist sweep in general gave more point to their analysis and theory, and commanded more consideration beyond their own ranks. Yet, despite the voluminous nature of their output in the United States, it was on the whole either narrowly orthodox or quarrelsome. Many theoreticians battled for the position of dominance among the faithful, and none attained undisputed preëminence. Sidney Hook, professor of philosophy in New York University, made studies of Marxism that displayed a command of the materials, but he was attacked more bitterly by men who claimed to possess the true faith than by professors called "bourgeois" in the everyday canon.

After the downfall of Trotsky in Russia, the school of Marxian commentators was splintered in America and the adepts devoted more energy, if possible, to the denunciation of one another than to the application of their scheme of thought to the American scene. No Kautsky, Lenin, or Bukharin arose in the United States to a place of intellectual mastery, and directed the swirl of petty controversy to any objectives of significance in either theory or practice. The nearest approach to this consummation was to be found in the articles printed in the magazine Science and Society. After all, the dogmatism apparently indigenous to central and eastern Europe seemed to evoke slight sympathy and less intellectual respect in the somewhat loose-jointed society of the American continent. Difficulties on this score were increased by the fact that one branch of the faithful was supposed to receive instructions respecting the correct line from Moscow, whereas the successors of Ivan the Terrible and Peter the Great were more concerned with the exigencies of Russian politics at home than with the logical and epistemological exactitude of Marxism in the United States.

Another invasion of orthodox thought was made by a group known as agrarians, for whom Herbert Agar spoke with knowledge and special persuasiveness. This school of thought, with its chief center in the south, at Vanderbilt University, attacked capitalism and its ethics as severely as did the Marxists, but offered another exit from the dilemma. Capitalism, it insisted, led to centralization, socialism, and servitude. Democracy, liberty, and security required a wider distribution of property, the multiplication of petty owners and industries, decentralization, handicrafts, and community sufficiency.

A few of the agrarians seemed to find their utopia realized in the golden age of the Old South where no capitalists disturbed rural bliss and the weary were at rest in their mansions. However, a touch of realistic history, imparted by other agrarians of the Old South, took most of the bloom off the Red Rose. Well aware of the illusions in the idyllic picture, the dissident agrarians offered a compromise. They understood that railways, electric power, and utilities in general might be useful in their ideal society to come but a redistribution of this kind of wealth was scarcely possible. Parcelling out railway ties, rails, power houses, and transformers among the populace, as Huey Long had seemed to suggest, was, indeed, not feasible at all. Conceding the point, the "forward looking" agrarians proposed to combine public ownership of great utilities with the redistribution of land and manufacturing. In emerging from manors and magnolias, agrarianism thus assumed a configuration by no means strange to the practice of American politics; nor was it entirely out of line with the humanistic tradition in the United States.

Some support for the agrarian scheme of thought was furnished by Catholic economists who refused to accept the matter-of-fact presuppositions underlying capitalist and Marxian economics. Catholic thinkers had never ruled ethics out of account or treated ethics as incidental to the main chance. With marked tenacity, the boldest economists among them had clung to mediaeval teachings relative to the just price and the fair wage, and their pertinacity had been reinforced by the various encyclicals of the Pope on labor and economy. No doubt the generality of the papal language permitted a great variety of views among the faithful in practical applications, and many Catholic economists did not differ materially from the classical school as far as practical upshot was concerned. In fact, wherever any conflict approached a line-up between fascism and communism, they showed a tendency to accept capitalistic fascism, if with reluctance. In the main, however, the Catholic economists were inclined to approve the distributionism of the agrarian school. Leaders in their grouping, such as John A. Ryan, continued undaunted in their emphasis on the ethical basis of economic policy, on the rights of labor, and on a wider distribution of wealth as a necessity of justice and social welfare. Here and there they encountered strenuous opposition from colleagues and members of the hierarchy but, within the limits of essential doctrine touching faith and morals, they enjoyed their liberty of thought and exercised their freedom to explore practice and propose policy.

Apart from group excursions into economic thought were individual forays. By his Folklore of Capitalism, issued in 1937, Thurman W. Arnold, professor in the Yale Law School, gave a considerable jolt to the purveyors of current maxims in business and economics. Though received as a systematic treatise done in the grand manner, Arnold's volume really did not belong within that designation. It was rather a realistic and ingenious analysis of the sayings of the marketplace and the schools, which often had little relevance to practice and generally stood in the way of understanding and manipulating concrete situations. Its merit lay in the application of the scientific, or clinical, method to the maladjustments and distresses of going concerns. For example, Arnold called attention to the fact that the staff of an insane asylum did not devote time to classifying the ideas of the inmates, but employed their skill in trying to make the patients comfortable. Of course, this was both amusing and suggestive; at the same time it revealed the author's method. The illustration was an analogy and came dangerously near to the kind of folklore that he was subjecting to destructive analysis. At bottom the Folklore of Capitalism was diagnostic, rather than systematic or therapeutic, but in an age of easy assumptions it was effective in exploding many unreal maxims of the counting house, the corner store, and the cloister.

Other individuals, such as Paul Douglas, Stuart Chase, Mary Van Kleek, Walton Hamilton, Broadus Mitchell, James Bonbright, and Harry Pratt Fairchild, also challenged the presuppositions of the logical faith in economics and, having done so, considered things deemed possible as well as necessary. Yet their work was, in the main, exploratory and piece-meal rather than systematic and universal in range. In substance it was primarily institutional, but without the amoral disclaimers of that persuasion. When Miss Van Kleek surveyed the coal industry, for instance, she gave "the essential facts" of the industry, but did not stop there. From the survey she proceeded to a constructive proposal running counter to the philosophy of automatic beneficence. Realizing that a good logician could get out of a major premise all that had been put into it, Miss Van Kleek avoided preliminary commitments that prevented her from seeing the coal industry as disorganized and demoralized. She assumed that the business of the industry was to mine and distribute coal and, after inquiring into its actual state, advanced to an examination of the methods most likely to sustain the function for which the industry was supposed to exist. If not iconoclastic, this was at least critical, for orthodoxy had assumed that the coal industry must work about as well as possible "in the natural course" or under the "invisible hand" of Providence. In time the multiplication of such inquiries was bound to have an effect on the most adamant system of insulated thought.

§

A similar influence was to be exerted by the work and memory of Thorstein Veblen. As if symbolically, in 1929, the year of the great crack in business enterprise, Veblen died in a little cabin near Stanford University, long the

scene of his labors and tribulations; but his work lived, and
five years later Joseph Dorfman gave it additional vitality
by publishing a comprehensive treatise on the life and setting
of this singular figure in the realm of economic analysis and
speculation. In all the history of American thought, few,
if any, had been as well equipped as Veblen by acquaintance
with foreign languages, by training in philosophy, by study
of cultural anthropology, and by scientific detachment from
the prestige of office, for dealing with economics in its social
affiliations as a phase of culture, rather than as a hypothetical mechanism. As early as 1899 he examined the limits
and probable consequences of the purely "scientific" or
matter-of-fact treatment of economic activities. After pointing out the cultural values which capitalist society had inherited from early systems, he sought to discover in current
tendencies the results that would flow from the preëminence
of pecuniary considerations in American thought and practice, especially the effect of this preëminence upon the hitherto disciplined mass of machine workers. Although Ruskin
and Carlyle in England had raised this problem near the
middle of the nineteenth century, Veblen was the first American writer to treat it broadly in the language of academic
scholarship.

Having called attention to the cultural context in which
economic activities were carried on, Veblen discussed the
epistemology of economic thought. He insisted that economic science of the most accepted and rigorous type took
for granted, without suspicion or inquiry, subjective presuppositions respecting the nature and course of all things.
By historical analysis, he related these unexamined "verities" to the intellectual and moral "axioms" of the handicraft and merchant economy which prevailed near the middle
of the eighteenth century. In one essay after another Veblen
brought under scrutiny such grand phrases as "the natural
order," "the natural course," "the normal rule," "the beneficence of nature," "natural rights," and "the system of
natural liberty." After he had finished his work of dissec-

tion, little was left of the delusion that the axioms of economic science were inescapable deductions drawn from the
observed phenomena of the twentieth-century marketplace.
Inherited thought and preliminary assumptions, Veblen
showed, had exerted a profound influence in shaping the
image of things supposed to exist in the world of practice —
the appearance of the reality.

With a philosophic groundwork firmly laid, Veblen made
an analysis of the theory of business enterprise, published
in 1904. A central point of economic orthodoxy had been
the contention that all economic activity except consumption was productive in nature, excluding, of course, mere
criminal undertakings penalized by the code. This, Veblen
maintained, was too simple for the facts in the case. The
interest of modern business enterprise was essentially pecuniary, as distinguished from the productive interest of the
craftsman, the manager, or the directing industrialist as
owner in a strict sense. Innumerable activities pertained
to the combination of existing concerns, the destruction of
competitors, the wrecking and reorganization of going enterprises. Such activities did not enlarge physical plant, increase production, or add to the output of wealth. Often
by closing competing works, business men actually reduced
output, enhanced prices, and destroyed capital goods. In
other words, a large number of business enterprisers were
not engaged in production at all, but were working in the
interstices between going industries, and their huge accumulations of riches flowed from interstitial operations rather
than from additions to national wealth or from personal
sacrifices.

Concerning the extent of subtractive and sabotaging activities as compared with the totality of genuinely productive
activities, Veblen was not dogmatic. Up to that time other
economists, if they considered interstitial activity at all, had
regarded it as practically negligible for economic science. But
Veblen emphasized it as a striking, persistent, and pervasive
characteristic of business enterprise. He did not live to

examine the multitude of illustrations produced by congressional investigations of foreign loans, banking, investment practices, security exchanges, the merchant marine, railroads, and naval construction after the great explosion of 1929, but years before his death he had divined the significance of such potentials in business enterprise for economy and social ethics.

In an analysis of business enterprise as practice, it was only a step to the consideration of competition as fact — competition which Richard T. Ely, John Bates Clark, and other economists had praised in the optimistic vein of Herbert Spencer, as the beneficent force that kept economy running at high speed. Veblen took the step. After a detailed examination of actual conduct under the head of competition, he discovered elements of cunning, dissimulation, and stratagem in business, such as prevailed in the jungle — in the materialist struggle for existence. Here again Veblen resorted to emphasis rather than to the measurement of exact proportions, but even a mere recognition of the facts seemed to the orthodox almost like a wanton riot in a Sunday school.

Other current maxims of the academicians Veblen subjected to observational tests. The automatic working and the beneficence of the price system were brought under scrutiny. Over against assumptions and theories, Veblen placed evidence of the restraining operations of the price system — the limitation as well as the promotion of production. As he saw it, the price system did not always assure the highest possible production of goods, but often checked and sabotaged production. As a kind of side remark, he pointed out that the country had never been in a state of high productive prosperity except in war periods and in times when business men were engaged in intense speculative activities, expanding credit and liquid claims to wealth, and that such periods were mere preliminaries to liquidating collapses. With economy so conceived, the business cycle as a phase of productive activity in itself took on the shadowy form of a myth. Capitalism, save for war and speculation,

ran on a low level of production, not on the highest possible
level. That finding was decidedly heterodox.

Holding that cultural values and institutional sentiments
furnished an essential part of the very cement of society, in
which economic activities were carried on, Veblen inquired
into the effects of advertising, promotional psychology, the
machine process, and competition in prestige upon real or
sustaining morality and conventional morality. Here likewise his conclusions ran contrary to the theory that everything is good in the course of nature under the propulsion of
the acquisitive instinct. If so, he inquired, what of the
prospects?

With all the prescience he could command, Veblen sought
to penetrate the future. After calculating probabilities as
things stood in 1904, he thought it likely that business enterprise would become more and more entangled in the imperialist quest for foreign trade, markets, and raw materials, with
wars and occasional prosperities as consequences. Out of the
imperialist quest was likely to come a growing power of the
State over business. With inherited moralities weakening
under the machine process and the increasing dominance of
pecuniary valuations, business might take flight to the military State and join it in restoring by force the loyalty,
obedience, and subordination of labor which had been dissolved by the preceding emphasis on the motive of gain, the
main chance, and the jungle law. Rejecting the "inevitability" of social democracy, while making occasional use of the
Marxian analysis, Veblen thought in 1904 that the immediate future was more likely to comprise war, a growth of military force in society, the recrudescence of arbitrary discipline,
the decline of laissez faire and civil liberties.

Although Veblen was widely regarded as a satirist, writing
for the pleasure of the jest, instead of a truth-seeker in the
correct line, the imputation was unjust. Occasionally his
style seemed ironical, but it was the irony which was necessary to an accurate description of the difference between
theory and practice. By the time Dorfman's life of Veblen

appeared in 1934, a motif that once seemed derisive was discovered to be predictive rather than quizzical, and his method of intellectual procedure was more widely understood. At all events, a few younger economists found more substance and light in his economic science than, for instance, in J. Laurence Laughlin's dehumanized edition of John Stuart Mill's political economy.

Still, with the notable exception of Wesley Mitchell, most of the elders who had taken the place of the ancients continued to maintain an attitude of criticism or skepticism. When Dr. Alan R. Sweezy, a young instructor in Harvard University, proposed to take up the study of finance capital in Veblen's manner, he found that the Department of Economics believed Veblen "not worth studying," and in a short time this youthful preceptor of wayward inclination was dropped from the faculty by the authorities of the University. That may have been indicative — or merely an accident of academic readjustment.

§

As a result of the searching, inquiring, and thinking, coupled with the impact of events, the simple orthodoxy of the classical school seemed to be gradually losing its undisputed sovereignty in the academies and outside. To this fact there was impressive testimony. When, for instance, the editors of the Encyclopaedia of the Social Sciences, economists of unquestioned rank in the gild, came to planning their main article on Economics, published in 1931, they abandoned, if they ever entertained, the idea of covering the whole subject in a systematic and coherent manner within the scope of a single conspectus. Instead they opened with an introduction on the discipline of economics written by Professor E. R. A. Seligman, in which he stated that economics "has long been and will perhaps ever continue to be the battle ground of rationalizations for group and class interests. . . . The modern student regards these controversies not as dispassionate attempts to attain by logical means to eternal verities, but as the reflection in one field of changes in *Zeitgeist* and of shifts in the class structure of economic society." Having disposed of finality in this fashion, the editors then printed ten articles on economic thought: on the physiocrats, the classical school, marginal utility economics, mathematical economics, the Cambridge (England) school, the historical school, socialist economics, socio-ethical schools, romantic and universalist economics, and the institutional school.

Although a playful critic called economists "the astrologers of the machine age," the phrase was more amusing than just. Despite the conflicts of schools and all the dispersive forces, there were two or three signs of concentration on a higher level than that of scholastic contests in verbalism. Events, as well as thought, suggested revisions and new conclusions. Something like a free hand had been given to economic enterprisers during the beneficence of the golden glow and they had enjoyed the powerful patronage of government in the pursuit of their interests. Nevertheless, a cataclysm had shaken the capitalist system. On the assumption that minor modifications and the elimination of "abuses" would make the system run better, if not well, the Roosevelt administration, with much advice from economists compelled to grant concessions to a people distraught by the evident disequilibrium, made many experiments not contemplated by classical theory, without departing essentially from its presuppositions and predilections. All this was conducive to thought as well as hope and anger in academies and marketplaces, and economic discussion came to closer quarters with fundamentals in a freer spirit of inquiry.

Commenting on the state of economic thought in 1938, nine years after the great blizzard of 1929, Broadus Mitchell, professor of economics in Johns Hopkins University, declared in the Virginia Review: "The most significant thing in economic writing . . . is the increasingly important place occupied by collectivism of one sort or another. As recently as twenty years ago, in all but heretic quarters, the capitalist system was taken for granted. It rested upon private property, was motivated by private profit, functioned by means of prices competitively determined. . . . Capitalism is [now] on the defensive. Collectivism is no longer treated in footnotes, as a dangerous or engaging proposal, as a chance or minor variant, but occupies the text. Even in the meticulous descriptions of industry, major economic premises obtrude. Economic literature, for all the haste of its preparation and the fervor of its issuance, has reached a higher plane than it has occupied since the great days of Marx and Mill and George. Uneventful textual criticism, crossing of verbal swords, precious theory have given way to discussions in the large."

§

Perhaps even more tenaciously than in economics, institutionalists held the center of thought and research in what was called political science. The founders of the republic had been both theorists and practitioners and had united economic interests and corresponding policies in their operating philosophy. For a time in the middle period of American history realism had continued to mark the course of political thinking. But orthodox economics and the classes whose interests it fitted pushed government into a corner, if not entirely out of the domain, of social theory. Government was to do nothing — except define and protect property, which was something substantial, and perhaps to add protective tariffs, subsidies, and bounties. In the circumstances political science as a grand subject for thought and inquiry sank in the scale of esteem. After the destruction of the landed gentry in the South, from whose ranks had come such masters of political exposition as Madison, Jefferson, John Taylor, and Calhoun, no more great contributions to political thought came from that source. In the North, lawyers, as a rule, took charge of the subject and attention was focused on the outward trappings of government —

constitutions, forms of executive and legislative departments, statutes, administrative machinery, bureaus, offices, civil service, and similar externals of politics.

Though a profession devoted to the study of politics had arisen in the universities, interest in legal institutions and practices remained uppermost. In the main, the great contributions to politics, such as they were, assumed the garb of descriptions — accounts of the words and visible signs. No Veblen had appeared in that field to examine the very presuppositions on which adepts proceeded. The everlasting perdurance of "the American form of government" was generally taken for granted, and the probabilities of profound developments in government were neglected. Seldom were the historic forces of which government was an expression subjected to fine analyses. So hard-set was this mold of thought that even the battering effects of the world crisis failed to break entirely the sovereignty of formalism over the exploration of politics and the contemplation of political experience. No doubt it was safer for professors to stay within the sphere of symbolism, but the love of safety alone could not explain the supremacy of institutionalism in political science.

The ingrained dislike of English-speaking people for "grand theory," their distrust of it, an inveterate suspicion that it was a prime source of dangerous bigotry and tyranny, partly accounted for the tendency of American investigators to stick close to the description of particularities and to pragmatic tests. Besides there was an immense amount of work to be done in the realm of the matter-of-fact as legislatures enacted statutes by the thousands, courts handed down opinions by the cubic yard, and new boards, commissions, and other institutions were set up to deal with specific issues arising from day to day. So analysis, description, comparison, and criticism in detail proceeded apace, rendering immense services to practitioners and piling up knowledge in voluminous texts, treatises, reports, and monographs. Meanwhile political theorists, few in number, devoted their powers to surveys of the classics rather than to attempts to scale Parnassus themselves, not so much perhaps from lack of native ability as from qualms respecting the utility of the effort.

For all that, formalism did not pass undisputed. Nor did institutionalism escape criticism. Perhaps inevitably, the shocks of the time induced a consideration of fascism. At all events Charles E. Merriam, William Y. Elliott, Herbert Schneider, and Henry Spencer brought up for re-examination the politics of power, restored to the center of thought about the State the ambitions, passions, ferocities, and lusts of men. Machiavelli had taken note of these human qualifications for government. John Adams and Alexander Hamilton had given such uniformities their places in the scheme of things. But laissez faire economics, with its calculating man engaged in the peaceful pursuit of self-interest, had minimized or discarded the obvious experience of past politics. And the natural rights school, with its gratuitous assumption that man was "good by nature," or at least "decent," had pushed the Caesars and Napoleons of history out at the back door of political speculation. In democracies, politicians could hardly tell the voters that the people were irrational and loved evil; nor could they confess that they were themselves motivated by ambition and avarice. But the insurgency of Stalin, Hitler, and Mussolini in Europe, accompanied by more or less secret longings for "strong men" in the United States, suggested a re-exploration of power politics, based on ferocity and ambition, in which economic interests were bent to the ends of the dictator and his cohorts.

Other deep-seated conflicts affected the course of political thought. The temerity with which the Supreme Court struck down acts of Congress and asserted its "power to govern" invited a re-appraisal of the constitutional process itself. Interest in the matter was quickened by a revised edition of Charles Grove Haines' The American Doctrine of Judicial Supremacy, by Edward S. Corwin's The Twilight of the Supreme Court, and by Irving Brant's Storm over the Constitution. These and other studies in the same field were enlarged by numerous technical essays on the economic theories and affiliations of Supreme Court judges in times past. Having access to the Hamilton Fish papers, Sidney Ratner, in an article in The Political Science Quarterly, September, 1935, exploded the fiction that President Grant had not "packed" the Supreme Court in connection with a movement to secure a reversal of its decision in the Legal Tender Cases in 1871. Works and essays dealing with former justices, such as Taney, Miller, and Field, placed them in their economic setting and disposed of the assumption that the Constitution was a treatise in mathematical or symbolic logic and that judges were mere adepts in ratiocination. Thus the conception of the struggle for power broke into juris-prudence, much to the alarm of professional lawyers who were sticklers for propriety in language, while quite practical in matters of clients, retainers, and legal maneuvers.

Proceeding on lines already defined and piqued no doubt by the successful use of symbols and mythology by fascism in Europe, a few students of politics took up the psychological aspects of human conduct in and under government — the worship of power and the love of prostration. Appropriately enough, at Chicago, Harold D. Lasswell inquired into the psycho-pathology of political manipulations. Having a prac-tical type of mind, he asked a pertinent, if impertinent, question in politics: "Who Gets What?" At Yale Univer-sity, Thurman W. Arnold, while teaching law, was impressed by its ceremonials and myths and, after exploring the laby-rinth, emerged with a volume entitled The Symbols of Government. That Yale, which had given Chief Justice Taft to public life, could later add Professor Arnold seemed strange on the surface of things, but it happened that Arnold had been a practicing lawyer and politician in the Far West before mounting the rostrum in New Haven. In Wyoming the face of jurisprudence had been less highly polished than in the East.

A similar realism was introduced into political thought by

a small group occupied in examining the operating forces of government. As a result more was learned about back-stairs manipulations, to which Peter Odegard gave the name of Pressure Politics. From parliamentary halls, antechambers, and caucus rooms, E. P. Herring, of Harvard, carried the technique of inquiry into administrative offices where the galvanism of the lobby was persistent and effective, if less open to observation than in the legislative branches of government. Reaching out into the occupations, interests, and activities of the people, Arthur Holcombe, also of Harvard, sought the ultimate sources of political power in the United States. His economic analysis of party composition and tactics, The Political Parties of Today, published in 1924, Holcombe crowned by a supplementary volume, The New Party Politics, in which he showed the essentially middle-class character of the dominant strata in American life and suggested that tacticians and prognosticators had better reckon with this invincible fact.

The realistic sense displayed here and there in the exploration of domestic politics seemed to pause, however, at the gates of grand policy in world affairs, touching war and peace. Although armament expenditures in the United States steadily mounted until they rose above a billion dollars a year, students of government continued to neglect the role of the army and the navy in American society and in the formulation of public policies. Other countries, according to the common credo, might be militaristic, but never the United States.

Given this assumption, treatises on government and economics practically ignored military institutions as interests. Economists sometimes railed at war as if it were a kind of inexplicable madness that interfered with an otherwise almost perfect free market and price mechanism; academic works on government gave a few pages to the organization of the military and naval establishments; but the business of war, with its collateral military and naval interests, backed by the avarice of supply surveyors and the passions of men,

received relatively little attention, save in occasional pacifist pamphlets which were usually sentimental instead of
informative.

From the schools of warfare came no von Clausewitz to
reconsider the art and science. Though the loose and sentimental system of thought on sea power put forth by Admiral
Alfred T. Mahan at the turn of the century disintegrated
under analysis and the impacts of practice, no successor tried
to gather up the fragments and provide a more tenable
substitute. Nevertheless there were signs that the nature,
trappings, symbols, and interests of armed force were to be
carefully examined rather than taken for granted and celebrated. Beginnings were made in Silas B. McKinley's Democracy and Military Power, in Mauritz A. Hallgren's The
Tragic Fallacy, in the work of Stephen and Joan Rauschenbush based on the reports of the Nye munitions committee,
and in Alfred Vagts' History of Militarism. Such volumes
indicated a drift of inquiry and thought, a concern with
war as an institution, with military establishments as vested
interests, with the relations between the rise of military
power and the decline of civil society. The subject had
evoked trenchant thought among the founders of the republic
and it might again recover its rightful place in what was
called political science.

In the sphere of foreign affairs — aspects of domestic
economy and policy — academic inquiries ran mainly along
institutional lines. No one appeared to reaffirm Archibald
Coolidge's unquestioning faith in America as a World Power.
Indeed, devotion to the imperialism of Manifest Destiny was
diminishing, not mounting into a more holy zeal. Nor did
political literature show a notable recrudescence of isolationist
philosophy in the manner that had prevailed generally from
1789 to 1898. Edwin Borchard and W. P. Lage exposed the
inner nature of American neutrality from 1914 to 1917 and
made a plea for sturdy resistance to entanglements. But they
seemed to speak for a minority among professors and ideologues. Since 1917 the discussion of "foreign affairs" had

turned mainly around Woodrow Wilson's system of universal philanthropy. Societies had been established to promote it. Chairs had been founded in universities to advance it, under the protection, to be sure, of "scientific detachment."

Verily the exposition of foreign affairs became a kind of vested interest. Accepting at face value the thesis that world peace could be effected by governments, that the world image constructed by Woodrow Wilson was a truism, and that the going systems of economy would continue to go as in the past, writers on foreign relations were more inclined to recite than to reconsider. After all, as they were committed by faith to dogmas of internationalism, an application of the Socratic elenchus to their assumptions would have been profanation — and perhaps catastrophic to schools, lecture-ships, endowments, and other sources of supply and prestige. It was no accident, then, that Clark Foreman's The New Internationalism and Jerome Frank's Save America First — demands for a sound internal economy and for abstention from political entanglements abroad — came from men who had graduated from colleges to enjoy the privileges of freedom from academic constrictions.

§

Broader in scope than economics and politics, sociology had for its domain of thought and inquiry all human activities, institutions, and relations — family, church, community, economy, war, politics, and all other phases of civilization in statu quo and presumably in long-time development. But no American sociologist sought to grasp the scheme of things entire and to subdue the voluminous and intractable masses of fact to any comprehensive and coherent frame of thought. No single person or group of persons occupied the center of the stage as Lester Ward, William Graham Sumner, Franklin Giddings, Simon Patten, and Edward A. Ross had done in past years, and carried on in their style. No sociologist, aspiring to Newtonian simplicity, proclaimed a new formula such as "the consciousness of kind as the basis of society," which Giddings had put forward long before. Instead of presenting the subject as a unified discipline, R. M. MacIver devoted the article on Sociology for The Encyclopaedia of the Social Sciences to a history of the sociological schools, their characteristics, and their centers of interest, and showed that heavy emphasis had been laid in the United States upon "classifications and descriptions of particular social processes, such as assimilation, accommodation, adjustment." These were aspects of society especially considered by Charles Ellwood, Robert Park, and Ernest Burgess.

Something like a positive school controlled by a single conception emerged at the University of Chicago and was called by a biological name, "ecological," indicating that social patterns and differences were or might be determined by the influences of environment. But the majority of the sociologists, even those who conceded that they were working under some hypothesis respecting the nature of all things, confined their attention to classifying and describing particular phases or communities of society, urban and rural — habits, customs, institutions, and relationships in microcosm. Their work was well illustrated by Robert and Helen Lynd's two intensive studies of Muncie, Indiana, under the head of Middletown; by the surveys of Southern economy, culture, and regionalism carried out under Howard Odum and his associates at the University of North Carolina; and by the statistical studies of William F. Ogburn of the University of Chicago.

Such work was in sum and substance what MacIver called "an extensive and intensive mapping of the contemporary social scene," that is, essentially reportorial in the best sense of the word. It largely ignored historical perspective and the issues of prognosis. Disclaiming all assumptions except perhaps the assumption that such work was worth doing and that the notations of appearances corresponded with the realities, the institutional and folkway sociologists adhered tightly to "facts" and in so doing gave to the public an enlarged knowledge of American communities and behaviors, incidentally destroying many dream pictures in the process. Almost any student trained in the "techniques" of the school could pursue this kind of sociology; foundations provided generous grants of money to finance it; the results brought no basic disturbances to the five or six primary articles of the American credo.

Whenever a professor got far off this well-worn and well-oiled track, discarded the neutrality of the institutional school, and took up the ethical aspects of society, either directly or by intended implication, he was likely to run into severe criticism from his "scientific" colleagues and to be regarded as a kind of preacher, theologically inclined. By insisting upon the existence of ethical motives and the necessity of bringing ethical considerations into account in any comprehensive treatment of human society, Charles Ellwood and Charles Cooley drew upon their heads this imputation from some of their brethren who imagined that they themselves had harder heads. A worse fate befell Jerome Davis of The Divinity School of Yale University. Under the heading of Capitalism and Its Culture, he pointed out an intimate relationship between two aspects of civilization which other sociologists had been inclined to neglect, and documented the relationship by a wealth of citations, warmed to intense heat by a moral indignation presumably appropriate to a professor of sociology in a divinity school. Not long afterward, the connections of Professor Davis with the University were severed, "on other grounds," the authorities explained.

The process of intellectual catalysis encouraged by analytical research in the branches of social study was partly offset by the completion of The Encyclopaedia of the Social Sciences in 1935, under the editorship of E. R. A. Seligman and Alvin Johnson, with the counsel of representatives from all cognate professional associations. Designed to cover the whole "field," all schools of thought, and all fundamental presuppositions and methods, it was of necessity sociological in nature and the authors of its articles, however specialized in their own researches, were more or less affected by the requirements of system and comprehensiveness. Representing as a rule contemporary scholarship at its best, these articles rose above traditional naïveté and contributed to the elevation of social thought in many spheres.

Even so, just as economists shrank from correcting theory by the fruits of institutional research and from emulating Adam Smith, Ricardo, or Alfred Marshall, sociologists declined to grasp at the universal in the manner of Auguste Comte or Herbert Spencer. In the establishment of The Journal of Social Philosophy in 1935, awareness of the larger challenge seemed imminent but the display of awareness was not accompanied by great efforts on the part of American scholars to meet it by coming to grips with "the ultimate design of the universe." That commission was left to writers of European origins. Pitirim Sorokin undertook it and reported his observations, conclusions, and frame of social thought in four large volumes entitled Social and Cultural Dynamics. Although at the time Sorokin was professor of sociology at Harvard University, he had been born, reared, and educated in Tsarist Russia, had lived through the Bolshevik revolution, and had not reached the United States until 1923. He had experienced immense history and he brought to sociology the historical perspective so widely neglected by surveyors of contemporary scenes; but his thought was colored by his concrete experience and he dyed his treatise with strains of absolutism and mysticism out of harmony with the pragmatic thought, the democratic susceptibilities, and prevailing experiences of American scholars.

Another effort to overcome the American "deficiency" in breadth and depth of conception was the translation into English and the publication in New York City of Vilfredo Pareto's treatise on general sociology under the title of Science and Society. By emphasizing the role of the irrational in human affairs, Pareto, like Sorokin, gave a certain jolt to fact-finders and compilers, but at the same time he suggested the imputation that he was also primarily a fact-finder bolstering up his own preconceptions. Less heralded as startling or epoch-making, but in truth more relevant to realistic thought about all societies, including the American, was the publication of another continental treatise in English, in 1935, namely, Karl Mannheim's Ideology and Utopia, a work on the nature of social knowledge and a study of the principal controlling conceptions under which the writing up of social facts and thinking about them could proceed. It asked in effect : Just what do you think you are doing when you are collecting, classifying, and writing about the behaviors and linguistic expressions of human beings in society ?

§

To educational thought the perpendicular and collateral strokes of the economic depression brought troubled dreams. In the evening of the golden glow all seemed serene and secure. With utmost confidence many educators spoke of "the science of education." The future of American institutions, of the sustaining environment, of the nourishing cultural heritage, could be taken for granted. If anything was needed it was more of the same things — more school buildings, larger appropriations, and the multiplication of "research" projects.

Under the appearance of eternal prosperity, the function of education was to prepare boys and girls for the professions, trades, occupations, and crafts, which would provide unending and adequate demand for the human output of the schools. By precise psychological and occupational measurements educators were supposed to discover the quantities of whatever was needed for each of the multitudinous niches into which graduates were to be fitted. Specialists presumably could also find out by research just the kind of courses, methods, and instructional apparatus required to fit the several candidates for their several callings. Expert testers, employing scientific "techniques" and "batteries" of blanks, questionnaires, and instrumentalities, could show with mathematical precision, it was thought, how far each of the millions of graduates would or could go in making a "success" in his or her pecuniary enterprise. All this was to be done without obliterating the notion of democratic opportunity and equalitarianism which had distinguished American education from, let us say, the stratified occupational therapy of old Prussian institutions of learning. In reality the matter was not quite so simple but, when boiled down, educational thought in the golden glow amounted to little more, and dissenters could be lightly brushed aside as "radicals" lacking in scientific and pedagogical discipline.

This dream of an educational science was interrupted by the crash of the economic depression, by the sharp curtailment of the employment for which the schools had been preparing their charges, by conflicts over New Deal legislation, by the breaking up of orthodoxy in many places, and by fascist upheavals and wars in Europe and Asia. Such events wrenched the business of education out of the groove and made the "science" of education appear far less scientifically sound. Teachers streamed out into the ranks of the unemployed. Schools by the thousands were closed. Bills were unpaid, even in the rich city of Chicago. Millions of graduates, correctly instructed and precisely tested according to the rigid canons of indubitable masters, could find no places in the scheme of things pecuniary. "Here we come, WPA!" was the cry of one graduating class. As the promoters of the New Deal made fierce attacks on "economic royalists" and pushed through Congress legislation different in purpose and upshot from the laws of the Full Dinner Pail or the New Freedom, and as the critics of the New Deal blasted away at such legislation and administration, calling it an emanation from Moscow, educators once safely ensconced in their solid science found the walls of their theory falling about their heads. They began to wonder whether their science was sufficient unto the day.

Commissions and individuals, equipped with knowledge and methods of inquiry, set to work zealously to take stock of education in the new situation and to find for it a philosophy and program more appropriate to the exigencies of the time. Through the stoutest ivory of the strongest towers swept reverberations from the marketplace and the forum, stirring active minds in the educational world to greater energy. Reports, volumes, essays, monographs, and learned papers began to jostle the old literature of education already mountainous in proportions.

In 1934 a Commission on the Social Studies, working under the auspices of the American Historical Association, completed a series of volumes, crowned by Conclusions and Recommendations, in which was set forth a collectivistic frame of reference for controlling the construction of curricula, methods, and expectations of education. In vital respects this report called for a reappraisal of the individualistic concepts on which "the science of education" had rested. Later the Educational Policies Commission of the National Education Association came to similar conclusions and, far from taking for granted the future of American democracy, asserted the obligation of public education to make positive contributions to strengthening, upholding, and developing that democracy, including the precious heritage of civil liberties, then so violently assailed by theory and practice. Indeed the persistent efforts of professional educators to think through the problems thrown upon them by actions and reactions in the secular world were spirited and courageous, displaying both vitality and comprehension.

On the upper level of education, called the "higher" learning for reasons not altogether conclusive, educational thought was apparently less agitated than on the lower level where teachers who managed to hold their positions came into direct contact with underfed children from the homes of the unemployed. Defaults in bonds curtailed incomes in college and university; great donations diminished in volume; graduates found fewer opportunities selling stocks and bonds or in the

professions. But honorary degrees and commencement orations brought continuous revelations of the fact that educational interest and thought on college campuses were substantially unchanged by the jars of the depression. The
tercentenary of Harvard University was conducted in the
spirit of the tradition and an effort to use it as a springboard
from which to launch a concentration of science and the
humanities upon the pressing problems of the contemporary
world died on the morrow of the hopeful day.

Only a few incidents whipped up the calm sea of educational thought in the "higher" ranges. In 1930 Abraham
Flexner brought out a comparative study of Universities,
American, English, German, in which he protested against
the invasion of learning by trivial, occupational, and pecuniary interests and found ideal contrasts abroad, especially in
Germany. The book made a temporary sensation, but the
charm of its constructive proposals was marred by the subsequent conduct of properly trained and conditioned professors
in Germany, after the advent of Hitler and his "Aryan"
learning. A few years later Norman Foerster assayed a similar
theme in The American State University, outlined a gloomy
picture of learning under the pressures of democratic politics,
and hinted at an escape through a new unity on a basis somewhat metaphysical. A still bigger discord was raised when
Robert Hutchins, president of Chicago University, issued his
reflections on the state of colleges and universities under a
title which Thorstein Veblen had made famous — The Higher
Learning in America.

On the one side President Hutchins' treatise was severely
critical. Without mercy he assailed the profusion, specialization, and "chaos" in the multitude of schools and courses
prevailing in the institutions of higher learning, and above
all the devotion to occupational and pecuniary interests. On
the constructive side, he proposed to introduce order and
simplicity by cleaning out a huge pile of courses in scientific
and humanistic studies, especially those directed to occupational and pecuniary ends, and substituting for them instruc-

tion in a few "principles." In substance he declared that "the heart of education will be, if education is rightly understood, the same at any time, in any place, under any political, social, or economic conditions," and the very center of the very heart should be metaphysics, that is, instruction in things highest by nature, first principles, and first causes.

As to upshot, if not specific intention, President Hutchins' scheme meant throwing overboard nearly everything that had been thought and done in the domain of the higher learning since the middle ages and returning to the apparent simplicities of the seven liberal arts adopted for Christendom — grammar, rhetoric, logic, arithmetic, geometry, astronomy, and music — with perhaps some alterations and condensations. This proposal, in effect, merely stopped a bit short of taking over the Roman Catholic view of the universe and the function of university learning — the truth, that is, our truth, is everywhere the same, good always, whatever change the years may bring.

In a critique, published in The Social Frontier, one of the prime leaders in the socialization of learning, John Dewey, replied to President Hutchins, by contrasting his proposed educational philosophy with that of Lancelot Hogben, the English author of The Retreat from Reason. "To Mr. Hutchins," Dewey explained, "the sciences represent in the main the unmitigated empiricism which is a great curse of modern life, while to Mr. Hogben the conceptions and methods which Mr. Hutchins takes to be the true and final definition of rationality are obscurantist and fatally reactionary, while their survival in economic theory and other branches of social 'science' is the source of the intellectual irrelevance of the latter to the fundamental problems of our present culture. Indeed, these disciplines are more than irrelevant and futile. They are literally terrible in their distraction of social intelligence and activity from genuine social problems and from the only methods by which these problems can be met."

Dewey might have added, had he been so inclined, a query

in respect of the great white hope contained in Hutchins' hypothesis: How did it happen that the higher learning of the liberal arts imposed on young minds in mediaeval Europe failed to bring order out of feudal chaos or to prevent the little western world, which ever imagines itself to be all civilization, from developing under God's providence into the modern world which seems so chaotic to believers who say they know and have "the" truth?

Nevertheless President Hutchins' volume struck into an issue of thought which had long occupied the western mind — unity amid diversity, permanence amid change, order against liberty, peace against war, the true, the beautiful, and the good against the false, the ugly, and the evil. The issue had never been resolved; and skeptics, even while pursuing the quest, suspected that the human mind was not equal to the task of resolution. However that might be, a nation seeking to bend the multiplicity and conflicts of things to the uses of a good life did call for operating postulates, strong affirmations, and coördinating forces in education conceived as a preparation for heroic endeavors and achievements in practice. But if anything was known at all, a return to the middle ages, in which the seven liberal arts occupied the center of instruction, was as impossible as an escape from the pull of gravitation.

It might be that the work of framing the postulates, making the strong affirmations, and providing the coördinating forces would not fall to any single division of learning, and that leadership in the process of uniting the Emotional and the Intellectual would be taken by the scientists so cavalierly treated by President Hutchins and his school. Not, of course, by the simple adherents of Newton and Darwin, or the followers of the theological physicists, Jeans and Eddington, but, as Herbert J. Muller pointed out in The Southern Review for the summer of 1938, by "the scientists who on naturalistic grounds are bursting through the abstractions once identified with Reality, scrapping the absolutes that have tyrannized thought, pointing to an organic synthesis in which philosophy, art, and science may be reconciled again after some centuries of specialization in different kinds of 'knowledge' and dispute over different levels of 'truth.'"

When educational thought left the school room and invaded the world of practice it took the form of concern with what was loosely called adult education. Although the covering tradition ran far back into the days of the lyceum, this concern now turned particularly to a consideration of education in relation to the exigencies of social living. Vocational extension went on as before, to be sure, with perhaps less confidence as vocational opportunities diminished or at least failed to expand with the increase in the number of applicants. Yet interest was enlarged in matters of social adjustment and great public issues; and, in the application of adult education, forums of discussion sprang up over the country, in private and public buildings, under private and public auspices.

Underlying this movement was a conviction that if the major questions of the time could be examined and debated in the light of reason, in the relative quiet of auditoriums, the likelihood of resorting to the methods of violence would be diminished. Impressed by the opportunities and tensions of the political and economic scene, the United States Office of Education, under the direction of John W. Studebaker, formulated programs, aided in the organization of procedures and methods, and stimulated the growth of systematic discussion among adults from one end of the country to the other. If somewhat overlooked by those engaged in formal and higher instruction, thought in this division of educational interest was directed with increasing sophistication and zeal to the exploration of democracy, its operating methods, and its sustaining economy.

§

Called of old the crown of all learning, philosophy continued its quest for unity and order through the toss and pitch of "matter and spirit" and, in so doing, took somewhat into account the events, experiences, and spirit of the mid-passage. One historian disputed its right to the crown and called it a mere phase of history but that had slight, if any, effect upon adepts. They would insist upon standing outside history, they thought, more or less emancipated from the conditioning or determining influences of mundane, secular, and economic interests and conflicts. Perhaps in fact the philosopher, like other thinkers, was dominated by the social frame of his own memory; still, when the idea was suggested, it was not welcomed by universal acclaim, for it made the philosopher a little lower than the angels.

As of old, there were still open to the philosopher the four ways traced by Irwin Edman: "philosophy as logical faith, as social criticism, as mystical insight, and as nature understood." These, at least, were the well-traveled highroads and, while banks crashed, multitudes searched for work and bread, and dictators threatened the "peace and order" of the world, such as it was, most philosophers either re-explored the ancient paths or sat and whittled away at fine points of minor doctrine.

For the philosophers of logical faith there was little to do except to restate historic maxims with new trimmings. They asserted, that is, assumed, the existence of absolute truth and the power of their minds to grasp it after attaining faith in the assertion or presupposition. Karl Mannheim had maintained that social relationships influence the course of the most abstract thought, that thinking does not develop in accordance with imminent laws, pre-logic, inner dialectic, or any other timeless or contentless process. But that meant little or nothing to the possessors of logical faith. Their chosen way was good enough for them. In fact if they left it, they well knew that they might soon be sunk in the bog of relativism or caught up in the drift of social action. The main highway seemed more secure.

Philosophers of the Catholic persuasion were guided by great masters of logical faith, especially the learned doctor, Thomas Aquinas. Scarcely able to transcend the work of the

Church fathers, they were mainly content to expound and explain to new generations that which they had received from their predecessors, often with new illustrations more or less ingeniously picked and presented. Nor did things change much on the Protestant side. Josiah Royce had no successor to preach as effectively in the name of the absolute as he had done; and philosophers who accepted that faith seemed more inclined to polish and refine it than to restate it in language more penetrating, vital, and comprehensive. As for mystical insight, that belonged in the realm of personal experience. When expressed in terms of logic, facts, and "earthly discourse," the reports of mystical insight fell short of an independent philosophy. Experiments in telepathy, mind reading, and supersensory perception, although they created an excitement similar to that raised by spirit-rappings in the Millerite age, disclosed little or no knowledge that was not more easily ascertained by direct observation.

There remained the two other ways: social criticism and the understanding of nature, which certainly crossed at many points, if they did not entirely blend. Philosophers of these directions kept on making the pragmatic assertion: Words, declarations, syllogisms have no meaning for us apart from the things done under them by the professors, expounders, and true believers. How can an idea be true if one cannot find it as a tangible in reality or express it in life and conduct? What is the use of proclaiming a theory to be absolutely true when practices contradict it every day? These questions, although certainly pertinent, did not materially disturb the possessors of logical faith; nor did this line of inquiry itself lead to "constructive formulations." Just where it would lead no one seemed able to say and there was no tribunal for passing unequivocal judgment upon its merits. If regular attendance at church services was a test of the popular concern, then a majority was on the side of the skeptics. Yet in a pinch a majority might be found in favor of the proposition that words uttered on Sunday were truer than things done on the other six days.

Although it was not always openly admitted, the philosophy of social criticism involved an interpretation of "nature" and indeed of all history, which Hegel sought to rationalize as revealing the ultimate design of the universe. It was doubtless a sign of the times that John Dewey, called the Dean of the American Philosophers by naturalists, sometimes accused of being an "atheist" by clergymen, became increasingly interested in the social implications of thought and in efforts to construct a social system more in harmony with conceptions of justice, truth, and beauty. From the academic chair he stepped out into the sphere of hazardous actions, seeking to apply the formulas of his thought. At another seat of learning Sidney Hook tried to bring the critique of Karl Marx to bear on the consideration of truth and action, theory and practice — philosophy in its largest reaches. Other philosophers, T. V. Smith, of Chicago, and William E. Hocking, of Harvard, for example, also ventured away from the cloister to test words uttered, "syntactical sentences," in the forum where practitioners strove, not always successfully, to combine virtue and the main chance.

In the realm of the concrete, strange things happened to philosophers. Amid the dust of the forum and the marketplace, where programs were drawn up and action taken, were often associated philosophic thinkers who differed diametrically in the calmer atmosphere of academies. For example, at opposite poles in metaphysical fundamentals stood John Dewey, the naturalist, and John A. Ryan, indomitable defender of the logical faith. Yet in matters of social procedure they had more in common than in dispute. If Morris Cohen, who held mediaeval philosophy in deep respect, found Dewey's pragmatism incomplete, perchance wholly unsatisfactory, he could join Dewey in any bitter struggle for the maintenance of civil liberties.

Upon occasion, as a cynic had remarked, it might be the duty of the philosopher, as of the historian or economist, to make the worse cause appear the better; yet as the golden glow paled to shadows, many of those leaders among American philosophers who commanded national consideration chose no such course. Criticizing the metaphysical aristocracy for aloofness, even when agreeing with its assumptions and syllogisms, they went into the highways and byways where men and women were battling for bread, struggling to hold families intact, and striving to employ the engines of organization and government in the interest of social security. After all, neither the founder of the logical faith nor the inventor of naturalism had ignored common clay and common purpose. And perhaps the best that philosophers could do was to accept the basic human values of civilization which had been asserted against sheer force and empty speculation in ages past, and reassert them amid the encircling menaces of tyranny and intolerance in their own times.

§

All thought about economics, politics, sociology, education, and philosophy, indeed all theory and practice in government and business, in entertainment, letters, the arts, and sciences, were in fact but phases of history, were enmeshed in history as actuality. The golden glow, the dissolutions, and the New Deal, however construed in terms of advancing or declining civilization, were outcomes of history and forerunners of destiny to come. And since this is true, out of the study of history, near and distant, was to flow such fundamental understanding of American society and its fortunes among the nations as human intelligence and knowledge could supply to prognosis and provision, in shaping the fleeting present and the oncoming future. If any facts known to the human mind were irreducible, this fact was certainly among them. What, then, were historians in the academies and beyond the campuses doing with it?

Committed by their craft to the study of the past, historians were not ostensibly so concerned with thought about contemporary affairs as were the professors of economics, politics, or sociology, and could, if they wished, keep on their way unperturbed by the events which impinged so sharply upon their colleagues. For a long time they had operated on the assumption that they could write history in a "scientific" manner and describe the past "as it actually had been," somewhat as the chemist correctly pictures by exact formulas the reactions in his test tube, and they had confined their attention mainly to political and military events. It was not their business, according to the maxims of the gild, to serve any practical needs of a society feverishly hunting solutions for its pressing problems.

This style of research and composition, called Historism, had been derived mainly from German scholasticism of the nineteenth century, itself largely an outcome of the inhibitions placed upon German historians by their bureaucratic status and by their rivalry for advancement, that is, competition in the mass of accumulated data, the multiplicity of footnotes and illustrations, the weight of their volumes. Impressive scholarship of that kind continued to control historical writing in the United States. Documentary research and indefatigable industry, coupled with extreme caution about the open admission of controlling conceptions, were its principal characteristics. What Alfred Cohn looked for in straight scientific thought, namely, the attainment of the simple generalization of a Newton or a Faraday or a Darwin, was not set as the goal of labors by historians of the scientific school. On the contrary they were inclined to regard as queer any member of the gild, such as Henry Adams, who sought to arrive at brief formulas in historical studies. Like minor workers in natural science, they restricted their activities principally to the collection and analysis of records and the meticulous piecing together of "facts" regarded as well authenticated. When true to form, they crowded their work with details, avoided colorful phrases, and aimed at a severity of style appropriate to a treatise on physics or chemistry, all in unquestioning faith, apparently, that such patterns of words faithfully described the past actuality which they were supposed to know.

Working more or less in this style, under such a theory of their function, historians continued to produce solid and scholarly volumes of high quality in matters of exactness and documentation. Shrinking from the mammoth enterprises requiring ten or fifteen volumes in the tradition of Gibbon, Mommsen, and Bancroft, they confined their attention to special periods or to particular phases and personalities. Charles McLean Andrews went forward with his meticulous survey of the colonial period in America; Tyler Dennett reconstructed the historic figure of John Hay; Douglas Southall Freeman completed a microscopic biography of Robert E. Lee; Allan Nevins reworked the life of Grover Cleveland and wrote a massive biography of Hamilton Fish; Samuel Flagg Bemis illuminated dark corners of American diplomacy in its historical development; John D. Hicks, after painstaking researches and journeys to and fro over the continent, portrayed The Populist Revolt in an urbane manner which Mark Hanna and Joseph Choate in 1896 might have called revolutionary; Henrietta Larson revamped the history of Jay Cooke, the financier of the civil war, on the basis of materials that had eluded the older biographers; George Clinton, Andrew Jackson, and Andrew Johnson were revived again in new configurations. These and other historical works done in the style of the craft displayed both vitality and critical energy which showed no signs of weariness or relaxation.

Nevertheless historians did not pursue their peaceful course without meeting groundswells of considerable proportions. Their main thesis that they really could describe history as it actually had been was denied by some members of the gild. Their claim to Olympian impartiality was subjected to inquiry and drastic revision. Since facts do not select and order themselves on the printed page, the historian, critics insisted, selects his own facts and arranges them according to some scheme of values and, in choosing the linguistic forms, sees them from some angle of social vision. In the spirit of this criticism, the president of the American Historical Association declared in 1933, the great year of the banking crisis and New Deal inauguration, that written history is not a science or an art, but contemporary thought about the past, instructed and delimited by the records and documents of history as actuality — "record and knowledge authenticated by criticism and ordered with the help of the scientific method."

On another flank James Harvey Robinson created a commotion by asserting that it was one of the prime functions of historiography to throw light upon "our present quandaries" by tracing the rise and development of the circumstances from which they sprang. Historical research and construction done in this spirit, with due respect for the authenticity of documents and for scientific exactitude in respect of details, was bound, in the nature of things, to give a different appearance to the past and the present. Although when expressed without adornment, this idea seemed heretical to keepers of orthodoxy, what it actually suggested was that historians do consciously what they had been doing more or less unconsciously.

Likewise disturbing to professors of political and military history was the widening of historical inquiries to include in the stream of history other aspects — business, the arts, medicine, literature, science, manners, customs, and commonplace ways of life in all ranks of society. Arthur M. Schlesinger and Dixon Ryan Fox brought near to the conclusion their editing of their twelve-volume coöperative series, A History of American Life. Albert Deutsch, in his history of The Mentally Ill in America, covered a long-neglected phase of barbarism and humanism in theory and practice. Richard H. Shryock, in The Development of Modern Medicine, related medicine to its social setting, and dealt with the reciprocal influences of the relationships. Applying a similar method, Vernon Parrington brought literature into the Main Currents in American Thought, demonstrating the shallowness of any criticism merely concerned with style and form and at the same time putting secular history in a new perspective.

More alarming to gild orthodoxy was the increasing emphasis on the economic interpretation of history, especially as the origin of this type of empirical realism was falsely ascribed to Karl Marx in spite of his disclaimers. Cautiously applied, with a sense of its limitations, the economic interpretation merely meant the persistent association of ideas and personalities in historical writing with the relevant economic interests in which they were entangled in history as actuality. An excellent example of this style was afforded by J. Franklin Jameson's The American Revolution Considered as a Social Movement, published in 1926. Since Jameson was in fact the beloved dean of the Historical Association, it was clear that the economic "taint" had gone rather deeply into the ranks of the fraternity. Dealing with a narrower field, Western Lands and the American Revolution, Thomas P. Abernethy showed the intimate affiliation of politics and land speculation in the heroic days of winning and establishing independence. In the extreme form employed by communist writers, the economic interpretation became materialist determinism, and history was written merely "from the class angle," but this type of historiography gained few if any adherents in the academies.

Either as mild reasonableness or closed dogma, the economic interpretation played havoc with the pleasing conceptions of history entertained by patriotic societies and bar associations and supplied fuel for contemporary politics and economics. Accordingly at the fiftieth anniversary of the American Historical Association, it received a severe drubbing at the hands of the professor chosen to review past achievements and present troubles.

While adepts were debating the theory of history writing, individual historians were illustrating the intellectual dilemma in works of many grades. How, for instance, should the civil struggle between Americans at the middle of the nineteenth century be viewed as human experiences? That struggle had been described in various terms: correct Whiggery, abolitionist idealism, planters' philosophy, Southern Democracy, the Republican conception of cause and effect, and judicious mixtures of the several assumptions, with emphasis somewhere. Now two professors, Francis B. Simkins and James W. Patton, found fundamental support for the Southern cause among the Women of the Confederacy. Remembering or discovering that a yeomanry, as well as the planters' caste, had existed in the South, other historians interpreted the civil conflict in terms of a Southern class struggle, in part at least, as the American revolution had been interpreted by J. Franklin Jameson. Into this reverie and assertion, William Burghart DuBois injected a Negro's opinion of the conflict, selecting his facts from facts which other versions had missed or discarded, making his own emphasis, and demonstrating that Negroes had played a larger role in the great drama than white historians had assigned to them. And a group of new writers on history, among whom Louis Hacker was a prominent representative, sought to remind readers of history that working people, white and black, agricultural and industrial, had been involved in that social upheaval so sweeping and revolutionary in character. What then was "the whole truth" of this immense social war conceived precisely "as it had been"?

Certainly all this writing from various "angles" influenced historical thought in general and in particular. Its effects were clearly traceable, for example, in J. G. Randall's The Civil War and Reconstruction — a work by a Northern historian which was warmly commended, for its treatment of the civil conflict, by a Southern historian, B. B. Kendrick. After referring at the outset to the narrow and partisan character of traditional writing on that vexatious subject, Randall declared that "on many a scholarly front the boundary of research has been extended; what is more significant is that there have come upon the historical world a fresh interpretative power, a new insight, a greater resourcefulness, a growing appreciation of human factors, an understanding of social and economic forces, and a sharpened sophistication in facing time-worn assumptions, which have given to historical writing a new tone and a new orientation."

When the geography of ideas was taken into account, it was perhaps just to say that the most fertile and penetrating historical writing of the midpassage was produced by Southern investigators, such as F. L. Owsley, B. B. Kendrick, A. M. Arnett, D. D. Wallace, Rupert Vance, and C. Vann Woodward, to make a selection. In some respects, Southerners were well fitted by experience and temper for writing history at a time when industrial civilization was suffering from pangs of disorder and twinges of conscience. In spite of the railroads, cotton mills, and blast furnaces in the South, the region remained essentially agrarian in economy and sentiments.

By 1933 the earlier generation of Southern historians who felt impelled to write romantically on the Old South, or to paint the Reconstruction blacker than it may have been on the whole, had passed away or done their work. The time for more critical thought was at hand. From the beginning Southern thinkers had refused to accept at face value the capitalist system and its maxims of virtue in the fashion of their Northern colleagues. They had been in opposition — not proletarian but agrarian. They could not swallow, without gagging at least, many aphorisms so palatable above the Mason and Dixon line, and they brought to the selection and arrangement of facts, called historiography, a frame of reference marked by many local peculiarities. Of this generalization innumerable illustrations were provided; for instance, in Wallace's History of South Carolina, in Woodward's Tom Watson, Agrarian Rebel, and in the long line of articles and reviews published in the Virginia Quarterly, The Southern Review, and other magazines of the region. The solid mentality of the solid South was dissolving "like mists before the morning sun," as Henry W. Grady might have put the case.

While reports on human experience from various angles of experience were coming into the thought of history, woman's experience through the ages received more critical attention and consideration. Largely composed and taught by men, written history had mainly represented the ambitions of men — of warriors, politicians, lords of creation, labor leaders, planters, and proletarians. If women appeared at all in the lectures and pages, they did so in identical or subsidiary capacities or as abstractions such as "women in industry" or as persons but newly introduced to society through the triumph of the suffrage movement. But studies on other than conventional lines indicated that the history of men alone was partial history; that men and women had shared human experiences throughout the past; that women had always been at or near the center of private and public affairs where history was made; that women also had distinctions and contributions to record. Thus the superficial notion that women had been a passive sex in history, counting for nothing in the molding of their own lives and in the molding of the common life, uneducated until they got the chance to attend modern colleges, was supplanted by a larger and more accurate view. Out of nothing, could something leap into being?

However useful the notion had been as a weapon of feminist agitation for enlarged civil and political advantages, its inadequacy was now shown in numerous and striking forms of historical writing. One instance illustrates the point: Dr. Kate C. Hurd-Mead's History of Women in Medicine — the work of a physician trained at Johns Hopkins, a linguist, a scholar accustomed to the precisions of research, and a researcher over a period of more than thirty years not only in the great libraries of the western world but out in the byways of the world where primitive medicine is still the rule. Writing on women in medicine called for writing on medicine itself, and writing on medicine required descriptions of social settings for the art of healing.

Historical documents were of course essential instruments for developing the knowledge required for realistic thought. Recognizing this requirement, interested women organized a movement having for its purpose to establish a World

Center for Women's Archives in New York City and began the systematic collection, listing, and calendaring of letters, journals, programs, speeches, and other materials bearing on the activities and thought of women. They had not gone far when they came to the conclusion that the vaunted "equal education" in colleges and universities was little more than coeducation in men's thought of their own history. To the growing concern with history as the great all-human experience the records of women's interests and activities could not fail to add substance and essentials.

If to persons busy at polite letters or practical affairs, the controversies and ferments among historians seemed like battles of kites and crows, such was not the case. Whatever the primary nature of other divisions of thought, such as economics, politics, or ethics, they were all phases of general history and enclosed in that enveloping medium. Every interpretation of economic conflicts and trends at the same time made an interpretation of history and rested on assumptions relative to the nature of history as actuality or positive human experience. Every formulation of public policy, domestic or foreign, was also an interpretation of history, that is, expressed calculations respecting things probable, possible, and necessary within the heritage from the past, within the borders of history ever in the process of becoming. Historical writing had been employed by Catholics and Protestants in their long struggle for possession of the human mind in the West. Voltaire had made it a dynamic force for the French Revolution. Under the guise of romanticism, history had served the reaction. Other illustrations were abundant. If historians working in the scientific spirit, seeking emancipation from the tyranny of old assumptions, persisted in the effort to bring all schemes of selection into some kind of articulation and stronger consensus, and could perform this function in historiography, even to a limited extent, then all divisions of contemporary thought and all formulations of public policy were bound to receive a higher and wider illumination.

CHAPTER XVII

Toward a Reconsideration of Democracy

ALL the major events and tendencies of the midpassage — the economic crisis, political conflicts arising out of national efforts to grapple with it, the multiplication of public functions and responsibilities, increased centralization in economy and government, the expansion of military and naval establishments, the rise of dictators and the spread of wars abroad, official declarations of foreign policies involving participation in the quarrels of Europe, tumult in the labor movement at home, outbursts of the vigilante spirit, degrading tendencies in commercialized entertainment, growing dissidence in literature, standardization and conservatism of the press, popular affirmations in the arts, the forces of science and invention, and the forms of social thought — all bore upon the fortunes of democracy and at every turn called for a reconsideration of its nature, its perduring power, its ability to cope with the complexities of a disjointed yet great society. In consequence, popular institutions long taken for granted were reëxamined and analyses once lightly dismissed were seriously reviewed as Americans became more conscious of democracy — of the contrasts opposing it and bidding for supreme favor everywhere.

From the close of the civil war to the end of the world war, democracy, or "the American way," had been loosely, though by no means universally, accepted as a fact and seldom probed to the bottom in journals and forums of public opinion. That it might pass, as other systems of government had passed, and within the time of living men and women, was generally deemed so improbable as to be unworthy of grave thought and discourse. Henry Adams and Brooks Adams might spend laborious days tracing the degradation of the democratic dogma but for the main body of the people nothing remained save the hymning of "further progress in democracy." Philosophic doubts were entertained and expressed by many politicians; but such doubts, if noticed, were taken to be the curious vagaries of nervous persons rather than sober reasoning and warning. Admittedly there were blemishes on the bright escutcheon; but education and the invincible spread of enlightenment would overcome them, gradually.

However, after 1929, in the midst of turbulence and shocks, the theory and practice of democracy confronted unequivocal denunciation abroad and wide-open questioning at home. An upheaval was due and it arrived. Individuals and groups that had never been associated with popular movements called democratic in the progressive era and the age of normalcy suddenly blossomed out as the "true custodians of democracy," as its defenders to the last trench. Individuals and groups that had set themselves down as democratic all along began to reinterpret their political philosophy in terms of the issues defined by centralization in capitalism and by its obvious inadequacies over a long period of years, with no promise of permanent security for individuals or groups in sight. For this conflict George S. Counts of the Teachers' College at Columbia University drew up in 1938 an impressive balance sheet of assets and liabilities in The Prospects of American Democracy, laid down a program for constructive action, and issued a call for a concert of the popular powers in America. Within the framework of an agrarian philosophy, Herbert Agar reinforced Counts' plea, by telling the story of American democracy in The Pursuit of Happiness.

In one sector of the celebration directed by the "true custodians of democracy" were leaders of bar associations, apologetic columnists of conservative newspapers, representatives of publishers, big industrialists, financiers, officers of the American Legion and other professional patriotic societies, and ideologues at large. These exponents of the democratic creed commonly identified it with the philosophy of "let us alone" and appointed themselves as its protectors against the "dictatorship" of the Roosevelt administration. With kindred vehemence Roosevelt and his supporters nominated themselves as true guardians of the democratic faith against "economic royalists." If words meant anything, both factions were strong upholders of democracy. Syntactical unanimity was almost perfect. It seemed no longer a question of representative government against democracy, as in the early days of the republic, but a matter of the best means for sustaining the democracy that now existed and was to be praised to the end of the world. If to the broad public this appeared to be in accord with the settled custom of the country, to Americans familiar with its background the situation was an interesting and significant novelty.

For at no time, at no place, in solemn convention assembled, through no chosen agents, had the American people officially proclaimed the United States to be a democracy. The Constitution did not contain the word or any word lending countenance to it, except possibly the mention of "we, the people," in the preamble. Nor, indeed, did the Constitution even proclaim a republic. It did guarantee a republican form of government in the states, but as John Adams wrote to Mercy Warren, during their heated controversy over political aims, nobody knew just what that meant. As a matter of fact, when the Constitution was framed no respectable person called himself or herself a democrat. The very word then had low connotations, though it was sometimes mentioned with detachment; and the connotations became distinctly horrible to Respectability after the outbreak of the reign of terror in France. Though denounced as a Jacobin by Federalists, Jefferson did not call his party "democratic," and was chary about mentioning the term even in private correspondence. As was said long afterward, the founders of the republic in general, whether Federalist or Republican, feared democracy more than they feared original sin. Not until Andrew Jackson had retired from the presidency did his followers completely discard the old name "Republican" and officially call themselves "Democrats." After that date references to democracy usually meant "the Democracy," that is, Jackson's party which, strange to relate, soon passed largely under the control of slave owners.

The Whigs and their successors, the Republicans, whatever their popular inclinations, could hardly style themselves democrats, or the United States a democracy, after Jackson's partisans seized the title and identified democracy with their peculiar organization. Moreover one strong wing of the Whig-Republican combination was just as much opposed to everything that savored of democracy as any slaveholder or as any good Federalist of the Hamilton school had been in the latter days of the eighteenth century. If a "sound Republican" had been asked to characterize the United States between 1865 and the end of the century, he would doubtless have called it "a representative republic." Democracy he would have identified with direct government, the initiative, the referendum, popular election of Senators, majority rule, and disrespect for the Supreme Court. As the battle over "more democracy" intensified in the early years of the twentieth century, conservative Republicans grew still more suspicious of democracy. If they mentioned it with any favor, they were quick to make a distinction between "the true democracy" which they espoused and "the false democracy" which "demagogues" were trying to promote.

Not until the United States entered the world war was the conception of the nation as a democracy given something that looked like official sanction and general approval, if often in the form of lip-service only. Whatever may have been the real reason for opening the war on the German government, President Wilson declared it to be a war for democracy, to make the world safe for democracy as against autocratic power. Wilson was, it is true, a Democratic president, but in the fury of the conflict his war cry was little disputed in public if not whole-heartedly accepted in private by conservatives who cheered his war. At last the United States was somewhat officially and generally proclaimed to be in fact a democracy, engaged in a conflict to save democracy from the force of authoritarian States. Even the most strenuous opponents of the initiative, referendum, popular election of Senators, woman suffrage, and other features of "more democracy" were found sanctioning Wilson's official ideology. The word once so hated and feared, so long reprobated, so reluctantly accepted in the United States, became for the hour the sign and symbol of American unity and government, for which the people were to pay, fight, and suffer. Could George Washington, John Adams, Thomas Jefferson, and James Madison have witnessed the scene and heard the chorus they certainly would have been surprised to find their representative republic universally and vociferously hailed as a democracy.

After the war was over objections became more articulate and doubts were entertained. In its manual for the instruction of young men in the art and science of military tactics, the War Department repudiated the doctrine proclaimed by President Wilson, namely, that the United States was a democracy. It did more than reject. It assailed democracy as a form of mobocracy leading to attacks upon property and to communistic heresies — a true-blue Federalist-Whig view of the peril, now put forth by the military. While the United States army derided the idea of democracy for which it had just been ostensibly fighting, communists also attacked democracy and condemned it root and branch as a mere "bourgeois dictatorship" for the oppression of the proletariat. The communist version was also approved by fascists. Mussolini called democracy a "mask for capitalism" and "rotten" besides, ready for burial. So for different reasons, official directors of the United States army, communists, and fascists agreed on one proposition : democracy is a menace or a farce. What is more : neither President Harding nor President Coolidge nor President Hoover resorted to any official action designed to offset the criticisms or to refurbish the symbol under which Wilson's war had been fought.

It took the great economic depression, the domestic conflict, the rise of Hitler, and the consolidation of fascist forces abroad, to arouse what appeared to be a fierce affection for democracy and to produce a tumult of praise for the idea and its institutional embodiments. Another Democratic President, Franklin D. Roosevelt, who liked especially to remember his predecessor, Andrew Jackson, in official addresses formally and solemnly identified the United States with democracy and suggested a second union of all the faithful against the autocracies of the earth. His opponents likewise seized upon democracy as the device under which to wage war at home on the Roosevelt "dictatorship."

Yet few if any of the contemporary disputants took pains to define the term, democracy, in any comprehensive manner. From the view of the White House anything done by the administration was for the purpose of safeguarding and perfecting democracy. In the eyes of the Liberty League or the National Manufacturers Association or Alfred M. Landon, nearly everything done by the Roosevelt administration, except its call for larger and larger armaments, violated the canons of democracy and savored of fascist or authoritarian ambitions. In an age of confusion, defeatism, myths, and symbols, this verbal tempest seemed appropriate. Moreover, besides being effective party politics, it was "safe," in that it raised no fundamental questions.

Any exploration of the reality beneath the term democracy would have led below equal suffrage, popular elections, public education, majority rule, "let us alone," and freedom of the press into the real basis of American civilization, into the forms and distribution of property which conditioned, and to some extent determined, the rise and growth of any democracy that existed. It would have meant a re-reading or, perhaps more correctly stated, a first reading of the papers and letters left by the founders who established American institutions, and also a re-examination of the Declaration of Independence. And such an intellectual labor would have been ruinous to the patois of the new debate or at least to the glibness with which its idioms were put into circulation.

§

Unlike the classical economists who later dominated academic thinking, the leaders in public affairs who drafted the Constitution of the United States and the first state constitutions regarded government and economics as things intimately associated, not as separable and separated. They did not assume that property is something definite, an independent invariable, fixed by nature, and having no relation to the forms and functions of government or to the structures and operations of political parties. Nor were they subject to the illusion that government is a mere matter of popular will — the counting of heads equal and alike, whether of a class or the whole population. On the contrary they recognized that the form of every government, whether tyranny, monarchy, aristocracy, or democracy, is closely connected with the forms and distribution of wealth. They knew that all fundamental actions of governments reflect and affect diverse interests in society and that such interests appear inexorably in every complex and civilized society. Hamilton and his school deliberately sought to attach powerful interests to the Federal Government. Jefferson clung tenaciously to the proposition that freehold agriculture bore a vital relation to the independence of spirit essential to popular rule. All these concepts John Marshall understood and employed in policy and action. Within the schemes of early republican thought, wealth and its distribution were central to law and administration.

Speaking later, after the industrial revolution was well under way in the United States and mechanics and artisans were demanding and winning equal suffrage, Daniel Webster grasped the unity of economics and politics as firmly as Hamilton and Jefferson had done long before. He went still further and made economics the determining force in shaping the forms and processes of government. "The idea is as old as political science itself," Webster observed, ". . . It seems to me to be plain that, in the absence of military force, political power naturally and necessarily goes into the hands which hold the property. In my judgment, therefore, a republican form of government rests, not more on political constitutions, than on those laws which regulate the descent and transmission of property. . . . It would be monstrous to give even the name of government to any association in which the rights of property should not be competently secured. The disastrous revolutions which the world has witnessed, those political thunderstorms and earthquakes which have overthrown the pillars of society from their very deepest foundations, have been revolutions *against property*" [Webster's italics]. In sum and substance, this was saying that property is the true basis of political power, and that political revolutions spring from conflicts over property. If this was not thorough-going determinism, it would be difficult to characterize it.

Calling attention concretely to the American scene, Webster declared that the frame and form of government were "fixed" by economic realities. "Our New England ancestors," he said, "brought hither no great capitals from Europe; and, if they had, there was nothing productive in which they could have been invested. They left behind them the whole feudal policy of the other continent. . . . They

came to a new country. There were as yet no lands yielding
rent, and no tenants rendering service. The whole soil was
unreclaimed from barbarism. They were themselves, either
from their original condition, or from the necessity of their
common interest, nearly on a general level in respect to
property. Their situation demanded a parcelling out and
division of the lands, and it may be fairly said that this
necessary act *fixed the future frame and form of their government* [Webster's italics]. The character of their political
institutions was *determined* [our italics] by the fundamental
laws respecting property. . . . The consequence of all these
causes has been a great subdivision of the soil and a great
equality of condition ; the true basis, most certainly, of popular government." So Webster, differing from Jefferson in
party politics, agreed with him in making a wide distribution
of landed property the foundation and hope of popular government in America.

Webster likewise agreed with Jefferson in holding that concentrated property and political democracy are incompatible
and point in the direction of a revolution of some kind. "The
freest government," continued Webster, "if it could exist
would not be long acceptable, if the tendency of the laws
were to create a rapid accumulation of property in few hands
and to render the great mass of the population dependent and
penniless. . . . Universal suffrage, for example, could not
long exist in a community where there was great inequality
of property. . . . In the nature of things those who have not
property, and see their neighbors possess much more than
they think them to need, cannot be favorable to laws made
for the protection of property. When this class becomes
numerous, it grows clamorous. It looks on property as its
prey and plunder, and is naturally ready, at all times, for
violence and revolution. It would seem, then, to be the part
of political wisdom to found government on property ; and to
establish such distribution of property, by the laws which
regulate its transmission and alienation, as to interest the
great majority of society in the protection of the government.

This is, I imagine, the true theory and the actual practice of our republican institutions."

Here Webster departed from economic determinism and spoke of "political wisdom," in other words, of that enlightened statesmanship which refuses to be a mere reflection of economic interests, and by act of will "establishes" a "distribution of property" calculated to maintain the economic basis of popular institutions. Yet in emphasizing the possibilities of such positive policy, Webster insisted that it be directed to appropriate economic ends.

§

Given this realistic combination of politics and economics, what upshot may be expected in case there is a serious maldistribution of property? One answer to this question was made by John Adams, Alexander Hamilton, and James Madison; namely, prevent the majority from attaining actual power by establishing an "independent" Executive, Senate, and Judiciary — agencies that do not bend to election returns but firmly defend the rights of property against democratic, or leveling, tendencies. This was, indeed, the kind of government which the majority of the men in the constitutional convention of 1787 intended to establish, although none was exactly satisfied with the Constitution as finally drafted.

While popular mythology had to some extent obscured this original conception of the negative aspects of the Constitution, it had never been lost to the sight of informed practitioners on either side, or of the more acute thinkers among academicians. John W. Burgess long taught the doctrine from his chair in Columbia University. Woodrow Wilson, as an academician, before he saw his star of political destiny, upheld it, especially in his opposition to popular election of United States Senators and his defense of judicial independence. This conception of constitutional checks on democracy appeared continuously in debates over the popular election of Senators, over the initiative and referendum, over "assaults on the judiciary," and over efforts of radicals and progressives to block the confirmation of conservatives nominated for the Supreme Court. Those concerned with the instant need of things, as distinguished from the arm-chair philosophers, still understood, if they did not always praise openly, the conception of the Constitution as a barrier in the way of the majority of the people who have no property.

Nowhere was the doctrine stated with more force and precision than by the President of Yale University, A. T. Hadley, in 1907. Writing of the position of property owners, he said that "the sum of the conditions which affect their standing for the long future and not for the immediate present is far stronger in the United States [than elsewhere]. The general status of the property-owner under the law cannot be changed by the action of the legislature, or the executive, or the people of a state voting at the polls, or all three put together. It cannot be changed without either a consensus of opinion among the judges, which should lead them to retrace their old views, or an amendment of the Constitution of the United States by the slow and cumbersome machinery provided for that purpose, or, last — and I hope most improbable — a revolution.

"When it is said, as it commonly is, that the fundamental division of powers in the modern State is into legislative, executive, and judicial, the student of American institutions may fairly note an exception. The fundamental division of powers in the Constitution of the United States is between voters on the one hand and property owners on the other. The forces of democracy on one side, divided between the executive and the legislature, are set over against the forces of property on the other side, with the judiciary as arbiter between them; the Constitution itself not only forbidding the legislature and executive to trench upon the rights of property, but compelling the judiciary to define and uphold those rights in a manner provided by the Constitution itself.

"This theory of American politics has not often been stated. But it has been universally acted upon. One reason why it has not been more frequently stated is that it has been acted upon so universally that no American of earlier generations ever thought it necessary to state it. It has had the most fundamental and far-reaching effects upon the policy of the country. To mention but one thing among many, it has allowed the experiment of universal suffrage to be tried under conditions essentially different from those which led to its ruin in Athens and Rome. The voter was omnipotent — within a limited area. He could make what laws he pleased, as long as those laws did not trench upon property right. He could elect what officers he pleased, as long as those office-holders did not try to do certain duties confided by the Constitution to the property holders."

Here was the negative philosophy of Hamilton, Adams, and Madison as conceived and set forth at the beginning of the twentieth century by an eminent university president. Its historicity and nuances were evident. It was accurate in that it showed how Hamilton, Adams, and Madison wished to block by checks and balances the encroachment of the propertyless majority upon the rights of the rich and well-born. It was correct in so far as it stated that democracy had been tried under peculiar conditions, namely, under a Constitution which, in a line of judicial decisions, had been interpreted to mean that political democracy could not alter in any fundamental way the distribution and accumulation of property. To what extent, however, the framers of the Constitution intended to rely upon the judiciary, as barrier or arbiter, as contrasted with the Senate and the Executive, was a matter of historical doubt.

Perhaps in 1907, when President Hadley wrote his essay, popular election of presidential electors, established long before, and the growing demand for popular election of Senators led him to lay undue emphasis upon the last bulwark — the judiciary. Moreover, in emphasizing negation, he lost sight of the fact that the framers of the Constitution also

intended the Federal Government to act strongly upon
property, in the interests of commerce and manufacturing
as against agriculture, to the detriment, it was charged, of
agriculture. Yet the central thesis was true: There is an
opposition between the voters at large and property owners
and the very form of government serves as a moderating
check on the hasty exercise of majority rule under the theory
of democracy.

A similar antithesis between "our representative republic"
and democracy was made by President Nicholas Murray
Butler of Columbia University, in an address on Why Should
We Change Our Form of Government? delivered before the
Commercial Club of St. Louis in 1911. Although the address
was directed especially against the initiative, referendum, and
recall, or direct democracy, it reviewed the larger aspects of
the American system. The makers of the Constitution, said
President Butler, "built a representative republic." He
called democracy an antithesis to this conception, and referred to Aristotle "who first told us how a democracy as
well as a tyranny may become a despotism." He quoted
John C. Calhoun: "The government of the uncontrolled
numerical majority is but the absolute and despotic form of
popular government, just as the uncontrolled will of one man
is monarchy."

Then President Butler drew his conclusion: "If democracy
is not to become a tyranny, it must recognize and build upon
those constitutional limitations and guaranties that are so
precious to the individual citizen and that protect him in his
life, his liberty, and his property." These limitations and
guaranties are contained in the American Constitution; but
their sanction transcends law; it partakes of natural law;
these fundamental guaranties "are beyond the legitimate
reach of any majority because they are established in the
fundamental laws of human nature upon which all government and civilization and progress rest. Sweep them away,
if you will; a majority may have that power, but with the
power does not go the right. If they are swept away, all

government and all liberty go with them, and anarchy, in which might alone makes right and power alone gives place, will rise upon their ruins."

According to this view of things, the Constitution of the United States incorporates "the fundamental laws of human nature" and the judiciary enforces these laws. "The judges," President Butler consistently argued, "are primarily the servants not of the people, but of the law. It is their duty to interpret the law as it is, and to hold the law-making bodies to their constitutional limitations, not to express their own personal opinions on matters of public policy."

The antithesis to this system, President Butler made "a socialistic democracy." He did not repudiate democracy entirely; for the time had passed in American history when that could be done with Federalist brusqueness by any person with political ambitions. On the contrary he made his principles "the principles of true democracy," thus distinguishing between his kind, which is "true," and the other kind, which is "false." "It may be, perhaps," he conceded, "that under the institutions of a socialistic democracy mankind would be happier, opportunity more free, property more equally distributed, and the satisfaction of man's wants more easily accomplished than now. All these things may be; but if a socialistic democracy is to be substituted for a representative republic, please do not overlook the fact that it can only be so substituted by revolution" — a revolution in our political beliefs, accustomed forms of political action, our ambitions, and aspirations.

In short American history and political philosophy were identified by President Butler with the Federalist interpretation of that history and political philosophy: the Constitution embodies the laws of human nature; the judges guard the laws and say what they are; this is "our" form of government; the antithesis is false democracy — a socialistic democracy — which seeks to make "opportunity more free, property more equally distributed, and the satisfaction of man's wants more easily accomplished than now" — a false democracy opposed to "principles of true democracy and representative government."

§

Early thinkers and writers in the domain of politics nevertheless expressed doubts respecting the perpetuity of the system of checks and balances as safeguards against the movement of events. In their conceptions of the problem, doubts took two forms. Gouverneur Morris and John Adams, for example, feared plutocracy about as much as they did democracy. In opposing the plan of the Constitution which placed no property qualifications on voters and office holders, Morris declared his principal objection : "It threatens this country with an Aristocracy. The Aristocracy will grow out of the House of Representatives. Give the votes to people who have no property, and they will sell them to the rich who will be able to buy them. We should not confine our attention to the present moment. The time is not distant when this country will abound with mechanics and manufacturers [industrial workers], who will receive their bread from their employers. . . . The man who does not give his vote freely is not represented. It is the man who dictates the vote [who is represented]."

On similar grounds, John Adams likewise sought safeguards against the dangers of a plutocracy rising in America. "In every society where property exists," he warned his contemporaries, "there will ever be a struggle between the rich and poor. . . . There is a constant effort and energy in the minds of the former to increase the advantages they possess over the latter, and to augment their wealth and influence at their expense. . . . As the former have most address and capacity, they gain more and more continually, until they become exorbitantly rich and the others miserably poor." This, Adams continued, is the source of parties, tumults, and war ; the masses look for a leader and protector ; here is "the history of that progress of passions and feeling which has produced every simple monarchy in the world ; and if nature and its feelings have their course without reflection, they will produce a simple monarchy forever." A constitution, a powerful executive, and an independent judiciary might hold the balance, but Adams was not certain of the outcome. He despised the speculative plunderers who gathered around Hamilton's system; he feared the predatory poor who rallied around Jefferson; he fell between two stools and was driven from the White House a disappointed and bitter man.

In developing his conception of the problem presented by the antithesis between the possessors of property and the propertyless, Madison shaded his emphasis according to time and circumstances. Speaking in 1787 behind the closed doors of the convention he said frankly: "Viewing the subject in its merits alone, the freeholders of the country would be the safest depositories of Republican liberty. In future times a great majority of the people will not only be without landed, but any other sort of property. These will either combine under the influence of their common situation; in which case [if the authority be in their hands by the rule of suffrage — (crossed out)] the rights of property and the public liberty will not be secure in their hands; or, which is more probable, they will become the tools of opulence and ambition, in which case there will be equal danger on another side. . . . The greatest part [of the representatives in the British Commons] are chosen by the cities and boroughs, in many of which the qualification of suffrage is as low as it is in any one of the United States, and it was in the boroughs and cities rather than the counties that bribery most prevailed and the influence of the Crown on elections was more dangerously exerted." Here was the positive fear, expressed by Gouverneur Morris and John Adams, that American society would in time be composed mainly of the propertyless and that opulence, through bribery and intrigue, would marshal indigent voters behind a dictatorship dangerous to the middle class.

However, these passages did not contain all of Madison's system of thought. Shortly after he entered the first Congress under the Constitution, he associated himself with Jefferson's party, which was appealing to the masses against "the rich and well born." Later in life, when the passions of the political conflict had diminished and Madison had contemplated anew the central problem of government, he set forth a modified scheme of politics. In his final program, Madison stated that his speech in the convention, as quoted above, did not convey his "more full and matured view of the subject."

This matured view, however, presented the old problem in all its original force. The antithesis between the concentration of wealth and political equality was still recognized and stress was laid upon it. The inexorable increase in the population, including those without property, was taken as the basis of his thought about the problem. Writing in 1829-30, Madison predicted that the population of the United States would probably be ninety-six millions in seventy-five years, that is in 1905, and one hundred and ninety-two millions in a hundred years, that is by 1930. Directing his attention especially to the members of the Virginia constitutional convention, he warned them that "as we are to prepare a system of government for a period which it is hoped will be a long one, we must look to the prospective changes in the condition and composition of the society on which it is to act."

A great density of population, Madison was sure, lay ahead and an increased mass of laborers. Not only this. "It is a lot of humanity, that of this surplus [of people beyond those having an immediate interest in the soil] a large proportion is necessarily reduced by a competition for employment to wages which afford them the bare necessaries of life. The proportion being without property, or the hope of acquiring it, cannot be expected to sympathize sufficiently with its rights to be safe depositories of power over them. What is to be done with this unfavored class of the community?"

Madison pondered his own query. "If it be, on one hand, unsafe to admit them to a full share of political power, it must be recollected, on the other, that it cannot be expedient to rest a republican government on a portion of the society having a numerical and physical force excluded from, and liable to be turned against it, and which would lead to a standing military force, dangerous to all parties and to liberty itself. This view of the subject makes it proper to embrace in the partnership of power every description of citizens having a sufficient stake in the public order and the stable administration of the laws, and particularly the house-keepers and heads of families, most of whom 'having given hostages to fortune,' will have given them to their country also." Thus Madison's latest solution of the contradiction was to grant the suffrage to "housekeepers and heads of families," that is, freeholders, and to "those who, although not possessed of a share of the soil, are deeply interested in other species of property," that is, to merchants and capital-ists not owning land.

Only so far was Madison prepared to go. "It would be happy," he conceded, "if a state of society could be found or framed in which an equal voice in making the laws might be allowed to every individual bound to obey them." But this theory of happiness required "limitations and modifications." The conflict remained; the suffrage must be restricted in some degree.

The future opened before the seer. The majority will be without landed or other property. There will be "a depend-ence of an increasing number on the wealth of a few." It will spring from the relations between landlords and tenants, between "wealthy capitalists and indigent laborers . . . from the connection between the great capitalists in manu-factures and commerce, and the numbers employed by them. Nor will accumulations of capital for a certain time be pre-cluded by our laws of descent and distribution." Still, Madison mused, in the future this tendency to concentration "may be diminished and the permanency defeated by the equalizing tendencies of the laws." Of this no one could speak with certainty: "How far this view of the subject will be affected by the republican laws of descent and distribution, in equalizing the property of the citizens . . . cannot be inferred from any direct and adequate experiment."

Nevertheless the challenge will press upon American society in times to come. "To effect these changes, intellectual, moral, and social, the institutions and laws of the country must be adapted; and it will require for the task all the wisdom of the wisest patriots." Into the nature of the legislation adapting the institutions of the country to this economic conjuncture — legislation touching the descent, distribution, and equalization of property — Madison did not venture. The problem he stated. The economic conflict he described. The political implications he frankly faced. The solution of the contradiction, if there was to be one, he left to coming generations. Hesitant in dealing with remedies, Madison was certainly prescient in foreshadowing the crisis likely to be at hand a hundred years later, in 1930. The population was not as large as he had predicted, but the concentration and indigence he had foretold certainly called for "all the wisdom of the wisest patriots."

Like Madison, his neighbor and successor in the White House, Jefferson scanned the long future in America, even while he dealt with the instant need of things. He accepted the dictum that politics and economics are inseparable and based his hopes for popular government on a wide distribution of freehold farms. Primogeniture was to be abolished; a diffusion of estates was to be facilitated; and the people were to be educated to know their rights and obligations. There were perils to democracy in commerce, manufacturing, and banking, which work for the concentration of wealth and "paper" claims to wealth; the distant future was uncertain and doom might lie ahead. The outlook for popular government was only good, Jefferson wrote to Madison, "as long as we remain virtuous; and I think we shall be so, as long as agriculture is our principal object, which will be the case while there remain vacant lands in any part of America." Beyond that was darkness. "When we get piled upon one another in large cities, as in Europe, we shall become corrupt as in Europe, and go to eating one another as they do there." While Madison hoped that "wise" statesmanship might do something effective in this crisis, Jefferson was pessimistic and saw no certain exit from the dilemma.

On the other hand, Webster's prediction respecting the outcome of the contradiction between accumulated wealth and democratic equality was positive. The element of military force, he recognized, was always present or imminent. "Numbers, nevertheless, constitute, ordinarily, the most important consideration, unless indeed there be *military force* [his italics] in the hands of the few, by which they can control the many." In case there is a "rapid accumulation of property in few hands," the great mass of the population is "dependent and penniless," and universal suffrage exists, then "popular power must break in upon the rights of property, or else the influence of property must limit and control the exercise of popular power. . . . The holders of estates would be obliged in such case, either in some way to restrain the right of suffrage, or else such right of suffrage would ere long divide the property."

There was the lesson of a Caesar. "Let it never be forgotten," Webster admonished his auditors, "that it was the popular magistrates, elevated to office where the bad outnumbered the good, where those who had no stake in the Commonwealth, by clamor, and noise, and numbers, drowned the voice of those who had, that laid the neck of Rome at the foot of her conqueror." The Senate sought to declare Caesar a public enemy. "To this decree the popular tribunes, the sworn protectors of the people, interposed their negative; and thus opened the high road of Italy, and the gates of Rome herself, to the approach of her conqueror." The application was obvious. If in such circumstances Rome was overcome by Caesar, America might, in similar circumstances, encounter the same fate. This message Webster bequeathed to posterity.

Far more systematic than the thought of either Madison or Jefferson was the political science of a contemporary, John

Taylor, of Virginia, who may be called the philosopher of agrarianism, although now almost forgotten. Like his Virginia friends, he believed freehold agriculture to be the only secure basis for popular government. Before Webster, he recognized the antithesis between the concentration of wealth and the diffusion of political power. But his solution of the contradiction differed from their replication. It did not rely vaguely on the hope of future wisdom in statecraft; it did not display the pessimism of Jefferson; nor did it present the choice between general confiscation and a military dictatorship implicit in Webster's speculations on the future.

Taylor's system made a distinction between "legal, factitious or fraudulent property" and "substantial, real or honest property" — between "that species of private property founded only in law, such as is gained by privilege, hierarchy, paper [public debts and bank money, for instance], charter [corporations], and sinecure; and that founded in nature, arising from industry, arts, and sciences." Taylor insisted that there was danger in uniting "these two opposite moral beings in a defensive war" against confiscatory measures.

The economic conflict, so evident in politics, was not, according to Taylor, a struggle between the propertied and the propertyless; it was essentially a conflict between "privileged, stipendiary, or factitious property" and property "founded in nature, arising from industry, arts, and sciences." Holders of the latter, he urged, should dispossess the former, thus breaking up the concentration effected through liquid claims to wealth, and bringing about the wide diffusion of wealth so essential to popular government.

This drastic action, Taylor contended, was justified by history. "All societies," he wrote, "have exercised the right of abolishing privileged, stipendiary, or factitious property, whenever they have become detrimental to them; nor have kings, churches, or aristocracies ever hesitated to do the same thing, for the same reason. The king of England joined the people and judges, in abolishing the tenures and perpetuities of the nobles; the king and nobles united in abolishing the property of the popish clergy; the consistory of Rome suppressed the order of Jesuits and disposed of its property; and several of these states [in the American union] have abolished entails, tithes, and hierarchial establishments. What stronger ground can be occupied by any species of law-begotten wealth than by these?"

Taylor's remedy, therefore, was to sweep away property rights founded on paper, corporation bank notes, protective tariffs, and "factitious" claims to wealth, and preserve property founded on nature, industry, sciences, and arts. By uniting with holders of the former kind of property in defense of all property, holders of the latter would make a fatal error, and jeopardize their own position.

§

Running through the years beside the cold and fatalistic analysis of the relations between economies and forms of government, between the nature and distribution of wealth on the one side and the institutions of politics on the other, was a broad stream of thought which furnished the dynamic of what may be called, with fair precision, humanistic democracy. This thought was concerned with the resolution of contradictions by democratic methods in the interest of human welfare and social stability. Its sources lay far back in western history, in the Christian tradition and the older humanism of the Greeks.

In colonial times it was represented by such thinkers and spokesmen as John Wise and John Woolman. Its widest and deepest formulation in the revolutionary period was made by Thomas Paine, especially in his Rights of Man and Agrarian Justice, wherein he set forth the principles of a leveling democracy in terms economic and political. Within Paine's scheme of thought, laid down in the Rights of Man — the counterblast to Edmund Burke's plea for the status quo in England — came a wide distribution of landed property, old age pensions, free and universal education, subsidies for maternal care, workshops for the employment of the casual poor, a "plan of progressive tax" operating to extirpate the unjust and unnatural law of primogeniture and the vicious influence of the aristocratical system, and international agreements for the reduction of armaments and promotion of peace. War, he said, "serves to keep up deceitful expectations, which prevent people from looking into the defects and abuses of government. It is the *lo here!* and the *lo there!* that amuses and cheats the multitude."

For a time humanistic democracy showed a tendency to rally around Thomas Jefferson, to whom Federalists applied the epithet of "atheist" as well as "Jacobin," but it never collected completely under the banner of his party. The truth seems to be that Jefferson himself was more an agent of popular forces than a creator and was prodded into leadership and action by spontaneous and wide-spread outbursts of democratic fervor among "the plain people." After the slave-owning planters got possession of the party machinery, a left-wing, loyal to the humanistic tradition, split off, especially in the North, and men calling themselves "Democratic" denounced the humanists as communists, anarchists, and feminists.

Then it was that a host of men and women not whole-heartedly committed to either party undertook to make America conscious of human values, alive to the dangers of a purely acquisitive economy, and willing to carry out programs of reform ranging from hard money to free schools, from agrarianism to utopian socialism. The names of this host would fill a bulky volume but in a selection from the long list of orators, lecturers, writers, organizers, and political leaders may be cited Horace Greeley, Charles A. Dana, Wendell Phillips, Dorothea Dix, Ralph Waldo Emerson, William Lloyd Garrison, Elizabeth Cady Stanton, Hinton Rowan Helper, George Henry Evans, Lydia Maria Child, Susan B. Anthony, Andrew Johnson, and William H. Sylvis — all powerful personalities. Year after year they discussed with their countrymen the problem of realizing the democratic ideal in the rearrangement of human affairs, institutions, and economic practices.

When the pall of the slavery conflict settled over other issues, leaders of humanistic democracy concentrated, for the time being, on abolition as the supreme task of the hour. A combination of Whigs and Democrats was formed and to this combination was given, in full recognition of its appeal, the title of Jefferson's old party, namely, Republican. Humanistic sentiments then gathered around Abraham Lincoln, whose expressed opinions were in harmony with the "democratic" as distinguished from the "aristocratic" tradition.

In democratic spirit Lincoln was Jeffersonian. "The principles of Jefferson," he said, "are the definitions and axioms of free society." To the agrarians and their affiliated labor reformers, the Republican party promised a distribution of the public domain in the form of free homesteads for free families. To industrial workers, then engaged in desperate efforts at unionism involving strikes disagreeable to the public, Lincoln, in a speech at Hartford, Connecticut, in March, 1860, extended his sympathies; he "thanked God that we have a system of labor where there can be a strike. Whatever the pressure, there is a point where the workman may stop." At Cincinnati, he exclaimed at a mass meeting: "I agree with you, Mr. Chairman, that the working men are the basis of all governments, for the plain reason that they are the more numerous." When Lincoln wavered on the question of slavery it was the democratic humanists who prodded him, as humanists had prodded Jefferson, brought pressure on him, and rallied popular support for emancipation — women taking a leading part in this form of pressure politics, especially the feminists, with their strong emphasis on general equality.

After the civil conflict, amid the upswing of industrialism in economy, with its shadowing philosophy of Darwinism and tooth-and-claw laissez faire, exponents of humanistic democracy turned from the slavery issue to the consideration

of the social problems raised by the ruthless advance of capitalism. The ink was scarcely dry on the Proclamation of
Emancipation when Elizabeth Cady Stanton challenged the
common assumption that "the new birth of freedom" had
closed American history, raised the broad question of labor
in industrial society, and started to make, year after year,
long journeys up and down the land discussing the issue from
the lecture platforms, indefatigably, until near the close of
her long life in 1902.

In the year 1868 she sounded the keynote of her humanistic
philosophy : "A knowledge of the history of the past teaches
us that the law governing human affairs is change, progress,
development in the world of thought as well as action. . . .
A healthy discontent is the first step of progress. . . . In the
long battle we have fought in this country for the emancipation and enfranchisement of the African race, the principles of
slavery and freedom have been so fully described that it does
not require much discrimination to see that the condition of
the laboring classes at the North differs little from that of the
colored race under the old system of the plantations of the
South. I ask those in the full enjoyment of all the blessings
that wealth can give to look around you in the filthy lanes
and byways of our cities, at the surging multitudes, ragged,
starving, packed in dingy cellars and garrets where no ray of
sunshine or hope can penetrate, no touch of light or love to
cheer their lives. Look in the factories and workshops where
young and old work side by side with tireless machines from
morn to night through all the days, the weeks, the months,
the years that make up the long sum of life, impelled by that
inexorable necessity that knows no law — toil or starvation. . . .

"Under all forms of government about seven-tenths of
the human family are doomed to incessant toil, living in
different degrees of poverty, from the man who hopes for
nothing but daily bread for himself and family to the one
who aims at education and accumulation. . . . Self-
preservation was considered the first law of nature prior to

all duties to neighbors, society, government. This principle is, however, theoretically and practically reversed in civilization. The individual, it is now said, must be sacrificed to society, the one to the good of the whole. The higher idea, it seems to me, is that the interests of the individual and society lie in the same direction, that the highest good of the individual is the highest good of society. . . . Those who believe that poverty is a part of the divine plan will consider their duty done in the manifestation of sympathy and charity. But for those who believe that it is the result of human ignorance and selfishness and can be remedied, a widely different course of action must be pursued. To the last class I belong."

Three years after Elizabeth Cady Stanton sounded her tocsin, Wendell Phillips went over to the labor reform movement and at a labor convention in Worcester, Massachusetts, presented a set of resolutions approving "the overthrow of the whole profit-making system, . . . the abolition of privileged classes," and the same public aid "to coöperative efforts that has hitherto been given to railroads and other enterprises." In his address to the convention, Phillips advanced to what he believed to be the central concern of the republic and uttered formulas that were to ring through the coming years: "The land [the landed aristocracy] of England has ruled it for six hundred years. The corporations of America mean to rule it in the same way and, unless some power more radical than that of ordinary politics is found, will rule it inevitably. I confess that the only fear I have in regard to republican institutions is whether, in our day, any adequate remedy will be found for this incoming flood of the power of incorporated wealth. . . . The great cities are the arsenals of great wealth, where wealth manages everything in its own way."

At this very moment, far out in California, Henry George was turning over in his mind the problem that troubled Stanton and Phillips and the other thinkers of their direction. In 1879 he offered to mankind his solution in Progress and

Poverty and profoundly moved the humanists of the world by his vigor and logic. The next great upsurge of humanistic democracy was well under way. A forceful leader of the Knights of Labor, Terence V. Powderly, while adhering to the party of Lincoln and revolutionary emancipation of the Negroes, carried on an agitation for the abolition of the wages system and the substitution of coöperative production. The militant spokesman of industrial workers and agrarians, John P. Altgeld, "the forgotten eagle," became governor of a major state, Illinois. Socialistic and populistic parties entered the arena and all the "lunatic fringes," as their censors characterized them, were fused into the democratic movement led by William Jennings Bryan in 1896. Blocked in the campaign of that year and depressed by the *lo here! lo there!* of the Spanish-American war and by the headlong plunge into imperialism, the old democratic currents emerged soon afterward and sapped away at the foundations of conservatism.

In the "progressive era," the ferment of humanistic democracy continued to work everywhere in the country — as expressed by innumerable personalities, notably by Robert M. La Follette, Theodore Roosevelt, Jane Addams, Oswald Garrison Villard, Graham Taylor, Florence Kelley, Harriot Stanton Blatch, Eugene V. Debs, John R. Commons, Julia Lathrop, Edith Abbott, Grace Abbott, Louis Post, Judson King, James Weldon Johnson, Hamlin Garland, and William S. U'Ren, selections from the huge who's who in "reform." By 1912 the popular movement had become so strong that it split, not the Democratic party, but the Republican party with its heritage from Lincoln and revolutionary emancipation. In the upheaval, the Progressive party was formed and Theodore Roosevelt was chosen as its candidate for the presidency. This spokesman of progressive democracy had been educated by events, he confessed, and took the position that the Republican party had been founded in the days of Lincoln as "the radical progressive party."

In the political dissolution, provoked by the revolt within

the Republican ranks, Woodrow Wilson, who, as professor, had hitherto not ventured far beyond Edmund Burke and Richard Ricardo in his political and economic thought, modified most of his philosophy and, as a politician, made a direct bid for the votes of "progressives." Aided by the dissension among the Republicans, Wilson won the presidency but soon afterward came the world war and its attendant holocaust, followed by the interlude of normalcy and the golden glow.

§

During the entire interlude the tide of humanistic democracy still beat upon the strongholds of the mighty and kept Congress in turmoil, until the detonations of the depression shook apart the fabric of complacency. Out of that convulsion emerged Franklin D. Roosevelt, who, also educated by events, finally combined in his thinking the severe economic analysis of the Hamilton-Webster tradition with the humanistic democracy of the parallel tradition. Whatever his merits or demerits as statesman or administrator, he eventually gave expression to the two most powerful tendencies in American history. In his second inaugural he took cognizance of the fundamental conflict of Western civilization, the antithesis between the ideal and the real — the conflict that perplexed philosophy, science, art, and letters, as well as every other interest of mankind; and having accepted this conflict as a challenge, President Roosevelt expressed the conviction that it was the function of statesmanship to bring the real into closer conformity to the ideal — the conception of humanistic democracy.

And the major measures of the Roosevelt regime, however open to criticism in details or in execution, looked in the direction of strengthening the economic foundations of democracy — salvaging agriculture, fortifying the bargaining power of industrial workers, minimum wages, social insurance, old age pensions, employment for the idle, security of livelihood and home, protection against the hazards of economic defeat. In presenting to Congress, on April 29, 1938, his message on the problem of so-called monopoly, a central issue of American political economy, President Roosevelt described factually the growing concentration of economic and financial power. He quoted Daniel Webster's dictum that free government is incompatible with a rapid accumulation of property in a few hands, thus bringing together, in a single state paper, the economic analysis and the affirmation of humanistic democracy.

It was well within the circle of factual description to say that in his numerous discourses Franklin D. Roosevelt discussed the basic human and economic problems of American society with a courage and range displayed by no predecessor in his office; that he thrust their challenges into spheres hitherto indifferent or hostile; that he set in swift circulation, through the use of the radio, ideas once confined to groups more or less esoteric; that he both reflected and stirred the thought of the nation to the uttermost borders of the land. And in doing this he carried on the tradition of humanistic democracy which from colonial times had been a powerful dynamic in the whole movement of American civilization and culture — economic, political, literary, scientific, and artistic.

After all the criticisms brought against him, justly and unjustly, had been weighed and assayed, that much remained written in the record and implanted in the accumulating heritage of thought and aspiration. Moreover the popular response to his appeal, which gave him forty-six of the forty-eight states in the election of 1936, bore witness to a profound moral and intellectual disturbance such as had characterized great epochs of the past. Even the relative failure of his effort to eliminate conservative Democrats in the congressional campaign of 1938 did not mean a material decline in the influence of his thought upon the broad masses of the people.

Important as was the role of directors and counselors in the development of American civilization, however, the destiny of coming years turned upon the fortunes of no single personality or group of personalities, of no political parties, for they were all passing particulars in the great movements of history, manifesting in thought and action forces that had long been at work in American society and were working for the future. As the speeches of candidates and the platforms of the parties demonstrated in the campaign of 1936, American democracy was engaged in bending the strength of talents, skills, natural resources, and property to humanistic purposes publicly declared and in process of realization however tedious and painful the procedure. Critical leaders of this democracy had no illusions about the peril of sheer force and cruelty, exalting the irrational, despising justice and mercy — despite noble professions on all sides. That terror, they well knew, had haunted the framers of the Constitution and had been condemned by George Washington when he rejected the suggestion of a dictatorship for himself as a crown of the American revolution; returning his sword, in sign of his fidelity, to the civilian Congress which had entrusted it to him, he surrendered, as he said, "with satisfaction the appointment I accepted with diffidence," to take up in time of peace the burdens of civilian public service. Aware that Caesar's empire of blood, if it came, would perish, as did even the colossal monument of Ozymandias the mighty with the sneer of cold command upon his lips, and fortified by a long and tenacious tradition, the humanistic wing of American democracy sought to provide the economic and cultural foundations indispensable to a free society, by rational methods of examination, discussion, legislation, administration, and coöperation, employing the sciences, letters, and arts in efforts to fulfill the promises of its heritage and aspirations.

INDEX

Weir, E. T., 304.
Welles, Orson, 638 f.
Wendell, Barrett, 656.
Werfel, Franz, 637.
Werner, M. R., cited, 174.
West, Benjamin, 758.
Western Lands and the American Revolution, Abernethy, cited, 915.
Wettereau, James O., 243.
Wexley, John, 625.
Whalen, Grover, 816.
Wharton, Edith, 655, 668, 686, 708, 712, 720, 725.
Wheeler, Burton K., 294, 352, 354, 355, 358, 542.
Whipple, G. H., 826.
White, Leonard D., 346.
White, Walter, 685.
White, William Allen, 125 ff., 303 f., 568.
White, W. L., 676.
White House conferences, 60, 211, 253 f., 371, 372, 565 f., 867 f.
Whither Mankind, symposium, cited, 840.
Whitman, Walt, 655, 656, 680, 687.
Whitney, George, 167 ff.
Whitney, Richard, 57, 164 f.
Whitney Museum of Modern Art, N. Y. C., exhibitions, 805, 807.
Wickwire, Arthur M., cited, 163.
Wiggin, Albert H., 109 f., 186, 862, 866.
Wilbur, Ray Lyman, 835.
Wilcox, O. W., 831.
Wilder, Thornton, 660.
Willard, Daniel, 99, 100.
Williams, Aubrey, 865.
Williams, William Carlos, 672.
Wilson, Edmund, 700, 724 f.
Wilson, M. L., 144, 868.
Wilson, Woodrow, 7, 27, 45, 48, 116, 126, 128, 134, 212, 242, 295, 323, 326, 336, 433, 448, 454, 455, 469, 476, 483, 486, 897, 924, 929, 947. *See also* New Freedom; Munitions industry.
Wilson dam, Supreme Court upholds, 273.
Winchell, Walter, 605.
Wisconsin, Progressives supported by farmer-labor, 551.
Wise, John, 941.
With Eyes of the Past, Ladd, cited, 753 f.
Wolfe, Bertram, 737.
Wolfe, Thomas, 669.
Wolff, Virginia, 640.
Woll, Matthew, 99 f., 530.
Women, and the golden glow, 3 ff.; 183; in the dissolution, 98; not to be forgotten, 139; as followers of Townsend, 198; as backers of Hitler, 202;

on the land, 240, 253, 556 f.; in industry, 556 f.; and political economy, 506; and the labor movement, 509, 533, 541; and the minimum wage, 280 ff., 306, 311, 359; in little business, 372, 565; and the war psychosis, 461 ff., 563; and campaign expenses, 329 f.; and middle-class ideology, 556 ff.; and entertainment, 578 ff.; and letters, 653 ff.; and esthetics, 745 ff.; and social thought, 875, 898, 918 ff.; and humanistic democracy, 922 ff. *See* Families; Housing.
Women of the Confederacy, Simkins and Patton, cited, 916.
Wood, Grant, 789, 796.
Woodberry, George Edward, 656.
Woodcarvings, 789, 798 f.
Woodin, William H., 146, 167, 169 f.
Woodring, Harry, 498, 569 ff., 598, 864.
Woodward, C. Vann, 917.
Woodward, Ellen S., 778.
Woolman, John, 941.
Works Progress Administration, 288 f., 541, 633, 707, 777 f., 811.
World, the Arts and the Artist, The, Edman, cited, 761.
World Center for Women's Archives, N. Y. C., 918 f.
World Court, U. S. interest in, 47; 1932 party platforms on, 119, 133; 1936 Republican platform on, 311; U. S. membership in, rejected, 314, 447, 474 f., 485.
World History of Art, A, Cheney, cited, 747.
World Imagism, 456, 464. *See also* Collective Internationalism; Neutrality Act.
World Peace Foundation, 430.
World Resources and Industries, Zimmermann, cited, 450.
World's Fair, Chicago, 1933, 775, 795, 816; N. Y. C., 1939, 816; San Francisco, 1939, 816.
World War, debts, 9, 20, 93 ff., 415, 421; and 1929 depression, 87, 123; 1932 Democratic platform on, 134, 463; problem facing Roosevelt, 204, 205; 1936 Republican platform on, 311; financing of, history, 407 ff.; origins of, 431 ff.; motion pictures as propaganda for, 596, 599 f. *See also* Moratorium; Veterans; Munitions industry; Johnson Act of 1934.
Worthington Pump and Machinery Company, 52.
Wright, Frank Lloyd, 818.
Wright, Quincy, 449.
Writers, subjects used by predepression,

653 ff.; 1926–35, 659 f., 661 ff.; 1936–38, 660 f., 661 ff.; humorous, 684 ff.; proletarian, 686 ff., 689 f.; on the American scene, 691 ff., 695 ff., 699 ff., 703 f., 704 ff.; on futility, 707 ff.; imaginative compared with newspaper and magazine, 743 f. *See also* Novels; Short stories; Poetry; Biographies; Literary criticism; Columnists; Reporting.

Writers' Congress, N. Y. C., 1937, 720 f.

Writers Project, of F. A. P., 788 f.

Wynn, Ed, 630.

Yale Review, The, cited, 556, 741.

Yale University, Workshop in drama, 642 f.; Institute of Human Relations, 824; social thought at, 894, 899.

Yeaman, Elizabeth, 614.

You Can't Do That, Seldes, cited, 567 f.

Young, Owen D., 103 f., 371.

Young, Stark, 677.

Yountz, Philip N., 763.

Zimmermann, Erich, 450.

Zugsmith, Leane, 666.